MEANINGFUL HELP AND FEEDBACK

- Personalized interactive learning aids are available for point-of-use help and immediate feedback. These learning aids include:

  - Help Me Solve This walks students through solving an algorithmic version of the questions they are working, with additional detailed tutorial reminders. These informational cues assist the students and help them understand concepts and mechanics.

  - Demo Docs are entire problems worked through step by step from start to finish, replicating the in-class experience for students anytime, anywhere.

  - Accounting Simplified videos give students a 3- to 5-minute lesson on concepts. Our new videos are engaging whiteboard animations that help illustrate concepts for students.

  - NEW! Accounting Cycle Tutorial provides students with an interactive and simulated exercise to reinforce the concepts critical to success in Accounting.

  - eText links students directly to the concept covered in the problem they are completing.

  - Homework and practice exercises with additional algorithmically generated problems are available for further practice and mastery.

  - NEW! Worked Out Solutions—now available to students when they are reviewing their submitted and graded homework. The Worked Out Solutions provide step-by-step explanations on how to solve select problems using the exact numbers and data that were presented to the student in the problem.

- NEW! Dynamic Study Modules—Using a highly personalized, algorithmically driven process, Dynamic Study Modules continuously assess students' performance and provide additional practice in the areas where they struggle the most.

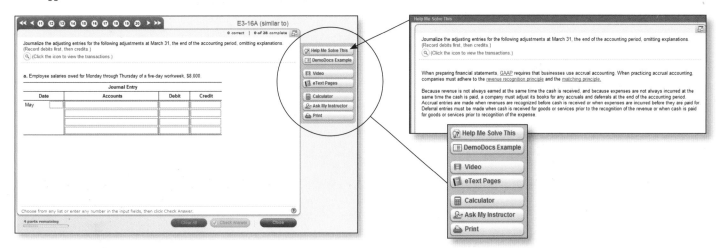

PERSONALIZED AND ADAPTIVE STUDY PATH

- Assist students in monitoring their own progress by offering them a customized study plan powered by Knewton, based on Homework, Quiz, and Test results.

- Regenerated exercises offer unlimited practice and the opportunity to prove mastery through Quizzes on recommended learning objectives.

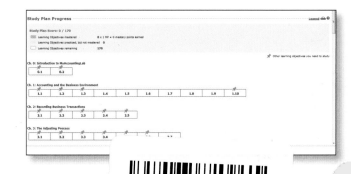

Financial Accounting

Financial Accounting

Third Edition

Robert Kemp
University of Virginia

Jeffrey Waybright
Spokane Community College

PEARSON

Boston   Columbus   Indianapolis   New York   San Francisco   Upper Saddle River
Amsterdam   Cape Town   Dubai   London   Madrid   Milan   Munich   Paris   Montréal   Toronto
Delhi   Mexico City   São Paulo   Sydney   Hong Kong   Seoul   Singapore   Taipei   Tokyo

Editor in Chief: Donna Battista
Acquisitions Editor: Lacey Vitetta
Senior Editorial Project Manager: Karen Kirincich
Development Editor: Mignon Tucker, JD,
    Brava 360° Solutions
Editorial Assistant: Christine Donovan
Marketing Manager: Alison Haskins
Marketing Assistant: Kimberly Lovato
Managing Editor: Jeff Holcomb
Senior Production Project Manager:
    Roberta Sherman

Manufacturing Buyer: Carol Melville
Art Director: Anthony Gemmellaro
Cover Designer: Joel Gendron, PreMediaGlobal
Cover Photo: Style_TTT/Shutterstock
Media Producer: James Bateman
Supplements Editor: Jill Kolongowski
Full-Service Project Management, Composition,
    and Text Design: Integra
Printer/Binder: Courier Kendallville
Cover Printer: Lehigh-Phoenix Color/Hagerstown
Text Font: 10/12 Meridian

Credits and acknowledgments borrowed from other sources and reproduced, with permission, in this textbook appear on the appropriate page within text [or on page 723].

Library of Congress Cataloging-in-Publication Data
Waybright, Jeffrey.
    Financial accounting/Robert Kemp, University of Virginia, Jeffrey
Waybright, Spokane Community College.—Third edition.
        pages cm
    Includes index.
    ISBN 978-0-13-342788-2
1. Accounting. 2. Accounting—Textbooks. I. Kemp, Robert S. II. Title.
    HF5636.W39 2015
    657—dc23

                                    2013042428

10 9 8 7 6 5 4 3

ISBN 10:   0-13-342788-9
ISBN 13: 978-0-13-342788-2

Dedication

I dedicate this book to my beloved children: Adam, Meg, and Sarah. I also dedicate this book to their spouses and children. They give meaning to my life and are my dream come true.

Robert Kemp

I would like to dedicate this book to my colleagues in the Business Department at Spokane Community College.

Jeffrey Waybright

About the Authors

Robert S. Kemp, DBA, CPA Professor Kemp is the Ramon W. Breeden, Sr. Research Professor at the McIntire School of Commerce, University of Virginia. He is a certified public accountant and possesses a baccalaureate, master's, and doctorate in business administration.

Professor Kemp is an accomplished scholar, conducting research and writing in the theory and practice of contemporary business. He currently is conducting research in the funding of pensions, the management of financial institutions, and corporate finance. His scholarly works include 70 completed projects, including monographs, articles, cases, research presentations, and working papers. His work is published in, among other places, *The Financial Review; The Journal of Financial Research; Advances in Accounting, A Research Journal; Benefits Quarterly; The Journal of Mathematics Applied in Business and Industry; The Journal of Accountancy; The Journal of Commercial Bank Lending; The Journal of Bank Accounting and Auditing;* and *The Journal of Business Economics.*

Professor Kemp is likewise an accomplished teacher, to both University students and executives throughout the world. During his 34 years at the University of Virginia, he has taught numerous undergraduate and graduate courses. He has taught classes using lectures, case studies, discussion groups, and distance learning. His consistently high evaluations by students reflect his devotion to the classroom. This high quality is likewise seen in his teaching of business executives. He has worked with and taught for organizations such as Bank of America, the FDIC, Navigant—Tucker Alan, the Siberian Banking Institute, the Barents Group, KPMG, Gerson Lehrman, Wellington Management, the Russian Bankers Association, the Central Asian American Enterprise Fund, the American Institute of Certified Public Accountants, and the Consumer Bankers Association.

Jeffrey Waybright teaches accounting at Spokane Community College, which is part of a multi-college district in eastern Washington. He has been a full-time, tenured community college instructor for more than 21 years. In addition to teaching at the community college level, he has also taught upper division courses for Linfield College. Jeffrey is a co-recipient of the Washington Society of CPA's Outstanding Educator Award.

Jeffrey received his BA in business administration (emphasis in accounting) and MBA from Eastern Washington University. Before becoming a professor, Jeffrey spent eight years as a practicing CPA in Washington State and still holds his license. During his teaching career, he has taught in many disciplines of accounting including financial, managerial, computerized, and payroll accounting as well as in the disciplines of economics, business math, and general business. Jeffrey developed online courses in accounting, teaches online and traditional courses for financial and managerial accounting, and advises students. Jeffrey is passionate about teaching students the subject of accounting.

Brief Contents

Contents

Preface

Changes to this Edition

Chapter 1 Business, Accounting, and You

- Added Real World Accounting Video summary of David Hitchner, owner and manager of ABC Wine, to set the chapter content in a real world business context for students.
- Added two questions to the Self Checks that assess student understanding of the Real World Accounting Videos.
- Changed 50% of the exercises and problems to provide diverse practice and teaching opportunities for students and teachers.
- EXCEL is now in MyAccountingLab. For every chapter, instructors have the option to assign students 2 end-of-chapter problems that can be completed in an Excel-simulated environment, auto graded and visible in the grade book. Excel remediation will be available to students.

Chapter 2 Analyzing and Recording Business Transactions

- Changed chapter introduction company from Best Buy to Target.
- Added Real World Accounting Video of Julie Gaines, owner and manager of Fishs Eddy, to set the chapter content in a real world business context for students.
- Animated each hybrid equation example so that students can drill themselves as many times as needed on the interrelationship of the journal entries, t-accounts, and general ledger when posting transactions. Available in the eText only, located in MyAccountingLab®.
- Changed 50% of the exercises and problems to provide diverse practice and teaching opportunities for students and teachers.
- Added two questions to the Self Checks that assess student understanding of the Real World Accounting Videos.
- Updated Continuing Financial Statement Analysis featuring Target using the 2012 annual report.
- Designated two Excel problems and exercises that can be automatically graded in MyAccountingLab. These materials are designated by a "Try It In Excel" icon.
- Updated the end of chapter material related to Under Armour and Columbia Sportswear using the 2012 annual reports.

Chapter 3 Adjusting and Closing Entries

- Changed chapter introduction company from Best Buy to Disney.
- Added Real World Accounting Video of Jeanette Cebollero, the chief financial officer (CFO) of Rosa Mexicano Restaurants, to set the chapter content in a real world business context for students.

- Animated each hybrid equation example so that students can drill themselves as many times as needed on the interrelationship of the journal entries, t-accounts, and general ledger when posting transactions. Available in the etext only, located in MyAccountingLab.
- Changed 50% of the exercises and problems to provide diverse practice and teaching opportunities for students and teachers.
- Added two questions to the Self Checks that assess student understanding of the Real World Accounting Videos.
- Updated Continuing Financial Statement Analysis featuring Target using the 2012 annual report.
- Designated two Excel problems and exercises that can be automatically graded in MyAccountingLab. These materials are designated by a "Try It In Excel" icon.
- Updated the end of chapter material related to Under Armour and Columbia Sportswear using the 2012 annual reports.

Chapter 4   Accounting for a Merchandising Business

- Changed chapter introduction company from Best Buy to Toys R Us.
- Added Real World Accounting Video of Noah Lenovitz, a partner and chief operating officer of Fishs Eddy, to set the chapter content in a real world business context for students.
- Changed 50% of the exercises and problems to provide diverse practice and teaching opportunities for students and teachers.
- Added two questions to the Self Checks that assess student understanding of the Real World Accounting Videos.
- Updated Continuing Financial Statement Analysis featuring Target using the 2012 annual report.
- Designated two Excel problems and exercises that can be automatically graded in MyAccountingLab. These materials are designated by a "Try It In Excel" icon.
- Updated the end of chapter material related to Under Armour and Columbia Sportswear using the 2012 annual reports.

Chapter 5   Inventory

- Changed chapter introduction company from Best Buy to Toys R Us.
- Added Real World Accounting Video of Keith Beavers, owner and operator of ABC Wines, to set the chapter content in a real world business context for students.
- Changed 50% of the exercises and problems to provide diverse practice and teaching opportunities for students and teachers.
- Added two questions to the Self Checks that assess student understanding of the Real World Accounting Videos.
- Updated Continuing Financial Statement Analysis featuring Target using the 2012 annual report.
- Designated two Excel problems and exercises that can be automatically graded in MyAccountingLab. These materials are designated by a "Try It In Excel" icon.
- Updated the end of chapter material related to Under Armour and Columbia Sportswear using the 2012 annual reports.

Chapter 6   The Challenges of Accounting: Standards, Internal Control, Audits, Fraud, and Ethics

- Added Real World Accounting Video of Vince Molinari, CEO and founder of Gate Technologies, to set the chapter content in a real world business context for students.
- Changed 50% of the exercises and problems to provide diverse practice and teaching opportunities for students and teachers.

- Added two questions to the Self Checks that assess student understanding of the Real World Accounting Videos.
- Updated Continuing Financial Statement Analysis featuring Target using the 2012 annual report.
- Designated two Excel problems and exercises that can be automatically graded in MyAccountingLab. These materials are designated by a "Try It In Excel" icon.
- Updated the end of chapter material related to Under Armour and Columbia Sportswear using the 2012 annual reports.

Chapter 7 Cash and Receivables

- Changed chapter introduction company from Best Buy to Hershey.
- Added Real World Accounting Video of Zachary Mack, owner and founder of Alphabet City Beer Company, to set the chapter content in a real world business context for students.
- Changed 50% of the exercises and problems to provide diverse practice and teaching opportunities for students and teachers.
- Added two questions to the Self Checks that assess student understanding of the Real World Accounting Videos.
- Updated Continuing Financial Statement Analysis featuring Target using the 2012 annual report.
- Designated two Excel problems and exercises that can be automatically graded in MyAccountingLab. These materials are designated by a "Try It In Excel" icon.
- Updated the end of chapter material related to Under Armour and Columbia Sportswear using the 2012 annual reports.

Chapter 8 Long-Term and Other Assets

- Changed chapter introduction company from Best Buy to AT&T.
- Added Real World Accounting Video of Jason Berry of Rosa Mexicano Restaurants to set the chapter content in a real world business context for students.
- Changed 50% of the exercises and problems to provide diverse practice and teaching opportunities for students and teachers.
- Added two questions to the Self Checks that assess student understanding of the Real World Accounting Videos.
- Updated Continuing Financial Statement Analysis featuring Target using the 2012 annual report.
- Designated two Excel problems and exercises that can be automatically graded in MyAccountingLab. These materials are designated by a "Try It In Excel" icon.
- Updated the end of chapter material related to Under Armour and Columbia Sportswear using the 2012 annual reports.

Chapter 9 Current Liabilities and Long-Term Debt

- Changed chapter introduction company from Best Buy to Ford.
- Added Real World Accounting Video of Bill Mercer, Controller of Sheffield Pharmaceuticals, to set the chapter content in a real world business context for students.
- Changed 50% of the exercises and problems to provide diverse practice and teaching opportunities for students and teachers.
- Added two questions to the Self Checks that assess student understanding of the Real World Accounting Videos.
- Updated Continuing Financial Statement Analysis featuring Target using the 2012 annual report.
- Designated two excel problems and exercises that can be automatically graded in MyAccountingLab. These materials are designated by a "Try It In Excel" icon.

- Updated the end of chapter material related to Under Armour and Columbia Sportswear using the 2012 annual reports.

Chapter 10   Corporations: Paid-In Capital and Retained Earnings

- Changed chapter introduction company from Best Buy to Apple.
- Added Real World Accounting Video of Howard Greenstone, President and CEO of Rosa Mexicano Restaurants, to set the chapter content in a real world business context for students.
- Changed 50% of the exercises and problems to provide diverse practice and teaching opportunities for students and teachers.
- Added two questions to the Self Checks that assess student understanding of the Real World Accounting Videos.
- Updated Continuing Financial Statement Analysis featuring Target using the 2012 annual report.
- Designated two Excel problems and exercises that can be automatically graded in MyAccountingLab. These materials are designated by a "Try It In Excel" icon.
- Updated the end of chapter material related to Under Armour and Columbia Sportswear using the 2012 annual reports.

Chapter 11   The Statement of Cash Flows

- Changed chapter introduction company from Best Buy to Delta Airlines.
- Added Real World Accounting Video of Peter Kranes, managing director of Fishs Eddy, to set the chapter content in a real world business context for students.
- Changed 50% of the exercises and problems to provide diverse practice and teaching opportunities for students and teachers.
- Added two questions to the Self Checks that assess student understanding of the Real World Accounting Videos.
- Updated Continuing Financial Statement Analysis featuring Target using the 2012 annual report.
- Designated two Excel problems and exercises that can be automatically graded in MyAccountingLab. These materials are designated by a "Try It In Excel" icon.
- Updated the end of chapter material related to Under Armour and Columbia Sportswear using the 2012 annual reports.
- Added an all new comprehensive problem that would make an excellent capstone problem for the course.

Chapter 12   Financial Statement Analysis

- Added Real World Accounting Video of David Drake of LDJ Capital to set the chapter content in a real world business context for students.
- Changed 50% of the exercises and problems to provide diverse practice and teaching opportunities for students and teachers.
- Added two questions to the Self Checks that assess student understanding of the Real World Accounting Videos.
- Updated Continuing Financial Statement Analysis featuring Target using the 2012 annual report.
- Designated two Excel problems and exercises that can be automatically graded in MyAccountingLab. These materials are designated by a "Try It In Excel" icon.
- Updated the end of chapter material related to Under Armour and Columbia Sportswear using the 2012 annual reports.

Dear Colleagues,

We are very excited about the newest edition of Kemp and Waybright's *Financial Accounting*. After you have had a chance to look at this edition's changes, we think you will be as excited about our latest edition as we are.

Practical Approach: Accounting from a Business Perspective
The goal and focus of the third edition of *Financial Accounting* is all about helping students learn. We believe the text and supporting materials tackle challenging topics in a pragmatic, easily understood manner so that they understand not only accounting but its critical role in the business world. After this course ends, it is our hope that your students will have mastered the basic concepts of financial accounting and can apply them to everyday business decisions.

Execution: Ensuring Student Success
Every feature in *Financial Accounting* is about helping you, the faculty, help your students achieve this goal. Based on our years of teaching, we believe we have created a complete package of instructional materials, using traditional and digital methods. For example, examine how each topic is introduced, explained, and demonstrated. Notice how students not only learn the topic, but also see how it is applied in the real world. Moreover, the end of chapter exercises, problems, and cases, prepared by us, create a progressive and appropriately challenging learning experience. For this edition, we developed more than 15 hybrid equation simulations, so that students can test their understanding of the relationship between the general journal, journal entries, and the impact on the accounting equation. These materials were all crafted carefully to help you ensure that your students have more of those "I get it" moments.

Assessment: Ensuring Your Success
We are first and foremost teachers. It's our passion. We understand the challenges you face as teachers. For example, in order to assure continuity between the text and the assessments, we prepared the test bank and solutions manual. In addition to all the updated, automatically graded homework assignments in MyAccountingLab, we added gradable Excel simulation problems so that you can easily evaluate student performance using Excel.

We love this text. Every day, we see how this text and supporting materials help students learn in and out of the classroom. We believe you too will love this text. We believe you will quickly see how *Financial Accounting*, with all of its supporting materials, creates success in your students.

Thank you for looking at *Financial Accounting*. We believe the third edition of *Financial Accounting* is unique. It's special. We hope you'll look at it, compare it to other books, and think about what is best for your students and you. If you do, we think there is one obvious choice. It's Kemp and Waybright's *Financial Accounting*. It's all about success for you and your students.

Best wishes,

Bob Kemp
Robert S. Kemp, DBA, CPA
Ramon W. Breeden Senior Research Professor
McIntire School of Commerce
The University of Virginia

Jeffrey Waybright
Jeffrey Waybright, CPA, MBA
Accounting Instructor
Spokane Community College

Visual Walk-Through

Chapter Openers
Business, Accounting, and You ties the business concept directly to the accounting topics covered in the chapters using a variety of well-known US and international companies as examples.

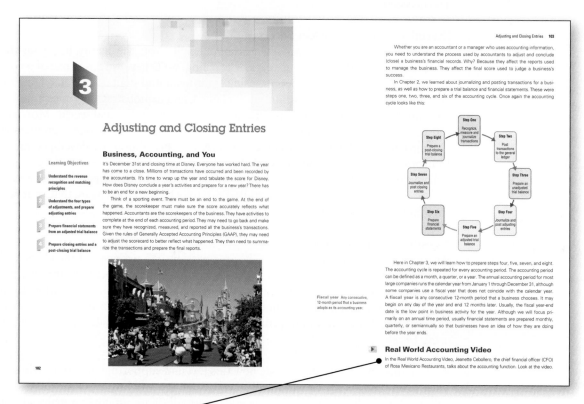

 Real Business Videos
Real Business Videos bring accounting to life in the business world. Denoted by an icon in the chapter openers and developed by the author, interviews with CFOs, financial analysts, investment bankers, and small business owners highlight chapter concepts and help students understand that accounting is the language of business. Self-check questions, two in each chapter, assess student understanding of the real business videos and the concepts illustrated.

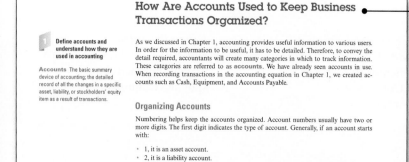

Question & Answer Format mirrors those valuable teachable moments in the classroom when a student asks a question that gets straight to the heart of the topic.

Hybrid Approach Animations
The authors introduce unique hybrid visuals to illustrate the connection between the accounting equation and journalizing transactions. In Chapters 2 and 3 of the eText, students can journalize transactions, create T-Accounts, and test their understanding of the relationship between journal entries and the accounting equation. Eighteen animations will allow students to practice over and over again until they comprehend these critical accounting concepts.

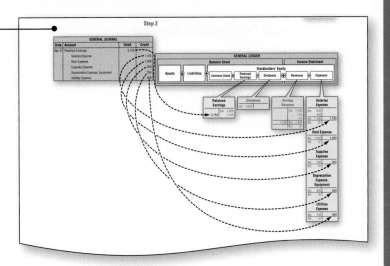

of sales revenue and net income for the second quarter of this year as compared to the second quarter of last year. Brent knew it had been a good quarter, but didn't think it had been spectacular. Suddenly, Brent realized that he failed to close out the revenue and expense accounts for the prior quarter, which ended in March. Because those temporary accounts were not closed out, their balances were included in the second quarter amounts for the current year. Brent then realized that the banker had the financial statements but not the general ledger or any trial balances. Thus, the banker would not be able to see that the accounting cycle from the first quarter was not properly closed and that this failure was creating a misstated income statement for the second quarter of the current year. The banker then commented that the business appeared to be performing so well that he would approve a line of credit for the business. Brent decided to not say anything because he did not want to lose the line of credit. Besides, he thought, it really did not matter that the income statement was misstated because his business would be sure to repay any amounts borrowed.

Should Brent have informed the banker of the mistake made, and should he have redone the second quarter's income statement? Was Brent's failure to close the prior quarter's revenue and expense accounts unethical? Does the fact that the business will repay the loan matter?

Know Your Business

Financial Analysis

Purpose: To help familiarize you with the financial reporting of a real company in order to further your understanding of the chapter material.

This case will help you to better understand the effect of adjusting journal entries on the financial statements. You know that adjusting journal entries are entered in the journal and then posted to the ledger accounts. We do not have access to the journals and ledgers used by Columbia Sportswear, but we can see some of the adjusted accounts on the company's financial statements. Refer to the Columbia Sportswear income statements, "Statements of Operations," and the Columbia Sportswear balance sheets, in Appendix A. Also find footnote 6 titled "Property, Plant, and Equipment, Net" and footnote 9 titled "Accrued Liabilities," which are two of the many footnotes included after the financial statements.

3. Post the journal entries to the T-accounts you set up. Check the updated ending balances in each account against the balances reported by Columbia Sportswear as of December 31, 2012.

Industry Analysis

Purpose: To help you understand and compare the performance of two companies in the same industry.

Go to the Columbia Sportswear Company Annual Report located in Appendix A . Now access the 2012 Annual Report for Under Armour, Inc. For instructions on how to access the report online, see the Industry Analysis in Chapter 1.

Requirement

1. By reviewing the financial statements of both companies, can you determine which method of accounting, cash or accrual basis, each of the companies used? How did you determine this? If one of the companies used the cash basis and the other used the accrual basis, would it affect your ability to compare the two companies? Explain your answer.

Small Business Analysis

Purpose: To help you understand the importance of cash flows in the operation of a small business.

It's the end of the month, and cash flow has been a little slow, as it usually is during this time of the accounting period. It just seems to be a little slower this month. You know that Wednesday the 31st is payday, which always requires a large cash outlay. However, you also know that your bank is looking for a set of financial statements as of the end of the month because the loan on your building is coming up for renewal soon. Based on some of the previous meetings with your bankers, they are always concerned with the cash balance, so you want to have your cash balance as high as possible.

You come up with a tentative plan you believe will not only preserve some of your cash balance at the end of the month but also will help your bottom line, your net income. That's the other thing that the bankers are always concerned about. You don't want to make any mistakes

The Perfect Balance of Small Business Perspective and Corporate Coverage Not every student will graduate and become part of a large corporation, which is why it's important for students to understand how financial accounting applies in small business scenarios as well as corporate ones.

Focus On Decision Making

How Does Accounting Report Business Transactions?

Think of the school you are attending. What are some of the transactions that are conducted every day at your school? How would the following transactions be recorded? Make sure you think through each of these transactions and understand that you need to acknowledge the total transaction.

1. You enroll in class and pay the school your tuition.
2. Your school hires your teacher, who teaches your class.
3. Your school pays the utilities that make your classroom comfortable.
4. You buy a ticket to an athletic event, concert, or other special activity.
5. Your school pays for advertising to promote the athletic event, concert, or other special activity.

Managers need good information about all the aspects of a business transaction. They need accounting systems to recognize, measure, record, and report the entire transaction. Financial statements must report the total transaction and how everything in a business works together.

How They Do It: A Look at Business

Businesses produce income by using assets financed with money. Think about Target, the large discount retailer. Target buys and sells goods such as clothing, groceries, electronics, and toys. Target sells these goods in large buildings. To earn more net income, Target tries to sell more goods. However, as sales increase, Target needs more assets. The more assets Target has, the more financing it needs. It needs money to finance the growing amount of clothing, groceries, electronics, and toys it sells. It also needs money to finance new and bigger buildings. Target gets this money from either borrowing the money (which increases Target's liabilities) or from its owners (stockholders' equity). For the year ended February 2, 2013, Target had revenues of $73.3 billion, expenses of $70.3 billion, and net income of $3 billion. As of February 2, 2013, Target had assets of $48.2 billion. These assets were financed with liabilities of $31.6 billion and stockholders' equity of $16.6 billion. As can be seen by comparing its 2012 and 2013 financial statements, Target grew its assets. For the year ended January 28, 2012, Target had revenues of $69.9 billion, expenses of $66.9 billion, and net income of $3 billion. As of January 28, 2012, Target had assets of $46.6 billion, liabilities of $30.8 billion, and stockholders equity of $15.8 billion. Target increased its assets, and thus its financing, in hopes of seeing net income increase in the future.

Focus on Decision Making shows students how to make financially sound business decisions and to evaluate risk and the impact of those decisions on a company.

Decision Guidelines focus students on the key business decisions that require a firm understanding of the accounting concepts in each chapter. UPDATED!

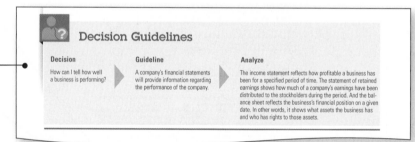

Decision Guidelines

Decision	Guideline	Analyze
How can I tell how well a business is performing?	A company's financial statements will provide information regarding the performance of the company.	The income statement reflects how profitable a business has been for a specified period of time. The statement of retained earnings shows how much of a company's earnings have been distributed to the stockholders during the period. And the balance sheet reflects the business's financial position on a given date. In other words, it shows what assets the business has and who has rights to those assets.

a. Record the expired rent.
b. Supplies on hand, $250.
c. Depreciation; $180 equipment, $50 furniture, $420 vehicles.
d. Services performed but unbilled, $2,200.
e. Accrued salaries, $625.
f. Unearned service revenue earned as of July 31, $1,100.

5. Prepare an adjusted trial balance for Aqua Magic, Inc., at the end of July.
6. Prepare the income statement and statement of retained earnings for the three-month period May 1 through July 31, 2014. Also prepare a balance sheet at July 31, 2014.
7. Prepare and post closing entries.
8. Prepare a post-closing trial balance at July 31, 2014.

Continuing Financial Statement Analysis Problem

Let's look at Target again. Think about the business of Target. Now return to that place on Target's website called "investor relations." Look at Target's 2012 financial statements contained in its 2012 annual report. Go to: *http://investors.target.com/phoenix.zhtml?c=65828&p=irol-reportsAnnual.* On page 33 of the financial statements, you'll find Target's income statement for the year ending February 2, 2013 (called the Consolidate Statement of Operations). On page 35, you'll find Target's balance sheet as of February 2, 2013 (called the Consolidated Statement of Financial Position). On page 37, you'll find Target's statement of retained earnings for the year ending February 2, 2013. It's a part of Target's statement titled Consolidated Statements of Shareholders' Investment. Now answer the following questions:

1. Look at Target's income statement. Is Target profitable? Does it have a positive net income or a negative net income (loss) for the year ending February 2, 2013? How does that compare with the year ending February 2, 2013?
2. Look at Target's statement of shareholders' investment. How does Target's net income flow into its balance sheet?
3. Look at Target's balance sheet. What assets does Target own? How much has Target invested in each type of assets and in total assets?
4. Look at Target's balance sheet. How does Target finance its assets? How much liabilities and shareholders' equity does Target have?

Continuing Financial Statement Analysis Problem uses Target's 2012 annual report to familiarize students with reading and interpreting financial statements in each chapter. By the end of the text, they have completely analyzed the financial statements.

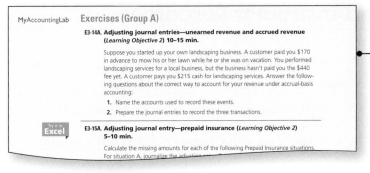

MyAccountingLab | **Exercises (Group A)**

E3-14A. Adjusting journal entries—unearned revenue and accrued revenue (*Learning Objective 2*) **10–15 min.**

Suppose you started up your own landscaping business. A customer paid you $170 in advance to mow his or her lawn while he or she was on vacation. You performed landscaping services for a local business, but the business hasn't paid you the $440 fee yet. A customer pays you $215 cash for landscaping services. Answer the following questions about the correct way to account for your revenue under accrual-basis accounting:

1. Name the accounts used to record these events.

2. Prepare the journal entries to record the three transactions.

E3-15A. Adjusting journal entry—prepaid insurance (*Learning Objective 2*) **5–10 min.**

Calculate the missing amounts for each of the following Prepaid Insurance situations. For situation A, journalize the adjusting entry.

End of Chapter 50% of problems and exercises (A and B sets) have been revised.

Test Bank and Solutions Manual prepared by author, Jeffrey Waybright.

Problems (Group B)

P3-48B. Common adjusting journal entries (*Learning Objective 2*) **15–20 min.**

Journalize the adjusting entries needed at December 31, the end of the current accounting year, for each of the following independent cases affecting Mountain Mania, Inc. No other adjusting entries have been made for the year.

a. Prior to making the adjusting entry on December 31, the balance in Prepaid Insurance is $1,200. Mountain Mania, Inc., pays liability insurance each year on April 30.

b. Mountain Mania, Inc., pays employees each Friday. The amount of the weekly payroll is $12,500 for a five-day workweek. December 31, the fiscal year-end, is a Monday.

c. Mountain Mania, Inc., received notes receivable from some customers for services provided. For the current year, accrued interest amounts to $640 and will be collected next year.

NEW!

EXCEL® in MyAccountingLab

- Now students can get real-world Excel practice in their classes.
- Instructors have the option to assign students selected end-of-chapter questions that can be completed in an Excel-simulated environment.
- Questions will be auto-graded and reported to and visible in the grade book.
- Excel remediation will be available to students.

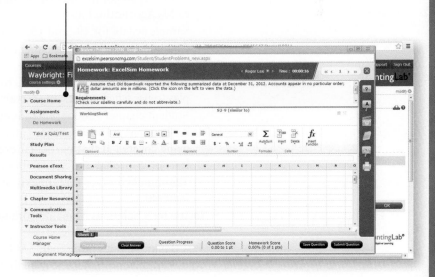

Student and Instructor Resources

MyAccountingLab

For Students

myaccountinglab.com online Homework and Assessment Manager

- Pearson eText
- Data Files
- Videos
- Demo Docs
- Working Papers

- Audio and Student PowerPoint® Presentations
- Accounting Cycle Tutorial
- MP3 Files with Chapter Objectives and Summaries
- Flash Cards

Student resource Web site: pearsonhighered.com/kemp

The book's Web site contains the following:

- Data Files: Select end-of-chapter problems have been set up in different software applications, including Excel, QuickBooks 2012, and General Ledger software.
- Working Papers

MyAccountingLab

For Instructors

myaccountinglab.com online Homework and Assessment Manager

For the instructor's convenience, the instructor resources can be downloaded from the textbook's catalog page (pearsonhighered.com/kemp) and MyAccountingLab. Available resources include the following:

- **Online Instructor's Manual:** Includes chapter summaries and the additional resources below:
    - Introduction to the Instructor's Manual with a list of resources and a roadmap to help navigate what's available in MyAccountingLab.
    - Instructor tips for teaching courses in multiple formats—traditional, hybrid, or online.
    - "First Day of Class" student handout that includes tips for success in the course, as well as an additional document that shows students how to register and log on to MyAccountingLab
    - Sample syllabi for 10- and 16-week courses.
    - Chapter overview and teaching outline that includes a brief synopsis and overview of each chapter.
    - Key topics that walk instructors through what material to cover and what examples to use when addressing certain items within the chapter.
    - Student chapter summary handout.
    - Assignment grid that outlines all end-of-chapter exercises and problems, the topic being covered in that particular exercise or problem, estimated completion time, level of difficulty, and availability in Excel templates.
    - Ten-minute quizzes that quickly assess students' understanding of the chapter material.
- **Instructor's Solutions Manual:** Contains solutions to all end-of-chapter questions, including short exercises, exercises, and problems.
- **Test Bank:** Includes more than 3,000 questions. Both objective-based questions and computational problems are available.

- **PowerPoint Presentations:** These presentations help facilitate classroom discussion by demonstrating where the numbers come from and what they mean to the concept at hand. Includes NEW Demonstration Problem slides.
  - Instructor PowerPoint Presentations—complete with lecture notes
  - Student PowerPoint Presentations
  - Audio Narrated PowerPoint Presentations
  - Clicker Response System (CRS) PowerPoint Presentations
- **Working Papers and Solutions in Excel and PDF Format.**
- **Image Library.**
- **Data and Solution Files:** Select end-of-chapter problems have been set up in different software applications, including QuickBooks 2012 and General Ledger. Corresponding solution files are also provided.

Acknowledgments

Thank you to Mignon Tucker for all of her hard work and support, Jill Kolongowski for her dedication to the supplements, and Linda Hajek for her careful eye and in grateful appreciation to you, our colleagues and reviewers:

Reviewers

The authors gratefully acknowledge the following reviewers of all editions of this text for their insightful comments and suggestions:

Dawn Addington, Central New Mexico Community College
Gary Adna, Ames Brigham Young University–Idaho
Sheila Ammons, Austin Community College
John Babich, Kankakee Community College
Beverly Beatty, Anne Arundel Community College
George Bernard, Seminole Community College
Joseph Berry, Campbell University
Swati Bhandarkar, University of Georgia
Donald Bond, Texas Southern University
Anna Boulware, St. Charles Community College
Amy Bourne, Oregon State University
Dr. Linda Bressler, University of Houston–Downtown
Jerold Braun, Daytona State College
Robert Braun, Southeastern Louisiana University
Kathleen Brenan, Ashland University
Molly Brown, James Madison University
Nina Brown, Tarrant County College, Northwest Campus
Ann K. Brooks, University of New Mexico
Kelley Butler, Ivy Tech Community College Lafayette
Marci L. Butterfield, University of Utah
Ernest Carraway, North Carolina State University
Sandra Cereola, James Madison University
Dr. Joan A. Cezair, Fayetteville State University
Yunhao Chen, Florida International University
Bea Chiang, the College of New Jersey
Leslie Cohen, University of Arizona
Barry N. Cooper, Borough of Manhattan Community College (BMCC)
Dori Danko, Grand Valley State University
John Daugherty, Pitt Community College
Vaun Day, Central Arizona College
Patricia Doherty, Boston University School of Management
Jimmy Dong, Sacramento City College
Jap Efendi, University of Texas at Arlington
Robert S Ellison, Texas State University–San Marcos

Kim Everett, East Carolina University
Janice Fergusson, University of South Carolina
Patricia Feller, Nashville State Community College
Richard Filler, Franklin University
Calvin Fink, Bethune-Cookman University
Philip Fink, University of Toledo
Linda Flowers, Houston Community College
Donald Foster, Tacoma Community College
Brenda Fowler, Alamance Community College
Donna Free, Oakland University
Andy Garcia, Bowling Green State University
Lisa Gillespie, Loyola University–Chicago
Marina Grau, Houston Community College
Ann Gregory, South Plains College
Anthony Greig, Purdue University
Michael Gurevitz, Montgomery College
Patrick A. Haggerty, Lansing Community College
Becky Hancock, El Paso Community College
Bowe Hansen, University of New Hampshire
Jerry W. Hanwell, Robert Morris University
Rob Hochschild, Ivy Tech Community College
Marsha Huber, Youngstown State University
Carol Hutchinson, AB Tech
Frank Ilett, Boise State University
Janice Klimek, University of Central Missouri
Jerry Kreuze, Western Michigan University
Ron Lazer, University of Houston
Patsy Lee, University of Texas at Arlington
Patti Lopez, Valencia Community College
Donald Lucy, Indian River State College
Lois S. Mahoney, Eastern Michigan University
Diane Marker, University of Toledo
Jim Martin, Washburn University
Michele Martinez, Hillsborough Community College
Suzanne McCaffrey, University of Mississippi
Bruce McClain, Cleveland State University
Florence McGovern, Bergen Community College
Heidi H. Meier, Cleveland State University
Terri Meta, Seminole Community College
Jeanine Metzler, Northampton Community College
Melanie Middlemist, Colorado State University
Susan Minke, Indiana Purdue University at Ft Wayne
Birendra Mishra, University of California Riverside
Earl Mitchell, Santa Ana College
Carol A. Murphy, Quinsigamond Community College
Khursheed Omer, University of Houston–Downtown
Deborah Pauly, Loras College
Sandra Pelfrey, Oakland University
Stanley M. Quon, Sacramento City College
Allan M Rabinowitz, Pace University
Judy Ramage, Lawrence Christian Brothers University
Rama Ramamurthy, College of William & Mary
Nancy Rochman, University of Arizona
Patrick Rogan, Cosumnes River College
Miles Romney, University of San Diego

Louis Rosamilia, Hudson Valley Community College
Christine Schalow, University of Wisconsin–Stevens Point
Tracy Schmeltzer, Wayne Community College
Randy Serrett, University of Houston–Downtown
Sheila Shain, Santa Ana College
Carol Shaver, Louisiana Tech University
Margaret L. Shelton, University of Houston–Downtown
Lily Sieux, California State University East Bay
Joanie Sompayrac, UT–Chattanooga
Nancy Snow, University of Toledo
Dennis Spector, Naugatuck Valley Community College
Barbara Squires, Corning Community College
Rick Street, Spokane Community College
Joe Standridge, Sonoma State University
Dennis Stovall, Grand Valley State University
Gloria Stuart, Georgia Southern University
Gracelyn Stuart-Tuggle, Palm Beach State College
Karen Sturm, Loras College
Ellen L. Sweatt, Georgia Perimeter College
Jan Sweeney, Baruch College CUNY
William Talbot, Montgomery College
Pavani Tallapally, Slippery Rock University
Samantha Ternes, Kirkwood Community College
Peter Theuri, Northern Kentucky University
Steven Thoede, Texas State University–San Marcos
Robin E. Thomas, North Carolina State University
Jack Topiol, Community College of Philadelphia
Jinhee Trone, Santa Ana College
John Trussel, University of West Florida
Terri Walsh, Seminole State College of Florida
Suzanne Ward, University of Louisiana at Lafayette
Marvin Williams, University of Houston–Downtown
Jan Workman, East Carolina University
Christian Wurst Jr., Temple University
James Yang, Montclair State University
Laura Young, University of Central Arkansas
Judith Zander, Grossmont College

Supplements Authors and Reviewers

Courtney Baillie, Nebraska Wesleyan University
Cheryl Bartlett, Central New Mexico Community College
Michelle Berube, Corinthian Colleges
Nabanita Bhattacharya, Northwest Florida State College
Robert Braun, Southern Louisiana University
Laurie Hays, Western Michigan University
Dr. Anna Lusher, Slippery Rock University School of Business
Michelle Maggio, Westfield State College
Donna Mallery, Florida State College at Jacksonville, Kent Campus
Sucharita Mandal, ansrsource
Diane Marker, University of Toledo
Jamie McCracken, Saint Mary-of-the-Woods College
Allan Sheets, International Business College
Ferdinand Siagian, Minnesota State University
Rick Street, Spokane Community College

Samantha Ternes, Kirkwood Community College
Nagaraj VL, ansrsource
Judith Zander, Grossmont College
Bob Kemp and Jeffrey Waybright would especially like to thank the individuals below for their support and guidance throughout the project:
Lacey Vitetta
Alison Haskins
Karen Kirincich
Roberta Sherman
Jeff Holcomb
Anthony Gemmellaro
Jill Kolongowski
Michele Somody
Mignon Tucker, Brava 360° Solutions

Financial Accounting

Business, Accounting, and You

Business, Accounting, and You

You are about to study accounting. What is accounting, and why is it so important? Why does the study of business typically start with accounting?

Accounting is the language of business. Can you think of living in a foreign country and not being able to read and speak the native language? It would be very hard. Accounting is the process business people use to communicate what they've been doing. To be successful in business, you need to be able to understand, speak, and use the language of business.

In addition to being the language of business, accounting is the scorekeeping aspect of business. Think of the last sporting event you watched or played in. Can you imagine the end of the game without someone saying who scored, when they scored, and even how they scored? Accounting lets business managers know if they are winning or losing.

Learning Objectives

1. Understand the nature of business and the role of accounting in business

2. Know how a business operates

3. Know the different types and forms of businesses

4. Know the key accounting principles and concepts

5. Know how accounting functions in a business

6. Understand and be able to prepare basic financial statements

Accounting is at the heart of business. Whether you become an accountant or a business manager, understanding the foundation and process of accounting is critical to your success. If you are to be successful in business, your success starts with accounting. At the beginning of each chapter in the section *Business, Accounting, and You*, we will focus on how accounting keeps track of a business's transactions and helps you, as a manager, make good business decisions.

 Real World Accounting Video

In the Real World Accounting Video, David Hitchner, owner and manager of ABC Wine, talks about what it means to own and operate a business. Look at the video. Think about what David is saying. And then realize how important accounting is to the success of a business.

What Is a Business, and Why Study Accounting?

1 Understand the nature of business and the role of accounting in business

Accounting Accounting is the process of recognizing, measuring, recording, and reporting information about a business's transactions.

You want to be successful in business. But why study accounting? The answer is what accounting reveals. **Accounting** is the process of recognizing, measuring, recording, and reporting information about a business's transactions. Understanding accounting enables you to recognize and understand business transactions. Understanding business transactions enables you to manage them successfully.

Think about going to a sporting event where you know nothing about the sport. You would probably have many questions. Your questions might include:

- What is the objective of this sport?
- Who are the players, and what are they doing to compete?
- How do players win or lose the competition?
- Who keeps score, and how is the score kept?

Business is a competition. Businesses compete for customers, employees, profits, and much more. To successfully compete in business you need to understand the objective of business, the players and their roles in business, the rules of business, and who keeps score and how it is kept.

If accounting is the scorekeeper of business, let's first talk about the game of business. When you look at business, you see people and organizations creating, producing, and selling products. Businesses, both for-profit and not-for-profit businesses, are everywhere. But have you ever stopped and thought about business? Think about it. What is a business? Why does a business exist? How does a business operate?

Business A business is a legal organization that attempts to create value by exchanging products with customers for money.

Product A good or service purchased or produced by a business to be sold.

Goods A good is a physical item that can be touched and felt. Goods are tangible.

The Definition of a Business

A **business** is a legal organization that attempts to create value by exchanging products with customers for money. An organization must have three elements to be called a business:

1. *Businesses are legal entities.* Businesses are empowered to operate by the law.

2. *A business must exchange a **product**,* often referred to as either a good or a service, for money or money substitutes.

    a. **Goods** are physical items that we can touch and feel. Goods are tangible. Examples include food, cars, and clothing.

Services A service is an activity that exists but cannot be touched and felt. Services are intangible.

b. Services are activities that we know exist but we cannot touch and feel. Services are intangible. Examples include medical services, car repairs, and education.

However, providing products is not sufficient criteria for a business to be called a business. Someone must buy these products for money or money substitutes (for example, a receivable or promise to pay later). So who buys the products for money or money substitutes? The answer is **customers**. To succeed, a business must create an exchange with a customer. The exchange is called a **sale**.

Customer A person or organization that purchases a product from a business.

Sale The exchange between a business and customer where the business provides a customer a product and the business receives money or money substitutes.

3. *Businesses create value.* Customers get value from the benefits of a product. However, the other stakeholders in a business should also receive value. Owners get value from the profits a business earns. Employees get value from their wages. Lenders get value from the interest they charge.

The purpose of any business is to create and increase value. In a for-profit business, this value is often measured as the market price of the business, or what you'd pay if you wanted to buy and own the business.[1] All too often people assume that a business exists to create products, sales, profits, and jobs. All these things are important; however, the purpose of a business is to create value. So what is value? What determines value? How does value differ from profit?

The General Concept of Value

Value The price someone is willing to pay for an item.

The **value** of an item is what someone is willing to pay for it. As such, value depends on:

1. What the owner of an item expects to receive.

2. When the owner expects to receive it.

3. How certain the owner is about what he or she will receive and when it will be received.

For example, imagine you plan to cook a very special dinner tonight with a very special person. You need groceries. Where do you go? You think of a grocery store such as Kroger. It's late in the day, and you need food now. You are certain that Kroger will have the food you want and need. So what are you doing? You are entering into an exchange with Kroger. Kroger will provide you food and you will pay Kroger money.

When we go to make an exchange, we seek an exchange *where the value we receive exceeds the value that we give up*. In other words, we want a "good deal." In the Kroger example, you go to the store and ask the grocer how much you would pay for its food. If you believe the value of Kroger's food is greater than the value of the money you must pay, you agree to the exchange. If you believe the value of Kroger's food is less than the value of the money you must pay, you keep your money and do not agree to the exchange. You're basically comparing the value of the food and the value of the money, seeking the greatest value for yourself.

Cost The amount of money or money substitutes that a business pays to receive an item used in operating a business.

Revenue The amount of money or money substitutes that a business receives from the sale of a product.

Profit The revenue from a sale less the cost of the sale.

Businesses behave in the same way. A business attempts to create value by exchanging a product with a customer. Businesses buy or make products at one value (**cost**) and try to sell these products to their customers at a higher value (**revenue**). This exchange creates a **profit** (net benefit) to the business. An example of this is Kroger's grocery business. If done well, Kroger makes a profit by paying less for the food (cost) than it charges you for the food (revenue). Making a profit is very important in a for-profit business and

---

[1]For-profit businesses attempt to earn a profit. The concept of profit is discussed later. Examples of for-profit businesses are Target, Southwest Airlines, and many smaller businesses in your community. Not-for-profit businesses attempt to break even, neither experiencing a profit or loss. Examples of not-for-profit businesses are charities, government, and religious organizations. This text will focus on for-profit businesses. However, many of the concepts discussed are applicable to not-for-profit businesses.

drives the value of the business. Accountants are responsible for measuring revenue, costs, and profits.

In addition to the amount of profit, businesspeople also worry about *when* they make a profit and the *risk* they take to generate a profit. As we'll see in later chapters, the old adage that "time is money" is true. Time does affect the value of an item. The quicker a business like Kroger earns a profit, the more valuable it is. The longer a business takes to earn a profit, the less valuable it is. Think about it. Would you pay extra to have Kroger prepare your special meal? The answer is probably yes, given that it is late in the day. As we'll see throughout the book, accountants worry about *when* to recognize business transactions such as revenue, cost, and profit.

Risk Risk is the uncertainty that could result in an outcome not desired.

Risk is also important. **Risk** is the uncertainty that an outcome we do not expect or desire could result. An example is Kroger's success. Do the owners of Kroger know that their business will succeed? The answer is they hope and believe Kroger will succeed but are not certain of its success. Think about Kroger's grocery business. What happens if you and others do not buy Kroger's food? Kroger incurs a **loss**, where revenue is less than cost. If Kroger continues to lose money, it will fail. Risk hurts value. Businesspeople must recognize, understand, measure, and manage risk. To compensate for taking a risk, businesses expect higher profits. Accountants help managers and other decision makers understand risk with accounting information. An example of such accounting information is whether a business can pay its debts on time or at all. In every chapter, specifically in Chapter 12, Financial Statement Analysis, we'll see how accounting information helps managers and other stakeholders understand risk.

Loss A loss is a negative profit, which occurs when the cost of a sale is greater than the revenue from the sale.

Business Owners and Other Stakeholders

Stakeholder A stakeholder is a person or organization that is affected by a business.

A business has many **stakeholders**, or people and organizations that are affected by a business. These stakeholders include customers, employees, suppliers, regulators, society, lenders, and owners. All stakeholders are important. All stakeholders should believe that they are receiving value from the business. In other words, each of the stakeholders in a business gives and receives value through an exchange. Ideally, each stakeholder believes that the value he or she receives exceeds the value he or she gives up. An employee gives a business his or her labor for a paycheck. A supplier sells products to a business, ideally at a profit. A customer buys a product from a business at a price. Society, and regulators appointed by society, benefit from a business through jobs, taxes, and hopefully a better quality of life. In a free-market economy, all stakeholders are free to enter into an exchange, are important, and should not be taken for granted.

However, the providers of money are free to provide their money as they deem appropriate. Nobody forces a bank to make a loan to a business. Nobody forces an owner to put money in a business. There is an old saying that goes "It takes money to make money." What that means is it takes money to form and operate a business. To attract that money, lenders and owners must believe they will receive value greater than they give.

The Goal of a Business

The goal of a business is to create value for its owners. Owners expect a profit that compensates them for the use of their money over time and for the risk they assume. If the business does not create value, owners will not provide the money needed to operate the business. Without the business, customers, suppliers, employees, and society will not receive the value they seek. A business must create value for its owners. However, to do so, owners must appreciate that the other stakeholders must also receive value.

So if the objective of the firm is to create value, and we need to focus on creating value for owners, how does a business create value for its owners? How does a business generate profits, over time, at risk?

How Does a Business Operate?

2 **Know how a business operates**

Operating a business is not simple or easy. It takes a lot of resources. It also takes the ability to use those resources wisely. So what are the resources a business needs, and how does a business use those resources to generate profits, over time and at risk?

Resources Needed to Start and Operate a Business

To operate, businesses need to acquire money and use that money to make a profit. A firm acquires money by:

Liabilities A liability is an amount owed to a lender or other creditor.

Stockholders' equity Money provided to the business by owners either through an initial investment or the retention of profits, also known as **owners' equity**.

1. Borrowing money from lenders (called **liabilities**).

2. Getting owners to put in their money (called **owners'** or **stockholders' equity**) in exchange for a percentage of ownership.

A liability is a financial claim, or debt, that the business owes to a party that is not an owner of the business. Owners' equity represents money provided to the business by owners, either through an initial investment or the retention of profits. Often people will say the owners *invested* their money in the business.

Operating the Business

Asset An economic resource that a business owns and can use to operate the business.

Employees People, hired by a business, for a period of time to operate the business.

Expense Money or other value surrendered due to the sale of goods or services or the operating of the business.

Interest The expense of using borrowed money for a period of time.

Net income Operating profit less interest expense, computed as revenue, less operating expenses, less interest expense.

A business then uses the money to acquire assets and hire people. An **asset** is an economic resource that a business owns and can use to operate the business. Assets include cash, inventory, and buildings. The business also hires people, called **employees**, to operate the business for a period of time.

With the assets and employees, the business operates in hope of generating a profit, where revenue is greater than expenses. Remember, revenue is money or other value received that a business earns from the sale of goods or services. **Expenses**, often referred to as costs, are money or other value surrendered from the operating of the business. Part of operating the business is making sure lenders are paid interest. **Interest** is the expense of using borrowed money for a period of time.

After paying interest and other expenses, the owners of the business get what remains, referred to as profit or **net income**. Net income is revenue, less expenses (including interest expense).[2]

Net Income = Revenue − Expenses

---

[2]A business must also pay taxes. Taxes are an expense that will be explored later in this book. Net income is what is left after a business recognizes its tax expense and other expenses.

The question that owners must ask is whether the net income is worth the time and risk involved. Owners have many alternative uses for their money. They, like everyone else, seek the greatest value or return on their money.

Let's look at a simple example. You start a computer repair business. You invest $1,000 in your business, which will be used to start the business and is called owner's equity. You expect net income of $100, or a 10% return on your money ($100/$1000). However, you need $2,000 to start your business. You need equipment and other assets that cost you $2,000. So you go to a bank and ask to borrow $1,000 for one year. The bank looks at your loan application and agrees to lend you $1,000. However, for the time and risk associated with your loan, the bank requires you to pay simple interest of 6%. Thus, in one year you are required to repay the $1,000 loan plus $60 (6%) interest, or a total of $1,060. You borrow the $1,000 from the bank, combine it with your $1,000 equity, and start your business.

After one year, you close and liquidate the business. You are proud of your business because you have worked hard. You had revenue of $500, expenses such as supplies and rent of $400, and interest expense of $60 (6% × $1,000). You made net income of $40 ($500 − $400 − $60 = $40). The revenue from these sales exceeded the expenses by $40. How do you feel? Net income of $40 is good, but is it good enough? Would you have invested your $1,000 in the business if you thought you would only earn net income of $40?

The Cost of Money

Creating value is more than just generating net income by selling a product. Money has a cost. Businesses get money by borrowing it or having owners provide it. If a business borrows money, it must pay the lender rent on the money, called interest. It must also return the borrowed money at an agreed-upon time in the future. However, owners' money also has a cost. Owners are not going to provide their money without expecting to receive a benefit, or return, over time. Why should they? Why would an owner put money in a business for no return when they could deposit their money in a bank and earn interest? Never forget that money, whether borrowed or provided by owners, has a cost. The cost of the money is dependent on many things, but above all else is a function of the risk the lender or owner is taking. Remember, great risk must be compensated by great return.

We just learned that a business first acquires money from lenders (liabilities) and owners (equity). Lenders require the business to pay interest plus return the money they borrow. Owners expect to receive a benefit or return. This benefit or return is based on net income. Then a business uses the money to hire employees and acquire assets. Next, the employees use the assets to generate net income. If successful, the net income is equal to or exceeds the net income expected by owners. When it does, value for the owners is created. When it does not, value for the owners is destroyed.

How Are Businesses Organized?

3 **Know the different types and forms of businesses**

There are many types and forms of business organizations. The type of business relates to what it does to create value or, in other words, make a profit. The form of business organization relates to how it is legally organized.

The Types of Businesses

Businesses are typically divided into two broad categories, for-profit businesses and not-for-profit businesses. In this book, we'll focus on for-profit businesses that operate as corporations.

For-profit business A business that attempts to create an exchange, or sale, where revenue exceeds expenses, creating a profit.

- **For-profit businesses** attempt to create an exchange or sale where revenue exceeds expenses, creating a profit. Examples of for-profit businesses are Kroger, Facebook, Ford, Walmart, and Apple.

Not-for-profit business A business that attempts to create an exchange or sale where revenue equals costs.

Service business A business that sells a service to its customers.

Merchandise business A business that sells physical goods or products to its customers.

Manufacturing business A business that produces the physical goods that it sells to its customers.

Wholesale business A business that sells products to other businesses for resale.

Retail business A business that sells products to the final consumer of the product.

- **Not-for-profit businesses** attempt to create an exchange or sale where revenue equals costs. Examples of not-for-profit businesses are charities like The Red Cross or Habitat for Humanity, religious organizations, and governments. Although not-for-profit businesses are not the focus of this book, many of the principles and techniques discussed in this book also apply to not-for-profit businesses.

Within these two broad categories of business, there are three types of businesses: **service businesses**, **merchandising businesses**, and **manufacturing businesses**.

- A service business sells services to its customers. In other words, what it sells is time. Common types of service businesses include law firms, accounting firms, physical therapy offices, painting companies, and automotive repair shops.
- A merchandise business sells physical goods or products to its customers. Common types of merchandise businesses include grocery stores, automobile dealerships, and sporting goods stores. A merchandise business may be either a wholesale business or a retail business. A **wholesale business** is a business that sells products to other businesses for resale. The business that sells food products to a grocery store is an example of a wholesale business. A **retail business** is a business that sells products to the final consumer of the product. Target, Macy's, and Kroger are examples of retail businesses.
- A manufacturing business produces the physical goods that it sells to its customers. Common types of manufacturing businesses include automobile manufacturers, the makers of clothing, and soft drink manufacturers.

The Legal Forms of Businesses

A business can be legally organized as a sole proprietorship, partnership, corporation, or limited liability company. Most businesses in the United States are sole proprietorships. However, most business transactions are conducted in and among corporations. Why? The answer is most large businesses like Kroger, Facebook, Ford, Apple, and Target are corporations. But how do you know what type of business organization is best for your business?

Sole proprietorship A business entity that has one owner, where, for legal and tax purposes, the business and the owner are considered the same.

Partnership A business that has more than one owner, where, for legal and tax purposes, the business and the owners are considered the same.

Corporation A legal entity, chartered under state law, that is empowered to conduct business. The corporation and owners are considered as separate for legal and tax purposes.

Stockholder An owner of part of a corporation.

Dividend The payment of past and current profits, less losses, previously retained in the business.

- A **sole proprietorship** is a business entity that has one owner. For legal purposes and for tax purposes, the business and the owner are considered the same. The business owner is personally responsible or liable for all of the debts and obligations of the business. If somebody wants to sue the business, he or she would have to sue the owner. In addition, all of the income or loss generated by the business is reported on the owner's personal tax return and taxed at individual rates.
- A **partnership** is very similar to a sole proprietorship except that it has two or more owners. For legal purposes, the owners (partners) and the business are considered the same. If somebody sues the business, he or she would need to sue the business owners. For tax purposes, the partners divide all of the income or loss of the partnership and report it on their personal tax returns. Therefore, it is taxed at individual tax rates just like a sole proprietorship.
- A **corporation** differs from a sole proprietorship or a partnership because it is a separate legal entity from the owners. The business is incorporated under the laws of a state. When you see the abbreviation "Corp." for "Corporation" or "Inc." for "Incorporated," the business is a corporation. The owners of a corporation and the corporation itself are considered as separate under the law. This legal separation is very attractive to the business owners because it limits their personal liability to what they have invested in the corporation. The corporation's debts and obligations are not the debts and obligations of the owners. For tax purposes, the corporation is taxed as a separate entity from the owners. Therefore, income tax is imposed on the income of the corporation at corporate tax rates. If the business chooses to pay owners, called **stockholders**, any of the current or past net income, the business will pay a **dividend**. Stockholders must pay a tax on the dividends they receive. In effect, the income is taxed twice, double taxing the business owners. Many business

S-corporation A small corporation that has met the legal requirements to act as a corporation but elected to be taxed at individual rates.

Limited liability company A hybrid business entity having characteristics of both a *corporation* and a *partnership*.

owners desire to have the legal protection that the corporate form of organization offers. Owners can only lose what they have invested. They thus have limited liability. But they do not want to be subject to the "double taxation" that also occurs. Owners of small corporations are able to make an **S-corporation** election, which allows them to have limited liability and be taxed at individual rates, eliminating the double taxation.

- A **limited liability company** is a relatively new form of business organization. When you see the letters "LLC," the business is a limited liability company. The owners of a limited liability company enjoy the same legal separation that a corporation provides. For tax purposes, a limited liability company's income is treated similar to a sole proprietorship or a partnership. All of the income of the limited liability company is divided among the owners and is taxed at their personal rates. In many ways, a limited liability company is similar to an S-corporation. However, unlike an S-corporation, a limited liability company can be very flexible in how it distributes earnings among the owners.

Exhibit 1-1 summarizes the different types of business organizations.

Type of Business	Legal Status	Tax Status	Benefits	Drawbacks
Sole Proprietorship	Business and owner are considered to be the same entity	Business income is allocated to the owner and taxed at owner's personal tax rate	• Ease of formation • No double taxation	• Unlimited liability of owner • Difficult to raise capital • Limited life
Partnership	Business and owners are considered to be the same entity	Business income is allocated to the owners and taxed at owners' personal tax rates	• Ease of formation • No double taxation • Shared investment/knowledge	• Unlimited liability of owners • Disagreements between partners • Limited life
Corporation	Business and owners are considered to be **separate** entities	Business income is taxed at corporate tax rates. Any income distributed to the owners is also taxed at owners' personal tax rates. Also referred to as a C-corporation.	• Limited liability of owners • Easier to raise capital • Unlimited life	• More difficult and costly to form • Double taxation • More paperwork • More regulations
S-corporation	Business and owners are considered to be **separate** entities	Business income is allocated to the owners and taxed at owners' personal tax rates	• Limited liability of owners • No double taxation • Easier to raise capital • Unlimited life	• More difficult and costly to form • More paperwork • More regulations
Limited Liability Company	Business and owners are considered to be **separate** entities	Business income is allocated to the owners and taxed at owners' personal tax rates	• Limited liability of owners • No double taxation • More flexibility than with S-corporation	• More difficult and costly to form • Limited life

Exhibit 1-1 ▲

Although the process of accounting for the different types of business organizations is similar, there are slight variations depending on the type of organization. In this book, we will focus our attention on accounting for corporations.

Decision Guidelines

Decision	**Guideline**	**Analyze**

Decision

What form of business organization should be chosen?

Guideline

There are many ways to organize a business including the following: a sole proprietorship, partnership, corporation or S-corporation, or limited liability company. Each type of business organization has different advantages and disadvantages.

Analyze

Know the tax and legal treatments of each type of organization. Weigh the best treatment of taxes and legal liability of each type, and pick the format that is most advantageous for the business owners.

What Is Accounting, and What Are the Key Accounting Principles and Concepts?

4 Know the key accounting principles and concepts

Financial accounting The process of recognizing, measuring, recording, and reporting information about a business's transactions to stakeholders outside the business, including stockholders (owners) and lenders.

Have you noticed how many kids play little league sports these days and wondered why so many kids compete in these sports? Some kids play to get into better shape and some kids play just for the fun, but most kids play because they want to win. If you think about it, we live in a very competitive world. This competitiveness makes the job of the scorekeeper very important because, without the scorekeeper, nobody would know which team won the contest. In addition to keeping track of who wins, the scorekeeper in an athletic contest tracks many other statistics that help the coach and the players judge individual performances.

The world of business is very much like little league sports. Businesses exist to win, which is usually defined as generating profits and creating value. **Financial accounting** is the process of recognizing, measuring, recording, and reporting information about a business's transactions to stakeholders outside the business. Outside stakeholders include stockholders (owners) and lenders.

So what does it take to make a business "win" and create value? It takes many hard-working people performing the functions of the business. It takes people developing great products (for example, the research and development group or department); making great products (for example, the production or operations group or department); promoting, selling, and distributing products (for example, the sales and marketing group or department); and acquiring money (for example, the finance department). But it also takes people providing information about the business's financial condition and operations. Businesses run on information, and accounting is at the heart of providing useful information. In essence, accountants are the scorekeepers in the business world.

Generally Accepted Accounting Principles (GAAP) The rules, principles, and concepts established by the accounting profession that govern financial accounting.

Financial Accounting Standards Board (FASB) A seven-person group primarily responsible for the establishment of standards of financial accounting and reporting called GAAP.

Generally Accepted Accounting Principles

In sports there are established rules and principles that dictate how each game is to be played and how the score is to be kept. In the same way, the accounting profession has created a set of rules and principles that must be followed. This set of rules is codified and called **Generally Accepted Accounting Principles (GAAP)**.

In the United States, financial accounting must follow GAAP, which is the rules, principles, and concepts established by the accounting profession that govern financial accounting. GAAP helps existing and potential owners and creditors compare different companies. In the US, most GAAP is developed by the **Financial Accounting Standards Board (FASB)**. The FASB is a seven-person group primarily responsible for the establishment of GAAP. The main objective of financial accounting is to provide information useful for owners and lenders. To be useful, information must be understandable, relevant, and reliable; GAAP tries to ensure that accounting information follows these principles.

International Financial Reporting Standards

International Financial Reporting Standards (IFRS) Accounting standards developed by the International Accounting Standards Board for use throughout the world.

The globalization of business means that companies outside the US are not required to follow US GAAP. Therefore, what principles do companies based outside the United States follow to ensure the reliability of accounting information to investors and other stakeholders? **International Financial Reporting Standards (IFRS)** are accounting standards that are developed by the International Accounting Standards Board. IFRS were originally followed by businesses located in countries that did not have their own accounting standards. However, many countries that have their own accounting standards have started to allow the use of IFRS in addition to, or instead of, their own standards. The United States is currently considering a switch from US GAAP to IFRS. However, because the adoption of IFRS by the United States is not certain and in any event would be years away, this book will focus on US GAAP. Chapter 6 has a more in-depth discussion of IFRS.

The Business Entity Principle

Business entity principle The business entity principle dictates that the financial affairs of a business organization must be kept separate from the personal financial affairs of the business owners.

The most basic concept in accounting is that of the **business entity principle**. The business entity principle dictates that the financial affairs of a business organization must be kept separate from the personal financial affairs of the business owners. This separation is necessary because, if the owners of a business choose to place personal assets into the business, then those assets are now considered to belong to the business and no longer to the owners. For example, if a business owner invests a used car into his or her business, that car should no longer be used by the business owner for personal purposes.

The Reliability (Objectivity) Principle

Reliability principle Information should be verifiable, confirmable by any independent observer; also called **objectivity principle**.

The **reliability (or objectivity) principle** requires that the accounting information for a business be arrived at objectively so it may be relied upon by outside users. The information should be independently verifiable. For example, a company's checking account is supported by a statement from the bank. This statement provides objective evidence that the account exists. Without the reliability principle, accounting information might be based on what people think or feel it should be, rather than what it really is. This would make it easier to manipulate the information for fraudulent purposes.

The Cost Principle

Cost principle The cost principle states that when a business acquires assets or services, they should be recorded at their actual cost, also called historical cost.

Actual cost Actual cost of assets and services acquired, also referred to as **historical cost**.

The **cost principle** states that when a business acquires assets or services, they should be recorded at their **actual cost**, also called **historical cost**. In other words, the amount paid for the asset or service is the amount recorded as its value. Other values, such as market value and appraised value, are not used even if they are known at the time of the purchase. The cost principle also requires that the accounting records keep the historical cost of an asset throughout its useful life because this cost is a reliable measure.

Accounting Ethics: A Matter of Trust

Accountants are important. Accountants have considerable responsibility and, thus, power. They must worry about providing information that is understandable, relevant, and reliable. Stakeholders use the information provided by accountants to make very serious business decisions. Accountants must be trustworthy and perform their accounting duties in accordance with high ethical standards. They must provide clear and complete information, not manipulate the financial information so as to mislead stakeholders, and make their best efforts to prevent fraud.

Think about a sports event. Who do you ask to be the scorekeeper? First, you figure out who understands how the game is played. From that group, you ask the most trustworthy person available to keep score. Business is the same. Accountants must be knowledgeable, but they must also be trustworthy. In Chapter 6, we'll explore the challenges faced by the accounting profession, including ethics.

Accounting in Your World

How would you respond to the following situations?

- The company CEO asks you to falsify the company's accounting records. He or she says that the company cannot afford to report that it is performing poorly. If it does, some stores will likely have to be closed and people will lose their jobs. The CEO implies that if you are not a "team player" and fail to falsify the records, then it will be your fault these people are unemployed.

- At the end of the month, your supervisor asks you to create fictitious sales invoices. He or she tells you that your department is just a little bit shy of reaching the sales goal necessary for each member of the department to receive a quarterly bonus. Your supervisor says that you can just delete the fictitious sales at the beginning of the next month and that no one will ever know.

- A coworker confides that he or she has stolen several MP3 players from the store at which you work. Your coworker offers to give you one of the players. He or she says that you both deserve it for all of the long hours you have worked for the company lately.

You may find yourself faced with an ethical dilemma at any time during your career. You only have one chance to make the right decision.

What Is the Role of Accounting in a Business?

5 Know how accounting functions in a business

Remember our sports analogy where accounting is the "scorekeeper" of business? Accountants must:

- Recognize business transactions.
- Measure business transactions.
- Record business transactions.
- Report business transactions over a period of time.

Now, we will look more closely at what those scorekeeping activities are and how they are done.

The Roles of Accounting in Business

How Do You Recognize a Business Transaction?

Accountants must first recognize a business transaction. This may appear easy, but often it is not. Let's look at an example. You own a computer repair store. A customer brings in a computer for repair. Is this a sale that generates revenue? The customer promises to pay you $100 when you complete the repair. However, you have not repaired the customer's computer. There is no exchange. You have not earned the revenue yet. The customer's order is an important event, but it is not a completed business transaction. Thus the accountant will wait to recognize this as revenue until you repair the customer's computer and earn the revenue.

Let's look at another example using a computer repair store. You repair the customer's computer. You have completed your part of the transaction. But you have an agreement with your customer that he or she does not have to pay you for 30 days. In other words, you exchanged your repair service for the customer's promise to pay you $100 in 30 days. You have exchanged your repair service for a receivable. Is this $100 revenue when you repaired the customer's computer? Do we wait until you receive the $100 cash before we recognize the revenue?

Cash Accounting

Cash accounting Accounting that only recognizes business transactions when cash is received or disbursed.

Cash accounting only recognizes a business transaction when cash is received or disbursed. If your computer repair store used cash accounting, you would not recognize the revenue until you received the cash. However, most businesses do not use cash accounting. Most businesses, in accordance with GAAP, use accrual accounting.

Accrual Accounting

Accrual accounting Accounting that recognizes a business transaction when it occurs, whether or not cash is received or disbursed.

Accrual accounting recognizes a business transaction when it occurs, whether or not cash is received or disbursed. Using accrual accounting, your computer repair store would recognize the revenue when you repaired the customer's computer. You repaired the computer and were paid with a promise for the services performed. You now have money owed to you from the customer. You have completed a business transaction. When the customer pays you the $100, you would recognize another transaction where you now have $100 cash and no promise of future money.

Understanding when a business receives and disburses cash is very important. A business must be able to manage its cash flow in order to pay its bills and survive. However, waiting to recognize a business transaction until cash is received or paid can deny stakeholders very important information. An example is a liability. Just because a business has not paid a bill does not mean it does not owe it. Stakeholders want to know what a business owes now and must pay in the future. For that reason, businesses typically use accrual accounting. However, as noted later, accountants also provide users information about where a business gets and uses its cash.

How Do You Measure a Business Transaction?

After recognizing a business transaction, the accountant must then measure the transaction. This process presents several challenges.

Let's return to our example of your computer repair store. You repaired your customer's computer, and he or she now owes you $100. Will you collect $100? You may not collect the $100. Based on prior experience, you may believe that you will only collect 90% of the money, or $90. You estimate that you will not collect, and thus lose, $10 of the sale. Do you disclose that you are owed $100 or expect to receive $90? Under

US GAAP, you would estimate that you will lose $10 and your claim on your customer is only worth $90. Measuring transactions using accrual accounting requires the accountant to make estimates. These estimates may need to be adjusted over time.

Let's look at another example. You bought a building to house your computer repair store. The building cost you $100,000 five years ago. You still own and use the building, but the building was recently appraised to have a value of $200,000. Your wealth has increased by $100,000 because your building appreciated from $100,000 to $200,000 in value. But do accountants recognize this increase in value? The GAAP used in the United States would not. Why? Because US GAAP is conservative, it requires a sale of the building to recognize that it is now worth more than when you bought it. US GAAP is based on historical cost and is designed not to overstate the value of assets. However, accounting rules in other countries may be different from US GAAP. They may recognize that your building's value has increased even without a sale. Such rules are based on current or market values for assets. IFRS is a set of accounting rules that uses current or market values. In this book, we'll focus on US GAAP. However, in other chapters, particularly Chapter 6, we'll look at how different countries can have different accounting rules. This coverage in other chapters will be denoted by the icon at left.

GAAP-
Original Value not
New Value.

How Do You Record Business Transactions Using the Accounting Equation?

Accounting is the process of recognizing, measuring, recording, and reporting information about a business's transactions. But what is the process or method used by accountants? After business transactions are recognized and measured, how do accountants record the business transactions?

Remember, the accountant's job is really the job of being the scorekeeper for the business. The accountant needs to keep track of information so he or she can tell people about the operations of the business. The accountant must keep track of two main things. First, the accountant must track the resources a business owns that have value. These are called assets. In addition, the accountant must track where the business obtained the money to finance its assets. Remember, money comes from liabilities or stockholders' equity. The amount of assets that a business owns at a point in time must equal the amount of financing the business has at that point in time. In other words, assets must equal liabilities plus stockholders' equity. This concept can be expressed as an equation, referred to as the **fundamental accounting equation**:

Fundamental accounting equation The equation that states that total assets equal the sum of total liabilities and total stockholders' equity.

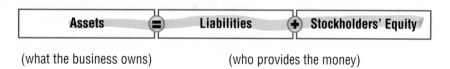

| **Assets** | **=** | **Liabilities** | **+** | **Stockholders' Equity** |

(what the business owns)   (who provides the money)

The parties who provide the money to finance a company's assets have an ownership interest in the assets of the company. Therefore, the liabilities and stockholders' equity also represent who has an ownership interest in, or claims to, a company's assets.

Transaction Analysis

Accountants will record a business transaction with this fundamental accounting equation. When the accountant records a transaction that affects the business, he or she will record what effect the transaction has on the assets of the business and what effect it has on the financing of the business. This process is called transaction analysis.

Stockholders' Equity

Before we start looking at how transactions affect the accounting equation, let's take a closer look at the stockholders' equity section of the equation. Stockholders' equity, sometimes called shareholders' equity, is the phrase used to describe owners' equity in a corporation. In order to provide more useful information to various people, the stockholders' equity section of the equation can be broken down into smaller subcategories:

Common stock The stockholders' equity that is the result of the owners of the business investing money (or other assets) into the business.

Retained earnings The stockholders' equity that is the result of the business having net income, or earnings, that have been retained in the business.

- **Common stock** is used to reflect stockholders' equity that is the result of the owners of the business investing money (or other assets) into the business.
- **Retained earnings** is used to reflect stockholders' equity that is the result of the business having net income, or earnings, that have been retained in the business. As we saw earlier (on page 5), net income is created when the business has revenue that exceeds expenses. A net loss is when a business has expenses that exceed revenue.

An expanded version of the accounting equation would look like this:

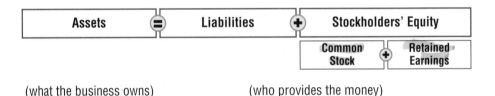

(what the business owns)   (who provides the money)

The retained earnings subcategory can now be further broken down into subcategories to help the accountant provide even better information. These are the subcategories and the information they reflect:

- *Revenue* is used to reflect an increase in retained earnings that is the result of the business providing goods and services.
- *Expenses* are used to reflect a decrease in retained earnings that is the result of the business incurring costs related to providing goods and services.
- *Dividends* are used to reflect a decrease in retained earnings that is the result of the owners receiving assets (usually cash) from the business.

An expanded version of the accounting equation would now look like this:

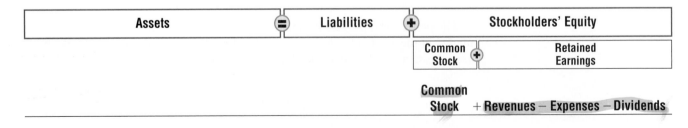

Retained Earnings and, therefore, Stockholders' Equity increases by adding amounts to Revenues. Retained Earnings and, therefore, Stockholders' Equity decreases by adding amounts to expenses and dividends. These subcategories will make more sense as we see how they are used to record the effects of business transactions. To illustrate, let's analyze the effects of several transactions on the accounting equation for the month of January 2014 for Osborne Consulting, Inc., a new computer consulting business started by Cindy Osborne.

1. **Sale of stock.** Cindy Osborne invests $10,000 to start the business. Osborne Consulting, Inc., sells Cindy $10,000 of common stock in exchange for her cash investment. The effect of this transaction on the accounting equation is to increase Assets and increase Stockholders' Equity as follows:

	Assets	=	Liabilities	+	Stockholders' Equity		
					Common Stock +		Retained Earnings
	Cash	=			Common Stock	+ Revenues − Expenses − Dividends	
(1)	+$10,000				+$10,000		
Bal	$10,000	=			$10,000		

Remember that, for each transaction, the amount on the left side of the equation must equal the amount on the right side. The amount of assets will be increased by $10,000 because the business now has $10,000 of cash that it did not have before. In order to keep track of what type of assets the business has, the accountant will create a subcategory under assets for each different type of asset that the business has, so a subcategory for Cash was created. Because the assets have increased, there is now a need to increase the ownership side of the equation. The business does not owe the $10,000 to a third party, so the $10,000 ownership interest must belong to Cindy and must be entered in the Stockholders' Equity section of the equation. If we look at the Stockholders' Equity side of the equation, we can see that there are two possible places the $10,000 can be entered in order to increase Stockholders' Equity: Common Stock and Retained Earnings. Based on the definitions of when each of these would be used, as discussed previously, we see that the $10,000 should be entered in the Common Stock section of Stockholders' Equity because this increase in Stockholders' Equity was the result of Cindy investing assets into the business.   *investing = CS*

2. **Purchase supplies on credit.** Osborne Consulting purchases office supplies, agreeing to pay $350 within 30 days. The effect of this transaction on the accounting equation is to increase Assets and increase Liabilities as follows:

	Assets			=	Liabilities	+	Stockholders' Equity		
							Common Stock +		Retained Earnings
	Cash	+	Supplies	=	Accounts Payable	+	Common Stock	+ Revenues − Expenses − Dividends	
Bal	$10,000			=			$10,000		
(2)			+$350		+$350				
Bal	$10,000	+	$350	=	$350	+	$10,000		

7. **Partial payment of accounts payable.** Osborne Consulting pays $150 to the store where it purchased $350 worth of supplies in Transaction 2. In accounting, this is referred to as "paying on account." The effect on the accounting equation is to decrease Assets and decrease Liabilities as follows:

	Assets				=	Liabilities			+	Stockholders' Equity			
										Common Stock		Retained Earnings	
	Cash	+ Accounts Receivable	+ Supplies	+ Equipment	=	Accounts Payable	+ Notes Payable	+	Common Stock	+ Revenues	− Expenses	− Dividends
Bal	$19,200	+ $1,900	+ $350	+ $4,000	=	$350	+ $12,000	+ $10,000	+ $3,100			
(7)	−$150					−$150						
Bal	$19,050	+ $1,900	+ $350	+ $4,000	=	$200	+ $12,000	+ $10,000	+ $3,100			

The payment of cash on account has no effect on Supplies because the payment does not affect the amount of supplies that the business has. Likewise, the payment on account does not affect Expenses because the business is paying off an amount owed, not using those supplies. The Cash account decreases because the business has less cash and the Accounts Payable account decreases because the business owes less to a third party.

8. **Payment of expenses.** During the month, Osborne Consulting paid $1,700 cash for expenses incurred such as wages, building rent, and utilities. Later on we will see that each different type of expense will be shown separately in the accounting equation, but for now we will lump them all together under the heading "Expenses." The effect on the accounting equation is to decrease Assets and decrease Stockholders' Equity as follows:

	Assets				=	Liabilities			+	Stockholders' Equity			
										Common Stock		Retained Earnings	
	Cash	+ Accounts Receivable	+ Supplies	+ Equipment	=	Accounts Payable	+ Notes Payable	+	Common Stock	+ Revenues	− Expenses	− Dividends
Bal	$19,050	+ $1,900	+ $350	+ $4,000	=	$200	+ $12,000	+ $10,000	+ $3,100			
(8)	−$1,700										+$1,700	
Bal	$17,350	+ $1,900	+ $350	+ $4,000	=	$200	+ $12,000	+ $10,000	+ $3,100	− $1,700		

For this transaction, Cash decreases and Expenses increase. Because Expenses are subtracted from Retained Earnings, Retained Earnings (and, therefore, Stockholders' Equity) will decrease. This decrease in Stockholders' Equity reflects that the assets for the business have decreased and, therefore, there has to be less ownership reported. Remember that Expenses are used to decrease Retained Earnings when needed as the result of the business incurring costs related to providing goods and services.

9. **Cash dividends.** Osborne Consulting pays $500 of cash dividends to Cindy Osborne, the stockholder. The effect on the accounting equation is to decrease Assets and decrease Stockholders' Equity as follows:

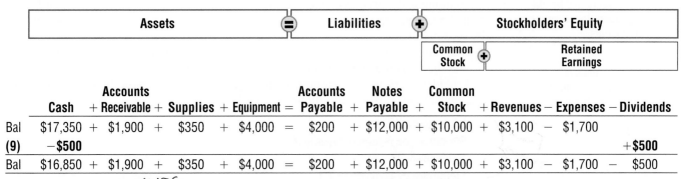

| | Assets | | | | | Liabilities | | | Stockholders' Equity | | | |
| | | | | | | | | | Common Stock | + | Retained Earnings | |

	Cash	+ Receivable +	Supplies +	Equipment =	Payable +	Payable +	Stock	+ Revenues −	Expenses −	Dividends
Bal	$17,350 +	$1,900 +	$350 +	$4,000 =	$200 +	$12,000 +	$10,000 +	$3,100 −	$1,700	
(9)	−$500									+$500
Bal	$16,850 +	$1,900 +	$350 +	$4,000 =	$200 +	$12,000 +	$10,000 +	$3,100 −	$1,700 −	$500

DIVIDENDS INCREASE

Salaries Payable is a Liabilitie

The payment of dividends causes a decrease in Cash of $500 and an increase in Dividends of $500. Because Dividends are subtracted from Retained Earnings, Retained Earnings (and, therefore, Stockholders' Equity) will decrease. This decrease in Stockholders' Equity reflects that the assets for the business have decreased and, therefore, there has to be less ownership interest reported. Dividends are different from expenses because the cash is paid directly to the owners rather than being paid for costs that were related to providing goods or services. Once again we can see that the total assets of $23,100 still equal the total liabilities of $12,200 plus stockholders' equity of $10,900, so the accounting equation continues to balance. Remember that total Stockholders' Equity equals the Common Stock of $10,000 plus the Retained Earnings of $900. Retained Earnings was arrived at by calculating net earnings of $1,400 (subtracting the Expenses from the Revenues) and then subtracting the Dividends.

Try It...

At the end of its first month of operations, Robinson Consulting, Inc., has assets totaling $57,000 and stockholders' equity totaling $32,000. What is the amount of Robinson Consulting's total liabilities at the end of the month?

Answer

We can use the fundamental accounting equation to figure out what Robinson Consulting's total liabilities are. First, it helps to restate the equation in a different format by subtracting stockholders' equity from both sides of the equation as follows:

| Assets | − | Stockholders' Equity | = | Liabilities |

Next, insert the amount of Robinson Consulting's total assets and the total stockholders' equity into the restated formula.

$57,000 − $32,000 = Liabilities

Finally, solve the equation to get the total liabilities of $25,000.

$57,000 − $32,000 = $25,000

How Do You Report Business Transactions Using Financial Statements?

6 **Understand and be able to prepare basic financial statements**

Financial statements Historical, objective reports, prepared according to GAAP, that communicate financial information about a business.

Accounting is the process of recognizing, measuring, recording, and reporting information about a business's economic transactions. But what is the process of reporting used by accountants?

To report the results of a business's transactions for a period, **financial statements** need to be prepared. These reports show the entity's financial information to interested stakeholders both inside and outside the organization. Four basic financial statements are prepared by most organizations:

Financial Statements

- Income statement
- Statement of retained earnings
- Balance sheet
- Statement of cash flows

The Income Statement

Income statement A financial statement that reports the revenue and expenses of a business during a given period of time.

An **income statement** answers the question, "Is the organization generating any net income?" Just as a scoreboard shows how many points a team earned for a specific period of time, a business prepares an income statement to show, for a specific time period, the revenue earned and the expenses incurred to produce that revenue. Like the scoreboard that shows whether the team is winning or losing, the income statement shows whether the business generated *net income* (total revenue was greater than total expenses, where total expenses are total operating expenses plus interest expense) or a *net loss* (total revenue is less than total expenses). To prepare an income statement, we set up a format that includes a heading and the body of the statement. The heading of all financial statements should show "who," "what," and "when." The "who" is the name of the business, the "what" is the name of the financial statement, and the "when" is the time period covered by the statement. The body of the income statement lists the revenue, then the expenses, and finally the net income or net loss. When revenue is greater than expenses, the business earns net income, or profit. When expenses are greater than revenue, the business has a net loss. We can prepare an income statement for Osborne Consulting for the month of January 2014 by referring to the ending balances in the accounting equation that we recently completed.

Fincial Statements heading.

Who
What
When

If we look at **Exhibit 1-2**, we can see what the income statement for Osborne Consulting looks like. In the first month of operations, Osborne Consulting, Inc., earned $3,100 in revenue and had $1,700 in expenses that resulted in net income of $1,400. This amount can remain part of the stockholders' equity in the business and can be used to "grow" or expand the business, or the business can distribute dividends to the stockholders.

Notice the dollar signs on the first and last amounts and the double underline under the last amount presented on the statement (Net Income). It is common practice to place a dollar sign on the first number and the last number in each column on a financial statement and to double underline the final amount.

Exhibit 1-2 ▶

Dividends are on Retained Earnings not income Statement.

Osborne Consulting, Inc.
Income Statement
Month Ended January 31, 2014

Revenue		$3,100
Expenses		1,700
Net Income		$1,400

Osborne Consulting, Inc.
Statement of Retained Earnings
Month Ended January 31, 2014

Retained Earnings, January 1, 2014	$ 0
Add: Net Income for the month	1,400
Subtotal	1,400
Less: Dividends	500
Retained Earnings, January 31, 2014	$ 900

Osborne Consulting, Inc.
Balance Sheet
January 31, 2014

ASSETS		LIABILITIES	
Cash	$16,850	Accounts Payable	$ 200
Accounts Receivable	1,900	Notes Payable	12,000
Supplies	350	Total Liabilities	12,200
Equipment	4,000		
		STOCKHOLDERS' EQUITY	
		Common Stock	10,000
		Retained Earnings	900
		Total Stockholders' Equity	10,900
		Total Liabilities &	
Total Assets	$23,100	Stockholders' Equity	$23,100

Osborne Consulting, Inc.
Statement of Cash Flows
Month Ended January 31, 2014

Cash flows from operating activities:		
Net income		$ 1,400
Adjustments to reconcile net income to net cash provided by operating activities:		
Increase in current assets	(2,250)	
Increase in current liabilities	200	(2,050)
Net cash used in operating activites		(650)
Cash flows from investing activities:		
Purchase of equipment	(4,000)	
Net cash used in investing activities		(4,000)
Cash flows from financing activities:		
Proceeds from issuance of commmon stock	10,000	
Proceeds from issuance of notes payable	12,000	
Payment of dividends	(500)	
Net cash provided by financing activities		21,500
Net increase in cash		16,850
Cash balance January 1, 2014		0
Cash balance January 31, 2014		16,850

The Statement of Retained Earnings

"How much net income has the corporation made and kept during the current accounting period?" The **statement of retained earnings** answers this question by presenting the amount of the retained earnings and the changes to it during a specific time period, such as a month or a year. Increases in retained earnings come from net income and decreases result from either a net loss or the payment of dividends.

To prepare the statement of retained earnings, we set up a format that includes a heading and body similar to the income statement. The heading includes the name of the business, the name of the financial statement, and the time period covered by the statement. The body of the statement lists the beginning retained earnings balance, any net income earned or net loss incurred, any dividends paid, and the ending balance of Retained Earnings. Using the information from the income statement that we just prepared and the dividend information from our accounting equation, we can prepare a statement of retained earnings.

Exhibit 1-2 shows what Osborne Consulting's statement of retained earnings looks like. Because this is the first month that Osborne Consulting has been in business, there is a zero balance in beginning Retained Earnings. During the first month of operations, Osborne Consulting, Inc., paid dividends of $500, which, when combined with the $1,400 of net income for January, leaves an ending Retained Earnings balance at January 31 of $900. Of the $1,400 that Osborne Consulting earned during January, we can see that $900 was retained in the business.

The Balance Sheet

"What assets does the company have, and who has ownership rights to those assets?" The **balance sheet** answers this question by listing all of an entity's assets, liabilities, and stockholders' equity as of a specific date, usually the end of a month or a year. Basically the balance sheet shows the accounting equation for a business and reflects the fact that assets equal liabilities plus stockholders' equity. The balance sheet is also known as the **statement of financial position**. Using the information from the statement of retained earnings that we just prepared and the ending balances from our accounting equation, we can prepare a balance sheet for Osborne Consulting. Exhibit 1-2 shows what Osborne Consulting's balance sheet will look like. Notice that total assets equal total liabilities and stockholders' equity.

The Statement of Cash Flows

"Where did the business get the money it needed to operate, and where did it spend its money?" The **statement of cash flows** answers this question by showing stakeholders all of the sources and all of the uses of cash by a business for a specified period of time. On the statement of cash flows, the sources and uses of cash are reported for three different types of business activities:

1. **Operating activities** are activities in the entity's major line of business to *generate revenue and/or expenses* such as providing goods or services.

2. **Investing activities** are the decisions made by management *to buy and sell long-term assets* such as buying equipment.

3. **Financing activities** are those actions that generate the receipt or payment of cash *to pay long-term liabilities or raise capital* such as selling common stock or borrowing money.

Exhibit 1-2 shows what Osborne Consulting's statement of cash flows will look like. Notice that the cash balance reported on the balance sheet equals the ending cash balance reported on the statement of cash flows. The statement of cash flows will be covered in more detail in Chapter 11.

Relationships Among the Financial Statements

The financial statements are prepared in the following order:

1. Income statement

2. Statement of retained earnings

3. Balance sheet

4. Statement of cash flows

The reason for this order is that the net income figure from the income statement is needed in order to prepare the statement of retained earnings. Likewise, the ending retained earnings balance from the statement of retained earnings is needed to prepare the balance sheet. Finally, information from both the income statement and the balance sheet is needed in order to prepare the statement of cash flows.

Focus on Decision Making

"What Is the Business?"

Think of a business. It may be a big business such as Kroger or Facebook, or a small business such as your local doctor. Now think about the following questions:

1. Why does the business exist?

2. What type of business is it?

3. What does the business sell?

4. What expenses does the business incur as it operates?

5. What assets and people are needed to operate the business?

6. Where could the business get the money to finance the assets and pay the employees?

Businesses all exist to create value for their stakeholders, especially for their owners. But each business tries to be different. Businesses compete. To be successful, they need to be special.

The Income Statement

The income statement of the business tells the owners and managers the revenues (or sales) and expenses a business has experienced during a period of time. Different businesses have different types of revenues and expenses. The revenues and expenses incurred by your doctor are different than the revenues and expenses incurred by Kroger or Facebook.

The Balance Sheet

Different businesses need different types of assets to be successful. Your doctor sells his or her services whereas Walmart sells clothing, tools, and other household products. Your doctor's office is small compared to the big buildings used by Kroger or even Facebook. The balance sheet of a business reflects the different assets a business needs to operate. Given that businesses are different, it is reasonable to expect that different businesses use different ways to finance their assets. Different businesses have different amounts and types of liabilities and owners' equity.

How They Do It: A Look at Business

Think about how different businesses operate. An example is a food store such as Kroger. Kroger sells food. It needs assets such as cash, food (called inventory), and buildings. Kroger finances these assets with liabilities and stockholders' equity. For the year ended

February 2, 2013, Kroger had sales of $96.8 billion, expenses of $95.3 billion, and net income of $1.5 billion. At February 2, 2013, Kroger had assets of $24.6 billion, financed with $20.4 billion in liabilities and $4.2 billion in stockholders' equity. Kroger's biggest assets were food and buildings. Compare that to Facebook, the Internet social media company. Facebook sells advertising and other Internet services. It needs cash, computers, and software to run the computers. For the year ended December 31, 2012, Facebook reported sales of $5.1 billion, expenses of $5.05 billion, and net income of just over $50 million. At December 31, 2012, Facebook reported assets of $15.1 billion, financed with $3.3 billion in liabilities and $11.8 billion in stockholders' equity. Facebook's biggest assets were marketable securities, short-term investments that can be quickly converted to cash.

Different businesses operate differently. Accountants must communicate these differences when they recognize, measure, record, and report business transactions using financial statements.

Decision Guidelines

Decision	Guideline	Analyze
How do I understand how a business operates?	The income statement reports the revenues and expenses of a business. Revenues represent what a business earns as a result of providing goods or services. Expenses represent the cost to the business of providing those goods or services.	If revenues exceed expenses, the business is profitable and has earned net income. However, if expenses exceed revenue, the business has incurred a net loss and is not profitable.
	The statement of retained earnings shows whether the net income of a business was paid out as dividends or retained in the business.	If a business is planning on growth, it will often issue low or no dividends to shareholders. This way, it retains the income in the business.
	The balance sheet reflects the assets, liabilities, and stockholders equity of the business.	The liabilities of a business reflect the claims of third parties to the assets of the business. Once those claims are settled, the remaining assets belong to the stockholders (the owners) of the business. This amount is reflected by the stockholders' equity on the balance sheet.
	The statement of cash flows reflects the sources and uses of cash over a period of time.	You can see whether a company's operations generated cash for the business and how much cash the business invested in the purchase of assets such as buildings and equipment. If a company's operations generated insufficient funds to finance its investments in assets, you can determine how the business financed these acquisitions.

Accounting, Business, and You—Putting It All Together

So what is accounting? Accounting is the process of recognizing, measuring, recording, and reporting information about a business's economic transactions. Accounting is the language of business.

So what is a business? A business is an organization, recognized under law, that attempts to create value by exchanging products with customers for money. Why does a business exist? A business exists to create value. How does a business create value? A business acquires money (liabilities and owners' equity) and uses money to hire people and acquire assets. The people (employees) then use the assets to generate revenue and expenses that hopefully result in enough net income to compensate owners for the use of their money.

It's not easy to create value. Managing a business is both challenging and rewarding. It's a challenge to blend all the parts of a business into a cohesive organization that delivers value for all stakeholders, particularly owners. A business is a team composed of people, assets, liabilities, and owners' equity. To compete successfully, a business must blend and manage all the parts or players in the business just right.

To be successful a business needs good information. That's the job of accounting. Accountants are the scorekeepers of business. Like all good scorekeepers, they have rules. The rules accountants use are called Generally Accepted Accounting Principles (GAAP). Accountants use GAAP to create financial statements. The four primary statements are the income statement, the statement of retained earnings, the balance sheet, and the statement of cash flows.

So look around. What do you see? You see businesses. You see people and organizations creating, producing, and selling products. And in doing so, you see businesses creating value. However, a very important part of that value-creating process is keeping track of your revenues, expenses, assets, liabilities, and owners' equity. In other words, as a business owner or manager, accounting is important to you.

Summary

MyAccountingLab

Here is what you should know after reading this chapter. MyAccountingLab will help you identify what you know and where to go when you need practice.

	Key Points	Key Accounting Terms
1 Understand the nature of business and the role of accounting in business	A business is a legal organization that attempts to create value by exchanging products with customers for money. Accounting is the process of recognizing, measuring, recording, and reporting business transactions.	**Accounting** (p. 2) **Business** (p. 2) **Cost** (p. 3) **Customer** (p. 3) **Goods** (p. 2) **Loss** (p. 4) **Product** (p. 2) **Profit** (p. 3) **Revenue** (p. 3) **Risk** (p. 4) **Sale** (p. 3) **Services** (p. 3) **Stakeholder** (p. 4) **Value** (p. 3)

		Key Points	**Key Accounting Terms**
2	**Know how a business operates**	A business obtains money from owners and lenders. Owners and lenders expect a return that compensates them for time and risk. Owners expect a profit, the difference between revenue and costs. Lenders expect interest. A business uses the money provided by owners and lenders to hire employees and invest in assets. Employees then use the assets to generate revenue and incur costs.	**Asset** (p. 5) **Employees** (p. 5) **Expense** (p. 5) **Interest** (p. 5) **Liabilities** (p. 5) **Net income** (p. 5) **Owners' equity** (p. 5) **Stockholders' equity** (p. 5)
3	**Know the different types and forms of businesses**	There are many types of businesses. A business is organized under the law as a sole proprietorship, a partnership, a corporation, or a limited liability company.	**Corporation** (p. 7) **Dividend** (p. 7) **For-profit business** (p. 6) **Limited liability company (LLC)** (p. 8) **Manufacturing business** (p. 7) **Merchandise business** (p. 7) **Not-for-profit business** (p. 7) **Partnership** (p. 7) **Retail business** (p. 7) **Service business** (p. 7) **Sole proprietorship** (p. 7) **Stockholder** (p. 7) **S-corporation** (p. 8) **Wholesale business** (p. 7)
4	**Know the key accounting principles and concepts**	Accounting is governed by rules, called Generally Accepted Accounting Principles (GAAP).	**Actual cost** (p. 10) **Business entity principle** (p. 10) **Cost principle** (p. 10) **Financial accounting** (p. 9) **Financial Accounting Standards Board (FASB)** (p. 9) **Generally Accepted Accounting Principles (GAAP)** (p. 9) **Historical cost** (p. 10) **International Financial Reporting Standards (IFRS)** (p. 10) **Objectivity principle** (p. 10) **Reliability principle** (p. 10)

	Key Points	Key Accounting Terms

5 ▶ Know how accounting functions in a business

Accounting is a critical part of a successful business. Accounting is the scorekeeping function of what the business is doing. Accounting must recognize, measure, record, and report the resources a business owns. These resources are called assets. Accounting must also account for the sources of the money to acquire the assets, money provided by owners or lenders. Last, accounting must account for how the business operates and whether it generates a profit, where revenue exceeds expenses, or a loss, where revenue is less than expenses.

Accounts payable (p. 16)

Accounts receivable (p. 17)

Accrual accounting (p. 12)

Cash accounting (p. 12)

Common stock (p. 14)

Fundamental accounting equation (p. 13)

Note payable (p. 16)

On account (p. 17)

Prepaid expenses (p. 16)

Retained earnings (p. 14)

6 ▶ Understand and be able to prepare basic financial statements

Accounting uses the accounting equation to produce four financial statements. These statements are the income statement, the balance sheet, the statement of retained earnings, and the statement of cash flows.

Balance sheet (p. 22)

Financial statements (p. 20)

Financing activities (p. 22)

Income statement (p. 20)

Investing activities (p. 22)

Operating activities (p. 22)

Statement of cash flows (p. 22)

Statement of financial position (p. 22)

Statement of retained earnings (p. 22)

Accounting Practice

Discussion Questions

1. The text states that accounting is the "language of business." What does this mean? Why is it important to know the language?

2. Would you describe accounting as primarily a technical discipline or primarily an ethical discipline? Why?

3. Financial statements are defined as "historical reports that communicate financial information about a business to people or organizations outside the company." Why is the word *historical* used?

4. What are some reasons why accounting has adopted "historical" financial statements as the model? What are some disadvantages associated with presenting "historical" financial statements?

5. What are some of the uses of financial statements?

6. What is the primary way in which corporations differ from proprietorships and partnerships? What are some of the factors that might affect a person's decision about the form of organization that would be best in a given situation?

7. What is the fundamental accounting equation? Define each of the components of this equation.

8. How is the accounting equation affected by each of these transactions?
   a. Owners contribute cash to start the business in exchange for common stock.
   b. The company borrows money from the bank.
   c. The company provides services for a client who promises to pay later.
   d. The company collects from the customer in transaction c.

9. In what order should the financial statements be prepared? Why?

10. Which financial statement would be most useful to answer each of the following questions?
    a. Does the corporation have enough resources to pay its short-term debts?
    b. What is the corporation's policy toward "growing the company" versus distributing its wealth to owners?
    c. Did the corporation pay its operating costs with resources generated from operations, money borrowed from banks, or money generated from selling off its buildings and equipment?
    d. Did the corporation make a profit last year?

Self Check

1. Which type of business organization is owned by its stockholders?
   a. Proprietorship
   b. Partnership
   c. Corporation
   d. All the above are owned by stockholders.

2. The majority of Generally Accepted Accounting Principles (GAAP) are created by the
   a. Institute of Management Accountants (IMA).
   b. Securities and Exchange Commission (SEC).
   c. American Institute of Certified Public Accountants (AICPA).
   d. Financial Accounting Standards Board (FASB).

3. Which accounting principle specifically states that we should record transactions at amounts that can be verified?

    a. Business entity principle
    b. Cost principle
    c. Reliability principle
    d. Going-concern principle

4. Wave Rider is famous for custom skateboards. At the end of a recent year, Wave Rider's total assets added up to $884 million and stockholders' equity was $187 million. How much did Wave Rider owe creditors?

    a. $1,071 million
    b. $884 million
    c. $697 million
    d. $187 million

5. Assume that Wave Rider sold skateboards to a department store for $28,000 cash. How would this transaction affect Wave Rider's accounting equation?

    a. Increase both assets and stockholders' equity by $28,000
    b. It will not affect the accounting equation because the effects cancel out.
    c. Increase both assets and liabilities by $28,000
    d. Increase both liabilities and stockholders' equity by $28,000

6. Assume that Wave Rider sold skateboards to another department store for $18,000 on account. Which parts of the accounting equation does a sale on account affect?

    a. Accounts Payable and Cash
    b. Accounts Receivable and Retained Earnings
    c. Accounts Receivable and Accounts Payable
    d. Accounts Payable and Retained Earnings

7. Assume that Wave Rider paid expenses totaling $32,000. How does this transaction affect Wave Rider's accounting equation?

    a. Increases assets and decreases liabilities
    b. Decreases both assets and stockholders' equity
    c. Increases both assets and stockholders' equity
    d. Decreases assets and increases liabilities

8. Consider the overall effects of the transactions in questions 5, 6, and 7 on Wave Rider. What is Wave Rider's net income or net loss?

    a. Net loss of $4,000
    b. Net income of $46,000
    c. Net income of $14,000
    d. It cannot be determined from the data given.

9. The balance sheet reports

    a. financial position on a specific date.
    b. results of operations on a specific date.
    c. results of operations for a specific period.
    d. financial position for a specific period.

10. The income statement reports

    a. financial position for a specific period.
    b. results of operations on a specific date.
    c. financial position on a specific date.
    d. results of operations for a specific period.

 11. According to the Real World Accounting Video, the objective of business is to create value. True or False?

12. According to the Real World Accounting Video, _____ are important reports business managers use in managing their business.

   a. balance sheets

   b. income statements

   c. both balance sheets and income statements

Answers are given after Written Communication.

MyAccountingLab

Short Exercises

S1-1. Accounting principles (*Learning Objective 4*) 5–10 min.

Place the corresponding letter of the definition next to the term.

_____ 1. Cost principle

_____ 2. Business entity principle

_____ 3. Generally Accepted Accounting Principles

_____ 4. Reliability principle

   a. An organization that stands as a separate economic unit must not have its financial affairs confused with that of other entities.

   b. Data must be verifiable.

   c. Standards developed by FASB.

   d. Acquired assets and services should be recorded at their actual cost.

S1-2. Accounting principles (*Learning Objective 4*) 5–10 min.

Jack Sanders owns and operates Jack's Java Coffee Shop. He proposes to account for the shop's assets at their current market value in order to have current amounts on the balance sheet. Which accounting concept or principle does Jack violate?

   a. Business entity principle

   b. Going-concern principle

   c. Reliability principle

   d. Cost principle

S1-3. Accounting terminology (*Learning Objectives 2 & 3*) 10–15 min.

Place the corresponding letter of the definition next to the term.

_____ 1. Liabilities

_____ 2. Assets

_____ 3. Corporation

_____ 4. Dividends

_____ 5. Sole proprietorship

_____ 6. Partnership

_____ 7. Transaction

   a. Any event that affects a firm's financial position.

   b. Organization form with a single owner.

   c. Organization form with two or more owners.

   d. Organization form that can have an indefinite life.

   e. Debt owed to outsiders.

   f. Economic resources of the business.

   g. Payment of cash to the owners of a corporation.

S1-4. Basic accounting equation (*Learning Objective 5*) 5–10 min.

Determine the missing amounts in the following accounting equations.

	Assets	=	Liabilities	+	Stockholders' Equity
a.	$106,000	=	$24,000	+	?
b.	?	=	$63,000	+	$28,000
c.	$94,000	=	?	+	$45,000

S1-5. Basic accounting equation (*Learning Objective 5*) 5–10 min.

Ellen Beach owns Ellen's Lawncare Service. The business has cash of $13,000 and equipment that costs $35,000. Debts of the business include accounts payable of $9,000 and a $5,000 note payable. Determine the amount of stockholders' equity Ellen has in the business. Write the accounting equation for Ellen's Lawncare Service.

S1-6. Basic accounting equation (*Learning Objective 5*) 5–10 min.

Boehms, Inc., has cash of $36,000, supplies costing $1,500, and stockholders' equity of $28,000. Determine the liabilities of the business. Write the accounting equation for Boehms, Inc.

S1-7. Basic accounting equation (*Learning Objective 5*) 5–10 min.

Qwick Care Clinic, Inc., started a business when Dr. Hamm purchased $15,000 of common stock in the business for cash. Before starting operations, Qwick Care Clinic, Inc., borrowed $18,000 cash by signing a note payable to 1st National Bank. Account for these two transactions in the accounting equation.

S1-8. Entering transactions in the accounting equation (*Learning Objective 5*) 5–10 min.

Sanchez Towing Service, Inc., earns service revenue by towing vehicles for AAA. Sanchez Towing Service's main expenses are the salaries paid to its employees. Account for the following transactions in the expanded accounting equation:

a. Sanchez Towing Service, Inc., earned $62,000 of service revenue on account.

b. Sanchez Towing Service, Inc., paid $33,000 in salaries expense.

S1-9. Basic accounting equation (*Learning Objective 5*) 5–10 min.

Match each of the following items with its location in the expanded accounting equation. Use the most detailed category appropriate:

_____ 1. Utilities Expense   a. Assets

_____ 2. Accounts Receivable   b. Liabilities

_____ 3. Common Stock   c. Stockholders' Equity

_____ 4. Office Supplies   d. Revenues

_____ 5. Lease Expense, Computer   e. Expenses

_____ 6. Salaries Expense

_____ 7. Cash

_____ 8. Rent Expense, Office

_____ 9. Service Revenue

_____ 10. Accounts Payable

_____ 11. Land

S1-10. Basic financial statements (*Learning Objective 6*) **5–10 min.**

Label each of the items listed with the abbreviation of the financial statement on which it appears. Items may appear on more than one statement.

Income Statement (IS)

Balance Sheet (BS)

Statement of Retained Earnings (RE)

_____ 1. Accounts Receivable

_____ 2. Notes Payable

_____ 3. Advertising Expense

_____ 4. Service Revenue

_____ 5. Retained Earnings

_____ 6. Office Supplies

S1-11. Entering transactions in the accounting equation (*Learning Objective 5*) **5–10 min.**

As a manager of a department store, you must deal with a variety of business transactions. Place the letter of each of the following transactions next to the effect it has on the accounting equation.

a. Paid cash to the stockholders as a distribution of earnings.

b. Paid cash to purchase land for building site.

c. Paid cash on an account payable.

d. Sold stock to stockholders.

e. Received cash from the bank in exchange for a note payable.

_____ 1. Increase an asset and increase stockholders' equity.

_____ 2. Increase an asset and increase a liability.

_____ 3. Increase one asset and decrease another asset.

_____ 4. Decrease an asset and decrease stockholders' equity.

_____ 5. Decrease an asset and decrease a liability.

S1-12. Transaction analysis (*Learning Objective 5*) **5–10 min.**

Action Powersports, Inc., a corporation, sells and services personal watercraft. The business experienced the following events. State whether each event (a) increased, (b) decreased, or (c) had no effect on the total assets of the business, and identify the asset(s) involved in each transaction.

1. Action Powersports, Inc., sold additional stock to stockholders.

2. Paid cash to purchase land as a building site.

3. Paid cash on accounts payable.

4. Purchased machinery and equipment; signed a promissory note in payment.

5. Performed service for a customer on account.

6. Paid cash to the stockholders as a distribution of earnings.

7. Received cash from a customer on account.

8. Sold land for a price equal to the cost of the land; received cash.

9. Borrowed money from the bank.

S1-13. Transaction analysis (*Learning Objective 5*) 5–10 min.

Presented here are nine transactions and the analysis used to account for them. Evaluate each of the suggested accounting treatments, and indicate whether it is true or false.

1. Received cash of $41,000 from the stockholders, who bought stock in the business.

   Answer: Increase asset, increase stockholders' equity. _____ True _____ False

2. Paid $600 cash to purchase supplies.

   Answer: Increase asset, increase stockholders' equity. _____ True _____ False

3. Earned service revenue on account, $1,200.

   Answer: Increase asset, increase retained earnings. _____ True _____ False

4. Purchased office furniture on account at a cost of $450.

   Answer: Increase asset, increase liability. _____ True _____ False

5. Received cash on account, $1500.

   Answer: Increase asset, decrease asset. _____ True _____ False

6. Paid cash on account, $175.

   Answer: Increase asset, increase liability. _____ True _____ False

7. Sold land for $68,000 cash, which was the cost of the land.

   Answer: Increase asset, decrease asset. _____ True _____ False

8. Performed services and received cash of $825.

   Answer: Increase asset, increase revenue. _____ True _____ False

9. Paid monthly office rent of $1,500.

   Answer: Decrease asset, increase stockholders' equity. _____ True _____ False

---

S1-14. Transaction analysis and calculating net income (*Learning Objective 5*) 5–10 min.

The analysis of Cunnington, Inc.'s first seven transactions follows. The business only sold stock once and paid no dividends.

		Assets		=	Liabilities		+	Stockholders' Equity	
	Cash	+ Accounts Receivable	+ Equipment	=	Accounts Payable	+ Notes Payable	+	Common Stock	+ Retained Earnings
1.	+ $40,000			=				+ $40,000	
2.	− 6,000		+ $ 6,000	=					
3.			+ 15,000	=		+ $15,000			
4.		+ $1,200		=					+ 1,200
5.	− 1,350			=					− 1,350
6.	+ 1,750			=					+ 1,750
7.	+ 350	− 350		=					

1. Label each of the transactions in the preceding analysis with the corresponding letter of the description that best fits it:
   a. Earned revenue for services provided, but customer will pay later.
   b. Customers paid cash for services completed earlier in the month.
   c. Received cash for revenue earned by providing services.
   d. Paid cash for expenses incurred to operate the business.
   e. Paid cash to purchase equipment.
   f. Sold stock to start the business.
   g. Purchased equipment with a bank loan.

2. If these transactions fully describe the operations of Cunnington, Inc., during the month, what was the amount of its net income or net loss?

MyAccountingLab
Exercises (Group A)

E1-15A. Basic accounting equation (*Learning Objective 5*) 10–15 min.

	Assets	=	Liabilities	+	Stockholders' Equity
Appleway Corp.	?	=	$48,700	+	$13,400
1st Choice Inc.	$ 82,000	=	?	+	$27,000
Hamilton Inc.	$127,300	=	$88,500	+	?

Quick solution:

$12,000 decrease

E1-16A. Basic accounting equation (*Learning Objective 5*) 10–15 min.

Mountain Drycleaners had $91,000 of total assets and $7,000 of total stockholders' equity at December 31, 2014. At December 31, 2015, Mountain Drycleaners had assets totaling $145,000 and stockholders' equity totaling $73,000.

After analyzing the data, answer the following questions:

1. What was the amount of the increase or decrease in liabilities?
2. Identify a possible reason for the change in liabilities during the year.

E1-17A. Basic accounting equation (*Learning Objective 5*) 10–15 min.

Lynne's Designs started business in 2014 with total assets of $37,000 and total liabilities of $16,000. At the end of 2014, Lynne's Designs' total assets were $82,000 and total liabilities were $28,000.

After analyzing the data, answer the following questions:

1. What was the amount of the increase or decrease in stockholders' equity?
2. Identify two possible reasons for the change in stockholders' equity during the year.

Try it in
Excel

E1-18A. Using the accounting equation to determine net income (*Learning Objectives 5 & 6*) 15–20 min.

The balance sheet data for Alan's Lightworks, Corp., at August 31, 2014, and September 30, 2014, follow:

	Aug 31, 2014	Sep 30, 2014
Total Assets	$135,000	$190,000
Total Liabilities	81,000	145,000
Common Stock	25,000	25,000
Total Stockholders' Equity	?	?

Requirement

1. The following are three *independent* assumptions about the business during September. For each assumption, compute the amount of net income or net loss during September 2014. Find the solution by preparing the statement of retained earnings. First, use the amounts of total assets, total liabilities, and common stock given previously and the accounting equation to determine the beginning and ending retained earnings amounts. Then plug those and the other amount given in each assumption into the statement of retained earnings to determine the net income or net loss.

   a. The business paid no dividends.
   b. The business paid $14,000 of dividends.
   c. The business paid $6,000 of dividends.

Retained Earnings + Dividends = Net

E1-19A. Transaction analysis (*Learning Objective 5*) 15–20 min.

Maria Lopez opened a medical practice titled Maria Lopez M.D., Inc. During August, the first month of operations, the business experienced the following events:

Aug	2	Lopez bought $90,000 of common stock in the business by opening a bank account in the name of Maria Lopez M.D., Inc.
	6	The business paid $53,000 cash for land with the intention of building an office building on the land.
	11	The business purchased medical supplies for $1,200 on account.
	15	The business officially opened for business.
	17	The business treated patients and earned service revenue of $9,400, receiving cash.
	19	The business paid office rent, $2,400.
	22	The business sold supplies to another doctor for $150 cash, the cost of those supplies.
	30	The business paid $800 on account related to the August 11 purchase.

Requirement

1. Analyze the effects of these events on the accounting equation of the medical practice of Maria Lopez M.D., Inc. Use headings for Cash, Medical Supplies, Land, Accounts Payable, Common Stock, Service Revenue, and Rent Expense.

E1-20A. Types of business organizations and balance sheet preparation (*Learning Objectives 3 & 6*) 10–15 min.

The following are the balances of the assets, liabilities, and equity of Happy Tots Gym at March 31, 2014:

Cash	$24,000	Office Equipment	$9,400
Retained Earnings	18,900	Common Stock	4,000
Accounts Payable	3,300	Note Payable	20,000
Accounts Receivable	12,500	Supplies	300

Requirements

1. What type of business organization is Happy Tots Gym?
2. Prepare the balance sheet of the business at March 31, 2014.
3. What does the balance sheet report?

E1-21A. Types of accounts and income statement preparation (*Learning Objectives 5 & 6*) 15–20 min.

Selected accounts of Cole Consulting, Inc., a financial services business, have the following balances at December 31, 2014, the end of its first year of operations. During the year, James Cole, the only stockholder, bought $20,000 of stock in the business.

Office Furniture	$ 26,500	Rent Expense	$28,000
Utilities Expense	6,300	Cash	4,200
Accounts Payable	4,100	Office Supplies	500
Note Payable	10,000	Salaries Expense	36,700
Service Revenue	116,600	Salaries Payable	1,500
Accounts Receivable	7,000	Property Tax Expense	1,600
Supplies Expense	2,700	Equipment	48,000

Requirements

1. Identify each as an asset, liability, revenue, or expense.

2. Prepare the income statement of Cole Consulting, Inc., for the year ended December 31, 2014. What is the result of operations for 2014?

3. Assuming the balance in Retained Earnings on December 31, 2014, was $9,300, what was the amount of the dividends during the year? Answer by preparing a statement of retained earnings to solve for the dividends. Recall that the business has just completed its first year and has no beginning balance for retained earnings.

E1-22A. Using the accounting equation to determine net income (*Learning Objectives 5 & 6*) 15–20 min.

Presented here is information for Earth, Inc., for the year ended August 31, 2014.

Earth, Inc.	
Beginning:	
Assets	$55,000
Liabilities	45,000
Ending:	
Assets	$114,000
Liabilities	25,000
Stockholders' Equity:	
Sale of Stock	$16,000
Payment of Dividends	50,000

Requirements

1. What is the beginning stockholders' equity of Earth, Inc.?
2. What is the ending stockholders' equity of Earth, Inc.?
3. What is the net income or net loss for the year?

Exercises (Group B)

E1-23B. Basic accounting equation (*Learning Objective 5*) 10–15 min.

Determine the missing amounts in the following accounting equations.

	Assets	=	Liabilities	+	Stockholders' Equity
Corner Grocery, Corp.	?	=	$45,000	+	$27,900
Sampson Hardware, Inc.	$104,000	=	?	+	$44,000
Perfect Cleaners, Inc.	$108,800	=	$92,600	+	?

E1-24B. Basic accounting equation (*Learning Objective 5*) 10–15 min.

Burnt Finger Restaurant had $84,000 of total assets and $56,000 of total stockholders' equity at July 31, 2014. At July 31, 2015, Burnt Finger Restaurant had assets totaling $153,000 and stockholders' equity totaling $91,000.

After analyzing the data, answer the following questions:

1. What was the amount of the increase or decrease in liabilities?
2. Identify a possible reason for the change in liabilities during the year.

E1-25B. Basic accounting equation (*Learning Objective 5*) 10–15 min.

Candy's Candies started a business in 2014 with total assets of $50,000 and total liabilities of $40,000. At the end of 2014, Candy's Candies' total assets were $57,000 and total liabilities were $8,000.

After analyzing the data, answer the following questions:

1. What was the amount of the increase or decrease in stockholders' equity?
2. Identify two possible reasons for the change in stockholders' equity during the year.

E1-26B. Using the accounting equation to determine net income (*Learning Objectives 5 & 6*) 15–20 min.

The balance sheet data for Cindy's Office Supplies, Co., at October 31, 2014, and November 30, 2014, follow:

	Oct 31, 2014	Nov 30, 2014
Total Assets	$127,000	$165,000
Total Liabilities	92,000	119,000
Common Stock	15,000	15,000
Total Stockholders' Equity	?	?

Requirement

1. The following are three *independent* assumptions about the business during November. For each assumption, compute the amount of net income or net loss during November 2014. Find the solution by preparing the statement of retained earnings. First, use the amounts of total assets, total liabilities, and common stock given previously and the accounting equation to determine the beginning and ending retained earnings amounts. Then plug those and the other amount given in each assumption into the statement of retained earnings to determine the net income or net loss.

   a. The business paid no dividends. $11,000
   b. The business paid $7,000 of dividends. $18,000
   c. The business paid $15,000 of dividends. $26,000

E1-27B. Transaction analysis (*Learning Objective 5*) 15–20 min.

Samantha Luden opened a medical practice titled Samantha Luden M.D., Inc. During March, the first month of operations, the business experienced the following events:

Mar 2	Luden bought $45,000 of common stock in the business by opening a bank account in the name of Samantha Luden M.D., Inc.
6	The business paid $20,000 cash for land with the intention of building an office building on the land.
11	The business purchased medical supplies for $1,000 on account.
15	The business officially opened for business.
17	The business treated patients and earned service revenue of $11,000, receiving cash.
19	The business paid office rent, $1,700.
22	The business sold supplies to another doctor for $350 cash, the cost of those supplies.
30	The business paid $700 on account related to the March 11 purchase.

Requirement

1. Analyze the effects of these events on the accounting equation of the medical practice of Samantha Luden M.D., Inc. Use headings for Cash, Medical Supplies, Land, Accounts Payable, Common Stock, Service Revenue, and Rent Expense.

E1-28B. Types of business organizations and balance sheet preparation (*Learning Objectives 5 & 6*) 10–15 min.

The following are the balances of the assets, liabilities, and equity of Julie's Coffee Shop at October 31, 2014:

Cash	$19,000	Office Equipment	$14,200
Retained Earnings	12,550	Common Stock	18,000
Accounts Payable	800	Note Payable	4,000
Accounts Receivable	1,400	Supplies	750

Requirements

1. What type of business organization is Julie's Coffee Shop?
2. Prepare the balance sheet of the business at October 31, 2014.
3. What does the balance sheet report?

E1-29B. Types of accounts and income statement preparation (*Learning Objectives 5 & 6***) 15–20 min.**

Selected accounts of Alden Consulting, Inc., a financial services business, have the following balances at December 31, 2014, the end of its first year of operations. During the year, Lorraine Alden, the only stockholder, bought $5,400 of stock in the business.

Office Furniture	$ 20,000	Rent Expense	$18,000
Utilities Expense	12,600	Cash	10,000
Accounts Payable	3,800	Office Supplies	500
Notes Payable	30,000	Salaries Expense	43,000
Service Revenue	161,000	Salaries Payable	2,200
Accounts Receivable	10,500	Property Tax Expense	2,400
Supplies Expense	3,400	Equipment	32,000

Requirements

1. Identify each as an asset, liability, revenue, or expense.

2. Prepare the income statement of Alden Consulting, Inc., for the year ended December 31, 2014. What is the result of operations for 2014?

3. Assuming the balance in Retained Earnings on December 31, 2014, was $21,600, what was the amount of the dividends during the year? Answer by preparing a statement of retained earnings to solve for the dividends. Recall that the business has just completed its first year and has no beginning balance for retained earnings.

E1-30B. Using the accounting equation to determine net income (*Learning Objectives 5 & 6***) 15–20 min.**

Presented here is information for Hastings, Inc., for the year ended October 31, 2014.

Hastings, Inc.	
Beginning:	
Assets	$ 83,000
Liabilities	36,000
Ending:	
Assets	$162,000
Liabilities	31,000
Stockholders' Equity:	
Sale of Stock	$ 20,000
Payment of Dividends	71,000

Requirements

1. What is the beginning stockholders' equity of Hastings, Inc.?

2. What is the ending stockholders' equity of Hastings, Inc.?

3. What is the net income or net loss for the year?

MyAccountingLab   ## Problems (Group A)

P1-31A. Transaction analysis and the calculation of net income (*Learning Objective 5*) **20–25 min.**

Jill Stevens worked as an accountant at a local accounting firm for five years after graduating from college. Recently, she opened her own accounting practice, which she operates as a corporation. The name of the new entity is Stevens and Associates, Inc. Jill experienced the following events during the first month of operations. Some of the events were personal and did not affect the accounting practice. Others were business transactions and should be accounted for by the business.

Apr	3	Received $65,000 cash proceeds from refinancing her house.
	5	$50,000 of common stock in the business was sold to Jill Stevens. The cash proceeds were deposited in a new business bank account titled Stevens and Associates, Inc.
	7	Paid $600 cash for office supplies for the new accounting practice.
	9	Purchased $4,300 of office furniture for the accounting practice and agreed to pay the vendor within three months.
	10	Jill sold 1,200 shares of Ford stock, which she had owned for several years, receiving $15,600 cash. The cash from the sale of stock was deposited in her personal bank account.
	14	A representative of a large company telephoned Jill and told her of the company's intention to hire Stevens and Associates, Inc., as its accountants.
	20	Finished accounting work for a client and sent the client a bill for $5,400. The client is expected to pay within two weeks.
	27	Paid office rent, $1,300.
	30	Paid $2,000 of dividends to shareholders of Stevens and Associates, Inc.

Requirements

1. Enter each transaction in the expanded accounting equation of Stevens and Associates, Inc., as needed, calculating new balances after each transaction.

2. Determine the following items:
   a. Total assets
   b. Total liabilities
   c. Total stockholders' equity
   d. Net income or net loss for April

P1-32A. Income statement and balance sheet transactions; prepare the income statement and balance sheet (*Learning Objectives 5 & 6*) **25–30 min.**

Dennise Geary started an interior design company called Interiors by Dennise, Inc., on November 1, 2014. The following amounts summarize the financial position of her business on November 14, 2014, after the first two weeks of operations:

Cash	+ Receivable	+ Supplies	+ Equipment	= Payable	+ Stock	+ Revenue	− Expense	− Dividends
$1,660	+ $3,210	+ 0	+ $26,000	= $4,700	+ $21,640	+ $6,300	− $1,770	− 0

During the remainder of November, the following events occurred:

a. Geary received $20,000 as a gift and used it to buy common stock in the business.

b. Paid off the beginning balance of Accounts Payable.

c. Performed services for a client and received cash of $4,000.

d. Collected cash from a customer on account, $1,100.

e. Purchased supplies on account, $500.

f. Consulted on the interior design of a major office building and billed the client for services performed, $3,500.

g. Sold an additional $8,000 of common stock in the business.

h. Incurred and paid salaries of $2,300.

i. Sold supplies at cost to another interior designer for $180 cash.

j. Paid dividends of $700 to Geary.

Requirements

1. Enter the remaining transactions for the month of November into the expanded accounting equation, calculating new balances after each transaction.

2. Prepare the income statement of Interiors by Dennise, Inc., for the month ended November 30, 2014.

3. Prepare the statement of retained earnings of Interiors by Dennise, Inc., for the month ended November 30, 2014.

4. Prepare the balance sheet of Interiors by Dennise, Inc., at November 30, 2014.

P1-33A. Prepare the income statement, statement of retained earnings, and balance sheet (*Learning Objective 6*) 20–25 min.

The Classy Chassis, Inc., restores antique automobiles. The retained earnings balance of the corporation was $32,400 at December 31, 2013. During 2014, the corporation paid $25,000 in dividends to its stockholders. At December 31, 2014, the business's accounting records show these balances:

Accounts Receivable	$12,500	Cash	$ 14,800
Note Payable	10,000	Accounts Payable	2,400
Retained Earnings	?	Advertising Expense	3,500
Salaries Expense	38,000	Service Revenue	106,000
Equipment	82,400	Common Stock	30,000
Insurance Expense	4,600		

Quick solution:

a. Net income = $59,900

b. Ending Retained earnings = $67,300

c. Total assets = $109,700

Requirement

1. Prepare the following financial statements for The Classy Chassis, Inc.:
   a. Income statement for the year ended December 31, 2014
   b. Statement of retained earnings for the year ended December 31, 2014
   c. Balance sheet at December 31, 2014

P1-34A. Prepare the income statement and balance sheet; identify certain financial information (*Learning Objective 6*) 25–30 min.

Presented here are the amounts of Assets, Liabilities, Stockholders' Equity, Revenues, and Expenses of Fast and Fit, Inc., at March 31, 2014. The items are listed in alphabetical order.

Accounts Payable	$ 16,000	Interest Expense	$ 6,000
Accounts Receivable	22,000	Land	35,000
Advertising Expense	15,000	Note Payable	62,000
Building	125,000	Property Tax Expense	3,500
Cash	16,000	Rent Expense	23,000
Common Stock	35,000	Salaries Expense	92,000
Dividends	28,000	Salaries Payable	3,000
Equipment	45,000	Service Revenue	166,000
Insurance Expense	2,300	Supplies	1,900

The retained earnings balance of the business was $132,700 at March 31, 2013.

Requirements

1. Identify each amount shown as an asset, liability, or stockholders' equity.

2. Prepare the company's income statement and statement of retained earnings for the year ended March 31, 2014.

3. Prepare the company's balance sheet at March 31, 2014.

4. Answer these questions about the company:
   a. What was the profit or loss for the year?
   b. What was the increase or decrease of retained earnings for the year?
   c. What is the amount of economic resources on March 31, 2014?
   d. What is the amount owed on March 31, 2014?

P1-35A. Error analysis and preparation of balance sheet (*Learning Objective 6*)
20–25 min.

The IT manager of Baldwin Realty, Inc., prepared the balance sheet of the company while the accountant was ill. The balance sheet contains numerous errors. In particular, the IT manager knew that the balance sheet should balance, so she plugged in the retained earnings amount to achieve this balance. The retained earnings amount, however, is not correct. All other amounts are accurate, but some are out of place.

Baldwin Realty, Inc.
Balance Sheet
Month Ended April 30, 2014

ASSETS		LIABILITIES	
Cash	$ 9,100	Accounts Payable	$ 650
Rent Expense	2,100	Utilities Expense	850
Supplies Expense	550	Accounts Receivable	2,300
Salaries Payable	1,800	Notes Payable	6,000
Equipment	21,000		
		STOCKHOLDERS' EQUITY	
		Common Stock	15,000
		Supplies	700
		Retained Earnings	9,050
		Total Stockholders' Equity	24,750
		Total Liabilities &	
Total Assets	$34,550	Stockholders' Equity	$34,550

Requirement

1. Prepare a new, corrected balance sheet for Baldwin Realty, Inc.

Problems (Group B)

P1-36B. Transaction analysis and the calculation of net income (*Learning Objective 5*) 20–25 min.

Davin Shore worked as an accountant at a local accounting firm for five years after graduating from college. Recently, he opened his own accounting practice, which he operates as a corporation. The name of the new entity is Shore and Associates, Inc. Davin experienced the following events during the first month of operations. Some of the events were personal and did not affect the accounting practice. Others were business transactions and should be accounted for by the business.

Jun	3	Received $60,000 cash proceeds from refinancing his house.
	5	$70,000 of common stock in the business was sold to Davin Shore. The cash proceeds were deposited in a new business bank account titled Shore and Associates, Inc.
	7	Paid $1,300 cash for office supplies for the new accounting practice.
	9	Purchased $3,500 of office furniture for the accounting practice and agreed to pay the vendor within three months.
	10	Davin sold 400 shares of Cooper stock, which he had owned for several years, receiving $40,000 cash. The cash from the sale of stock was deposited in his personal bank account.
	14	A representative of a large company telephoned Davin and told him of the company's intention to hire Shore and Associates, Inc., as its accountants.
	20	Finished accounting work for a client and sent the client a bill for $3,800. The client is expected to pay within two weeks.
	27	Paid office rent, $2,400.
	30	Paid $700 of dividends to shareholders of Shore and Associates, Inc.

Requirements

1. Enter each transaction in the expanded accounting equation of Shore and Associates, Inc., as needed, calculating new balances after each transaction.
2. Determine the following items:
    a. Total assets
    b. Total liabilities
    c. Total stockholders' equity
    d. Net income or net loss for June

P1-37B. Income statement and balance sheet transactions; prepare the income statement and balance sheet (*Learning Objectives 5 & 6*) **25–30 min.**

Jill Schultz started an interior design company called Interiors by Jill, Inc., on June 1, 2014. The following amounts summarize the financial position of her business on June 14, 2014, after the first two weeks of operations:

Assets					=	Liabilities	+	Stockholders' Equity				
								Common Stock	+	Retained Earnings		
Cash	+ Accounts Receivable	+ Supplies	+ Equipment	=	Accounts Payable	+	Common Stock	+	Service Revenue	−	Salaries Expense	− Dividends
$1,680	+ $4,130	+ 0	+ $32,000	=	$3,100	+	$30,000	+	$9,170	−	$4,460	− 0

During the remainder of June, the following events occurred:

a. Schultz received $10,000 as a gift and used it to buy common stock in the business.

b. Paid off the beginning balance of Accounts Payable.

c. Performed services for a client and received cash of $2,500.

d. Collected cash from a customer on account, $2,130.

e. Purchased supplies on account, $850.

f. Consulted on the interior design of a major office building and billed the client for services performed, $6,200.

g. Sold an additional $7,000 of common stock in the business.

h. Incurred and paid salaries of $4,600.

i. Sold supplies at cost to another interior designer for $250 cash.

j. Paid dividends of $1,500 to Schultz.

Requirements

1. Enter the remaining transactions for the month of June into the expanded accounting equation, calculating new balances after each transaction.

2. Prepare the income statement of Interiors by Jill, Inc., for the month ended June 30, 2014.

3. Prepare the statement of retained earnings of Interiors by Jill, Inc., for the month ended June 30, 2014.

4. Prepare the balance sheet of Interiors by Jill, Inc., at June 30, 2014.

P1-38B. **Prepare the income statement, statement of retained earnings, and balance sheet** (*Learning Objective 6*) **20–25 min.**

McKnight, Inc., restores antique automobiles. The retained earnings balance of the corporation was $23,500 at December 31, 2013. During 2014, the corporation paid $40,000 in dividends to its stockholders. At December 31, 2014, the business's accounting records show these balances:

Accounts Receivable	$ 8,000	Cash	$17,000
Note Payable	16,000	Accounts Payable	9,000
Retained Earnings	?	Advertising Expense	5,500
Salaries Expense	13,000	Service Revenue	88,000
Equipment	65,000	Common Stock	20,000
Insurance Expense	8,000		

Requirement

1. Prepare the following financial statements for McKnight, Inc.:
   a. Income statement for the year ended December 31, 2014
   b. Statement of retained earnings for the year ended December 31, 2014
   c. Balance sheet at December 31, 2014

P1-39B. **Prepare the income statement and balance sheet; identify certain financial information** (*Learning Objective 6*) **25–30 min.**

Presented here are the amounts of Assets, Liabilities, Stockholders' Equity, Revenues, and Expenses of Alpha, Inc., at October 31, 2014. The items are listed in alphabetical order.

Accounts Payable	$ 13,700	Interest Expense	$ 7,500
Accounts Receivable	15,100	Land	40,000
Advertising Expense	19,600	Note Payable	75,000
Building	142,000	Property Tax Expense	4,900
Cash	24,800	Rent Expense	24,000
Common Stock	75,000	Salaries Expense	91,300
Dividends	28,000	Salaries Payable	4,750
Equipment	51,000	Service Revenue	210,000
Insurance Expense	3,600	Supplies	2,250

The retained earnings balance of the business was $75,600 at October 31, 2013.

Requirements

1. Identify each amount shown as an asset, liability, or stockholders' equity.

2. Prepare the company's income statement and statement of retained earnings for the year ended October 31, 2014.

3. Prepare the company's balance sheet at October 31, 2014.

4. Answer these questions about the company:
   a. What was the profit or loss for the year?
   b. What was the increase or decrease of retained earnings for the year?
   c. What is the amount of economic resources on October 31, 2014?
   d. What is the amount owed on October 31, 2014?

P1-40B. Error analysis and preparation of balance sheet (*Learning Objective 6*)
20–25 min.

The IT manager of On Call Realty, Inc., prepared the balance sheet of the company while the accountant was ill. The balance sheet contains numerous errors. In particular, the IT manager knew that the balance sheet should balance, so she plugged in the retained earnings amount to achieve this balance. The retained earnings amount, however, is not correct. All other amounts are accurate, but some are out of place.

On Call Realty, Inc. Balance Sheet Month Ended November 30, 2014				
ASSETS			**LIABILITIES**	
Cash	$31,000		Accounts Payable	$ 2,500
Rent Expense	1,800		Utilities Expense	900
Supplies Expense	500		Accounts Receivable	3,200
Salaries Payable	1,100		Notes Payable	7,000
Equipment	8,100			
			STOCKHOLDERS' EQUITY	
			Common Stock	10,000
			Supplies	580
			Retained Earnings	18,320
			Total Stockholders' Equity	28,900
			Total Liabilities &	
Total Assets	$42,500		Stockholders' Equity	$42,500

Requirement

1. Prepare a new, corrected balance sheet for On Call Realty, Inc.

ON Call Reality, Inc.
Balance Sheet
November 30, 2014

Assets

Cash 31,000
Equip 8,100
AR 3,200
Supplies 580
        $42,880

Liabilities
AP 2,500
NP 7,000
SP 1,100
        $ 10,600

OE
CS 10,000
RE 22,280
        22,280
        $42,880

Continuing Exercise

This exercise is the first exercise in a sequence that begins an accounting cycle. The cycle is continued in Chapter 2 and completed in Chapter 3. Cole's Yard Care, Inc., began operations and completed the following transactions during April:

Apr	1	Received $2,000 and issued 500 shares of common stock. Deposited this amount in a bank account in the name of Cole's Yard Care, Inc.
	3	Purchased on account a mower, $1,200, and weed whacker, $400. The equipment is expected to remain in service for four years.
	5	Purchased $90 of gas. Wrote check #1 from the new bank account.
	6	Performed lawn services for client on account, $225.
	8	Purchased $85 of fertilizer from the lawn store. Wrote check #2 from the new bank account.
	17	Completed landscaping job for client, received cash $850.
	30	Received $175 on account from services performed on April 6.

Requirement

1. Analyze the effects of Cole's Yard Care, Inc.'s transactions on the accounting equation. Include these headings: Cash, Accounts Receivable, Lawn Supplies, Equipment, Accounts Payable, Common Stock, Retained Earnings, Service Revenue, and Fuel Expense. Determine the ending balances in each account on April 30.

In Chapter 2, we will account for these same transactions a different way—as the accounting is actually performed in practice.

Continuing Problem

This problem is the first problem in a sequence that begins an accounting cycle. The cycle is continued in Chapter 2 and completed in Chapter 3.

Greg Richards recently left his job at a local pool company to open his own pool and spa maintenance business. Greg Richards took all of the money he and his wife had in their personal savings account and used it to open Aqua Magic, Inc., on May 1, 2014. Presented next are the transactions for the first month of operations for Aqua Magic, Inc.:

May	1	Greg invested $35,000 cash and a used truck with a fair market value of $10,000 in the business in exchange for the company's common stock.
	3	Paid $1,800 cash to purchase office equipment.
	7	Purchased $600 of supplies on account.
	12	Performed services for cash customers and received $1,350.
	15	Incurred and paid salaries of $625 to the office receptionist.
	16	Sold the company truck for $10,000.
	18	Signed a note payable for $36,200 to purchase a new truck.
	21	Performed $4,500 of services on account for a local hotel chain.
	27	Paid $300 of the amount owed from the purchase of supplies on May 7.
	30	Received $2,200 on account from credit customers.
	31	Received the utility bill for the month of May, $740. The bill is not due until June 15.
	31	Paid $2,500 dividends to the shareholder, Greg Richards.

Requirements

1. Enter the transactions for Aqua Magic, Inc., for the month of May into the expanded accounting equation. Calculate the ending balances at May 31.

2. Prepare the income statement for Aqua Magic, Inc., for the first month of operations.

3. Prepare the statement of retained earnings for Aqua Magic, Inc., for the first month of operations.

4. Prepare the balance sheet for Aqua Magic, Inc., at May 31.

5. Did Greg make a wise decision leaving his job to start Aqua Magic, Inc.?

Continuing Financial Statement Analysis Problem

Let's look at Target, one of the largest retailers found throughout the United States. Think about Target, all its stakeholders, what products it sells, and how and where it sells its products. Think about all the employees that work for Target and the assets that Target needs. Think about the business of Target.

Now go to Target's Web site at www.target.com. Next, scroll to the bottom of the page and look for the heading "about Target" and click on "company information." There you'll find information about Target's business. Explore the menu options available in "Our Company" and in "Investors" in order to find the answers to these questions:

1. What is the mission statement of the business? What does it say about value?

2. What type of business is Target? Is it a service company, a merchandise company, or a manufacturing company?

3. What products does Target sell? Where does it get the products it sells?

4. Who are Target's customers?

5. Now look at Target's stock price. At the beginning of February 2013 you would pay approximately $62 to own one share of Target's stock. When you add all the shares of stock together, Target is valued at approximately $40 billion. That's a considerable amount of money. Do you think Target is worth $40 billion? What role do you think accounting plays in helping owners (stockholders) decide the value of Target?

Apply Your Knowledge

Ethics in Action

Case 1. Lisa Hill and her husband Mike were the owners of LM Enterprises, Inc. They applied for a small business loan, and the bank requested the most recent business financial statements. When Lisa compiled the balance sheet, she noticed that the business's assets and related stockholders' equity were small. Accordingly, she told Mike that they should contribute some of their personal assets to the business so the assets and equity would appear much larger and thus the bank would more likely agree to the business loan. Mike agreed that the balance sheet would appear stronger with more assets and equity, but his concern was with the income statement. The sales for the latest period were low, which resulted in a slight net loss because expenses were slightly higher than revenues. Mike reasoned that contributing assets would show a stronger balance sheet but felt something had to be done to also improve the income statement. He then told Lisa that their business could "sell" back some of the assets they had contributed and report higher sales on the income statement, which would result in net income rather than the actual net loss. Lisa did not feel comfortable buying back assets from their business just to increase reported sales.

Discuss any ethical concerns you may have with Lisa's proposal. Discuss any ethical concerns you may have with Mike's proposal. Do you think it is ethical for a business to "dress up" its financial statements when applying for a loan?

Case 2. Blackstone, Inc., was in the final phase of completing a land development project it started earlier in the year. Blackstone, Inc., had acquired 50 acres of raw land for $400,000 and then spent an additional $1,700,000 in land development costs to create a new subdivision with 100 residential lots. With a total cost of $2,100,000 and 100 lots, each lot had a cost of $21,000; however, the lots were listed for sale at $48,000 per lot. Blackstone, Inc., was applying for a business loan and needed to provide current financial statements to the bank. Amy Clark, the company president, wanted to report the total current value of the lots, $4,800,000 (100 lots x $48,000 per lot), rather than the total cost currently listed on the balance sheet, $2,100,000. Dan Sullivan, the company accountant, told Amy that the lots were inventory and that they should be reported on the balance sheet at the $2,100,000 rather than the fair market value.

Should the balance sheet for Blackstone, Inc., list the lots at the total cost of $2,100,000 or the total selling price of $4,800,000? Could Blackstone, Inc., provide one balance sheet using historical cost and another balance sheet using market value?

Know Your Business

Financial Analysis

Purpose: To help familiarize you with the financial reporting of a real company in order to further your understanding of the chapter material you are learning.

Each chapter will have a financial statement case that will focus on material contained in that chapter. You will be asked questions and will then refer to Appendix A at the end of the book where you will find the annual report for Columbia Sportswear Company. Use the annual report to answer these questions. As you progress through each chapter, you will gain a real understanding of actual corporate financial reporting in addition to the basic accounting concepts you are learning within each textbook chapter. This added learning experience will reinforce your understanding of accounting.

Requirements

1. Look at all the financial statements starting on page 656 of Appendix A and see whether you can identify the balance sheet, income statement, and statement of cash flows. (Note that the term *Consolidated* simply means "combined.")

2. What was the total amount of assets Columbia Sportswear reported as of December 31, 2012? (Keep in mind that the numbers are in thousands.) Did the total assets increase or decrease from December 31, 2011?

3. Did you see that Columbia Sportswear titled its income statement "Statements of Operations"? Were you able to identify it? (Note that some companies use this title.)

4. What was the total amount of revenues (net sales) Columbia Sportswear reported for the year ended December 31, 2012? (Keep in mind that the numbers are in thousands.) Did the revenues increase or decrease from the previous years presented?

Industry Analysis

Purpose: To help you understand and compare the performance of two companies in the same industry.

Go to the Columbia Sportswear Company Annual Report located in Appendix A and find the Consolidated Balance Sheets on page 000. Now access the 2012 Annual Report for Under Armour, Inc. To do this from the Internet, go to the company's Web page at http://www.underarmour.com. At the bottom of the page under **Business Info**, click on **Investor Relations**. Next, click on **Financials** on the left-hand side of the page and then click on **Annual Report and Proxy**. Now, on the right-hand side of the page, look for the link to download the 2012 annual report. The Consolidated Balance Sheet is located on page 48.

Columbia Sportswear Company and Under Armour, Inc., are in the same industry, which is manufacturing and selling sportswear. It is helpful to compare a company's financial data against other companies in their industry.

Requirement

1. Look at the data from the Consolidated Balance Sheets at December 31, 2012, for each of the companies. Which company's stockholders have a higher claim to their company's assets? To find out, divide the total stockholders' equity for each company by its total liabilities and stockholders' equity.

Small Business Analysis

Purpose: To help you understand the importance of cash flows in the operation of a small business.

You have just received your year-end financial statements from your CPA and you notice one very disturbing item. The net income from your income statement shows $36,000! Your very first thought is "where is it?" Then you look at your cash balance and see that it decreased $8,000 from last year to this year. You're thinking there has to be something wrong here. So you call up your CPA and ask for a meeting to discuss this obvious error. After all, how can you possibly have a positive net income and have your cash balance **decrease**?

At the meeting, the CPA lays out the financial statements in front of you and begins to explain how this would have happened. Following are a condensed income statement, statement of retained earnings, and balance sheet:

BCS Consultants, Inc.
Income Statement
For the Year Ended December 31, 2014

Total Revenue		$142,000
Total Expenses		106,000
Net Income		$ 36,000

BCS Consultants, Inc.
Statement of Retained Earnings
For the Year Ended December 31, 2014

Beginning Retained Earnings		$ 84,000
Net Income	$ 36,000	
Dividends Paid	(15,000)	21,000
Ending Retained Earnings		$105,000

BCS Consultants, Inc.
Balance Sheet
December 31, 2014 & 2013

	2014	2013
Assets:		
Cash	$ 30,000	$ 38,000
Equipment	158,000	146,000
Total Assets	$188,000	$184,000
Liabilities:		
Notes Payable—Bank	$ 58,000	$ 75,000
Stockholder's Equity:		
Common Stock	25,000	25,000
Retained Earnings	105,000	84,000
Total Stockholders' Equity	130,000	109,000
Total Liabilities and Stockholders' Equity	$188,000	$184,000

Requirement

1. By looking at the three financial statements, can you anticipate what the CPA is going to tell you about why the cash decreased even though you had net income for the year? What changed from 2013 to 2014? Are transactions that affect the income statement the only transactions that affect your cash balance?

Written Communication

You just received an e-mail from a potential new client who contacted you from your Web site. This client has indicated to you that he or she is planning to start a new business. The client would like to find out from you what different types of business organizations are available. Also, the client is wondering exactly what role an accountant would have in the running of his or her business.

Requirement

1. Prepare an e-mail to this potential client addressing his or her questions about the different types of business organizations and why he or she needs to have an accountant involved in the business.

Self Check Answers
1. c 2. d 3. c 4. c 5. a 6. b 7. b 8. c 9. a 10. d 11. true 12. c

Analyzing and Recording Business Transactions

Business, Accounting, and You

Walk into your local Target and look around. What do you see? You see people browsing, making decisions to buy or not to buy, and taking their purchases to the checkout. You see Target employees helping customers. You see many business transactions occurring simultaneously. You see business in action.

Now, think about it. How does Target keep up with the cause and effect of all those transactions? How does a business keep track of all its assets, liabilities, revenue, costs, and other activities? There must be a "scorekeeper" or systematic process that recognizes, measures, records, and reports these business transactions in an understandable, reliable, and relevant manner. That's the role of accounting in business.

To ensure accounting information is understandable, reliable, and relevant, accountants have rules. GAAP, as noted in Chapter 1, set the rules for recognizing

Learning Objectives

1 Define accounts and understand how they are used in accounting

2 Explain debits, credits, and the double-entry system of accounting

3 Demonstrate the use of the general journal and the general ledger to record business transactions

4 Use a trial balance to prepare financial statements

and measuring the business transactions. This part of the process will be explored throughout the book. However, the rules for recording and reporting business transactions are based on a set of proven techniques that have evolved over time. The result is a set of standard, universally accepted procedures that work. The key to using these techniques and procedures is understanding: (1) accounts and (2) double-entry accounting.

So why is this important to you? Whether you want to be an accountant or manager, you need to understand how business transactions are recorded. The final report card, good or bad, is a result of this recording process. Would you want to play a game where you do not understand how the score is recorded and ultimately reported? Probably not. Understanding how accountants record business transactions is very important.

 ## Real World Accounting Video

In the Real World Accounting Video, Julie Gaines, owner and manager of Fishs Eddy, talks about what it means to own and operate a business. Look at the video. Think about what Julie is saying. And then realize how important accounting is to the success of a business.

How Are Accounts Used to Keep Business Transactions Organized?

1 **Define accounts and understand how they are used in accounting**

Accounts The basic summary device of accounting; the detailed record of all the changes in a specific asset, liability, or stockholders' equity item as a result of transactions.

As we discussed in Chapter 1, accounting provides useful information to various users. In order for the information to be useful, it has to be detailed. Therefore, to convey the detail required, accountants will create many categories in which to track information. These categories are referred to as **accounts**. We have already seen accounts in use. When recording transactions in the accounting equation in Chapter 1, we created accounts such as Cash, Equipment, and Accounts Payable.

Organizing Accounts

Numbering helps keep the accounts organized. Account numbers usually have two or more digits. The first digit indicates the type of account. Generally, if an account starts with:

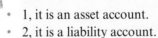

- 1, it is an asset account.
- 2, it is a liability account.
- 3, it is a stockholders' equity account other than a revenue or expense account.
- 4, it is a revenue account.
- 5, it is an expense account.

Accounts that start with 6, 7, 8, or 9 are used by some businesses to record special types of accounts such as other revenues and expenses.

After the first digit, the remaining digits in an account number are used to specify the exact account. For example, Cash may be numbered 101 and Accounts Receivable may be numbered 131. A gap in numbers is usually left between the different accounts to allow for additional accounts to be added later. A listing of all of the accounts is referred

Chart of accounts A list of all the accounts of a business and the numbers assigned to those accounts.

to as a **chart of accounts**. The accounts are typically listed in the chart of accounts in the order that they appear in the accounting equation. Therefore, assets would be listed first, followed by the liabilities, and then the stockholders' equity accounts. Typical types of accounts for many businesses are as follows:

Assets

As described in Chapter 1, assets represent things of value that a business has. Most businesses use the following asset accounts:

- **Cash.** Cash typically includes the business's bank account balance, paper currency, coins, and checks.
- **Accounts Receivable.** A business may sell goods or services in exchange for a promise of a future cash receipt. Such sales are said to be made on credit or on account. The Accounts Receivable account reflects the amounts that customers owe the business for goods or services that have already been provided. In other words, it shows how much money the company can expect to *receive* from customers in the future.
- **Notes Receivable.** A business may sell goods or services or loan money and receive a promissory note. A note receivable is a written promise that the customer or borrower will pay a fixed amount of money by a certain date. Notes Receivable reflects the amount of the **promissory notes** that the business expects to collect in cash at a later date.
- **Prepaid Expenses.** A business often pays certain expenses, such as rent and insurance, in advance. A prepaid expense is an asset because the prepayment provides a future benefit for the business. A separate asset account is used for each prepaid expense. Prepaid Rent and Prepaid Insurance are examples of prepaid expense accounts.
- **Land.** The Land account is used to keep track of the cost of land a business owns and uses in its operations.
- **Buildings.** The cost of a business's buildings, offices, warehouses, etc. is recorded in the Buildings account.
- **Equipment, Furniture, and Fixtures.** A business typically has a separate asset account for each type of equipment. Examples include Computer Equipment, Office Equipment, Store Equipment, and Furniture and Fixtures.

Promissory note A written pledge to pay a fixed amount of money at a later date.

Liabilities

As defined in Chapter 1, liabilities are amounts owed to third parties. A business generally has fewer liability accounts than asset accounts because a business's liabilities can be summarized in a few categories such as:

- **Accounts Payable.** A business may purchase goods or services in exchange for a promise of future payment. Such purchases are said to be made on credit or on account. The Accounts Payable account reflects how much cash the business must pay to suppliers for goods or services that have already been received.
- **Notes Payable.** Notes Payable represents amounts the business must pay because it signed promissory notes to borrow money or to purchase goods or services.
- **Accrued Liabilities.** An accrued liability is a liability for an expense that has been incurred but has not yet been paid. Taxes Payable, Interest Payable, and Salaries Payable are examples of accrued liability accounts.

Stockholders' Equity

As we saw in Chapter 1, the owners' claim to the assets of the business is called Stockholders' Equity. We have already discussed the different types of stockholders' equity accounts and what they're used for, but they are listed here again for review.

- **Common Stock.** The Common Stock account represents the investment of assets, usually cash, the stockholders have invested into a business in exchange for the company's stock.
- **Retained Earnings.** The Retained Earnings account tracks the cumulative earnings of the business since it began, less any dividends given to stockholders.
- **Revenues.** Increases in Retained Earnings (and, therefore, Stockholders' Equity) created by selling goods or services to customers are called revenues. This account represents amounts *earned* by the company even if the company has not yet been paid for the goods and services provided. A business may have several revenue accounts depending on how many ways it earns its revenue.
- **Expenses.** Expenses are decreases in Retained Earnings (and, therefore, Stockholders' Equity) from using resources to deliver goods and services to customers. A business needs a separate account for each type of expense, such as Insurance Expense, Rent Expense, Salaries Expense, and Utilities Expense. Businesses often have numerous expense accounts because many different types of costs are associated with providing goods and services to customers.
- **Dividends.** This account reflects the amount of earnings that have been distributed to the stockholders. Dividends decrease Retained Earnings (and, therefore, Stockholders' Equity).

What Is Double-Entry Accounting?

 Explain debits, credits, and the double-entry system of accounting

Double-entry accounting The rule of accounting that specifies every transaction involves at least two accounts and is recorded with equal amounts of debits and credits.

Debit The left side of any account; an entry made to the left side of an account.

Credit The right side of any account; an entry made to the right side of an account.

T-account An informal account form used to summarize transactions, where the top of the T holds the account title and the base divides the debit and credit sides of the account.

In Chapter 1, we learned that every time we entered a transaction in the accounting equation, it affected at least two accounts. In accounting, the requirement that every transaction affect at least two accounts is called **double-entry accounting**. In order to simplify the process of accounting, each account is broken down into two sides. This can be visualized as a large T. For each account, one side of the T will represent an increase to the account, while the other side represents a decrease. Whether it is the left side of the T or the right side that increases the account depends on the type of account. Some accounts will increase on the left side and some will increase on the right side. In accounting terms, the left side of an account is referred to as the **debit** side. The right side of an account is referred to as the **credit** side. An example of a **T-account** is as follows:

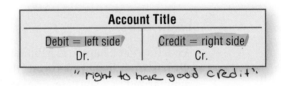

Although T-accounts are not an official accounting tool, accounting professors use them to help students visualize the accounts. When first learning accounting, it can be very confusing trying to understand why some accounts are increased with debits (on the left side) while other accounts are increased with credits (on the right side). However confusing this might be, it was designed this way for a purpose. In addition to the rule that states that assets must always equal liabilities plus stockholders' equity, another accounting rule states that in every transaction the dollar amount of debits must equal the dollar amount of credits. By requiring that the amount of debits always equals the amount of credits and having some accounts increase with debits and other accounts increase with credits, the accounting equation is automatically kept in balance. **Exhibit 2-1** shows the accounting equation with T-accounts under each type of account along with which side of the account increases it or decreases it.

When trying to learn which accounts are increased with debits and which accounts are increased with credits, it is helpful to think of the acronym ADE and the acronym LCR. In the acronym ADE, the A stands for Assets, the D for Dividends, and the E for Expenses. These accounts are increased on the debit side (think of the DE in ADE). In the acronym LCR, the L stands for Liabilities, the C stands for Common Stock, and the R stands for both Revenues and Retained Earnings. These accounts are increased on the credit side (think of the CR in LCR).

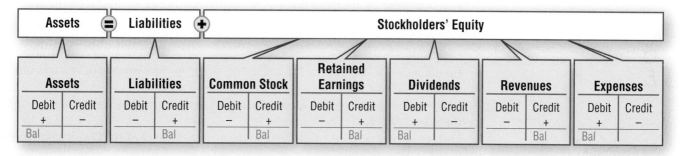

Exhibit 2-1 ▲

Accounting in Your World

Jill recently purchased something over the phone and used her debit card to pay for it. When she checked her bank account activity online, the bank "debited" her account when it took money out of her account to pay for the purchase. Jill read in the textbook that a debit would increase her cash account. Now Jill is really confused.

Many students feel this way when first introduced to debits and credits. It is really just a matter of perspective. You see, your bank account is an asset to you because it represents cash that is yours. However, your account is a liability to the bank because it represents money that the bank owes you. So, when the bank removes money from your account, it will debit the account to lower the liability because it no longer owes you the money. This is why it is called a *debit* card. You would actually need to credit your cash account, an asset, to show a decrease to your cash. Because you view your account as an asset and the bank views it as a liability, what you do (debit or credit) to the account to increase or decrease it will be exactly opposite of what the bank does.

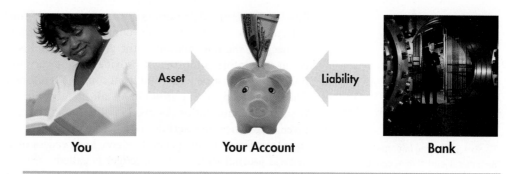

Normal Balance

You would expect an account to have a positive balance; therefore, the **normal balance** of an account is on the increase side of an account:

- Assets increase on the debit side, so the normal balance of an asset is on the debit side.
- Liabilities increase on the credit side, so the normal balance of a liability is on the credit side.
- Common Stock increases on the credit side, so the normal balance of this account is on the credit side.
- Retained Earnings increases on the credit side, so the normal balance of this account is on the credit side.
- Dividends increase on the debit side, so the normal balance of the Dividends account is on the debit side.
- Revenues increase on the credit side, so the normal balance of a revenue is on the credit side.
- Expenses increase on the debit side, so the normal balance of an expense is on the debit side.

How Are the General Journal and General Ledger Used to Keep Track of Business Transactions?

Demonstrate the use of the general journal and the general ledger to record business transactions

General journal The chronological accounting record of the transactions of a business.

Record Entering a transaction in a journal; also called **journalize**.

Transaction An event that has a financial impact on a business entity.

Although it would be possible to enter transactions directly into the T-accounts, if we were to try to do this for a real company, it would become very cumbersome and inefficient. Accountants need to enter transactions efficiently and in a timely manner. In order to do this, the **general journal** was created. The general journal is a chronological, or date order, record of the transactions of a business. The general journal can be compared to an individual person's diary. Like an individual person's diary, the general journal is a place to **record** events that have affected the business. Recording a **transaction** in the general journal is referred to as **journalizing** the transaction. To record a journal entry:

1. Record the date.
2. Record the debit part of the entry by entering the account title and then entering the amount in the debit column.
3. Record the credit part of the entry on the next line by indenting the account title and then entering the amount in the credit column.
4. Write an explanation describing the entry.

Exhibit 2-2, Panel A, describes a transaction, and Panel B shows how this transaction is entered in the journal. The page number of the journal appears in its upper-right corner.

Because the information in the general journal is organized by date and not by account, the information that it provides is not very useful. In order to be more useful, information must be organized by account. Therefore, the **general ledger** was created. The general ledger is a grouping of all the accounts of a business with their balances. It shows the amount of Assets, Liabilities, and the Stockholders' Equity accounts on a given date. Once transactions have been entered in the general journal, the information is then transferred to the general ledger. The process of transferring information from the general journal to the general ledger is called **posting**. Posting simply means copying the amounts from the journal to the ledger. Debits in the journal are posted as debits in

General ledger The accounting record summarizing, in accounts, the transactions of a business and showing the resulting ending account balances.

Posting Copying information from the general journal to accounts in the general ledger.

PANEL A—Illustrative Transaction:

DATE	TRANSACTION
Jan 1, 2014	Osborne Consulting, Inc., sold $10,000 of common stock to Cindy Osborne, who was investing cash in the business.

PANEL B—Journal:

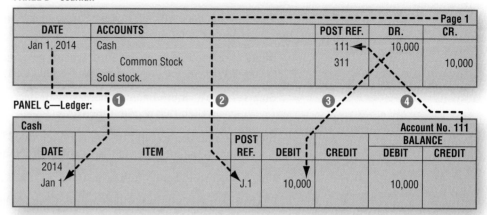

				Page 1
DATE	ACCOUNTS	POST REF.	DR.	CR.
Jan 1, 2014	Cash	111	10,000	
	Common Stock	311		10,000
	Sold stock.			

PANEL C—Ledger: ❶ ❷ ❸ ❹

Cash   Account No. 111

DATE	ITEM	POST REF.	DEBIT	CREDIT	BALANCE DEBIT	BALANCE CREDIT
2014 Jan 1		J.1	10,000		10,000	

Common Stock   Account No. 311

DATE	ITEM	POST REF.	DEBIT	CREDIT	BALANCE DEBIT	BALANCE CREDIT
2014 Jan 1		J.1		10,000		10,000

Exhibit 2-2 ▲

the ledger, and credits in the journal are posted as credits in the ledger. Exhibit 2-2, Panel C, demonstrates how an entry is posted from the journal to the ledger.

The posting process demonstrated in Exhibit 2-2 includes four steps. The four steps required to post the first part of the journal entry are as follows:

Arrow ❶ Copy the transaction date from the journal to the Cash account in the ledger.

Posting reference A notation in the journal and ledger that links these two accounting records together.

Arrow ❷ Copy the journal page number from the journal to the **posting reference** column in the Cash account in the ledger. "J.1" refers to Journal page 1. This provides a reference that links the entry in the ledger back to the journal.

Arrow ❸ Copy the dollar amount of the debit, $10,000, from the journal as a debit into the Cash account in the ledger.

Arrow ❹ Copy the account number, 111, from the Cash account in the ledger back to the posting reference column in the journal. This step indicates that the $10,000 debit to Cash was posted to the Cash account in the ledger.

The journal entry is posted to Cash first because this is the first account listed in the entry. Once posting to Cash is complete, repeat the process to post the entry to Common Stock. The account format that is utilized in Panel C of Exhibit 2-2 is called a four-column account. The first pair of debit and credit columns contains the individual transaction amounts that have been posted from journal entries, such as the $10,000 debit. The second pair of debit and credit columns is used to show the account's balance after each entry. Posting used to be performed on a periodic basis, such as daily or weekly. However, most modern computerized accounting systems post transactions immediately after they have been entered.

Transaction Analysis

To properly record, or journalize, transactions in the general journal, it is helpful to complete a five-step process. Steps 1 through 4 analyze the transaction for the journal entry and Step 5 reflects the journalizing of the transaction and the posting from the journal into the accounts in the general ledger. The five-step process is as follows:

Step 1 What accounts are involved? *Example*: Cash, Accounts Payable, Salaries Expense, etc.

Step 2 For each account involved, what type of account is it? Is it an asset, a liability, or one of the stockholders' equity accounts? *Example*: Cash is an asset.

Step 3 Is the account balance increasing or decreasing? *Example*: If you receive cash, then that account increases.

Step 4 Should the account be debited or credited? *Example*: Cash is an asset and it increases; increases in assets are recorded as debits.

Step 5 Record the entry and post to the accounts in the general ledger.

The five-step analysis looks like the following in chart form:

Step 1	Step 2	Step 3	Step 4	Step 5
Accounts Affected	Type	↑↓	Dr. or Cr.	Journalize entry and post to ledger

Applying Transaction Analysis

Check out how the transactions for the first month of operations for Osborne Consulting, Inc., are analyzed and recorded. These transactions were examined in Chapter 1 for a new computer consulting business. *For illustration purposes, journal entries are shown being posted to T-accounts within the accounting equation. In actual practice, the journal entries would be posted to four-column accounts in the general ledger.*

1. **Sale of stock.** The business sold Cindy Osborne $10,000 of common stock for cash.

   Analysis of Transaction (1)

   Step 1 What accounts are involved? The business received cash in exchange for stock, so the accounts involved are Cash and Common Stock.

   Step 2 What type of account is it? Cash is an asset. Common Stock is an account within stockholders' equity.

   Step 3 Does the account balance increase or decrease? Because cash was received, Cash is increased. Common Stock also increased because there has been more stock issued.

   Step 4 Do you debit or credit the account in the journal entry? According to the rules of debits and credits, an increase in an asset is recorded with a debit. An increase in Common Stock is recorded with a credit.

The first four steps can be summarized as follows:

1 **Accounts Affected**	2 **Type**	3 ↑↓	4 **Dr. or Cr.**
Cash	Asset	↑	Dr.
Common Stock	Stockholders' Equity	↑	Cr.

Step 5 Journalize and post the transaction as follows:

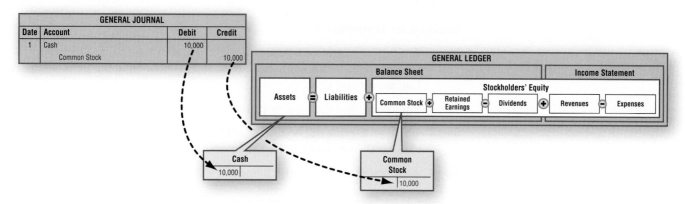

Notice that the name of the account being credited is indented in the journal. This format is a standard way to differentiate the accounts that are credited from the accounts that are debited. Also, note again that every transaction affects at least two accounts and that the total amount added to the debit side equals the total amount added to the credit side. This demonstrates double-entry accounting, which keeps the accounting equation in balance.

2. **Purchase supplies on credit.** Osborne Consulting purchases office supplies agreeing to pay $350 within 30 days.

Analysis of Transaction (2)

Step 1 The business received supplies in exchange for a promise to pay cash to the supplier next month. The accounts involved in the transaction are Supplies and Accounts Payable.

Step 2 Supplies is an asset; Accounts Payable is a liability.

Step 3 The asset Supplies is increased. The liability Accounts Payable is increased because the business owes more than it did before this transaction.

Step 4 An increase in the asset Supplies is a debit; an increase in the liability Accounts Payable is a credit.

1 Accounts Affected	2 Type	3 ↑↓	4 Dr. or Cr.
Supplies	Asset	↑	Dr.
Accounts Payable	Liability	↑	Cr.

Step 5 Journalize and post the transaction as follows:

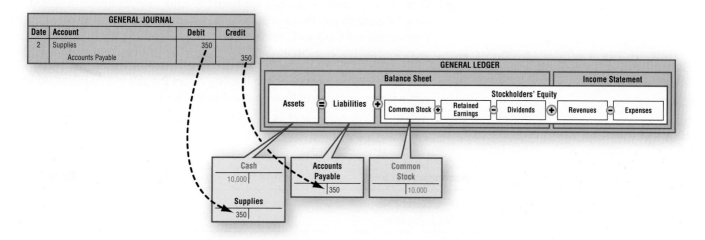

3. **Purchase equipment for cash.** The business purchases equipment, paying cash of $4,000.

Analysis of Transaction (3)

Step 1 The business received equipment in exchange for cash paid to the equipment manufacturing company. The accounts involved in the transaction are Equipment and Cash.

Step 2 Equipment and Cash are both assets.

Step 3 The asset Equipment is increased. The asset Cash is decreased because a check was written to pay for the equipment.

Step 4 An increase in the asset Equipment is a debit; a decrease in the asset Cash is a credit.

1 Accounts Affected	2 Type	3 ↑↓	4 Dr. or Cr.
Equipment	Asset	↑	Dr.
Cash	Asset	↓	Cr.

Step 5 Journalize and post the transaction:

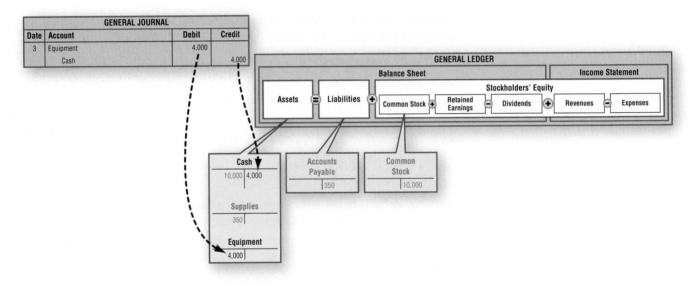

4. **Borrow cash from the bank.** Osborne Consulting borrows $12,000 cash from the bank and signs a two-year note payable to the bank.

Analysis of Transaction (4)

Step 1 Osborne Consulting received cash from the bank in exchange for a signed note agreeing to pay the cash back in two years. The accounts involved in the transaction are Cash and Notes Payable.

Step 2 Cash is an asset; Notes Payable is a liability.

Step 3 The asset Cash is increased. The liability Notes Payable is also increased because it represents an obligation owed to the bank.

Step 4 An increase in the asset Cash is a debit; an increase in the liability Notes Payable is a credit.

1 Accounts Affected	2 Type	3 ↑↓	4 Dr. or Cr.
Cash	Asset	↑	Dr.
Notes Payable	Liability	↑	Cr.

Step 5 Journalize and post the transaction as follows:

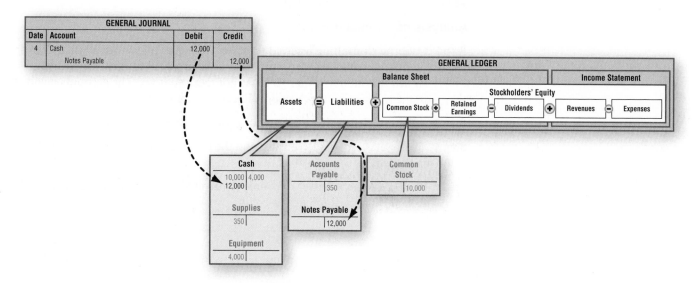

5. **Provide services for cash.** Osborne collects $1,200 of cash for services provided.

    Analysis of Transaction (5)

    Step 1 The business received cash in exchange for computer consulting services. The accounts involved in the transaction are Cash and Service Revenue.

    Step 2 Cash is an asset; Service Revenue is a revenue.

    Step 3 The asset Cash is increased. The revenue Service Revenue is increased also because the business has earned revenue by providing services.

    Step 4 An increase in the asset Cash is a debit; an increase in the revenue Service Revenue is a credit.

1 Accounts Affected	2 Type	3 ↑↓	4 Dr. or Cr.
Cash	Asset	↑	Dr.
Service Revenue	Revenue	↑	Cr.

    Step 5 Journalize and post the transaction as follows:

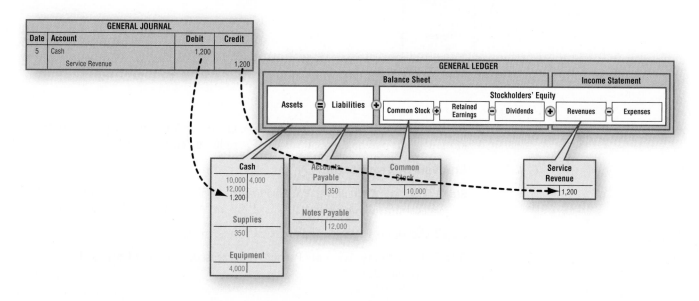

6. **Provide services on credit.** Osborne Consulting performs $1,900 of services on account.

Analysis of Transaction (6)

Step 1 Osborne Consulting received promises from customers to send cash next month in exchange for consulting services provided. Again, the business *earned* this money, although it has not received it yet. The accounts involved in the transaction are Accounts Receivable and Service Revenue.

Step 2 Accounts Receivable is an asset; Service Revenue is a revenue.

Step 3 The asset Accounts Receivable and the revenue Service Revenue are both increased.

Step 4 An increase in the asset Accounts Receivable is a debit; an increase in the revenue Service Revenue is a credit.

1 Accounts Affected	2 Type	3 ↑↓	4 Dr. or Cr.
Accounts Receivable	Asset	↑	Dr.
Service Revenue	Revenue	↑	Cr.

Step 5 Journalize and post the transaction as follows:

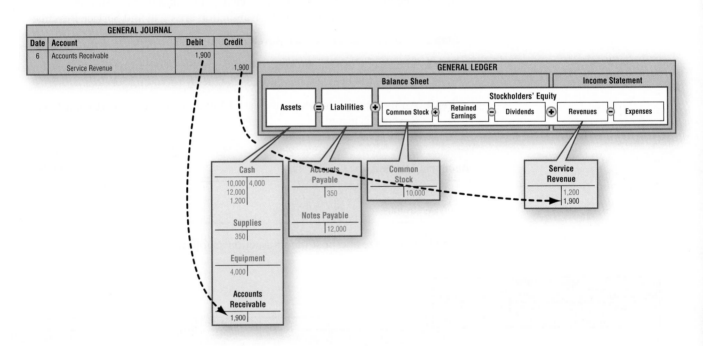

7. **Partial payment of accounts payable.** Osborne Consulting pays $150 to the store where it purchased $350 worth of supplies in Transaction (2).

Analysis of Transaction (7)

Step 1 Osborne Consulting paid $150 of the $350 that it owed to a supplier. The accounts involved in the transaction are Accounts Payable and Cash.

Step 2 Accounts Payable is a liability; Cash is an asset.

Step 3 The liability Accounts Payable is decreased. The asset Cash is also decreased.

Step 4 A decrease in the liability Accounts Payable is a debit; a decrease in the asset Cash is a credit.

1 Accounts Affected	2 Type	3 ↑↓	4 Dr. or Cr.
Accounts Payable	Liability	↓	Dr.
Cash	Asset	↓	Cr.

Step 5 Journalize and post the transaction as follows:

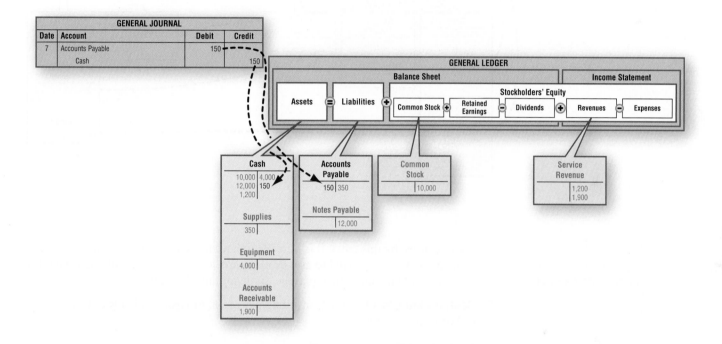

8. **Payment of expenses.** During the month, Osborne Consulting paid cash of $1,700 for expenses incurred such as salaries ($600), building rent ($900), and utilities ($200).

Analysis of Transaction (8)

Step 1 The business paid $1,700 in exchange for employee services, the use of the building, and for utilities consumed as part of operating the business. The accounts involved in the transaction are Salaries Expense, Rent Expense, Utilities Expense, and Cash.

Step 2 Salaries Expense, Rent Expense, and Utilities Expense are expenses; Cash is an asset.

Step 3 The expense accounts are increased. The asset Cash is decreased.

Step 4 An increase in an expense is a debit; a decrease in the asset Cash is a credit.

1 Accounts Affected	2 Type	3 ↑↓	4 Dr. or Cr.
Salaries Expense	Expense	↑	Dr.
Rent Expense	Expense	↑	Dr.
Utilities Expense	Expense	↑	Dr.
Cash	Asset	↓	Cr.

Step 5 Journalize and post the transaction:

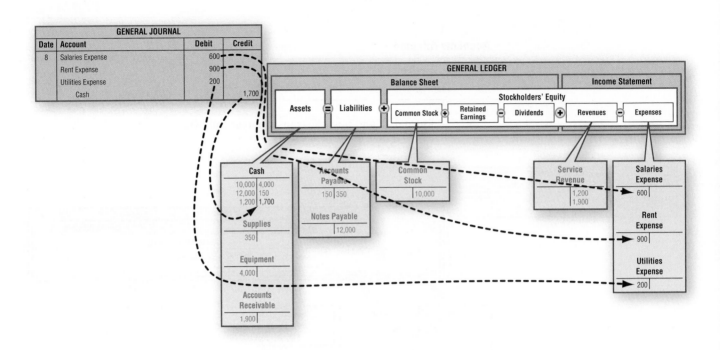

As we can see by this entry, it is possible to have more than two accounts utilized in an entry. This is referred to as a **compound journal entry**. Note that the total amount of debits must still equal the total amount of credits.

Compound journal entry A journal entry that affects more than two accounts.

9. **Cash dividends.** Osborne Consulting pays $500 of cash dividends to Cindy Osborne, the stockholder.

Analysis of Transaction (9)

Step 1 The stockholder received cash dividends. The business reduced the stockholders' equity interest because of dividends paid to the stockholder. The accounts involved in the transaction are Dividends and Cash.

Step 2 Dividends is an account within stockholders' equity and Cash is an asset.

Step 3 The Dividends account is increased because dividends have been paid. The asset Cash is decreased.

Step 4 An increase in Dividends is a debit; a decrease in the asset Cash is a credit.

1 Accounts Affected	2 Type	3 ↑↓	4 Dr. or Cr.
Dividends	Stockholders' Equity	↑	Dr.
Cash	Asset	↓	Cr.

Step 5 Journalize and post the transaction:

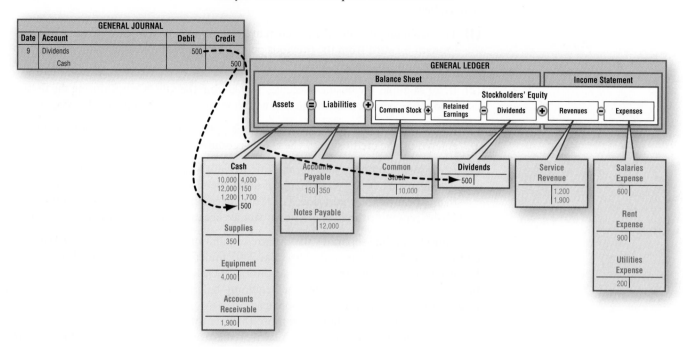

Decision Guidelines

Decision	Guideline	Analyze
When does a business recognize and record a transaction?	Examine the transaction to determine its impact, if any, on the company's accounting equation.	If the transaction immediately increases or decreases assets, liabilities, or stockholders' equity, then the transaction should be recorded in the company's accounting records.

Balancing the T-Accounts

Balance The difference between an account's total debit and total credit amounts; the ending value of an account.

After the transactions are recorded and posted to the T-accounts, you will calculate each account's **balance**. The ending balance is the difference between the account's total debits and its total credits. Every account has a beginning and ending balance as shown as "Bal" in the following T-account:

Cash			101
(1) Bal	0	(3)	300
(2)	1,000		
(4) Bal	700		

The numbers (1) through (4) for different entries in the Cash T-account above are explained below.

(1) The beginning balance for the current accounting period is the ending balance brought forward from the previous period. In this example, the business is new, so its beginning balance is $0.

(2) If, for example, the business receives $1,000 from the sale of stock during the first accounting period, this transaction will show up as a debit to the Cash account.

(3) If the company then pays $300 cash for supplies purchased, the amount will be entered on the credit side of the Cash account.

(4) Because the company just started, this account had a beginning debit balance of $0. Add increases of $1,000 that appear on the debit side, and subtract decreases of $300 that appear on the credit side. The resulting ending balance of Cash is $700. The Cash account normally has a debit balance because debits increase this account.

A horizontal line separates the transaction amounts from the account balance at the end of an accounting period. The "Bal 700" under the horizontal line shows that the balance in Cash at the end of the accounting period was $700. In the next accounting period, this balance will be the new beginning balance and will change as the business receives more cash and pays out more cash.

If an account's total debits are more than its total credits, then that account has a debit ending balance. If an account's total credits are more than its total debits, then that account has a credit ending balance. The ending balance of any T-account can be found in the same way that we just did for the Cash account.

The ending balances for Osborne Consulting are seen below. Please note that the ending balances for the T-accounts are indicated by double underlines.

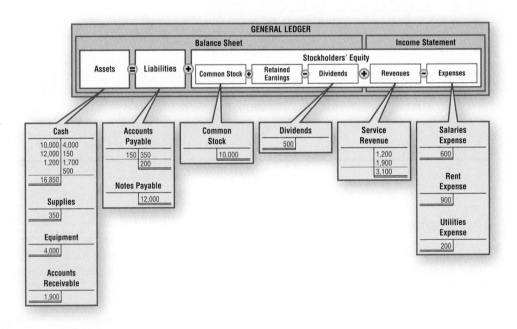

Try it...

During the month of September, Powers, Inc. had transactions that resulted in the following amounts being recorded in its Cash account; $1,200 debit, $250 credit, $875 debit, $2,125 credit, $350 credit, and a $400 debit. Powers, Inc.'s cash balance at the beginning of September was $2,450.

Enter the amounts from above in a T-account to determine Power's, Inc.'s cash balance at the end of September.

Answer:

Cash		
Bal	2,450	250
	1,200	2,125
	875	350
	400	
Bal	2,200	

How Is a Trial Balance Prepared, and What Is It Used For?

4   Use a trial balance to prepare financial statements

Trial balance A list of all the accounts of a business and their balances; its purpose is to verify that total debits equal total credits.

Accounting period Generally, the time period reflected by a set of financial statements.

Once transactions have been recorded in the journal and posted to accounts in the ledger, a **trial balance** is prepared. The first step in preparing a trial balance is to complete the heading. Similar to the financial statements that were prepared in Chapter 1, the heading should show the company name, the statement name, and the date of the trial balance. Next, the name of each account is entered into the first column of the trial balance in the order that the account appears in the general ledger. Now, two columns are created labeled "debit" and "credit," and the balance of each account is entered into the correct column. Finally, the debit and credit columns are totaled. As was done when preparing the financial statements in Chapter 1, the first and last amount in each column have a dollar sign placed before them, and the last amounts in both columns are double underlined. It should be noted that the trial balance is not an "official" financial statement. Its purpose is to summarize all account balances to be certain that total debits equal total credits after the entries have been journalized and posted. A trial balance can be prepared at any time, but is most commonly done at the end of the **accounting period**. An accounting period is usually defined as a month, a quarter, or a year. **Exhibit 2-3** shows the trial balance for Osborne Consulting, Inc., after all transactions have been journalized and posted for January 2014.

Osborne Consulting, Inc. Trial Balance January 31, 2014		
ACCOUNT	**DEBIT**	**CREDIT**
Cash	$16,850	
Accounts Receivable	1,900	
Supplies	350	
Equipment	4,000	
Accounts Payable		$ 200
Notes Payable		12,000
Common Stock		10,000
Dividends	500	
Service Revenue		3,100
Rent Expense	900	
Salaries Expense	600	
Utilities Expense	200	
Total	$25,300	$25,300

Exhibit 2-3 ▲

Stop and Think...

Jill just completed a problem that was assigned in her accounting class. She told Alan, one of her classmates, that she was confident that she did the problem correctly because the debits equal the credits on the trial balance. According to Alan, just because the debits equal the credits on the trial balance, it does not mean that everything was done correctly. Who is right, Jill or Alan?

Answer

Alan is correct. The following are some of the errors that can occur and yet the trial balance will still be in balance:

• A transaction can be recorded for the wrong amount in a journal entry.

• An entire journal entry can be recorded twice or not recorded at all.

• The wrong accounts can be debited or credited in a journal entry. For example, when recording a payment on an account payable, it is possible to debit Accounts Receivable instead of Accounts Payable.

Correcting Errors

If an error has occurred, the steps required to correct it depend on the type of error that was made. If a journal entry has been made to the wrong accounts or for the wrong amount, it is easiest to reverse, or undo, the incorrect entry. A new entry should then be prepared that contains the correct accounts or amount. To correct an entry that has been made twice, one of the entries should be reversed. If an entry was erroneously omitted, it simply needs to be entered.

Preparation of Financial Statements

After completing the trial balance, you can use it to prepare the financial statements because it shows all of the accounts with their balances. First, set up the financial statements as we did in Chapter 1. Now, using the account balances from the trial balance, insert the account names and their balances into the financial statements, starting with the income statement, then the statement of retained earnings, and finishing with the balance sheet. Make sure the balance sheet is in balance! That is, total Assets equal total Liabilities plus Stockholders' Equity.

Exhibit 2-4 on the following page shows the income statement and statement of retained earnings for the month ended January 31, 2014, and the balance sheet at January 31, 2014, for Osborne Consulting, Inc. You can see once again how the information flows from one statement to another.

Osborne Consulting, Inc.
Income Statement
Month Ended January 31, 2014

Revenue:		
Service Revenue		$3,100
Expenses:		
Rent Expense	$900	
Salaries Expense	600	
Utilities Expense	200	
Total Expenses		1,700
Net Income		$1,400

Osborne Consulting, Inc.
Statement of Retained Earnings
Month Ended January 31, 2014

Retained Earnings, January 1, 2014	$ 0
Add: Net Income for the month	1,400
Subtotal	1,400
Less: Dividends	500
Retained Earnings, January 31, 2014	$ 900

Osborne Consulting, Inc.
Balance Sheet
January 31, 2014

ASSETS		LIABILITIES	
Cash	$16,850	Accounts Payable	$ 200
Accounts Receivable	1,900	Notes Payable	12,000
Supplies	350	Total Liabilities	12,200
Equipment	4,000		
		STOCKHOLDERS' EQUITY	
		Common Stock	10,000
		Retained Earnings	900
		Total Stockholders' Equity	10,900
		Total Liabilities &	
Total Assets	$23,100	Stockholders' Equity	$23,100

Exhibit 2-4 ▲

These statements look the same as they did in Chapter 1, except now on the income statement we see detailed information for revenues and expenses. Also, notice that the income statement now has two columns. Many students assume, erroneously, that these columns represent debits and credits as they did on the trial balance. On financial statements, columns are used in order to make the statement more organized and easier to read; they are not used to signify debits and credits.

The process of analyzing transactions, entering them into the journal, posting them to the ledger, preparing a trial balance, and preparing financial statements is only a part of what is called the **accounting cycle**. This accounting cycle is completed by a business for every accounting period, and then it is repeated for the next accounting period, and the next, and the next, and so on. The following is a visual representation of the accounting cycle:

Accounting cycle The sequence of steps used to record and report business transactions.

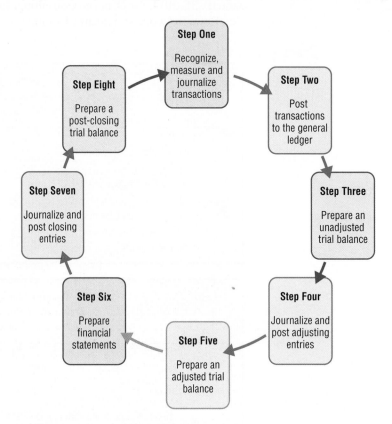

In the next chapter, you will learn the remaining steps in the accounting cycle, which include preparing adjusting and closing entries.

Focus On Decision Making

How Does Accounting Report Business Transactions?

Think of the school you are attending. What are some of the transactions that are conducted every day at your school? How would the following transactions be recorded? Make sure you think through each of these transactions and understand that you need to acknowledge the total transaction.

1. You enroll in class and pay the school your tuition.

2. Your school hires your teacher, who teaches your class.

3. Your school pays the utilities that make your classroom comfortable.

4. You buy a ticket to an athletic event, concert, or other special activity.

5. Your school pays for advertising to promote the athletic event, concert, or other special activity.

Managers need good information about all the aspects of a business transaction. They need accounting systems to recognize, measure, record, and report the entire transaction. Financial statements must report the total transaction and how everything in a business works together.

How They Do It: A Look at Business

Businesses produce income by using assets financed with money. Think about Target, the large discount retailer. Target buys and sells goods such as clothing, groceries, electronics, and toys. Target sells these goods in large buildings. To earn more net income, Target tries to sell more goods. However, as sales increase, Target needs more assets. The more assets Target has, the more financing it needs. It needs money to finance the growing amount of clothing, groceries, electronics, and toys it sells. It also needs money to finance new and bigger buildings. Target gets this money from either borrowing the money (which increases Target's liabilities) or from its owners (stockholders' equity). For the year ended February 2, 2013, Target had revenues of $73.3 billion, expenses of $70.3 billion, and net income of $3 billion. As of February 2, 2013, Target had assets of $48.2 billion. These assets were financed with liabilities of $31.6 billion and stockholders' equity of $16.6 billion. As can be seen by comparing its 2012 and 2013 financial statements, Target grew its assets. For the year ended January 28, 2012, Target had revenues of $69.9 billion, expenses of $66.9 billion, and net income of $3 billion. As of January 28, 2012, Target had assets of $46.6 billion, liabilities of $30.8 billion, and stockholders equity of $15.8 billion. Target increased its assets, and thus its financing, in hopes of seeing net income increase in the future.

Now think about IBM. IBM, the large technology firm, helps its customers implement solutions to technological challenges and opportunities. IBM sells physical goods such as computers. However, more than goods, IBM sells the services of its people. As IBM sells more goods, it needs more assets and thus financing. However, if IBM sells more services, it may not need more assets like Target does.

Today, IBM is shifting its focus to selling more services than goods. We can see that in its financial statements for the year ended December 31, 2012, IBM had revenues of $104.5 billion, expenses of $87.9 billion, and net income of $16.6 billion. At December 31, 2012, IBM had assets of $119.2 billion, liabilities of $100.2 billion, and stockholders' equity of $19 billion. For the year ended December 31, 2011, IBM had revenues of $106.9 billion, expenses of $91.0, and net income of $15.9 billion. At December 31, 2011, IBM had assets of $116.4 billion, liabilities of $96.2 billion, and stockholders' equity of $20.2 billion. Now think about it. IBM's total revenue decreased, but net income increased. IBM is changing how it does business by selling more services and fewer computers. IBM services have lower costs. This change is making IBM more competitive and valuable. IBM increased net income in 2012 by 4.4% by changing what it does and the resources it needs.

As you can see from the comparison of IBM and Target, each transaction affects the business in many ways. Accountants must communicate all these effects when they recognize, measure, record, and report business transactions using financial statements. Financial statements report how the transactions all come together.

Summary

Here is what you should know after reading this chapter. MyAccountingLab will help you identify what you know and where to go when you need practice.

	Key Points	Key Accounting Terms
1 Define accounts and understand how they are used in accounting	Numbered accounts are used to keep things organized. Account numbers starting with: • 1, assets • 2, liabilities • 3, stockholder's equity other than revenues and expenses • 4, revenues • 5, expenses • 6 through 9, other	**Accounts** (p. 54) **Chart of accounts** (p. 55) **Promissory note** (p. 55)
2 Explain debits, credits, and the double-entry system of accounting	Debits and credits are used to record changes in an account's balance. • Debits increase assets, expenses, and dividends. • Credits increase liabilities, common stock, retained earnings, and revenues. • Debits decrease liabilities, common stock, retained earnings, and revenues. • Credits decrease assets, expenses, and dividends.	**Credit** (p. 56) **Debit** (p. 56) **Double-entry accounting** (p. 56) **Normal balance** (p. 58) **T-account** (p. 56)
3 Demonstrate the use of the general journal and the general ledger to record business transactions	Business transactions are: • Entered into the general journal. • Posted from the general journal to the general ledger.	**Compound journal entry** (p. 66) **Balance** (p. 67) **General journal** (p. 58) **General ledger** (p. 58) **Journalize** (p. 58) **Posting** (p. 58) **Posting reference** (p. 59) **Record** (p. 58) **Transaction** (p. 58)
4 Use a trial balance to prepare financial statements	A trial balance: • Ensures that debits equal credits. • Is used to prepare the Income Statement, Statement of Retained Earnings, and Balance Sheet.	**Accounting cycle** (p. 72) **Accounting period** (p. 69) **Trial balance** (p. 69)

Accounting Practice

Discussion Questions

1. The order in which assets were listed and described in the text is the order in which you will see them listed on the balance sheet. What is the organizing principle behind the order in which assets are listed?

2. What type of transaction would result in the recording of a prepaid asset? What do you think will happen to that prepaid asset eventually?

3. How is revenue related to retained earnings?

4. Distinguish between an event and a transaction. Are all transactions events? Are all events transactions? Why or why not? What are the implications of your answers with respect to journal entries?

5. What is a "normal balance"? What are normal balances for the following accounts?
   a. Accounts Receivable
   b. Prepaid Expenses
   c. Notes Payable
   d. Retained Earnings
   e. Salaries Expense

6. You learned in this chapter that Cash is increased with a debit. When you deposit your paycheck in your account, however, the teller might say that he or she is going to credit your account. Why?

7. What would be the implications of a credit balance in the Cash account?

8. Distinguish between journalizing and posting.

9. True or false: If the trial balance is in balance, the financial statements will be accurate. Why or why not?

10. When it is time to prepare the financial statements, from where do the financial statement numbers come?

Self Check

1. Which sequence of actions correctly summarizes the accounting process?
   a. Prepare a trial balance, journalize transactions, post to the accounts
   b. Journalize transactions, post to the accounts, prepare a trial balance
   c. Post to the accounts, journalize transactions, prepare a trial balance
   d. Journalize transactions, prepare a trial balance, post to the accounts

2. The left side of an account is used to record
   a. debits.
   b. increases.
   c. credits.
   d. debits or credits, depending on the type of account.

3. Suppose Green Products, Inc., has cash of $41,000, receivables of $37,000, and furniture and fixtures totaling $174,000. Green Products, Inc., owes $64,000 on account and has a $125,000 note payable. How much is the stockholders' equity?
   a. $127,000
   b. $189,000
   c. $63,000
   d. $252,000

4. Cathy's Catering, Inc., purchased $200 of supplies on account. The journal entry to record this transaction is denoted by which of the following?

DATE		ACCOUNTS	POST REF.	DR.	CR.
a.		Supplies		200	
		Accounts Receivable			200
b.		Supplies		200	
		Accounts Payable			200
c.		Inventory		200	
		Accounts Payable			200
d.		Accounts Payable		200	
		Supplies			200

5. Posting a $500 purchase of supplies on account appears as which of the following?

a.

Supplies	
500	

Accounts Payable	
	500

c.

Cash	
	500

Supplies	
500	

b.

Supplies	
	500

Accounts Payable	
500	

d.

Supplies	
500	

Accounts Receivable	
	500

6. Which journal entry records obtaining a bank loan of $10,000?

DATE		ACCOUNTS	POST REF.	DR.	CR.
a.		Notes Payable		10,000	
		Cash			10,000
b.		Cash		10,000	
		Notes Payable			10,000
c.		Notes Payable		10,000	
		Accounts Receivable			10,000
d.		Cash		10,000	
		Accounts Payable			10,000

7. RV Wholesale, Inc., paid $1,200 for supplies and purchased additional supplies on account for $1,000. RV Wholesale, Inc., also paid $200 of the accounts payable. What is the balance in the Supplies account?

a. $1,200
b. $1,000
c. $2,400
d. $2,200

8. The Blue Ox Restaurant recorded a cash collection on account by debiting Cash and crediting Accounts Payable. What will the trial balance show for this error?

a. Too much for liabilities
b. Too much for assets
c. The trial balance will not balance.
d. Both a and b

9. Christopher Foley, an attorney, has a law corporation, Christopher Foley, Attorney, Inc., that began the year with total assets of $145,000, total liabilities of $70,000, and stockholders' equity of $75,000. During the year, Christopher Foley, Attorney, Inc., earned revenue of $125,000 and paid expenses of $35,000. Christopher Foley, Attorney, Inc., also sold an additional $24,000 of stock and paid $10,000 in dividends. How much is the stockholders' equity in Christopher Foley, Attorney, Inc., at year-end?

a. $235,000
b. $155,000
c. $179,000
d. $199,000

10. The entry to record the payment of $1,500 rent expense would be which of the following?

DATE	ACCOUNTS	POST REF.	DR.	CR.
a.	Rent Expense		1,500	
	Cash			1,500
b.	Cash		1,500	
	Rent Expense			1,500
c.	Rent Expense		1,500	
	Accounts Payable			1,500
d.	Accounts Payable		1,500	
	Rent Expense			1,500

11. According to the Real World Accounting Video, businesses take risks to earn a profit. True or False?

12. According to the Real World Accounting Video, _____ is a profitability measure that shows how much net income is earned on every dollar of sales.

a. sales ratio
b. expense ratio
c. asset financing ratio
d. profit margin ratio

Answers are given after Written Communication.

Short Exercises

S2-1. Accounting terms (*Learning Objective 1*) 5–10 min.

Match the accounting terms at the left with the corresponding definitions at the right.

____ 1. Account	a. Any economic event that has a financial impact on the business.
____ 2. Assets	b. The detailed record of the changes in a particular asset, liability, or stockholders' equity.
____ 3. Stockholders' Equity	c. Economic resources that provide a future benefit for a business.
____ 4. Expenses	d. Debts or obligations of a business.
____ 5. Liabilities	e. Stockholders' claim to the assets of a corporation.
____ 6. Revenues	f. Increases in stockholders' equity from selling goods or services to customers.
____ 7. Transactions	g. Decreases in stockholders' equity from using resources to sell goods or services.

S2-2. Account types (*Learning Objective 1*) 5–10 min.

For each of the following accounts, place the corresponding letter(s) of its account type in the space provided. Use the most detailed account type appropriate.

(A) Asset   (L) Liability   (SE) Stockholders' Equity   (R) Revenue   (E) Expense

___SE___	Dividends
_____	1. Accounts Payable
_____	2. Cash
_____	3. Service Revenue
_____	4. Prepaid Rent
_____	5. Rent Expense
_____	6. Common Stock

S2-3. Accounting cycle steps (*Learning Objectives 2, 3, & 4*) 5–10 min.

The following list names the activities involved in the accounting process of recording and summarizing business transactions. Place the number corresponding with the order the activity occurs next to the activity, starting with 1.

____1____	Transaction occurs.
_____	Prepare the financial statements.
_____	Prepare the trial balance.
_____	Post the transactions from the journal to the ledger.
_____	Record the transactions in the journal.

S2-4. Account types (*Learning Objective 1*) 5–10 min.

For each of the following accounts, indicate the account type by labeling it as an asset (A), liability (L), stockholders' equity (SE), revenue (R), or expense (E). Also give the digit each account number would begin with in the chart of accounts. Use the most detailed account type appropriate.

____A,1____   Land

_____   1. Service Revenue

_____   2. Dividends

_____   3. Accounts Receivable

_____   4. Salaries Expense

_____   5. Notes Payable

_____   6. Common Stock

_____   7. Rent Expense

S2-5. Accounting terminology (*Learning Objectives 2, 3, & 4*) 5–10 min.

Demonstrate your knowledge of accounting terminology by filling in the blanks to review some key definitions.

Dillon Baker is describing the accounting process for a friend who is a psychology major. Dillon states, "The basic summary device in accounting is the _____. The left side of an account is called the _____ side, and the right side is called the _____ side. We record transactions first in a _____. Then we post, or copy, the data to the _____. It is helpful to list all the accounts with their balances on a _____ _____."

S2-6. Effects of debits and credits on accounts (*Learning Objective 2*) 5–10 min.

For each of the following accounts, indicate if the account's normal balance is a debit balance (DR) or a credit balance (CR).

____DR____   Cash

_____   1. Rent Expense

_____   2. Accounts Payable

_____   3. Service Revenue

_____   4. Office Furniture

_____   5. Common Stock

_____   6. Land

_____   7. Dividends

S2-7. Balancing accounts and normal balances (*Learning Objective 2*) 5–10 min.

Calculate each account balance.

Supplies		132		Note Payable		221
3/8	250	3/27 400	3/20	1,250	3/5	9,500
3/17	800		3/31	4,500		

S2-8. Types of accounts and effects of debits and credits (*Learning Objective 2*)
5–10 min.

Complete the following table. For each account listed, identify the type of account, how the account is increased (debit or credit), and how the account is decreased (debit or credit). Use the most detailed account type appropriate.

Account	Type	↑	↓
Office Equipment	Asset	Dr.	Cr.
Dividends			
Service Revenue			
Accounts Payable			
Rent Expense			
Cash			

S2-9. Recreating journal entries from T-account postings (*Learning Objective 2*)
15–20 min.

Haskins, Inc., began operations on January 1, 2014. The seven transactions recorded during January by the company accountant are shown in the following T-accounts:

Cash			111
(1)	15,000	(2)	3,000
		(5)	250
		(6)	2,300
		(7)	1,000
Bal	8,450		

Accounts Receivable			112
(4)	4,500		
Bal	4,500		

Supplies			113
(3)	600		
Bal	600		

Equipment			114
(2)	3,000		
Bal	3,000		

Accounts Payable			211
(5)	250	(3)	600
		Bal	350

Common Stock			311
		(1)	15,000
		Bal	15,000

Dividends			322
(7)	1,000		
Bal	1,000		

Service Revenue			411
		(4)	4,500
		Bal	4,500

Operating Expenses			511–524
(6)	2,300		
Bal	2,300		

Complete the following table. For each transaction shown, determine the accounts affected, the type of account, whether the account increases or decreases, and whether it would be recorded in the journal on the debit or credit side.

Transaction	Accounts Affected	Type	↑↓	Dr. or Cr.
(1)	Cash	Asset	Increase	Dr.
	Common Stock	Stockholders' Equity	Increase	Cr.

S2-10. Journalizing transactions (*Learning Objective 3*) 10–15 min.

Cindy Anderson opened a dental practice in Spokane, Washington as a corporation. The following transactions took place in August:

Aug	1	Sold $50,000 of common stock to Anderson to start the business.
	5	Purchased dental supplies on account, $6,300.
	7	Paid monthly office rent of $1,000.
	10	Provided $3,800 of dental services to patients. Received cash of $1,200 for these services and sent bills to patients for the remainder.

Using the steps outlined in the five-step transaction analysis, record the transactions in the journal.

S2-11. Journalizing transactions (*Learning Objective 3*) **10–15 min.**

After operating for a month, Rosa Anderson's dental practice completed the following transactions during September:

Sep 3	The business borrowed $35,000 from the bank, signing a note payable.
9	Performed service for patients on account, $1,250.
16	Received cash on account from patients, $500.
22	Received a utility bill, $380, which will be paid during October.
30	Paid the monthly salary to its dental assistant, $2,250.
30	Paid interest expense of $170 on the bank loan.

Using the steps outlined in the five-step transaction analysis, record the transactions in the journal.

S2-12. Prepare trial balance (*Learning Objective 4*) **10–15 min.**

The accounting records for Audio Masters, Corp., contain the following amounts on April 30, 2014. The accounts appear in no particular order.

Service Revenue	$63,000	Utilities Expense	$18,400
Prepaid Rent	750	Note Payable	11,500
Accounts Payable	1,700	Cash	18,300
Equipment	21,000	Rent Expense	10,150
Dividends	22,600	Common Stock	15,000

Prepare the trial balance for Audio Masters at April 30, 2014. List the accounts in proper order.

S2-13. Preparation of financial statements from a trial balance (*Learning Objective 4*) **5–10 min.**

To the left of each account listed on the trial balance, indicate the financial statement that will include the account: income statement (IS), statement of retained earnings (RE), or balance sheet (BS).

Mylar, Inc.		
Trial Balance		
December 31, 2014		

	ACCOUNT	DEBIT	CREDIT
	Cash	$12,100	
	Accounts Receivable	1,900	
	Supplies	250	
	Equipment	6,000	
	Accounts Payable		$ 1,830
	Notes Payable		10,000
	Common Stock		8,500
	Dividends	700	
	Service Revenue		3,500
	Salaries Expense	1,740	
	Rent Expense	800	
	Utilities Expense	340	
	Total	$23,830	$23,830

S2-14. Accounting terminology (*Learning Objectives 1, 2, 3, & 4*) **5–10 min.**

Accounting has its own vocabulary and basic relationships. Match the accounting terms at the left with the corresponding phrase at the right.

____	1. Posting	a. Chronological record of transactions.
____	2. Normal balance	b. An asset.
____	3. Payable	c. Left side of an account.
____	4. Journal	d. Side of an account where increases are recorded.
____	5. Receivable	e. Copying data from the journal to the ledger.
____	6. Chart of accounts	f. List of all accounts with their balances.
____	7. Debit	g. A liability.
____	8. Trial balance	h. List of all of the accounts of a business.
____	9. Credit	i. Right side of an account.

MyAccountingLab

Exercises (Group A)

E2-15A. Journalizing transactions (*Learning Objectives 2 & 3*) **10–15 min.**

The following are six transactions for Hart Engineering, Inc., during the month of July:

Jul 1	Paid advertising expense, $225.
3	Performed service for customers and received cash, $2,000.
5	Purchased supplies on account, $400.
9	Received cash of $1,500 from credit customers on account.
12	Paid $700 on accounts payable.
17	Performed service for customers on account, $2,200.

Requirement

1. Complete the following table. For each transaction shown, determine the accounts affected, the type of account, whether the account increases or decreases, and whether it would be recorded in the journal on the debit or credit side.

Transaction Date	Accounts Affected	Account Type	↑↓	Dr. or Cr.
July 1	Advertising Expense	Stockholders' Equity	↑	Dr.
	Cash	Asset	↓	Cr.

E2-16A. Journalizing transactions (*Learning Objective 3*) **15–20 min.**

Using the steps outlined in the five-step transaction analysis, record the following transactions in the general journal for Pete's Plumbing, Inc. Explanations are not required.

Apr 1	Paid interest expense, $380.
5	Purchased office furniture on account, $3,200.
10	Performed service on account for a customer, $2,650.
12	Borrowed $25,000 cash, signing a note payable.
19	Sold for $53,000 land that had cost the company $53,000.
21	Purchased building for $250,000; signed a note payable.
27	Paid $1,800 on account.

E2-17A. Journalizing transactions (*Learning Objective 3*) **15–20 min.**

Walsh & Associates, Inc., completed the following transactions during November 2014, its first month of operations:

Nov	1	Sold $85,000 of common stock to Kenda Walsh to start the business.
	3	Purchased supplies on account, $400.
	5	Paid cash for a building to use for storage, $40,000.
	6	Performed service for customers and received cash, $1,600.
	11	Paid on accounts payable, $350.
	18	Performed service for customers on account, $2,600.
	24	Received cash from a customer on account, $1,300.
	30	Paid the following expenses: salaries, $700; and rent, $1,800.

Requirement

1. Using the steps outlined in the five-step transaction analysis, journalize the transactions of Walsh & Associates, Inc. List transactions by date. Use the following accounts: Cash, Accounts Receivable, Supplies, Building, Accounts Payable, Common Stock, Service Revenue, Salaries Expense, and Rent Expense.

E2-18A. Balance accounts and prepare trial balance (*Learning Objectives 3 & 4*) **10–15 min.**

The transactions for Tiny Tykes Daycare, Inc., for the month of October 2014 are posted in the following T-accounts.

Cash			111
Oct 1	25,000	Oct 4	13,500
6	6,700	9	300
23	1,400	29	1,600
Bal			

Accounts Receivable			112
Oct 17	2,300	Oct 23	1,400
Bal			

Supplies			113
Oct 2	450		
Bal			

Equipment			115
Oct 4	13,500		
Bal			

Accounts Payable			211
Oct 9	300	Oct 2	450
		Bal	

Common Stock			311
		Oct 1	25,000
		Bal	

Service Revenue			411
		Oct 6	6,700
		17	2,300
		Bal	

Salaries Expense			501
Oct 29	1,600		
Bal			

Quick solution:

1. Cash balance = $17,700

2. Trial balance totals = $34,150

Requirements

1. Calculate account balances at October 31, 2014.

2. Prepare the trial balance for Tiny Tykes Daycare, Inc., at October 31, 2014.

E2-19A. Record transactions and prepare a trial balance (*Learning Objectives 3 & 4*) **15–20 min.**

Baily Realty, Inc., had the following transactions for the month of March 2014.

Mar	2	Paid Rent Expense, $1,000.
	4	Performed service for a customer and received cash, $1,100.
	8	Purchased supplies on account, $100.
	11	Received cash from credit customers on account, $2,600.
	15	Sold an additional $45,000 of Common Stock.
	19	Paid $450 on account.
	27	Performed service for customers on account, $3,300.
	31	Made a payment on the Notes Payable, $6,000.

The following T-accounts have been set up for Baily Realty, Inc., with their beginning balances as of March 1, 2014.

Cash		111
Mar 1	5,000	

Accounts Receivable		112
Mar 1	2,800	

Supplies		113
Mar 1	550	

Office Furniture		114
Mar 1	2,900	

Building		116
Mar 1	30,000	

Accounts Payable		211
	Mar 1	400

Notes Payable		212
	Mar 1	9,000

Common Stock		311
	Mar 1	30,750

Service Revenue		411
	Mar 1	2,600

Rent Expense		511
Mar 1	1,500	

Requirements

1. Journalize the transactions for the month of March. Explanations are not required.
2. Post the journal entries to the appropriate T-accounts. Identify all items by date.
3. Calculate the balance of each account at March 31, 2014.
4. Prove that the total of all the debit balances equals the total of all of the credit balances by preparing a trial balance at March 31, 2014.

E2-20A. Journalize transactions, prepare a trial balance and balance sheet (*Learning Objectives 3 & 4*) 20–25 min.

The transactions for Rawlins Equipment, Inc., for the month of September 2014 have been posted to the accounts as follows:

Cash			
(1)	53,000	(4)	7,500
		(5)	5,500
		(6)	500

Supplies	
(2)	750

Equipment	
(4)	7,500

Building	
(3)	140,000

Accounts Payable		
(6)	500	(2) 750

Notes Payable		
(5)	5,500	(3) 140,000

Common Stock	
	(1) 53,000

Requirements

1. Prepare the journal entries that served as the sources for the six transactions.
2. Calculate the ending balance in each account.
3. Prepare the trial balance for Rawlins Equipment, Inc., at September 30, 2014.
4. Prepare a balance sheet for Rawlins Equipment, Inc., as of September 30, 2014.

E2-21A. Journalizing, posting, trial balance, income statement, and balance sheet (*Learning Objectives 3 & 4*) **25–30 min.**

Munro Consulting, Inc., completed the following transactions during November 2014, its first month of operations:

Nov	2	Sold $80,000 of common stock to Darryl Munro to start the consulting practice.
	3	Paid monthly office rent, $1,700.
	6	Paid cash for a new computer, $1,800.
	8	Purchased office furniture on account, $1,200.
	11	Purchased supplies on account, $400.
	19	Performed consulting service for a client on account, $2,600.
	20	Paid utility expenses, $500.
	28	Performed service for a client and received cash for the full amount of $1,600.

Requirements

1. Open, or set up, T-accounts in the ledger for the following accounts: Cash, Accounts Receivable, Supplies, Equipment, Furniture, Accounts Payable, Common Stock, Service Revenue, Rent Expense, and Utilities Expense.

2. Record transactions in the journal. Explanations are not required.

3. Post the journal entries to the T-accounts, identify all items by date. Calculate the ending balance in each account.

4. Prepare a trial balance at November 30, 2014.

5. Prepare the income statement, statement of retained earnings, and balance sheet.

E2-22A. Error correction (*Learning Objective 4*) **20–25 min.**

Allie Murphy has trouble keeping her debits and credits equal. During a recent month, Allie made the following errors:

a. Allie recorded a $450 payment of rent by debiting rent expense for $45 and crediting Cash for $45.

b. In recording an $800 payment on account, Allie debited Accounts Receivable and credited Cash.

c. Allie recorded the receipt of cash for service revenue by debiting Cash for $640 instead of the correct amount of $460. Allie also credited Service Revenue for $640, the incorrect amount.

d. Allie recorded a $275 purchase of supplies on account by debiting Accounts Payable and crediting Supplies.

e. In preparing the trial balance, Allie omitted a $30,000 note payable.

Requirements

1. For each of these errors, state whether Allie's mistake would cause the total debits and total credits on the trial balance to be unequal.

2. Identify each account with an incorrect balance, and indicate the amount and direction of the error.

Use the following format:

Effect on Trial Balance	Account(s) Misstated
Total debits = Total credits	Cash $405 too high Rent Expense $405 too low

Exercises (Group B)

E2-23B. Journalizing transactions (*Learning Objectives 2 & 3*) **10–15 min.**

The following are six journal entries KLP Engineering, Inc., made during the month of April.

Apr	1	Paid advertising expense, $340.
	3	Paid $7,800 cash to purchase a new piece of equipment.
	5	Issued common stock in exchange for $18,000 cash.
	9	Borrowed $12,000 on a note payable from the bank.
	12	Paid monthly telephone bill, $280.
	17	Purchased supplies for $165, paid cash.

Requirement

1. For each transaction shown, determine the accounts affected, the type of account, whether the account increases or decreases, and whether it would be recorded in the journal on the debit or credit side. The first transaction has been analyzed for you.

Transaction Date	Accounts Affected	Type	Increase/Decrease	Dr. or Cr.
April 1	Advertising Expense	Stockholders' Equity	Increase	Dr.
	Cash	Asset	Decrease	Cr.

E2-24B. Journalizing transactions (*Learning Objective 3*) **15–20 min.**

Using the steps outlined in the five-step transaction analysis, record the following transactions in the general journal for Washup Plumbing, Inc. Explanations are not required.

Apr	1	Paid interest expense, $1,000.
	5	Purchased office furniture on account, $3,000.
	10	Performed service on account for a customer, $2,400.
	12	Borrowed $20,000 cash, signing a note payable.
	19	Sold for $75,000 land that had cost the company $75,000.
	21	Purchased building for $300,000; signed a note payable.
	27	Paid $1,500 on account.

E2-25B. Journalizing transactions (*Learning Objective 3*) **15–20 min.**

Flores & Associates, Inc., completed the following transactions during December 2014, its first month of operations:

Dec	1	Sold $80,000 of common stock to Angela Flores to start the business.
	3	Purchased supplies on account, $160.
	5	Paid cash for a building to use for storage, $45,000.
	6	Performed service for customers and received cash, $3,700.
	11	Paid on accounts payable, $120.
	18	Performed service for customers on account, $2,650.
	24	Received cash from a customer on account, $2,100.
	31	Paid the following expenses: salaries, $1,100; and rent, $1,450.

Requirement

1. Using the steps outlined in the five-step transaction analysis, journalize the transactions of Flores & Associates, Inc. List transactions by date. Explanations are not required.

E2-26B. Balancing accounts and prepare trial balance (*Learning Objectives 2 & 3*)
10–15 min.

The transactions for Fun Time Daycare, Inc., for the month of May 2014 are posted in the following T-accounts.

Cash			111
May 1	35,000	May 4	12,700
6	3,000	9	600
23	750	29	1,500
Bal			

Accounts Receivable			112
May 17	5,100	May 23	750
Bal			

Supplies			113
May 2	900		
Bal			

Equipment			115
May 4	12,700		
Bal			

Accounts Payable			211
May 9	600	May 2	900
		Bal	

Common Stock			311
		May 1	35,000
		Bal	

Service Revenue			411
		May 6	3,000
		17	5,100
		Bal	

Salaries Expense			501
May 29	1,500		
Bal			

Requirements

1. Calculate account balances at May 31, 2014.

2. Prepare the trial balance for Fun Time Daycare, Inc., at May 31, 2014.

E2-27B. Record transactions and prepare a trial balance (*Learning Objectives 3 & 4*)
15–20 min.

Going Green, Inc., had the following transactions for the month of December 2014.

Dec	2	Paid Rent Expense, $1,600.
	4	Performed service for a customer and received cash, $900.
	8	Purchased supplies on account, $225.
	11	Received cash from credit customers on account, $1,500.
	15	Sold an additional $5,000 of Common Stock.
	19	Paid $375 on account.
	27	Performed service for customers on account, $1,640.
	28	Made a payment on the Notes Payable, $2,500.

The following T-accounts have been set up for Going Green, Inc., with their beginning balances as of December 1, 2014.

Cash		111
Dec 1	4,325	

Accounts Payable		211
	Dec 1	875

Accounts Receivable		112
Dec 1	2,200	

Notes Payable		212
	Dec 1	17,500

Supplies		113
Dec 1	450	

Common Stock		311
	Dec 1	30,000

Office Furniture		114
Dec 1	3,100	

Service Revenue		411
	Dec 1	5,300

Building		116
Dec 1	42,000	

Rent Expense		511
Dec 1	1,600	

Requirements

1. Journalize the transactions for the month of December. Explanations are not required.
2. Post the journal entries to the appropriate T-accounts. Identify all items by date.
3. Calculate the balance of each account at December 31, 2014.
4. Prove that the total of all the debit balances equals the total of all of the credit balances by preparing a trial balance at December 31, 2014.

E2-28B. Journalize transactions, prepare a trial balance and balance sheet (*Learning Objectives 3 & 4*) 20–25 min.

The transactions for Grinko, Inc., for the month of June 2014 have been posted to the accounts as follows:

Cash			
(1)	28,000	(4)	9,000
		(5)	2,500
		(6)	500

Supplies	
(2)	1,100

Equipment	
(4)	9,000

Building	
(3)	50,000

Accounts Payable			
(6)	500	(2)	1,100

Notes Payable			
(5)	2,500	(3)	50,000

Common Stock			
		(1)	28,000

Requirements

1. Prepare the journal entries that served as the sources for the six transactions.
2. Calculate the ending balance in each account.
3. Prepare the trial balance for Grinko, Inc., at June 30, 2014.
4. Prepare a balance sheet for Grinko, Inc., as of June 30, 2014.

E2-29B. Journalizing, posting, trial balance, income statement, and balance sheet (*Learning Objectives 3 & 4*) **25–30 min.**

Nolan Consulting, Inc., completed the following transactions during September 2014, its first month of operations:

Sep	2	Sold $50,000 of common stock to James Nolan to start the consulting practice.
	3	Paid monthly office rent, $1,750.
	6	Paid cash for a new computer, $1,400.
	8	Purchased office furniture on account, $2,700.
	11	Purchased supplies on account, $225.
	19	Performed consulting service for a client on account, $1,835.
	20	Paid utility expenses, $285.
	28	Performed service for a client and received cash for the full amount of $975.

Requirements

1. Open, or set up, T-accounts in the ledger for the following accounts: Cash, Accounts Receivable, Supplies, Equipment, Furniture, Accounts Payable, Common Stock, Service Revenue, Rent Expense, and Utilities Expense.

2. Record transactions in the journal. Explanations are not required.

3. Post journal entries to the T-accounts. Identify all items by date. Calculate the ending balance in each account.

4. Prepare a trial balance at September 30, 2014.

5. Prepare the income statement, statement of retained earnings, and balance sheet.

E2-30B. Error correction (*Learning Objective 4*) **20–25 min.**

Allison Meehan has trouble keeping her debits and credits equal. During a recent month, Allison made the following errors:

a. Allison recorded a $900 payment of rent by debiting Rent Expense for $90 and crediting Cash for $90.

b. In recording a $700 payment on account, Allison debited Accounts Receivable and credited Cash.

c. Allison recorded the receipt of cash for service revenue by debiting Cash for $230 instead of the correct amount of $320. Allison also credited Service Revenue for the $230, the incorrect amount.

d. Allison posted a $190 purchase of supplies on account by debiting Accounts Payable and crediting Supplies.

e. In preparing the trial balance, Allison omitted a $95,000 note payable.

Requirements

1. For each of these errors, state whether Allison's mistake would cause the total debits and total credits on the trial balance to be unequal.

2. Identify each account with an incorrect balance, and indicate the amount and direction of the error.

Effect on Trial Balance	Account(s) Misstated
Total debits = Total credits	Cash $810 too high Rent Expense $810 too low

During the remainder of September, Safe Systems, Inc., completed the following transactions:

Sep 16	Collected $3,200 cash from a client on account.
18	Performed services on account, $2,650.
21	Received $1,150 cash for services performed.
23	Purchased supplies on account, $215.
25	Paid $1,500 in dividends.
27	Paid $1,800 on account.
29	Received $3,200 cash for services performed.
30	Paid rent, $1,950.
30	Paid employees' salaries, $1,400.

Requirements

Quick solution:

1. Cash balance = $7,430

2. Trial balance totals = $40,455

1. Journalize the transactions that occurred September 16 to September 30 on page 6 of the journal.

2. Open the ledger accounts listed in the trial balance together with their beginning balances at September 15. Use the four-column account format illustrated in the chapter. Enter "Bal" for the September 15 balance in the Item column. Post the transactions to the ledger using dates, account numbers, and posting references. Calculate the new account balances at September 30, 2014.

3. Prepare the trial balance for Safe Systems, Inc., at September 30, 2014.

P2-35A. Prepare a trial balance, income statement, statement of retained earnings, and balance sheet (*Learning Objective 4*) **20–25 min.**

The accounts of Apex Consulting, Inc., follow with their normal balances at January 31, 2014. The accounts are listed in no particular order.

Account	Balance
Common Stock	$34,300
Insurance Expense	2,000
Accounts Payable	4,500
Service Revenue	126,500
Land	54,000
Supplies Expense	3,500
Cash	7,600
Salaries Expense	62,000
Building	99,000
Rent Expense	7,500
Dividends	14,000
Utilities Expense	5,400
Retained Earnings	10,400
Accounts Receivable	5,500
Notes Payable	85,000
Supplies	200

Requirements

1. Prepare the company's trial balance at January 31, 2014, listing accounts in the proper order. List the largest expense first, the second-largest expense next, and so on.

2. Prepare the year-end financial statements: income statement, statement of retained earnings, and balance sheet. The retained earnings balance of $10,400 is the beginning balance for the year; it has not been updated for the current year's income or loss.

3. Was it a profitable year for Apex Consulting, Inc.? Why or why not?

P2-36A. Error correction (*Learning Objective 4*) **15–20 min.**

The following errors occurred in the accounting records of Allied Security, Inc.:

a. The company accountant recorded the receipt of cash for service revenue by debiting Cash for $240 instead of the correct amount of $420. Service Revenue was also credited for $240, the incorrect amount.

b. A $375 purchase of supplies on account was recorded by debiting Accounts Payable and crediting Supplies.

c. The company accountant recorded a $1,375 payment of rent by debiting rent expense for $13,750 and crediting Cash for $13,750.

d. In recording a $1,100 payment on account, Accounts Receivable was debited and Cash was credited.

Requirements

1. Prepare the necessary journal entries to correct each of these errors.

2. For each of the errors, determine if the error would cause net income to be overstated, understated, or unchanged.

Problems (Group B)

P2-37B. Journalizing transactions (*Learning Objective 3*) **15–20 min.**

Tina Dalton practices law under the business title Tina Dalton, Attorney at Law, Inc. During September, her law practice engaged in the following transactions:

Sep	1	Sold $60,000 of common stock to Dalton to start the business.
	3	Paid $450 for the purchase of office supplies.
	8	Paid $43,000 cash to purchase land for an office site.
	12	Purchased office equipment on account, $4,300.
	17	Borrowed $65,000 from the bank. Dalton signed a note payable to the bank in the name of the business.
	26	Paid $2,800 on account.
	30	Revenues earned during the month included $12,000 cash and $16,500 on account.
	30	Paid employees' salaries, $3,240; office rent, $1,800; and utilities, $675.
	30	Paid $4,300 of dividends to stockholder, Dalton.

Dalton's business uses the following accounts: Cash, Accounts Receivable, Supplies, Land, Office Equipment, Accounts Payable, Notes Payable, Common Stock, Dividends, Service Revenue, Salaries Expense, Rent Expense, and Utilities Expense.

Requirement

1. Journalize each transaction. Omit explanations.

P2-38B. Journalizing transactions (*Learning Objective 3*) **15–20 min.**

Action Advertising, Inc., engaged in the following business transactions during May 2014:

May	1	Borrowed $150,000 from Northern Bank. The company president signed a note payable to the bank in the name of Action Advertising, Inc.
	3	Paid $135,000 cash to purchase an office building.
	6	Provided services to customers on account, $11,800.
	9	Purchased $1,100 of office supplies on account.
	13	Provided services to cash customers, $8,100.
	15	Paid $5,000 of dividends to company stockholders.
	17	Received payment on account from credit customers, $7,500.
	18	Paid property tax expense on office building, $1,250.
	22	Paid employee salaries, $3,350.
	26	Paid cash to purchase supplies, $1,300.
	31	Paid $5,000 on account.

Action Advertising, Inc., uses the following accounts: Cash, Accounts Receivable, Supplies, Building, Accounts Payable, Notes Payable, Common Stock, Dividends, Service Revenue, Salaries Expense, and Property Tax Expense.

Requirement

1. Journalize each transaction. Omit explanations.

P2-39B. Journalizing, posting, and trial balance preparation (*Learning Objectives 3 & 4*) **20–25 min.**

Tom Slater opened an accounting firm on July 1, 2014. During the month of July, the business completed the following transactions:

Jul	1	The business sold $100,000 of common stock to open the firm, Slater & Associates, Inc.
	3	Purchased supplies, $575, and furniture, $2,300, on account.
	5	Performed accounting service for a client and received cash, $1,600.
	8	Paid cash to acquire land for a future office site, $28,000.
	11	Prepared tax returns for a client on account, $1,850.
	14	Paid assistant's salary, $575.
	16	Paid for the furniture purchased July 3 on account.
	19	Received $2,450 cash for accounting services performed.
	23	Billed a client for $3,300 of accounting services.
	28	Received $1,450 from client on account.
	31	Paid secretary's salary, $575.
	31	Paid rent expense, $1,720.
	31	Paid $2,500 of dividends.

Requirements

1. Open, or set up, the following T-accounts: Cash, Accounts Receivable, Supplies, Furniture, Land, Accounts Payable, Common Stock, Dividends, Service Revenue, Salaries Expense, and Rent Expense.

2. Journalize transactions. Explanations are not required.

3. Post the transactions to the T-accounts that have been set up for you, using transaction dates as posting references.

4. Calculate the balance in each account.

5. Prepare the trial balance for Slater & Associates, Inc., at July 31, 2014.

P2-40B. Journalizing, posting, and trial balance preparation (*Learning Objectives 3 & 4*) **25–30 min.**

The trial balance for XYZ Systems, Inc., at January 15, 2014, follows:

	XYZ Systems, Inc. **Trial Balance** January 15, 2014		
ACCT #	**ACCOUNT**	**DEBIT**	**CREDIT**
110	Cash	$ 2,700	
112	Accounts Receivable	8,000	
115	Supplies	1,000	
140	Equipment	14,600	
210	Accounts Payable		$ 4,500
311	Common Stock		21,600
315	Dividends	2,800	
411	Service Revenue		6,600
511	Salaries Expense	2,300	
515	Rent Expense	1,300	
	Total	$32,700	$32,700

During the remainder of January, XYZ Systems, Inc., completed the following transactions:

Jan 16	Collected $3,400 cash from a client on account.
18	Performed services on account, $1,200.
21	Received $2,700 cash for services performed.
23	Purchased supplies on account, $400.
25	Paid $1,400 in dividends.
27	Paid $2,100 on account.
29	Received $3,800 cash for services performed.
30	Paid rent, $1,000.
30	Paid employees' salaries, $2,400.

Requirements

1. Journalize the transactions that occurred January 16 to January 30 on page 6 of the journal.

2. Open T-accounts for the ledger accounts listed in the trial balance and enter their beginning balances at January 15. Use the four-column account format illustrated in the chapter. Enter "Bal" for the January 15 balance in the item column. Post the transactions to the ledger, using dates, account numbers, and posting references. Calculate the new account balances at January 31, 2014.

3. Prepare the trial balance for XYZ Systems, Inc., at January 31, 2014.

P2-41B. Prepare a trial balance, income statement, statement of retained earnings, and balance sheet (*Learning Objective 4*) 20–25 min.

The accounts of Baker Consulting, Inc., follow with their normal balances at December 31, 2014. The accounts are listed in no particular order.

Account	Balance
Common Stock	$120,000
Insurance Expense	5,300
Accounts Payable	4,100
Service Revenue	101,700
Land	82,000
Supplies Expense	1,840
Cash	9,120
Salaries Expense	48,750
Building	135,000
Rent Expense	11,340
Dividends	15,000
Utilities Expense	6,750
Retained Earnings	12,320
Accounts Receivable	7,370
Notes Payable	85,000
Supplies	650

Requirements

1. Prepare the company's trial balance at December 31, 2014, listing accounts in the proper order. List the largest expense first, the second-largest expense next, and so on.

2. Prepare the year-end financial statements: income statement, statement of retained earnings, and balance sheet. The retained earnings balance of $12,320 is the beginning balance for the year; it has not been updated for the current year's net income or loss.

3. Was it a profitable year for Baker Consulting, Inc.? Why or why not?

P2-42B. Error correction (*Learning Objective 4*) 15–20 min.

The following errors occurred in the accounting records of Coral Cove, Inc.:

a. The company accountant recorded the receipt of cash for service revenue by debiting Cash for $470 instead of the correct amount of $740. Service Revenue was also credited for $470, the incorrect amount.

b. A $225 purchase of supplies on account was recorded by debiting Accounts Payable and crediting Supplies.

c. The company accountant recorded a $1,200 payment of rent by debiting Rent Expense for $12,000 and crediting Cash for $12,000.

d. In recording an $825 payment on account, Accounts Receivable was debited and Cash was credited.

Requirements

1. Prepare the necessary journal entries to correct each of these errors.

2. For each of the errors, determine if the error would cause net income to be overstated, understated, or unchanged.

Continuing Exercise

This exercise continues with the business of Cole's Yard Care, Inc., begun in the continuing exercise in Chapter 1. Instead of using T accounts as you did in Chapter 1, now you will account for Cole's Yard Care, Inc.'s transactions in the general journal. Cole's Yard Care, Inc., completed the following transactions during April:

Apr 1	Received $2,000 and issued 500 shares of common stock. Deposited this amount in a bank account in the name of Cole's Yard Care, Inc.
3	Purchased on account a mower, $1,200, and weed whacker, $400. The equipment is expected to remain in service for four years.
5	Purchased $90 of gas. Wrote check #1 from the new bank account.
6	Performed lawn services for client on account, $225.
8	Purchased $85 of fertilizer from the lawn store. Wrote check #2 from the new bank account.
17	Completed landscaping job for client, received cash $850.
30	Received $175 on account from services performed on April 6.

Requirements

1. Open T-accounts in the ledger: Cash, Accounts Receivable, Lawn Supplies, Equipment, Accounts Payable, Common Stock, Retained Earnings, Service Revenue, and Fuel Expense.

2. Journalize the transactions. Explanations are not required.

3. Post journal entries to the T-accounts. Key all items by date and denote an account balance as *Bal*. Formal posting references are not required. Determine ending balances in T-accounts on April 30, 2014.

4. Prepare a trial balance at April 30, 2014.

Continuing Problem

This problem continues with the business of Aqua Magic, Inc., begun in the continuing problem in Chapter 1. Here you will account for Aqua Magic, Inc.'s transactions using formal accounting practices. The trial balance for Aqua Magic, Inc., as of May 31, 2014, is presented below.

<table>
<tr><td colspan="3" align="center">**Aqua Magic, Inc.**
Trial Balance
May 31, 2014</td></tr>
<tr><td>**ACCOUNT**</td><td>**DEBIT**</td><td>**CREDIT**</td></tr>
<tr><td>Cash</td><td>$43,325</td><td></td></tr>
<tr><td>Accounts Receivable</td><td>2,300</td><td></td></tr>
<tr><td>Supplies</td><td>600</td><td></td></tr>
<tr><td>Equipment</td><td>1,800</td><td></td></tr>
<tr><td>Vehicles</td><td>36,200</td><td></td></tr>
<tr><td>Accounts Payable</td><td></td><td>$ 1,040</td></tr>
<tr><td>Notes Payable</td><td></td><td>36,200</td></tr>
<tr><td>Common Stock</td><td></td><td>45,000</td></tr>
<tr><td>Dividends</td><td>2,500</td><td></td></tr>
<tr><td>Service Revenue</td><td></td><td>5,850</td></tr>
<tr><td>Salaries Expense</td><td>625</td><td></td></tr>
<tr><td>Utilities Expense</td><td>740</td><td></td></tr>
<tr><td>Total</td><td>$88,090</td><td>$88,090</td></tr>
</table>

During June the following transactions occurred:

Jun	1	Paid receptionist's salary, $625.
	2	Paid cash to acquire land for a future office site, $25,000.
	3	Moved into a new location for the business and paid the first month's rent, $2,300.
	4	Performed service for a customer and received cash, $1,750.
	5	Received $450 on account.
	8	Purchased $725 of supplies on account.
	11	Billed customers for services performed, $3,250.
	13	Sold an additional $10,000 of common stock to Greg Richards.
	16	Paid receptionist's salary, $625.
	17	Received $1,500 cash for services performed.
	18	Received $1,025 from customers on account.
	19	Paid $450 to be listed in the Yellow Pages telephone directory.
	21	Paid $875 on account.
	22	Purchased office furniture on account, $4,000.
	24	Paid miscellaneous expenses, $275.
	26	Billed customers for services provided, $1,450.
	28	Received $1,800 from customers on account.
	30	Paid utility bill, $640.
	30	Paid receptionist's salary, $625.
	30	Paid $3,500 of dividends.

Requirements

1. Journalize the transactions that occurred in June, omit explanations.

2. Open the ledger accounts listed in the trial balance together with their beginning balances at May 31. Use the four-column account format illustrated in the chapter. Enter "Bal" for the May 31 balance in the Item column. Post the journal entries to the ledger creating new ledger accounts as necessary, omit posting references. Calculate the new account balances at June 30, 2014.

3. Prepare the trial balance for Aqua Magic, Inc., at June 30, 2014.

Continuing Financial Statement Analysis Problem

Let's look at Target some more. Think about Target. Think about accountants reporting what Target has, where it gets or receives its money, and what it has been doing to create value. Is Target earning net income or loss? What resources does Target need to operate? Think about the business of Target.

Return to Target's Web site at www.target.com. Next, scroll to the bottom of the page and look for the heading "about Target" and click on "company information." Now click on "Investors" and click on "Annual Reports." Finally, look for the link to the 2012 annual report and click on it. A lot of information is contained in Target's financial statements, which are located in the annual report. Look through the pages of the annual report. On page 33 of the annual report, you'll find Target's income statement for the year ending February 2, 2013 (called the Consolidated Statement of Operations). On page 35, you'll find Target's balance sheet as of February 2, 2013 (called the Consolidated Statement of Financial Position). After the income statement and balance sheet are other reports and explanations of the numbers on the reports. Now answer the following questions:

Look at the 2013 income statement and balance sheet of Target. How would the following transactions affect the financial statements?

a. What would happen to Target's balance sheet if it borrowed $50 million of cash from a bank?

b. What would happen to Target's balance sheet if it built a new store costing $50 million in cash?

    c. What would happen to Target's income statement and balance sheet if it had a big sale, increasing net income by $10 billion which all ended up as cash?

    d. What would happen to Target's income statement and balance sheet if it hired more employees? The salaries of these employees cost Target $1 billion paid in cash. The extra employees did not create any extra net income.

Apply Your Knowledge

Ethics in Action

Case 1. Lynne Jamison was recording the daily transactions of Liberty Physical Therapy, Inc., into the accounting records so she could prepare financial statements and apply for a bank loan. Some of the business expenses were higher than she had expected, and Lynne was worried about the effect of these expenses on net income. Lynne was recording a $3,800 payment for legal fees incurred by the business by debiting Legal Expense and crediting Cash to properly record the journal entry. She then thought that, rather than debiting the expense account for the $3,800 payment, she could debit the Dividends account, which also had a normal debit balance. Lynne knew that debits had to equal credits, so debiting the Dividends account instead of the Legal Expense account would not affect the trial balance. Further, the net income would be $3,800 higher because now no legal expense would be recorded. She thought that either way the retained earnings would be lower, and besides, it really didn't matter how the $3,800 payment was shown as long as she showed it somewhere.

    Should Lynne debit the Dividends account rather than the Legal Expense account? Do you agree with her thought that it really doesn't matter how the $3,800 payment is shown as long as it is shown somewhere? Considering that Lynne owns all of the Liberty Physical Therapy, Inc., common stock, does she have any ethical responsibilities to properly record each business transaction?

Case 2. Joe Reese is the accountant for Lawn Boyz Lawnservice, Inc. During the month, numerous payments were made for wages for which he was properly debiting the Wage Expense account and crediting Cash. Joe became concerned that if he kept debiting the Wage Expense account it would end up with a balance much higher than any of the other expense accounts. Accordingly, he began debiting other expense accounts for some of the wage payments and, thus, "spread the expenses around" to other expense accounts. When he was done posting all the journal entries to the ledger accounts, he printed a trial balance. He saw that the Wage Expense balance was $42,000 and the total of all the other expense accounts was $26,000. Had he properly posted all the wage expense transactions, Wage Expense would have totaled $54,000 and the other expense accounts would have totaled $14,000. Joe reasoned that his actions provided for "more balanced" expense account totals and, regardless of his postings, the total expenses were still $68,000, so the overall net income would be the same.

    Were Joe's actions justified? Do they cause any ethical concerns? If you were the owner of Lawn Boyz Lawnservice, Inc., would you have a problem with what Joe did?

Know Your Business

Financial Analysis

Purpose: To help familiarize you with the financial reporting of a real company in order to further your understanding of the chapter material you are learning.

    Although we do not have access to the journals used by Columbia Sportswear, we can still understand various business transactions on the financial statements in Columbia Sportswear's annual report. Refer to the Columbia Sportswear income statements, "Statements of Operations," and the Columbia Sportswear balance sheets in Appendix A. Assume Columbia Sportswear completed the following transactions during January 2012:

Jan	3	Purchased $583,000 of equipment for cash.
	7	Had cash sales of $27,480,000.
	10	Purchased $31,364,000 of inventory on account.
	15	Made $703,000 of sales on account.
	29	Paid $14,625,000 on account from the January 10 purchase.

Requirements

1. Prepare journal entries to record the transactions listed. Use the account titles found in the Columbia Sportswear financial statements: Cash; Accounts Receivable; Inventory; Property, Plant, and Equipment; Accounts Payable; and Net Sales.

2. Look at the financial statements and locate the accounts that you included in your journal entries. Note that the balances Columbia Sportswear reported include millions of dollars in transactions for the year. Imagine how much activity and how many transactions Columbia Sportswear has every day!

Industry Analysis

Purpose: To help you understand and compare the performance of two companies in the same industry.

Go to the Columbia Sportswear Company Annual Report located in Appendix A. Now access the 2012 Annual Report for Under Armour, Inc. For instructions on how to access the report online, see the Industry Analysis in Chapter 1.

Requirements

Answer these questions about the two companies:

1. In terms of net sales or net revenue, which is the larger company for the year ending December 31, 2012? Which financial statement did you look at to find that information?

2. In terms of total assets at December 31, 2012, which is the larger company? Which financial statement did you look at to find that information?

3. Which company has more total debt at December 31, 2012? Which financial statement did you look at to find that information?

4. Which company has the higher gross profit percentage for the year ending December 31, 2012? Don't know that one? On the Consolidated Statements of Operations/Income, divide Gross Profit by Net Sales (or Net Revenues). What exactly does this mean?

5. Which company paid more cash dividends to its stockholders in 2012? Which financial statement did you look at to find that information?

6. Which company's stock would you rather own? Why?

Small Business Analysis

Purpose: To help you understand the importance of cash flows in the operation of a small business.

You're sitting in your CPA office late on a Friday afternoon when you get an e-mail from a client. You know that she has been working on setting up a new accounting system in her office for a new business that she just started. You figured that this would eventually generate some communication between the two of you because you know that she has relatively limited accounting knowledge. Here's her e-mail to you:

"Brian, I'm pretty frustrated right now! As you know, I've been installing this new accounting system here in the office and I've run into a problem. I don't understand this Cash account.

I have purchased some items on my debit card, and I've purchased some items on my credit card. So, logically, when I purchased the items on my debit card, I debited the Cash account. But when I used my credit card, it made sense to credit my Cash account. And to make things even worse, my Cash account ends up with a credit balance, and I'm pretty sure that's not right. This is too confusing and it's Friday afternoon; I'm going home!"

The following journal entries were attached to your client's e-mail:

DATE	ACCOUNTS	POST REF.	DR.	CR.
May 5	Cash		320	
	Supplies			320
	Purchased supplies using debit card.			

DATE	ACCOUNTS	POST REF.	DR.	CR.
May 6	Utilities Expense		275	
	Cash			275
	Paid utilities bill using credit card.			

Requirement

1. Because Cash is the lifeblood of any business, having a correct balance in the Cash account is of utmost importance. Correctly entering cash transactions is equally important. Suggest to your client the corrections that need to be made to the journal entries she made.

Written Communication

Consider the situation that was presented in the Small Business Analysis. Your client had two concerns that she asked you about. The first one is that she was concerned that her Cash balance had a credit balance instead of a debit balance. And even after the corrections were made, the Cash balance was still a credit. The second concern she had was how to record transactions when she uses her debit card as opposed to transactions when she uses her credit card.

Write a short memo or letter to your client addressing these two situations and what you would consider to be the proper accounting treatment for each of the two. More specifically, if the Cash account was showing as a credit balance, how would that have happened? Is it possible for that to happen? And regarding the use of the debit card versus the credit card, from the information contained in the chapter, explain the difference between the two types of cards and how each transaction should be recorded from an accounting point of view.

Self Check Answers

1. b 2. a 3. c 4. b 5. a 6. b 7. d 8. d 9. c 10. a 11. true 12. d

3

Adjusting and Closing Entries

Business, Accounting, and You

Learning Objectives

1 Understand the revenue recognition and matching principles

2 Understand the four types of adjustments, and prepare adjusting entries

3 Prepare financial statements from an adjusted trial balance

4 Prepare closing entries and a post-closing trial balance

It's December 31st and closing time at Disney. Everyone has worked hard. The year has come to a close. Millions of transactions have occurred and been recorded by the accountants. It's time to wrap up the year and tabulate the score for Disney. How does Disney conclude a year's activities and prepare for a new year? There has to be an end for a new beginning.

Think of a sporting event. There must be an end to the game. At the end of the game, the scorekeeper must make sure the score accurately reflects what happened. Accountants are the scorekeepers of the business. They have activities to complete at the end of each accounting period. They may need to go back and make sure they have recognized, measured, and reported all the business's transactions. Given the rules of Generally Accepted Accounting Principles (GAAP), they may need to adjust the scorecard to better reflect what happened. They then need to summarize the transactions and prepare the final reports.

Whether you are an accountant or a manager who uses accounting information, you need to understand the process used by accountants to adjust and conclude (close) a business's financial records. Why? Because they affect the reports used to manage the business. They affect the final score used to judge a business's success.

In Chapter 2, we learned about journalizing and posting transactions for a business, as well as how to prepare a trial balance and financial statements. These were steps one, two, three, and six of the accounting cycle. Once again the accounting cycle looks like this:

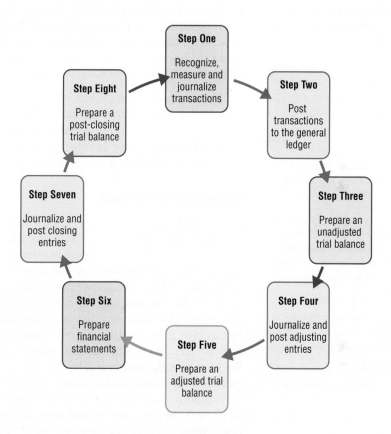

Here in Chapter 3, we will learn how to prepare steps four, five, seven, and eight. The accounting cycle is repeated for every accounting period. The accounting period can be defined as a month, a quarter, or a year. The annual accounting period for most large companies runs the calendar year from January 1 through December 31, although some companies use a fiscal year that does not coincide with the calendar year. A **fiscal year** is any consecutive 12-month period that a business chooses. It may begin on any day of the year and end 12 months later. Usually, the fiscal year-end date is the low point in business activity for the year. Although we will focus primarily on an annual time period, usually financial statements are prepared monthly, quarterly, or semiannually so that businesses have an idea of how they are doing before the year ends.

Fiscal year Any consecutive, 12-month period that a business adopts as its accounting year.

▶ Real World Accounting Video

In the Real World Accounting Video, Jeanette Cebollero, the chief financial officer (CFO) of Rosa Mexicano Restaurants, talks about the accounting function. Look at the video.

Think about what Jeanette is saying. Think about how important accounting is to the success of a business.

How Does a Company Accurately Report Its Income?

Revenue Recognition and Matching Principles

1 **Understand the revenue recognition and matching principles**

Accrual accounting Accounting method that records revenues when earned and expenses when incurred without regard to when cash is exchanged.

Revenue recognition principle Recording revenues when they are earned by providing goods or services to customers.

Matching principle Recording expenses in the time period they were incurred to produce revenues, thus matching them against the revenues earned during that same period.

Cash-basis accounting Accounting method that records revenues when cash is received and expenses when cash is paid.

Accruals Revenues earned or expenses incurred before cash has been exchanged.

Deferrals Cash received or paid before revenues have been earned or expenses have been incurred.

Adjusting entries Journal entries made at the end of the accounting period to measure the period's income accurately and bring the related asset and liability accounts to correct balances before the financial statements are prepared.

In Chapter 1, we learned that financial statements are prepared in order to provide useful information to various users. However, for financial statements to be useful, they must be accurate and up to date. To ensure that financial statements are up to date, GAAP requires the use of **accrual accounting**. To practice accrual accounting, a business must follow the next two accounting principles:

- The **revenue recognition principle** states that revenues should be recognized, or recorded, when they are earned regardless of when cash is received.
- The **matching principle** states that expenses should be matched with the revenues they helped generate. In other words, expenses should be recorded when they are incurred regardless of when they are paid for.

Accruals and Deferrals

It is possible for a business to record revenues only when cash is received and record expenses only when cash is paid. As discussed in Chapter 1, this is referred to as **cash-basis accounting**. In many instances, when a company uses cash-basis accounting, its financial statements do not present an accurate picture of how the company is performing. This is because a business may provide goods and services to customers "on account." In this case, the business has earned revenue prior to receiving cash from the customer. A business may also purchase goods and services from suppliers on account. In this case, expenses are incurred before cash is paid. When revenues are earned before cash is received or expenses are incurred before cash is paid, it is called an **accrual**. We have already seen accruals in Chapters 1 and 2 when we recorded transactions in Accounts Receivable and Accounts Payable.

Businesses may also receive cash from customers prior to the delivery of goods or services to the customer. In this case, cash is received before revenue is earned. In addition, businesses may pay for goods or services prior to receiving those goods or services from the supplier. In this case, cash is paid before an expense is incurred. When cash is received for goods or services prior to the recognition of a revenue or cash is paid for goods or services prior to the recognition of the expense, it is called a **deferral**. We have also seen deferrals in Chapters 1 and 2 when we purchased supplies and equipment. Accruals and deferrals can be summarized as follows:

	Now	Later
Accrued Revenue	Revenue is recognized	Cash is received
Accrued Expense	Expense is recognized	Cash is paid
Deferred Revenue	Cash is received	Revenue is recognized
Deferred Expense	Cash is paid	Expense is recognized

As we saw in Chapter 2, a business records transactions throughout the accounting period as the transactions occur. At the end of the period, the accountant prepares a trial balance and uses it to prepare financial statements. However, before most businesses can prepare accurate, up-to-date financial statements, the accountant will have to prepare **adjusting entries**.

Stop and Think...

If cash is so important to the well-being of a business, why does US GAAP require the use of accrual accounting instead of cash-basis accounting?

Answer

The goal of US GAAP is for financial statements to reflect accurate information regarding the performance of a business. The fact that a business has received cash from customers does not necessarily mean that the business is performing well. For example, let's assume that during the year a business received $20,000 from customers for services that it had provided during the same year. The business also received another $10,000 from customers for services that will not be provided until the following year. Under cash-basis accounting, the business would report $30,000 of revenues in the first year. Now, suppose during the second year the customers asked for (and received) a refund of the $10,000 before the services were provided. The $30,000 in revenues that were originally reported under cash-basis accounting during the first year now seems to be inaccurate because the business only ended up with revenues of $20,000. Under accrual accounting, the business would have only reported $20,000 of revenues in the first year, which would have reflected a more accurate picture of the business's performance. This is because, under accrual accounting, revenues are recorded when they are earned instead of when cash is received.

What Is the Role of Adjusting Entries, and When Are They Prepared?

2 Understand the four types of adjustments, and prepare adjusting entries

Adjusting entries are journal entries used to ensure that the revenue recognition principle and the matching principle are followed. Adjustments may be needed for accruals when revenues have been earned, or expenses have been incurred, before cash is exchanged. Because cash has not been exchanged, it is possible that the revenue or expense has not been recorded, so an adjusting entry is needed to record the revenue or expense.

- Two types of adjustments are made for accruals:

  1. Accrue, or record, unrecorded revenues. Revenues are recorded in the current period by debiting a receivable and crediting revenue.

  2. Accrue, or record, unrecorded expenses. Record the expenses in the current period by debiting an expense and crediting a liability.

A deferral is created when cash is exchanged before the related revenue or expense is recognized. Examples include receiving cash from customers prior to providing services or purchasing supplies that are not used immediately.

- Two types of adjustments are made for deferrals:

Unearned revenue A liability created when a business collects cash from customers in advance of providing goods or services; also called **deferred revenue**.

  1. Divide **unearned revenues** between periods. When payment is received in advance from a customer for goods or services, cash is debited. The liability account, Unearned Revenue, is credited because the customer is owed the goods or services. Once the customer receives the goods or services, an adjusting entry is prepared in which the Unearned Revenue account is debited to reduce it and a Revenue account is credited.

Prepaid expenses Amounts that are assets of a business because they represent items that have been paid for but will be used later; also called **deferred expenses**.

2. Divide **prepaid expenses**, supplies, buildings, equipment, and other assets between periods. These items are recorded as assets when they are purchased because the item that was paid for has not yet been used up. Therefore, an asset account is debited and cash is credited to record the purchase. Once part, or all, of the item is used up, an adjusting entry is prepared in which an expense account is debited and the related asset is credited to reduce it.

At the end of the accounting period, the accountant prepares a trial balance from the account information contained in the general ledger. This trial balance lists most of the revenues and expenses of the business, but these amounts are incomplete because the adjusting entries have not yet been prepared. Therefore, this trial balance is called an **unadjusted trial balance** (step three in the accounting cycle). Remember Osborne Consulting, Inc., from Chapter 2? **Exhibit 3-1** shows the unadjusted trial balance for Osborne Consulting, Inc., at the end of its first quarter of operations, at March 31, 2014. Now, we need to prepare adjusting entries at March 31, 2014.

Unadjusted trial balance A trial balance that is prepared at the end of the accounting period prior to the adjusting entries being made.

		BALANCE	
ACCOUNT TITLE		**DEBIT**	**CREDIT**
Cash		$26,300	
Accounts Receivable		3,100	
Supplies		900	
Prepaid Rent		3,000	
Equipment		12,600	
Accounts Payable			$13,100
Unearned Service Revenue			450
Common Stock			20,000
Retained Earnings			9,500
Dividends		3,200	
Service Revenue			7,000
Salaries Expense		550	
Utilities Expense		400	
Total		$50,050	$50,050

Osborne Consulting, Inc.
(Unadjusted) Trial Balance
March 31, 2014

Exhibit 3-1 ▲

Remember from Chapter 2 that transactions are recorded in the journal and posted to accounts in the general ledger. This process is still used when adjusting the accounts. In this chapter, we will show how to record adjusting entries and how to post them to accounts. However, instead of using the real ledger account form, we will post adjustments to T-accounts. We use this method because it is easier to see how these entries affect the specific accounts as well as the accounting equation.

Accruing Revenues

Accounts Receivable Businesses sometimes earn revenue by providing goods or services before they receive cash. Assume that a local car dealership hires Osborne Consulting, Inc., on March 15 as a computer consultant. Osborne Consulting agrees to a monthly fee of $500, which the car dealership pays on the 15th of each month, beginning on April 15. During March, Osborne earns half a month's fee, $250 ($500 × 1/2 month), for consulting work performed March 15 through March 31. On March 31, Osborne makes the following adjusting entry to reflect the accrual of the revenue earned during March (the beginning balance of each account is found on the unadjusted trial balance presented in Exhibit 3-1):

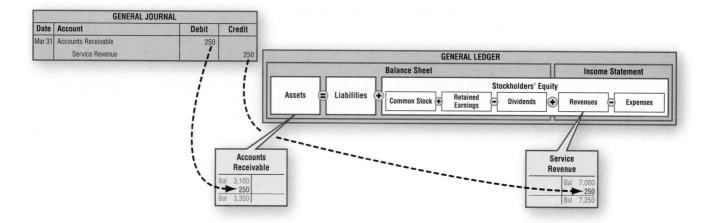

Without the adjustment, Osborne Consulting's financial statements are inaccurate because they would understate both Accounts Receivable and Service Revenue.

Accruing Expenses

Salaries Payable   Suppose Osborne Consulting pays the office assistant a monthly salary of $550. Osborne pays the assistant on the 15th of each month for the past month's work. On March 31, the following adjustment must be made to record the salaries expense for the month of March:

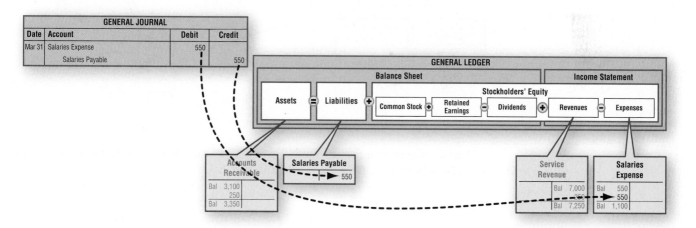

Accrued expenses Expenses that have been incurred prior to being paid for.

This is referred to as accruing the expense. **Accrued expenses**, such as the accrual for salaries expense, are expenses that the business has incurred but not paid. The adjusting entry to accrue the expense always creates a liability, such as Salaries Payable, Taxes Payable, or Interest Payable.

Adjusting Deferred Revenues

Unearned Revenues   It is possible for a business to collect cash from customers prior to providing goods or services. Receiving cash from a customer before earning it creates a liability called unearned revenue, or **deferred revenue**. It is classified as a liability because the company owes a product or service to the customer. Even though the account has the word *revenue* in its title, it is not a revenue account because the amount in the account represents what has not yet been earned.

Deferred revenue A liability created when a business collects cash from customers in advance of providing goods or services; also called **unearned revenue**.

Suppose a local real estate agency hires Osborne Consulting to provide consulting services, agreeing to pay $450 monthly, beginning immediately. Osborne Consulting collects the first amount from the real estate agency on March 21. Osborne Consulting records the cash receipt and a liability as follows:

DATE	ACCOUNTS	POST REF.	DR.	CR.
Mar 21	Cash		450	
	Unearned Service Revenue			450
	Collected revenue in advance.			

The liability account Unearned Service Revenue now shows that Osborne Consulting owes $450 of services because of its obligation to provide consulting services to the real estate agency.

During the last ten days of March, Osborne Consulting earned one-third of the $450, or $150 ($450 × 1/3). Therefore, Osborne Consulting makes the following adjustment to record earning $150 of the revenue:

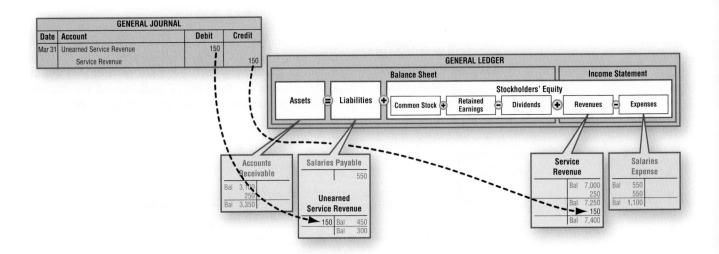

Service Revenue increases by $150, and Unearned Service Revenue decreases by $150. Now both accounts are up to date at March 31.

Adjusting Deferred Expenses

Prepaid Rent   Prepaid rent and prepaid insurance are examples of prepaid expenses, also called **deferred expenses**. Prepaid expenses represent items that are paid for before they are used. Often, renters are required to pay rent in advance. This prepayment creates an asset for the renter. Suppose Osborne Consulting, Inc., moves to a new office and prepays three months' office rent on March 1, 2014. If the lease specifies a monthly rental of $1,000, the amount of cash paid is $3,000 ($1,000 × 3 months). The entry to record the payment is as follows:

Deferred expenses Amounts that are assets of a business because they represent items which have been paid for but will be used later. Also called **prepaid expenses**.

DATE	ACCOUNTS	POST REF.	DR.	CR.
Mar 1	Prepaid Rent		3,000	
	Cash			3,000
	Paid three months' rent in advance.			

After posting, Prepaid Rent has a $3,000 debit balance. During March, Osborne Consulting uses the rented space for one month; therefore, the balance in Prepaid Rent is reduced by $1,000 (one month's rent). The required adjusting entry is as follows:

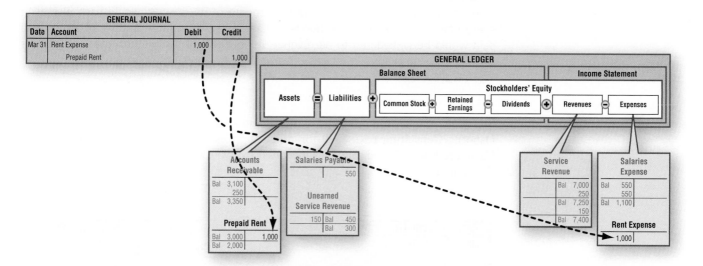

The Rent Expense account is increased with a debit, which reduces Retained Earnings and, therefore, Stockholders' Equity. The asset account Prepaid Rent is decreased with a credit for the same amount. After posting, Prepaid Rent and Rent Expense show the correct ending balances. If Osborne Consulting, Inc., had prepaid insurance, the same analysis would also apply to this asset account. The difference in the adjusting entry would be in the account titles, which would be Prepaid Insurance instead of Prepaid Rent and Insurance Expense instead of Rent Expense. The amount of the entry would also be different.

Accounting in Your World

In order to better understand the difference between a prepaid expense and an unearned revenue, consider this example:

At the start of this quarter or semester in school, you paid your school the tuition that was due for the upcoming term. Your tuition will ultimately be an expense to you. However, before the term began, the amount you paid was not yet an expense to you because the school had not yet provided any classes. In other words, you had not yet received anything for your payment. Instead, the amount you paid represented an asset known as a prepaid expense. It was an asset because the school owes you either the classes or a refund.

Once classes started, you began to incur an expense. Technically, the amount of your asset, prepaid expense, would have decreased and the amount of your expense would have increased every day. By the end of the quarter or semester, none of the tuition you paid would be considered to be a prepaid expense. Instead, it becomes an expense.

Now, let's look at the same example from the perspective of your school. When your school received the tuition payment from you, it did not have the right to record it as a revenue because it had not provided you with any classes. Instead, the school would record your tuition as a liability called unearned revenue. Unearned revenue represents a liability to the school because the school owes you either the classes or your money back.

Once classes started, your school began to earn revenue. The amount of its unearned revenue would have decreased and the amount of its revenue would have increased every day. By the end of the quarter or semester, the entire amount of tuition you paid would be considered to be revenue to your school. As you can see, one entity's prepaid expense is another entity's unearned revenue and vice versa.

Supplies Supplies receive the same treatment as prepaid expenses. On March 5, Osborne Consulting pays $900 for office supplies. The asset accounts, Supplies and Cash, are both affected. Supplies increased by $900, while Cash decreased by $900, as shown here:

DATE	ACCOUNTS	POST REF.	DR.	CR.
Mar 5	Supplies		900	
	Cash			900
	Purchased office supplies.			

The March 31 trial balance, as shown in Exhibit 3-1 on page 106, shows Supplies with a $900 debit balance. During March, Osborne Consulting uses some of these supplies to conduct business. Therefore, Osborne Consulting's March 31 Balance Sheet should *not* report supplies of $900. To figure out the amount of supplies used, Osborne Consulting counts the supplies on hand at the end of March. The supplies on hand are still an asset to the business. Assume that Osborne Consulting has supplies costing $600 at March 31. The supplies purchased ($900) minus the supplies on hand at the end of March ($600) equals the value of the supplies used during the month ($300). The amount of supplies used during the month will become supplies expense. The March 31 adjusting entry updates the Supplies account and records Supplies Expense for the month:

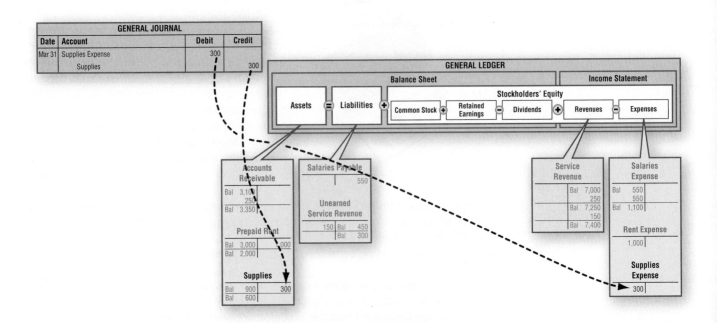

After the entry is posted to the general ledger, the correct account balances for Supplies and Supplies Expense will be reflected.

Depreciation of long-term assets

Long-term assets Long-lived, tangible assets such as land, buildings, equipment, and furniture used in the operation of a business lasting for more than a year.

Depreciation Allocation of the cost of a long-term asset to expense over its useful life.

Long-term assets, or fixed assets, are assets that last for more than one year. Examples include land, buildings, equipment, and furniture. All of these assets, except land, are used up over time. As a long-term asset is used up, part of the asset's cost becomes an expense, just as supplies become supplies expense when they are used up. The expensing of a long-term asset's cost over its useful life is called **depreciation**. No depreciation is recorded for land because it is never really used up.

We account for long-term assets in the same way as prepaid expenses and supplies because they are all assets. The major difference is the length of time it takes for the asset to be used up. Prepaid expenses and supplies are typically used within a year, while most long-term assets remain functional for several years. Suppose that, on March 1, Osborne Consulting purchases equipment on account for $12,600 and makes this journal entry:

DATE	ACCOUNTS	POST REF.	DR.	CR.
Mar 1	Equipment		12,600	
	Accounts Payable			12,600
	Purchased equipment on account.			

Straight-line depreciation A method of estimating depreciation (Cost of the Asset − Salvage Value)/ Useful Life of the Asset.

Salvage value The estimated value of a long-term asset at the end of its useful life.

After posting the entry, the Equipment account has a $12,600 balance. It is difficult to measure the amount of a long-term asset that has been used up over time, so the amount must be estimated. Several methods can be used to estimate the amount of depreciation. The most common method, which Osborne Consulting utilizes, is called the **straight-line depreciation** method. Osborne Consulting believes the equipment will be useful for three years and will be worthless and have no **salvage value** at the end of its life. Depreciation of this equipment is calculated using the straight-line method as follows:

$$\text{Depreciation Expense per Year} = \frac{\text{Cost of Asset} - \text{Salvage Value of Asset}}{\text{Useful Life of Asset}} = \frac{\$12,600}{3} = \$4,200$$

Osborne Consulting purchased the equipment on March 1, so the accountant needs to calculate one month's Depreciation Expense. To calculate one month's depreciation, divide the yearly depreciation by twelve ($4,200/12 months = $350).

Accumulated Depreciation A contra-asset account that reflects all of the depreciation recorded for an asset to date.

The Accumulated Depreciation Account

Depreciation expense for March is recorded by debiting Depreciation Expense. However, instead of crediting the asset account (as was done with supplies and prepaid expenses) to reduce it, an account called **Accumulated Depreciation**, Equipment will be credited.

The journal entry to record depreciation expense for the month of March is as follows:

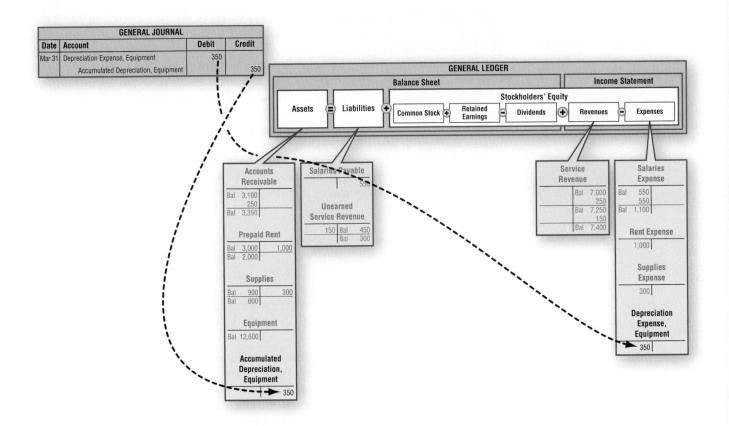

Contra-account An account that is linked to another account. A contra-account will have a normal balance opposite of the account it is linked to.

Net value The amount found by subtracting the balance of a contra-account from the balance of the account it is linked to.

Book value The asset's cost minus its accumulated depreciation; also called **carrying value**.

Accumulated Depreciation, Equipment is a contra-asset account. A **contra-account** has three main characteristics:

- A contra-account is linked to another account and will always appear with this account in the financial statements.
- A contra-account's normal balance is always opposite of the account it is linked to.
- The balance in a contra-account is subtracted from the balance of the account it is linked to in order to find the **net value** of the two accounts.

Because it is linked to Equipment, an asset account, Accumulated Depreciation, Equipment will appear on the balance sheet. Being an asset, the Equipment account has a debit balance, so the Accumulated Depreciation, Equipment account will have a credit balance because it is a contra-asset. Since it's a contra-account, the balance of Accumulated Depreciation, Equipment is subtracted from Equipment. The net amount of a long-term asset is called its **book value**, or **carrying value**, and is calculated as follows:

	Book Value of a Long-Term Asset	
Cost	Equipment	$12,600
− Accumulated Depreciation	Less: Accumulated Depreciation, Equipment	350
= Book (or Carrying) Value	Book Value	$12,250

Accumulated Depreciation, Equipment increases over the life of the asset as the asset is used up, which reduces the book value of the equipment. By keeping the cost of the equipment separate from its accumulated depreciation, financial statement users can look at the Equipment account to see how much the asset originally cost and also look at the Accumulated Depreciation, Equipment account to see how much of the original cost has been used up. A business usually keeps an accumulated depreciation account for each type of depreciable long-term asset. If Osborne Consulting, Inc., had both buildings and equipment, it would use two accumulated depreciation accounts, Accumulated Depreciation, Buildings and Accumulated Depreciation, Equipment. Depreciation will be covered more in depth in Chapter 8.

Try It!

Jim Oliver is the accountant for Crazy Critters, Inc., a local veterinary clinic. After Jim finished preparing the financial statements for the year, he realized that he failed to make an adjusting entry to record $1,800 of depreciation expense. What effect did this error have on Crazy Critters' financial statements?

Answer

In order to determine the effects of omitting an adjusting entry, we must examine what the adjusting entry should have been. The adjusting entry Jim should have made is:

DATE	ACCOUNTS	POST REF.	DR.	CR.
	Depreciation Expense		1,800	
	Accumulated Depreciation			1,800

As we can see from the journal entry, Depreciation Expense should have been debited (increased), which would have increased total expenses for the year. An increase in total expenses causes a decrease in Net Income. So, the omission of the adjusting entry for depreciation expense causes Net Income, and therefore Retained Earnings, to be overstated. We also see that the Accumulated Depreciation account should have been credited (increased), which would cause total assets to decrease because Accumulated Depreciation is a contra-asset account. So, the omission of the adjusting entry for depreciation expense also causes the total assets to be overstated.

How Are Financial Statements Prepared from an Adjusted Trial Balance?

The Adjusted Trial Balance

3 **Prepare financial statements from an adjusted trial balance**

Adjusted trial balance A list of all the accounts of a business with their adjusted balances.

Earlier in the chapter, the unadjusted trial balance in Exhibit 3-1 on page 106 showed the account balances for Osborne Consulting, Inc., before the adjustments had been made. After adjustment, Osborne Consulting's accounts would appear as presented in **Exhibit 3-2**.

Prior to preparing the financial statements, an **adjusted trial balance** is prepared to make sure total debits still equal total credits after adjusting entries have been recorded and posted. The adjusted trial balance for Osborne Consulting is presented in **Exhibit 3-3**.

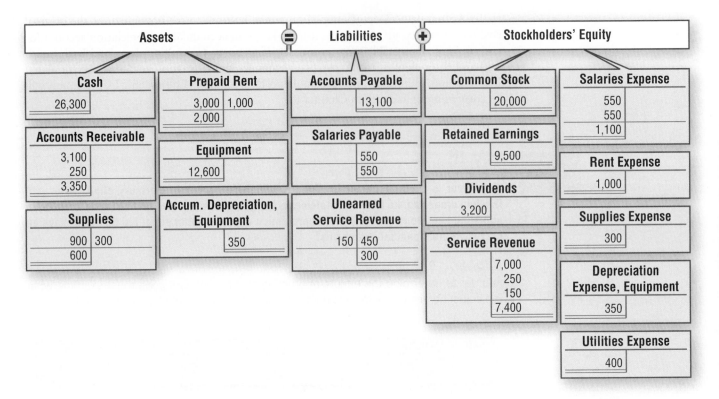

Exhibit 3-2 ▲

Osborne Consulting, Inc.		
Adjusted Trial Balance		
March 31, 2014		
ACCOUNT	**DEBIT**	**CREDIT**
Cash	$26,300	
Accounts Receivable	3,350	
Supplies	600	
Prepaid Rent	2,000	
Equipment	12,600	
Accumulated Depreciation, Equipment		$ 350
Accounts Payable		13,100
Salaries Payable		550
Unearned Service Revenue		300
Common Stock		20,000
Retained Earnings		9,500
Dividends	3,200	
Service Revenue		7,400
Salaries Expense	1,100	
Rent Expense	1,000	
Utilities Expense	400	
Depreciation Expense, Equipment	350	
Supplies Expense	300	
Total	$51,200	$51,200

Exhibit 3-3 ▲

Preparing the Financial Statements

The March financial statements of Osborne Consulting, Inc., are prepared from the adjusted trial balance in Exhibit 3-3. The financial statements should be prepared in the same order that we used in previous chapters:

1. The income statement (**Exhibit 3-4**) reports the revenues and the expenses to determine net income or net loss for a period of time.

2. The statement of retained earnings (**Exhibit 3-5**) shows the changes in retained earnings during the period and computes the ending balance of retained earnings. Notice that the Retained Earnings balance of $9,500 on the adjusted trial balance does *not* represent the ending Retained Earnings balance because the account has not yet been updated for the current period's earnings or dividends.

3. The balance sheet (**Exhibit 3-6**) reports the assets, liabilities, and stockholders' equity to see the financial position of the business at a specific point in time.

As we first discussed in Chapter 1, all financial statements include these elements:

- Heading

   1. Name of the entity, such as Osborne Consulting, Inc.

   2. Title of the statement: Income Statement, Statement of Retained Earnings, or Balance Sheet

   3. Date, or period, covered by the statement: Quarter ended March 31, 2014, or March 31, 2014

- Body of the statement

On the income statement, expenses may be listed in descending order from the largest amount to the smallest amount, as Osborne Consulting did, or they may be listed in some other order, such as alphabetical order.

Osborne Consulting, Inc. Income Statement Quarter Ended March 31, 2014		
Revenue:		
Service Revenue		$7,400
Expenses:		
Salaries Expense	$1,100	
Rent Expense	1,000	
Utilities Expense	400	
Depreciation Expense, Equipment	350	
Supplies Expense	300	
Total Expenses		3,150
Net Income		$4,250

Exhibit 3-4 ▲

Osborne Consulting, Inc. Statement of Retained Earnings Quarter Ended March 31, 2014	
Retained Earnings, March 1, 2014	$ 9,500
Add: Net Income	4,250
Subtotal	13,750
Less: Dividends	3,200
Retained Earnings, March 31, 2014	$10,550

Exhibit 3-5 ▲

Osborne Consulting, Inc. Balance Sheet March 31, 2014				
ASSETS			**LIABILITIES**	
Cash		$26,300	Accounts Payable	$13,100
Accounts Receivable		3,350	Salaries Payable	550
Supplies		600	Unearned Service Revenue	300
Prepaid Rent		2,000	Total Liabilities	13,950
Equipment	$12,600			
Less: Accumulated			**STOCKHOLDERS' EQUITY**	
Depreciation,			Common Stock	20,000
Equipment	350	12,250	Retained Earnings	10,550
			Total Stockholders' Equity	30,550
			Total Liabilities &	
Total Assets		$44,500	Stockholders' Equity	$44,500

Exhibit 3-6 ▲

Decision Guidelines

Decision		**Guideline**		**Analyze**
How can I tell how well a business is performing?		A company's financial statements will provide information regarding the performance of the company.		The income statement reflects how profitable a business has been for a specified period of time. The statement of retained earnings shows how much of a company's earnings have been distributed to the stockholders during the period. And the balance sheet reflects the business's financial position on a given date. In other words, it shows what assets the business has and who has rights to those assets.

How Does a Company Prepare for a New Accounting Period?

Completing the Accounting Cycle

4 Prepare closing entries and a post-closing trial balance

Closing entries Journal entries that are prepared at the end of the accounting period. Closing entries zero out the revenue, expense, and dividend accounts so accounting can begin for the next period.

We have now seen steps one through six in the accounting cycle completed for Osborne Consulting. The entire accounting cycle can be completed by finishing steps seven and eight. Step seven of the accounting cycle is the journalizing and posting of the closing entries, and step eight is the preparation of a post-closing trial balance.

In order to complete the accounting cycle, **closing entries** must be journalized and posted. Earlier in the chapter, we processed the transactions for Osborne Consulting and prepared the financial statements at the end of March. If we continue recording information in the revenue, expense, and dividend accounts, we will lose track of what activity happened prior to April compared to what happens in April and beyond, making it impossible to prepare accurate financial statements for the next accounting period.

In order to not confuse the transactions from the two different periods, the revenue, expense, and dividend accounts must be reset to zero before we start recording transactions for April. It is similar to resetting the scoreboard at the end of a game before you start a new game. Because we must keep the accounting equation in balance, we cannot just erase the balances in the revenue, expense, and dividend accounts because it would cause the equation to become unbalanced. To keep the accounting equation in balance and still be able to zero out these accounts, we will use closing entries. Closing entries are utilized to accomplish two things:

- The revenue, expense, and dividend account balances from the current accounting period are set back to zero so accounting for the next period can begin.
- The revenue, expense, and dividend account balances from the current accounting period are transferred into Retained Earnings so the accounting equation stays in balance. Transferring the revenue and expense account balances into Retained Earnings actually transfers the Net Income, or Net Loss, for the current period into Retained Earnings. Transferring the dividend account balance into Retained Earnings decreases Retained Earnings by the amount of dividends for the period.

Temporary accounts The revenue, expense, and dividend accounts; these accounts are closed at the end of the accounting period.

The revenue, expense, and dividend accounts are known as **temporary accounts**. They are called temporary because they are used temporarily to record activity for a specific period, the accounting period, and then they are closed into Retained Earnings. It is easy to remember the temporary accounts if you think of the color RED. The R in RED stands for revenues, the E stands for expenses, and the D stands for dividends. The RED accounts are closed at the end of each accounting period.

Before closing the temporary accounts, the accounting equation for a corporation would be as follows:

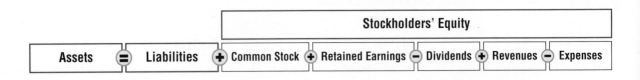

After closing the temporary accounts, the accounting equation would be as follows:

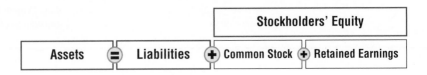

Permanent accounts The asset, liability, common stock and retained earnings accounts; these accounts are not closed at the end of the accounting period.

The accounts that remain in the accounting equation after closing are called **permanent accounts**. Assets, liabilities, common stock, and retained earnings are *not* closed at the end of the period because they are not used to measure activity for only one specific period. Consider Cash, Accounts Receivable, Accounts Payable, and Common Stock. These accounts do not represent business activity for a single period, so they are not closed at the end of the period. Their balances carry over to the next period. For example, the ending Cash balance at March 31, 2014, becomes the beginning balance on April 1, 2014.

The Three Closing Entries: Revenues, Expenses, and Dividends

To journalize closing entries, complete the following steps:

Step 1 Close the revenue accounts and move their balances into the Retained Earnings account. To close revenues, debit each revenue account for the amount of its credit balance. Transfer the revenue balances to Retained Earnings by crediting the Retained Earnings account for the total amount of the revenues. This closing entry transfers total revenues to the credit side of Retained Earnings.

Step 2 Close the expense accounts and move their balances into the Retained Earnings account. To close expenses, credit each expense account for the amount of its debit balance. Transfer the expense balances to Retained Earnings by debiting the Retained Earnings account for the total amount of the expenses. This closing entry transfers total expenses to the debit side of Retained Earnings.

Step 3 Close the Dividends account and move its balance into the Retained Earnings account. To close the Dividends account, credit it for the amount of its debit balance and debit the Retained Earnings account. This entry transfers the dividends to the debit side of Retained Earnings.

Remember that Net Income is equal to Revenues minus Expenses. So, closing the Revenues and Expenses into Retained Earnings (Steps 1 and 2) has the effect of adding Net Income for the period to, or deducting a Net Loss for the period from, Retained Earnings. Once the Dividends account has been subtracted from Retained Earnings, Step 3, the balance in the Retained Earnings account should match ending retained earnings on the statement of retained earnings.

The process for making closing entries is the same as it is for making any entry; record the entries in the journal and post them to the proper accounts in the ledger.

Now, let's apply this process to Osborne Consulting, Inc., at the end of March:

Step 1

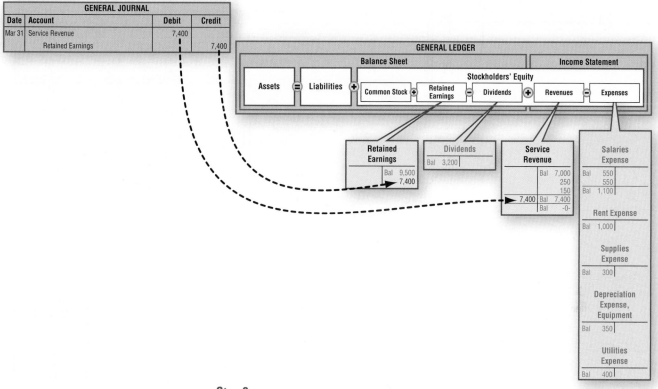

Step 2

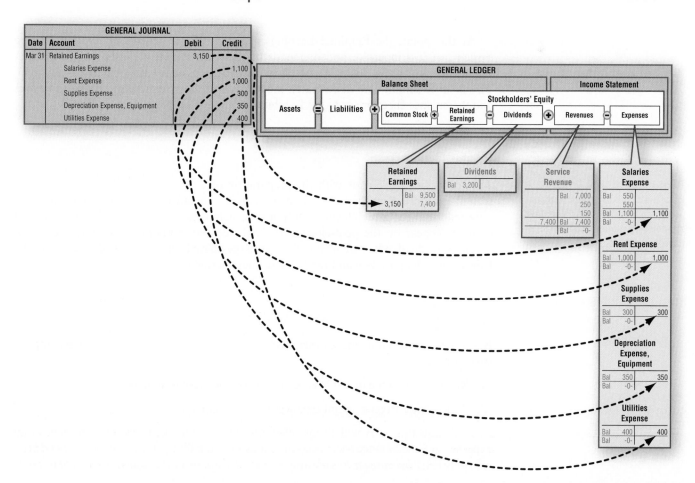

Step 3

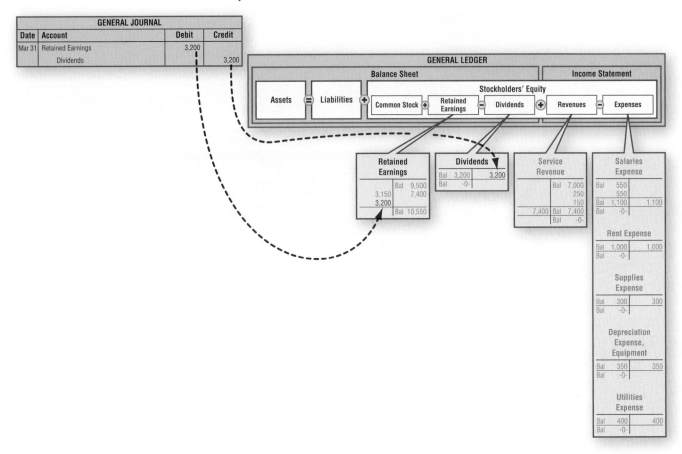

At this point, the Retained Earnings account balance reflects all the net income earned, net loss incurred, and dividends paid during the life of Osborne Consulting, Inc., to date. After the closing entries, Retained Earnings ends with a balance of $10,550. This balance should, and does, match the balance on the statement of retained earnings and the balance sheet presented in Exhibits 3-5 and 3-6 on page 116.

Post-Closing Trial Balance

Post-closing trial balance A list of the accounts and their balances at the end of the accounting period after closing entries have been journalized and posted.

The accounting cycle ends with the preparation of a **post-closing trial balance**, as seen in **Exhibit 3-7** on the following page. This trial balance lists the accounts and their adjusted balances after closing. Only assets, liabilities, common stock, and retained earnings appear on the post-closing trial balance. No temporary accounts—revenues, expenses, or dividends—are included because they have been closed. The accounts in the ledger are now up to date and ready for the next period's transactions.

Summary of the Adjusting and Closing Processes

Businesses record adjusting entries at the *end* of the accounting period to accomplish two purposes:

1. Report net income or net loss accurately on the income statement.

2. Reflect the correct account balances on the balance sheet.

Each adjusting entry will always affect one income statement account, a revenue or an expense, and one balance sheet account, an asset or a liability. *Cash is never included in an adjusting entry because cash is always recorded accurately at the time it is received or paid.*

				BALANCE	
		ACCOUNT TITLE		**DEBIT**	**CREDIT**
		Cash		$26,300	
		Accounts Receivable		3,350	
		Supplies		600	
		Prepaid Rent		2,000	
		Equipment		12,600	
		Accumulated Depreciation, Equipment			$ 350
		Accounts Payable			13,100
		Salaries Payable			550
		Unearned Service Revenue			300
		Common Stock			20,000
		Retained Earnings			10,550
		Total		$44,850	$44,850

Osborne Consulting, Inc.
Post-Closing Trial Balance
March 31, 2014

Exhibit 3-7 ▲

Accruals and deferrals can be summarized as follows:

1. With an *accrued revenue or expense*, a revenue or expense is recorded first when the revenue is earned or the expense is incurred and cash is received or paid later.

2. With a *deferred revenue or expense*, cash is received or paid first. The revenue or expense is recorded later as the revenue is earned or the expense is incurred.

Exhibit 3-8 summarizes the accrual and deferral adjustments.

	Accruals: Cash transaction comes later					
	First	**Dr.**	**Cr.**	**Later**	**Dr.**	**Cr.**
Accrued Expenses	*Accrue an expense and the related liability:*			*Pay cash and decrease the liability:*		
	Salaries Expense	XXX		Salaries Payable	XXX	
	Salaries Payable		XXX	Cash		XXX
Accrued Revenues	*Accrue a revenue and the related asset:*			*Receive cash and decrease the asset:*		
	Accounts Receivable	XXX		Cash	XXX	
	Service Revenue		XXX	Accounts Receivable		XXX
	Deferrals: Cash transaction comes first					
	First	**Dr.**	**Cr.**	**Later**	**Dr.**	**Cr.**
Prepaid Expenses, Depreciable Assets	*Pay cash and record an asset:*			*Record an expense and decrease the asset:*		
	Prepaid Rent	XXX		Rent Expense	XXX	
	Cash		XXX	Prepaid Rent		XXX
Unearned Revenues	*Receive cash and record a liability:*			*Record a revenue and decrease the liability:*		
	Cash	XXX		Unearned Service Revenue	XXX	
	Unearned Service Revenue		XXX	Service Revenue		XXX

Exhibit 3-8 ▲

Businesses record closing entries at the *end* of the accounting period to accomplish two purposes:

- Zero out the revenue, expense, and dividend accounts.
- Transfer the balances of the revenue, expense, and dividend accounts into Retained Earnings.

Closing entries are the end-of-period journal entries that get the temporary accounts—revenues, expenses, and dividends—ready for the next accounting period by zeroing them out. Closing entries also transfer the balances from the temporary accounts into the Retained Earnings account. The post-closing trial balance is the final step in the accounting cycle. The post-closing trial balance is prepared to ensure that total debits still equal total credits before a new accounting period is started.

Focus on Decision Making

"Who Owns Net Income and Where Does Income Go?"

What is net income? You can't touch it. You can't see it. You can't spend it. There's not even an account in the general ledger that is called Net Income. You can touch, see, and spend cash. But using accrual accounting, net income is not cash. So what is net income? Net income is the net of revenues less expenses. But who gets the net income? Who owns net income?

The answer is owners own net income. Think of revenues as something that benefits owners. Think of expenses as something that takes away some of that benefit that revenues provide. The net, whether net income or loss, belongs to the owners.

At the end of each accounting period, we want to close out the old measure and start a new measure of revenues, expenses, and net income. We have closing entries that zero out all the revenue and expense accounts so they start with a zero balance. However, we do not zero out the impact that revenues and expenses had on balance sheet accounts such as cash, accounts receivable, and accounts payable. To get this to work, we take the net income and recognize that it belongs to the business's owners. It's a part of the owners' equity. If the business does not distribute it to the owners, the net income is retained in the business. Earnings over time can be retained in the business or distributed to owners.

How They Do It: A Look At Business

Let's look at the Walt Disney Company. Disney operates amusement parks, makes movies, sells clothing, and a lot of other things related to the entertainment business. Some years are very good. Some years are not as good. At the end of 2011 and the beginning of 2012, Disney had retained earnings of $38.375 billion. This figure represents all of the net income and net losses earned by Disney, less any dividends to its stockholders, since the company was founded in 1923. In 2012, Disney had net income of $5.682 billion. However, it paid its stockholders $1.092 billion in dividends. So, at the end of 2012, Disney had retained earnings of $42.965 billion. Disney started out 2012 with retained earnings of $38.375 billion, added net income of $5.682 billion, and paid dividends of $1.092 billion, thus creating an ending retained earnings of $42.965 billion. During 2012, Disney had sales of $42.278 billion and expenses of $36.596 billion, creating net income of $5.682 billion. This net income belongs to Disney's owners and was reflected in the increase in retained earnings, which is a part of stockholders' equity.

Now what did Disney do with the net income it did not pay to its stockholders? Disney used the earnings to invest in new assets such as movies and attractions at its amusement parks. Disney also used some of the money to pay its liabilities. Disney paid its stockholders a dividend, but retained some of its earnings to help grow the business for the future.

Next, let's think about Under Armour, Inc. Under Armour manufactures and sells sporting apparel. From the year that it was founded, 1996, until the end of 2012, Under Armour had good and bad years. Under Armour had never paid dividends to its owners, its stockholders. At the end of 2011 and the beginning of 2012, the net of all of Under

Armour's income and losses throughout its life summed to $366.164 million. In 2012, Under Armour had net income of $128.778 million. Under Armour decided it needed to retain all its 2012 earnings to grow the business. It once again decided not to pay dividends to its stockholders. So at the end of 2012, Under Armour had retained earnings of $493.181 million. Under Armour started out 2012 with retained earnings of $366.164 million, had a special tax adjustment of $1.761 million, added net income of $128.778 million, thus creating an ending retained earnings of $493.181 million. During 2012, Under Armour had sales of $1,834,921,000 and expenses of $1,706,143,000, creating net income of $128,778,000. This net income belongs to Under Armour's owners and was reflected in the increase in retained earnings, which is a part of stockholders' equity.

Now what did Under Armour do with the net income? Under Armour used the money to invest in new assets such as cash, accounts receivable, and property and equipment. Under Armour did not pay its stockholders a dividend. Under Armour retained the earnings to help finance the business' growth.

Summary

MyAccountingLab

Here is what you should know after reading this chapter. MyAccountingLab will help you identify what you know and where to go when you need practice.

Key Points	Key Accounting Terms
Accrual versus cash accounting • Revenue recognition principle recognizes revenues when they are earned • Matching principle recognizes expenses when they are incurred	**Accrual accounting** (p. 104) **Accruals** (p. 104) **Adjusting entries** (p. 104) **Cash-basis accounting** (p. 104) **Deferrals** (p. 104) **Fiscal year** (p. 103) **Matching principle** (p. 104) **Revenue recognition principle** (p. 104)

1 ▶ **Understand the revenue recognition and matching principles**

Key Points	Key Accounting Terms
2 Understand the four types of adjustments, and prepare adjusting entries	

2 **Understand the four types of adjustments, and prepare adjusting entries**

Adjusting entries

- Are recorded at the end of the accounting period
- Always include one revenue *or* expense account *and* one asset *or* liability account
- Ensure that net income is reported properly
- Ensure that the proper balance is reflected in asset and liability accounts

Accrued expenses (p. 107)
Accumulated Depreciation (p. 111)
Book value (p. 112)
Carrying value (p. 112)
Contra-account (p. 112)
Deferred expenses (p. 108)
Deferred revenue (p. 107)
Depreciation (p. 111)
Long-term assets (p. 111)
Net value (p. 112)
Prepaid expenses (p. 106)
Salvage value (p. 111)
Straight-line depreciation (p. 111)
Unadjusted trial balance (p. 106)
Unearned revenue (p. 105)

3 **Prepare financial statements from an adjusted trial balance**

The adjusted trial balance

- Is prepared after all adjusting entries have been entered in the general journal and posted to the general ledger
- Is used to prepare the period-end financial statements

Adjusted trial balance (p. 113)

4 **Prepare closing entries and a post-closing trial balance**

Closing entries

- Are made at the end of an accounting period in order to prepare for a new accounting period
- Transfer the balances in all revenue accounts, all expense accounts, and the dividends account into the retained earnings account

Closing entries (p. 117)
Permanent accounts (p. 118)
Post-closing trial balance (p. 120)
Temporary accounts (p. 117)

Accounting Practice

Discussion Questions

1. If XYZ Consulting performs a consulting service and bills the customer on June 28 and receives payment from the customer on July 19, on what date would revenue be recorded if
   a. XYZ uses the cash basis of accounting?
   b. XYZ uses the accrual basis of accounting?

2. What does the matching principle require companies to match?

3. Why does the time period in which revenue is recognized matter?

4. What is a deferral? Under which basis of accounting, cash or accrual, would deferrals come into play? Under what circumstances would a company record a deferral?

5. Why do companies prepare adjusting entries?

6. What are some similarities and differences between assets and expenses?

7. What type of account (asset, liability, revenue, or expense) would Joe's Towing Company debit when it pays (credits) cash for each of the following transactions?
   a. Pays $100 to fill tow truck with gas
   b. Pays $1,000 to have a gas company deliver gas for its on-site refueling station
   Did you choose the same type of account or different ones? Why?

8. Describe the type of transaction that gives rise to a deferred revenue journal entry during the year. Why might deferred revenues require adjustment?

9. What kind of account is accumulated depreciation? How is it reported on the financial statements?

10. What are the objectives of the closing process? Which kind of accounts get closed? What is the only account that is affected by the closing process but not closed?

Self Check

1. The revenue recognition principle says
   a. divide time into equal periods to measure net income or net loss properly.
   b. record revenue only after you have earned it.
   c. match revenues and expenses in order to compute net income.
   d. record revenue only when you receive cash.

2. Adjusting the accounts is the process of
   a. subtracting expenses from revenues to measure net income.
   b. recording transactions as they occur during the accounting period.
   c. updating the accounts at the end of the accounting period.
   d. zeroing out account balances to prepare for the next accounting period.

3. Which of the following terms describe the types of adjusting entries?
   a. Expenses and revenues
   b. Prepaid expenses and prepaid revenues
   c. Deferrals and accruals
   d. Deferrals and depreciation

4. Assume that the weekly payroll of ASR, Inc., is $4,500. Employees work five days per week, Monday through Friday. December 31, the end of the year, falls on Wednesday, but the company won't pay employees for the full week until its usual payday, Friday. What adjusting entry will ASR, Inc., make on Wednesday, December 31?

DATE	ACCOUNTS	POST REF.	DR.	CR.
a.	Salaries Payable		2,700	
	Salaries Expense			2,700
b.	Salaries Expense		2,700	
	Accumulated Salaries			2,700
c.	Salaries Expense		2,700	
	Cash			2,700
d.	Salaries Expense		2,700	
	Salaries Payable			2,700

5. Unearned Revenue is always

   a. revenue.
   b. stockholders' equity.
   c. a liability.
   d. an asset.

6. The adjusted trial balance shows

   a. assets, liabilities, and common stock only.
   b. revenues and expenses only.
   c. amounts that may be out of balance.
   d. amounts that are ready for the financial statements.

7. Which of the following accounts is not closed?

   a. Salaries Expense
   b. Dividends
   c. Accumulated Depreciation, Equipment
   d. Service Revenue

8. What do closing entries accomplish?

   a. Bring the Retained Earnings account to its correct ending balance
   b. Transfer revenues, expenses, and dividends to retained earnings
   c. Zero out the revenues, expenses, and dividends to prepare them for the next accounting period
   d. All of the above

9. Which of the following is not a closing entry?

DATE	ACCOUNTS	POST REF.	DR.	CR.
a.	Salaries Payable		1,000	
	Retained Earnings			1,000
b.	Service Revenue		1,200	
	Retained Earnings			1,200
c.	Retained Earnings		1,500	
	Dividends			1,500
d.	Retained Earnings		800	
	Rent Expense			800

10. Which correctly represents the flow of information from one financial statement to another?

    a. Statement of retained earnings to the balance sheet

    b. Income statement to the statement of retained earnings

    c. Both a and b are correct.

    d. None of the above is correct.

11. According to the Real World Accounting Video, the excess of sales revenue over cost of goods sold is called _____.

    a. the sales margin or net sales

    b. the gross margin or gross profit

    c. net income or earnings after taxes

12. According to the Real World Accounting Video, GAAP is the term used for _____.

    a. Government Accredited Accounting Positions

    b. Generally Accepted Accounting Principles

    c. General and Accounting Procedures

Answers are given after Written Communication.

MyAccountingLab

Short Exercises

S3-1. **Accounting principles (*Learning Objectives 1 & 2*) 5–10 min.**

Match the accounting term with the corresponding definition.

____ 1. Accrual-basis accounting	a. Any consecutive 12-month period.
____ 2. Matching principle	b. Records the impact of a business event as it occurs regardless of whether the transaction affected cash.
____ 3. Revenue recognition principle	
____ 4. Fiscal period	c. Records expenses when incurred to sell goods or provide services.
	d. Records revenue when it is earned.

S3-2. **Accounting terminology (*Learning Objectives 2 & 3*) 5–10 min.**

Match the accounting term with the corresponding definition.

____ 1. Accumulated depreciation	a. An account whose normal balance is opposite that of its companion account.
____ 2. Adjusted trial balance	
____ 3. Adjusting entry	b. Entry made to assign revenues to the period in which they are earned and expenses to the period incurred.
____ 4. Book value	
____ 5. Contra-account	c. A list of accounts with their adjusted balances.
____ 6. Depreciation	
____ 7. Long-term asset	d. The cumulative sum of all depreciation recorded for an asset.
	e. The allocation of a long-term asset's cost to expense over its useful life.
	f. The asset's cost less its accumulated depreciation.
	g. Long-lived asset used to operate the business.

S3-3. Types of adjusting entries (*Learning Objective 2*) 5–10 min.

The trial balance of Allen & Associates includes the following balance sheet accounts. For each account, identify the type of adjusting entry that is typically made for the account (deferred expense, deferred revenue, accrued expense, or accrued revenue), and give the related income statement account used in that adjustment. Example: Prepaid Insurance: deferred expense; Insurance Expense

a. Interest Payable

b. Unearned Service Revenue

c. Accounts Receivable

d. Supplies

e. Accumulated Depreciation

S3-4. Adjusting journal entry—prepaid rent (*Learning Objective 2*) 5–10 min.

Julie's Flower Shop's Prepaid Rent balance is $4,500 on July 1. This prepaid rent represents six months' rent. Journalize and post the adjusting entry on July 31 to record one month's rent. Compute the balances of the two accounts involved on July 31.

S3-5. Adjusting journal entry—supplies (*Learning Objective 2*) 5–10 min.

Julie's Flower Shop's Office Supplies balance on October 1 is $1,200 and the balance in Office Supplies Expense is $0. On October 31, there is $480 of supplies on hand. Journalize and post the adjusting entry on October 31 for the supplies used. Compute the balances of the two accounts involved on October 31.

S3-6. Adjusting journal entry—interest expense (*Learning Objective 2*) 5–10 min.

In order to purchase equipment and supplies, Sinclair Bike Shop, Inc., borrowed $28,000 on August 1 by signing a note payable to Community One Bank. Interest expense for Sinclair Bike Shop, Inc., is $140 per month. Journalize an adjusting entry to accrue interest expense at December 31, assuming no other adjusting entries have been made for the year. Post to the two accounts affected by the adjustment.

S3-7. Adjusting journal entry—magazine subscriptions (*Learning Objective 2*) 5–10 min.

Backcountry, Inc., an outdoor magazine, collected $2,700 on June 1 for one-year subscriptions from subscribers in advance. Journalize and post the adjusting entry on December 31 to record the revenue that Backcountry, Inc., has earned, assuming no other adjusting entries have been made for the year. Compute the balances of the two accounts involved.

S3-8. Adjusting journal entry—salaries, accrued revenue, interest expense (*Learning Objective 2*) 5–10 min.

Journalize the following adjusting entries at August 31:

1. Services provided but not recorded, $2,700.

2. Salaries earned by employees but not recorded, $3,200.

3. Accrued interest on a note payable, $260.

S3-9. Adjusting journal entry—accrued service revenue (*Learning Objective 2*) 5–10 min.

Suppose you work summers mowing yards. Most of your customers pay you immediately after their lawn is mowed, but a few customers ask you to bill them at the end of the month. It is now July 31 and you have collected $750 from cash-paying customers for services performed in July. Your remaining customers owe you $165 for services performed in July. How much service revenue would you record in July according to accrual-basis accounting?

S3-10. Closing entries (*Learning Objective 4*) 5–10 min.

From the following list of accounts from the adjusted trial balance, identify each as an asset, liability, stockholders' equity, revenue, or expense. Use the most detailed account type appropriate. Also, state whether each account is a permanent or temporary account and whether it is an account that gets closed at the end of the accounting period. Following the accounts is a sample of the format to use.

1. Depreciation Expense
2. Sales Revenue
3. Building
4. Cash

5. Unearned Service Revenue
6. Prepaid Rent
7. Dividends

Account	Type of Account	Permanent/Temporary	Closed
Supplies	Asset	Permanent	No

S3-11. Financial statements and closing entries (*Learning Objectives 3 & 4*) 10–15 min.

The following selected accounts and balances appear on the adjusted trial balance for Waverly, Inc., on July 31, 2014:

Service Revenue	$ 1,800
Rent Expense	650
Salaries Expense	575
Dividends	300
Common Stock	25,000
Retained Earnings	4,100

1. What is the net income or net loss?
2. What is the change in Retained Earnings?
3. Journalize the closing entries required.

S3-12. Adjusting and closing entries (*Learning Objectives 2 & 4*) 5–10 min.

For the following series of journal entries, indicate whether each is an adjusting entry (ADJ) or a closing entry (CL).

TYPE OF ENTRY (ADJ OR CL)	ACCOUNTS	POST REF.	DR.	CR.
	Salaries Expense		725	
	Salaries Payable			725
	Service Revenue		4,200	
	Retained Earnings			4,200
	Retained Earnings		1,500	
	Dividends			1,500
	Unearned Revenue		940	
	Service Revenue			940

S3-13. Preparing a post-closing trial balance (*Learning Objective 4*) **5–10 min.**

After closing its accounts at July 31, 2014, Anderson Realty, Inc., had the following account balances:

Notes Payable	$ 5,000	Cash	$ 3,800
Prepaid Rent	1,600	Service Revenue	0
Accounts Receivable	2,300	Retained Earnings	10,700
Prepaid Insurance	4,200	Common Stock	35,000
Accounts Payable	2,100	Salaries Expense	0
Equipment	45,500	Accumulated Depreciation, Equipment	4,600

Prepare Anderson Realty's post-closing trial balance at July 31, 2014. List accounts in proper order.

MyAccountingLab

Exercises (Group A)

E3-14A. Adjusting journal entries—unearned revenue and accrued revenue (*Learning Objective 2*) **10–15 min.**

Suppose you started up your own landscaping business. A customer paid you $170 in advance to mow his or her lawn while he or she was on vacation. You performed landscaping services for a local business, but the business hasn't paid you the $440 fee yet. A customer pays you $215 cash for landscaping services. Answer the following questions about the correct way to account for your revenue under accrual-basis accounting:

1. Name the accounts used to record these events.

2. Prepare the journal entries to record the three transactions.

E3-15A. Adjusting journal entry—prepaid insurance (*Learning Objective 2*) **5–10 min.**

Calculate the missing amounts for each of the following Prepaid Insurance situations. For situation A, journalize the adjusting entry. Consider each situation separately.

	Situation			
	A	**B**	**C**	**D**
Beginning Prepaid Insurance	$ 350	$ 800	?	$ 700
Payments for Prepaid Insurance during the year	1,300	?	2,200	?
Total amount to account for	?	?	3,600	2,300
Ending Prepaid Insurance	300	400	?	?
Insurance Expense	$?	$1,300	$2,600	$1,400

E3-16A. Common adjusting journal entries (*Learning Objective 2*) **10–15 min.**

Journalize the adjusting entries for the following adjustments at March 31, the end of the accounting period, omitting explanations.

a. Employee salaries owed for Monday through Thursday of a five-day workweek, $4,300.

b. Unearned service revenue now earned, $840.

c. Depreciation, $1,800.

d. Prepaid rent expired, $950.

e. Interest revenue accrued, $275.

E3-17A. Error analysis (*Learning Objective 2*) **10–15 min.**

The adjusting entries for the following adjustments were omitted at period-end:

a. Prepaid rent expired, $3,000.

b. Depreciation, $1,300.

c. Employee salaries owed for Monday through Wednesday of a five-day workweek, $4,000.

d. Supplies used during the period, $800.

e. Unearned service revenue now earned, $4,200.

Requirement

Compute the amount that net income for the year is overstated or understated for each omitted entry. Use the following format to help analyze the transactions.

Transaction	Overstated/Understated	Amount
Sample a., b., etc.	Overstated	$5,000

E3-18A. Common adjusting journal entries (*Learning Objective 2*) **15–20 min.**

Journalize the adjusting entry needed at March 31, the fiscal year-end, for each of the following independent situations. No other adjusting entries have been made for the year.

a. On January 1, $4,200 rent was collected in advance. Cash was debited and Unearned Rent Revenue was credited. The tenant was paying six months' rent in advance.

b. The business holds a $25,000 note receivable. Interest revenue of $475 has been earned on the note but not yet received.

c. Salaries expense is $3,700 per day, Monday through Friday, and the business pays employees each Friday. This year, March 31 falls on a Thursday.

d. The unadjusted balance of the Supplies account is $900. Supplies on hand total $175.

e. Equipment was purchased two years ago at a cost of $25,000. The equipment's useful life is four years.

f. On September 1, when $1,800 was paid for a one-year insurance policy, Prepaid Insurance was debited and Cash was credited.

E3-19A. Common adjusting journal entries (*Learning Objective 2*) **15–20 min.**

The accounting records of Media Unlimited include the following unadjusted balances at September 30: Accounts Receivable, $1,800; Supplies, $900; Salaries Payable, $0; Unearned Service Revenue, $900; Service Revenue, $4,300; Salaries Expense, $2,500; and Supplies Expense, $0. The following data pertain to the September 30 adjusting entries:

a. Service revenue accrued, $1,600.

b. Unearned service revenue that has been earned, $300.

c. Supplies on hand, $50.

d. Salaries owed to employees, $1,400.

Requirement

Record the adjustments, then post them to T-accounts, labeling each adjustment by letter. Calculate each account's adjusted balance.

E3-20A. Income statement preparation (*Learning Objective 3*) 15–20 min.

The accountant for Halco, Inc., posted adjusting entries (a) through (e) to the accounts at December 31, 2014. Selected balance sheet accounts and all the revenues and expenses of the entity follow in T-account form.

Accounts Receivable		
	7,000	
(e)	1,100	

Supplies		
2,500	(a)	800

Accumulated Depreciation, Equipment		
		3,600
	(b)	1,400

Accumulated Depreciation, Building		
		50,000
	(c)	3,600

Salaries Payable		
	(d)	2,300

Service Revenue		
		15,700
	(e)	1,100

Salaries Expense		
	10,500	
(d)	2,300	

Supplies Expense		
(a)	800	

Depreciation Expense, Equipment		
(b)	1,400	

Depreciation Expense, Building		
(c)	3,600	

Quick solution:

Net Loss = $1,800

Requirements

1. Explain the purpose for each adjusting entry.
2. Calculate ending balances in the accounts and use the appropriate accounts to prepare the income statement of Halco, Inc., for the year ended December 31, 2014. List expenses in order from largest to smallest.
3. Were the 2014 operations successful? Give the reason for your answer.

E3-21A. Statement of retained earnings preparation (*Learning Objective 3*) 10–15 min.

Delta Alarm, Inc., began the year with $20,000 of common stock and $32,000 of retained earnings. On May 5, investors bought $12,000 of additional stock in the business. On August 22, the business purchased land valued at $80,000. The income statement for the year ended December 31, 2014, reported a net loss of $9,000. During this fiscal year, the business paid $300 each month for dividends.

Requirements

1. Prepare Delta Alarm's statement of retained earnings for the year ended December 31, 2014.
2. Did the retained earnings of the business increase or decrease during the year? What caused this change?

E3-22A. Recreating adjusting journal entries (*Learning Objective 2*) 10–15 min.

The adjusted trial balances of Rimrock, Inc., at March 31, 2014, and March 31, 2015, include these amounts:

	2014	2015
Supplies	$ 1,600	$4,100
Salaries Payable	2,700	1,800
Unearned Service Revenue	14,500	8,200

Analysis of the accounts at March 31, 2015, reveals these transactions for the past twelve months:

Purchase of supplies	$ 7,300
Cash payments for salaries	51,400
Cash receipts in advance for service revenue	74,000

Requirement

Compute the amount of supplies expense, salaries expense, and service revenue Rimrock, Inc., will report for the year ended March 31, 2015. Solve by making T-accounts and posting the information to solve for the unknown amounts.

E3-23A. Financial statement preparation (*Learning Objective 3*) 15–20 min.

The adjusted trial balance for Sweet Home Catering, Inc., is presented next. Prepare the income statement and statement of retained earnings for Sweet Home Catering, Inc., for the month ended March 31, 2014. Also prepare a balance sheet at March 31, 2014.

Sweet Home Catering, Inc. Adjusted Trial Balance March 31, 2014		
ACCOUNT	**DEBIT**	**CREDIT**
Cash	$16,000	
Accounts Receivable	4,700	
Supplies	500	
Equipment	24,300	
Accumulated Depreciation, Equipment		$ 5,400
Accounts Payable		4,500
Salaries Payable		1,000
Unearned Service Revenue		3,000
Common Stock		13,000
Retained Earnings		8,200
Dividends	1,900	
Service Revenue		21,000
Salaries Expense	5,100	
Rent Expense	1,800	
Depreciation Expense, Equipment	1,500	
Supplies Expense	300	
Total	$56,100	$56,100

E3-24A. Prepare closing entries (*Learning Objective 4*) 10–15 min.

Requirements

1. Using the following selected accounts of Allied Electrical, Inc., at November 30, 2014, prepare the entity's closing entries:

Common Stock	$25,000	Accounts Receivable	$ 4,400
Service Revenue	90,000	Retained Earnings	16,800
Unearned Revenues	2,500	Salaries Payable	2,375
Salaries Expense	24,400	Depreciation Expense	5,100
Accumulated Depreciation	33,600	Rent Expense	8,300
Supplies Expense	2,800	Dividends	20,000
Interest Revenue	750	Supplies	825
Interest Expense	3,650		

2. What is Allied Electrical's ending Retained Earnings balance at November 30, 2014?

E3-25A. Statement of retained earnings preparation (*Learning Objective 3*) 10–15 min.

From the following accounts of Waves Salon, Inc., prepare the business's statement of retained earnings for the year ended July 31, 2014:

Retained Earnings					Dividends			
Clo	150,000	Aug 1	92,000	Oct 31	24,000			
Clo	77,000	Clo	299,000	Jan 31	10,000			
		Bal	164,000	Apr 30	25,000			
				Jul 31	18,000			
				Bal	77,000	Clo	77,000	

E3-26A. Prepare a post-closing trial balance (*Learning Objective 4*) 10–15 min.

The following post-closing trial balance was prepared for Perfect Portraits, Inc., but some balances were entered in the wrong column. Prepare a corrected post-closing trial balance. Assume all accounts have normal balances and the amounts are correct.

Perfect Portraits, Inc.
Post-Closing Trial Balance
May 31, 2014

ACCOUNT	DEBIT	CREDIT
Cash	$ 8,100	
Accounts Receivable	4,300	
Supplies		$ 800
Equipment		70,000
Accumulated Depreciation, Equipment	11,500	
Accounts Payable	5,600	
Salaries Payable		1,700
Unearned Service Revenue	3,200	
Common Stock		35,000
Retained Earnings	26,200	
Total	$58,900	$107,500

E3-27A. Prepare closing entries (*Learning Objective 4*) **10–15 min.**

The following is the adjusted trial balance of Lending Hand, Inc., for December 31, 2014.

Requirement

1. Journalize the closing entries at December 31, 2014.

Lending Hand, Inc. Adjusted Trial Balance December 31, 2014		
ACCOUNT	**DEBIT**	**CREDIT**
Cash	$ 5,400	
Accounts Receivable	15,000	
Supplies	400	
Furniture	6,500	
Accumulated Depreciation, Furniture		$ 3,180
Equipment	39,000	
Accumulated Depreciation, Equipment		3,000
Accounts Payable		1,100
Salaries Payable		1,200
Unearned Service Revenue		2,200
Common Stock		21,000
Retained Earnings		40,170
Dividends	17,000	
Service Revenue		66,000
Salaries Expense	45,000	
Rent Expense	6,000	
Depreciation Expense, Equipment	2,600	
Depreciation Expense, Furniture	600	
Supplies Expense	350	
Total	$137,850	$137,850

Exercises (Group B)

E3-28B. Adjusting journal entries—unearned revenue and accrued revenue (*Learning Objective 2*) **10–15 min.**

Suppose you started up your own landscaping business. A customer paid you $170 in advance to mow his or her lawn while he or she was on vacation. You performed landscaping services for a local business, but the business hasn't paid you the $375 fee yet. A customer pays you $80 cash for landscaping services. Answer the following questions about the correct way to account for your revenue under accrual-basis accounting:

1. Name the accounts used to record these events.
2. Prepare the journal entries to record the three transactions.

**E3-29B. Adjusting journal entry—prepaid insurance (*Learning Objective 2*)
5–10 min.**

Calculate the missing amounts for each of the Prepaid Insurance situations.

For situation A, journalize the adjusting entry. Consider each situation separately.

	Situation			
	A	**B**	**C**	**D**
Beginning Prepaid Insurance	$ 400	$ 600	?	$ 800
Payments for Prepaid Insurance during the year..........	1,500	?	2,200	?
Total amount to account for.....................................	?	?	3,300	1,700
Ending Prepaid Insurance	700	400	?	?
Insurance Expense..	?	$1,200	$3,000	$ 500

E3-30B. Common adjusting journal entries (*Learning Objective 2*) 10–15 min.

Journalize the adjusting entries at July 31, the end of the accounting period. Omit explanations.

a. Employee salaries owed for Monday through Thursday of a five-day workweek, $4,500.

b. Unearned service revenue now earned, $1,250.

c. Depreciation, $1,900.

d. Prepaid rent expired, $350.

e. Interest revenue accrued, $980.

E3-31B. Error analysis (*Learning Objective 2*) 10–15 min.

The adjusting entries for the following adjustments were omitted at period-end:

a. Prepaid rent expired, $1,400.

b. Depreciation, $2,600.

c. Employee salaries owed for Monday through Wednesday of a five-day workweek, $3,750.

d. Supplies used during the period, $450.

e. Unearned service revenue now earned, $2,200.

Requirement

Compute the amount that net income for the year is overstated or understated for each omitted entry. Use the following format to help analyze the transactions.

Transaction	Overstated/Understated	Amount
Sample a., b., etc.	Overstated	$5,000

E3-32B. Common adjusting journal entries (*Learning Objective 2*) **15–20 min.**

Journalize the adjusting entry needed at March 31, the fiscal year-end, for each of the following independent situations. No other adjusting entries have been made for the year.

a. On February 1, we collected $6,600 rent in advance. We debited Cash and credited Unearned Rent Revenue. The tenant was paying six months' rent in advance.

b. The business holds a $5,000 note receivable. Interest revenue of $520 has been earned on the note but not yet received.

c. Salaries expense is $3,100 per day, Monday through Friday, and the business pays employees each Friday. This year, March 31 falls on a Thursday.

d. The unadjusted balance of the Supplies account is $1,000. Supplies on hand total $700.

e. Equipment was purchased two years ago at a cost of $4,000. The equipment's useful life is five years.

f. On November 1, when $936 was paid for a one-year insurance policy, Prepaid Insurance was debited and Cash was credited.

E3-33B. Common adjusting journal entries (*Learning Objective 2*) **15–20 min.**

The accounting records of Activities Unlimited, Inc. include the following unadjusted balances at September 30: Accounts Receivable, $2,100; Supplies, $900; Salaries Payable, $0; Unearned Service Revenue, $750; Service Revenue, $4,100; Salaries Expense, $1,850; and Supplies Expense, $0. The following data pertains to September 30 adjusting entries:

a. Service revenue accrued, $1,650.

b. Unearned service revenue that has been earned, $350.

c. Supplies on hand, $240.

d. Salaries owed to employees, $980.

Requirement

Record the adjustments, then post them to T-accounts, labeling each adjustment by letter. Calculate each account's adjusted balance.

E3-34B. Income statement preparation (*Learning Objective 3*) **15–20 min.**

The accountant for Cyclone Construction, Inc., posted adjusting entries (a) through (e) to the accounts at July 31, 2014. Selected balance sheet accounts and all the revenues and expenses of the entity follow in T-account form.

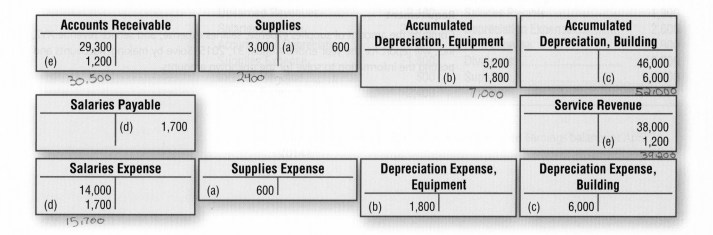

3. Prepare the adjusted trial balance at April 30, 2014.

4. Journalize and post the closing entries at April 30. Denote each closing amount as *Clo* and an account balance as *Bal*.

5. Prepare a post-closing trial balance at April 30, 2014.

Continuing Problem

This problem continues the accounting process for Aqua Magic, Inc., from the continuing problem in Chapter 2. The trial balance for Aqua Magic, Inc., at June 30, 2014, should look like this:

<table>
<tr><td colspan="3" align="center">**Aqua Magic, Inc.**
Trial Balance
June 30, 2014</td></tr>
<tr><th>ACCOUNT</th><th>DEBIT</th><th>CREDIT</th></tr>
<tr><td>Cash</td><td>$ 24,935</td><td></td></tr>
<tr><td>Accounts Receivable</td><td>3,725</td><td></td></tr>
<tr><td>Supplies</td><td>1,325</td><td></td></tr>
<tr><td>Land</td><td>25,000</td><td></td></tr>
<tr><td>Furniture</td><td>4,000</td><td></td></tr>
<tr><td>Equipment</td><td>1,800</td><td></td></tr>
<tr><td>Vehicles</td><td>36,200</td><td></td></tr>
<tr><td>Accounts Payable</td><td></td><td>$ 4,890</td></tr>
<tr><td>Notes Payable</td><td></td><td>36,200</td></tr>
<tr><td>Common Stock</td><td></td><td>55,000</td></tr>
<tr><td>Dividends</td><td>6,000</td><td></td></tr>
<tr><td>Service Revenue</td><td></td><td>13,800</td></tr>
<tr><td>Salaries Expense</td><td>2,500</td><td></td></tr>
<tr><td>Rent Expense</td><td>2,300</td><td></td></tr>
<tr><td>Utilities Expense</td><td>1,380</td><td></td></tr>
<tr><td>Advertising Expense</td><td>450</td><td></td></tr>
<tr><td>Miscellaneous Expense</td><td>275</td><td></td></tr>
<tr><td>Total</td><td>$109,890</td><td>$109,890</td></tr>
</table>

During July, the following transactions occurred:

Jul	1	Paid four months' rent, $9,200.
	4	Performed service for a customer and received cash, $2,700.
	9	Received $2,300 from customers for services to be performed later.
	12	Purchased $800 of supplies on account.
	15	Billed customers for services performed, $2,800.
	16	Paid receptionist's salary, $625.
	22	Received $2,950 on account.
	25	Paid $2,100 on account.
	28	Received $1,725 cash for services performed.
	30	Paid $1,400 of dividends.

Requirements

1. Journalize the transactions that occurred in July. Omit explanations.

2. Using the four-column accounts from the continuing problem in Chapter 2, post the transactions to the ledger creating new ledger accounts as necessary. Omit posting references. Calculate the new account balances at July 31.

3. Prepare the unadjusted trial balance for Aqua Magic, Inc., at July 31.

4. Journalize and post the adjusting entries for July based on the following adjustment information.

   a. Record the expired rent.

   b. Supplies on hand, $250.

   c. Depreciation; $180 equipment, $50 furniture, $420 vehicles.

   d. Services performed but unbilled, $2,200.

   e. Accrued salaries, $625.

   f. Unearned service revenue earned as of July 31, $1,100.

5. Prepare an adjusted trial balance for Aqua Magic, Inc., at the end of July.

6. Prepare the income statement and statement of retained earnings for the three-month period May 1 through July 31, 2014. Also prepare a balance sheet at July 31, 2014.

7. Prepare and post closing entries.

8. Prepare a post-closing trial balance at July 31, 2014.

Continuing Financial Statement Analysis Problem

Let's look at Target again. Think about the business of Target. Now return to that place on Target's website called "investor relations." Look at Target's 2012 financial statements contained in its 2012 annual report. Go to: *http://investors.target.com/phoenix.zhtml?c=65828&p=irol-reportsAnnual*. On page 33 of the financial statements, you'll find Target's income statement for the year ending February 2, 2013 (called the Consolidate Statement of Operations). On page 35, you'll find Target's balance sheet as of February 2, 2013 (called the Consolidated Statement of Financial Position). On page 37, you'll find Target's statement of retained earnings for the year ending February 2, 2013. It's a part of Target's statement titled Consolidated Statements of Shareholders' Investment. Now answer the following questions:

1. Look at Target's income statement. Is Target profitable? Does it have a positive net income or a negative net income (loss) for the year ending February 2, 2013? How does that compare with the year ending February 2, 2013?

2. Look at Target's statement of shareholders' investment. How does Target's net income flow into its balance sheet?

3. Look at Target's balance sheet. What assets does Target own? How much has Target invested in each type of assets and in total assets?

4. Look at Target's balance sheet. How does Target finance its assets? How much liabilities and shareholders' equity does Target have?

Apply Your Knowledge

Ethics in Action

Case 1. Jilian Carter was preparing the adjusting journal entries for Jilian's Java, a business that uses the accrual basis of accounting, in order to prepare the adjusted trial balance and financial statements. She knew that $610 of salaries related to the current accounting period had accrued but wouldn't be paid until the next period. Jilian thought that simply not including the adjustment for these salaries would mean that salaries expense would be lower and reported net income would be higher than it would have been if she had made the adjustment. Further, she knew that the Salaries Payable account would be zero, so the liabilities reported on the balance sheet would be less and her business would look even better. Besides, she reasoned that these salaries would be reported eventually, so it was merely a matter of showing them in one period instead of another. Dismissing the reporting as just a timing issue, she ignored the adjustment for the additional salaries expense.

Is Jilian acting unethically by failing to record the adjustment for accrued salaries? Does it matter that, shortly into the new accounting period, the salaries will ultimately be paid? Is it really simply a matter of timing? What are the potential problems of failing to include all the adjusting journal entries?

Case 2. Brent Robertson and his banker were reviewing the quarterly income statements for his consulting business, Robertson and Associates, Inc. The banker was impressed with the growth of sales revenue and net income for the second quarter of this year as compared to the second quarter of last year. Brent knew it had been a good quarter, but didn't think it had been spectacular. Suddenly, Brent realized that he failed to close out the revenue and expense accounts for the prior quarter, which ended in March. Because those temporary accounts were not closed out, their balances were included in the second quarter amounts for the current year. Brent then realized that the banker had the financial statements but not the general ledger or any trial balances. Thus, the banker would not be able to see that the accounting cycle from the first quarter was not properly closed and that this failure was creating a misstated income statement for the second quarter of the current year. The banker then commented that the business appeared to be performing so well that he would approve a line of credit for the business. Brent decided to not say anything because he did not want to lose the line of credit. Besides, he thought, it really did not matter that the income statement was misstated because his business would be sure to repay any amounts borrowed.

Should Brent have informed the banker of the mistake made, and should he have redone the second quarter's income statement? Was Brent's failure to close the prior quarter's revenue and expense accounts unethical? Does the fact that the business will repay the loan matter?

Know Your Business

Financial Analysis

Purpose: To help familiarize you with the financial reporting of a real company in order to further your understanding of the chapter material.

This case will help you to better understand the effect of adjusting journal entries on the financial statements. You know that adjusting journal entries are entered in the journal and then posted to the ledger accounts. We do not have access to the journals and ledgers used by Columbia Sportswear, but we can see some of the adjusted accounts on the company's financial statements. Refer to the Columbia Sportswear income statements, "Statements of Operations," and the Columbia Sportswear balance sheets, in Appendix A. Also find footnote 6 titled "Property, Plant, and Equipment, Net" and footnote 9 titled "Accrued Liabilities," which are two of the many footnotes included after the financial statements.

Requirements

1. Open T-accounts for the following accounts and their balances as of December 31, 2011. (Note that amounts from the Columbia Sportswear financial statements are in thousands.)

Accumulated Depreciation	$275,886
Accrued Salaries, Bonus, Vacation, and Other Benefits	$ 55,958
Accrued Import Duties	$ 11,258
Accrued Product Warranties	$ 10,452
Other Accrued Liabilities	$ 26,828

2. Using the following information for Columbia Sportswear's 2012 operations, make the appropriate journal entries.
   a. Full payment of the December 31, 2011, balances in the accrued liability accounts.
   b. Depreciation expense, $27,157.
   c. Accrued salaries and benefits expense, $55,728.
   d. Accrued import duty expense, $15,023.
   e. Accrued product warranty expense, $10,209.
   f. Accrued other (miscellaneous) expenses, $24,230.

3. Post the journal entries to the T-accounts you set up. Check the updated ending balances in each account against the balances reported by Columbia Sportswear as of December 31, 2012.

Industry Analysis

Purpose: To help you understand and compare the performance of two companies in the same industry.

Go to the Columbia Sportswear Company Annual Report located in Appendix A . Now access the 2012 Annual Report for Under Armour, Inc. For instructions on how to access the report on-line, see the Industry Analysis in Chapter 1.

Requirement

1. By reviewing the financial statements of both companies, can you determine which method of accounting, cash or accrual basis, each of the companies used? How did you determine this? If one of the companies used the cash basis and the other used the accrual basis, would it affect your ability to compare the two companies? Explain your answer.

Small Business Analysis

Purpose: To help you understand the importance of cash flows in the operation of a small business.

It's the end of the month, and cash flow has been a little slow, as it usually is during this time of the accounting period. It just seems to be a little slower this month. You know that Wednesday the 31st is payday, which always requires a large cash outlay. However, you also know that your bank is looking for a set of financial statements as of the end of the month because the loan on your building is coming up for renewal soon. Based on some of the previous meetings with your bankers, they are always concerned with the cash balance, so you want to have your cash balance as high as possible.

You come up with a tentative plan you believe will not only preserve some of your cash balance at the end of the month but also will help your bottom line, your net income. That's the other thing that the bankers are always concerned about. You don't want to make any mistakes with your financial statements at this crucial point, so you decide to contact your CPA to run the idea by her. The conversation goes something like this:

"Good morning, Sherry. This is Bill Conan from Conan Consultants, Inc. Our financial statements have to look really good this month because the bank is going to be scrutinizing them pretty closely for our pending loan renewal. I know that the two things they concentrate on are the cash balance and the net income. So, I've got a plan to help in both of those areas. I'm going to hold off paying my employees until after the first of the month. Plus, last month, I made a big insurance payment to cover me for the next six months, so I won't need to show any insurance expense this month. Both of those will help my net income because I won't be showing those expenses on my income statement. Plus, by not writing the paychecks until the first of the month, I'll be helping to show a higher cash balance. It's really only one day, but the bank won't know that my cash balance should be lower. These certainly sound like some good ideas that would help with my situation, but just in case, I wanted to check with you to see what you thought. Any comments?"

The first words out of the CPA's mouth are "Bill, you know that your financial statements are prepared using the accrual basis of accounting."

Requirement

1. Complete the thought process of the CPA concerning Bill's plan. What does she mean by the accrual basis of accounting? What effect will that have on the net income? Is Bill correct in his assessment of the big insurance payment he made last month covering the next six months? What effect will that have on the net income? And in regard to the last item, what about Bill's plan to keep the cash balance as high as possible and his statement "the bank won't know that my cash balance should be lower"?

Written Communication

You have received a letter from a disgruntled client concerning this year's tax return that your firm recently completed for his or her company. The client's business is in the second year of operations, and you remembered that it seemed to be much more profitable this year than during the first year of operations. You also recall that this particular client's year-end work was assigned to one of your relatively new staff accountants, which might be part of the problem. The gist of the letter is that last year's taxable net income was about $32,000, and according to the company's calculations, the net income from this year should have been about $55,000. The client is wondering why the company is showing taxable net income of $87,130 on this year's return and paying income tax on that amount. You retrieve the file to review it and immediately see the problem. Your staff accountant failed to make the closing entries at the end of the first year of operations!

Requirement

1. Prepare a letter to this client explaining the situation and, most importantly, explaining the importance of preparing closing entries at the end of each and every year. Also, suggest a solution to this problem for the client, knowing that just explaining the accounting issue might not be enough to retain this client in the future.

Self Check Answers
1. b 2. c 3. c 4. d 5. c 6. d 7. c 8. d 9. a 10. c 11. b 12. b

Comprehensive Problem

Journalizing, Posting, Adjusting, Preparing, and Closing Financial Statements

Brava Landscaping, Inc., completed the following transactions during its first month of operations for January 2014:

a. Gabrielle Brava invested $8,500 cash and a truck valued at $16,000 to start Brava Landscaping, Inc. The business issued common stock in exchange for these assets.

b. Purchased $450 of supplies on account.

c. Paid $1,800 for a six-month insurance policy.

d. Performed landscape services for a customer and received $925 cash.

e. Completed a $5,300 landscaping job on account.

f. Paid employee salary, $820.

g. Received $1,560 cash for performing landscaping services.

h. Collected $1,350 in advance for landscaping service to be performed later.

i. Collected $2,800 cash from a customer on account.

j. Purchased fuel for the truck, paying $110 with a company credit card. Credit Accounts Payable.

k. Performed landscaping services on account, $2,130.

l. Paid the current month's office rent, $1,150.

m. Paid $400 on account.

n. Paid cash dividends of $1,000.

Requirements

1. Record each transaction in the general journal. Use the letter corresponding to each transaction as the transaction date. Explanations are not required.

2. Post the transactions that you recorded in Requirement 1 in the following T-accounts.

Cash	Salaries Payable	Service Revenue
Accounts Receivable	Unearned Service Revenue	Salaries Expense
Supplies	Common Stock	Depreciation Expense
Prepaid Insurance	Retained Earnings	Insurance Expense
Truck	Dividends	Fuel Expense
Accumulated Depreciation		Rent Expense
Accounts Payable		Supplies Expense

3. Prepare an unadjusted trial balance as of January 31, 2014.

4. Journalize and post the adjusting journal entries on January 31, 2014, based on the following information:
   a. Accrued salaries expense, $470.
   b. Depreciation expense, $330.
   c. Record the expiration of one month's insurance.
   d. Supplies on hand, $85.
   e. Earned 2/3 of the Unearned Service Revenue during January.

5. Prepare an adjusted trial balance as of January 31, 2014. Use the adjusted trial balance to prepare Brava Landscaping's income statement and statement of retained earnings for the month ending January 31, 2014, and balance sheet at January 31, 2014. On the income statement list expenses in decreasing order by amount—that is, the largest expense first, the smallest expense last.

6. Journalize and post the closing entries.

7. Prepare a post-closing trial balance at January 31, 2014.

4

Accounting for a Merchandising Business

Business, Accounting, and You

Walk into a Toys R Us. Look around. What do you see? You see employees, products, and customers. You see employees unloading products, called inventory, from trucks of suppliers. You see other employees placing the products on display shelves. You see employees demonstrating products and helping customers make informed decisions. You see customers taking products from the shelves, going to check-out stations, and purchasing products. You see thousands of business transactions.

So how does a business like Toys R Us account for operating its business? How does Toys R Us recognize, measure, record, and report the purchase and sale of inventory? How does Toys R Us account for employee wages, advertising, and

Learning Objectives

1. Describe the relationships among manufacturers, wholesalers, retailers, and customers

2. Define periodic and perpetual inventory systems

3. Journalize transactions for the purchase of inventory

4. Journalize transactions for the sale of inventory

5. Understand shipping terms and journalize transactions for freight charges and other selling expenses

6. Prepare a multi-step income statement and a classified balance sheet

7. Compute earnings per share, the gross profit percentage, and the net income percentage

other operating expenses such as utilities? How does Toys R Us account for customers buying inventory and giving Toys R Us, in exchange for the inventory, cash or promises to pay cash? How does Toys R Us account for the merchandising of products?

Business is about operating and earning net income. Net income starts with buying and selling products. As an accountant or manager, you need to understand how products flow from suppliers to customers. You need to understand how accountants keep score and determine whether the sale of a product results in net income or net loss.

▶ Real World Accounting Video

In the Real World Accounting Video, Noah Lenovitz, a partner and chief operating officer of Fishs Eddy, talks about what it means to operate a business. Look at the video. Think about what Noah is saying. Now realize how important accounting is to the success of a business.

What Are the Relationships Among Manufacturers, Wholesalers, Retailers, and Customers?

1 Describe the relationships among manufacturers, wholesalers, retailers, and customers

Merchandise inventory Goods purchased for resale to customers in the normal course of merchandising operations; also called **inventory**.

Wholesalers Businesses that buy goods from manufacturers and resell them to retailers.

Retailers Businesses that buy goods from manufacturers or wholesalers and resell them to the general public.

In Chapters 1–3, you learned how to account for a service business. In this chapter, you will learn how to account for a merchandising business. A merchandising business buys and sells products, called **merchandise inventory**, instead of services. Throughout the remainder of the book, we will refer to merchandise inventory simply as **inventory**. Inventory is a very important asset to a merchandising business because it reflects the amount of goods the business has available to sell to its customers.

A merchandising business can be either a **wholesaler** or a **retailer**. Wholesalers generally purchase large lots of products from manufacturers and resell them to retailers. Retailers buy goods from wholesalers and resell them to the final consumers, the general public. It is also possible for a retailer to purchase products directly from a manufacturer. **Exhibit 4-1** shows the relationships among manufacturers, wholesalers, retailers, and customers.

The discount chain Walmart and the Internet merchandiser Amazon.com are well-known examples of retailers. In this chapter, a fictitious merchandiser named Cellular

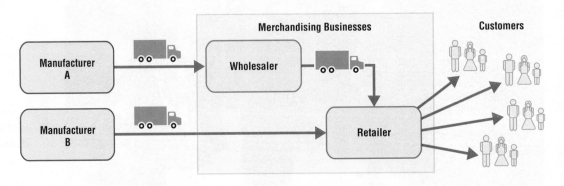

Exhibit 4-1 ▲

Connect, Inc., is used to illustrate merchandising operations. Cellular Connect is a mall retailer that sells cell phones and accessories. We will learn how Cellular Connect records entries related to purchases of inventory from its suppliers. In addition, we will learn the entries Cellular uses to record sales of merchandise to its customers. We will also learn how the type of inventory tracking system chosen by Cellular will affect the journal entries that it must make.

How Do Periodic and Perpetual Inventory Systems Differ?

2 **Define periodic and perpetual inventory systems**

Periodic inventory system An inventory system in which the business does not keep a continuous record of inventory on hand. At the end of the accounting period, a physical count of inventory is taken and is used to determine the cost of ending inventory and the cost of the goods sold.

Merchandisers use one of two inventory tracking systems:

- The **periodic inventory system** is a system of accounting for inventory that does *not* keep a continuous, running record of inventory as it is bought and sold. Instead, the business physically counts the goods in inventory at the end of the accounting period. It then multiplies the quantity of each item by its cost to get the total value of the ending inventory. Once the cost of ending inventory has been determined, a business will calculate the cost of the inventory it has sold during the period using the following formula:

$$
\begin{array}{l}
\text{Beginning Inventory} \\
+ \text{ Purchases} \\
\hline
= \text{Cost of Goods Available for Sale} \\
- \text{ Ending Inventory} \\
\hline
= \text{Cost of Goods Sold}
\end{array}
$$

Historically, businesses that sold large quantities of relatively inexpensive goods used the periodic inventory system because it was too costly and time consuming to track the inventory items that were sold. Currently, thanks to innovations in inventory tracking technology, most businesses utilize a perpetual inventory system.

Perpetual inventory system An inventory system in which the business keeps a continuous record of inventory on hand and the cost of the goods sold.

- The **perpetual inventory system** is a system of accounting for inventory that keeps a running record of inventory as it is bought and sold. Every time the business engages in a transaction involving inventory, the balance in the inventory account is immediately updated. By doing this, the inventory balance is *perpetually* up to date. However, the business must still physically count inventory at least once a year to see whether any goods have been lost, damaged, or stolen. Just because the accounting records indicate that a certain amount of inventory exists, it doesn't mean that this amount is actually on hand. If the actual inventory count is different than the perpetual records indicate, the perpetual records are adjusted to reflect the physical count. The general ledger is also updated by debiting or crediting the inventory account as needed. The offsetting debit or credit is to the Cost of Goods Sold account. Technology makes it easier for almost any business to use the perpetual system. Usually, a cash register used in a perpetual system is connected to a bar code scanner. When an inventory item is scanned, not only is the sale recorded, but the inventory records are simultaneously updated. Because the perpetual inventory system is more commonly used, we will use it to illustrate the transactions for Cellular Connect.

How Do You Account for the Purchase of Inventory?

Journalize transactions for the purchase of inventory

Throughout the year, merchandisers engage in a number of inventory transactions with suppliers including cash purchases, credit purchases, purchase returns and allowances, and purchase discounts. Let's examine how Cellular Connect, Inc., accounts for these types of transactions.

Cash and Credit Purchases

Cellular Connect purchases 300 cell phone cases from Accessories Unlimited on account at a cost of $25 each. Therefore, the total value of Cellular's purchase is $7,500 (300 cases × $25). Cellular Connect receives the goods on February 1 and records this purchase as follows:

DATE	ACCOUNTS	POST REF.	DR.	CR.
Feb 1	Inventory		7,500	
	Accounts Payable—Accessories Unlimited			7,500
	Record purchase of inventory on account.			

The purchase of inventory on account increases both Cellular Connect's assets and liabilities. The Inventory account reflects the cost of goods purchased for resale. The balance increases every time inventory is purchased. Inventory is an asset until it is sold because, as discussed in Chapter 1, assets represent things of value that the business owns.

Notice that the name of the supplier is listed in the journal entry following Accounts Payable. The supplier's name is used because the amount owed to each individual supplier will be posted to a **subsidiary ledger** in addition to the Accounts Payable account in the general ledger. The subsidiary ledger contains a record for each separate supplier. If everything has been posted correctly, the total of the account balances in the accounts payable subsidiary ledger will equal the Accounts Payable account balance in the general ledger. This way, a merchandiser can keep track of the amount of accounts payable owed to each individual supplier.

Some suppliers may require cash to be paid at the time of shipment. If Accessories Unlimited required cash payment for the 300 cell phone cases at the time of sale, Cellular Connect would record the cash purchase as follows:

Subsidiary ledger An accounting record that contains details, such as a list of customers and the accounts receivable due from each or a list of suppliers and the accounts payable due to each.

DATE	ACCOUNTS	POST REF.	DR.	CR.
Feb 1	Inventory		7,500	
	Cash			7,500
	Record purchase of inventory for cash.			

Purchase Returns and Allowances

Occasionally, merchandisers buy goods that are not satisfactory. In these cases, most suppliers allow the goods to be returned. They may also allow the merchandiser to keep the unsuitable goods and receive a deduction, or allowance, from the amount they owe for the merchandise. Both **purchase returns and allowances** decrease the merchandiser's cost of the inventory.

Suppose Cellular Connect buys 20 hands-free headsets for $20 each from Mega Mobile. Upon receipt of the headsets, Cellular Connect determines that Mega Mobile

Purchase returns and allowances A reduction in the amount owed for a purchase due to returning merchandise or accepting unsatisfactory goods.

shipped the wrong headsets and, after notifying Mega Mobile, returns the headsets. Because Cellular Connect no longer owes Mega Mobile for the headsets, it will reduce Accounts Payable by debiting the account. Cellular Connect also no longer has the inventory, so it will reduce the Inventory account by crediting it.

Cellular records the purchase return on April 5 as follows:

DATE	ACCOUNTS	POST REF.	DR.	CR.
Apr 5	Accounts Payable—Mega Mobile		400	
	Inventory			400
	Record inventory returned to manufacturer.			

Now, assume that instead of returning the headsets, Cellular Connect had been granted a $50 reduction in the total purchase price (an allowance) as an incentive to keep the headsets. In this case, Cellular Connect would make the same entry that was made to record the return but the amount of the entry would be for $50.

Purchase Discounts

Sales invoice A bill that documents the sale of goods to a customer.

Credit terms The payment terms for customers who buy on account.

n/30 Credit term specifying that payment for a purchase is due within 30 days after the date of the invoice.

n/eom Credit term specifying that payment for a purchase is due by the end of the month; also referred to as **eom**.

Purchase discount Discount received on purchases by paying early within a discount period.

Exhibit 4-2 illustrates Accessories Unlimited's sales invoice for Cellular's $7,500 purchase of inventory. A **sales invoice** is a bill that documents the sale of goods to a customer. The invoice includes **credit terms**, or the payment terms, for customers who buy on account. A customer may pay cash when it receives the goods or it may pay within a period of time following the receipt of those goods. Credit terms are used on sales invoices to communicate to the customer when payment is due. Often, merchandisers will use the term **n/30**, which means that the sales price for the goods must be paid within 30 days after the date of the invoice. If the amount is due at the end of the month, the invoice will include the phrase **n/eom** or just **eom**.

All businesses want to have enough cash to pay their bills on time. Therefore, businesses often offer customers **purchase discounts** for early payment in order to improve

	Invoice	
	Date	Number
	2/1/14	644

Accessories UNLIMITED
Accessories Unlimited
P.O. Box 873
Redding, CA

Shipped to:	Cellular Connect
	1471 E. Union St.
	Seattle, WA

Terms: 3/15, n/30

Quantity	Item	Unit Price	Total
300 each	Cell phone cases	$ 25	$ 7,500
		Subtotal	$ 7,500
		Shipping Charge	–
		Tax	–
		Total	$ 7,500

Exhibit 4-2 ▲

their cash inflow. By rewarding the customer for paying amounts before the due date, these companies get cash sooner. The time period in which the customer may pay and receive the discount is called the **discount period**. If the customer takes advantage of this offer and pays early, then these discounts represent a reduction in the cost of the merchandise purchased.

Review Accessories Unlimited's sales invoice in Exhibit 4-2. Accessories Unlimited's credit terms of "3/15, n/30" mean that Cellular Connect may deduct 3% of the total amount due to Accessories Unlimited if it pays within 15 days of the invoice date. Otherwise, the full amount is due in 30 days. In this case, the discount period covers 15 days. However, if Accessories Unlimited listed terms of "n/30" instead of "3/15, n/30," it would mean that it was not offering a discount at all and payment is due 30 days after the invoice date.

If Cellular Connect pays within the discount period, it will pay $7,275, or 97% of the invoice amount of $7,500:

Invoice Total	$7,500	(100% of invoice amount)
− Purchase Discount	(225)	(3% of invoice amount, or 0.03 × $7,500)
= Cash Paid	$7,275	(97% of invoice amount, or 0.97 × $7,500)

Cellular records its payment on February 13, which is within the discount period:

DATE	ACCOUNTS	POST REF.	DR.	CR.
Feb 13	Accounts Payable—Accessories Unlimited		7,500	
	Cash			7,275
	Inventory			225
	Record payment of inventory purchases within the			
	discount period.			

Note that the discount is credited to the Inventory account. This is because the discount decreases the cost of the cell phone cases that Cellular Connect bought from Accessories Unlimited. However, if Cellular Connect pays this invoice after the discount period, it pays the full amount of $7,500. In this case, it records the payment as:

DATE	ACCOUNTS	POST REF.	DR.	CR.
Feb 24	Accounts Payable—Accessories Unlimited		7,500	
	Cash			7,500
	Record payment of inventory purchases after the			
	discount period.			

It is important to note that discounts are not granted on any purchase returns or allowances.

How Do You Account for the Sale of Inventory?

4 Journalize transactions for the sale of inventory

Merchandisers engage in several different types of business transactions with customers:

- Cash sales: Goods are sold for cash.
- Credit sales: Goods are sold on account.

Discount period Period in which the customer can make early payment for a purchase and receive a discount on that purchase.

- Sales returns and allowances: Damaged goods are returned by a customer for a refund. However, sometimes the customer keeps the damaged goods and accepts an allowance (price reduction) on the goods.
- Sales discounts: Suppliers grant customers a reduction in the amount owed as an incentive for paying within a discount period.

Let's examine how Cellular Connect accounts for these types of transactions.

Cash Sales

Sales Revenue The amount that a business earns from selling its inventory.

Merchandisers, such as Cellular Connect, often receive cash at the time they sell merchandise. The journal entry to record a cash sale increases the asset, Cash, and also increases the revenue account, **Sales Revenue**. Sales Revenue is the account used by merchandisers to track the value of merchandise sold to customers at the price that the merchandiser charges those customers.

Cost of Goods Sold The cost of the inventory that the business has sold to customers.

Remember that Cellular Connect uses the perpetual inventory system to account for its inventory. At the time of a sale, in addition to recording the sales revenue, Cellular also reduces the Inventory balance for the cost of the merchandise sold. By doing this, the Inventory account is updated so that it always, or perpetually, reflects the current balance. The cost of the merchandise sold is accounted for in the **Cost of Goods Sold** account. This income statement account reflects the cost of merchandise sold during the period. The Cost of Goods Sold is deducted from Sales Revenue as a step in determining the amount of net income or loss for the period.

Assume that on June 9, Cellular Connect sells $3,000 of merchandise to customers for cash. The goods that Cellular sold its customers cost Cellular $1,900. The journal entry to record the sale is as follows:

DATE	ACCOUNTS	POST REF.	DR.	CR.
Jun 9	Cash		3,000	
	Sales Revenue			3,000
	Cost of Goods Sold		1,900	
	Inventory			1,900
	Record sale of inventory for cash.			

Remember that when a product is sold, a merchandiser recognizes the following:

1. Sales revenue for the selling price of the product to the customer
2. Cost of goods sold for the merchandiser's cost of the product

Compound journal entry A journal entry affecting more than two accounts; an entry that has more than one debit and/or more than one credit.

A journal entry that involves more than two accounts is called a **compound journal entry**. A compound entry may include more than one debit amount or more than one credit amount.

Some merchandisers allow customers to use credit cards and debit cards rather than currency. These transactions are treated as cash sales because the merchandiser receives cash from the credit/debit card company. The credit/debit card company then collects the amount due from the customer. The merchandiser, however, usually must pay a service charge to the credit/debit card company in exchange for its processing of the transactions. Accounting for debit and credit card sales is discussed in Chapter 7 in more detail.

Credit Sales

Many merchandisers establish charge accounts for their customers. Assume that Cellular Connect sold a cell phone and accessories to Jim Kahl on account, n/30 on June 11 for $500. The goods cost Cellular $290. The entry to record this transaction is similar to accounting for a cash sale except Accounts Receivable is debited instead of Cash. Cellular records this sale on account and the cost of goods sold as follows:

DATE	ACCOUNTS	POST REF.	DR.	CR.
Jun 11	Accounts Receivable—Jim Kahl		500	
	Sales Revenue			500
	Cost of Goods Sold		290	
	Inventory			290
	Record sale of inventory on account, invoice no. 322.			

When Jim sends Cellular his payment for this merchandise, Cellular records the cash receipt on account as follows:

DATE	ACCOUNTS	POST REF.	DR.	CR.
Jun 19	Cash		500	
	Accounts Receivable—Jim Kahl			500
	Record payment received on invoice no. 322.			

Notice that the name of the customer is listed in the journal entry following Accounts Receivable. This is similar to what is done for Accounts Payable. A separate account is kept in an accounts receivable subsidiary ledger for each charge customer. Each entry affecting accounts receivable is posted to the customer's account in the subsidiary ledger as well as to the Accounts Receivable account in the general ledger. After all entries are posted, the total of the account balances in the accounts receivable subsidiary ledger will equal the Accounts Receivable account balance in the general ledger. This way, the merchandiser can keep track of the amount of accounts receivable owed by each individual customer.

Sales Returns and Allowances

Sales Returns and Allowances A reduction in the amount of sales due to customers returning merchandise or accepting unsatisfactory goods; a contra-account to Sales Revenue.

Credit memorandum A document that supports the return of goods from the customer or an allowance for unsatisfactory goods and the adjustment to the customer's account balance.

Merchandisers may allow customers to return unwanted merchandise, or they may let customers keep the goods and request an allowance. A business tracks these returns and allowances so it can analyze and manage the causes behind the returns and allowances and measure the related costs to the business. To track returns and allowances accurately, the amount of returns and allowances is recorded in a contra-account called **Sales Returns and Allowances**. Remember from Chapter 3 that a contra-account is an account with a balance opposite of the account to which it is linked. Sales Returns and Allowances is linked to Sales Revenue, which has a credit balance. Therefore, Sales Returns and Allowances will have a debit balance. As we will see later, Sales Returns and Allowances appears on the income statement and is deducted from Sales Revenue to arrive at Net Sales.

Exhibit 4-3 illustrates a **credit memorandum**, a document that acknowledges the return of goods from a customer or the granting of an allowance. The credit memo gets its name from the effect that it has on the balance of the customer's account. Because the credit memo decreases the amount due from the customer, the merchandiser *credits* the accounts receivable balance for that customer. The merchandiser sends a credit memorandum to the customer as notification that an adjustment has been made to the amount the customer owes the merchandiser.

CELLULAR CONNECT

1471 E. Union St.
Seattle, WA

CREDIT MEMORANDUM #14

To: Jill Harris   Date: August 15, 2014
2194 S.E. 31st Ave.
Olympia, WA

We credit your account balance for the following:

3 car chargers @ $25 each	**$75**

Exhibit 4-3 ▲

Sales Returns

When a customer returns goods, the merchandiser will:

* Decrease net sales revenue by increasing Sales Returns and Allowances, and decrease the customer's Accounts Receivable account balance for the sales price of those goods.
* Decrease Cost of Goods Sold and increase Inventory for the cost of the returned goods.

Let's see how Cellular records the return illustrated in the credit memo in Exhibit 4-3. The credit memo reflects the return of three car chargers, originally purchased for $75, by Jill Harris, a customer. The returned car chargers cost Cellular $30. Cellular Connect records the sales return as follows:

DATE	ACCOUNTS	POST REF.	DR.	CR.
Aug 15	Sales Returns and Allowances		75	
	Accounts Receivable—Jill Harris			75
	Inventory		30	
	Cost of Goods Sold			30
	Record receipt of returned goods, credit memo no. 14.			

Accounts Receivable decreases because the customer no longer owes Cellular for the returned goods. Cellular also updates its inventory because its perpetual inventory system needs to reflect the increase to Inventory because of the return of the goods. Cellular also decreases the Cost of Goods Sold because the goods are no longer sold.

Sales Allowances

Rather than return goods to the merchandiser, some customers may be willing to keep unwanted goods and accept an allowance. Assume Cellular Connect grants credit customer Bill Logan a $100 sales allowance for damaged goods. Cellular records the sales allowance as follows:

DATE	ACCOUNTS	POST REF.	DR.	CR.
Aug 29	Sales Returns and Allowances		100	
	Accounts Receivable—Bill Logan			100
	Record sales allowance for damaged goods, credit memo no. 15.			

Notice that the journal entry for a sales allowance does not affect Inventory or Cost of Goods Sold because the customer did not return any goods to the merchandiser.

Sales Discounts

Do you recall the discount that Cellular Connect received from Accessories Unlimited for early payment? It is possible for Cellular to offer discounts to its credit customers for early payment. Let's assume that Cellular sells merchandise to Kelly Harding for $450. The sale is made on account with credit terms of 2/15, n/30. If Kelly chooses to pay the invoice within the 15-day discount period, she will get a 2%, or $9, discount on her $450 purchase ($450 × 0.02). Kelly will pay $441, or 98% of the invoice amount of $450. This discount represents a reduction in the value of sales to Cellular.

Businesses track the amount of these sales discounts so they can measure the impact on their sales revenue. To do so, businesses record these discounts in a contra-account called **Sales Discounts**. Because Sales Discounts is linked to Sales Revenue, it will normally have a debit balance. The Sales Discounts account tracks decreases in sales revenue, which result from a discount to customers. Similar to the treatment of Sales Returns and Allowances, Sales Discounts appears on the income statement and is deducted from Sales Revenue to arrive at Net Sales. Because the Sales Returns and Allowances and the Sales Discount accounts have debit balances, they will be closed along with the expense accounts at the end of the period.

Assume that Cellular receives payment of $441 from Kelly on February 13 within the discount period. The journal entry to record the receipt of cash and the sales discount is as follows:

Sales Discount Discount granted on sales for the customer's early payment within a discount period; a contra-account to Sales Revenue.

DATE	ACCOUNTS	POST REF.	DR.	CR.
Feb 13	Cash		441	
	Sales Discounts		9	
	Accounts Receivable—Kelly Harding			450

If Kelly fails to pay within the 15-day discount period, she will have to pay the full invoice price of $450. If Cellular receives payment from Kelly on February 24, it records the payment as follows:

DATE	ACCOUNTS	POST REF.	DR.	CR.
Feb 24	Cash		450	
	Accounts Receivable—Kelly Harding			450

Try It...

If a customer returned $2,500 of merchandise and the transaction was recorded by debiting Sales and crediting Accounts Receivable, instead of debiting Sales Returns and Allowances and crediting Accounts Receivable, would the net income on the income statement be incorrect?

Answer

No. Let's assume that the company has $20,000 of total sales at the time the return is made and that this is the first time merchandise is returned during the period. If the transaction is recorded by debiting Sales, the Sales balance will be reduced to $17,500. As there have been no other sales returns, the balance in the Sales Returns and Allowances will be zero. Therefore, the amount of Net Sales will be $17,500. If instead of debiting Sales, the Sales Returns and Allowances account is debited, the Sales account will have a balance of $20,000 and the Sales Returns and Allowances account will have a balance of $2,500. Therefore, the amount of Net Sales will still be $17,500 ($20,000 − $2,500). If the amount of Net Sales is $17,500 regardless of which way the transaction is recorded, the net income will be the same. The reason for using the Sales Returns and Allowances account is simply to keep track of the amount of merchandise returned during the period. Managers often use this information to determine if there are quality issues with their products.

How Do You Account for Freight Charges and Other Selling Expenses?

5 **Understand shipping terms and journalize transactions for freight charges and other selling expenses**

Freight charges The cost of shipping merchandise from the seller to the buyer.

Title Legally recognized rights to the possession and ownership of property.

Free on board (FOB) shipping point A shipping term specifying that title to goods passes to the buyer when the goods are shipped at the seller's place of business; thus, the buyer pays the cost of shipping the goods to its location.

Free on board (FOB) destination A shipping term specifying that title to goods passes to the buyer when the goods are received at the buyer's destination; thus, the seller pays the cost of shipping the goods to this destination.

In addition to purchases and sales transactions, a merchandiser also accounts for shipping costs and other selling expenses. Merchandisers often pay costs related to:

* Receiving goods from suppliers.
* Delivering goods to customers.
* Advertising and other selling costs.

When merchandisers order items, they often pay the cost of shipping the items to their place of business. These shipping costs are often referred to as **freight charges**.

Buyers and sellers specify who pays shipping costs by agreeing to shipping terms. In addition to dictating who is responsible for paying shipping costs, shipping terms also specify the point at which ownership of the goods, or **title**, transfers from seller to buyer. Shipping terms may be **free on board (FOB) shipping point** or **free on board (FOB) destination**.

* Under free on board (FOB) shipping point, ownership transfers from the seller to the buyer at the point when the goods *leave the seller's place of business*. Also, this term means that the buyer pays the shipping charges to have the merchandise delivered to its place of business. The buyer adds the shipping costs to inventory by debiting Inventory because these amounts increase the cost of the goods purchased.
* Free on board (FOB) destination denotes the opposite arrangement. Ownership transfers from the seller to the buyer when the goods *reach their destination*. This means that the seller must pay to ship goods to that point. The seller records the shipping costs with a debit to Delivery Expense.

Exhibit 4-4 summarizes FOB terms.

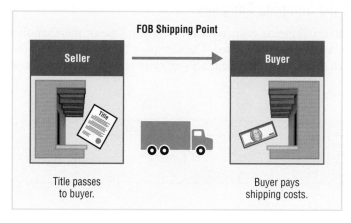

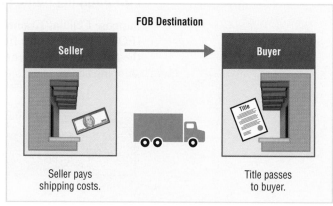

Exhibit 4-4 ▲

Accounting in Your World

Have you ever purchased something online or from a catalog and thought you received a really great deal until you received the bill and realized that the company charged you a significant amount for "shipping"? The reason that you were required to pay these shipping charges is because the merchandise was sold with shipping terms of "FOB Shipping Point." Next time, you should purchase items from a company that offers "FOB Destination" shipping terms.

Costs Related to the Receipt of Goods from Suppliers

Let us see how Cellular Connect records shipping costs when it purchases goods. When it buys products under FOB shipping point, Cellular either pays the shipping company directly or reimburses the seller for the freight charges if they have been prepaid by the seller. When Cellular buys products under FOB destination, the supplier pays the freight charges.

FOB Shipping Point, Pay the Shipping Company

Suppose Cellular Connect incurs shipping costs related to the purchase of merchandise (FOB shipping point) from Accessories Unlimited. Cellular pays $60 to the carrier for the February 1 shipment seen earlier. Cellular Connect's entry to record payment of the shipping charge is as follows:

DATE	ACCOUNTS	POST REF.	DR.	CR.
Feb 1	Inventory		60	
	Cash			60
	Record payment of shipping bill for the February 1 purchase.			

Cellular debits Inventory to increase the cost of the merchandise bought and credits Cash for the shipping costs.

FOB Shipping Point, Repay the Seller for Prepaid Shipping Costs

Under FOB shipping point, the seller sometimes prepays the shipping costs as a convenience to the buyer. These costs are added to the invoice for the merchandise.

Let's see how Cellular records the following purchase transactions. On July 15, Cellular buys $1,000 of goods on account from CellTel, Inc. The terms of the purchase are 2/10, n/30, FOB shipping point. CellTel prepaid $80 of shipping costs and added the charges to the invoice for an invoice total of $1,080. Cellular then returns $100 of these goods for credit on July 20. On July 25, Cellular makes payment in full for the purchase. First, Cellular records the purchase of goods:

DATE	ACCOUNTS	POST REF.	DR.	CR.
Jul 15	Inventory		1,080	
	Accounts Payable—CellTel, Inc.			1,080
	Record purchase of inventory on account.			

Next, Cellular records the return of inventory, as follows:

DATE	ACCOUNTS	POST REF.	DR.	CR.
Jul 20	Accounts Payable—CellTel, Inc.		100	
	Inventory			100
	Record inventory returned to the manufacturer.			

Finally, it records the payment for the purchase by calculating the purchase discount and the balance due. Cellular pays on July 25, which is within the 10-day discount period, so it receives a discount of $18: 2% of the $1,000 original cost of the goods minus $100 of returned goods, or $0.02 \times \$900$. Although shipping costs increase the invoice amount of the merchandise purchased, they are not included in the calculation of any purchase discount. The purchase discount is computed only on the amount due to the supplier for the goods purchased. The calculation of the payment amount is as follows:

Purchase Amount	$1,000	
+ Shipping Costs	80	
− Purchase Return	(100)	
− Purchase Discount	(18)	($1,000 − $100 = $900; $900 × 0.02 = $18)
= Cash Paid	$ 962	

The journal entry to record the cash payment is as follows:

DATE	ACCOUNTS	POST REF.	DR.	CR.
Jul 25	Accounts Payable—CellTel, Inc. ($1,000 + $80 − $100)		980	
	Inventory [($1,000 − $100) × 0.02]			18
	Cash ($1,000 + $80 − $100 − $18)			962
	Record payment of inventory puchases within the			
	discount period.			

FOB Destination

Under FOB destination, the seller pays to ship the goods to the destination requested by the customer. If Cellular Connect purchased goods under these terms, it has no shipping costs to record because the supplier pays the freight.

Costs Related to Delivering Goods to Customers

The cost of shipping goods to customers is recorded in an expense account titled Delivery Expense. This cost occurs when the seller agrees to shipping terms of FOB destination. Delivery Expense is an expense on the income statement and, as an expense account, normally has a debit balance.

Let's see how the sale of goods and payment of shipping costs affect Cellular Connect in different situations. Rob Macklin, a frequent customer at Cellular Connect, has an account with the store. Rob buys a bluetooth headset as a Christmas gift for his sister who lives in Las Vegas. Cellular purchases the headset for $45 and sells it to Rob for $100. Shipping costs to Las Vegas total $15.

FOB Destination

Let's assume that Cellular advertises that shipping costs are free with any purchase of $100 or more. Assume Rob buys the headset on November 30 and charges it to his account. He asks Cellular to ship it to Las Vegas. Cellular records the sale and payment of shipping costs as follows:

DATE	ACCOUNTS	POST REF.	DR.	CR.
Nov 30	Accounts Receivable—Rob Macklin		100	
	Sales Revenue			100
	Cost of Goods Sold		45	
	Inventory			45
	Record sale of inventory on account.			

DATE	ACCOUNTS	POST REF.	DR.	CR.
Nov 30	Delivery Expense		15	
	Cash			15
	Record shipping costs on sale.			

In this case, income from the sale is $40 ($100 − $45 − $15).

FOB Shipping Point

Now, let's assume that Cellular does not offer free shipping. Because Cellular sold the goods FOB shipping point, Rob pays for the shipping costs. Rob purchases the headset on November 30 and takes it home to wrap and send with another gift. Cellular would record the sale as follows:

DATE	ACCOUNTS	POST REF.	DR.	CR.
Nov 30	Accounts Receivable—Rob Macklin		100	
	Sales Revenue			100
	Cost of Goods Sold		45	
	Inventory			45
	Record sale of inventory on account.			

In this situation, income from sale would be $55 ($100 − $45).

FOB Shipping Point, Seller Agrees to Prepay the Shipping Costs

Now assume that Rob buys the headset on November 30 and asks Cellular to ship it to Las Vegas for him. Again, because the goods are sold FOB shipping point, Rob is responsible for the shipping charges. In this case, Cellular pays for shipping the goods and adds the cost to Rob's invoice. Cellular records the sale, including the payment of shipping costs, as follows:

DATE	ACCOUNTS	POST REF.	DR.	CR.
Nov 30	Accounts Receivable—Rob Macklin		100	
	Sales Revenue			100
	Cost of Goods Sold		45	
	Inventory			45
	Record sale of inventory on account.			

DATE	ACCOUNTS	POST REF.	DR.	CR.
Nov 30	Accounts Receivable—Rob Macklin		15	
	Cash			15
	Record prepayment of shipping costs.			

Income from the sale is again $55 ($100 – $45). The $15 Cellular paid to ship the headset to Las Vegas is not an expense as it will be reimbursed by Rob. A comparison reveals that the income from the sale under FOB shipping point remains the same whether or not Cellular prepays the shipping charges:

	FOB destination	FOB Shipping Point	FOB Shipping Point, Seller Prepays
Sales Revenue	$100	$100	$100
– Cost of Goods Sold........	(45)	(45)	(45)
– Delivery Expense	(15)	—	—
= Income from Sale	$ 40	$ 55	$ 55

Other Selling Costs

Selling expenses represent the costs associated with advertising and selling inventory. Examples of selling expenses usually found on a merchandiser's income statement include the following:

- Sales salaries, wages, and commissions
- Advertising and promotion
- Depreciation on stores, parking lots, counters, displays, shelves, vehicles of salespeople, and storage space (such as warehouses and refrigerators)
- Delivery costs of merchandise to customers

As we will see in the next section, selling expenses are a deduction when arriving at the net income of a merchandiser.

Selling expenses Expenses related to advertising and selling products including sales salaries, sales commissions, advertising, depreciation on items used in sales, and delivery expense.

Stop and Think...

If freight charges paid by a merchandiser to ship merchandise to a customer are expensed as a delivery expense, why are freight charges paid by the merchandiser to have goods it purchased delivered added to the Inventory account?

Answer

It has to do with the matching principle that was discussed in Chapter 3. By expensing the freight charges of delivering merchandise to a customer, the freight costs are being matched with the revenue that was earned when the merchandise was sold. The freight charges associated with the receipt of purchased goods are added to the cost of inventory so that they are not expensed until the inventory is sold. Because the freight costs become part of the cost of the inventory, they will be expensed through cost of goods sold once the inventory is sold and therefore the matching principle is better observed.

How Do You Prepare a Merchandiser's Financial Statements?

The Income Statement

6 **Prepare a multi-step income statement and a classified balance sheet**

Single-step income statement Income statement format that groups all revenues together and lists all expenses together, subtracting total expenses from total revenues and calculating net income or net loss without computing any subtotals.

In earlier chapters, you learned how to complete the financial statements for a service business. Many service businesses use a **single-step income statement**. The single-step income statement groups all revenues together and all expenses together. Then the total expenses are subtracted from total revenues in a single step without calculating any subtotals. The advantage of the single-step format is that it clearly distinguishes revenues from expenses. Although Cellular Connect is a merchandiser, **Exhibit 4-5** illustrates its income statement for the year ended December 31, 2014, prepared using the single-step format.

Cellular Connect, Inc.
Income Statement
Year Ended December 31, 2014

Revenues:		
Net Sales Revenue		$167,900
Expenses:		
Cost of Goods Sold	$90,300	
Selling Expenses	1,200	
General and Administrative Expenses	19,650	
Interest Expense	1,100	
Total Expenses		112,250
Net Income		$ 55,650

Exhibit 4-5 ▲

Multi-step income statement Income statement format that calculates net income or net loss by listing important subtotals, such as gross profit and operating income.

Net Sales Revenue Sales revenue less sales discounts and sales returns and allowances.

Most merchandisers use a **multi-step income statement**. The multi-step income statement is prepared in steps. Important subtotals are computed as part of the calculation of net income or net loss. Investors prefer this format because it provides step-by-step information about the profitability of the business. This format makes it more useful for managers within the business as well as investors outside of the business. The multi-step income statement for most merchandisers will contain most, but not necessarily all, of the following items:

- **Net Sales Revenue** is presented first and is calculated by subtracting both Sales Returns and Allowances and Sales Discounts from Sales Revenue. Keep in mind that a company may not offer its customers any sales discounts. Also, even if sales discounts are offered, customers may not take advantage of them. Therefore, it is possible that no sales discounts will appear on a company's income statement.

- The cost of the merchandise that is sold appears next as Cost of Goods Sold.
- **Gross Profit**, also called **Gross Margin**, is a subtotal computed next. The gross profit equals Net Sales Revenue minus Cost of Goods Sold.
- **Operating Expenses** are the expenses, other than cost of goods sold, of operating the business. Operating Expenses are listed after Gross Profit. Many companies report operating expenses in two categories:

> **1.** Selling Expenses include sales salaries, commissions, advertising, promotion, depreciation for items used in sales, and delivery costs to customers.
>
> **2.** **General and Administrative Expenses** include office expenses, such as the salaries of the company president and office employees, depreciation of items used in administration, rent, utilities, and property taxes on the office building.

- On the multi-step income statement, Gross Profit minus Operating Expenses equals **Operating Income**, or **Income from Operations**. Operating income measures the results of the entity's primary, ongoing business activities.
- The last section of a multi-step income statement is **Other Revenues and Expenses**. This category reports revenues and expenses that fall outside of a business's main operations. Examples include interest revenue, interest expense, dividend revenue, and gains and losses on the sale of long-term assets. As not every business has revenues and expenses outside its main operations, not all income statements will include this section.
- The last line of the multi-step income statement is Net Income or Net Loss. To calculate, add Other Revenues and subtract Other Expenses from Operating Income. The final results of operations, net income or net loss, is a company's *bottom line,* a commonly used business term.

Cellular Connect's multi-step income statement for the year ended December 31, 2014, appears in **Exhibit 4-6** on page 176 along with the Statement of Retained Earnings and the Balance Sheet.

After you review Cellular Connect's multi-step income statement in Exhibit 4-6, look again at its single-step version in Exhibit 4-5. Notice that in both formats net income is exactly the same. The format of the income statement does not change the net income or net loss of a business. It simply changes how the calculation of net income or net loss is presented.

Gross Profit Net sales revenue minus cost of goods sold; also called **Gross Margin.**

Operating Expenses Expenses of operating a business other than cost of goods sold. Examples include depreciation, rent, salaries, utilities, advertising, delivery expense, property taxes, and supplies expense.

General and Administrative Expenses Office expenses, such as the salaries of the company president and office employees, depreciation of items used in administration, rent, utilities, and property taxes on the office building.

Operating Income Gross profit minus operating expenses. Also called **Income from Operations**.

Other Revenues and Expenses Revenues and expenses that fall outside the main operations of a business, such as interest expense and a loss on the sale of long-term assets.

Decision Guidelines

Decision	**Guideline**	**Analyze**
When should a financial statement user expect to see a single versus multi-step format for the income statement?	It depends on how the information will be used by the user.	The single-step format shows the calculation of net income or net loss by subtracting all expenses from all revenues in a single step. The single-step format typically shows summary information and is intended for users who do not need much detail. This format would not be a good format for creditors or investors to use, but it would be great to use in a press release or newspaper article. The multi-step format shows the calculation of net income or net loss in a series of steps with subtotals for gross profit and operating income. This format shows detailed information and is best suited for creditors and investors.

Cellular Connect, Inc.
Income Statement
Year Ended December 31, 2014

Sales Revenue		$171,300	
Less: Sales Returns and Allowances		3,400	
Net Sales Revenue			$167,900
Cost of Goods Sold			90,300
Gross Profit			77,600
Operating Expenses:			
Selling Expenses:			
Advertising Expense	$ 1,000		
Delivery Expense	200	1,200	
General and Administrative Expenses:			
Salaries Expense	10,200		
Rent Expense	7,300		
Insurance Expense	1,000		
Depreciation Expense, Office Equipment	600		
Supplies Expense	550	19,650	20,850
Operating Income			56,750
Other Revenues and (Expenses):			
Interest Expense			(1,100)
Net Income			$ 55,650

Cellular Connect, Inc.
Statement of Retained Earnings
Year Ended December 31, 2014

Retained Earnings, December 31, 2013	$20,900
Add: Net Income	55,650
Subtotal	76,550
Less: Dividends	55,900
Retained Earnings, December 31, 2014	$20,650

Cellular Connect, Inc.
Balance Sheet
December 31, 2014

ASSETS			LIABILITIES		
Current Assets:			Current Liabilities:		
Cash	$ 7,150		Accounts Payable	$30,000	
Accounts Receivable	4,600		Salaries Payable	400	
Inventory	15,700		Unearned Sales Revenue	700	
Supplies	100		Total Current Liabilities		$31,100
Prepaid Insurance	200		Long-Term Liabilities:		
Total Current Assets		$27,750	Mortgage Payable		10,000
Long-term Assets:			Total Liabilities		41,100
Office Equipment	52,000				
Less: Accumulated			**STOCKHOLDERS'**		
Depreciation, Office			**EQUITY**		
Equipment	3,000	49,000	Common Stock	15,000	
			Retained Earnings	20,650	
			Total Stockholders' Equity		35,650
			Total Liabilities &		
Total Assets		$76,750	Stockholders' Equity		$76,750

Exhibit 4-6 ▲

The Statement of Retained Earnings

A merchandiser's statement of retained earnings looks exactly like that of a service business. Cellular's statement of retained earnings is presented in Exhibit 4-6.

The Balance Sheet

Classified balance sheet A balance sheet that separates assets and liabilities into current and long-term classes.

Liquidity The ability to convert an asset to cash quickly.

In order to provide more useful information, merchandisers, as well as most service businesses, usually prepare a **classified balance sheet**. A classified balance sheet lists assets in classes in the order of their **liquidity**. Liquidity refers to how close an asset is to becoming cash or being used up. Similar to the assets, the liabilities are listed in classes based on how soon the obligation will be paid or fulfilled. By listing the assets and liabilities in these classes, financial statement users can better analyze the business's ability to pay its bills on time.

Assets

Current Assets Assets that are expected to be converted to cash, sold, or consumed within one year or the business's operating cycle if the cycle is longer than a year.

Operating cycle The time span during which the business obtains resources, uses them to sell goods and services to customers, and collects cash from these customers.

The most liquid assets are presented on a classified balance sheet in a class called **Current Assets**. Current Assets are assets that will be converted to cash, sold, or used up during the next twelve months or within a business's normal **operating cycle** if longer than one year.

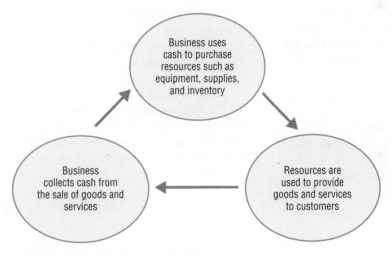

The Operating Cycle

Long-term assets Assets other than those that are current.

Fixed assets The long-lived assets of a business including land, buildings, furniture, fixtures, and equipment; also called **plant assets** and commonly shown on the balance sheet as property, plant, and equipment.

Property, plant, and equipment A heading often seen on the balance sheet used to describe fixed, or plant, assets.

For most businesses, the operating cycle is a few months. Cash, Accounts Receivable, Notes Receivable due within one year, and Prepaid Expenses are all current assets. If the business is a merchandiser, then the major difference between its balance sheet and that of a service business is that it also shows Inventory as a current asset.

All assets other than current assets are reported in a class called **long-term assets**. One category of long-term assets is called **fixed assets** or **plant assets**. This category is often labeled on the balance sheet as **property, plant, and equipment**. Land, buildings, furniture, fixtures, and equipment are examples of these assets.

Liabilities

Current liabilities Debts due to be paid with cash or fulfilled with goods and services within one year or the entity's operating cycle if the cycle is longer than a year.

The debts or obligations of a business that must be paid for or fulfilled within one year (or within the entity's operating cycle if the cycle is longer than a year) are reported in a class called **current liabilities**. Accounts Payable, Notes Payable due within one year, Salaries Payable, Interest Payable, and Unearned Revenue are current liabilities.

Long-term liabilities Liabilities other than those that are current.

Account form A balance sheet format that lists assets on the left of the report and liabilities and stockholders' equity on the right, just as those accounts appear in the accounting equation.

Report form A balance sheet format that reports assets at the top of the report, followed by liabilities, and ending with stockholders' equity at the end of the report.

Obligations that extend beyond one year are reported as **long-term liabilities**. Often, a business owner signs a contract to repay a note or mortgage over several years. The portion of the note or mortgage that must be paid within one year is classified as a current liability. However, the remaining balance is a long-term liability.

The balance sheet for Cellular Connect is presented in Exhibit 4-6. Cellular's balance sheet is presented in **account form**. The account form lists the assets on the left and the liabilities and stockholders' equity on the right, just as these accounts appear in the accounting equation. It is also acceptable to present the balance sheet in **report form**, which lists the assets at the top and the liabilities and stockholders' equity on the bottom.

Focus On Decision Making

"Is the Business Profitable?"

Think about being the manager of Cellular Connect, Inc. Look at Exhibit 4-6. Are you doing a good job or bad job? Is your business profitable? How profitable is your business? Three measures often used to evaluate profitability are the earnings per share, gross profit percentage, and net income percentage.

7 Compute earnings per share, the gross profit percentage, and the net income percentage

Earnings per share (EPS) The portion of a company's earnings allocated to each outstanding share of common stock. Earnings per share serves as an indicator of a company's profitability.

Earnings per Share

Earnings per share (EPS) is a measure of the profitability or loss of each unit of ownership. In a corporation, each unit of ownership is called a share of stock. As noted in Chapter 1, the owners of a corporation are called stockholders. Stockholders own shares of a corporation's stock.

Earnings per share is computed by dividing the corporation's net income or net loss by the average number of shares outstanding during a year. Assume Cellular Connect has 1,875 average shares of stock outstanding during the year. Based on information provided from the income statement in Exhibit 4-6, Cellular Connect's earnings per share is $29.68, calculated as follows:

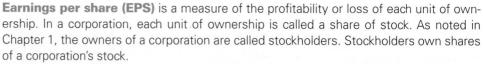

Earnings Per Share = $55,650/1,875 = $29.68

A $29.68 earnings per share means that Cellular Connect earned $29.68 for each share of stock outstanding during the year.[1,2]

---

[1] Earnings per share is computed by dividing net income or loss by the average number of shares outstanding during the year. All corporations have common stock. Sometimes a corporation has common stock and preferred stock. Owners of preferred stock have priority in receiving a stated amount of dividends. What remains belongs to the owners of the corporation's common stock. Stockholders that own common stock control the business by voting for management and other major decisions. If a company has preferred stock, earnings per share is computed by subtracting preferred dividends from net income, resulting in *net income available for common stockholders*. This net income available to common stockholders is then divided by the average number of common shares outstanding during the year.

[2] Earnings per share is computed by dividing net income or loss by the average number of shares outstanding during the year. This earnings per share number is called *basic earnings per share*. If a corporation has certain contingencies that have a high probability of occurring in the future, accountants will compute a *diluted earnings per share*. An example of such a contingency is when a company gives its senior executives the option to buy its stock at a very attractive price. Diluted earnings per share is computed by re-computing the net income and average number of shares outstanding, assuming the contingency occurred. The recomputed net income is then divided by the recomputed average number of shares outstanding during the year. The result is diluted earnings per share.

The Gross Profit Percentage

Gross profit, also called gross margin, is a key tool in evaluating merchandising operations. Remember that gross profit is net sales revenue minus the cost of goods sold. Thus, gross profit is the amount left over from sales after deducting the cost of the merchandise sold. Merchandisers strive to maximize gross profit in order to help maximize net income. The **gross profit percentage**, also called the **gross margin percentage**, shows how well a merchandising business meets this goal. The gross profit percentage measures the relationship between gross profit and sales.

Gross profit percentage A measure of profitability equal to gross profit divided by net sales revenue; also called **gross margin percentage**.

The gross profit percentage is one of the most carefully watched measures of profitability by investors and business managers. This information is used to compare changes in gross profit from year to year for the business. Also, it is used to compare the company to other businesses in the same industry. For most businesses, the gross profit percentage changes little from year to year. To investors, a significant change in the gross profit percentage signals a significant change in the business's operations, meriting further investigation.

To compute the gross profit percentage, divide gross profit by net sales revenue. Based on information provided in the income statement in Exhibit 4-6, the gross profit percentage for Cellular Connect is 46.2%, calculated as follows:

$$\text{Gross Profit Percentage} = \frac{\text{Gross Profit}}{\text{Net Sales Revenue}} = \frac{\$77,600}{\$167,900} = 0.462 = 46.2\%$$

A 46.2% gross margin percentage means that each dollar of net sales generates $0.462 of gross profit. Every time Cellular Connect sells $1 of merchandise, it produces $0.462 of gross profit that hopefully covers operating expenses, interest expense, and generates net income.

The Net Income Percentage

Net income is the difference between sales (plus other revenues) and all the expenses the business incurs during a certain period. These expenses include the cost of inventory sold, but also include operating expenses such as salaries, rent, advertising, and utilities, as well as other expenses such as interest. Another way to look at it is that net income is gross profit (sales less the cost of merchandise sold) less operating expenses (which equals operating income) plus or minus other revenues and expenses a business experiences in a set accounting period. Net income is very important because it is the return that stockholders earn.

Net income percentage A measure of profitability equal to net income divided by net sales revenue.

Now ask yourself, "How much of every dollar of sales ends up as net income?" The **net income percentage** answers that question. The net income percentage is the percent of every dollar of net sales that ends up as net income. To compute the net income percentage, divide net income by net sales revenue. The formula for calculating the net income percentage is:

$$\text{Net Income Percentage} = \text{Net Income/Net Sales Revenue}$$

Based on the information provided from the income statement in Exhibit 4-6, the net income percentage for Cellular Connect is 33.1%, calculated as follows:

$$\text{Net Income Percentage} = \frac{\$55,650}{\$167,900} = 33.1\%$$

Cellular Connect makes a little over $0.33 on every dollar of sales. That's pretty good. The stockholders should be pleased with the management of Cellular Connect. Cellular Connect appears to be doing a very good job of keeping expenses low relative to sales.

How They Do It: A Look at Business

Think about how different businesses operate and make a profit. Some businesses sell a lot of products and make a modest profit on each sale. An example is a toy store such as Toys R Us. Think of all the customers that come into a toy store. Think of all the toys each customer buys. Toys R Us only makes a few cents on each item sold, but it sells a lot of items. For the year ending February 2, 2013, Toys R Us' gross profit margin percentage was 37%, but its net income percentage was less than 1%. This resulted in Toys R Us earning net income of only $39 million and earnings per share of $0.39 for the year ending February 2, 2013.

Other businesses sell only a few items but make a lot of profit on each sale. An example is the very expensive jewelry store Tiffany & Co. Although Tiffany does not have a lot of customers and sales, it makes a large profit on each sale. This also results in a large net income. As of January 31, 2013, Tiffany's gross profit margin percentage was 57% and net income percentage was 11%. This resulted in Tiffany & Co. earning net income of $416 million and earnings per share of $3.28 for the year ending January 31, 2013.

Now, think; all businesses want to earn a profit or net income. However, different businesses earn that profit in different ways. Toys R Us made its profit by selling a lot of toys, making a small profit on each toy sale. Tiffany's made its profit by selling a few items, making a large profit on each sale.

Decision Guidelines

Decision	Guideline	Analyze
Am I charging enough for my product?	Consider the gross profit on the income statement.	A business must have sufficient gross profit after paying for the cost of the goods that it sold in order to pay its operating expenses and other expenses and provide sufficient net income to satisfy its stockholders.
Am I earning a profit for my owners (stockholders)?	Consider the business' net income and its earnings per share (EPS)	A business needs to reward its owners for providing money. This reward is net income. To measure the net income for each share of stock outstanding we compute the earnings per share (EPS). EPS is computed by dividing net income by the average number of shares outstanding during the period.

Summary

MyAccountingLab

Here is what you should know after reading this chapter. MyAccountingLab will help you identify what you know and where to go when you need practice.

Key Points	Key Accounting Terms
How do customers get their goods?	**Inventory** (p. 160)
• Manufacturers usually sell inventory to wholesalers or sometimes directly to retailers.	**Merchandise inventory** (p. 160)
• Wholesalers sell to retailers.	**Retailers** (p. 160)
• Customers usually buy from retailers.	**Wholesalers** (p. 160)

 1 Describe the relationships among manufacturers, wholesalers, retailers, and customers

		Key Points	Key Accounting Terms
2	Define periodic and perpetual inventory systems	Types of inventory systems: • Perpetual inventory system keeps a running record of inventory as it is bought and sold. • Periodic inventory system only updates the inventory balance at the end of each period based on a physical count.	**Periodic inventory system** (p. 161) **Perpetual inventory system** (p. 161)
3	Journalize transactions for the purchase of inventory	Accounting for merchandise inventory purchases: • Cash and credit purchases are recorded as increases to the Inventory account. • Purchase returns and allowances are recorded as decreases to the Inventory account. • Purchase discounts are recorded as decreases to the Inventory account.	**Credit terms** (p. 163) **Discount period** (p. 164) **eom** (p. 163) **Purchase discount** (p. 163) **Purchase returns and allowances** (p. 162) **n/30** (p. 163) **n/eom** (p. 163) **Sales invoice** (p. 163) **Subsidiary ledger** (p. 162)
4	Journalize transactions for the sale of inventory	Accounting for merchandise sales: • Merchandise sales require a compound entry that increases Cash or Accounts Receivable, increases Sales, increases Cost of Goods Sold, and decreases Inventory. • The returns of merchandise (or sales allowances) are recorded in a contra-account titled Sales Returns and Allowances. • Sales discounts received for the prompt payment of an invoice are recorded in a contra-account titled Sales Discounts.	**Compound journal entry** (p. 165) **Cost of Goods Sold** (p. 165) **Credit memorandum** (p. 166) **Sales Discount** (p. 168) **Sales Returns and Allowances** (p. 166) **Sales Revenue** (p. 165)
5	Understand shipping terms and journalize transactions for freight charges and other selling expenses	Accounting for freight and other charges: • Freight charges incurred on the delivery of goods from a vendor are recorded in the Inventory account. • Freight charges incurred on the delivery of goods to a customer are recorded in an expense account such as Delivery Expense. • The shipping terms dictate when title to goods (ownership) transfers.	**Free on board (FOB) destination** (p. 169) **Free on board (FOB) shipping point** (p. 169) **Freight charges** (p. 169) **Selling expenses** (p. 173) **Title** (p. 169)

6 **Prepare a multi-step income statement and a classified balance sheet**

Key Points

Financial statements for a merchandiser:

- Multi-step income statements are usually detailed and show important subtotals such as Gross Profit and Operating Income.

- Classified balance sheets show more useful information because assets and liabilities are classified as either current or long-term. The time frame used by most businesses to define current is one year or less.

Key Accounting Terms

Account form (p. 178)

Classified balance sheet (p. 177)

Current Assets (p. 177)

Current liabilities (p. 177)

Fixed assets (p. 177)

General and Administrative Expenses (p. 175)

Gross Margin (p. 175)

Gross Profit (p. 175)

Income from Operations (p. 175)

Liquidity (p. 177)

Long-term assets (p. 177)

Long-term liabilities (p. 178)

Multi-step income statement (p. 174)

Net Sales Revenue (p. 174)

Operating cycle (p. 177)

Operating Expenses (p. 175)

Operating Income (p. 175)

Other Revenues and Expenses (p. 175)

Plant assets (p. 177)

Property, plant, and equipment (p. 177)

Report form (p. 178)

Single-step income statement (p. 174)

7 **Compute earnings per share, the gross profit percentage, and the net income percentage**

Ratios often used to help make decisions:

- Earnings per share (EPS) is a measure of the profitability or loss of each unit of ownership. In a corporation, each unit of ownership is called a share of stock.

- Gross profit percentage measures the percentage of each dollar of sales that a business has left to pay its operating and other expenses and provide net income.

- Net income percentage measures the percentage of net sales that results in net income.

Earnings per share (p. 178)

Gross margin percentage (p. 179)

Gross profit percentage (p. 179)

Net income percentage (p. 179)

Accounting Practice

Discussion Questions

1. What accounts will appear on the financial statements of a merchandiser that will not appear on those of a service-oriented company?

2. What are some reasons why a merchandiser might prefer to use a perpetual inventory system over a periodic inventory system?

3. Why do businesses use subsidiary ledgers?

4. What do the terms 2/10, n/30 mean? If you were advising a company that bought goods under these terms, what would you advise it to do with respect to payment? Why?

5. How many accounts are involved in recording the sale of merchandise on credit?

6. What kind of account is Sales Returns and Allowances? Where would it appear on the financial statements?

7. What is a credit memorandum? Give an example of the type of transaction in which it would be used.

8. What does the term "free on board" mean? Why is this an important term to understand if you are involved in making decisions about the purchasing of inventory or the setting of prices for your products?

9. What is the difference between a single-step and multi-step income statement? For what type of business is a multi-step income statement most appropriate?

10. What situation might explain why a company's gross profit percentage went down from 60% to 40% from one year to the next?

Self Check

1. Which account does a merchandiser use that a service company does not use?
   a. Cost of goods sold
   b. Inventory
   c. Sales revenue
   d. All of the above

2. The two main inventory accounting systems are the
   a. perpetual and periodic.
   b. cash and accrual.
   c. returns and allowances.
   d. purchase and sale.

3. Which of the following represents the journal entry to record the purchase of $1,500 of inventory on account?

DATE	ACCOUNTS	POST REF.	DR.	CR.
a.	Cost of Goods Sold		1,500	
	Accounts Payable			1,500
b.	Inventory		1,500	
	Cash			1,500
c.	Accounts Payable		1,500	
	Inventory			1,500
d.	Inventory		1,500	
	Accounts Payable			1,500

4. Water Works Pool Supply, Inc., purchased inventory for $2,700 and also paid $70 freight to have the inventory delivered. Water Works Pool Supply, Inc., returned $125 of the goods to the seller and later took a 3% purchase discount. What is the final cost of the inventory that Water Works Pool Supply, Inc., kept? (Round your answer up to the next whole number.)

   a. $2,645
   b. $2,566
   c. $2,498
   d. $2,568

5. Suppose Riley Electronics, Inc., had sales of $280,000 and sales returns of $26,000. Cost of goods sold was $112,000. How much gross profit did Riley Electronics, Inc., report?

   a. $168,000
   b. $142,000
   c. $194,000
   d. $254,000

6. Suppose Perfect Picture Photography Supply's Inventory account showed a balance of $44,700. A physical count showed $43,300 of goods on hand. To adjust the inventory account, Picture Perfect Photography Supply, Inc., would make which of the following entries?

DATE	ACCOUNTS	POST REF.	DR.	CR.
a.	Cost of Goods Sold		1,400	
	Inventory			1,400
b.	Inventory		1,400	
	Accounts Payable			1,400
c.	Accounts Payable		1,400	
	Inventory			1,400
d.	Inventory		1,400	
	Cost of Goods Sold			1,400

7. If Holiboards, Inc., returned $2,750 of snowboards to a supplier, which of the following entries would be used to record the transaction?

DATE	ACCOUNTS	POST REF.	DR.	CR.
a.	Accounts Payable		2,750	
	Inventory			2,750
b.	Accounts Payable		2,750	
	Sales Returns and Allowances			2,750
c.	Inventory		2,750	
	Accounts Payable			2,750
d.	Cost of Goods Sold		2,750	
	Inventory			2,750

8. An asset is classified as current if it

   a. will last longer than one year.
   b. will become cash, be sold, or be used up within twelve months.
   c. was purchased within the last six months.
   d. was purchased with cash.

9. The income statement format that shows important subtotals is referred to as

 a. a subtotaled income statement.

 b. a single-step income statement.

 c. a multi-step income statement.

 d. a classified income statement.

10. Suppose Acme Electronics, Inc., had sales of $195,000 and sales returns of $15,000. Cost of goods sold was $108,000. What was Neilson Electronics' gross profit percentage (rounded) for this period?

 a. 37%

 b. 40%

 c. 45%

 d. 34%

11. According to the Real World Accounting Video, the cost of merchandise inventory that the business has sold to customers is called _____.

 a. inventory shrinkage

 b. cost of business

 c. cost of goods sold

 d. cost of inventory

12. According to the Real World Accounting Video, vendors generally sell merchandise expecting to be paid in _____ days.

 a. 0

 b. 30

 c. 90

 d. 180

Answers are given after Written Communication.

MyAccountingLab

Short Exercises

S4-1. **Inventory methods (*Learning Objective 2*) 5–10 min.**

The following characteristics are related to either periodic inventory or perpetual inventory systems.

 1. A physical count of goods on hand at year-end is required.

 2. Inventory records are continuously updated.

 3. Purchases of inventory are recorded in an asset account at the time of purchase.

 4. Bar code scanners are often utilized when using this inventory system.

 5. It is necessary to calculate the cost of goods sold at the end of the year with this inventory system.

Match each characteristic with one of the following:

 a. Periodic inventory

 b. Perpetual inventory

 c. Both periodic and perpetual inventory

 d. Neither periodic nor perpetual inventory

S4-2. **Adjusting inventory based on a physical count (*Learning Objective 2*) 5–10 min.**

Cole's Furniture uses the perpetual inventory method. At the end of the year, Cole's Furniture's Inventory account had a ledger balance of $163,000. A physical inventory count revealed that the actual inventory on hand totaled $161,800. Journalize the transaction necessary to adjust the Inventory account at the end of the year.

S4-3. Journalizing inventory purchases (*Learning Objective 3*) 5–10 min.

Suppose A-1 Sports purchases $83,000 of sportswear on account from Outdoor Wear, Inc., on December 1, 2014. Credit terms are 2/10, net 45. A-1 Sports pays Outdoor Wear, Inc., on December 8, 2014.

1. Journalize the transactions for A-1 Sports on December 1, 2014, and December 8, 2014.
2. What was the final cost of this inventory for A-1 Sports?

S4-4. Inventory purchases and returns (*Learning Objective 3*) 5–10 min.

Regal Spas, Inc., purchased $17,400 worth of inventory from the Pool Palace on account, terms of 1/10, n/30. Some of the goods are damaged in shipment, so Regal Spas, Inc., returns $1,600 of the merchandise to the Pool Palace.
How much must Regal Spas, Inc., pay the Pool Palace

a. after the discount period?
b. within the discount period?

S4-5. Journalizing inventory purchases and returns (*Learning Objective 3*) 5–10 min.

Regal Spas, Inc., purchased $11,800 worth of inventory from the Pool Palace on account, terms of 2/10, n/30. Some of the goods are damaged in shipment, so Regal Spas, Inc., returns $2,300 of the merchandise to the Pool Palace.

Journalize the following transactions for Regal Spas, Inc. Explanations are not required.

a. Purchase of the goods
b. Return of the damaged goods
c. Payment for the goods within the discount period

S4-6. Journalizing inventory purchases and freight charges (*Learning Objectives 3 & 5*) 5–10 min.

Journalize the following transactions for Jammin' Joe's music store.

a. Purchased $4,200 of merchandise on account, terms 3/15, n/30, FOB shipping point.
b. Paid $140 to the freight company for the delivery of the merchandise purchased.
c. Paid for the inventory purchased in part a. within the discount period.

S4-7. Journalizing sales transactions (*Learning Objective 4*) 5–10 min.

Journalize the following transactions for the Pool Palace. Explanations are not required.

a. The Pool Palace sold $81,000 of merchandise to Regal Spas, Inc., on account, terms 4/15, n/60. The merchandise cost the Pool Palace $44,500.
b. Received payment for the goods from Regal Spas, Inc., within the discount period.

S4-8. Journalizing sales and return transactions (*Learning Objective 4*) 5–10 min.

Suppose Peter's Hardware sells merchandise on account, terms 2/10, n/30, for $640 (cost of the inventory is $360) on March 17, 2014. Peter's Hardware later received $185 of goods (cost, $110) as sales returns on March 21, 2014. The customer paid the balance due on March 26, 2014. Journalize the March 2014 transactions for Peter's Hardware.

S4-9. Calculate income statement items (*Learning Objective 6*) 5–10 min.

Suppose Paul's Hardware sells merchandise on account, terms 1/10, n/45, for $920 (cost of the inventory is $550) on March 17, 2014. Peter's Hardware later received $290 of goods (cost, $175) as sales returns on March 21, 2014. The customer paid the balance due on March 26, 2014.

1. Calculate net sales revenue for March 2014.

2. Calculate gross profit for March 2014.

S4-10. Calculate classified balance sheet amounts (*Learning Objective 6*) 5–10 min.

Selected account balances for Maria's Mocha at the end of the month are listed below in random order:

Accounts Payable	$14,800
Unearned Revenue	7,300
Equipment	43,000
Inventory	27,000
Accounts Receivable	5,700
Salaries Payable	2,150
Note Payable, Long-Term	46,000
Accumulated Depreciation, Equipment	4,200
Common Stock	28,000
Supplies	1,950
Building	121,000
Cash	6,400
Accumulated Depreciation, Building	53,000
Prepaid Rent	2,400
Retained Earnings	11,800

Identify or compute the following amounts for Maria's Mocha:

a. Total current assets

b. Total current liabilities

c. Book value of plant assets

d. Total long-term liabilities

S4-11. Prepare a multi-step income statement (*Learning Objective 6*) 10–15 min.

The accounting records for The Skate Shed, Inc., reflected the following amounts at the end of January 2014:

Cash	$2,750	Cost of Goods Sold	$21,000
Total Operating Expense	6,475	Equipment, Net	25,700
Accounts Payable	4,800	Accrued Liabilities	2,475
Total Stockholders' Equity	6,025	Net Sales Revenue	41,500
Long-Term Notes Payable	23,000	Accounts Receivable	3,100
Inventory	4,700	Prepaid Rent	1,200
Salaries Payable	1,150	Interest Expense	375

Prepare The Skate Shed's multi-step income statement for the fiscal year ended January 31, 2014.

S4-12. Prepare a classified balance sheet (*Learning Objective 6*) 10–15 min.

Use the data from S4-11 to prepare the classified balance sheet for The Skate Shed, Inc., at January 31, 2014. Use the report format.

E4-29B. Journalizing inventory sales, returns, and freight transactions (*Learning Objectives 4 & 5*) **10–15 min.**

Journalize the following transactions for Wolfe Wholesale, Inc., that occurred during the month of November. Wolfe Wholesale's cost of inventory is 55% of the sales price.

Nov	3	Sold $1,800 of merchandise on account, terms 2/15, n/45, FOB shipping point. Wolfe Wholesale, Inc., prepaid $75 of shipping costs and added the amount to the customer's invoice.
	7	Issued a credit memo to the customer acknowledging the return of $150 of unwanted goods.
	16	Received payment in full from the customer for the November 3 invoice.

E4-30B. Journalizing inventory purchases, sales, returns, and freight transactions (*Learning Objectives 3, 4, & 5*) **15–20 min.**

The following transactions occurred during June 2014 for Valley Gift and Collectables, Inc.:

Jun	3	Purchased $3,900 of goods on account. Terms, 2/10, n/30. FOB shipping point.
	6	Returned $400 of defective merchandise purchased on June 3.
	8	Paid freight charges of $70 for delivery of goods purchased on June 3.
	11	Sold $1,900 of inventory to a customer on account. Terms, 3/15, n/45, FOB shipping point. The cost of the goods was $800.
	12	Paid amount owed on the June 3 purchase.
	18	Granted a $200 sales allowance on the June 11 sale because the goods were the wrong color.
	25	Received payment in full from customer for the June 11 sale.

Requirement

1. Journalize the June transactions for Valley Gift and Collectables, Inc. Omit explanations.

E4-31B. Calculate multi-step income statement items (*Learning Objective 6*) **10–15 min.**

Consider the following incomplete table of a merchandiser's profit data:

Sales	Sales Discounts	Net Sales	Cost of Goods Sold	Gross Profit
(a)	3,100	(b)	72,500	27,200
71,000	2,600	(c)	43,900	(d)
112,000	(e)	98,400	(f)	43,600
(g)	1,200	106,500	37,600	(h)

Requirement

1. Complete the table by computing the missing amounts.

E4-32B. Prepare a single-step income statement (*Learning Objective 6*) 10–15 min.

The account balances for Borden's Furniture, Inc., for the year ended August 31, 2014, are presented next in random order:

Cash	$ 11,600	Cost of Goods Sold	$128,700
Equipment	32,000	Accumulated Depreciation,	
Accounts Payable	5,100	Equipment	12,700
Common Stock	15,000	Unearned Revenues	3,100
Long-Term Notes Payable	60,000	Sales Revenue	249,000
General Expenses	13,800	Accounts Receivable	6,300
Salaries Payable	2,600	Accumulated Depreciation,	
Supplies	2,400	Building	38,700
Building	155,000	Mortgage Payable	
Sales Returns and		(Long-Term)	21,500
Allowances	2,500	Dividends	65,200
Prepaid Rent	1,900	Sales Discounts	1,900
Retained Earnings	56,000	Selling Expenses	32,400
		Inventory	8,300
		Interest Expense	1,700

Requirements

1. Prepare Borden's Furniture's *single-step* income statement.

2. Would you recommend the use of the single-step income statement format by a merchandiser? Why?

E4-33B. Prepare a multi-step income statement; calculate gross profit percentage (*Learning Objectives 6 & 7*) 15–20 min.

Use the data for Borden's Furniture, Inc., from E4-32B.

Requirements

1. Prepare Borden's Furniture Inc.'s multi-step income statement.

2. Calculate the gross profit percentage.

3. The gross profit percentage for 2013 was 41.3%. Did the gross profit percentage improve or deteriorate during 2014?

E4-34B. Prepare a classified balance sheet (*Learning Objective 6*) 15–20 min.

Use the data for Borden's Furniture, Inc., from E4-32B.

Requirement

1. Prepare Borden's Furniture's classified balance sheet. Use the account format. The balance shown for retained earnings represents the balance prior to closing the temporary accounts for the year.

E4-35B. Calculate earnings per share, gross profit percentage, and net income percentage (*Learning Objective 7*) 10–15 min.

Alliance Software, Inc., had Sales Revenue of $67 million, Sales Returns and Allowances of $2.8 million, and Sales Discounts of $1.6 million in 2014. Cost of goods sold was $31 million, and net income was $9 million for the year. The average number of shares of common stock outstanding during the year was 600,000 shares.

Requirement

1. Compute Alliance Software's earnings per share, gross profit percentage, and net income percentage for 2014.

MyAccountingLab **Problems (Group A)**

P4-36A. Journalizing inventory purchases, returns, and freight transactions (*Learning Objectives 3 & 5*) 15–20 min.

The following purchase-related transactions for Bailey, Inc., occurred during the month of June.

Jun	3	Purchased $6,900 of merchandise, paid cash.
	9	Purchased $550 of supplies on account from Slater Unlimited. Terms, n/30, FOB destination.
	16	Purchased $7,100 of merchandise on account from Tire, Inc. Terms, 2/15, n/30, FOB shipping point.
	22	Received a credit memo in the amount of $1,400 from Tire, Inc., for damaged goods from the June 16 purchase that were returned.
	28	Paid for the supplies purchased on June 9.
	28	Paid Tire, Inc., in full for the June 16 purchase.

Requirement

1. Journalize the transactions for Bailey, Inc. Omit explanations.

P4-37A. Journalizing inventory sales, returns, and freight transactions (*Learning Objectives 4 & 5*) 15–20 min.

The following sale-related transactions for Handyman Hardware, Inc., occurred during the month of April.

Apr	3	Sold $4,400 (cost $2,340) of merchandise on account to F. Adams. Terms, 1/15, n/45, FOB destination.
	4	Paid $115 to ship the goods sold on April 3 to F. Adams.
	10	Sold $2,350 (cost $1,410) of merchandise to cash customers.
	17	Received payment in full from F. Adams for the April 3 sale.
	22	Sold $5,900 (cost $3,540) of merchandise on account to B. Osborne. Terms, 2/10, n/30, FOB shipping point.
	26	Granted B. Osborne a $850 allowance on the April 22 sale due to minor defects in the goods shipped.
	30	Received payment in full from B. Osborne for the April 22 sale.

Requirement

1. Journalize the transactions for Handyman Hardware, Inc. Omit explanations.

P4-38A. Journalizing inventory purchases, sales, returns, and freight transactions (*Learning Objectives 3, 4, & 5*) **20–25 min.**

The following transactions occurred between Tucker's Fine Furnishings and K & B Furniture Warehouse during August of the current year:

Aug 4	Tucker's Fine Furnishings purchased $12,000 of merchandise from K & B Furniture Warehouse on account. Terms, 3/15, n/30, FOB shipping point. The goods cost K & B Furniture Warehouse $7,200.
7	Tucker's Fine Furnishings paid a $150 freight bill for delivery of the goods purchased on August 4.
10	Tucker's Fine Furnishings returned $1,300 of the merchandise purchased on August 4. The goods cost K & B Furniture Warehouse $750.
18	Tucker's Fine Furnishings paid $2,000 of the August 4 invoice less the discount.
31	Tucker's Fine Furnishings paid the remaining amount owed on the August 4 invoice.

Requirements

1. Journalize these transactions on the books of Tucker's Fine Furnishings.
2. Journalize these transactions on the books of K & B Furniture Warehouse.

P4-39A. Journalizing inventory purchases, sales, returns, and freight transactions; calculate gross profit (*Learning Objectives 3, 4, 5, & 6*) **25–30 min.**

The following transactions for Tireboyz Tire, Inc., occurred during June:

Jun 4	Purchased $6,500 of merchandise on account from Westcoast Tire. Terms, 3/15, n/45, FOB shipping point. Westcoast Tire prepaid the $450 shipping cost and added the amount to the invoice.
7	Purchased $350 of supplies on account from Office Express. Terms, 2/10, n/30, FOB destination.
9	Sold $1,350 (cost, $760) of merchandise on account to P. Haskins. Terms, 2/15, n/45, FOB destination.
11	Paid $60 freight charges to deliver goods to P. Haskins.
13	Returned $1,200 of the merchandise purchased on June 4 and received a credit.
15	Sold $840 (cost, $505) of merchandise to cash customers.
16	Paid for the supplies purchased on June 7.
18	Paid Westcoast Tire the amount due from the June 4 purchase in full.
20	P. Haskins returned $650 (cost, $390) of merchandise from the June 9 sale.
22	Purchased $4,800 of inventory. Paid cash.
23	Received payment in full from P. Haskins for the June 9 sale.

Requirements

1. Journalize the transactions on the books of Tireboyz Tire, Inc.
2. What was Tireboyz Tire, Inc.'s gross profit for the month of June?

Quick solution:

2. Gross Profit for the month of June = $651

P4-40A. Prepare a multi-step income statement; calculate gross profit percentage (*Learning Objectives 6 & 7*) 20–25 min.

The adjusted trial balance for Great Gadget, Inc., as of April 30, 2014, is presented next:

		ACCOUNT	DEBIT	CREDIT
		Great Gadget, Inc.		
		Trial Balance		
		April 30, 2014		
		Cash	$ 10,100	
		Accounts Receivable	31,900	
		Inventory	20,100	
		Supplies	2,400	
		Equipment	75,000	
		Accumulated Depreciation, Equipment		$ 6,100
		Accounts Payable		6,300
		Unearned Sales Revenue		2,400
		Note Payable, Long-Term		15,000
		Common Stock		40,000
		Retained Earnings		43,700
		Dividends	41,000	
		Sales Revenue		221,600
		Sales Returns and Allowances	3,500	
		Sales Discounts	3,100	
		Cost of Goods Sold	98,900	
		Selling Expense	32,600	
		General Expense	16,100	
		Interest Expense	400	
		Total	$335,100	$335,100

Requirements

1. Prepare the multi-step income statement for April for Great Gadget, Inc.

2. Calculate the gross profit percentage for April for Great Gadget, Inc.

3. What does Great Gadget, Inc.'s gross profit percentage mean?

P4-41A. Prepare a multi-step income statement, a statement of retained earnings, and a classified balance sheet (*Learning Objective 6*) 25–30 min.

The account balances for the year ended July 31, 2014, for Wilson Industries, Inc., are listed next:

Sales Revenue	$315,000		Cost of Goods Sold	$121,700
Equipment	142,000		Accumulated Depreciation,	
Accounts Payable	12,700		Equipment	27,300
Sales Discounts	3,500		Unearned Sales Revenue	6,200
Advertising Expense	13,700		Prepaid Rent	2,850
Interest Expense	1,200		Office Salaries Expense	53,000
Salaries Payable	1,750		Accumulated Depreciation,	
Accounts Receivable	7,600		Building	39,700
Building	180,000		Utilities Expense	4,200
Sales Returns and			Dividends	12,000
Allowances	7,200		Cash	14,200
Common Stock	125,000		Retained Earnings, 7/31/2013	97,550
Depreciation Expense			Delivery Expense	1,800
(General)	18,000		Insurance Expense	4,400
Inventory	31,500		Mortgage Payable	
Commission Expense	43,000		(Long-Term)	37,500
			Supplies	850

Requirements

1. Prepare Wilson Industries, Inc.'s *multi-step* income statement.
2. Prepare Wilson Industries, Inc.'s statement of retained earnings.
3. Prepare Wilson Industries, Inc.'s classified balance sheet in *report form*.

P4-42A. Calculate earnings per share, gross profit percentage, and net income percentage (*Learning Objective 7*) 20–25 min.

Use the data for Wilson Industries, Inc., from P4-41A.

Requirements

1. Calculate the earnings per share for Wilson Industries for the year. Assume that the average number of common shares outstanding during the year was 7,500 shares.
2. The earnings per share for 2013 was $8.04. Did the earnings per share improve or deteriorate during 2014?
3. Calculate the gross profit percentage for Wilson Industries, Inc., for the year.
4. The gross profit percentage for 2013 was 58.6%. Did the gross profit percentage improve or deteriorate during 2014?
5. Calculate the net income percentage for Wilson Industries, Inc.
6. The net income percentage for 2013 was 21.3%. Did the net income percentage improve or deteriorate during 2014?

Problems (Group B)

P4-43B. Journalizing inventory purchases, returns, and freight transactions (*Learning Objectives 3 & 5*) **15–20 min.**

The following purchase-related transactions for Penestrie, Inc., occurred during the month of June.

Jun	3	Purchased $7,700 of merchandise, paid cash.
	9	Purchased $650 of supplies on account from Supplies Unlimited. Terms, n/30, FOB destination.
	16	Purchased $5,600 of merchandise on account from Brown International, Inc. Terms, 2/15, n/30, FOB shipping point.
	22	Received a credit memo in the amount of $450 from Brown International, Inc., for damaged goods from the June 16 purchase that were returned.
	30	Paid for the supplies purchased on June 9.
	30	Paid Brown International, Inc., in full for the June 16 purchase.

Requirement

1. Journalize the transactions for Penestrie, Inc. Omit explanations.

P4-44B. Journalizing inventory sales, returns, and freight transactions (*Learning Objectives 4 & 5*) **15–20 min.**

The following sale-related transactions for Budget Decor, Inc., occurred during the month of April.

Apr	3	Sold $3,200 (cost $1,400) of merchandise on account to B. Levin. Terms, 1/15, n/45, FOB destination.
	4	Paid $85 to ship the goods sold on April 3 to B. Levin.
	10	Sold $2,300 (cost $1,025) of merchandise to cash customers.
	17	Received payment in full from B. Levin for the April 3 sale.
	22	Sold $4,800 (cost $2,800) of merchandise on account to A. Klecans. Terms, 2/10, n/30, FOB shipping point.
	26	Granted A. Klecans a $900 allowance on the April 22 sale due to minor defects in the goods shipped.
	30	Received payment in full from A. Klecans for the April 22 sale.

Requirement

1. Journalize the transactions for Budget Decor, Inc. Omit explanations.

P4-45B. Journalizing inventory purchases, sales, returns, and freight transactions (*Learning Objectives 3, 4, & 5*) **20–25 min.**

The following transactions occurred between Tanaka's Antique Furniture and R. S. Furniture Warehouse during August of the current year:

Aug 4	Tanaka's Antique Furniture purchased $7,100 of merchandise from R.S. Furniture Warehouse on account. Terms, 2/15, n/30, FOB shipping point. The goods cost R.S. Furniture Warehouse $3,900.
7	Tanaka's Antique Furniture paid a $275 freight bill for delivery of the goods purchased on August 4.
10	Tanaka's Antique Furniture returned $1,300 of the merchandise purchased on August 4. The goods cost R.S. Furniture Warehouse $700.
18	Tanaka's Antique Furniture paid $1,800 of the August 4 invoice less the discount.
31	Tanaka's Antique Furniture paid the remaining amount owed on the August 4 invoice.

Requirements

1. Journalize these transactions on the books of Tanaka's Antique Furniture.

2. Journalize these transactions on the books of R. S. Furniture Warehouse.

P4-46B. Journalizing inventory purchases, sales, returns, and freight transactions; calculate gross profit (*Learning Objectives 3, 4, 5, & 6*) **25–30 min.**

The following transactions for Bestbuy Tire, Co., occurred during November:

Nov 4	Purchased $5,100 of merchandise on account from Salem Tire. Terms, 2/15, n/45, FOB shipping point. Salem Tire prepaid the $75 shipping cost and added the amount to the invoice.
7	Purchased $600 of supplies on account from Office Maxx. Terms, 3/10, n/30, FOB destination.
9	Sold $1,250 (cost, $750) of merchandise on account to T. Thompson. Terms, 1/15, n/45, FOB destination.
11	Paid $50 freight charges to deliver goods to T. Thompson.
13	Returned $700 of the merchandise purchased on November 4 and received a credit.
15	Sold $1,300 (cost, $780) of merchandise to cash customers.
16	Paid for the supplies purchased on November 7.
18	Paid Salem Tire the amount due from the November 4 purchase in full.
20	T. Thompson returned $250 (cost, $170) of merchandise from the November 9 sale.
22	Purchased $3,500 of inventory. Paid cash.
23	Received payment in full from T. Thompson for the November 9 sale.

Requirements

1. Journalize the transactions on the books of Bestbuy Tire, Co.

2. What was Bestbuy Tire's gross profit for the month of November?

P4-47B. Prepare a multi-step income statement; calculate gross profit percentage (*Learning Objectives 6 & 7*) **20–25 min.**

The adjusted trial balance Fresh Foods, Inc., as of November 30, 2014, is presented next:

	ACCOUNT	DEBIT	CREDIT
	Fresh Foods, Inc. **Trial Balance** **November 30, 2014**		
	Cash	$ 14,200	
	Accounts Receivable	16,500	
	Inventory	27,600	
	Supplies	2,800	
	Equipment	74,000	
	Accumulated Depreciation, Equipment		$ 13,800
	Accounts Payable		6,100
	Unearned Sales Revenue		4,900
	Note Payable, Long-term		35,700
	Common Stock		35,000
	Retained Earnings		28,250
	Dividends	45,000	
	Sales Revenues		214,700
	Sales Returns and Allowances	3,800	
	Sales Discounts	4,300	
	Cost of Goods Sold	102,600	
	Selling Expense	25,400	
	General Expense	20,900	
	Interest Expense	1,350	
	Total	$338,450	$338,450

Requirements

1. Prepare the multi-step income statement for November for Fresh Foods, Inc.
2. Calculate the gross profit percentage for November for Fresh Foods, Inc.
3. What does Fresh Foods, Inc.'s gross profit percentage mean?

P4-48B. Prepare a multi-step income statement, a statement of retained earnings, and a classified balance sheet (*Learning Objective 6*) 25–30 min.

The accounts for the year ended October 31, 2014, for Ramirez Industries, Inc., are listed next:

Sales Revenue	$325,800	Cost of Goods Sold	$171,600
Equipment	97,000	Accumulated Depreciation,	
Accounts Payable	17,700	Equipment	13,000
Sales Discounts	4,600	Unearned Sales Revenue	4,100
Advertising Expense	14,600	Prepaid Rent	3,500
Interest Expense	1,300	Office Salaries Expense	53,200
Salaries Payable	1,700	Accumulated Depreciation,	
Accounts Receivable	8,800	Building	41,300
Building	125,000	Utilities Expense	5,300
Sales Returns and		Dividends	10,000
Allowances	6,800	Cash	12,200
Common Stock	45,000	Retained Earnings, 10/31/2013	88,250
Depreciation Expense		Delivery Expense	1,400
(General)	13,500	Insurance Expense	10,200
Inventory	16,400	Mortgage Payable	
Commission Expense	25,700	(Long-Term)	45,000
		Supplies	750

Requirements

1. Prepare Ramirez Industries, Inc.'s *multi-step* income statement.
2. Prepare Ramirez Industries, Inc.'s statement of retained earnings.
3. Prepare Ramirez Industries, Inc.'s classified balance sheet in *report form*.

P4-49B. Calculate earnings per share, gross profit percentage, and net income percentage (*Learning Objective 7*) 20–25 min.

Use the data for Ramirez Industries, Inc., from P4-48B.

Requirements

1. Calculate the earnings per share for Ramirez Industries for the year. Assume that the average number of common shares outstanding during the year was 5,000.
2. The earnings per share for 2013 was $3.27. Did the earnings per share improve or deteriorate during 2014?
3. Calculate the gross profit percentage for Ramirez Industries for the year.
4. The gross profit percentage for 2013 was 42.6%. Did the gross profit percentage improve or deteriorate during 2014?
5. Calculate the net income percentage for Ramirez Industries for the year.
6. The net income percentage for 2013 was 4.9%. Did the net income percentage improve or deteriorate during 2014?

Continuing Exercise

Let's continue our accounting for Cole's Yard Care, Inc., from Chapter 3. Starting in May, Cole's Yard Care, Inc., has begun selling plants that it purchases from a wholesaler. During May, Cole's Yard Care, Inc., completed the following transactions:

May 2	Completed lawn service and received cash of $450.
5	Purchased 120 plants on account for inventory, $345, plus freight-in of $15. Freight-in was added to the invoice by the seller. Credit terms were n/30.
15	Sold 30 plants on account, $215 (cost $90).
17	Consulted with a client on landscaping design for a fee of $165 on account.
20	Purchased 110 plants on account for inventory, $352.
21	Paid on account, $1,900.
25	Sold 120 plants for cash, $840 (cost $366).
31	Recorded the following adjusting entries: Accrued salaries for the month of May equal $225 Depreciation on equipment $33 Lawn supplies used during May were $8 Physical count of plant inventory, 75 plants (cost $240)

Refer to the T-accounts for Cole's Yard Care, Inc., from the Continuing Exercise in Chapter 3. Use the ending balances on April 30 to set up T-accounts for the month of May.

Requirements

1. Journalize and post the May transactions to the T-accounts. Omit explanations. Compute each account balance, and denote the balance as *Bal*. Open additional accounts as necessary.

2. Prepare the May income statement of Cole's Yard Care, Inc., using the single-step format.

Continuing Problem

In this problem, we continue the accounting for Aqua Magic, Inc. from Chapter 3. On August 1, Aqua Magic, Inc., expanded its business and began selling and installing swimming pools and spas. The post-closing trial balance for Aqua Magic, Inc., as of July 31, 2014, is presented next.

Aqua Magic, Inc.
Trial Balance
July 31, 2014

ACCOUNT	DEBIT	CREDIT
Cash	$ 21,285	
Accounts Receivable	5,775	
Supplies	250	
Prepaid Rent	6,900	
Land	25,000	
Furniture	4,000	
Accumulated Depreciation, Furniture		$ 50
Equipment	1,800	
Accumulated Depreciation, Equipment		180
Vehicles	36,200	
Accumulated Depreciation, Vehicles		420
Accounts Payable		3,590
Salaries Payable		625
Unearned Service Revenue		1,200
Notes Payable (long-term)		36,200
Common Stock		55,000
Retained Earnings		3,945
Total	$101,210	$101,210

The following transactions occurred during the month of August:

Aug	2	Paid the receptionist's salary, which was accrued on July 31.
	3	Purchased $21,500 of merchandise on account from the Tranquil Spa. Terms, 3/15, n/45, FOB shipping point.
	5	Purchased $950 of supplies. Paid cash.
	6	Paid freight charges of $475 related to the August 3 purchase.
	8	Sold a spa for $6,000 (cost, $3,500) on account to J. Nelson. Terms, 1/15, n/30, FOB shipping point.
	10	Purchased office furniture for $1,800. Paid cash.
	11	Paid advertising expense, $550.
	12	Returned a defective spa, which was purchased on August 3. Received a $3,000 credit from the Tranquil Spa.
	13	Sold a spa for $7,000 (cost, $3,450) to a cash customer.
	15	Granted J. Nelson a $400 allowance because of imperfections she detected upon receiving her spa.
	16	Paid receptionist's salary, $625.
	17	Paid the Tranquil Spa the amount due from the August 3 purchase in full.
	19	Purchased $12,500 of inventory on account from Apex Pools. Terms, 2/10, n/30, FOB destination.
	21	Sold an above ground pool for $14,500 (cost, $9,250) on account to R. Jimenez. Terms, 2/10, n/30, FOB destination.
	22	Received payment in full from J. Nelson for the August 8 sale.
	24	Paid freight charges of $575 to have the pool sold to R. Jimenez on August 21 delivered.
	25	Purchased equipment on account from Sonic City, Inc., for $6,000. Terms, n/30, FOB destination.
	27	Received payment in full from R. Jimenez for the August 21 sale.
	28	Paid in full the invoice from the August 19 purchase from Apex Pools.
	30	Paid monthly utilities, $650.
	31	Paid sales commissions of $2,800 to the sales staff.

Requirements

1. Journalize the transactions that occurred in August.

2. Using the four-column accounts from the Continuing Problem in Chapter 3, post the transactions to the ledger, creating new ledger accounts as necessary; omit posting references. Calculate the new account balances.

3. Prepare the unadjusted trial balance for Aqua Magic, Inc., at August 31.

4. Journalize and post the adjusting entries for August based on the following adjustment information.
    a. Record the expired rent.
    b. Supplies on hand, $640.
    c. Depreciation; $60 equipment, $80 furniture, $475 vehicles.
    d. A physical count of inventory revealed $14,280 of inventory on hand.

5. Prepare an adjusted trial balance for Aqua Magic, Inc., at August 31.

6. Prepare the multi-step income statement and statement of retained earnings for the month ended August 31. Also, prepare a classified balance sheet at August 31.

7. Prepare and post closing entries.

8. Prepare a post-closing trial balance at August 31.

Continuing Financial Statement Analysis Problem

Let's look at Target again. Think about the business of Target.

Return to Target's 2012 annual report. For instructions on how to access the report online, see the Continuing Financial Statement Analysis Problem in Chapter 2. On page 33 of the annual report, you'll find Target's income statement for the year ending February 2, 2013 (called the Consolidated Statement of Operations). Now answer the following questions:

1. Look at Target's income statement. What are Target's sales for the past three years? Are sales increasing or decreasing compared with the previous year?

2. Look at Target's income statement. Target had 1778 stores in 2012 and 1763 stores in 2011. What are Target's sales per store in 2012 and 2011? (Divide total sales by the number of stores Target operated in each year.) Are sales per store increasing or decreasing?

3. Look at Target's income statement. What is Target's gross profit margin for the years ending January 28, 2012, and February 2, 2013? Is Target's gross profit margin increasing or decreasing?

4. Look at footnotes 2 and 3 of the financial statements (pages 38 and 39 of the financial statements found in the 2012 annual report). How is Target accounting for sales (revenue) and costs?

5. What is Target's net income percentage for the years ending January 28, 2012, and February 2, 2013? Is Target's net income percentage increasing or decreasing?

6. Looking back over your answers to questions 1 through 5, how do you think Target is performing? What do you think is causing the changes in Target's sales, costs, and margins?

Apply Your Knowledge

Ethics in Action

Case 1. Rob Peterson works as a salesperson at Consolidated Systems, Inc. In addition to a base monthly salary, Rob receives a commission that is based on the amount of sales that he makes during the month. Rob was hoping to have enough money for a down payment on a new car, but sales have been low due to a downturn in the economy. Rob was aware that Consolidated Systems, Inc., granted credit terms of 2/10, n/30 to its credit customers. In addition, Rob knew that Consolidated Systems, Inc., had a "no questions asked" return policy. Based on this knowledge, Rob had an idea. Rob contacted a regular customer and convinced the customer to make a substantial purchase of merchandise so that he could earn the commission on the sale. Rob explained to the customer that he would not have to pay for the goods for 30 days and that he could return part, or all, of the goods prior to paying for them. However, Rob asked the customer not to return any of the goods until the following month to ensure that he would earn the full commission.

Requirements

1. Do you feel Rob acted unethically? Why or why not?
2. How can Consolidated Systems, Inc., deter actions like Rob's?

Case 2. Dolly Harding owns and operates Dolly Jo's Café. Dolly has requested a credit application from LRM, Inc., a major food supplier from which she hopes to begin purchasing inventory. LRM, Inc., has requested that Dolly submit a full set of financial statements for Dolly Jo's Café with the credit application. Dolly is concerned because the most recent balance sheet for Dolly Jo's Café reflects a current ratio of 1.24. Dolly has heard that most creditors like to see a current ratio that is 1.5 or higher. In order to increase Dolly Jo's Café's current ratio, Dolly has convinced her parents to loan the business $25,000 on an 18-month long-term note payable. Dolly's parents are apprehensive about having their money "tied up" for over a year. Dolly reassured them that even though the note is an 18-month note, Dolly Jo's Café can, and probably will, repay the $25,000 sooner.

Requirements

1. Discuss the ethical issues related to the loan from Dolly's parents?
2. Why do you think creditors like to see current ratios of 1.5 or higher?

Know Your Business

Financial Analysis

Purpose: To help familiarize you with the financial reporting of a real company in order to further your understanding of the chapter material.

This case uses both the income statement (statement of operations) and the balance sheet of Columbia Sportswear in Appendix A at the end of the book.

Requirements

1. What income statement format does Columbia Sportswear use? How can you tell?
2. Calculate the gross profit percentage for Columbia Sportswear for 2010, 2011, and 2012. Has the gross profit percentage been improving or deteriorating?
3. Calculate the net income percentage for Columbia Sportswear for 2010, 2011, and 2012. Has the net income percentage improved or deteriorated?
4. Does Columbia Sportswear report a classified balance sheet? How can you tell?

Industry Analysis

Purpose: To help you understand and compare the performance of two companies in the same industry.

Find the Columbia Sportswear Company Annual Report located in Appendix A, and go to the financial statements starting on page 656. Now access the 2012 Annual Report for Under Armour, Inc., from the Internet. For instructions on how to access the report online, see the Industry Analysis in Chapter 1. The company's financial statements start on page 48.

Which of these companies would be considered to be merchandising businesses? If your answer was "both companies are merchandising businesses," you would be correct. But how did you know that? If you didn't know anything about either of these two companies (maybe you're already familiar with them through their advertising campaigns), how would you know that they are merchandising businesses? Can you tell that by looking at the consolidated balance sheets for both companies? What about the consolidated statements of income (or operations)? Which accounts on these two financial statements tell you that these companies are merchandising businesses?

Small Business Analysis

Purpose: To help you understand the importance of cash flows in the operation of a small business.

The end of the year is approaching. You're going to meet with your CPA next week to do some end-of-the-year tax planning, so in preparation for that meeting, you look at your last month's income statement. You know that you've had a pretty good year, which means that you're going to have to pay some income taxes. But you know if you can get your taxable income down, you won't have to pay as much in income taxes.

You remember that one of your suppliers was offering a pretty good discount if you purchased from the company in bulk. The only problem is you have to pay for the purchases at the time of purchase. Knowing that you want to decrease your taxable income, you call up the supplier, place a large order, and write the supplier a check.

At your meeting with the CPA, you tell her of the large inventory purchase for cash that you just made and how much income tax that will save you on this year's income tax return. The CPA has a rather troubled look on her face; that look usually means you've made some kind of an error. So you pose this question to her:

"Trish, you got that look on your face right after I told you about the big inventory purchase that I made. Even though I used up a lot of my available cash, the reason I did it was to save money on my tax return. A big purchase like that has to knock down my taxable income pretty good, huh? And besides, I got these products for a really good price, which means I'll make more profit when I sell them. So why do you have that look? Did I mess up?"

Requirement

1. If you were the CPA, how would you respond to this client? Is the large inventory purchase going to have any effect on his income statement? What about the fact that he paid for this large purchase in cash? Was it a good idea to use a large portion of available cash for a purchase like this? Keeping in mind that inventory can have a significant amount of carrying cost (storage, personnel, opportunity cost of the money, etc.), would you tell your client that he acted wisely or not?

Written Communication

You just received a letter from one of your good customers complaining about the shipment of your product that she just received. Football season is approaching, and the customer had ordered a large shipment of regulation-size footballs. Instead, she received youth-size footballs for half of the order. The customer is asking you what can be done about this mistake. Knowing that this client is located halfway across the country, it's not feasible to just have her drop by your facility and trade out the footballs.

The customer also had a question about a line item on her invoice under shipping terms. It said "FOB Destination" and the customer noticed that she was charged freight, which the customer normally doesn't have to pay. The customer wants to know if that is correct.

Requirement

1. Write a letter to your customer explaining how you intend to handle this purchase return or this purchase allowance (you choose which one you're going to do). Explain the accounting forms that will need to be prepared to document this transaction. Also address the customer's concern about the shipping terms.

Self Check Answers
1. d 2. a 3. d 4. d 5. b 6. a 7. a 8. b 9. c 10. b 11. c 12. b

5

Inventory

Business, Accounting, and You

Walk down the aisles of a Toys R Us®. Look at all the products. There are dolls, bicycles, video games, crafts, and much more. There are thousands of items of inventory. Now blink. What happened? The inventory changed. Customers are constantly buying and removing inventory from Toys R Us. Employees are constantly restocking inventory with new items.

Inventory is at the heart of operating a merchandise business. Businesses like Toys R Us purchase inventory hoping that customers will buy it at a price above the cost to the business. If this occurs, the business earns net income, if it can cover operating expenses. If this does not occur, the business incurs a net loss. Inventory is important and is at the center of creating a return by taking risks.

Now ask yourself: How does Toys R Us keep up with its inventory? Who counts the inventory? How does Toys R Us figure out the cost of all the items sold? How does Toys R Us determine the cost of the items that it owns and hopes to sell in the

future? These concerns are complicated when prices constantly change. Toys R Us must have a method to account for the quantity and cost of the thousands of items it buys, owns, and sells.

Business is about earning net income. Net income is revenues less costs. How a business accounts for the cost of the items it buys and sells is very important. As an accountant or manager, you need to understand how merchandising businesses recognize, measure, record, and report the cost of inventory. It's all about the scorecard of business and figuring out whether the merchandise business is winning or losing; that is, if the business is making a profit or loss.

Real World Accounting Video

In the Real World Accounting Video, Keith Beavers, owner and operator of ABC Wines, talks about what it means to operate a business. Look at the video. Think about what Keith is saying. Now realize how important accounting is to the success of a business.

What Inventory Costing Methods Are Allowed?

1 Describe the four different inventory costing methods

Finished goods Inventory of goods ready to sell.

Raw materials Inventory items used in the production of goods.

Work in process Inventory of partially completed goods.

As discussed in Chapter 4, merchandise inventory represents the goods that a merchandiser has available to sell to its customers. A manufacturer also has goods it holds for sale to its customers. These goods are called **finished goods** inventory. In addition, a manufacturer maintains two other types of inventory: **raw materials** inventory, which it uses to produce the goods it sells, and **work in process** inventory, which represents partially completed goods. In other words, work in process inventory represents goods that are in the process of becoming finished goods. A more detailed discussion of the inventory accounts of a manufacturer will be left to a managerial or cost accounting course. In this chapter, we focus on managing and accounting for inventory in merchandise businesses. Inventory represents a key asset for a merchandiser and is probably the business's largest current asset.

Recall from Chapter 4 that most companies utilize a perpetual inventory system. Under a perpetual system, the cost of goods purchased is added to the Inventory account in the general ledger when goods are purchased. When the goods are sold, the cost of the goods is removed from the Inventory account and added to the Cost of Goods Sold account. Most merchandisers purchase large quantities of identical items. Due to inflation and other market forces, the cost the merchandiser pays for the items often differs from one purchase to the next. This raises an important accounting dilemma. If the goods are identical, but have different costs, how does the business know which costs to remove from the Inventory account and transfer to Cost of Goods Sold when the merchandise is sold?

According to Generally Accepted Accounting Principles (GAAP), a business can assign costs using one of four different inventory costing methods. The four costing methods allowed by GAAP are:

Specific-identification Inventory costing method in which a business uses the specific cost of each unit of inventory; also called the *specific-unit-cost* method.

1. **Specific-identification** method—Assumes that the cost assigned to an inventory item when it is sold is the actual cost paid for that item. Therefore, the Cost of Goods Sold represents the actual cost of the items that were sold. Also, the Ending Inventory represents the actual cost of the goods remaining in inventory. Under

First-in, first-out (FIFO) Inventory costing method in which the first inventory costs incurred are the first costs to be assigned to cost of goods sold. FIFO leaves in ending inventory the last, most recent costs incurred.

Last-in, first-out (LIFO) Inventory costing method in which the last inventory costs incurred are the first costs to be assigned to cost of goods sold. LIFO leaves in ending inventory the first, oldest costs incurred.

Average cost Inventory costing method where, after each purchase of inventory, a new weighted average cost per unit is computed and is used to value ending inventory and cost of goods sold.

specific-identification, the cost flow of the goods through the accounting records will *exactly* match the physical flow of the goods through the business. This method is also called the **specific-unit-cost** method.

2. **First-in, first-out (FIFO)** method—Assumes that the earliest inventory costs are assigned to items as they are sold. The Cost of Goods Sold represents the oldest costs incurred to purchase inventory items. The Ending Inventory represents the most recent costs incurred to purchase inventory items. Under FIFO, the cost flow of the goods through the accounting records will closely match the physical flow of the goods through the business.

3. **Last-in, first-out (LIFO)** method—Assumes that the most recent inventory costs are assigned to items as they are sold. The Cost of Goods Sold represents the latest costs incurred to purchase inventory items. The Ending Inventory represents the earliest costs incurred to purchase inventory. Under LIFO, the cost flow of the goods through the accounting records will be nearly opposite of the physical flow of the goods through the business.

4. **Average cost** method—Assumes that a weighted-average cost per item of the entire inventory purchased is assigned to items as they are sold. Both the Cost of Goods Sold and the Ending Inventory represent an average of the cost incurred to purchase inventory items. Under the average cost method, the Cost of Goods Sold and the Ending Inventory will fall between the amounts arrived at using FIFO and LIFO assuming that costs are steadily rising or falling.

Accounting in Your World

Does this taste funny to you?

Jill was at the grocery store the other day picking up a gallon of milk when she started thinking about LIFO, which she had been learning about in her accounting class. It did not make sense to her that any company would want to use LIFO. After all, she reasoned, if the grocery store used LIFO, it would be selling milk that it just purchased first, which would leave older milk on the shelves. Jill wonders how she can be sure that the gallon of milk she took off the shelf is fresh and not one that has been on the shelf for weeks or even months.

Jill is confusing the flow of costs through the accounting records with the physical flow of inventory through a store. LIFO refers to the flow of costs through the accounting records and not to the physical flow of goods. The flow of costs through the accounting records can match, or be exactly opposite of, the physical flow of goods through a store. Jill can rest assured that even if the store uses LIFO, her milk is likely to be fresh.

Cost Flow Versus Physical Flow of Inventory

The inventory costing method (FIFO, LIFO, etc.) refers to the flow of costs through a merchandiser's accounting records rather than to the physical flow of the goods through the business. The physical flow of the goods through the business will depend on how the goods are stocked and in what order customers, or employees, remove the goods from the shelves when they are sold. The flow of the *costs* through the accounting records will depend upon which inventory costing method the business chooses.

Imagine that every inventory item that is purchased has a "yellow sticky note" attached to it with the price that was paid for the item written on the "sticky note." Next, assume that when the business receives a shipment of inventory items, the "sticky notes" reflecting the cost of the items are removed from each item and given to the Accounting Department. The Accounting Department will keep track of the "sticky notes" for each separate purchase in what is referred to as an **inventory layer**. The quantity purchased of each item along with the purchase price is tracked as an inventory layer for every separate purchase.

The physical inventory will most likely be managed in a manner that causes the oldest inventory to be sold first followed by more recent purchases and so on. The physical flow of the inventory is maintained in this manner to prevent inventory items from spoiling if they are perishable or to prevent having items that look outdated should the manufacturer choose to change the packaging. The Accounting Department calculates the cost flow of the inventory without any consideration of the actual physical flow of the merchandise (unless the specific-identification inventory method is used). The Accounting Department only needs to know *how many* units were sold, not *which* units were sold. The Accounting Department then applies the cost flow method (FIFO, LIFO, etc.) to the inventory layers that it has recorded. In other words, the inventory costs are assigned based on the layers of "sticky notes." **Exhibit 5-1** demonstrates the difference between cost flow and physical flow.

Inventory layer A record of the quantity of and the cost of inventory items made in a single purchase.

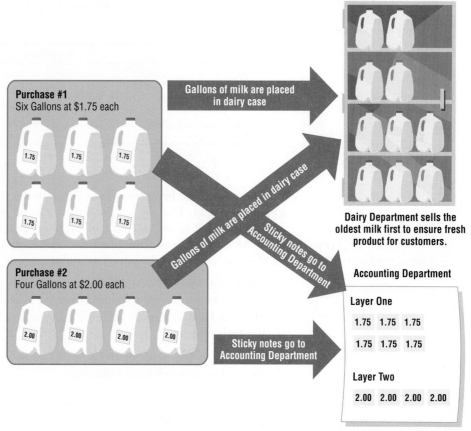

Exhibit 5-1 ▲

Stop and Think...

James Washington has decided to open a produce business named Prime Produce, Inc. Because produce spoils quickly, James wants to sell the oldest produce first so that it doesn't spoil while sitting on the shelves. Does Prime Produce, Inc., have to use FIFO as its inventory costing method?

Answer

No. Remember that the inventory costing method refers to the flow of the inventory costs through the company's accounting records, not to the physical flow of the inventory items through the business. The flow of costs through the accounting records may be the same as, closely follow, or be totally opposite of the physical flow of the inventory items through the business.

How Are the Four Inventory Costing Methods Applied?

Inventory Cost Flows

2 Compute inventory costs using first-in, first-out (FIFO), last-in, first-out (LIFO), and average cost methods and journalize inventory transactions

Recall from Chapter 4 that, in a perpetual inventory system, purchases of goods for resale increase the balance of the Inventory account, while sales of goods to customers decrease the account. The Inventory account also reflects purchase discounts, purchase returns and allowances, and shipping costs related to the purchase of goods

Inventory			
Bal	XX		
Purchases	XX	Purchase Discounts	XX
Shipping Costs	XX	Purchase Returns and Allowances	XX
		Sales	XX
Bal	XX		

Cost of goods available for sale The cost of inventory on hand at the beginning of the period plus the net cost of inventory purchased during the period.

The cost of the inventory flows through the Inventory account as items are purchased and sold. The cost of the units on hand in inventory at the beginning of the period is added to the net cost of units purchased for the period to determine the **cost of goods available for sale**. The objective of tracking the inventory cost is to allocate the cost of the goods available for sale between the following:

- Units sold, which is recorded as Cost of Goods Sold and is subtracted from net sales revenue on the income statement to arrive at gross profit
- Units on hand, or unsold, which is reflected as Ending Inventory, a current asset on the balance sheet

Let's follow the September inventory activity for ski parkas sold by Northwest Outfitters, Inc., assuming the following:

Sep	1	One parka costing $40 is on hand, unsold from the previous month.
	5	Purchased six parkas for $45 each.
	15	Sold four parkas for $80 each.
	26	Purchased seven parkas for $50 each.
	30	Sold eight parkas for $80 each.
	30	Two parkas are on hand, unsold.

During September, Northwest Outfitters had 14 parkas available for sale: 1 unit on hand in beginning inventory, plus 13 units purchased during the month. The cost of goods available for sale for Northwest Outfitters would be calculated as follows:

Beginning Inventory	(1 @ $40)	= $ 40
+ Purchases	(6 @ $45)= $270	
	(7 @ $50)= 350	620
= Cost of Goods Available for Sale		$660

Of the 14 parkas available for sale, Northwest sold 12 parkas and still had 2 parkas on hand in ending inventory at the end of the month. What would be the cost of the goods sold for the month and the ending inventory balance for that month? The answer depends on which inventory costing method Northwest Outfitters elects to use. **Exhibit 5-2** illustrates the objective of calculating inventory costs for Northwest Outfitters.

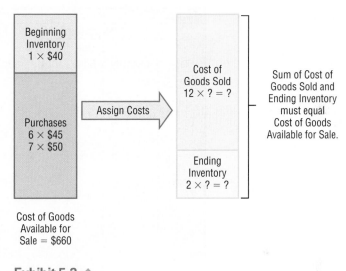

Exhibit 5-2 ▲

As we shall see, the various inventory costing methods produce different values for ending inventory and cost of goods sold.

Specific-Identification Method

The specific-identification method is also called the specific-unit-cost method. This method values inventory according to the specific cost of each item of inventory. This method is used predominately by businesses that sell unique items with very different costs. Some examples are businesses that sell automobiles, houses, and artwork. For instance, an automobile dealer may have two vehicles on its car lot, a "basic" model that costs $22,000 and a "fully equipped" model that costs $29,000. Accordingly, the sales price of the basic model would be less than the sales price for the fully equipped model. It would not make sense for the dealer to assign the cost of the fully equipped model to the basic model when the basic model is sold. This would cause gross profit to be inaccurately stated because the higher cost of the fully equipped model would be subtracted from the lower selling price of the basic model. The dealer would want to specifically identify which model it sold and assign the actual cost of that model to the cost of goods sold. In order to utilize the specific-identification method, each inventory item must be able to be distinguished from other items with some identifying mark such as a serial number. Because the specific-identification method of inventory valuation is not widely used, we will focus on the more popular inventory costing methods. Let's see how to compute inventory amounts using the FIFO, LIFO, and average cost methods for Northwest Outfitters.

First-In, First-Out (FIFO) Method

Assume that Northwest Outfitters uses the FIFO method to account for its inventory. Under FIFO, the first inventory costs incurred by Northwest each period are the first costs to be assigned to cost of goods sold. *Simply put, FIFO assumes that the first inventory items Northwest purchased are the first inventory items it sold.* In order to track inventory costs efficiently, a **perpetual inventory record** is often utilized. The perpetual inventory record maintains the detail supporting the quantity of, and costs assigned to, the inventory items as they are purchased and sold. It also maintains a running balance of the inventory on hand. When preparing the perpetual inventory record, it is critical that the inventory "layers" are kept in the proper order. An inventory layer consists of the quantity of inventory and its purchase cost. **Exhibit 5-3** illustrates the FIFO perpetual inventory record for Northwest Outfitters, while **Exhibit 5-4** illustrates the flow of costs using FIFO.

Perpetual inventory record A record that tracks the quantity of, and cost assigned to, inventory items as they are purchased and sold.

Parkas									
	Purchases			**Cost of Goods Sold**			**Inventory on Hand**		
Date	**Quantity**	**Unit Cost**	**Total Cost**	**Quantity**	**Unit Cost**	**Total Cost**	**Quantity**	**Unit Cost**	**Total Cost**
Sep 1							1	$40	$ 40
5	6	$45	$270				1	$40	$ 40
							6	$45	$270
15				1	$40	$ 40			
				3	$45	$135	3	$45	$135
26	7	$50	$350				3	$45	$135
							7	$50	$350
30				3	$45	$135			
				5	$50	$250	2	$50	$100
30	**13**		**$620**	**12**		**$560**	**2**		**$100**

Exhibit 5-3 ▲

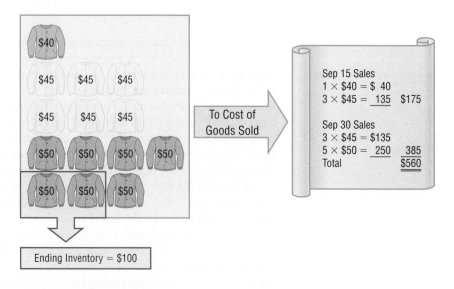

Exhibit 5-4 ▲

Northwest began September with one parka that cost $40. After the September 5 purchase, the inventory on hand consists of seven units: one at $40 plus six at $45. On September 15, Northwest sold four units. Under FIFO, the cost of the first unit sold is the oldest cost, $40 per unit. The next three units sold come from the layer that cost $45 per unit. That leaves three units in inventory on hand, and these units cost $45 each. The remainder of the perpetual inventory record is completed in the same manner.

The FIFO monthly summary on September 30 is as follows:

- Cost of Goods Sold: 12 units that cost a total of $560
- Ending Inventory: 2 units that cost a total of $100

Look for these amounts in the last row of the perpetual inventory record in Exhibit 5-3 as well as in Exhibit 5-4. If Northwest uses the FIFO method, it will use these amounts for the cost of goods sold and ending inventory in its financial statements. Notice that the sum of the cost of goods sold plus ending inventory equals the cost of goods available for sale, $660 ($560 + $100).

Last-In, First-Out (LIFO) Method

Now, imagine that Northwest uses the LIFO method instead of FIFO. Under the LIFO method, the last, most recent costs incurred are the first costs assigned to the cost of goods sold. *Accordingly, LIFO assumes that the last inventory items purchased are the first inventory items sold.* The ending inventory's cost comes from the oldest, earliest purchases of the inventory. Remember, LIFO costing does not follow the actual physical flow of goods for most companies. LIFO is simply a method of *assigning* costs to the physical units that were sold. The LIFO method perpetual inventory record for Northwest Outfitters is presented in **Exhibit 5-5**. **Exhibit 5-6** illustrates the assignment of costs using LIFO.

Parkas									
	Purchases			Cost of Goods Sold			Inventory on Hand		
Date	Quantity	Unit Cost	Total Cost	Quantity	Unit Cost	Total Cost	Quantity	Unit Cost	Total Cost
Sep 1							1	$40	$ 40
5	6	$45	$270				1	$40	$ 40
							6	$45	$270
15				4	$45	$180	1	$40	$ 40
							2	$45	$ 90
26	7	$50	$350				1	$40	$ 40
							2	$45	$ 90
							7	$50	$350
30				7	$50	$350			
				1	$45	$ 45	1	$40	$ 40
							1	$45	$ 45
30	**13**		**$620**	**12**		**$575**	**2**		**$ 85**

Exhibit 5-5 ▲

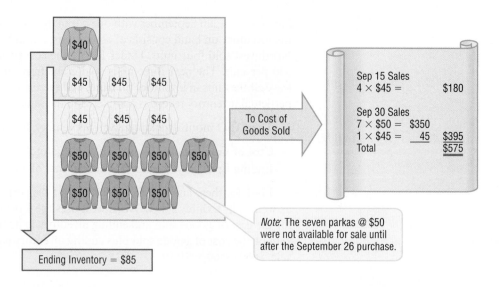

Exhibit 5-6 ▲

Again, Northwest had one parka at the beginning of September. After the purchase on September 5, Northwest holds seven units of inventory: one at $40 plus six at $45. Northwest then sells four units on September 15. Under LIFO, the cost of goods sold always comes from the latest purchase. That leaves three parkas in inventory on September 15: one at $40 plus two at $45. The purchase of seven units on September 26 adds a new $50 layer to inventory. Then the sale of eight units on September 30 removes units from inventory in LIFO order.

The LIFO monthly summary on September 30 is as follows:

- Cost of Goods Sold: 12 units that cost a total of $575
- Ending Inventory: 2 units that cost a total of $85

These amounts can be seen in the last row of the perpetual inventory record in Exhibit 5-5 as well as in Exhibit 5-6. If Northwest uses the LIFO method, it will use these amounts for the cost of goods sold and ending inventory in its financial statements. Notice that the sum of cost of goods sold and ending inventory still equals the cost of goods available for sale, $660 ($575 + $85).

Average Cost Method

Suppose Northwest Outfitters uses the average cost method to account for its inventory of parkas. *With this method, the business computes a new, weighted-average cost per unit after each purchase* based on the number of items purchased at each price. Ending inventory and cost of goods sold are then based on the average cost per unit. **Exhibit 5-7** shows a perpetual inventory record for the average cost method. We round average unit cost to the nearest cent and total cost to the nearest dollar.

Parkas									
	Purchases			**Cost of Goods Sold**			**Inventory on Hand**		
Date	**Quantity**	**Unit Cost**	**Total Cost**	**Quantity**	**Unit Cost**	**Total Cost**	**Quantity**	**Unit Cost**	**Total Cost**
Sep 1							1	$40.00	$ 40
5	6	$45	$270				7	$44.29	$310
15				4	$44.29	$177	3	$44.29	$133
26	7	$50	$350				10	$48.30	$483
30				8	$48.30	$386	2	$48.30	$ 97
30	**13**		**$620**	**12**		**$563**	**2**		**$ 97**

Exhibit 5-7 ▲

The average unit cost on September 5 is based on the cost of the unit on hand at the beginning of September plus the cost of the six units purchased on September 5:

		Number of Units	**Unit Cost**	**Total Cost**
Sep 1	Beginning Inventory	1	$40	$ 40
5	Purchase	6	$45	$270
Total		7		$310

Total Cost of Inventory on Hand ÷ Number of Units on Hand = Average Cost per Unit		
$310	7 Units	$44.29

The four items sold on September 15 are assigned a cost of $44.29 per unit, and the remaining three units are carried forward at a cost of $44.29 each. Northwest then computes a new average cost after the September 26 purchase in the same manner.

The average cost monthly summary on September 30 is as follows:

- Cost of Goods Sold: 12 units that cost a total of $563
- Ending Inventory: 2 units that cost a total of $97

Once again, these amounts can be seen in the last row of the perpetual inventory record presented in Exhibit 5-7. If Northwest uses the average cost method, it will use these amounts to prepare its financial statements. Yet again, the sum of the cost of goods sold and ending inventory equals the cost of goods available for sale, $660 ($563 + $97).

Journalizing Inventory Transactions

The journal entries to record the inventory transactions for Northwest Outfitters for the month of September are presented in **Exhibit 5-8** using the following information:

- All purchases and sales in September were made on account.
- The sales price of a parka charged to a customer was $80.

			FIFO		LIFO		AVERAGE COST	
	DATE	ACCOUNTS	DR.	CR.	DR.	CR.	DR.	CR.
Purchase inventory on account (six parkas @ $45 each)	Sep 5	Inventory	270		270		270	
		Accounts Payable		270		270		270
Sold four parkas for $80 each	15	Accounts Receivable	320		320		320	
		Sales Revenue		320		320		320
		Cost of Goods Sold	175		180		177	
		Inventory		175		180		177
Purchased inventory on account (seven parkas @ $50 each)	26	Inventory	350		350		350	
		Accounts Payable		350		350		350
Sold eight parkas for $80 each	30	Accounts Receivable	640		640		640	
		Sales Revenue		640		640		640
		Cost of Goods Sold	385		395		386	
		Inventory		385		395		386

Exhibit 5-8 ▲

Notice that the journal entries to record the purchases of inventory on account are the same, regardless of the costing method chosen. *The differences occur in the second part of the sales entries that removes the cost of the parkas sold from the inventory account and transfers it to cost of goods sold.*

What Effect Do the Different Costing Methods Have on Net Income?

3 **Compare the effects of the different costing methods on the financial statements**

The choice of inventory costing method often has an effect on the amount of net income a company reports on its income statement.

Exhibit 5-9 compares the FIFO, LIFO, and average cost methods of costing inventory assuming that, over time, inventory costs are *increasing*. As you can see, different

Inventory Costing Method	Description	Benefit
First-In, First-Out (FIFO)	Cost of goods sold has older, lower costs. Ending inventory has the newer, higher costs.	Most closely matches actual flow of goods in most cases. Maximizes net income. Use method to attract investors or borrow money.
Last-In, First-Out (LIFO)	Cost of goods sold has newer, higher costs. Ending inventory has the older, lower costs.	Minimizes net income and income taxes and minimizes ending inventory. Use method to reduce income taxes and cash needed to pay taxes.
Average Cost	Averages costs in ending inventory and cost of goods sold.	A "middle-ground solution" for reporting net income and ending inventory and paying income taxes.

Exhibit 5-9 ▲

methods have different benefits. FIFO is the most popular inventory costing method, followed by LIFO, and then by average cost.

Exhibit 5-10 summarizes the results of the three inventory methods as used for Northwest Outfitters. It shows Sales Revenue, Cost of Goods Sold, and Gross Profit for FIFO, LIFO, and average cost. The Cost of Goods Sold data comes from Exhibits 5-3, 5-5, and 5-7.

	FIFO	LIFO	Average Cost
Sales Revenue [(4 + 8) × $80]	$960	$960	$960
Cost of Goods Sold	560	575	563
Gross Profit	$400	$385	$397

Exhibit 5-10 ▲

Exhibit 5-10 shows that FIFO produces the lowest cost of goods sold and the highest gross profit. Net income is also the highest under FIFO when inventory costs are rising. Many companies choose this method when they want to report high income in order to attract investors and borrow on attractive terms.

LIFO results in the highest cost of goods sold and, therefore, the lowest gross profit when inventory costs are increasing. Lower gross profit results in lower net income and lower income taxes. A drawback to using LIFO when inventory costs are rising is that the company reports lower net income.

The average cost method generates gross profit, net income, and income tax amounts that fall between the extremes of FIFO and LIFO. Therefore, companies that seek a "middle-ground" solution choose the average cost method for valuing inventory.

Consistency principle
Accounting principle that states that a business should use the same accounting methods and procedures from period to period.

Based upon the previous information, it appears that a business could "manage its income" by switching back and forth between costing methods depending upon the circumstances. This is not the case due to the **consistency principle** mandated by GAAP. The consistency principle states that businesses should use the same accounting methods and procedures from period to period. The consistency principle does not mean that a company can never change its accounting methods, for instance changing from the LIFO to FIFO inventory valuation method, but that it can only do so if it can justify the change. Also, any changes in accounting methods must be disclosed to the financial statement users.

Suppose you are analyzing a company's net income pattern over a two-year period and costs are rising. If the company switched from LIFO to FIFO during that time, its net income likely increased significantly. The problem is that much, if not all, of the increase in income could be the result of the change in inventory method. If you were unaware of the change, you might believe that the company's income increased because of improved operations. Therefore, companies must report any changes in the accounting methods they use and they generally must retrospectively apply the impact of the change as an adjustment to beginning retained earnings, unless it is impractical to do so. Consistency helps investors compare a company's financial statements from one period to the next and make better decisions.

Try It...

Anderson's Outdoor Equipment, Inc., has recently opened for business. The owners are trying to determine which inventory costing method to choose. They would like to pay the least amount of income taxes possible. Which inventory method will allow Anderson's Outdoor Equipment, Inc., to pay the least amount of taxes?

Answer

It depends on whether the cost of inventory is expected to increase or decrease during the period. If inventory costs are expected to increase, Anderson's Outdoor Equipment, Inc., should choose LIFO. However, if inventory costs are expected to decrease, Anderson's Outdoor Equipment, Inc., should choose FIFO. If inventory costs are expected to remain constant, the choice of inventory costing method will have no effect on the net income for the period.

Decision Guidelines

Decision	Guideline	Analyze
Which inventory costing method should a company choose?	The physical and cost flow of the inventory can differ. The choice of inventory method depends on the type of inventory being sold, whether inventory costs are rising or declining, and whether you want to report higher or lower net income.	A company should choose: Specific-identification method when it sells unique items with varying costs.
		FIFO if inventory costs are rising and the company wants to report higher net income.
		FIFO if inventory costs are declining and the company wants to report the lowest net income.
		LIFO if inventory costs are rising and the company wants to report the lowest net income.
		LIFO if inventory costs are declining and the company wants to report the highest net income.
		Average cost method if costs are continually fluctuating and the company wants to stabilize net income.

What Else Determines How Inventory Is Valued?

 4 **Value inventory using the lower-of-cost-or-market (LCM) rule**

Conservatism Accounting principle that states that a business must report all items in the financial statements at amounts that lead to the most cautious immediate results.

Another important accounting principle is the principle of **conservatism**. Conservatism in accounting means reporting items in the financial statements at amounts that lead to the most cautious immediate results. A conservative approach will mean that, when there are two reasonable options present, the option should be chosen that causes assets and income to be understated, rather than overstated. A conservative approach will also mean that liabilities and expenses are overstated, rather than understated. The goal is for financial statements to report figures that minimize the risk of overstating the company's assets and understating liabilities.

Lower-of-cost-or-market (LCM) rule The rule that a business must report inventory in the financial statements at whichever is lower, the historical cost or the market value, of each inventory item.

Merchandisers are often faced with a situation where the cost of replacing an inventory item is lower than what was originally paid for the item. In order to take a conservative approach when these situations arise, businesses will apply the **lower-of-cost-or-market (LCM) rule**. The LCM rule requires businesses to report inventory in the financial statements at whichever is lower, the amount originally paid (the historical cost) or the replacement cost (the current market value) of each inventory item. If the replacement cost of inventory is less than its historical cost, a company writes down the inventory value by decreasing inventory and increasing cost of goods sold. In this way, net income is decreased in the period in which the decrease in the market value of the inventory occurred.

Let's look at the process of valuing inventory according to the lower-of-cost-or-market rule for the inventory in **Exhibit 5-11**.

- Prepare a table listing each inventory item, its quantity, unit cost, and unit market value.
- Calculate the total cost and total market value for each item. Inventory Item 122A, for example, has a total cost of $2,000 (40 units × $50 cost per unit) and a total market value of $2,080 (40 units × $52 market value per unit).
- Place the lower of the cost or market value for each item in the "Lower of Cost or Market" column. Item 122A would have a value of $2,000.
- Add the amounts in each column to obtain the total cost, total market value, and total lower-of-cost-or-market amounts.
- Adjust the inventory balance to reflect the lower-of-cost-or-market amount. The total cost is $14,800 and the total LCM amount is $14,425, so a journal entry is made to reduce the inventory amount by the difference of $375 ($14,800 – $14,425).

Inventory Item	Inventory Quantity	Unit Cost	Unit Market Value	Total Cost	Total Market	Lower of Cost or Market
122A	40	$ 50	$ 52	$ 2,000	$ 2,080	$ 2,000
1587L	75	$ 80	$ 75	6,000	5,625	5,625
394CZ	68	$100	$101	6,800	6,868	6,800
				$14,800	$14,573	$14,425

Exhibit 5-11 ▲

The application of LCM is actually more complex than is demonstrated in Exhibit 5-11; however, more in-depth coverage will be left to a more advanced accounting course. The LCM rule may be applied to inventory on an item-by-item basis as in Exhibit 5-11, to broad categories of items, or to the entire inventory taken as a whole. Application of the LCM rule is a continuation of the process of valuing inventory. Businesses will record inventory transactions, assigning a cost to each inventory item sold using the specific-identification, FIFO, LIFO, or average cost method. Then, at the end of the accounting period, they will apply the LCM rule to the ending inventory. In this way, businesses report conservative values for inventory and net income.

Materiality Accounting principle that states that a company must perform strictly proper accounting *only* for items that are significant for the business's financial statements. Information is significant, or material, when its presentation in the financial statements would cause someone to change a decision.

Most businesses will report inventory on the balance sheet at the lower-of-cost-or-market value; however, others will use the concept of **materiality** to decide whether inventory needs to be written down to its current replacement cost. The materiality concept states that a company must perform strictly proper accounting *only* for items that have a material effect on the company's financial statements. An item is considered to have a material *effect* when it would cause someone to change a decision; stated differently, a material amount is one large enough to make a difference to a user of the financial statements. For example, if the lower-of-cost-or-market comparison in Exhibit 5-11 resulted in a difference between total cost and total LCM of $3, the company would have been appropriate in ignoring any adjustment to inventory for the $3. So, the materiality concept frees accountants from having to report every account in strict accordance with GAAP, while still reporting items properly.

How Is Inventory Reported on the Balance Sheet?

 Illustrate the reporting of inventory in the financial statements

Full-disclosure principle
Accounting principle that states that a company's financial statements should report enough information for users to make knowledgeable decisions about the company.

Footnotes Disclosures that accompany the financial statements.

Inventory is reported as a current asset and is often listed after receivables on the balance sheet. In addition to showing the inventory amount, a business must disclose the costing method used to value inventory (specific-identification, FIFO, LIFO, or average cost) and the application of LCM. This disclosure helps a business adhere to the **full-disclosure principle**. The full-disclosure principle requires that a company's financial statements report enough information for outsiders to make knowledgeable decisions about the company. To provide this information, accountants typically include a set of **footnotes** that accompany the financial statements. Footnote disclosures help ensure that companies report relevant, reliable, and comparable financial information. A common footnote related to inventory would look like this:

> NOTE 2: Statement of Significant Accounting Policies:
> *Inventory*. Inventory is carried at the *lower of cost or market*. Cost is determined using the first-in, first-out method.

Suppose a banker is comparing two companies, one using LIFO and the other FIFO. When inventory costs are rising, the company using the FIFO inventory costing method reports higher net income, but only because it uses FIFO. Without knowledge of the accounting methods the companies are using, the banker could lend money to the wrong business or lend the wrong amount of money to each.

Inventory Shrinkage

Inventory shrinkage The loss of inventory.

The perpetual inventory method keeps a continuous record of the inventory on hand at all times. However, the actual amount of inventory on hand may differ from the amount on hand according to the accounting records due to errors in recording inventory-related transactions or due to **inventory shrinkage**. Inventory shrinkage represents a loss of inventory. Inventory shrinkage is most often the result of employee theft, customer theft, and the damage, spillage, or spoilage of inventory items.

A physical inventory count is used to determine the amount of inventory actually on hand at the end of the accounting period. A number of commonly used procedures help ensure the accuracy of the count. A count usually occurs when the store is closed. Individuals assigned to the count can use maps of inventory locations, pre-numbered count sheets, and ink pens and may count in pairs. The count may also involve pre-written inventory instructions and tags to identify merchandise to be counted and is typically supervised. To save time and increase objectivity for the count, an outside inventory-taking firm may be used to take counts instead of, or in addition to, employees. If the entity has its financial statements audited, a representative of the audit firm will usually be present at the count to take test counts and determine whether inventory instructions are being adequately followed. This allows the auditor to evaluate whether inventory and cost of goods sold are fairly presented in the statements.

The inventory value derived from the physical inventory count is used as the inventory account balance on the balance sheet. The accounting records are adjusted for any difference between the inventory value determined by the count and the value according to the perpetual records. The Inventory account is debited or credited as necessary with a corresponding credit or debit to the Cost of Goods Sold account.

How Do Inventory Errors Affect the Financial Statements?

6 **Determine the effect of inventory errors on the financial statements**

A correct count of the inventory items on hand is necessary to ensure the accurate reporting of the inventory's value. However, errors in the inventory count can and do occur, such as:

- Counting inventory inaccurately.
- Double counting inventory; for example, counting it in one location and then moving it to another location where it is counted again.
- Not counting one section of the storeroom or excluding incoming goods shipped FOB shipping point.
- Failure to recognize obsolete or damaged goods, resulting in failure to write down their value accordingly.

What is the impact of a counting error? Remember that in a perpetual inventory system, the inventory account balance is adjusted to reflect the value arrived at by the physical count. A wrong count, a count that disagrees with the accounting records of inventory, will result in making a journal entry that causes both the Inventory balance and the Cost of Goods Sold to be incorrect.

To demonstrate, let's look at the income statements for a company for two consecutive years. In order to keep the example simple, we will assume that the company has a $20,000 balance in both beginning inventory and ending inventory for the first year. We will also assume that it has a $20,000 balance in ending inventory in the second year (remember that the beginning balance in the inventory account in year 2 is the ending inventory balance from year 1). In addition, assume that the company made purchases of $75,000 and that it had sales of $160,000 and operating expenses of $40,000 in both years. In other words, the activity for both years is exactly the same. **Exhibit 5-12**, Panel A, illustrates the income statements for both years assuming that inventory was properly counted.

Panel A—Ending Inventory correctly stated		Year 1		Year 2
Sales Revenue		$160,000		$160,000
Cost of Goods Sold:				
Beginning Inventory	$20,000	→ $ 20,000		
Purchases	75,000	75,000		
Cost of Goods Available for Sale	95,000	95,000		
Ending Inventory	20,000	20,000		
Cost of Goods Sold		75,000		75,000
Gross Profit		85,000		85,000
Operating Expenses		40,000		40,000
Net Income		$45,000		$45,000

Panel B—Ending Inventory overstated by $5,000		Year 1		Year 2
Sales Revenue		$160,000		$160,000
Cost of Goods Sold:				
Beginning Inventory	$20,000	→ $ 25,000		
Purchases	75,000	75,000		
Cost of Goods Available for Sale	95,000	100,000		
Ending Inventory	25,000	20,000		
Cost of Goods Sold		70,000		80,000
Gross Profit		90,000		80,000
Operating Expenses		40,000		40,000
Net Income		$ 50,000		$ 40,000

Exhibit 5-12 ▲

Now, let's assume that the ending inventory in year 1 was incorrectly valued at $25,000 (instead of the correct amount of $20,000) due to an error in the physical count. Exhibit 5-12, Panel B, illustrates the income statements for both years assuming that ending inventory in year 1 was overstated by $5,000.

A comparison of the statements in Panel A and Panel B of Exhibit 5-12 reveals the following for year 1:

- Cost of Goods Sold is understated by $5,000.
- Gross Profit is overstated by $5,000.
- Net Income is overstated by $5,000.
- Retained Earnings will be overstated because Net Income is closed into Retained Earnings.

Recall from Chapter 3 that Inventory, as an asset, is a permanent account that carries its balance over to the next period. So, one period's ending inventory becomes the next period's beginning inventory. Thus, the error in ending inventory in year 1 carries over as an error in the beginning inventory in year 2. A comparison of the statements in Panel A and Panel B of Exhibit 5-12 reveals the following for year 2:

- Cost of Goods Available for Sale is overstated by $5,000.
- Cost of Goods Sold is overstated by $5,000.
- Gross Profit is understated by $5,000.
- Net Income is understated by $5,000.
- Retained Earnings will now be correctly stated because the understatement in Net Income in year 2 will offset the overstatement from year 1 when the Net Income from year 2 is closed into Retained Earnings.

As you can see, the error cancels out after two periods. The total net income, $90,000, from Panel B for the two periods combined when there is an error is the same as it is in Panel A for the two periods when there are no errors. The effects of inventory errors are summarized in **Exhibit 5-13**.

	Period 1		Period 2	
Inventory Error	**Cost of Goods Sold**	**Gross Profit and Net Income**	**Cost of Goods Sold**	**Gross Profit and Net Income**
Period 1 Ending Inventory *Overstated*	Understated	Overstated	Overstated	Understated
Period 1 Ending Inventory *Understated*	Overstated	Understated	Understated	Overstated

Exhibit 5-13 ▲

Is It Possible to Estimate the Value of Inventory If the Inventory Is Accidentally Destroyed?

7 Use the gross profit method to estimate ending inventory

Often a business must estimate the value of its inventory. Suppose the company suffers a fire loss. To collect insurance, it must estimate the cost of the inventory destroyed, that is, it must estimate the ending inventory.

Gross profit method A way to estimate ending inventory by using the gross profit percentage.

The **gross profit method** estimates ending inventory by using the format for the Cost of Goods Sold:

> Beginning Inventory
> + Purchases (Net of Discounts and Returns and Allowances, Plus Shipping Costs)
> = Cost of Goods Available for Sale
> − Ending Inventory
> = Cost of Goods Sold

Rearranging ending inventory and cost of goods sold helps to estimate ending inventory. Let's look at an example. We can estimate ending inventory through the following steps and amounts, as shown in **Exhibits 5-14** and **5-15**:

Step 1 Calculate the cost of goods available for sale. Add the beginning balance of inventory and the net cost of purchases for the accounting period ($14,000 + $66,000 = $80,000).

Step 2 Estimate the cost of goods sold. Do you remember calculating the gross profit percentage in Chapter 4? The historical gross profit percentage of a business can be used to estimate the current period's gross profit. Calculate the estimated gross profit by multiplying the net sales revenue by the historical gross profit percentage ($100,000 × 40% = $40,000). Subtract the estimated gross profit from the net sales revenue to get the estimated cost of goods sold ($100,000 − $40,000 = $60,000).

Step 3 Estimate the ending inventory. Subtract estimated cost of goods sold from the cost of goods available for sale ($80,000 − $60,000 = $20,000).

Step 1	Beginning Inventory		$ 14,000
	+ Purchases (net)		66,000
	= Cost of Goods Available for Sale		80,000
Step 2	Estimated Cost of Goods Sold:		
	Net Sales Revenue	$100,000	
	− Estimated Gross Profit of 40% ($100,000 × 40%)	(40,000)	
	= Estimated Cost of Goods Sold		(60,000)
Step 3	Estimated Ending Inventory		$ 20,000

Exhibit 5-14 ▲

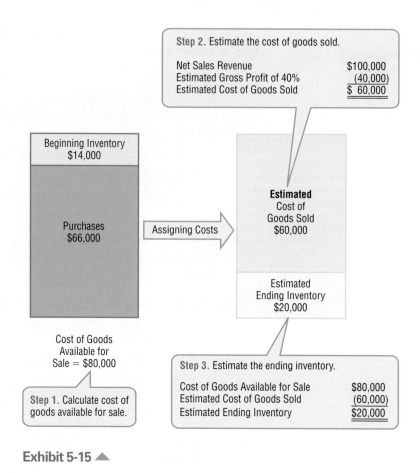

Step 2. Estimate the cost of goods sold.

Net Sales Revenue	$100,000
Estimated Gross Profit of 40%	(40,000)
Estimated Cost of Goods Sold	$ 60,000

Beginning Inventory
$14,000

Purchases
$66,000

Assigning Costs

Estimated
Cost of
Goods Sold
$60,000

Estimated
Ending Inventory
$20,000

Cost of Goods
Available for
Sale = $80,000

Step 1. Calculate cost of goods available for sale.

Step 3. Estimate the ending inventory.

Cost of Goods Available for Sale	$80,000
Estimated Cost of Goods Sold	(60,000)
Estimated Ending Inventory	$20,000

Exhibit 5-15 ▲

Focus On Decision Making

"How Much Inventory Does a Business Need?"

What do you think about when you think of a merchandise business like Toys R Us? Most likely, it's the things you buy; in other words, inventory. Inventory is the most important asset in a merchandise business. But how much inventory does a business need? A business does not want too little or too much inventory. If it has too little, the business will lose sales and profit. But having too much inventory is also a problem. Inventory is expensive to maintain. It takes up space and it ties up money. Remember that the money used to finance assets (liabilities or shareholders' equity) comes at a cost. Likewise, inventory may become obsolete and lose value. The bottom line is merchandise businesses want enough inventory to meet future sales, but not too much inventory that it incurs excessive costs to maintain it.

The Rate of Inventory Turnover and Days-Sales-in-Inventory

So how do managers determine the right amount of inventory? Often they look at inventory turnover and days-sales-in-inventory. **Inventory turnover** is the ratio of cost of goods sold to the average inventory. Inventory turnover tells the manager how many times in a year the average inventory sold. Inventory turnover is computed as:

8 **Compute the inventory turnover and days-sales-in-inventory**

Inventory turnover The ratio of cost of goods sold to average inventory.

$$\text{Inventory Turnover} = \frac{\text{Cost of Goods Sold}}{\text{Average Inventory}} = \frac{\text{Cost of Goods Sold}}{(\text{Beginning Inventory} + \text{Ending Inventory})/2}$$

Inventory turnover is usually computed for an annual period, so the cost of goods sold figure is the amount for the entire year. Average inventory is computed by adding the beginning inventory balance to the ending inventory balance and dividing the total by two. Remember that balance sheet accounts, such as Inventory, carry their balances from one period to the next. The ending inventory for one year becomes the beginning inventory for the next year.

Days-sales-in-inventory looks at the same issue with a slightly different measure. **Days-sales-in-inventory** measures how much inventory a business sells in a day and compares that amount with how much inventory a business owned on average during the year. Days-sales-in-inventory is computed as:

Days-sales-in-inventory The average number of days that it took to sell the average inventory held during the year.

$$\text{Days-Sales-In-Inventory} = \text{Average Inventory/ (Cost of Goods Sold/365 Days)}$$

To demonstrate inventory turnover and days-sales-in-inventory, we will use the financial statements for Cellular Connect, Inc., from Exhibit 4-6 in Chapter 4. Cellular Connect's rate of inventory turnover is calculated:

$$\text{Inventory Turnover} = \frac{90,300}{(13,900^* + 15,700)/2} = 6.10 \text{ Times Per Year (rounded)}$$

*The $13,900 beginning inventory balance is the ending inventory balance for the prior period and is not shown in Exhibit 4-6.

Cellular Connect's days-sales-in-inventory is calculated as:

$$\text{Days-Sales-in-Inventory} = \frac{(13,900 + 15,700)/2}{(90,300/365)} = 60 \text{ days (rounded)}$$

Cellular Connect's inventory turnover shows that it is selling its merchandise inventory a little more than six times a year. Cellular Connect's days-sales-in-inventory shows it had enough inventory, during 2014, for 60 days of sales. Cellular Connect could operate for 60 days without buying any more inventory.

A high turnover rate and low days-sales-in-inventory is desirable because it indicates that the inventory is turning over, or being sold, quickly. An increase in the turnover rate usually means increasing profits will result from increasing sales.

Regardless of the turnover rate, merchandisers need to keep sufficient levels of inventory on hand to meet sales demand. However, they also need to avoid purchasing too much inventory. Inventory management is about meeting customer demand with the least amount of inventory.

How They Do It: A Look at Business

Go back to Chapter 4 and look at *Focus on Decision Making*. Remember how some businesses have small net income percentages and some businesses have large net income percentages? If a business has a small net income percentage, it needs to sell a lot of items to earn a large net income. To do this, the business must have a high inventory turnover and low days-sales-in-inventory. If a business has a large net income percentage, it does not need to sell a lot of items to earn a large net income. It can have a low inventory turnover and a high days-sales-in-inventory.

Now once again think about Toys R Us and Tiffany & Co. In Chapter 4, we saw that Toys R Us had a low net income percentage and Tiffany had a high net income percentage. However, both businesses earned net income. How did they do it? For the year ending February 2, 2013, Toys R Us had an inventory turnover of 3.85 times a year and an average of 95 days-sales-in-inventory. For the year ending January 31, 2013, Tiffany had an inventory turnover of only 0.76 times a year and an average of 482 days-sales-in-inventory.

Toys R Us, compared with Tiffany, operates with a lower net income percentage but a higher inventory turnover. Toys R Us makes a little profit on each sale, but has a lot of sales. Tiffany, compared with Toys R Us, operates with a higher net income percentage and a lower inventory turnover. Tiffany has few sales, but makes a lot of profit on each sale. Although they operate differently, both Toys R Us and Tiffany are successful businesses.

Summary

MyAccountingLab

Here is what you should know after reading this chapter. MyAccountingLab will help you identify what you know and where to go when you need practice.

Key Points	Key Accounting Terms
Inventory costing methods:	**Average cost** (p. 210)
• Determine the flow of costs through the accounting records.	**Cost of goods available for sale** (p. 213)
• Specific-identification assigns the actual cost of each item to the units sold.	**First-in, first-out (FIFO)** (p. 210)
• FIFO assigns the oldest costs to the units sold.	**Finished goods** (p. 209)
	Inventory layer (p. 211)
• LIFO assigns the most recent costs to the units sold.	**Last-in, first-out (LIFO)** (p. 210)
• Average cost assigns a weighted average cost of the inventory on hand to the units sold.	**Perpetual inventory record** (p. 214)
	Raw materials (p. 209)
	Specific-identification (p. 209)
	Specific-unit-cost (p. 209)
	Work in process (p. 209)
The choice of inventory costing method can affect net income:	**Consistency principle** (p. 219)
• In times of rising prices, FIFO will result in the highest net income and LIFO will result in the lowest net income.	
• In times of declining prices, FIFO will result in the lowest net income and LIFO will result in the highest net income.	

1 Describe the four different inventory costing methods

2 Compute inventory costs using first-in, first-out (FIFO), last-in, first-out (LIFO), and average cost methods and journalize inventory transactions

3 Compare the effects of the different costing methods on the financial statements

4 Value inventory using the lower-of-cost-or-market (LCM) rule

5 Illustrate the reporting of inventory in the financial statements

6 Determine the effect of inventory errors on the financial statements

7 Use the gross profit method to estimate ending inventory

Key Points

Reporting inventory in the financial statements

- The lower-of-cost-or-market (LCM) rule is used in inventory valuation. LCM requires that inventory be valued at current market value if lower than historical cost.

- The ending inventory balance is always adjusted to equal the value according to a physical count taken at year-end.

- The full-disclosure principle requires that the methods used to value inventory be disclosed in the financial statements. This is usually done in footnotes added to the financial statements.

- A misstatement in ending inventory will cause net income on the income statement to be incorrect in the year of the misstatement as well as in the following year. The assets and retained earnings on the balance sheet will be incorrect in the year of the misstatement but will be correctly reported in the year following the misstatement.

- The value of ending inventory can be estimated using the gross profit method in cases where the inventory has been lost or destroyed.

Key Accounting Terms

Conservatism (p. 221)

Footnotes (p. 222)

Full-disclosure principle (p. 222)

Gross profit method (p. 225)

Inventory shrinkage (p. 222)

Lower-of-cost-or-market (LCM) rule (p. 221)

Materiality (p. 222)

8 Compute the inventory turnover and days-sales-in-inventory

Ratios often used to help make decisions:

- Inventory turnover measures how quickly a business sells its inventory.

- Days-sales-in-inventory measures how many days worth of sales is held in inventory.

Days-sales-in-inventory (p. 227)

Inventory turnover (p. 226)

Accounting Practice

Discussion Questions

1. The introduction to this chapter suggests that the chapter will explore the answers to some questions about inventory. Did you get the answers to those questions? Specifically,
   a. why does inventory need to be counted?
   b. what would happen if the count was done incorrectly?
   c. what do the terms FIFO and LIFO have to do with inventory?

2. How are the financial statements of a manufacturer different from those of a merchandiser with respect to inventory?

3. What is a cost-flow assumption? Why is a cost-flow assumption necessary in accounting for inventory?

4. If a company had two units that cost $1 each in its beginning inventory and purchased two more units for $2 each, what would be the cost of goods sold associated with a sale of three units under each of the following assumptions?
   a. FIFO
   b. LIFO
   c. Average cost

5. If a company had two units that cost $1 each in its beginning inventory and purchased two more units for $2 each, what would be the gross profit reported on the income statement under each of the following assumptions if three units were sold for $3 each?
   a. FIFO
   b. LIFO
   c. Average cost

6. In a period of rising inventory costs, which cost-flow assumption would produce the highest net income? Why?

7. Let's say that two companies, identical in every way except that one used FIFO and one used LIFO, went into a bank on the same day to get a loan to deal with the rising cost of acquiring inventory. Despite the fact that they both engaged in the same transactions at the same dollar values, one company reported higher net income and higher total assets on the financial statements. Which one was it? If the banker made the decision based on the company that would have higher cash flow associated with the inventory costing method choice, which company would have received the loan?

8. Describe some business and economic conditions that might make the lower-of-cost-or-market rule more likely to result in a write-down of inventory.

9. Under which of the inventory methods, periodic or perpetual, would a company be better equipped to detect inventory shrinkage? Why?

10. If a company is having a harder time selling its products, even at discounted prices compared to last year, would this year's inventory turnover rate be higher or lower than last year's rate? What about the gross profit rate?

Self Check

1. During April, Bargain Hardware made sales of $42,300 and ended the month with inventories totaling $5,400. Cost of Goods Sold was $21,900. Total operating expenses were $10,800. How much net income did Bargain Hardware earn for the month?
   a. $4,200
   b. $20,400
   c. $9,600
   d. $15,000

2. Which inventory costing method assigns the newest, most recent costs incurred during the period to ending inventory?

   a. Last-in, first-out (LIFO)
   b. Specific-unit cost
   c. Average cost
   d. First-in, first-out (FIFO)

3. Which inventory costing method results in the lowest net income during a period of declining inventory costs?

   a. Last-in, first-out (LIFO)
   b. Specific-unit cost
   c. Average cost
   d. First-in, first-out (FIFO)

4. Assume BAL, Inc., began March with 95 units of inventory that cost a total of $1,710. During March, BAL, Inc., purchased and sold goods as follows:

   95 @ $18

Mar	6	Purchased 120 units @ $16 each
	15	Sold 135 units @ $30 each
	22	Purchased 135 units @ $14
	30	Sold 95 units @ $29 each

   BAL, Inc., uses perpetual inventory. Under the FIFO inventory method, how much is BAL's cost of goods sold for the sale on March 15?

   a. $2,190
   b. $2,430
   c. $2,350
   d. $1,280

5. Assume BAL, Inc., began March with 95 units of inventory that cost a total of $1,710. During March, BAL, Inc., purchased and sold goods as follows:

   95 @ $18   −15

Mar	6	Purchased 120 units @ $16 each —
	15	Sold 135 units @ $30 each
	22	Purchased 135 units @ $14 each −
	30	Sold 95 units @ $29 each

   BAL, Inc., uses perpetual inventory. Under the LIFO inventory method, how much is BAL's cost of inventory on hand after the sale on March 30?

   a. $1,920
   b. $2,160
   c. $1,680
   d. $2,000

6. Assume BAL, Inc., began March with 95 units of inventory that cost a total of $1,710. During March, BAL, Inc., purchased and sold goods as follows:

   95 @ 18 = 1,710

Mar	6	Purchased 120 units @ $16 each	*1920*
	15	Sold 135 units @ $30 each	
	22	Purchased 135 units @ $14 each	
	30	Sold 95 units @ $29 each	

   BAL, Inc., uses perpetual inventory. Under the average cost inventory method, how much is BAL's cost of goods sold for the sale on March 15? Round unit cost to the nearest cent.

   a. $1,800.90
   b. $2,278.80
   c. $2,000.00
   d. $2,295.00

7. Which of the following prevents a company from switching its inventory costing method to a different method each year?

   a. Consistency principle
   b. Materiality concept
   c. Matching principle
   d. Disclosure principle

8. Which of the following is most closely linked to the accounting principle of conservatism?

   a. Consistency principle
   b. Disclosure principle
   c. Lower-of-cost-or-market rule
   d. Materiality concept

9. At December 31, 2012, Island Equipment understated ending inventory by $2,500. How does this error affect cost of goods sold and net income for 2012?

   a. Understates costs of goods sold and overstates net income
   b. Leaves both cost of goods sold and net income correct because the errors cancel each other
   c. Overstates cost of goods sold and understates net income
   d. Overstates both cost of goods sold and net income

10. Suppose Rocky Mountain, Inc., lost its entire inventory in a hurricane. Beginning inventory was $49,000, net purchases totaled $530,000, and sales came to $880,000. Rocky Mountain's normal gross profit percentage is 42%. Use the gross profit method to estimate the cost of the inventory lost in the hurricane.

    a. $301,000
    b. $19,600
    c. $68,600
    d. $209,400

    530,000
    + 49,000
    - (510,400)
    ⎯⎯⎯⎯⎯⎯⎯
    68,600

11. According to the Real World Accounting Video, a _____ is a profitability measure that is computed as net income/net sales.

    a. gross profit margin ratio
    b. profit margin ratio
    c. net income ratio
    d. net sales ratio

12. According to the Real World Accounting Video, ABC Wines has a supply chain that is composed of its _____.

    a. landlords
    b. importers and distributors
    c. customers
    d. employees

    Answers are given after Written Communication.

MyAccountingLab

Short Exercises

S5-1. Inventory methods (*Learning Objective 1*) 5 min.

Hasse Landscaping would like to assign the oldest costs of inventory items to its ending inventory.

Which inventory costing method should Hasse Landscaping choose?

S5-2. Inventory methods (*Learning Objective 1*) 5–10 min.

Cunnington Furniture doesn't expect prices to change dramatically and wants to use a method that averages price changes.

1. Which inventory method would best meet Cunnington Furniture's goal?

2. What if Cunnington Furniture wanted to expense out the newer purchases of goods instead? Which inventory would best meet that need?

S5-3. FIFO (*Learning Objective 2*) 5–10 min.

Score More Sports uses the FIFO inventory method. Score More Sports started December with 10 helmets that cost $54 each. On December 19, Score More Sports bought 15 helmets at $52 each. On December 28, Score More Sports sold 12 helmets.

Prepare a perpetual inventory record for Score More Sports.

S5-4. LIFO (*Learning Objective 2*) 5–10 min.

Score More Sports uses the LIFO inventory method. Score More Sports started December with 10 helmets that cost $54 each. On December 19, Score More Sports bought 15 helmets at $52 each. On December 28, Score More Sports sold 12 helmets. Prepare a perpetual inventory record for Score More Sports.

S5-5. Average cost (*Learning Objective 2*) 5–10 min.

Score More Sports uses the average cost inventory method. Score More Sports started December with 10 helmets that cost $54 each. On December 19, Score More Sports bought 15 helmets at $52 each. On December 28, Score More Sports sold 12 helmets.

Prepare a perpetual inventory record for the average cost method. Round average cost per unit to the nearest cent and all other amounts to the nearest dollar.

S5-6. Recording inventory transactions (*Learning Objective 2*) 5–10 min.

Score More Sports uses the (perpetual) LIFO inventory method. Score More Sports started December with 10 helmets that cost $54 each. On December 19, Score More Sports bought 15 helmets at $52 each. On December 28, Score More Sports sold 12 helmets.

1. The December 19 purchase of inventory was on account.
2. The December 28 sale of inventory was on account. Score More Sports sold each helmet for $106.

Prepare the required journal entries for the purchase and sale of inventory.

S5-7. FIFO versus LIFO (*Learning Objective 3*) 5–10 min.

Consider the FIFO, LIFO, and average cost inventory costing methods. Answer the following questions assuming that inventory costs are increasing:

1. Which method of inventory costing will produce the lowest cost of goods sold?
2. Which method of inventory costing will produce the highest cost of goods sold?
3. If prices had been declining instead of rising, which inventory method will produce the highest cost of goods sold?

S5-8. Inventory terms (*Learning Objectives 4 & 5*) 5–10 min.

Match the terms with the definitions.

_____ 1. A company must perform strictly proper accounting only for items that are significant to the business's financial statements.

_____ 2. Reporting the least favorable figures in the financial statements.

_____ 3. A business's financial statements must report enough information for users to make knowledgeable decisions about the company.

_____ 4. A business should use the same accounting methods and procedures from period to period.

a. Full-disclosure
b. Materiality
c. Consistency
d. Conservatism

S5-9. Lower-of-cost-or-market (*Learning Objective 4*) 5–10 min.

Assume that Bob's Boards has the following LIFO perpetual inventory record for skateboards for the month of March:

Skateboards			
Date	Purchases	Cost of Goods Sold	Inventory on Hand
Mar 1			$ 9,460
8	$1,670		$11,130
19		$2,140	$ 8,990
30	$1,810		$10,800

At March 31, the accountant for Bob's Boards determines that the current replacement cost of the ending inventory is $10,640. Make any adjusting entry needed to apply the lower-of-cost-or-market rule. Inventory would be reported on the balance sheet at what value on March 31?

S5-10. Reporting inventory on the balance sheet (*Learning Objective 5*) 5–10 min.

At the end of the current year, Cottage Cafe's inventory account balance was $13,550. A physical count of the inventory revealed that inventory on hand totaled $13,480.

What amount should Cottage Cafe report on its balance sheet for inventory?

S5-11. Inventory principles and terminology (*Learning Objectives 1, 4, & 5*) 5–10 min.

Match the accounting terms on the left with the corresponding definitions on the right.

_____1. Assigns the most recent inventory costs to ending inventory.

_____2. Results in cost of goods sold that falls between what FIFO and LIFO produce assuming rising prices.

_____3. This principle is the basis for using the lower-of-cost-or-market rule.

_____4. Principle that prevents a company from using a different inventory costing method each year.

_____5. Identifies exactly which inventory item was sold. Usually used for unique inventory items.

_____6. Requires that a company report enough information for outsiders to make decisions.

_____7. Treats the most recent/newest purchases as the first units sold.

_____8. Principle that states significant items must conform to GAAP.

a. Conservatism
b. Full-disclosure
c. LIFO
d. Average cost
e. FIFO
f. Consistency
g. Materiality
h. Specific-Identification

S5-12. Inventory errors (*Learning Objective 6*) **5–10 min.**

Inland Industrial Supply's income statement data for the year ended October 31, 2014, follow.

Sales Revenue	$253,700
Cost of Goods Sold	136,400
Gross Profit	$117,300

Assume that the ending inventory was accidentally overstated by $2,800.

What are the correct amounts for cost of goods sold and gross profit?

S5-13. Inventory errors (*Learning Objective 6*) **10–15 min.**

Inland Industrial Supply's income statement data for the year ended December 31, 2014, follow.

Sales Revenue	$253,700
Cost of Goods Sold	136,400
Gross Profit	$117,300

Assume that the ending inventory was accidentally overstated by $3,200. How would the inventory error affect Inland Industrial Supply's cost of goods sold and gross profit for the year ended December 31, 2015, if the error is not corrected in 2014?

S5-14. Estimating ending inventory (*Learning Objective 7*) **10–15 min.**

Haskin's Wholesale began the year with inventory of $51,600 and made purchases of $326,800 during the year. Sales for the year are $505,300, and Haskin's Wholesale's gross profit percentage is 38% of sales.

Compute Haskin's Wholesale's estimated cost of ending inventory using the gross profit method.

S5-15. Inventory turnover (*Learning Objective 8*) **5–10 min.**

Swanson, Incorporated's sales for the year ended March 31, 2014, were $1,275,000, and cost of goods sold amounted to $728,000. Beginning inventory was $55,000, and ending inventory was $68,000.

Compute Swanson, Incorporated's rate of inventory turnover for the year ended March 31, 2014. Round answer to the nearest tenth.

MyAccountingLab **Exercises (Group A)**

E5-16A. FIFO (*Learning Objective 2*) 10–15 min.

Riley's Sports Shop carries a line of waterproof cameras. Riley's Sports Shop uses the FIFO method and a perpetual inventory system. The sales price of each camera is $380. Company records indicate the following activity for waterproof cameras for the month of August:

Date	Item	Quantity	Unit Cost
Aug 1	Balance	10	$240
7	Purchase	14	$252
11	Sale	16	
19	Purchase	12	$256
28	Sale	9	

Requirements

1. Prepare a perpetual inventory record for the waterproof cameras to determine the amount Riley's Sports Shop should report for ending inventory and cost of goods sold using the FIFO method.

2. Journalize Riley's Sports Shop's inventory transactions using the FIFO method. Assume that all purchases and sales are on account.

E5-17A. LIFO (*Learning Objective 2*) 10–15 min.

Refer to the data for E5-16A. However, instead of the FIFO method, assume Riley's Sports Shop uses the LIFO method.

Requirements

1. Prepare a perpetual inventory record for the cameras on the LIFO basis to determine the cost of ending inventory and cost of goods sold for the month.

2. Journalize Riley's Sports Shop's inventory transactions using the perpetual LIFO method. Assume that all purchases and sales are on account.

E5-18A. Average cost (*Learning Objective 2*) 10–15 min.

Refer to the data for E5-16A. However, instead of the FIFO method, assume Riley's Sports Shop uses the average cost method.

Requirements

1. Prepare a perpetual inventory record for the cameras on the average cost basis to determine the cost of ending inventory and cost of goods sold for the month. Round average cost per unit to the nearest cent and all other amounts to the nearest dollar.

2. Journalize Riley's Sports Shop's inventory transactions using the perpetual average cost method. Assume that all purchases and sales are on account.

E5-19A. FIFO versus LIFO (*Learning Objective 2*) **10–15 min.**

Assume that Brazington Bikes bought and sold a line of mountain bikes during May as follows:

Date	Item	Quantity	Unit Cost
May 1	Balance	12	$480
5	Sale	8	
12	Purchase	18	$460
21	Sale	6	
30	Sale	7	

Brazington Bikes uses the perpetual inventory system.

Requirements

1. Compute the cost of ending inventory under FIFO.

2. Compute the cost of ending inventory under LIFO.

3. Which method results in higher cost of ending inventory?

E5-20A. FIFO versus LIFO (*Learning Objective 2*) **10–15 min.**

Refer to the data for Brazington Bikes in E5-19A.

Quick solution:

*1. FIFO cost of goods sold =
$9,900; 2. LIFO cost of goods sold
= $9,820*

Requirements

1. Compute the cost of goods sold under FIFO.

2. Compute the cost of goods sold under LIFO.

3. Which method results in the higher cost of goods sold?

E5-21A. FIFO versus LIFO versus average cost (*Learning Objectives 2 & 3*) **15–20 min.**

Assume that McCormack Tire completed the following perpetual inventory transactions for a line of tires.

Beginning Inventory...	28 tires @ $193
Purchase...	35 tires @ $185
Sale...	42 tires @ $284

Requirements

1. Compute cost of goods sold and gross profit under FIFO.

2. Compute cost of goods sold and gross profit using LIFO.

3. Compute cost of goods sold and gross profit using average cost. Round average cost per unit to the nearest cent and all other amounts to the nearest dollar.

4. Which method results in the largest gross profit and why?

E5-22A. Lower of cost or market (*Learning Objective 4*) 10–15 min.

Vermont Resources has the following account balances at March 31, 2014. The inventory balance was determined using FIFO.

Inventory		Cost of Goods Sold		Sales Revenue	
Beg Bal 10,000					
End Bal 21,000		Bal 101,000		Bal 186,000	

Vermont Resources has determined that the replacement cost (current market value) of the March 31, 2014, ending inventory is $20,200.

Requirements

1. What value would Vermont Resources report on the balance sheet at March 31, 2014, for inventory assuming the company uses the lower-of-cost–or-market rule?

2. Prepare any adjusting journal entry required from the information given.

E5-23A. Reporting inventory on the balance sheet (*Learning Objective 5*) 5–10 min.

Sundaze Sunglasses had the following FIFO perpetual inventory record at November 30, the end of the fiscal year.

Date	Purchases Quantity	Purchases Unit Cost	Purchases Total Cost	Cost of Goods Sold Quantity	Cost of Goods Sold Unit Cost	Cost of Goods Sold Total Cost	Inventory on Hand Quantity	Inventory on Hand Unit Cost	Inventory on Hand Total Cost
Nov 1							150	$6.00	$900.00
Nov 3	140	$6.05	$847.00				150	$6.00	$900.00
							140	$6.05	$847.00
Nov 7				130	$6.00	$ 780.00	20	$6.00	$120.00
							140	$6.05	$847.00
Nov 13	90	$6.15	$ 553.50				20	$6.00	$120.00
							140	$6.05	$847.00
							90	$6.15	$553.50
Nov 18				20	$6.00	$ 120.00	55	$6.05	$332.75
				85	$6.05	$ 514.25	90	$6.15	$553.50
Nov 25				55	$6.05	$ 332.75			
				60	$6.15	$ 369.00	30	$6.15	$184.50
Nov 30	230		$1,400.50	350		$2,116.00	30		$184.50

A physical count of the inventory performed at year-end revealed $178.35 of inventory on hand.

Requirements

1. Journalize the adjusting entry for inventory, if any is required.

2. What could have caused the value of the ending inventory based on the physical count to be lower than the amount based on the perpetual inventory record?

E5-24A **Inventory errors** (*Learning Objective 6*) **10–15 min.**

Old Time Bakery reported sales revenue of $134,000 and cost of goods sold of $89,000.

Requirements

1. Compute Old Time Bakery's correct gross profit assuming the company's ending inventory is overstated by $1,100. Show your work.

2. Compute Old Time Bakery's correct gross profit assuming the company's ending inventory is understated by $2,200. Show your work.

E5-25A. **Inventory errors** (*Learning Objective 6*) **10–15 min.**

Apex Auto Parts, Inc., reported the following comparative income statement for the years ended September 30, 2014 and 2013.

		2014		2013
Apex Auto Parts, Inc.				
Comparative Income Statements				
For the Years Ended September 30, 2014 and 2013				
Sales Revenue		$157,000		$148,300
Cost of Goods Sold:				
Beginning Inventory	$18,400		$11,800	
Net Purchases	72,000		71,300	
Cost of Goods Available	90,400		83,100	
Ending Inventory	17,900		18,400	
Cost of Goods Sold		72,500		64,700
Gross Profit		84,500		83,600
Operating Expenses		25,300		25,800
Net Income		$ 59,200		$ 57,800

During 2014, Apex Auto Parts, Inc., discovered that the 2013 ending inventory, as previously reported, was understated by $3,200.

Requirements

1. Prepare the corrected comparative income statement for the two-year period, complete with a heading for the statement.

2. What was the effect of the error on net income for the two years combined? Explain your answer.

E5-26A. **Estimating ending inventory** (*Learning Objective 7*) **5–10 min.**

Sounds on Wheels sells and installs audio equipment. During a recent fire that occurred at its warehouse, Sounds on Wheels' entire inventory was destroyed. Sounds on Wheels' accounting records reflect the following information.

Beginning Inventory	$ 54,000
Net Purchases	280,400
Net Sales	425,000
Gross Profit Rate	35%

Requirement

1. Use the gross profit method to estimate the amount of Sounds on Wheels' inventory loss.

E5-27A. Inventory turnover (*Learning Objective 8*) **10–15 min.**

Outdoor Adventure, Inc., has the following information as of December 31, 2014:

Sales Revenue		$1,675,400
Cost of Goods Sold:		
Beginning Inventory	$ 36,200	
Net Purchases	760,400	
Cost of Goods Available	796,600	
Ending Inventory	48,400	
Cost of Goods Sold		748,200
Gross Profit		927,200
Operating Expenses		67,300
Net Income		$ 859,900

Requirements

1. Compute the rate of inventory turnover for Outdoor Adventure, Inc., for the year ended December 31, 2014. Round the result to two decimal places.

2. The rate of inventory turnover for Outdoor Adventure, Inc., was 17.42 in 2013. Has the rate improved or deteriorated?

Exercises (Group B)

E5-28B. FIFO (*Learning Objective 2*) **10–15 min.**

Underwater World carries a line of waterproof watches. Underwater World uses the FIFO method and a perpetual inventory system. The sales price of each watch is $185. Company records indicate the following activity for waterproof watches for the month of March:

Date	Item	Quantity	Unit Cost
Mar 1	Balance	6	$100
7	Purchase	8	$108
11	Sale	10	
19	Purchase	13	$112
28	Sale	9	

Requirements

1. Prepare a perpetual inventory record for the waterproof watches to determine the amount Underwater World should report for ending inventory and cost of goods sold using the FIFO method.

2. Journalize Underwater World's inventory transactions using the FIFO method. Assume that all purchases and sales are on account.

E5-29B. LIFO (*Learning Objective 2*) **10–15 min.**

Refer to the data for E5-28B. However, instead of the FIFO method, assume Underwater World uses the LIFO method.

Requirements

1. Prepare a perpetual inventory record for the watches on the LIFO basis to determine the cost of ending inventory and cost of goods sold for the month.

2. Journalize Underwater World's inventory transactions using the perpetual LIFO method. Assume that all purchases and sales are on account.

E5-30B. Average cost (*Learning Objective 2*) **10–15 min.**

Refer to the data for E5-28B. However, instead of the FIFO method, assume that Underwater World uses the average cost method.

Requirements

1. Prepare a perpetual inventory record for the watches on the average cost basis to determine the cost of ending inventory and cost of goods sold for the month. Round average cost per unit to the nearest cent and all other amounts to the nearest dollar.

2. Journalize Underwater World's inventory transactions using the perpetual average cost method. Assume that all purchases and sales are on account.

E5-31B. FIFO versus LIFO (*Learning Objective 2*) **10–15 min.**

Assume that North Country Bike World bought and sold a line of mountain bikes during August as follows:

Date	Item	Quantity	Unit Cost
Aug 1	Balance	17	$267
5	Sale	11	
12	Purchase	16	$271
21	Sale	10	
30	Sale	7	

North Country Bike World uses the perpetual inventory system.

Requirements

1. Compute the cost of ending inventory under FIFO.

2. Compute the cost of ending inventory under LIFO.

3. Which method results in a higher cost of ending inventory?

E5-32B. FIFO versus LIFO (*Learning Objective 2*) **10–15 min.**

Refer to the data for North Country Bike World in E5-31B.

Requirements

1. Compute the cost of goods sold under FIFO.

2. Compute the cost of goods sold under LIFO.

3. Which method results in a higher cost of goods sold?

E5-33B. FIFO versus LIFO versus average cost (*Learning Objectives 2 & 3*) **15–20 min.**

Assume that Performance Tire, Inc., completed the following perpetual inventory transactions for a line of tires.

Beginning Inventory	34 tires @ $ 88
Purchase	29 tires @ $ 90
Sale	38 tires @ $160

Requirements

1. Compute cost of goods sold and gross profit under FIFO.

2. Compute cost of goods sold and gross profit using LIFO.

3. Compute cost of goods sold and gross profit using average cost. Round average cost per unit to the nearest cent and all other amounts to the nearest dollar.

4. Which method results in the largest gross profit and why?

E5-34B. Lower of cost or market (*Learning Objective 4***) 10–15 min.**

Ridgeview Resources has the following account balances at January 31, 2014. The inventory balance was determined using FIFO.

Inventory		Cost of Goods Sold		Sales Revenue	
Beg Bal 18,300					
End Bal 29,700		Bal 132,600			Bal 297,800

Ridgeview Resources has determined that the replacement cost (current market value) of the January 31, 2014, ending inventory is $30,600.

Requirements

1. What value would Ridgeview Resources report on the balance sheet at January 31, 2014, for inventory assuming the company uses the lower-of-cost-or-market rule?

2. Prepare any adjusting journal entry required from the information given.

E5-35B. Reporting inventory on the balance sheet (*Learning Objective 5***) 5–10 min.**

Sunglass Bungalow had the following FIFO perpetual inventory record at April 30, the end of the fiscal year.

	Purchases			Cost of Goods Sold			Inventory on Hand		
Date	Quantity	Unit Cost	Total Cost	Quantity	Unit Cost	Total Cost	Quantity	Unit Cost	Total Cost
Apr 1							180	$9.00	$1,620.00
Apr 3	110	$9.10	$1,001.00				180	$9.00	$1,620.00
							110	$9.10	$1,001.00
Apr 7				160	$9.00	$1,440.00	20	$9.00	$ 180.00
							110	$9.10	$1,001.00
Apr 13	80	$9.25	$ 740.00				20	$9.00	$ 180.00
							110	$9.10	$1,001.00
							80	$9.25	$ 740.00
Apr 18				20	$9.00	$ 180.00	20	$9.10	$ 182.00
				90	$9.10	$ 819.00	80	$9.25	$ 740.00
Apr 25				20	$9.10	$ 182.00			
				70	$9.25	$ 647.50	10	$9.25	$ 92.50
Apr 30	190		$1,741.00	360		$3,268.50	10		$ 92.50

A physical count of the inventory performed at year-end revealed $64.75 of inventory on hand.

Requirements

1. Journalize the adjusting entry for inventory, if any is required.

2. What could have caused the value of the ending inventory based on the physical count to be lower than the amount based on the perpetual inventory record?

E5-36B. Inventory errors (*Learning Objective 6*) 10–15 min.

Titan Trucks reported sales revenue of $343,000 and cost of goods sold of $246,000.

Requirements

1. Compute Titan Trucks' correct gross profit assuming the company's ending inventory is overstated by $3,600. Show your work.

2. Compute Titan Trucks' correct gross profit assuming the company's ending inventory is understated by $1,800. Show your work.

E5-37B. Inventory errors (*Learning Objective 6*) 10–15 min.

Gomez Auto Parts, Inc., reported the following comparative income statement for the years ended April 30, 2014 and 2013.

	Gomez Auto Parts, Inc. Comparative Income Statements For the Years Ended April 30, 2014 and 2013				
		2014		**2013**	
Sales Revenue		$143,000		$119,000	
Cost of Goods Sold:					
Beginning Inventory	$12,000		$12,500		
Net Purchases	79,000		71,000		
Cost of Goods Available	91,000		83,500		
Ending Inventory	18,000		12,000		
Cost of Goods Sold		73,000		71,500	
Gross Profit		70,000		47,500	
Operating Expenses		29,000		23,000	
Net Income		$ 41,000		$ 24,500	

During 2014, Gomez Auto Parts, Inc., discovered that the 2013 ending inventory, as previously reported, was overstated by $3,000.

Requirements

1. Prepare the corrected comparative income statement for the two-year period, complete with a heading for the statement.

2. What was the effect of the error on net income for the two years combined? Explain your answer.

E5-38B. Estimating ending inventory (*Learning Objective 7*) 5–10 min.

Mobile Audio sells and installs audio equipment. During a recent fire that occurred at its warehouse, Mobile Audio's entire inventory was destroyed. Mobile Audio's accounting records reflect the following information.

Beginning Inventory	$ 58,000
Net Purchases	287,000
Net Sales	486,000
Gross Profit Rate	43%

Requirement

1. Use the gross profit method to estimate the amount of Mobile Audio's inventory loss.

E5-39B. Inventory turnover (*Learning Objective 8*) 10–15 min.

Pete's Plants has the following information as of July 31, 2014:

Sales Revenue...		$980,000
Cost of Goods Sold:		
Beginning Inventory	$ 44,300	
Net Purchases..	257,000	
Cost of Goods Available	301,300	
Ending Inventory..	21,200	
Cost of Goods Sold		280,100
Gross Profit..		699,900
Operating Expenses		70,000
Net Income		$629,900

Requirements

1. Compute the rate of inventory turnover for Pete's Plants for the year ended July 31, 2014. Round the result to two decimal places.

2. The rate of inventory turnover for Pete's Plants was 10.24 in 2013. Has the rate improved or deteriorated?

MyAccountingLab **Problems (Group A)**

P5-40A. Computing LIFO and journalizing inventory transactions (*Learning Objectives 1 & 2*) 15–20 min.

Watkins Equipment sells hand-held engine analyzers to automotive service shops. Watkins Equipment started April with an inventory of 140 units that cost a total of $22,120. During the month, Watkins Equipment purchased and sold merchandise on account as follows:

Apr	6	Purchased 60 units @ $160
	13	Sold 50 units @ $310
	19	Purchased 80 units @ $162
	25	Sold 60 units @ $310
	29	Sold 110 units @ $310

Watkins Equipment uses the LIFO method. Cash payments on account totaled $18,400. Operating expenses for the month were $16,200, with two-thirds paid in cash and the rest accrued as Accounts Payable.

Requirements

1. Which inventory method (excluding specific-unit) most likely mimics the physical flow of Watkins Equipment's inventory?

2. Prepare a perpetual inventory record, using LIFO cost, for this merchandise.

3. Journalize all transactions using LIFO. Record the payments on account and the operating expenses on April 30.

P5-41A. Computing average cost and preparing a multi-step income statement (*Learning Objectives 2 & 5*) 15–20 min.

Refer to the data for Watkins Equipment in P5-40A. However, assume Watkins Equipment uses the average cost method.

Requirements

1. Prepare a perpetual inventory record using average cost. Round the average unit cost to the nearest cent and all other amounts to the nearest dollar.

2. Prepare a multi-step income statement for Watkins Equipment for the month of April.

P5-42A. FIFO, LIFO, and average cost (*Learning Objectives 2 & 3*) 15–20 min.

Horizon Furnishings, Inc., completed the following inventory transactions during the month of March:

Date	Item	Quantity	Unit Cost
Mar 1	Balance	15	$110
4	Purchase	45	$107
12	Sale	53	
22	Purchase	60	$104
31	Sale	32	

Requirements

1. Without resorting to calculations, determine which inventory method will result in Horizon Furnishings, Inc., paying the lowest income taxes.

2. Prepare a perpetual inventory record using FIFO.

3. Prepare a perpetual inventory record using LIFO.

4. Prepare a perpetual inventory record using average cost. Round average cost per unit to the nearest cent and all other amounts to the nearest dollar.

P5-43A. Lower of cost or market (*Learning Objective 4*) 10–15 min.

Raleigh Golf Pros uses the LIFO inventory method and values its inventory using the lower-of-cost-or-market (LCM) rule. Raleigh Golf Pros has the following account balances at December 31, 2014, prior to releasing the financial statements for the year:

Inventory		Cost of Goods Sold		Sales Revenue	
Beg Bal 39,000					
End Bal 63,300		Bal 231,000			Bal 325,000

The accountant for Raleigh Golf Pros has determined that the replacement cost (current market value) of the ending inventory as of December 31, 2014, is $61,700.

Requirements

1. Which accounting principle or concept is most relevant to Raleigh Golf Pros' decision to utilize LCM?

2. What value would Raleigh Golf Pros report on the balance sheet at December 31, 2014, for inventory?

3. Prepare any adjusting journal entry required from the information given.

P5-44A. Lower of cost or market (*Learning Objective 4*) 10–15 min.

Due to a nationwide recession, Liquidation World's merchandise inventory is gathering dust. It is now October 31, 2014, and the $189,400 that Liquidation World paid for its ending inventory is $13,200 higher than current replacement cost. Before any adjustments at the end of the period, Liquidation World's Cost of Goods Sold account has a balance of $728,600. Liquidation World uses lower of cost or market to value its ending inventory.

Requirements

1. What amount should Liquidation World report for inventory on the balance sheet?
2. What amount should Liquidation World report for cost of goods sold?
3. Journalize any required entries.

P5-45A. Inventory errors (*Learning Objective 6*) 20–25 min.

Evergreen Supply, Co., shows the following financial statement data for 2012, 2013, and 2014. Prior to issuing the 2014 statements, auditors found that the ending inventory for 2012 was understated by $5,000 and that the ending inventory for 2014 was overstated by $8,000. The ending inventory at December 31, 2013, was correct.

(In thousands)	2014		2013		2012	
Sales Revenue		$206		$193		$182
Cost of Goods Sold:						
Beginning Inventory	$ 32		$ 23		$ 25	
Net Purchases	125		129		120	
Cost of Goods Available	157		152		145	
Ending Inventory	20		32		23	
Cost of Goods Sold		137		120		122
Gross Profit		69		73		60
Operating Expenses		37		35		36
Net Income		$ 32		$ 38		$ 24

Requirements

1. State whether each year's net income before corrections is understated or overstated and indicate the amount of the understatement or overstatement.
2. Prepare corrected income statements for the three years.
3. What is the impact on the 2014 income statement if the 2012 inventory error is left uncorrected?

Quick solution:

1. October 31 estimated inventory = $69,288; 2. Gross Profit = $286,188.

P5-46A. Estimating ending inventory (*Learning Objective 7*) 15–20 min.

Pugliese Enterprises lost its entire inventory in a hurricane that occurred on October 31, 2014. Over the past five years, gross profit has averaged 42% of net sales. The company's records reveal the following data for the month of October:

Beginning Inventory	$ 43,600
Net Purchases	420,900
Sales	743,200
Sales Returns and Allowances	58,300
Sales Discounts	3,500

Requirements

1. Estimate the October 31 inventory, using the gross profit method.
2. Prepare the October income statement through gross profit for Pugliese Enterprises.

P5-47A. Inventory turnover and days-sales-in-inventory (*Learning Objective 8*)
10–15 min.

Sanchez Wholesale, Inc., has the following information for the years ending May 31, 2014 and 2013:

(In thousands)	2014		2013	
Sales Revenue		$228		$226
Cost of Goods Sold:				
Beginning Inventory	$ 32		$ 35	
Net Purchases	139		140	
Cost of Goods Available	171		175	
Ending Inventory	25		32	
Cost of Goods Sold		146		143
Gross Profit		82		83
Operating Expenses		39		41
Net Income		$ 43		$ 42

Requirements

1. Compute the rate of inventory turnover for Sanchez Wholesale, Inc., for the years ended May 31, 2014 and 2013. Round the result to two decimal places.

2. Compute the days-sales-in-inventory for Sanchez Wholesale, Inc., for the years ended May 31, 2014 and 2013.

3. What is a likely cause for the change in the rate of inventory turnover from 2013 to 2014?

Problems (Group B)

P5-48B. Computing LIFO and journalizing inventory transactions (*Learning Objectives 1 & 2*) **15–20 min.**

Top Line Equipment sells hand-held engine analyzers to automotive service shops. Top Line Equipment started November with an inventory of 95 units that cost a total of $11,400. During the month, Top Line Equipment purchased and sold merchandise on account as follows:

Nov	6	Purchased 105 units @ $134
	13	Sold 100 units @ $280
	19	Purchased 150 units @ $136
	25	Sold 110 units @ $280
	29	Sold 105 units @ $280

Top Line Equipment uses the LIFO method. Cash payments on account totaled $16,300. Operating expenses for the month were $9,000, with two-thirds paid in cash and the rest accrued as Accounts Payable.

Requirements

1. Which inventory method (excluding specific-unit) most likely mimics the physical flow of Top Line Equipment's inventory?

2. Prepare a perpetual inventory record, using LIFO cost, for this merchandise.

3. Journalize all transactions using LIFO. Record the payments on account and the operating expenses on November 30.

P5-49B. Computing average cost and preparing a multi-step income statement
(*Learning Objectives 2 & 5*) **15–20 min.**

Refer to the data for Top Line Equipment in P5-48B. However, assume Top Line Equipment uses the average cost method.

Requirements

1. Prepare a perpetual inventory record using average cost. Round the average unit cost to the nearest cent and all other amounts to the nearest dollar.

2. Prepare a multi-step income statement for Top Line Equipment for the month of November.

P5-50B. FIFO, LIFO, and average cost (*Learning Objectives 2 & 3*) **15–20 min.**

Lakeside Industries completed the following inventory transactions during the month of August:

Date	Item	Quantity	Unit Cost
Aug 1	Balance	35	$90
4	Purchase	70	$92
12	Sale	81	
22	Purchase	56	$95
31	Sale	44	

Requirements

1. Without resorting to calculations, determine which inventory method will result in Lakeside Industries paying the lowest income taxes.

2. Prepare a perpetual inventory record using FIFO.

3. Prepare a perpetual inventory record using LIFO.

4. Prepare a perpetual inventory record using average cost. Round average cost per unit to the nearest cent and all other amounts to the nearest dollar.

P5-51B. Lower of cost or market (*Learning Objective 4*) **10–15 min.**

SoCal Sporting Goods uses the LIFO inventory method and values its inventory using the lower-of-cost-or-market (LCM) rule. SoCal Sporting Goods has the following account balances at December 31, 2014, prior to releasing the financial statements for the year:

Inventory		Cost of Goods Sold		Sales Revenue	
Beg Bal 43,200					
End Bal 75,230		Bal 360,450			Bal 514,340

The accountant for SoCal Sporting Goods has determined that the replacement cost (current market value) of the ending inventory as of December 31, 2014, is $73,850.

Requirements

1. Which accounting principle or concept is most relevant to SoCalSporting Goods' decision to utilize LCM?

2. What value would SoCal Sporting Goods report on the balance sheet at December 31, 2014, for inventory?

3. Prepare any adjusting journal entry required from the information given.

P5-52B. Lower of cost or market (*Learning Objective 4*) 10–15 min.

Due to a nationwide recession, Freeze It Corp.'s merchandise inventory is gathering dust. It is now July 31, 2014, and the $160,500 that Freeze It Corp., paid for its ending inventory is $11,200 higher than current replacement cost. Before any adjustments at the end of the period, Freeze It Corp.'s Cost of Goods Sold account has a balance of $671,000. Freeze It Corp. uses lower of cost or market to value its ending inventory.

Requirements

1. What amount should Freeze It Corp. report for inventory on the balance sheet?
2. What amount should Freeze It Corp. report for cost of goods sold?
3. Journalize any required entries.

P5-53B. Inventory errors (*Learning Objective 6*) 20–25 min.

Ling Supply, Co., shows the following financial statement data for 2012, 2013, and 2014.

(In thousands)	2014	2013	2012
Net Sales Revenue	$198	$177	$179
Cost of Goods Sold:			
Beginning Inventory	$ 16	$ 19	$ 6
Net Purchases	145	112	132
Cost of Goods Available	161	131	138
Ending Inventory	23	16	19
Cost of Goods Sold	138	115	119
Gross Profit	60	62	60
Operating Expenses	42	41	43
Net Income	$ 18	$ 21	$ 17

Prior to issuing the 2014 statements, auditors found that the ending inventory for 2012 was understated by $5,000 and that the ending inventory for 2014 was overstated by $8,000. The ending inventory at December 31, 2013, was correct.

Requirements

1. State whether each year's net income before corrections is understated or overstated, and indicate the amount of the understatement or overstatement.
2. Prepare corrected income statements for the three years.
3. What is the impact on the 2014 income statement if the 2012 inventory error is left uncorrected?

P5-54B. Estimating ending inventory (*Learning Objective 7*) 15–20 min.

Inland Empire Supply, Inc., lost its entire inventory in a hurricane that occurred on July 31, 2014. Over the past five years, gross profit has averaged 39% of net sales. The company's records reveal the following data for the month of July:

Beginning Inventory	$ 43,400
Net Purchases	287,300
Sales	488,400
Sales Returns and Allowances	81,500
Sales Discounts	5,900

Requirements

1. Estimate the July 31 inventory using the gross profit method.
2. Prepare the July income statement through gross profit for Inland Empire Supply, Inc.

P5-55B. **Inventory turnover and days-sales-in-inventory** (*Learning Objective 8*)
10–15 min

Keystone Electronics, Inc., has the following information for the years ending January 31, 2014 and 2013:

(In thousands)	2014		2013	
Sales Revenue		$226		$218
Cost of Goods Sold:				
Beginning Inventory	$ 24		$ 28	
Net Purchases	147		147	
Cost of Goods Available	171		175	
Ending Inventory	18		24	
Cost of Goods Sold		153		151
Gross Profit		73		67
Operating Expenses		47		43
Net Income		$ 26		$ 24

Requirements

1. Compute the rate of inventory turnover for Keystone Electronics, Inc., for the years ended January 31, 2014 and 2013. Round the result to two decimal places.

2. Compute the days-sales-in-inventory for Keystone Electronics, Inc., for the years ended January 31, 2014 and 2013.

3. What is a likely cause for the change in the rate of inventory turnover from 2013 to 2014?

Continuing Exercise

This exercise continues the Cole's Yard Care, Inc., exercise begun in Chapter 1. Consider the May transactions for Cole's Yard Care that were presented in Chapter 4. (Cost data has been removed from the sale transactions.)

May	2	Completed lawn service and received cash of $450.
	5	Purchased 120 plants on account for inventory, $345, plus freight-in of $15. Freight-in was added to invoice by seller. Credit terms were n/30.
	15	Sold 30 plants on account, $215.
	17	Consulted with a client on landscaping design for a fee of $165 on account.
	20	Purchased 110 plants on account for inventory, $352.
	21	Paid on account, $1,900.
	25	Sold 120 plants for cash, $840.
	31	Recorded the following adjusting entries: Accrued salaries for the month of May equal $225. Depreciation on equipment $33. Lawn supplies used during May were $8. Physical count of plant inventory, 75 plants

Refer to the T-accounts for Cole's Yard Care, Inc., from the Continuing Exercise in Chapter 3. Use the ending balances in T-accounts at April 30.

Requirements

1. Prepare perpetual inventory records for Plant Inventory for May for Cole's Yard Care, Inc., using the FIFO method.

2. Journalize and post the May transactions using the perpetual inventory record created in Requirement 1. Omit explanations. Key all items by date. Compute each account balance, and denote the balance as *Bal*.

3. Journalize and post the adjusting entries. Denote each adjusting amount as *Adj*. Compute each account's ending balance and denote the balance as *Bal*.

4. Journalize and post closing entries. Denote each closing amount as *Clo*. Compute each account's ending balance and denote the balance as *Bal*. Prove the equality of debits and credits by preparing a post closing trial balance.

Continuing Problem

This continues our accounting for Aqua Magic, Inc. As stated in the Continuing Problem in Chapter 4, Aqua Magic, Inc., began selling pools and spas in August. For this problem, we will focus on the purchase and sales of spas during the month of September. The purchases and sales of spa inventory for the month of September are as follows:

Spa Inventory		
	Unit @ Cost	**Total Cost**
August 31 balance	5 units @ $2,750 each	$13,750
September 5 purchase	4 units @ $2,600 each	$10,400
September 11 sale	6 units	
September 17 purchase	7 units @ $2,500 each	$17,500
September 21 sale	5 units	
September 25 purchase	4 units @ $2,350 each	$ 9,400
September 29 sale	3 units	

Requirements

1. Assuming that Aqua Magic, Inc., uses the FIFO inventory cost flow assumption, what is the September 30 ending spa inventory balance and September cost of goods sold for spas?

2. Assuming that Aqua Magic, Inc., uses the LIFO inventory cost flow assumption, what is the September 30 ending spa inventory balance and September cost of goods sold for spas?

3. Assuming that Aqua Magic, Inc., uses the average cost inventory cost flow assumption, what is the September 30 ending spa inventory balance and September cost of goods sold for spas? Round average cost per unit to the nearest cent and all other amounts to the nearest dollar.

Continuing Financial Statement Analysis Problem

Look again at Target's financial statements contained in its 2012 annual report. For instructions on how to access the report online, see the Continuing Financial Statement Analysis Problem in Chapter 2. On page 33 of the annual report, you'll find Target's income statement for the year ending February 2, 2013 (called the Consolidated Statement of Operations). On page 35, you'll find Target's balance sheet as of February 2, 2013 (called the Consolidated Statement of Financial Position). Now answer these questions:

1. What makes up Target's inventory? Look at footnote 12 of the financial statements (footnote 12 on page 45 of the financial statements found in Target's 2012 annual report). What inventory method (such as FIFO and LIFO) does Target use?

2. Look at Target's balance sheet. How much has Target invested in inventory as of February 2, 2013, and January 28, 2012?

3. Look at Target's balance sheet. How much inventory does Target have per store as of February 2, 2013, and January 28, 2012? (Divide total inventory by the number of stores Target operated in each of these years [1778 stores at February 2, 2013, and 1763 stores at January 28, 2012].) Is inventory per store increasing or decreasing?

4. Look at Target's balance sheet and income statement. What is Target's inventory turnover rate for the year ending February 2, 2013? What does this tell you?

5. Look at Target's balance sheet and income statement. What is Target's days-sales-in-inventory ratio for the year ending February 2, 2013? What does this tell you?

6. Looking back over your answers to questions 1 through 5, how do you think Target is performing?

Apply Your Knowledge

Ethics in Action

Case 1. Susan Hopkins recently went to work for RJ Enterprises as the accounting manager. At the end of the year, Bill Harrison, the CEO, called Susan into his office for a meeting. Mr. Harrison explained to Susan that RJ Enterprises was in the midst of obtaining a substantial investment of cash by a major investor. Mr. Harrison explained that he was concerned that the investor would decide not to invest in RJ Enterprises when it saw the current year's results of operations. Mr. Harrison then asked Susan to revise the current year's financial statements by increasing the value of the ending inventory in order to decrease cost of goods sold and increase net income. Mr. Harrison tried to reassure Susan by explaining that the company is undertaking a new advertising campaign that will result in a significant improvement in the company's income in the following year. Susan is concerned about the future of her job, as well as others within the company, if the company does not receive the investment of cash.

Requirements

1. What would you do if you were in Susan's position?

2. If Susan increases the value of the current year's ending inventory, what will be the effect on the following year's net income?

Case 2. Pacific Equipment, which sells industrial handling equipment, values its inventory using LIFO. During the recent year, Pacific Equipment has experienced a significant increase in the cost of its inventory items. Although the net income for the current year has been fairly good, Lynne Jamison, the company president, wishes it was higher because the company has been considering borrowing money to purchase a new building. Mrs. Jamison has heard that a company's choice of inventory valuation method can affect the net income of the company. Mrs. Jamison has asked the controller, Lisa Adams, to explore the possibility of changing the company's inventory valuation method.

Requirement

1. If you were in Lisa's position how would you respond to Mrs. Jamison? Address potential ethical implications and applicable accounting principles in your answer.

Know Your Business

Financial Analysis

Purpose: To help familiarize you with the financial reporting of a real company in order to further your understanding of the chapter material you are learning.

This case continues our examination of the financial statements of Columbia Sportswear. In addition to the income statement (statement of operations) and the balance sheet of Columbia Sportswear in Appendix A, you will also be investigating the notes to the financial statements.

Requirements

1. Which footnote discusses the inventory costing method used by Columbia Sportswear?
2. What inventory method does Columbia Sportswear use to value its inventory?
3. Calculate the rate of inventory turnover for Columbia Sportswear for 2012 and 2011 (the 2010 ending balance in inventory was $314,298,000). Has the rate of inventory turnover improved or deteriorated?

Industry Analysis

Purpose: To help you understand and compare the performance of two companies in the same industry.

Find the Columbia Sportswear Company annual report located in Appendix A, and go to the financial statements starting on page 656. Now access the 2012 annual report for Under Armour, Inc., from the Internet. For instructions on how to access the report online, see the Industry Analysis in Chapter 1. The company's financial statements start on page 48.

Requirement

1. Calculate the inventory turnover for both companies for 2012. Who has the highest inventory turnover? Is that good or bad? Is it better to have a high inventory turnover or a low inventory turnover?

Small Business Analysis

Purpose: To help you understand the importance of cash flows in the operation of a small business.

It's the end of the year, and your warehouse manager just finished taking a physical count of the inventory on hand. Because you are utilizing the perpetual inventory method with a relatively sophisticated inventory software program, you expect that the ending inventory balance will be fairly close to the balance on your general ledger. In the past, you've had to make some pretty large adjustments for inventory shrinkage, but with the new security measures you've installed to safeguard your inventory, you're hoping that any shrinkage adjustment this year will be minimal. At least you hope that's the case because your net income can't take many more adjustments. This year's financial statements are very important to your banker because of the loan renewal coming up early next year.

You look at the amount from the final inventory count and it reads $465,375. You go to the general ledger Merchandise Inventory account and it reads $493,240. You look at the preliminary income statement, which doesn't reflect any of these adjustments yet, and the net income is $176,600. You remember that the banker said that he really wanted to see a net income of at least $150,000 this year.

Requirements

1. Calculate the effect that the required inventory adjustments will have on the net income for the year. Would your banker be happy or not so happy when you presented the financial statements to him after these adjustments?
2. If the adjustment you made for inventory shrinkage last year was only about $10,000, should that cause you any concern for the amount of adjustment you have to make this year?
3. In addition to the impact that the inventory adjustment might have on your loan renewal, what effect did it have on your cash flow during the year?

Written Communication

You just finished a telephone conversation with one of your clients, who has decided to expand her business by beginning to offer some merchandise for sale. Previously the company had only been a consulting business, but now it has an opportunity to sell some product from a new line offered by one of its clients.

The client's question to you seems rather simple, at least in her eyes. Which inventory costing method should the client use that will give the highest amount of net income? Because the consulting part of the business has not been doing very well lately, the company wants to have a lot of net income from this new side of the business so that the income statement will look good at the end of the year. The company has heard that either the LIFO or FIFO inventory method will result in higher net income, but it is not certain which one it is. Plus, the company definitely plans to always sell the oldest merchandise first, so will this have any impact on which method it chooses? The question does seem simple, but is the answer simple?

Requirement

1. Respond to your client either with a memo, a letter, or an e-mail.

Self Check Answers
1. c 2. d 3. d 4. c 5. d 6. b 7. a 8. c 9. c 10. c 11. b 12. b

Comprehensive Problem

The Accounting Cycle for a Merchandiser, Including Inventory Valuation

Bike World, Inc., wholesales a line of custom road bikes. Bike World's inventory, as of November 30, 2014, consisted of 22 mountain bikes costing $1,650 each. Bike World's trial balance as of November 30 appears as follows:

Bike World, Inc. Trial Balance November 30, 2014		
ACCOUNT	**DEBIT**	**CREDIT**
Cash	$ 9,150	
Accounts Receivable	12,300	
Inventory	36,300	
Supplies	900	
Office Equipment	18,000	
Accumulated Depreciation, Office Equipment		3,000
Accounts Payable		1,325
Note Payable, Long-Term		5,000
Common Stock		8,500
Retained Earnings		21,425
Dividends	4,250	
Sales Revenue		150,950
Sales Returns and Allowances	1,700	
Sales Discounts	1,275	
Cost of Goods Sold	78,900	
Sales Commissions Expense	11,300	
Office Salaries Expense	7,425	
Office Rent Expense	5,500	
Shipping Expense	3,200	
Total	$190,200	$190,200

During the month of December 2014 Bike World, Inc., had the following transactions:

Dec	4	Purchased 10 bikes for $1,575 each from Truspoke Bicycle, Co., on account. Terms, 2/15, n/45, FOB destination.
	6	Sold 14 bikes for $2,100 each on account to Allsport, Inc. Terms, 3/10, n/30, FOB destination.
	8	Paid $375 freight charges to deliver goods to Allsport, Inc.
	10	Received $7,200 from Cyclemart as payment on a November 17 sale. Terms were n/30.
	12	Purchased $450 of supplies on account from Office Express. Terms, 2/10, n/30, FOB destination.
	14	Received payment in full from Allsport, Inc., for the Dec 6 sale.
	16	Purchased 15 bikes for $1,600 each from Truspoke Bicycle, Co., on account. Terms, 2/15, n/45, FOB destination.
	18	Paid Truspoke Bicycle, Co., the amount due from the December 4 purchase in full.
	19	Sold 18 bikes for $2,125 each on account to Columbia Cycle, Inc. Terms, 2/15, n/45, FOB shipping point.
	20	Paid for the supplies purchased on December 12.
	22	Paid sales commissions, $1,850.
	30	Paid current month's rent, $500.

Requirements

1. Using the transactions previously listed, prepare a perpetual inventory record for Bike World, Inc., for the month of December. Bike World, Inc., uses the FIFO inventory costing method. (Bike World records inventory in the perpetual inventory record net of any discounts as it is company policy to take advantage of all purchase discounts.)

2. Open four-column general ledger accounts and enter the balances from the November 30 trial balance.

3. Record each transaction in the general journal. Explanations are not required. Post the journal entries to the general ledger, creating new ledger accounts as necessary. Omit posting references. Calculate the new account balances.

4. Prepare an unadjusted trial balance as of December 31, 2014.

5. Journalize and post the adjusting journal entries based on the following information, creating new ledger accounts as necessary:
   a. Depreciation expense on office equipment, $1,875.
   b. Supplies on hand, $245.
   c. Accrued salary expense for the office receptionist, $845.

6. Prepare an adjusted trial balance as of December 31, 2014. Use the adjusted trial balance to prepare Bike World, Inc.'s multi-step income statement and statement of retained earnings for the year ending December 31, 2014. Also, prepare the balance sheet at December 31, 2014.

7. Journalize and post the closing entries.

8. Prepare a post-closing trial balance at December 31, 2014.

Control Environment

The **control environment** is the foundation for all other components of internal control. The control environment reflects management and staff attitudes regarding internal control and sets the tone for the entire organization. Control environment factors include the following:

- Leadership philosophy and operating style (an effective control environment cannot exist if management has a "do as I say, not as I do" attitude).
- The competency of the employees within an organization.
- The integrity and ethical values of the company personnel.
- The organizational structure of the company, namely the delegation of authority and responsibility.

Risk Assessment

Risk is a fact of life. Every day a company will face a variety of risks from both internal and external sources. **Risk assessment** is an ongoing process that identifies and analyzes risks and takes steps to reduce them. For example, a fast food restaurant like McDonald's that hires predominately younger workers would be at a higher risk of violating child labor laws. Also, a company that has a large amount of cash on hand will have a higher risk of having cash stolen from it.

Control Activities

There are two elements related to **control activities**:

- Policies establishing what should be done.
- The procedures that should be followed to implement the policies.

The control activities of an organization vary from company to company. Control activities occur at all levels and in all functions throughout the entire organization. Generally, the controls chosen for an organization are based on its control environment, its assessment of risk, the size and structure of the organization, and the nature of its operations. Examples of common control activities include the following:

- Proper training and supervision: Employees should have written job descriptions and be properly trained and adequately supervised.
- Separation of duties: Responsibility for more than one of the following functions should not be given to any one employee:

  1. Authorizing transactions

  2. Maintaining custody of assets

  3. Keeping accounting records

Assigning an individual responsibility for more than one of these duties creates an opportunity for fraud. For example, if an employee has access to cash or other assets and he or she can record transactions, then he or she can steal from the company and falsify financial information to hide the theft.

- Mandatory vacations: Employees should be required to take annual vacations. If an employee knows that another person will be performing his or her duties while he or she is on vacation, there is less perceived opportunity to commit fraud. The vacationing employee will be concerned that any improper activities will be detected.
- Restricted access: Limit the number of employees who have access to company assets, such as cash, inventory, and supplies. For instance, use cash registers, vaults, and locked storage units to control access to assets. Also, access to computerized accounting records should be restricted to authorized personnel through the use of passwords. Allowing too many people access to assets and records creates an opportunity for fraud to occur. It also makes it more difficult to find the perpetrator should fraud occur.

- Security measures: Proper security measures should be implemented to deter theft. These measures can include the use of security cameras and alarm systems. Cash registers that print a receipt should also be utilized with a requirement that all customers receive a receipt.
- Proper authorization: Requiring proper authorization for certain activities. For example, requiring proper authorization for all sales returns can help prevent improper refunds from being issued.
- Maintain adequate documents and records: A trail of business documents and records, called an **audit trail**, should be maintained. The audit trail provides evidence of, and the details supporting, business transactions. Documents should be pre-numbered so gaps in the numbered sequence draw attention. Creating an effective audit trail lowers the chance that inappropriate activity will go unnoticed.

Audit trail A trail of business documents and records that provides evidence of transactions.

Accounting in Your World

Have you ever eaten at a food court in a mall and seen a sign that says, "If you do not get a receipt your meal is free"? Why would the business care if you get a receipt? This is actually part of the business's internal control activities. You see, the company doesn't really care if you get a receipt; it just cares that a receipt is printed. This practice prevents an employee from taking your money and pocketing it because once the receipt is printed, the sale is recorded. If the employee pockets your payment, the daily cash count will not match the daily record of sales and the theft will be detected. This example is just one of many control activities that businesses utilize as part of their internal control systems.

Information and Communication

To maximize the effectiveness of an internal control system, information about the control environment, the risk assessment, and the control activities must be communicated at all levels of the organization. This information should be communicated up, down, and across the organizational structure of the company. It is also critical that management communicates to all personnel that internal control must be taken seriously.

Monitoring

The internal control system must be continually monitored to locate weaknesses in the system. Monitoring can be accomplished through ongoing activities or through separate evaluations. Ongoing monitoring activities include regular management and supervisory activities. It also includes the assessment of the performance of the internal control system by employees as they perform their required duties. The need for separate evaluations depends on the effectiveness of the ongoing monitoring procedures.

Internal Control Limitations

A good internal control system reduces the risk of undetected errors and irregularities. However, an internal control system cannot provide absolute assurance that no errors will occur. It also does not guarantee that fraud will be prevented or detected. The effectiveness of an internal control system is limited because:

- Employees can become tired, careless, or distracted and make mistakes. They may also use poor judgment or misunderstand policies and procedures.
- Controls can be poorly designed.
- Staff size limitations may hinder efforts to properly segregate duties.
- Two or more people can work together to circumvent controls. This is known as **collusion**.
- Management can override controls.
- The cost of implementing some internal controls may exceed the benefits of these controls.

Collusion Two or more individuals working together to commit fraud.

Some examples of these limitations are:

- An employee may forget to check authorization for the extension of credit to a customer when the phone rings in the middle of the transaction.
- A disgruntled employee may convince another employee to help steal from the company.
- Management may override controls and direct the accounting staff to record revenue for services that have not yet been performed.
- In small businesses, the cost of employing enough people for a separation of duties may exceed the benefits of the segregation.

Stop and Think...

Goodguys Tire Company is a small retail tire outlet located in Portland, Oregon. Bill Hanson, the president of Goodguys Tire Company, has assigned the bookkeeper the responsibility of processing all cash receipts as well as all cash disbursements. The bookkeeper also prepares the daily cash deposits and takes them to the bank. Bill knows that he has not achieved a very good separation of duties, but the limited number of employees (due to the size of the company) did not allow it. Is there anything Bill can do, in light of the fact that there is not a good separation of duties, to help prevent fraud from occurring?

Answer

Yes, although there is no substitute for proper separation of duties, some of the steps Bill could take to help detect and deter fraud include, but are not limited to:

- Ensure that someone other than the bookkeeper receives the unopened bank statement and prepares a bank reconciliation on a monthly basis.
- Require that all adjustments to customer accounts be authorized by someone other than the bookkeeper. A periodic review of the customer account detail should also be performed by someone other than the bookkeeper. Any unauthorized adjustments to the accounts should be noted and investigated.
- Require that someone other than the bookkeeper authorize all cash disbursements. The cash disbursement detail should also be reviewed for unusual disbursements periodically by someone other than the bookkeeper.

What Is Fraud, and Who Commits It?

Define fraud and describe the different types of fraud in business

Fraud Deceit or trickery involving intentional actions that cause harm to a business, its stakeholders, or both.

Errors occur. Errors hurt a business. But were the errors unintentional, or were they intended to deceive and defraud? What exactly is fraud? Although there are many definitions, in its broadest sense, **fraud** can be defined as the use of deception or trickery for personal gain. In the United States, fraud is one of the fastest-growing crimes. It accounts for more losses than robbery. In the business world, fraud is either committed by a business organization or against a business organization.

Management Fraud

Management fraud Management's intentional misstatement of the financial statements, driven by greed or the pressure to show that a business is more profitable than it really is.

An organization's top management is usually responsible for fraud that is committed by a business organization. This **management fraud** typically involves fraudulent financial reporting. Fraudulent financial reporting most often makes a company's earnings look better than they are. The goal of overstating earnings is to help increase a company's stock price or to ensure larger year-end bonuses for upper management. Fraudulent financial reporting is achieved when management does the following:

- Overstates revenues by:

  1. Overstating receivables related to revenue that has not yet been earned.

  2. Understating unearned revenue (recording revenue when cash is received even though goods or services have not yet been provided).

- Understates expenses by:

  1. Overstating the value of assets such as inventory, equipment, and buildings or recording assets that do not exist.

  2. Understating amounts owed to suppliers, employees, or creditors.

Employee Embezzlement

Employee embezzlement Fraud where employees steal from employers by taking assets or engaging in disbursement schemes to steal cash.

Disbursement schemes A form of employee embezzlement in which an employee tricks a company into giving up cash for an invalid reason. Examples include check tampering, cash register schemes, and expense schemes.

Check tampering A fraud scheme in which an employee writes a fraudulent check and makes the check payable to himself or herself, or obtains a check intended for an outside party, endorses the check, and then cashes it.

Cash register schemes A fraud scheme in which an employee steals cash by processing false refunds.

Expense schemes A fraud scheme in which an employee over-charges the company for travel and other business-related expenses, such as lunches, hotels, parking fees, and cab fares.

The primary form of fraud committed against a business organization is **employee embezzlement**. Employee embezzlement usually involves the misappropriation of business assets by an employee. Employees can:

- Steal cash, inventory, tools, supplies, or other assets from the employer.
- Establish fake companies, have the employer pay these phony companies for goods or services that are never delivered, and then intercept and fraudulently cash the checks.
- Engage in **disbursement schemes**. Employee embezzlement involving disbursement schemes takes place when an employee tricks a company into giving up cash for an invalid reason. Examples of disbursement schemes include the following:

  1. **Check tampering**: The employee writes a fraudulent check and makes the check payable to himself or herself. Alternatively, the employee obtains a check intended for an outside party, endorses the check, and then cashes it.

  2. **Cash register schemes**: The employee gives a false refund for returned merchandise by filling out a refund form and putting it in the cash register. The employee then pockets the cash. Another related scheme happens when the employee accepts cash from a customer for a purchase but does not record the transaction in the cash register. The employee then keeps the cash for personal use.

  3. **Expense schemes**: The employee overbills the company for travel or other business-related expenses, such as lunches, hotels, parking fees, and cab fares.

Bribe The payment of money in order to influence the conduct of a person; also referred to as a **kickback**.

Employee dishonesty also occurs when an employee takes **bribes** or **kickbacks** from:

- Suppliers in exchange for the employee turning a blind eye to a supplier charging the employer higher purchase prices.
- Suppliers in exchange for the employee turning a blind eye to the delivery of inferior goods.
- Suppliers in exchange for the employee authorizing payments to the supplier for goods not delivered to the employer.
- Customers in exchange for granting the customer a lower sales price.
- Customers in exchange for giving the customer goods or services for which the employer is never paid.

The Factors Usually Present When Fraud Is Committed

Fraud triangle The combination of perceived pressure, rationalization, and perceived opportunity necessary to commit fraud.

Anyone who has done much camping knows that it takes three things to build a fire: fuel, oxygen, and ignition. For fraud to occur, three factors must also exist: perceived pressure, rationalization, and perceived opportunity. **Exhibit 6-2** presents the **fraud triangle**, which shows the connection of the three factors necessary to commit fraud.

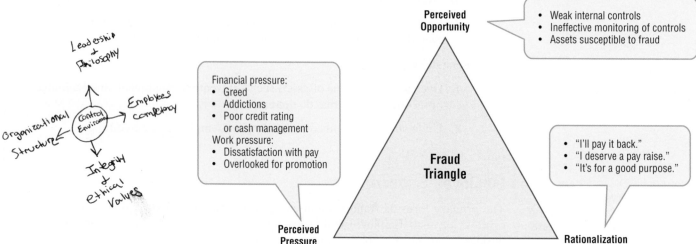

Exhibit 6-2 ▲

Let us take a closer look at the three elements of the fraud triangle.

Perceived Pressure

Perceived pressure An element of the fraud triangle in which the employee feels a need to obtain cash or other assets.

Numerous reasons exist that could cause an individual to feel pressured to commit fraud. However, the most likely source of **perceived pressure** is usually financial pressure or work-related pressure. Financial pressure can be caused by, but is not limited to, the following:

- Unexpected financial needs, such as medical bills
- A drug or alcohol habit
- Living beyond one's means
- A gambling addiction
- Unanticipated financial losses
- Excessive bills or personal debt

Work-related pressure also has several possible causes. An employee might feel dissatisfied with his or her job because of a sense of being underpaid or underappreciated.

Or an employee might have recently been overlooked for a promotion. Either of these things can motivate an employee to "get even" with the company by committing fraud. Also, if a company is performing poorly, it is possible for people within management to feel they are personally responsible. The perceived pressure caused by this feeling of personal responsibility can lead them to commit management fraud by falsifying the financial statements.

Rationalization

Rationalization An element of the fraud triangle in which the employee justifies his or her actions and convinces himself or herself that fraud is not wrong.

The next element of the fraud triangle that must be present in order for fraud to occur is **rationalization**. Rationalization is simply finding good reasons for doing things that we really know are wrong. Rationalization is human nature and very few people, if any, do not rationalize their behavior at some time or another. For example, you may have rationalized going out to a movie with your friends last night when you knew that you really needed to study for an important quiz. Employees who commit fraud attempt to justify their actions and convince themselves that fraud is not wrong by rationalizing their behavior. Common rationalizations used by individuals involved in fraud include the following:

- "I didn't steal the money; I only borrowed it, and I will pay it back."
- "I deserve a pay raise. The company owes this to me."
- "It won't hurt anyone."
- "Once the company gets over its financial difficulties, I will correct the books."

Perceived Opportunity

Perceived opportunity An element of the fraud triangle in which the employee believes a chance exists to commit fraud, conceal it, and avoid punishment.

The third and final element of the fraud triangle is **perceived opportunity**. An individual who commits fraud must perceive that an opportunity exists to commit the fraud, conceal it, and avoid punishment. An opportunity to commit fraud is often perceived when there is easy access to assets or when assets are poorly accounted for by an organization.

Removing any one of the three elements of the fraud triangle makes it much less likely that fraud will occur. Consider the following examples:

- No perceived pressure: An employee may see an opportunity to steal a company computer. He or she may even be able to justify taking the computer by telling himself or herself that the computer is an older one the company no longer uses. However, if he or she can afford to purchase a new computer, the employee will have a low incentive to commit fraud.
- No rationalization: An employee may desperately need cash to pay overdue bills and may see a way to steal money without detection. However, the employee's moral beliefs may make it impossible for him or her to justify taking the money.
- No perceived opportunity: An employee may feel pressured to steal money to cover a gambling debt. He or she may rationalize the theft by convincing himself or herself that he or she will repay the company next month. However, if it is not possible for the employee to steal money without detection, it is unlikely that he or she will commit fraud. This situation arises because the employee sees no opportunity to engage in fraudulent activity without discovery.

Out of the three elements of the fraud triangle, a business can have the most influence over the element of perceived opportunity. A business generally has limited control over perceived pressure felt by an employee or an employee's ability to rationalize unethical behavior. So, the most effective way for a business to prevent fraud is to reduce, or eliminate, the perceived opportunity for an employee to misappropriate company assets or for a manager to falsify financial information. Perceived opportunity can be reduced through a good system of internal control.

What Is a Certified Public Accountant (CPA)?

4 **Know what a Certified Public Accountant (CPA) is and does**

Certified Public Accountant (CPA) An accountant, licensed by a state, who serves the general public by auditing businesses and reporting whether the business's financial statements are in accordance with Generally Accepted Accounting Principles (GAAP).

American Institute of Certified Public Accountants (AICPA) The professional organization that supports and improves the practice of public accounting in the United States.

Internal audit (managerial audit) An audit and assessment of a company's compliance with laws and regulations, operating controls, and policies and procedures. An internal audit is performed by employees of the company.

External audit An audit of a company's financial statements performed by independent Certified Public Accountants (CPAs).

Generally Accepted Auditing Standards (GAAS) The procedures used by CPAs to audit companies.

Accountants in a company recognize, measure, record, and report business transactions in accordance with GAAP. But who validates that the accountants have done a good job and the information provided in financial reports is in accordance with GAAP? The answer is **Certified Public Accountants (CPAs)**.

A CPA is a person who has had extensive education and experience in the area of business and accounting. CPAs have passed a series of rigorous exams and must continuously update their education. CPAs are licensed to practice by states. To discover how to become a CPA, visit the Web sites of the **American Institute of Certified Public Accountants**, referred to as the AICPA (www.aicpa.org) and the National Association of State Boards of Accountancy, referred to as NASBA (www.nasba.org).

Audits

An audit is an examination of the validity and reliability of accounting information. Testing a business's internal controls is a big part of an audit. Often, businesses use employees to conduct **internal or managerial audits**. However, businesses also hire external accountants to conduct audits. This external accountant must be a CPA and independent of the business. The purpose of an **external audit** is to assure users that a business's financial statements conform to GAAP. The US Securities and Exchange Commission (SEC) requires that all companies that sell stocks and bonds to the general public in the United States be audited by independent CPAs. **Exhibit 6-3** illustrates a typical organizational chart of a large business and how the external auditor relates to management.

CPAs who conduct external audits must use **Generally Accepted Auditing Standards (GAAS)**. These standards were developed by the AICPA to ensure that auditors use good procedures and judgment.

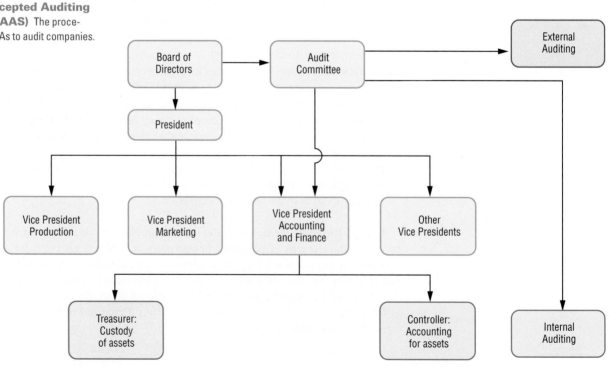

Exhibit 6-3 ▲

Audit Opinions

Audit opinion The opinion, issued by the CPA auditing a business, which indicates whether the financial statements are prepared in accordance with Generally Accepted Accounting Principles.

The outcome of an external audit is the issuance of an opinion by the independent CPA. **Exhibit 6-4** describes the four different types of **audit opinions**. The CPA can issue one of four types of opinions. The CPA may issue:

- An unqualified or "clean" opinion.
- A qualified or "except for" opinion.
- An adverse opinion.
- A disclaimer.

Type of Opinion	Reason Supporting the Opinion	Impact as a Result of the Opinion
Unqualified (also called a "clean" opinion)	An unqualified opinion means that, in the auditors' opinion, the financial statements are fairly presented. In addition, they are free of material misstatements and have been prepared in accordance with Generally Accepted Accounting Principles, unless otherwise noted.	This is the best type of opinion. It gives the financial statement users assurance that the financial statements can be relied upon.
Qualified (also called an "except for" opinion)	A qualified opinion is issued when one of the following occurs: • The auditors have taken exception to an accounting application or treatment the company being audited used. • The auditors were unable to gather the information they felt was necessary in order to issue an unqualified opinion. • The auditors were unable to determine the outcome of an uncertainty, which could have an effect on the financial statements.	A qualified opinion includes a separate paragraph outlining the reason for the qualification. A qualified opinion is used to help financial statement users make more informed decisions about the company. It allows the auditor to bring to the attention of the users circumstances or situations that may affect the user's reliance on the financial statements.
Adverse	By issuing an adverse opinion, the auditors are stating that in their opinion one of the following situations exists: • The financial statements are not fairly presented in accordance with GAAP. • There are material misstatements in the financial statements.	An adverse opinion will be accompanied by a paragraph explaining the reason for the negative opinion. An adverse opinion is very detrimental to a company as it basically informs users that the financial statements should not be relied upon.
Disclaimer	A disclaimer indicates that the auditors are unable to express an opinion based on their audit. A disclaimer of opinion may be issued because of the following: • A lack of independence on the auditors' part. • The inability to obtain the evidence needed to support a different type of opinion. • The existence of substantial doubts regarding the business's ability to continue as a "going concern." • Material uncertainties for which the auditors are unable to determine the outcome.	Because the auditors are unable, or unwilling, to express an opinion on the financial statements, investors will give considerable thought before investing in a company that has been issued a disclaimer of opinion.

Exhibit 6-4 ▲

Decision makers, such as lenders and stockholders, use the audit opinion to decide whether they can rely on the financial statements. When an unqualified opinion is issued, users can have confidence that the financial statements report what the business has been doing.

Look at Appendix A containing the Columbia Sportswear Annual Report. Look at the audit opinion which is located right before the financial statements. It looks complicated, but read it slowly. Notice how it talks about the audit. See how it concludes in an unqualified or clean opinion. The CPA firm that audits Columbia Sportswear, Deloitte and Touche, certifies that the financial statements fairly present the financial position and results of operations in conformity with GAAP.

If a CPA issues an incorrect opinion and users suffer losses, the users have the right to sue the CPA for damages. A CPA has a lot of responsibility.

Decision Guidelines

Decision	Guideline	Analysis
How do I know that I can rely on a business's financial statements?	Look to see if a business's financial statements have been audited by independent Certified Public Accountants.	Although unaudited financial statements are not necessarily unreliable, there is no third-party assurance that the information contained in the financial statements is accurate. Audited financial statements provide reasonable assurances that the information contained in the statements conforms to GAAP, is accurate, and can be relied upon.

What Are the Legal and Ethical Responsibilities of Accountants?

5 Know the legal and ethical responsibilities of an accountant, including the requirements of the Sarbanes-Oxley Act (SOX)

Accountants are very important. Accountants have a lot of responsibility. The success or failure of a business depends on the decisions of its stakeholders. Those decisions are based on accounting information. Because of their importance, accountants have legal and ethical responsibilities.

The law specifies the responsibilities of accountants and CPAs. Society also expects accountants to act ethically. Ethical behavior is conduct that requires adherence to higher standards than is required by law. The law states how we *require* people to act. Ethics state how we *expect* people to act. An example is an accountant who commits fraud. The law says this is illegal and specifies the penalties for committing the fraud. However, what happens if the accountant does not participate in the fraud, but suspects the fraud? We'd expect the accountant to inform the business's stakeholders that fraud could be occurring. The accountant has not committed a crime. However, the accountant has committed an unethical act if he or she does not inform the stakeholders that they could lose money. A person who reports illegal or unethical behavior is often called a **whistleblower**. Doing the right thing is often hard. People sometimes feel pressure not to report illegal or unethical acts. What would you do if you saw a boss steal, knowing your boss had the ability to fire you? There are laws that protect whistleblowers. Look at the US Department of Labor's Web site regarding the protection of whistleblowers (www.dol.gov/compliance/laws/comp-whistleblower.htm).

Whistleblower A person who reports illegal or unethical behavior.

The Legal Responsibilities of Accountants

Information is power. Accountants have information that others do not. Accountants must be very careful in what they do and say.

How powerful are accountants? Think about it. What would you do if you, as the accountant, knew that a company was about to announce an unexpected increase in profit?

After announcing the profit, the price of the company's stock would increase. You could make a lot of money by buying the stock before the information was announced and became public. That's power. If you acted on information the general public did not have, you would be participating in insider trading, a form of fraud, which is against the law.

Accountants that participate in fraud are subject to the same penalties as everyone else. They can be convicted. If convicted, accountants could be required to pay substantial amounts of money and, in some situations, go to jail. If the accountant is a CPA, he or she could lose his or her license to practice as a CPA.

Sarbanes-Oxley (SOX): Accountability of Accountants and Management

In response to a rash of accounting fraud cases, the United States enacted a special law in 2002 called the **Sarbanes-Oxley Act (SOX)**. SOX requires a company's management to take responsibility for a company's financial statements. The Sarbanes-Oxley Act:

- Applies to publicly traded companies.
- Established the **Public Company Accounting Oversight Board (PCAOB)**. The PCAOB is a private sector, nonprofit corporation that oversees the auditors of publicly traded companies. The PCAOB protects the interests of investors by helping ensure that fair, independent audit reports are issued. The PCAOB reports to the Securities and Exchange Commission (SEC).
- Requires that external auditors report to an audit committee, rather than to an organization's management. Prior to Sarbanes-Oxley, the external auditors often reported to a company's upper management.
- Requires that a company's Chief Executive Officer (CEO) and Chief Financial Officer (CFO) certify all annual, or quarterly, reports filed by an organization. By signing the reports, the executives certify the following:

    1. They have reviewed the report.

    2. The report does not contain any materially untrue statements.

    3. The financial statements and related information contained in the report fairly present the financial condition and the results of operations in all material respects of the organization.

    4. The signing officers are responsible for internal controls, have evaluated these internal controls within the previous 90 days, and have reported on their findings.

    5. They have disclosed:

        a. A list of all deficiencies in the internal controls and information on any fraud that involves employees who are involved with internal activities.

        b. Any significant changes in internal controls or related factors that could have a negative impact on the internal controls.

While SOX has been costly to implement for many companies, it has had a definite impact on improving internal controls in corporate America. As is true in any relationship, once trust has been broken, it takes time to rebuild. The implementation of SOX, along with the business community's heightened awareness of the need for proper ethical behavior, has started to restore the public's trust in corporate America.

Ethical Responsibilities of Accountants

Ethics are the set of moral values an individual or society holds that specify how people and organizations should act or behave. The law specifies the minimum level of behavior. An example is that you cannot steal. However, many decisions people face are not directly addressed by the law. The law cannot specify how people and organizations act in every situation. However, we expect people and organizations to act ethically, be fair, and do the right thing for all stakeholders.

Sarbanes-Oxley Act (SOX) A law passed in 2002 by the US Congress requiring a business's management to accept responsibility for providing the information needed by stakeholders outside the business.

Public Company Accounting Oversight Board (PCAOB) A private sector, nonprofit corporation that oversees the auditors of publicly traded companies. The PCAOB reports to the US Securities and Exchange Commission (SEC).

Ethics The set of moral values an individual or society holds that specify how people and organizations should act.

Accountants are expected to have very high ethical standards. We expect accountants to be competent, objective, responsible, and concerned for the welfare of all stakeholders. We expect accountants to have integrity. The American Institute of Certified Public Accountants (AICPA) addresses these issues in its Code of Professional Conduct (www.aicpa.org/Research/Standards/CodeofConduct/Pages/default.aspx). Likewise, many states require CPAs to pass exams and participate in continuing education programs dealing with ethics.

Accountants must make a lot of judgments. We must trust accountants to make good judgments and be responsible for their decisions. Accountants have considerable power. Accountants must know the law, abide by the law, and act ethically in all matters. Accountants must be trustworthy.

Focus on Decision Making

"How Much Is the Business Worth?"

How much is a business worth to its owners? Is it worth what the owners paid for the business? Is the business worth what the owners could receive if they sold the business? How should the accountant report the worth of the business?

6 Know the difference between book value and market value of stockholders' equity

A balance sheet reports the value of what a business owns (assets) and how it finances those assets (liabilities and stockholders' equity). Remember, the accounting equation states that assets equal liabilities plus stockholders' equity. If we use algebra to rearrange the terms, we see that stockholders' equity is equal to assets less liabilities. The value reported as stockholders' equity is based on the values reported for assets and liabilities.

$$\text{Stockholders' Equity} = \text{Assets} - \text{Liabilities}$$

Book Value and Market Value of Stockholders' Equity

Using GAAP, accountants report most assets and liabilities at historical cost. The value of most assets is what the business paid for them. The value of most liabilities is the amount the business owed when the liabilities were incurred less any payments that have been made. The difference between assets and liabilities is stockholders' equity. Stockholders' equity reflects what the stockholders paid the business for the stock plus the profits retained in the business. This is called the book value of a company or the **book value of stockholders' equity**. Book value is the value of stockholders' equity reported on a balance sheet created using GAAP. Book value is the result of recording past transactions at historical costs.

Book value of stockholders' equity The book value of assets minus the book value of liabilities. The value reported on a company's balance sheet for stockholders' equity.

But how much would the stockholders receive if they sold the business in the current market? It's probably not what the stockholders paid in the past. The amount stockholders expect to receive for their stock is based on the expected profits to be earned in the future. This amount is called the business's **market value** or **market capitalization**. The market value of a business is what future owners will pay present owners for the business. That amount is based on the profits prospective owners believe the business will earn in the future.

Market value or market capitalization The current market price per share times the number of shares outstanding.

The market value of stockholders' equity is equal to the market value of the assets less the market value of the liabilities. Now look back at the accounting standards provided by the IASB. Remember that these accounting standards use current or market values for assets and liabilities. This results in a reported value for stockholders' equity that more closely reflects market value.

Using US GAAP, the book value of stockholders' equity is typically lower than the market value of stockholders' equity. It's because US GAAP is conservative and uses the cost principle. International accounting standards are less conservative and report stockholders' equity at a value that is closer to market value.

How They Do It: A Look at Business

So is the difference between book and market values of stockholders' equity big or small? The difference between book and market values can be very large.

Let's look at two examples, Google and McDonald's. On December 31, 2012, Google's reported book value of stockholders' equity using US GAAP was $71.7 billion. Based on what you'd pay to buy a share of Google at the same time, the market value of Google's stock was $239 billion. The market believes Google is worth almost twice what the balance sheet reports. The reason is that US GAAP is conservative and focuses on past transactions. The market is valuing Google based on the net income it believes Google will earn in the future.

Now think about McDonald's, the fast food restaurant company. On December 31, 2012, its reported book value of stockholders' equity using US GAAP was $15.3 billion. Based on what you'd pay to buy a share of McDonald's at the same time, the market value of its stock was $89.2 billion. The market believes McDonalds is worth almost four times what the balance sheet reports. Once again, the reason is book value reports the past while market value focuses on the future.

Summary

MyAccountingLab

Here is what you should know after reading this chapter. The Study Plan in MyAccountingLab will help you identify what you know and where to go when you need practice.

Key Points	Key Accounting Terms
1 Understand the importance of US GAAP and how it differs from accounting standards in other countries (IFRS)	US accounting standards are designed to produce financial information that is understandable, relevant, and reliable. The Financial Accounting Standards Board (FASB) determines the standards used in the United States. US accounting standards are conservative, reporting most information using historical cost. Accounting standards differ around the world due to differences in culture and law. Many countries use accounting standards issued by the International Accounting Standards Board (IASB). These standards are referred to as International Financial Reporting Standards (IFRS) and use current or market prices instead of historical costs.	**Accounting Standards Codification (ASC)** (p. 258) **Audit** (p. 258) **Financial Accounting Standards Board (FASB)** (p. 258) **Generally Accepted Accounting Principles (GAAP)** (p. 257) **International Accounting Standards Board (IASB)** (p. 259) **International Financial Reporting Standards (IFRS)** (p. 259) **Securities and Exchange Commission (SEC)** (p. 258)
2 Understand the importance and role of internal control	Internal control is a comprehensive system that helps an organization safeguard assets, operate efficiently and effectively, ensure proper reporting of financial information, and ensure compliance with applicable laws and regulations.	**Audit trail** (p. 263) **Collusion** (p. 264) **Control activities** (p. 262) **Control environment** (p. 262) **Internal control** (p. 261) **Risk assessment** (p. 262)

5. Separation of duties refers to separating all of these functions *except* which of the following?

   a. Keeping accounting records
   b. Hiring personnel
   c. Authorizing transactions
   d. Maintaining custody of assets

6. Which of the following is *not* a control activity?

   a. Proper authorization
   b. Security measures
   c. Risk assessment
   d. Mandatory vacations

7. Darice Goodrich receives cash from customers as part of her job duties. Her other duty is to post the receipts to customer accounts receivable. Based on these duties, her company has (a) weak

   a. disbursement schemes.
   b. fraud triangle.
   c. ethics.
   d. separation of duties.

8. Which of the following is *not* a limitation of internal control?

   a. Rationalization
   b. Tired employees
   c. Poorly designed controls
   d. Collusion

9. Internal auditors focus on _____; external auditors are more concerned with _____. (Fill in the blanks.)

   a. financial statements; laws and regulations
   b. company policies and procedures; financial statements
   c. e-commerce; fraud
   d. financial statements; risk assessment

10. Which of the following is *false* regarding the Sarbanes-Oxley act?

    a. It requires that external auditors report to the company president.
    b. It established the PCAOB.
    c. It applies to publicly traded companies.
    d. It requires that the company CEO certify annual reports.

11. According to the Real World Accounting Video, Generally Accepted Accounting Principles (GAAP) provide all of the following except _____.

    a. standardization
    b. investor confidence
    c. comparability
    d. confusion

12. According to the Real World Accounting Video, CPAs are very special people in the accounting world. The initials CPA stand for _____.

    a. Chartered Public Auditor
    b. Certified Public Accountant
    c. Certified Pubic Auditor
    d. Commerce Practicing Accountant

Answers are given after Written Communication.

MyAccountingLab   ## Short Exercises

S6-1. Internal controls (*Learning Objective 2*) 5–10 min.

Indicate by letters the type of fraud committed:

Check tampering (CT)

Cash register scheme (CR)

Expense scheme (E)

Bribe (B)

Fraudulent financial reporting (F)

Here is an example:

__CT__   Employee writes a fraudulent check, making it payable to herself.

_____ 1. At the end of the year, the chief financial officer for Montgomery International recorded $80,000 in sales that had not been made.

_____ 2. Bill is a cashier at a local restaurant. Once a day, he leaves the cash register open and does not record the sale in the cash register when he takes the customer's cash.

_____ 3. Janet's major customer in California asked Janet to take 15% off of the sales price on the next shipment of jeans to his stores. In return, the customer will give her part of the money saved from the reduced sales price. Janet agrees to lower the price.

_____ 4. Sherri Smith, owner of Smith's Real Estate, asked the accountant to ignore any depreciation that should be recorded on assets owned.

_____ 5. Ashley submits a cash reimbursement for a cab ride she never took.

S6-2. Fraud triangle (*Learning Objective 3*) 5–10 min.

Identify each of the following as an example of a perceived pressure (P), perceived opportunity (O), or rationalization (R) in the fraud triangle:

_____ 1. Job dissatisfaction

_____ 2. Greed

_____ 3. "It's for a good purpose."

_____ 4. Weak internal control

_____ 5. Gambling addiction

S6-3. Internal controls (*Learning Objective 2*) 5–10 min.

Internal controls are designed to safeguard assets, encourage employees to follow company policies, promote operational efficiency, and ensure accurate records.

Which objective is most important? What must the internal controls accomplish for the business to survive? Give your reason.

S6-4. Internal controls (*Learning Objective 2*) 5–10 min.

Indicate by letters which of the following control activities match with the following descriptions:

Separation of duties (SD)

Restricted access (RA)

Proper authorization (PA)

Adequate documents and records (ADR)

_____ 1. Pre-numbered invoices

_____ 2. Locking inventory in a warehouse

_____ 3. Manager approval of sales returns

_____ 4. Password protection of accounting software

_____ 5. Not allowing the accounts payable clerk to sign checks

S6-5. Internal controls (*Learning Objective 2*) 10–15 min.

Explain in your own words why separation of duties is often described as the cornerstone of internal control for safeguarding assets. Describe what can happen if the same person has custody of an asset and also accounts for the asset.

S6-6. Fraud triangle (*Learning Objective 3*) 5–10 min.

Look at each of the following employees of Anthony's Restaurant. Which of the elements of the fraud triangle apply?

Perceived pressure (P)

Perceived opportunity (O)

Rationalization (R)

_____ 1. As the bartender puts $20 in tips in her pocket, she thinks, "Nobody will get hurt."

_____ 2. Jim uses money stolen from the company to pay for his mother's high medical bills.

_____ 3. Kirk knows he will be fired if he doesn't record some fictitious sales.

_____ 4. Trish, the night shift manager, knows that upper management does not monitor internal control.

_____ 5. Alan, a waiter, drove to work in a BMW and bragged about his recent vacation to Hawaii.

_____ 6. Brian, a cashier for the past five years, was caught stealing cash. When questioned about the theft, he said that he had not received a promotion and deserved more pay.

S6-7. Internal controls (*Learning Objective 2*) 5–10 min.

Identify each of the following as an internal control objective (O), an internal control activity (A), or a limitation of internal control (L).

_____ 1. Separation of duties

_____ 2. Collusion

_____ 3. Proper authorization

_____ 4. Report financial information properly

_____ 5. Mandatory vacations

_____ 6. Management override

_____ 7. Complies with laws and regulations

_____ 8. Adequate documents and records

_____ 9. Poorly designed controls

_____10. Operates efficiently and effectively

S6-8. Internal controls (*Learning Objective 2*) 5–10 min.

Peter's Hardware maintains the following policies/procedures with regard to internal control. Indicate by letter which of the following control activities applies to each of the following policies/procedures:

_____ 1. Every day, all checks written are recorded in the accounting records using the information on the check stubs.

_____ 2. The store utilizes electronic theft detection systems.

_____ 3. Purchases of new equipment must be approved by the store manager.

_____ 4. Daily sales are recorded in the accounting records by someone other than the sales associates.

_____ 5. The company maintains passwords that limit access to its computerized accounting records.

a. Proper authorization

b. Adequate documents and records

c. Restricted access

d. Security measures

e. Separation of duties

S6-9. Internal controls (*Learning Objective 2*) 5–10 min.

The following situations suggest a strength or a weakness in internal control. Identify each as a strength or weakness, and give the reason for your answer.

a. All employees must take at least five consecutive days off each year.

b. The accounting department orders merchandise and approves invoices for payment.

c. Cash received over the counter is controlled by the sales clerk, who rings up the sale and places the cash in the register. The daily sales are recorded in the accounting records by the accounting department.

d. The officer who signs the checks need not examine the payment packet because he is confident the amounts are correct.

S6-10. Internal controls (*Learning Objective 2*) **5–10 min.**

Identify the missing internal control in the following situations. Select from these activities:

- Proper authorization
- Separation of duties
- Adequate documents and records

a. While reviewing the records of Discount Drug, you find that the same employee orders merchandise and approves invoices for payment.

b. Business is slow at Play Time Amusement Park on Tuesday, Wednesday, and Thursday nights. To reduce expenses, the owner decides not to use a ticket taker on those nights. The ticket seller is told to keep the tickets as a record of the number sold.

c. When business is brisk, Shop Mart does not give customers a written receipt unless they ask for it.

d. Lynne has worked for Watkins Electric Supply for more than 12 years. Due to her length of employment, she has been allowed to grant sales returns at her discretion.

e. At a grocery store, the manager decides to reduce paperwork. He eliminates the requirement that the receiving department prepare a receiving report.

S6-11. Fraud and internal controls (*Learning Objectives 2 & 3*) **15–20 min.**

Each of the following situations has an internal control weakness.

a. Crystal Lund has been your trusted employee for 25 years. She performs all cash-handling and accounting duties. Crystal just purchased a new Lexus and a new home in an expensive suburb. As owner of the company, you wonder how she can afford these luxuries because you pay her only $42,000 a year and she has no sources of outside income.

b. Sanchez Hardwoods allows its sales staff to grant credit to any customer. As a result, it has had several large write-offs in Accounts Receivable recently.

c. The office supply company where Power's Sporting Goods purchases its business forms recently notified Power's Sporting Goods that its documents were no longer going to be pre-numbered. Bill Powers, the owner, replied that he never uses the receipt numbers anyway.

d. Discount stores, such as Target, make most of their sales in cash, with the remainder in credit card sales. To reduce expenses, one store manager allows the cashiers to record sales in the accounting records.

Identify the missing internal control in each situation. Answers should include authorization, documentation, and separation of duties. Identify the possible problem caused by each control weakness. Answers should include theft and financial loss. Propose a solution to each internal control problem.

S6-12. Accounting terminology (*Learning Objectives 1 & 4*) **5–10 min.**

Place the corresponding letter of the definition next to the term.

_____ 1. Unqualified opinion

_____ 2. Audit

_____ 3. IFRS

_____ 4. GAAP

_____ 5. External audit

_____ 6. CPA

_____ 7. FASB

_____ 8. Qualified opinion

_____ 9. IASB

_____10. GAAS

a. An audit opinion that brings attention to special circumstances.

b. Accounting standards issued by FASB and used in the United States.

c. Auditing standards developed by the AICPA.

d. Issues accounting standards that are used in the United States.

e. An audit performed by an independent CPA.

f. An examination of the financial statements.

g. An accountant who is licensed to practice by one of the states.

h. Issues accounting standards that are utilized internationally.

i. An audit opinion that states that the financial statements are fairly presented.

j. International accounting standards issued by the IASB.

S6-13. Sarbanes-Oxley Act (*Learning Objective 5*) **20–25 min.**

What are the main provisions of the Sarbanes-Oxley Act? Be specific.

S6-14. IFRS (*Learning Objective 1*) **20–25 min.**

Describe the major differences between US GAAP and International Financial Reporting Standards.

Continuing Financial Statement Analysis Problem

Return to Target's 2012 annual report. For instructions on how to access the report online, see the Continuing Financial Statement Analysis Problem in Chapter 2. Now, answer the following questions:

1. Look at Target's latest audit opinion. It can be found on page 31 of Target's 2012 annual report. Which CPA firm audits Target? Is its audit opinion unqualified, qualified, adverse, or a disclaimer?

2. What does the auditor's opinion say about the accounting standards used by Target? What does the opinion say about how the audit was conducted? What does the audit opinion say about Target's internal control?

3. Look at management's statement on internal control found on page 32 of the financial statements, found in Target's annual report. Look at the auditor's statement on internal control found on that same page. What do these statements tell you?

4. Look at Target's balance sheet as of February 2, 2013. Do Target's financial statements reflect current or historical values? What is the value of stockholders' equity reported on the latest balance sheet? On the same date as the latest financial statements, Target's stock sold for approximately $60 per share for a total market value of approximately $40 billion. Why is there a difference?

5. Look over Target's financial statements and footnotes. Look at your answers to questions 1 through 4 above. Do you think Target's financial statements are understandable, relevant, and reliable?

7

Cash and Receivables

Business, Accounting, and You

Walk into a candy store. Look at customers buying candy such as Hershey chocolate bars or Hershey chocolate kisses. Stop at the front of the store and watch the employees operating cash registers. What are they doing? They are helping customers to pay for products. Now, look at *how* customers are paying for their purchases. They often pay with cash or credit cards. A credit card is a promise to pay cash in the future. It's a receivable to the candy store. Hopefully, it's a good receivable and the candy store will collect the entire amount when it is due. Now think about Hershey, the candy manufacturer. Hershey sold the candy to the candy store. The candy store bought the candy with a promise to pay Hershey in the future. Hershey has a receivable from the candy store. That receivable may or may not be good. The candy store may or may not pay Hershey.

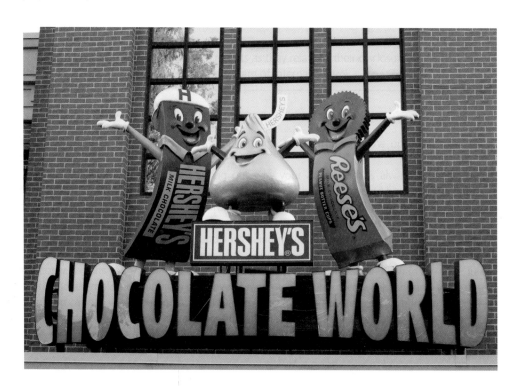

So what does the candy store do with its cash? The candy store uses its cash to pay its bills. The candy store must pay for the candy it purchased from Hershey, the wages it owes its employees, and the other liabilities that it incurs to operate. If it cannot pay its bills, it cannot stay in business. Being in business is about taking risks. Managing cash is a very important part of managing risk.

Accountants use accrual accounting to recognize, measure, record, and report business transactions. But managing cash and the promise of future cash is very important in operating a successful business. Business is about earning net income, but to earn net income, you need to be able to pay the bills. As an accountant or manager, you need to understand how businesses account for cash transactions and receivables.

In earlier chapters, we have seen that net income is the result of deducting all of a business's expenses from its revenues. Therefore, it makes sense that in order to increase net income a business must either reduce its expenses or increase its revenues. The choice of what methods of payment a business is willing to accept from its customers can have a significant effect on the amount of revenue it is able to generate. The method of payment a business accepts is determined by the type of sales it makes.

▶ Real World Accounting Video

In the Real World Accounting Video, Zachary Mack, owner and founder of Alphabet City Beer Company, talks about operating a business. Look at the video. Think about what Zachary is saying. Now realize how important cash management is to the success of a business.

What Are the Different Types of Sales?

Cash Sales

Cash sales are the most desirable form of sales because the business receives cash immediately upon delivering goods or services. Cash sales are also the easiest type to track because customers hand over currency or a check at the time of sale. The business does not need to keep records of the individual customers. As demonstrated in earlier chapters, a cash sale is recorded as follows (assume the sale amount is $500 and ignore cost of goods sold):

DATE	ACCOUNTS	POST REF.	DR.	CR.
	Cash		500	
	Sales			500

Although cash sales are easy to account for, businesses may limit their sales potential by not providing options for customers to buy now and pay later.

Credit Card Sales

Accepting credit cards as an alternative to cash helps businesses attract more customers. There are two main types of credit cards:

- Credit cards issued by a financial institution such as a bank or a credit union. The most common types of these cards are Visa and MasterCard.
- Credit cards issued by a credit card company. Discover and American Express are the most common credit card companies.

One of the primary benefits of credit cards is that they allow customers to buy now and pay later. Retailers who accept credit card payments do not have to worry about collecting from the customer or keeping accounts receivable records because the entity that issued the card bears the responsibility of collecting the amounts due from the customers. Instead of collecting cash from the customer, the retailer will receive payment from the issuer of the card. Another benefit of credit card sales is that they facilitate purchases made via telephone or online due to the fact that no cash has to change hands at the time of sale. One drawback to accepting credit card payments is that retailers typically pay a service fee to cover the cost of processing the transactions.

Debit Card Sales

Businesses can also attract customers by accepting debit card payments in addition to cash and credit card payments. From the retailer's perspective, debit cards are nearly identical to credit cards and have the same benefits and drawbacks. The primary difference between a debit card and a credit card is how and when the cardholder must pay the card issuer.

Credit/Debit Card Processing

Most businesses hire a third party to process credit and debit card transactions. As previously mentioned, there is a fee associated with credit and debit card transactions; the fees vary depending on the type of card processed and the specific agreement the business has with the card processor. The agreement also specifies when and how fees are paid. The most common methods of fee payment are:

- The fees are deducted from the proceeds of each sale at the time the sale proceeds are deposited into the business's bank account.
- The fees for all transactions processed are deducted from the business's bank account on a monthly basis.

Proceeds from credit and debit card transactions are typically deposited into a business's bank account within a one- to three-day period after the sale. Therefore, credit and debit card sales are journalized in a manner similar to cash sales. Assume a business has credit/debit card transactions that total $500 for the day and that $8 of processing fees are deducted from the proceeds. The journal entry to record the day's card sales is:

DATE	ACCOUNTS	POST REF.	DR.	CR.
	Cash		492	
	Service Fee Expense		8	
	Sales			500

The expense associated with processing the transactions is recorded at the same time the sale proceeds are recorded. Now, assume that instead of having the processing fees deducted from the sales proceeds, the business has the fees deducted from its bank account at the end of each month. The journal entry to record the day's card sales would now look like this:

DATE	ACCOUNTS	POST REF.	DR.	CR.
	Cash		500	
	Sales			500

Notice that this entry is exactly the same as the entry required for cash sales. The expense associated with processing the transactions will be recorded at the time a statement is received from the processor or at the time the monthly bank reconciliation is prepared.

Sales on Account

Bad debt An account receivable that is unable to be collected; also called an **uncollectible account**.

In Chapter 4, we discussed sales of merchandise on account. When businesses agree to sell on credit, sales increase, but so does the risk of not being able to collect what is owed as a result of these sales. Accordingly, companies bear the risk of **bad debts**, or **uncollectible accounts**, which occur when a customer does not pay for the goods or services it received. Regardless of its size, a business must manage its customer relationships to avoid bad debts. We will account for bad debts later in the chapter.

Decision Guidelines

Decision		**Guideline**		**Analyze**
Should a company accept forms of payment other than cash?		A business needs to weigh the costs of accepting alternative forms of payment against the income generated by increased sales.		When a company accepts alternative forms of payment, it incurs additional costs. If those costs exceed the additional income generated from increased sales, then it is not in the best interest of the company to accept alternative forms of payment.

What Internal Control Procedures Should Be Used for Cash?

 Discuss internal controls for cash and prepare a bank reconciliation

Regardless of whether sales are cash sales, credit/debit card sales, or sales on account, ultimately a business will collect cash from the transactions. Cash is one of the most vulnerable assets a business has. Cash is easy to conceal and has no identifying marks that link it to its owner, making it relatively easy to steal. Transactions that affect the cash account also affect other accounts, so any misstatement of cash can result in the misstatement of other items. As a result, it is important to have good internal controls over cash.

Internal Controls over Cash Receipts

Companies typically receive cash over the counter and through the mail. Good internal control dictates that all cash receipts be deposited in the bank quickly. Each source of cash needs its own security measures.

Over-the-Counter Cash Receipts

The cash register provides control over the cash receipts for a retail business. Consider a Target store. Target issues a receipt for each transaction to ensure that every sale is recorded; a customer cannot receive a receipt unless the register records the transaction. When the sales associate enters a transaction in the register, the machine records it and the cash drawer opens to receive cash. At the end of the day, the cash in the drawer is reconciled against the machine's record of cash sales to ensure the proper amount of cash is on hand. The machine's record of sales is then used as the source for the journal entry to record sales.

At the end of the day, or several times daily if the company is making a lot of sales, cash should be deposited in the bank. Any cash not in a cash register should be kept in a locked location within the business, such as a safe, until it can be deposited in the bank. These measures, coupled with oversight by management, help discourage theft.

Cash Receipts by Mail

Many companies receive cash by mail, especially if they sell products or services on credit. **Exhibit 7-1** shows how companies can control cash received by mail. Generally, an employee who has no other involvement in the sales or collection process, often a mailroom employee, opens all incoming mail and prepares a control listing of amounts received. At this time, a remittance advice is prepared if one did not accompany the payment. The mailroom then sends all customer checks to the treasurer, who oversees having the money deposited in the bank. The remittance advices, often check stubs, go to the Accounting Department and serve as a basis for making journal entries to Cash and the customers' accounts receivable. As a final step, the controller compares the bank deposit amount from the treasurer with the debit to Cash from the Accounting Department.

The amount of cash received according to the mailroom should match the debit to Cash and equal the amount deposited in the bank. This procedure ensures that cash receipts are safe in the bank and that the company accounting records are up to date.

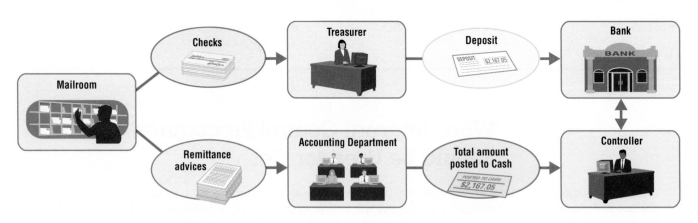

Exhibit 7-1 ▲

Internal Control over Cash Payments

A good separation of duties between operations and cash payments provides internal control over those payments. Also, making payments by check is another important control for several reasons:

- The check provides a written record of the payment.
- An authorized official studies the evidence supporting the payment.
- The official approves the payment by signing the check.

Purchase and Payment Process

To illustrate the internal control over cash payments by check in a company large enough to separate duties, suppose Top Ten Sporting Goods buys snowboard inventory from Taylor Snowboards. This purchase and payment process will generally follow steps similar to those shown in **Exhibit 7-2**:

Purchase order A document showing details of merchandise being ordered from a supplier.

1. Top Ten Sporting Goods sends a **purchase order** to Taylor Snowboards, its supplier. By preparing this document, Top Ten is placing an order to buy snowboards.

2. Taylor Snowboards ships the goods and sends an invoice back to Top Ten.

Receiving report A document evidencing the receipt of goods purchased.

3. Top Ten receives the snowboards and prepares a **receiving report** as evidence that it received the goods.

4. After matching the information on these documents, Top Ten sends a check to Taylor Snowboards to pay for the goods.

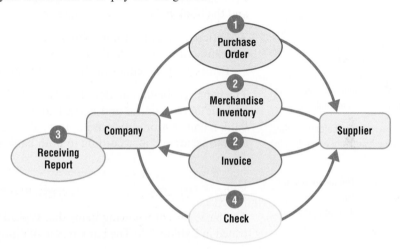

Exhibit 7-2 ▲

Purchasing agent The individual in an organization responsible for placing orders to purchase goods for that organization.

Controller The individual in an organization responsible for the accounting system and financial statements.

Treasurer The individual in an organization responsible for the custody of assets, such as cash.

For good internal control, the **purchasing agent**, the individual who places the order, should neither receive the goods nor approve the payment. Otherwise, the purchasing agent could buy goods and have them shipped to his or her home. Or he or she could receive kickbacks from suppliers by having the supplier bill his or her employer too much, approving the payment and splitting the excess with the supplier. The **controller**, as the person responsible for the accounting function, should not sign the checks for similar reasons. He or she could sign a check payable to himself or herself and then manipulate the accounting records to hide this improper payment.

Before signing the check, the **treasurer**, who usually assumes responsibility for the custody of cash, should examine each set of documents including the purchase order, receiving report, purchase invoice, and check to prove that they agree. This helps the company ensure that:

1. The goods it received were the goods it ordered, as proved by the purchase order and receiving report.

2. It is paying only for the goods ordered and received, as proved by the purchase order, receiving report, invoice, and check.

After payment, the check signer should deface the set of documents. This can be accomplished by punching a hole through the payment packet or stamping the documents "PAID." This hole or stamp confirms the bill has been paid and prevents the documents from being used to generate a second payment.

Streamlined Payment Procedures

Electronic data interchange (EDI) Direct electronic communication between suppliers and retailers.

For many companies, the purchase and payment process is made more efficient through the use of **electronic data interchange (EDI)**. EDI is a streamlined process that

Electronic funds transfer (EFT) System that transfers cash by electronic communication rather than by paper documents.

bypasses people and documents altogether. For example, in electronic data interchange, Costmart's computers communicate directly with the computers of suppliers such as Energize Soft Drinks, Inc., and Husky Foods. When Costmart's inventory of Husky chocolate candy reaches a low level, the computer sends a purchase order to Husky. Husky ships the candy and invoices Costmart electronically. Then an **electronic funds transfer (EFT)** sends Costmart's payment to Husky via electronic communication.

The Bank Reconciliation

Bank reconciliation A document that identifies and explains the differences between a depositor's record of a cash account and a bank's record of the same cash account.

Bank statement A document the bank prepares to report the changes in the depositor's cash account for a period of time. It shows the beginning bank account balance, lists the month's cash transactions, and shows the ending bank account balance.

Bank balance The balance in the company's bank account according to the bank.

Book balance The balance in a company's bank account according to the company's accounting records, or books.

Preparing a **bank reconciliation** is an important internal control that should be performed regularly. On a monthly basis a company will receive a **bank statement** from its bank that shows the **bank balance**, the cash balance in the company's account according to the bank. This balance usually does not agree with the **book balance**, the cash balance according to the company's records. Differences between the bank balance and the book balance arise because of:

- Differences, called timing differences, between the time when the bank records a transaction and when the business records it.
- Errors made by either the bank or the business.

The bank reconciliation identifies and explains the differences between the bank balance and the book balance and is used to arrive at the actual "true" balance of cash. The bank reconciliation serves as an internal control because it allows the correct amount of cash to be arrived at according to both bank and book records.

Preparing the Bank Reconciliation

The basic format, showing items that typically appear on a bank reconciliation, is illustrated in **Exhibit 7-3**. The bank reconciliation is divided into two sides, the bank side and

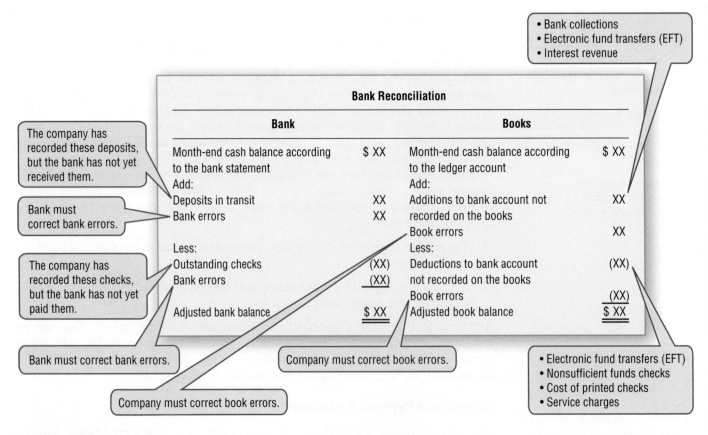

Exhibit 7-3 ▲

the book side. When establishing the procedures for a bank reconciliation, keep in mind our discussion of separation of duties; the person who prepares the bank reconciliation should have no other responsibilities related to cash. Otherwise, the bank reconciler could steal cash and manipulate the reconciliation to conceal the theft.

Bank Side of the Reconciliation

When preparing a bank reconciliation, the following items are included on the bank side of the reconciliation:

Deposits in transit Deposits that have been recorded by a company but not yet by its bank.

Outstanding checks Checks that have been issued by a company and recorded in its books but have not yet been paid by its bank.

1. **Deposits in transit** are deposits that the business has recorded but the bank has not. Deposits in transit are added to the bank balance.

2. **Outstanding checks** are checks that the business has recorded but the bank has not yet paid. Outstanding checks are subtracted from the bank balance.

3. Bank errors include the bank recording a deposit or a check for the wrong amount. The bank may also record a deposit or check that belongs in another bank customer's account. The bank must correct the errors that it has made. Adjust the bank balance for the amount of the error, adding or subtracting as necessary depending on the nature of the error.

Book Side of the Reconciliation

When preparing a bank reconciliation, the following items are included on the book side of the reconciliation:

Bank collection Collection of money by the bank on behalf of a depositor.

Lock-box system A system in which customers send payments to a post office box of a business. The bank collects payments from the box and deposits them into the business's account.

1. **Bank collections** are cash collections made by the bank on behalf of the business. Many businesses have their customers pay their bank directly. One way customers make payment is through a **lock-box system** in which they send their payments to a business's post office box. The bank then collects payments from the box and deposits them in the business's account, thus reducing the chance of theft. Another example is a bank collection of a depositor's note receivable. Because the bank statement is often the first communication that cash was received, the business has not yet recorded the receipt. These collections are added to the book balance.

2. Electronic fund transfers occur when the bank receives or pays cash on the depositor's behalf electronically. Because the bank statement is often the first communication of the transactions, the book balance may need to be adjusted accordingly for the cash receipt or cash payment.

3. Interest revenue may be earned on an account depending on the balance in that account. Interest revenue is added to the book balance.

Nonsufficient funds (NSF) check A check drawn against a bank account that has insufficient money to pay the check.

4. **Nonsufficient funds (NSF) checks** represent customer checks that the business has previously deposited that have turned out to be worthless. In other words, there were not sufficient funds in the customers' bank accounts to pay the checks. These amounts are subtracted from the book balance to reverse the deposit amount made earlier.

5. Service charges represent bank fees for processing transactions, printing checks, etc. These amounts are subtracted from the book balance.

6. Book errors include mistakes made in recording cash transactions. For example, an error might involve recording a check in the accounting records for a different amount than what the check was written for. Another mistake might be failing to record a deposit that was made. The book balance is adjusted for the amount of the error, adding or subtracting as necessary depending on the nature of the error.

Accounting in Your World

I don't need a check register; I use online banking.

Chris got a job his senior year in high school and opened a bank account to put the money he earns in. Chris deposits his paychecks into the account and then uses a debit card to make purchases. Chris's dad encouraged him to keep track of his finances using a check register and to reconcile his account balance each month when his bank statement arrives. Instead, Chris decided to just check his account activity every few days online to see that the deductions from his account agree with what he remembers purchasing. A few days after going out for pizza with friends, Chris was looking at his account activity online. Chris happened to have his receipt from the pizza parlor in his wallet, which was unusual as he normally throws them away, and decided to check it against his account activity. The receipt from the pizza parlor showed that the cost of the pizza was $18.53 and that Chris had added a $2 tip bringing the total amount to $20.53. However, the amount deducted from Chris's account was $22.53. It appeared that the amount of the tip was, accidentally or purposefully, added into the total amount charged twice. Chris feels lucky that he caught this mistake but wonders how many mistakes like this have occurred in the past that he didn't catch. Now, Chris understands why it is important to maintain a check register and to reconcile the account activity each month when he receives his bank statement.

Bank Reconciliation Illustrated

The January bank statement of Acrofab, Inc., is presented in **Exhibit 7-4**. The summary at the top shows the beginning balance, total deposits, total withdrawals, service charges, and the resulting ending balance. Details of the transactions for the month appear on the statement following this summary. The statement shows that the January 31 bank balance of Acrofab, Inc., is $5,875.

Acrofab's Cash account has a balance of $3,147 at January 31, 2014 as shown in **Exhibit 7-5**. Notice that the cash payments appear as one deduction, or credit, to the Cash account in the general ledger to make the process more efficient because businesses often write and record many checks at once.

The bank reconciliation in **Exhibit 7-6** identifies and explains the differences between the balance according to the bank statement and the balance according to Acrofab's records, thus determining the correct Cash balance at the end of January. Exhibit 7-6, Panel A, lists the reconciling items, and Panel B shows the completed reconciliation.

INWNB
INLAND NORTHWEST NATIONAL BANK.

Acrofab, Inc.
721 Front Street
Seattle, WA 98058

CHECKING ACCOUNT 136-213733

CHECKING ACCOUNT SUMMARY AS OF 1/31/2014

BEGINNING BALANCE	TOTAL DEPOSITS	TOTAL WITHDRAWALS	SERVICE CHARGES	ENDING BALANCE
6,500	4,362	4,972	15	5,875

DEPOSITS	DATE	AMOUNT
Deposits	4-Jan	1,000
Deposits	4-Jan	112
Deposits	8-Jan	200
EFT-Rent	17-Jan	905
Bank collection	26-Jan	2,115
Interest	31-Jan	30

CHARGES	DATE	AMOUNT
Service charges	31-Jan	15

CHECKS		DAILY BALANCE				
Number	Amount	Date	Balance		Date	Balance
956	100	31-Dec	6,500		20-Jan	4,845
732	3,000	4-Jan	7,560		26-Jan	6,960
733	160	6-Jan	7,360		31-Jan	5,875
734	100	8-Jan	7,560			
735	100	10-Jan	7,460			
736	1,100	17-Jan	5,205			

OTHER CHARGES	DATE	AMOUNT
NSF	4-Jan	52
EFT-Insurance	20-Jan	360

MONTHLY SUMMARY

Withdrawals: 9	Minimum Balance: 4,845	Average Balance: 6,085

Exhibit 7-4 ▲

General Ledger:

Cash   Account No. 111

		POST			BALANCE	
DATE	ITEM	REF.	DEBIT	CREDIT	DEBIT	CREDIT
2014						
Jan 1	Balance				6,500	
2		J. 30	1,112		7,612	
7		J. 30	200		7,812	
31		J. 32		6,265*	1,547	
31		J. 32	1,600		3,147	

Cash Payments: *Supporting Detail for Jan 31 Credit to Cash

CHECK NO.	AMOUNT	CHECK NO.	AMOUNT
732	$3,000	738	$ 320
733	610	739	85
734	100	740	205
735	100	741	460
736	1,100		
737	285	Total	$6,265

Exhibit 7-5 ▲

PANEL A—Reconciling Items

a. Deposit in transit: $1,600
b. Bank error: The bank mistakenly deducted $100 for a check written by another company. Add $100 to bank balance because this balance will be $100 higher once the bank fixes its error.
c. Outstanding checks:

Check No.	Amount
737	$285
738	320
739	85
740	205
741	460

d. EFT receipt of rent revenue: $905
e. Bank collection of a note receivable: $2,115, which includes interest revenue of $115
f. Interest revenue earned on bank balance: $30
g. Book error: Check no. 733 for $160 paid to Brown Company on account was recorded as $610; add $450 to the book balance.
h. Bank service charge: $15
i. NSF check from L. Ross: $52
j. EFT payment of insurance expense: $360

PANEL B—Completed Reconciliation

Acrofab, Inc.
Bank Reconciliation
January 31, 2014

BANK		BOOKS	
Bal, Jan 31	$5,875	Bal, Jan 31	$3,147
Add:		Add:	
a. Deposit of January 31 in transit	1,600	d. EFT receipt of rent revenue	905
b. Correction of bank error	100	e. Bank collection of note receivable,	
	7,575	$2,000 plus interest revenue of $115	2,115
		f. Interest revenue earned on bank balance	30
Less:		g. Correction of book error—overstated	
c. Outstanding checks		our check no. 733 ($610 − $160)	450
No. 737	(285)		6,647
No. 738	(320)	Less:	
No. 739	(85)	h. Service charge	(15)
No. 740	(205)	i. NSF check	(52)
No. 741	(460)	j. EFT payment of insurance expense	(360)
Adjusted bank balance	$6,220	Adjusted book balance	$6,220

These amounts must agree, or the reconciliation is not complete.

Here is a summary of how to treat the reconciling items encountered most often:

Bank Balance—Always:
- *Add* deposits in transit.
- *Subtract* outstanding checks.
- *Add* or *subtract* corrections of bank errors.

Book Balance—Always:
- *Add* bank collections, interest revenue, and EFT receipts.
- *Subtract* NSF checks, the cost of printed checks, service charges, and EFT payments.
- *Add* or *subtract* corrections of book errors.

Exhibit 7-6 ▲

Journalizing Transactions from the Reconciliation

Once the bank reconciliation has been prepared, the true balance of cash is known. However, the Cash account in the general ledger still reflects the original book balance. Journal entries must be made and posted to the general ledger so it reflects the updated cash balance. *All items on the book side of the bank reconciliation require journal entries, whereas none of the items on the bank side require journal entries.*

The journal entries listed here bring the Cash account up to date as a result of completing the reconciliation. The letters of the entries correspond to the letters of the reconciling items listed in Exhibit 7-6, Panel A. Entry (i), the entry for the NSF check, needs explanation. When L. Ross's check was first deposited, Inland Northwest National Bank added $52 to Acrofab's account. When L. Ross's check was returned to Inland Northwest National Bank due to insufficient funds, the bank deducted $52 from Acrofab's account. Because the funds are still receivable from Ross, Accounts Receivable—L. Ross is debited to re-establish the amount due from Ross.

DATE	ACCOUNTS	POST REF.	DR.	CR.
d.	Cash		905	
	Rent Revenue			905
	Record receipt of monthly rent.			
e.	Cash		2,115	
	Notes Receivable			2,000
	Interest Revenue			115
	Record note receivable and interest collected by bank.			
f.	Cash		30	
	Interest Revenue			30
	Record interest earned on bank balance.			
g.	Cash		450	
	Accounts Payable—Brown Co.			450
	Correct recording of check no. 733			
h.	Miscellaneous Expense		15	
	Cash			15
	Record bank service charge.			
i.	Accounts Receivable—L. Ross		52	
	Cash			52
	Record NSF check returned by bank.			
j.	Insurance Expense		360	
	Cash			360
	Record payment of monthly insurance premium.			

Online Banking

Online banking allows businesses to pay bills and view account activity electronically. The company doesn't have to wait until the end of the month to get a bank statement. The account history is like a bank statement because it lists all transactions including deposits, checks, EFT receipts and payments, ATM withdrawals, and interest earned on the bank balance. Because of this, it can be used instead of a bank statement to reconcile the bank account at any time.

Stop and Think...

Jill and Ramon were working on their accounting homework together. Their instructor had given them a problem that required them to prepare a bank reconciliation. He then asked them, "What balance would the company report on its balance sheet for the period?" Jill thought it should be the book balance from the bank reconciliation because that is the amount of cash the company's records reflected. Ramon disagreed. He thought it should be the bank balance from the reconciliation because that is the amount of cash reflected on the bank statement, which is a formal document received from the bank. Which student is correct?

Answer

Neither student is correct. This is because neither the book balance nor the bank balance reflects all of the transactions that have affected the company's cash balance during the period. The balance that would be reported on the balance sheet would be the reconciled balance from the bank reconciliation, as this represents the true amount of cash the company has at the end of the period.

How Is Cash Reported on the Balance Sheet?

Report cash on the balance sheet

Petty cash Fund containing a small amount of cash that is used to pay for minor expenditures.

Cash equivalents Highly liquid, highly safe investments that so closely resemble cash that they may be shown with cash on the balance sheet.

Remember from our discussion of the classified balance sheet in Chapter 4 that Cash is the first asset listed because it's the most liquid. Businesses often have several bank accounts, but they customarily combine all cash amounts into a single total. On the balance sheet, this total may be called Cash, or it may be called Cash and Cash Equivalents.

Cash on the balance sheet includes coin, currency, checks on hand, **petty cash** (discussed in Appendix 7A), checking accounts, money orders, and traveler's checks. In short, cash consists of anything that a bank will take as a deposit.

Cash equivalents include very liquid, very safe short-term investments. Generally, investments with original maturities of three months or less qualify as cash equivalents. They often include time deposits, money market funds, certificates of deposit, and U.S. Treasury bills. These items are liquid because they can readily be converted into cash, and they are safe because they have little risk of losing their value. Cash equivalents so closely resemble cash that they are included with cash on the balance sheet.

How Do You Account for Receivables?

Types of Receivables

Identify the different types of receivables and discuss related internal controls for accounts receivable

As discussed earlier in the chapter, companies often make sales on account that create a receivable from the customer. The two major types of receivables are accounts receivable and notes receivable. Remember from Chapter 1 that a business's accounts receivable are current assets that reflect the amounts due from customers for credit sales of goods or services. Also recall from Chapter 2 that notes receivable are written promises by customers to pay an amount of cash to the business in the future. Notes receivable are more formal and usually longer in term than accounts receivable. Notes also usually include a charge for interest. A detailed discussion of notes receivable will follow later in the chapter.

A company may also have other receivables, such as loans to employees and interest receivable. These other receivables may be either current or long-term assets, depending on if they are due within one year or less.

Internal Control over Accounts Receivable

Most companies have a Credit Department to evaluate customers' credit applications. The extension of credit requires a balancing act. The company wants to avoid receivables that will never be collected while at the same time granting credit to as many customers as possible. Also, companies that sell on credit often receive the related payment by mail, so internal control over collections is important. Remember, a critical element of internal control is the separation of cash-handling and cash-accounting duties.

Write off Removing a customer's receivable from the accounting records because it is considered uncollectible.

Good internal control over Accounts Receivable dictates that the granting of credit, the receipt of cash, and the recording of Accounts Receivable transactions are done by different individuals, preferably from different departments. For example, if the employee who handles the daily cash receipts also records the Accounts Receivable transactions, the company would have no separation of duties. The employee could pocket money received from a customer. He or she could then label the customer's account as uncollectible, and the company would write off the account receivable, as discussed in the next section. The company would stop billing that customer, and the employee would have covered his or her theft. For this reason, separation of duties is important.

Accounting for Uncollectible Accounts Receivable

Unfortunately, when a business chooses to sell goods or services on account, there will likely be customers who fail to pay the amount owed. When this happens, the customer's account is referred to as an uncollectible account or a bad debt. Uncollectible accounts reflect a cost associated with selling goods and services on account. Companies who make sales on account expect that the benefit of granting credit to customers outweighs the cost.

Bad debt expense Selling expense caused by uncollectible accounts; also called **uncollectible accounts expense**.

- **The benefit:** Increased revenues and profits from making sales to a wider range of customers.
- **The cost:** Some customers don't pay, and that creates an expense called **Bad Debt Expense**. Bad Debt Expense is also called **Uncollectible Accounts Expense**. Both account names mean the same thing—a customer did not pay his or her account balance.

There are two methods of accounting for uncollectible accounts receivable:

- The direct write-off method
- The allowance method

We will examine the direct write-off method first.

Direct write-off method The method of accounting for uncollectible accounts in which a customer's account is written off as uncollectible when the business determines that the customer will not pay.

How Do You Account for Uncollectible Accounts?

The Direct Write-Off Method

4 **Use the direct write-off and allowance methods to account for uncollectible accounts**

The simplest way to account for uncollectible accounts is to use the **direct write-off method**. Under the direct write-off method, at the time it is determined the business will not collect from a specific customer, the business writes off that customer's Account Receivable. The Account Receivable is written off by debiting Bad Debt Expense and crediting the customer's Account Receivable. For example, on March 5, 2015, assume that Allied Enterprises determined that Bill Johnson's $400 Account Receivable was uncollectible. The entry to write off Bill Johnson's account under the direct write-off method would be:

DATE	ACCOUNTS	POST REF.	DR.	CR.
Mar 5	Bad Debt Expense		400	
	Accounts Receivable—Bill Johnson			400
	Wrote off Bill Johnson's account.			

The direct write-off method is generally not allowed by GAAP because it does not always adhere to the matching principle that was discussed in Chapter 3. For example, let's assume Bill Johnson's $400 account, which was written off, originated from a credit sale that occurred in 2014. In this instance, Allied Enterprises would have recorded sales revenue in 2014. However, Allied Enterprises wrote off the bad debt by recording the bad debt expense in 2015, a different year. As a result, Allied Enterprises fails to correctly match expenses with related revenues. The materiality principle, discussed in Chapter 5, allows companies who experience low amounts of bad debt expense to utilize the direct write-off method.

Direct Write-Off Method: Recovery of Accounts Previously Written Off

Occasionally after a company has written off a customer's account, the customer will unexpectedly pay part, or all, of the amount owed. There is a two-step process used to record the receipt of cash from the customer when this happens. First, the customer's Account Receivable is reinstated. This step is required as the customer's account no longer exists within the company's records. Next, the payment on the account is recorded. Let's assume that on August 10, 2015, Bill Johnson unexpectedly sent Allied Enterprises a check for $250 as payment on his account, which had previously been written off. Allied Enterprises would first reinstate the Account Receivable as follows:

DATE	ACCOUNTS	POST REF.	DR.	CR.
Aug 10	Accounts Receivable—Bill Johnson		250	
	Bad Debt Expense			250
	Reinstate Bill Johnson's account.			

Observe that only $250 of the account was reinstated. If Allied Enterprises believes Mr. Johnson will pay the remaining $150 owed on the account, the entire $400 could have been reinstated. Also, notice that the accounts debited and credited in this entry are exactly opposite of those used in the entry to write off the account. Now that the account has been reinstated, Allied Enterprises records the receipt of cash as follows:

DATE	ACCOUNTS	POST REF.	DR.	CR.
Aug 10	Cash		250	
	Accounts Receivable—Bill Johnson			250
	Collected cash on account.			

Another method of accounting for uncollectible accounts that does adhere to the matching rule is the allowance method.

The Allowance Method

Allowance method A method of accounting for uncollectible accounts that utilizes estimates of the amount of Accounts Receivable that are not expected to be collected in the future.

Allowance for Uncollectible Accounts A contra-asset account that holds the estimated amount of uncollectible accounts receivable; also called **Allowance for Doubtful Accounts**.

Net realizable value The net amount that the business expects to collect; the net realizable value of receivables is calculated by subtracting Allowance for Uncollectible Accounts from Accounts Receivable.

The **allowance method** is a method of accounting for bad debts in which bad debt expense is recorded in the same period as sales revenue. For this reason, the allowance method adheres to the matching principle and is, therefore, required by GAAP. Under the allowance method, a business will use an adjusting entry at the end of the period to record the bad debt expense for the period. Because the business does not know which customers will eventually not pay it, it must estimate the amount of bad debt expense based on past experience. The debit side of the adjusting entry will be to the Bad Debt Expense account. This is the same account that was debited when an account was written off using the direct write-off method. However, instead of crediting Accounts Receivable, a contra-account called **Allowance for Uncollectible Accounts** or **Allowance for Doubtful Accounts** will be credited. The Allowance for Uncollectible Accounts is "tied" to the Accounts Receivable account and is subtracted from Accounts Receivable to arrive at the **net realizable value** of the Accounts Receivable. The adjusting entry will look like this:

DATE	ACCOUNTS	POST REF.	DR.	CR.
Dec 31	Bad Debt Expense		XXX	
	Allowance for Uncollectible Accounts			XXX
	To record estimated bad debts.			

Control account An account in the general ledger that summarizes the details of an account balance.

The Allowance for Uncollectible Accounts is utilized because the specific customers who will ultimately not pay are unknown at the time the adjusting entry is made. Remember from Chapter 4 that, in addition to the Accounts Receivable **control account** in the general ledger, each customer also has an account in the Accounts Receivable subsidiary ledger. In order to reduce Accounts Receivable, the specific customer would have to be known so that his or her Account Receivable could be reduced in the subsidiary ledger. As we will demonstrate later in the chapter, once it is known that a specific customer's account is uncollectible, his or her Account Receivable will be written off. The offset to this entry will be to reduce the Allowance for Uncollectible Accounts by an equal amount.

Estimating the Amount of Uncollectible Accounts

In order to estimate the amount of bad debt expense, a company will use its past bad debt experience to make an educated guess of how much will be uncollectible. The state of the economy, the industry the business operates in, and other variables are also used in order to arrive at the best estimate possible. There are two basic ways to estimate the amount of uncollectible accounts:

Percent of sales method The method of estimating uncollectible accounts that focuses on net credit sales; also called the *income statement approach*.

Net credit sales The total credit sales less sales discounts and sales returns and allowances related to the credit sales.

- Percent of sales method
- Aging method

Percent of Sales Method The **percent of sales method** computes the estimated amount of uncollectible accounts as a percentage of **net credit sales**. To demonstrate, let's assume that Allied Enterprises has the following selected account balances as of December 31, 2014, prior to adjusting for bad debts:

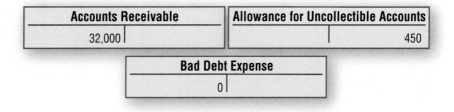

It is important to note that when using the allowance method, the Allowance for Uncollectible Accounts will almost always have a balance at the end of the period. The balance in the account may have a debit or a credit balance depending on the amount of the adjusting entry from the prior period and the amount of uncollectible accounts that have been written off during the current period. Also, note that the Bad Debt Expense account will always have a zero balance before the adjusting entry. This is because, as an expense account, it was closed at the end of the prior period.

Now, let's assume that Allied Enterprises estimates uncollectible accounts to be 1/2 of 1% of net credit sales, which totaled $300,000 during 2014. The estimated amount of uncollectible accounts is $1,500 ($300,000 × 0.005). Under the percent of sales method, once the estimated amount of uncollectible accounts has been determined, the adjusting entry is made for that amount. The required journal entry at December 31, 2014, would be as follows:

DATE	ACCOUNTS	POST REF.	DR.	CR.
Dec 31	Bad Debt Expense		1,500	
	Allowance for Uncollectible Accounts			1,500
	To record estimated bad debts.			

After posting the adjusting entry, Allied Enterprises' accounts would look like this:

Accounts Receivable		Allowance for Uncollectible Accounts	
32,000			450
			1,500
			1,950

Bad Debt Expense	
0	
1,500	
1,500	

The net realizable value of Allied Enterprises' Accounts Receivable is $30,050 at December 31, 2014 ($32,000 Accounts Receivable less $1,950 Allowance for Uncollectible Accounts). Notice that Bad Debt Expense reflects the calculated amount of uncollectible accounts ($1,500), whereas Allowance for Uncollectible Accounts reflects a different amount ($1,950). This reflects why this method is also called the **income statement approach**. This method focuses more on the income statement than on the balance sheet. After the adjusting entry has been posted, the income statement account (Bad Debt Expense) reflects the calculated amount of uncollectible accounts rather than the balance sheet account (Allowance for Uncollectible Accounts).

Income statement approach The method of estimating uncollectible accounts that focuses on net credit sales; also called the *percent of sales method*.

Aging method The method of estimating uncollectible accounts that focuses on accounts receivable; the accountant calculates the end-of-period allowance balance based on an aging of the Accounts Receivable; also called the *balance sheet approach*.

Aging Method   The other method for estimating uncollectible accounts is the **aging method**. Once again, let's assume Allied Enterprises had the following account balances at December 31, 2014, prior to adjusting for bad debts.

Accounts Receivable		Allowance for Uncollectible Accounts	
32,000			450

Bad Debt Expense	
0	

When using the aging method, a schedule is created that reflects all of the company's individual credit customers with their account balances broken down based on how long they've been outstanding. This is known as an Accounts Receivable aging report. **Exhibit 7-7** reflects the Accounts Receivable aging report for Allied Enterprises at December 31, 2014.

	Customer	Balance	Current	Days Past Due				
				1–30	31–60	61–90	91–180	> 181
1	B. Ashford	$ 450		150	300			
2	L. Clark	875	875					
32	M. Reynolds	575	575					
33	R. Turlock	225						225
34	K. Wilson	950				125	825	
	Total	$32,000	26,850	2,800	475	325	1,250	300

Exhibit 7-7 ▲

Once the aging report has been prepared, an estimated percentage of uncollectible accounts is determined for each age category. This percentage is then multiplied by the balance for each age category to determine the estimated uncollectible amount for that category. These amounts are then added together to arrive at the total estimated amount of uncollectible accounts for the period. The calculation for Allied Enterprises would look like this:

Account Age	Balance	Estimated Percent Uncollectible	Estimated Uncollectible Amount
Current	$26,850	2%	$ 537
1–30	2,800	5%	140
31–60	475	20%	95
61–90	325	40%	130
91–180	1,250	50%	625
> 181	300	80%	240
Total	$32,000		$1,767

Now that we know the total estimated amount of uncollectible accounts, $1,767, we are ready to make the adjusting entry. Unlike when using the percent of sales method, we do not simply take the calculated amount of uncollectible accounts and use this as the amount of the journal entry (this is the biggest difference between the two methods). Instead, we must look at the existing balance in Allowance for Uncollectible Accounts and perform a calculation to determine the amount to use in the adjusting entry. When using the aging method, the goal is for Allowance for Uncollectible Accounts to reflect the calculated amount of uncollectible accounts *after* the adjusting entry has been recorded and posted. The easiest way to determine the correct amount of the required adjusting entry is to do a T-account analysis of Allowance for Uncollectible Accounts:

Allowance for Uncollectible Accounts	
	450
	?
	1,767

The first step in the analysis is to enter the Allowance for Uncollectible Accounts balance that existed prior to making the adjusting entry. Next, skip a line and enter the desired ending balance in the T-account. This balance will be the calculated amount of the uncollectible accounts, $1,767. The question mark represents the adjusting entry amount that is required. This amount is determined by calculating the credit needed to bring the ending balance up to the desired amount. It is very important to pay attention to whether the Allowance for Uncollectible Accounts balance that existed prior to making the adjusting entry was a debit or a credit. Also, remember that the ending balance in the account will always be a credit balance. By looking at the T-account analysis, we can see that the required adjusting entry amount is $1,317 ($1,767 – $450). The required journal entry at December 31, 2014, would be:

DATE	ACCOUNTS	POST REF.	DR.	CR.
Dec 31	Bad Debt Expense		1,317	
	Allowance for Uncollectible Accounts			1,317
	To record estimated bad debts.			

After posting the adjusting entry, Allied Enterprises' accounts would look like this:

Accounts Receivable	
32,000	

Allowance for Uncollectible Accounts	
	450
	1,317
	1,767

Bad Debt Expense	
0	
1,317	
1,317	

The net realizable value of Allied Enterprises' Accounts Receivable is $30,233 at December 31, 2014 ($32,000 Accounts Receivable less $1,767 Allowance for Uncollectible Accounts). Notice that Allowance for Uncollectible Accounts reflects the calculated amount of uncollectible accounts ($1,767), whereas Bad Debt Expense reflects a different amount ($1,317). This reflects why this method is also called the **balance sheet approach**. This method focuses more on the balance sheet than on the income statement. After the adjusting entry has been posted, the balance sheet account (Allowance for Uncollectible Accounts) reflects the calculated amount of uncollectible accounts rather than the income statement account (Bad Debt Expense).

Balance sheet approach The method of estimating uncollectible accounts that focuses on accounts receivable. The accountant calculates the end-of-period allowance balance based on an aging of the Accounts Receivable; also called the *aging method.*

Writing Off Uncollectible Accounts Under the Allowance Method

The entry to write off a customer's account under the allowance method is similar to the entry used under the direct write-off method. At the time a company determines a customer's account is uncollectible, the Accounts Receivable will be credited to remove it from the company's books. However, the offsetting debit will not be made to Bad Debt Expense as it was under the direct write-off method. Instead, it will be made to Allowance for Uncollectible Accounts. Assume that on March 5, 2015, Allied Enterprises determined that Bill Johnson's $400 Account Receivable was uncollectible.

The entry to write off Bill Johnson's account under the allowance method would be as follows:

DATE	ACCOUNTS	POST REF.	DR.	CR.
Mar 5	Allowance for Uncollectible Accounts		400	
	Accounts Receivable—Bill Johnson			400
	Wrote off Bill Johnson's account.			

Remember that the expense related to writing off Bill Johnson's account was recognized in 2014 when Allied Enterprises made the adjusting entry to record the estimated bad debts.

Allowance Method: Recovery of Accounts Previously Written Off

The entries required to record the receipt of cash from a customer whose account was previously written off are similar under the allowance method to those used under the direct write-off method. First, the customer's Account Receivable is reinstated. Then the payment on the account is recorded. Let's assume once again that on August 10, 2015, Bill Johnson unexpectedly sent Allied Enterprises a check for $250 as payment on his previously written-off account. Allied Enterprises would first reinstate the Account Receivable:

DATE	ACCOUNTS	POST REF.	DR.	CR.
Aug 10	Accounts Receivable—Bill Johnson		250	
	Allowance for Uncollectible Accounts			250
	Reinstated Bill Johnson's account.			

Notice again that the accounts debited and credited in this entry are exactly opposite of those used in the entry to write off the account. Allied Enterprises now records the receipt of cash in the same manner as was done under the direct write-off method as:

DATE	ACCOUNTS	POST REF.	DR.	CR.
Aug 10	Cash		250	
	Accounts Receivable—Bill Johnson			250
	Collected cash on account.			

Exhibit 7-8 summarizes the differences between the entries required when using the direct write-off method and those required when using the allowance method.

Event	Direct Write-off Method			Allowance Method		
Period-end adjusting entry	None required			Bad Debt Expense	XXXX	
				Allowance for Uncollectible Accounts		XXXX
Entry to write off customer account	Bad Debt Expense	XXXX		Allowance for Uncollectible Accounts	XXXX	
	Accounts Receivable—customer name		XXXX	Accounts Receivable—customer name		XXXX
Entries to record receipt of payment on an account previously written off	Accounts Receivable—customer name	XXXX		Accounts Receivable—customer name	XXXX	
	Bad Debt Expense		XXXX	Allowance for Uncollectible Accounts		XXXX
	Cash	XXXX		Cash	XXXX	
	Accounts Receivable—customer name		XXXX	Accounts Receivable—customer name		XXXX

Exhibit 7-8 ▲

Try It...

Will writing off Bill Johnson's $400 account reduce the net realizable value of Allied Enterprises' Accounts Receivable?

Answer

No, under the allowance method, the write-off of uncollectible receivables has no impact on the net realizable value of Accounts Receivable. Remember that the net realizable value of Accounts Receivable equals the balance in the Accounts Receivable account less the balance in the related contra account, Allowance for Uncollectible Accounts. When Bill Johnson's account was written off, the asset account, Accounts Receivable, was reduced by $400. However, the Allowance for Uncollectible Accounts was also reduced by $400, so the total change in the net realizable value of the Accounts Receivable is zero.

How Are Accounts Receivable Reported on the Balance Sheet?

5 Report accounts receivable on the balance sheet

Accounts receivable are reported at "net realizable value" in the current assets section of the balance sheet. There are two ways to show Accounts Receivable at net realizable value. For example, assume that at December 31, 2014, Allied Enterprises' Accounts Receivable balance is $32,000 and its Allowance for Uncollectible Accounts balance is $1,767. Allied Enterprises could report its accounts receivable in either of the two ways shown here:

Allied Enterprises Balance Sheet (partial): December 31, 2014	
Accounts Receivable	$32,000
Less: Allowance for Uncollectible Accounts	1,767
Accounts Receivable, Net	$30,233

Allied Enterprises Balance Sheet (partial): December 31, 2014	
Accounts Receivable, Net of Allowance for Uncollectible Accounts of $1,767	$30,233

Most companies use the second method, but either is acceptable. The key is to show Accounts Receivable at net realizable value.

How Do You Account for Notes Receivable?

6 Account for notes receivable

Notes receivable are more formal than accounts receivable. The debtor signs a promissory note as evidence of the transaction. Before launching into the accounting, let's define the terms related to notes receivable.

Promissory note A written promise to pay a specified amount of money at a particular future date.

Maker of a note The entity that promises future payment; also called the **debtor.**

Payee of a note The entity to whom the debtor promises future payment; also called the **creditor.**

Principal The amount loaned out by the payee and borrowed by the maker of the note.

Interest The fee for using money; revenue to the creditor for loaning money; expense to the debtor for borrowing money.

Interest rate The percentage rate of interest specified by the note; almost always stated for a period of one year.

Maturity date The date when final payment of a note is due; also called the **due date.**

Maturity value The sum of the principal of a note plus interest due at maturity.

Note term The time span of the note during which interest is computed; it extends from the original date of the note to the maturity date.

- **Promissory note**: A written promise to pay a specified amount of money on a particular future date.
- **Maker of a note**: The entity that signs the note and promises to pay the required amount; the maker of the note is the **debtor.**
- **Payee of a note**: The entity to whom the maker promises future payment; the payee of the note is the **creditor.**
- **Principal**: The amount loaned out by the payee and borrowed by the maker of the note.
- **Interest**: The amount charged for loaning money. Interest is expense to the debtor and revenue to the creditor.
- **Interest rate**: The percentage rate of interest specified by the note. Interest rates are almost always stated for a period of one year. A 10% note means that the amount of interest for *one year* is 10% of the note's principal.
- **Maturity date**: This is the date when final payment of the note is due. Also called the **due date.**
- **Maturity value**: The sum of the principal plus interest due at maturity.
- **Note term**: The period of time during which interest is earned. It extends from the original date of the note to the maturity date.

Exhibit 7-9 illustrates a promissory note. As you study the promissory note, look for the items mentioned previously.

Identifying the Maturity Date

Some notes specify the maturity date. For example, March 31, 2015, is the maturity date of the note shown in Exhibit 7-9. Other notes state the period of the note in days or months. When the period is given in months, the note's maturity date falls on the same

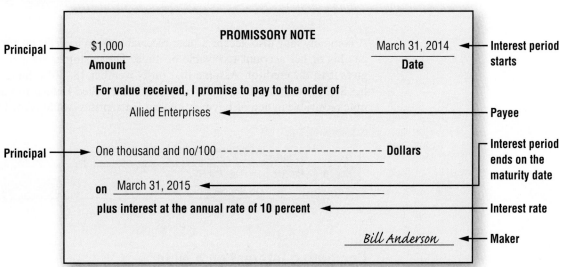

Exhibit 7-9 ▲

day of the month as the date the note was issued. For example, a three-month note dated March 1, 2014, would mature on June 1, 2014.

When the period is given in days, the maturity date is determined by counting the actual days from the date of issue. A 180-day note dated March 16, 2014, matures on September 12, 2014.

When counting the days for a note term, remember to:

- Count the maturity date.
- Omit the date the note was issued.

Origination of Notes Receivable

Notes receivable typically originate from a company doing one of the following:

- Lending money.
- Providing goods or services in exchange for a promissory note.
- Accepting a promissory note as payment on an account receivable.

Assume that, on August 1, 2014, Allied Enterprises lent $800 to Kim Simmons on a six-month, 8% promissory note. The journal entry to record the note would be:

DATE	ACCOUNTS	POST REF.	DR.	CR.
Aug 1	Note Receivable—K. Simmons		800	
	Cash			800

Next, assume that on September 5, Allied Enterprises sells goods for $2,500 to Don Hammond. Hammond signs a nine-month promissory note at 10% annual interest. Allied Enterprises' entry to record the sale (ignore cost of goods sold) is:

DATE	ACCOUNTS	POST REF.	DR.	CR.
Sep 5	Note Receivable—D. Hammond		2,500	
	Sales			2,500

A company may also accept a note receivable from a credit customer who is unable to pay his or her account receivable on time. The customer signs a promissory note and gives it to the creditor. Assume that on November 18, 2014, Sandra Fisher cannot pay her $1,200 account when it comes due and that Allied Enterprises accepts a 60-day, 12% note receivable in lieu of payment. Allied Enterprises would record this as follows:

DATE	ACCOUNTS	POST REF.	DR.	CR.
Nov 18	Note Receivable—S. Fisher		1,200	
	Accounts Receivable—S. Fisher			1,200

Computing Interest on a Note

The formula for computing the interest is:

$$\text{Amount of interest} = \text{Principal} \times \text{Interest rate} \times \text{Time}$$

In the formula, multiplying by "Time" adjusts for the fact that the interest rate represents a year's worth of interest. The "Time," or time period, represents the portion of a year for which interest has accrued on the note. It may be expressed as a fraction of a year in months (x/12) or a fraction of a year in days (x/360 or x/365). When the interest period is stated in days, interest may be computed based on either a 360-day year or a 365-day year. Using the data in Exhibit 7-9, Allied Enterprises computes interest revenue for one year:

$$\text{Amount of interest} = \text{Principal} \times \text{Interest rate} \times \text{Time}$$
$$\$100 = \$1,000 \times 0.10 \times 12/12$$

The maturity value of the note is $1,100 ($1,000 principal + $100 interest). The time element is 12/12 or 1 because the note's term is 1 year.

Interest on a $2,000 note at 6% for nine months is computed as:

$$\text{Amount of interest} = \text{Principal} \times \text{Interest rate} \times \text{Time}$$
$$\$90 = \$2,000 \times 0.06 \times 9/12$$

Interest on a $4,000 note at 8% for 90 days (assuming a 360 day year) is computed as:

$$\text{Amount of interest} = \text{Principal} \times \text{Interest rate} \times \text{Time}$$
$$\$80 = \$4,000 \times 0.08 \times 90/360$$

Accruing Interest Revenue

Notes receivable are often outstanding at the end of an accounting period. The interest revenue earned on the notes up to year-end should be recorded as part of that year's earnings. Recall that interest revenue is earned over time, not just when cash is received. Because of the matching principle, we want to record the interest revenue from notes in the year in which it was earned.

Let's continue with the Allied Enterprises' note receivable from Exhibit 7-9. Allied Enterprises' accounting period ends December 31.

• How much of the total interest revenue does Allied Enterprises earn in 2014 (from March 31 through December 31, 2014)?

$$\text{Amount of interest} = \text{Principal} \times \text{Interest rate} \times \text{Time}$$
$$\$75 = \$1,000 \times 0.10 \times 9/12$$

Allied Enterprises makes the following adjusting entry at December 31, 2014:

DATE	ACCOUNTS	POST REF.	DR.	CR.
Dec 31	Interest Receivable		75	
	Interest Revenue			75
	Accrue interest revenue.			

• How much interest revenue does Allied Enterprises earn in 2015 (from January 1 through March 31, 2015)?

$$\text{Amount of interest} = \text{Principal} \times \text{Interest rate} \times \text{Time}$$
$$\$25 \qquad = \$1,000 \times \qquad 0.10 \qquad \times 3/12$$

On the note's maturity date, Allied Enterprises makes the following entry:

DATE	ACCOUNTS	POST REF.	DR.	CR.
Mar 31	Cash (Maturity Value)		1,100	
	Note Receivable—B. Anderson			1,000
	Interest Receivable			75
	Interest Revenue			25
	Record repayment of note at maturity.			

Earlier we determined that total interest on the note was $100 ($1,000 × 0.10 × 12/12). These entries assign the correct amount of interest to each year.

$$2014 = \$\ 75$$
$$2015 = \$\ 25$$
$$\text{Total Interest} = \$100$$

Focus on Decision Making

"Can a Business Pay Its Bills?"

How much cash, and assets that can be quickly turned into cash, should a business have? A business needs enough cash to pay its bills in normal times. It also needs enough cash to face unexpected challenges and opportunities.

Just because a business is profitable does not mean that it can pay its bills. Remember, accrual accounting does not wait to recognize revenue or expense until the cash is received or paid. Thus, net income is not the same as cash. Likewise, an unprofitable business may be able to pay its bills in the short term.

Like any asset, a business can have too little or too much cash. A business wants enough cash to pay its bills. But unneeded cash does not help the business's profitability. So how can you tell when a business has the right amount of cash and assets that quickly turn into cash? The term often used to describe this issue is "liquidity management." **Liquidity management** examines how a business manages its cash so it can pay its bills.

Current Ratio and Quick Ratio

Two ratios often used to measure a business's liquidity are the current ratio and the quick ratio. The **current ratio** is the ratio of current assets to current liabilities. Current assets are cash and assets that are expected to turn into cash or be sold or consumed within the next year. **Current assets** include cash, short-term investments, accounts receivable, inventory, and prepaid expenses. Current liabilities are liabilities that must be paid in one year. Current liabilities include accounts payable, accrued liabilities, and other debts due in the next year. The formula for the current ratio is:

$$\text{Current Ratio} = \frac{\text{Current Assets}}{\text{Current Liabilities}}$$

7 **Calculate the current ratio, quick ratio, accounts receivable turnover, and receivable collection period**

Liquidity management The management of cash, specifically the amount and timing of cash receipts and payments.

Current ratio The ratio of current assets to current liabilities.

Current assets Cash, short-term investments, accounts receivable, inventory, and prepaid expenses.

A more stringent measure of a company's ability to pay current liabilities is the quick ratio. The **quick ratio**, also called the **acid-test ratio**, compares a company's quick assets to its current liabilities. **Quick assets** include cash, short-term investments, and accounts receivable. The quick ratio reveals whether the entity could pay all of its current liabilities with quick assets if they were to become due in the near future. The formula for the quick ratio is:

> **Quick ratio** Ratio that reveals how well the entity can pay its current liabilities; also called the **acid-test ratio**.
>
> **Quick assets** Cash, short-term investments, and accounts receivable.

$$\text{Quick Ratio} = \frac{\text{Quick Assets}}{\text{Current Liabilities}}$$

Let's assume that Mackay Industries has the following current assets as of December 31, 2013: cash, $3,100; net current receivables, $2,500; inventory, $6,300; and short-term investments, $1,600. Current liabilities are $4,300. The current ratio for Mackay Industries is calculated as:

$$\text{Current Ratio} = \frac{\$3{,}100 + \$2{,}500 + \$1{,}600 + \$6{,}300}{\$4{,}300} = 3.14$$

The quick ratio for Mackay Industries is calculated as:

$$\text{Quick Ratio} = \frac{(\$3{,}100 + \$2{,}500 + \$1{,}600)}{\$4{,}300} = \frac{\$7{,}200}{\$4{,}300} = 1.67$$

Notice the $6,300 of inventory was not considered in the calculation of the quick ratio. This is because, although inventory is a current asset, it is not considered to be a "quick" asset.

The higher the current and quick ratios, the more able the business is to pay its current liabilities. Mackay Industries has a very strong current ratio and quick ratio. Mackay Industries' current ratio of 3.14 means that it has $3.14 of current assets to pay each $1.00 of current liabilities. Mackay Industries' quick ratio of 1.67 means that it has $1.67 of quick assets to pay each $1.00 of current liabilities.

Accounts Receivable Turnover and Receivable Collection Period

Why would a business have accounts receivable? Every business would prefer to receive cash from a sale. The answer is competition. Businesses have accounts receivable to attract customers. Accounts receivable are a way customers finance their purchases. Would you shop at Best Buy if it did not accept credit cards? Credit cards are a form of accounts receivable. So how much accounts receivable should a business have? It's a balancing act. A business wants enough accounts receivable to attract customers and have sales. However, businesses do not want unnecessary accounts receivable. The money to finance accounts receivable is expensive. The business must also work to collect the accounts receivable and worry about bad debts.

To help manage accounts receivable, a business often looks at two measures, the accounts receivable turnover and the receivable collection period. The **accounts receivable turnover** measures the ability to collect cash from customers who buy on credit. The higher the turnover, the more successful the business is in collecting cash. However, an accounts receivable turnover that is too high may indicate that a company is not extending credit freely enough to make sales to all potentially good customers. The accounts receivable turnover is calculated as:

> **Accounts receivable turnover** Net Credit Sales divided by average Net Accounts Receivable; it measures a company's ability to collect cash from its credit customers.

$$\text{Accounts Receivable Turnover} = \frac{\text{Net Credit Sales}}{\text{Average Net Accounts Receivable}} = \frac{\text{Net Credit Sales}}{(\text{Beginning Net Accounts Receivable} + \text{Ending Net Accounts Receivable})/2}$$

The accounts receivable turnover is usually computed for an annual period, so the sales figure is the amount for the entire year. Average accounts receivable is computed by adding the beginning balance and ending balance of net accounts receivable and dividing the total by two. Remember that balance sheet accounts, such as accounts receivable, carry their balances from one period to the next. The ending accounts receivable for one year becomes the beginning accounts receivable for the next year.

The receivable collection period looks at the same issue with a slightly different measure. The **receivable collection period** measures how many days it takes to collect the average balance of accounts receivable. The receivable collection period is computed as follows:

Receivable collection period Average Net Accounts Receivable divided by daily credit sales. It measures how many days it takes to collect accounts receivable.

$$\text{Receivable Collection Period} = \frac{\text{Average Net Accounts Receivable}}{(\text{Net Credit Sales}/365 \text{ Days})}$$

To demonstrate the accounts receivable turnover and receivable collection period, assume that Mackay Industries has net credit sales for the year of $486,000; beginning net accounts receivable of $64,000; and ending net accounts receivable of $52,000. Mackay Industries would calculate the accounts receivable turnover and receivable collection period for the year as:

$$\text{Accounts Receivable Turnover} = \frac{\$486,000}{((\$64,000 + \$52,000)/2)} = \frac{\$486,000}{\$58,000} = 8.38$$

$$\text{Receivable Collection Period} = \frac{(\$64,000 + \$52,000)/2}{(\$486,000/365 \text{ Days})} = \frac{\$58,000}{\$1,331.51} = 44 \text{ Days}$$

The determination of whether a company's accounts receivable turnover is good or bad depends on the company's credit terms. If Mackay Industries grants 30-day credit terms, its 8.38 accounts receivable turnover and 44 day receivable collection period would be viewed as poor. With 30-day credit terms, you would expect a turnover of closer to 12 (365 days divided by 30 days). If Mackay Industries grants 45-day credit terms, its 8.38 accounts receivable turnover and 44 day receivable collection period would be viewed as good. With 45-day credit terms, you would expect an accounts receivable turnover of closer to 8 (365 days divided by 45 days).

How They Do It: A Look at Business

So, what are acceptable current and quick ratios? What are a good accounts receivable turnover and receivable collection period? It depends on the business. Let's look at Hershey and Walmart.

First, let's look at Hershey. Hershey makes and sells candy to wholesalers and retailers. When the economy is doing well, customers buy a lot of Hershey's products. When the economy is not doing well, customers do not buy as much Hershey candy. Making and selling these products is a volatile and thus risky business. To make sure it can pay its bills, Hershey has a considerable amount of cash. On December 31, 2012, Hershey's had $728 million in cash and cash equivalents. But Hershey also had a current ratio of 1.4 and a quick ratio of 0.8. The management of Hershey has significant liquidity to make sure it can pay its bills in good and bad times.

A part of Hershey's liquidity is the management of accounts receivable. Hershey sells to wholesalers and retailers, allowing them to pay later. Hershey has accounts receivable. Hershey's accounts receivable turnover for its 2012 fiscal year was 15.4 times a year. It takes Hershey an average of 23.6 days to collect its average level of accounts receivable.

Now, let's look at Walmart. Walmart buys and resells clothing and household products. Walmart is a discount retailer that sells the basic goods that people need to live in good and bad times. Its sales and costs are very predictable. Its business is risky, but not as risky as Hershey's. To make sure it can pay its bills, Hershey has a lot of cash. On January 31, 2013, Walmart had $7.8 billion in cash. But Walmart also had a current ratio of 0.8 and a quick ratio of 0.2 at the end of the 2012 fiscal year. Walmart is a business that has less risk than Hershey. Because of the higher certainty of Walmart's sales and operations, the management of Walmart does not believe Walmart needs as much liquidity as Hershey.

A part of Walmart's liquidity is the management of accounts receivable, particularly its credit card receivables. Walmart doesn't loan money to its customers directly. However, Walmart accepts credit cards issued by banks. When Walmart accepts a credit card for payment, it takes several days for the bank to pay Walmart. Until the bank pays Walmart, credit card transactions are receivables. Walmart's accounts receivable turnover for the fiscal year ending January 31, 2013, was 73.4 times a year. In other words, it takes Walmart an average of 5 days to collect its credit card receivables.

Now think about and compare Hershey and Walmart. Each have accounts receivables. Accounts receivable are important in how each does business. However, Hershey and Walmart use accounts receivables differently and thus have different accounts receivable turnovers and collect periods.

Summary

MyAccountingLab

Here is what you should know after reading this chapter. The Study Plan in MyAccountingLab will help you identify what you know and where to go when you need practice.

Key Points	Key Accounting Terms
1 **Discuss internal controls for cash and prepare a bank reconciliation**	Maintaining internal controls over cash is critical: • Cash receipts should be deposited promptly. • A payment process that ensures separation of duties is very important. • Bank reconciliations should be prepared regularly.	**Bank balance** (p. 294) **Bank collection** (p. 295) **Bank reconciliation** (p. 294) **Bank statement** (p. 294) **Book balance** (p. 294) **Controller** (p. 293) **Deposits in transit** (p. 295) **Electronic data interchange (EDI)** (p. 293) **Electronic funds transfer (EFT)** (p. 294) **Lock-box system** (p. 295) **Nonsufficient funds (NSF) check** (p. 295) **Outstanding checks** (p. 295) **Purchase order** (p. 293) **Purchasing agent** (p. 293) **Receiving report** (p. 293) **Treasurer** (p. 293)

		Key Points	**Key Accounting Terms**
2	**Report cash on the balance sheet**	Most companies report cash and cash equivalents together on the balance sheet: • Cash consists of most things a bank will take as a deposit. • Cash equivalents are very liquid, short-term investments such as money market funds.	**Cash equivalents** (p. 300) **Petty cash** (p. 300)
3	**Identify the different types of receivables and discuss related internal controls for accounts receivable**	Granting credit to customers can generate more sales, but it comes at a cost if customers don't pay: • GAAP requires the use of the allowance method to account for uncollectible accounts. • The direct write-off method is generally not allowed by GAAP because it violates the matching principle. • On the balance sheet, the allowance for uncollectible accounts is subtracted from the accounts receivable balance to report the "net realizable value" of Accounts Receivable.	**Aging method** (p. 304) **Allowance for Doubtful Accounts** (p. 303) **Allowance for Uncollectible Accounts** (p. 303) **Allowance method** (p. 303) **Bad debt expense** (p. 301) **Balance sheet approach** (p. 306) **Control account** (p. 303) **Direct write-off method** (p. 301) **Income statement approach** (p. 304) **Net credit sales** (p. 303) **Net realizable value** (p. 303) **Percent of sales method** (p. 303) **Uncollectible Accounts Expense** (p. 301) **Write off** (p. 301)
4	**Use the direct write-off and allowance methods to account for uncollectible accounts**		
5	**Report accounts receivable on the balance sheet**		
6	**Account for notes receivable**	Notes receivable are generally longer in term than accounts receivable and are supported by a promissory note • Notes are recorded in the accounting records at face value, which is the principal amount of the note. • The maturity value of a note equals the principal amount of the note plus the interest due on the note.	**Creditor** (p. 309) **Debtor** (p. 309) **Due date** (p. 309) **Interest** (p. 309) **Interest rate** (p. 309) **Maker of a note** (p. 309) **Maturity date** (p. 309) **Maturity value** (p. 309) **Note term** (p. 309) **Payee of a note** (p. 309) **Principal** (p. 309) **Promissory note** (p. 309)

7   **Calculate the current ratio, quick ratio, accounts receivable turnover, and receivable collection period**

Key Points	Key Accounting Terms
Ratios frequently used to help make decisions: • The current ratio and quick ratio help a company determine its ability to pay current liabilities. • The accounts receivable turnover and receivable collection period measure how quickly a business collects its accounts receivable.	**Accounts receivable turnover** (p. 313) **Acid-test ratio** (p. 313) **Current assets** (p. 312) **Current ratio** (p. 312) **Liquidity management** (p. 312) **Quick assets** (p. 313) **Quick ratio** (p. 313) **Receivable collection period** (p. 314)

Accounting Practice

Discussion Questions

1. Which duties should be segregated in the purchasing process? Why? That is, what could go wrong if two or more of those duties are not segregated?

2. After preparing a bank reconciliation, which reconciling items will require journal entries? Why?

3. What would be the surest way to eliminate the possibility of having any bad debts? Why don't companies operate this way if it could help them eliminate this costly expense?

4. Why does the allowance method of accounting for bad debts conform to GAAP while the direct write-off method does not?

5. How is Allowance for Doubtful Accounts reported on the financial statements? Why is it important for companies to report net realizable value of Accounts Receivable on the balance sheet?

6. Why is the percent of sales method called the "income statement approach" while the aging method is called the "balance sheet approach"?

7. Under which method, percent of sales or aging, would the balance in Allowance for Doubtful Accounts, just before the adjusting entry, affect the amount of the adjusting entry? Why?

8. How would the net realizable value of Accounts Receivable change when an account is written off under the allowance method?

9. If a company with a 12/31 year-end lends money in the form of a six-month note on 11/1, which accounts will be credited when the note is paid off on 4/30?

10. Recently the United States was in a recession. What would be the expected effect of a recession on accounts receivable turnover ratios?

Self Check

1. The document that identifies and explains all differences between the company's record of cash and the bank's record of that cash is the

   a. bank reconciliation.
   b. electronic fund transfer.
   c. bank collection.
   d. bank statement.

2. Which item(s) appears as a reconciling item(s) to the book balance in a bank reconciliation?

   a. Outstanding checks
   b. Deposits in transit
   c. Both a and b
   d. None of the above

3. Which item(s) appears as a reconciling item(s) to the bank balance in a bank reconciliation?

   a. Outstanding checks
   b. Deposits in transit
   c. Both a and b
   d. None of the above

4. On its books, Nile Valley Company's Cash account shows an ending balance of $950. The bank statement for the current period shows a $22 service charge and an NSF check for $140. A $220 deposit is in transit, and outstanding checks total $380. What is Nile Valley's adjusted book balance for Cash?

   a. $626
   b. $788
   c. $818
   d. $1,168

5. After performing a bank reconciliation, journal entries are required for

   a. all items on the book side of the reconciliation.
   b. all items on the bank side of the reconciliation.
   c. all items on the reconciliation.
   d. no items from the reconciliation because the Cash account needs no adjustment.

6. Uncollectible accounts are the same as

   a. notes receivable.
   b. bad debts.
   c. both a and b.
   d. none of the above.

7. Which method of estimating uncollectible receivables focuses on net credit sales?

   a. Aging approach
   b. Net realizable value approach
   c. Percent-of-sales approach
   d. All of the above

8. Your business uses the allowance method to account for uncollectible receivables. At the beginning of the year, Allowance for Uncollectible Accounts had a credit balance of $1,800. During the year you wrote off bad receivables of $2,000 and recorded Bad Debt Expense of $2,900. What is your year-end balance in Allowance for Uncollectible Accounts?

   a. $2,700
   b. $3,800
   c. $4,700
   d. $3,300

9. Which of the following is *true* regarding the direct write-off method of accounting for uncollectibles?

   a. The direct write-off method does not adhere to GAAP.
   b. The direct write-off method does not use an allowance for uncollectible accounts and, thus, overstates assets on the balance sheet.
   c. The direct write-off method does not match expenses against revenues very well.
   d. All of the above are true.

10. On December 31, you have a $15,000 note receivable from a customer. Interest of 5% has also accrued for eight months on the note. What will your financial statements report for this situation?

    a. The balance sheet will report the note receivable of $15,000 and interest receivable of $500.
    b. The balance sheet will report the note receivable of $15,000.
    c. Nothing will be reported because you haven't received the cash yet.
    d. The income statement will report a note receivable of $15,000.

 11. In the Real World Accounting Video, Zachery Mack talks about the challenges of cash management. He was able to survive a catastrophe due to Hurricane Sandy. He was able to pay his bills and keep his business operating. He attributed his survival to which trait:

    a. being organized
    b. being optimistic
    c. being patient
    d. being positive

12. According to the Real World Accounting Video, cash sales account for approximately _____ of all sales at Alphabet City Beer.

    a. half, or 50%
    b. a quarter, or 25%
    c. none, or 0%
    d. all, or 100%

Answers are given after Written Communication.

Short Exercises

S7-1. Bank reconciliation adjustments (*Learning Objective 1*) 5–10 min.

For each of the following, indicate whether the item is an adjustment to the bank balance or the book balance:

_____ 1. Bank service charge

_____ 2. Deposit in transit

_____ 3. Bank collection of amount due from customer

_____ 4. Interest revenue on bank balance

_____ 5. Outstanding check

S7-2. Bank reconciliation adjustments (*Learning Objective 1*) 10–15 min.

Classify each of the following items as one of the following:

Addition to the book balance (+ Book)

Subtraction from the book balance (– Book)

Addition to the bank balance (+ Bank)

Subtraction from the bank balance (– Bank)

_____ 1. Outstanding checks

_____ 2. Deposits in transit

_____ 3. NSF check

_____ 4. Bank collection of our note receivable

_____ 5. Interest earned on bank balance

_____ 6. Bank service charge

_____ 7. Book error: We credited Cash for $200. The correct amount of the check was $2,000.

_____ 8. Bank error: The bank decreased our account for a check written by another customer.

S7-3. Prepare a bank reconciliation (*Learning Objective 1*) 5–10 min.

The T-account for cash and the bank statement of Sinclair Food Services for the month of October 2014 follows:

Cash			
Oct 1	3,310	Check #704	640
Oct 10 deposit	925	Check #705	300
Oct 31 deposit	240	Check #706	930
Pre-adjusted Bal @ Oct 31	2,605		

Bank Statement:				
Bal, Oct 1				$3,310
Deposits:				
Deposits			$925	
Bank collection			630	
Interest			5	1,560
Checks:	No.	Amount		
	704	640		
	705	300		(940)
Other Charges:				
Service charge			$ 40	(40)
Bal, Oct 31				$3,890

Prepare Sinclair Food Services' bank reconciliation at October 31.

S7-4. Prepare bank reconciliation journal entries (*Learning Objective 1*) 5–10 min.

Make the necessary journal entries arising from Greenacres Auto Center's bank reconciliation presented next. Date each entry May 31 and include an explanation with each entry.

Greenacres Auto Center **Bank Reconciliation** **May 31**			
BANK		**BOOKS**	
Bal, May 31	$ 678	Bal, May 31	$ 785
Add:		Add:	
Deposit in transit	300	Interest revenue	5
	978		790
		Less:	
Less:		Service charge	(25)
Outstanding checks	(345)	NSF Checks	(132)
Adjusted bank balance	$ 633	Adjusted book balance	$ 633

S7-5. Balance sheet presentation of cash (*Learning Objective 2*) 5–10 min.

Prepare the current assets section of the balance sheet as of May 31, 2014, for Spices and More, Inc., using the following information:

Accounts Receivable	$54,200
Petty Cash	300
Cash in Bank Accounts	21,400
Inventory	85,800

S7-12. Internal controls—credit sales (*Learning Objective 3*) 10–15 min.

Claire Billiot, the office manager of a local office supply company, is designing its internal control system. Billiot proposes the following procedures for credit checks on new customers, sales on account, cash collections, and write-offs of uncollectible receivables:

a. The Credit Department runs a credit check on all customers who apply for credit. When an account proves uncollectible, the Credit Department authorizes the write-off of the account receivable.

b. Cash receipts come into the Credit Department, which separates the cash received from the customer remittance slips. The Credit Department lists all cash receipts by customer name and the amount of cash received.

c. The cash goes to the treasurer for deposit in the bank. The remittance slips go to the Accounting Department for recording of the collections.

d. The controller compares the daily deposit slip to the total amount of the collections recorded. Both amounts must agree.

For each of the four procedures, indicate whether the procedure includes an internal control weakness. Explain how employee fraud could occur because of the weakness. What can Claire do to strengthen the internal control system?

S7-13. Notes receivable terms (*Learning Objective 6*) 10–15 min.

Match the term with its definition by placing the corresponding letter in the space provided:

_____1. A written promise to pay a specified amount of money at a particular future date.

_____2. The date when final payment of the note is due; also called the due date.

_____3. The percentage rate of interest specified by the note for one year.

_____4. The entity to whom the maker promises future payment.

_____5. The period of time during which interest is earned.

_____6. The amount loaned out by the payee and borrowed by the maker of the note.

_____7. The sum of the principal plus interest due at maturity.

_____8. The entity that signs the note and promises to pay the required amount.

_____9. The revenue to the payee for loaning money; the expense to the debtor.

a. Interest
b. Note term
c. Interest rate
d. Maker of the note
e. Maturity date
f. Maturity value
g. Payee of the note
h. Principal
i. Promissory note

S7-14. Accounting for notes receivable (*Learning Objective 6*) 10–15 min.

For each of the following notes receivable, compute the amount of interest revenue earned during 2014. Use a 360-day year, and round to the nearest dollar.

	Principal	Interest Rate	Interest Period During 2014
Note 1	$ 25,000	9%	11 months
Note 2	42,000	8%	75 days
Note 3	10,000	6%	45 days
Note 4	125,000	4%	9 months

S7-15. Accounting for notes receivable (*Learning Objective 6*) **10–15 min.**

Pacific Bank lent $125,000 to Robert Simmons on a 30-day, 6% note. Record the following transactions for Pacific Bank (explanations are not required):

1. Lending the money on June 12.
2. Collecting the principal and interest at maturity. Specify the date. For the computation of interest, use a 360-day year and round to the nearest dollar.

S7-16. Quick ratio (*Learning Objective 7*) **5–10 min.**

Calculate the quick assets and the quick ratio for each of the following companies:

	Rhodes	Peters
Cash	$15,000	$ 23,000
Short-term Investments	6,000	13,000
Net Receivables	41,000	51,000
Current Liabilities	40,000	108,750

S7-17. Accounts receivable turnover (*Learning Objective 7*) **5–10 min.**

Calculate accounts receivable turnover for the following two companies:

	Simpson	Martinez
Net Credit Sales	$90,000	$48,000
Net Accounts Receivable, Beginning	18,000	21,000
Net Accounts Receivable, Ending	15,000	23,000

MyAccountingLab

Exercises (Group A)

E7-18A. Bank reconciliation adjustments (*Learning Objective 1*) **10–15 min.**

Calculate the answers for the missing data:

BANK		BOOKS	
Bal, Jan 31	$1,045	Bal, Jan 31	(c)
Add:		Add:	
Deposit in transit	620	Bank collection	635
	(a)	Interest revenue	15
			(d)
Less:		Less:	
Outstanding checks	(b)	Service charge	(45)
Adjusted bank balance	$1,310	Adjusted book balance	$1,310

E7-19A. Prepare a bank reconciliation and journal entries (*Learning Objective 1*)
20–25 min.

Chester's Produce's checkbook lists the following:

Date	Check No.	Item	Check	Deposit	Balance
6/1					$1,420
5	922	West St. Kitchen	$ 15		1,405
10		Dividends received		$ 340	1,745
14	923	Kingpin Products	48		1,697
15	924	Fauna (payment on account)	68		1,629
19	925	Cash	99		1,530
27	926	Staples	144		1,386
28	927	Miller Properties	667		719
29		Monthly Sales		4,220	4,939

Chester's Produce's June bank statement shows the following:

Bal, Jun 1					$1,420
Deposits:					340
Checks:	No.	Amount			
	922	$ 15			
	923	48			
	924	78*			
	925	99			(240)
Other Charges:					
Printed checks			$12		
Service charge			22		(34)
Bal, Jun 30					$1,486

*This amount is correct for check no. 924.

Requirements

1. Prepare Chester's Produce's bank reconciliation on June 30, 2014. How much cash does Chester's Produce actually have on June 30?

2. Prepare all necessary journal entries for Chester's Produce to update the Cash account as a result of the bank reconciliation.

E7-20A. Prepare a bank reconciliation (*Learning Objective 1*) **20–25 min.**

Information from Pring's Picture Frames' Cash account as well as the July bank statement are presented next.

Cash			
Jul 1	2,106	Check #210	28
Jul 30	1,430	Check #211	500
		Check #212	63
		Check #213	270
		Check #214	145
Pre-adjusted			
Bal @ Jul 31	2,530		

Bank Statement:				
Bal, Jul 1				$2,106
Deposits:				
EFT—rent				850
Checks:	No.	Amount		
	210	280		
	211	500		
	212	63		(843)
Other Charges:				
Service charge			$ 35	
Check printing			28	
NSF check #201			75	(138)
Bal, Jul 31				$1,975

Check #210 was written for $280 to pay salaries expense.

Requirements

1. Prepare the bank reconciliation on July 31.
2. Prepare all necessary journal entries for Pring's Picture Frames to update the Cash account as a result of the bank reconciliation.

Quick solution:

1. Adjusted cash balance = $2,990

E7-21A. Direct write-off method (*Learning Objective 4*) 5–10 min.

Blue Mountain, Inc., uses the direct write-off method to account for bad debts. Record the following transactions that occurred during the year:

May 3	Provided $4,450 of services to Ken Reeve on account.
Nov 8	Wrote off Ken Reeve's $4,450 account as uncollectible.
Dec 10	Unexpectedly collected $1,000 from Ken Reeve on the account that had been written off. Blue Mountain, Inc., does not expect to collect the remaining balance.

E7-22A. Percent of sales allowance method (*Learning Objective 4*) 10–15 min.

Charly's Automotive ended December 2013 with Accounts Receivable of $72,000 and a credit balance in Allowance for Uncollectible Accounts of $2,800. During January 2014, Charly's Automotive completed the following transactions:

a. Sales of $273,000, which included $141,000 in credit sales and $132,000 of cash sales. Ignore cost of goods sold.
b. Cash collections on account, $128,000.
c. Write-offs of uncollectible receivables, $2,300.
d. Bad debt expense, estimated as 1% of credit sales.

Requirements

1. Prepare journal entries to record sales (ignore cost of goods sold), collections, write-offs of uncollectibles, and bad debt expense by the percent-of-sales method.
2. Calculate the ending balances in Accounts Receivable, Allowance for Uncollectible Accounts, and net Accounts Receivable at January 31, 2014. How much does Charly's Automotive expect to collect?

E7-23A. Aging of accounts receivable allowance method (*Learning Objective 4*) 15–20 min.

On January 31, 2014, the Accounts Receivable balance of Advanced Automotive Technology is $270,000. The Allowance for Uncollectible Accounts has a $4,100 credit balance. Advanced Automotive Technology prepares the following aging schedule for its accounts receivable:

	Age of Accounts			
	1–30 Days	31–60 Days	61–90 Days	Over 90 Days
Accounts Receivable..............................	$120,000	$75,000	$65,000	$10,000
Estimated Percentage Uncollectible	0.4%	2.0%	10.0%	45%

Requirements

1. Journalize the year-end adjusting entry for uncollectible accounts on the basis of the aging schedule. Calculate the resulting ending balance of the Allowance account based on the account aging. Show the T-account for the Allowance on January 31, 2014.

2. Assume that instead of a $4,100 credit balance, there is a $900 debit balance in the Allowance account prior to adjustment. Journalize the year-end adjusting entry for uncollectible accounts on the basis of the aging schedule. Calculate the resulting ending balance of the Allowance account based on the account aging. Show the T-account for the Allowance on January 31, 2014.

E7-24A. Percent of sales and aging of accounts receivable allowance methods (*Learning Objective 4*) 15–20 min.

EasternTextile uses the allowance method to account for uncollectible accounts. On December 31, 2014, Allowance for Uncollectible Accounts has a $1,475 credit balance. Journalize the year-end adjusting entry for uncollectible accounts assuming the following *independent* scenarios:

1. Eastern Textile estimates uncollectible accounts as 1/5 of 1% of net credit sales. Net credit sales for the year equal $1,475,000.

2. Based on an aging of Accounts Receivable, Eastern Textile estimates that uncollectible accounts will equal $4,250.

E7-25A. Accounting for notes receivable (*Learning Objective 6*) 15–20 min.

On September 30, 2014, Citibank loaned $800,000 to George Wells on a one-year, 9% note.

Requirements

1. Compute the interest for the years ended December 31, 2014 and 2015, on the Wells note. Round interest calculations to the nearest dollar.

2. Which party has
   a. a note receivable?
   b. a note payable?
   c. interest revenue?
   d. interest expense?

3. How much in total would Wells pay the bank if he pays off the note early on April 30, 2015?

E7-26A. Accounting for notes receivable (*Learning Objective 6*) 15–20 min.

Journalize the following transactions of Alegro Inc., which ends its accounting year on April 30:

Feb 1	Loaned $65,000 cash to Doug Gaston on a one-year, 4% note.
Apr 6	Sold goods to Turf Pro, receiving a 90-day, 5% note for $7,200. Ignore cost of goods sold.
30	Made a single entry to accrue interest revenue on both notes.
	Use a 360-day year for interest computations and round to the nearest dollar.

E7-27A. Accounting for notes receivable (*Learning Objective 6*) 15–20 min.

Jonah Enterprises sells on account. When a customer account becomes four months old, Jonah converts the account to a note receivable. During 2014, Jonah completed these transactions:

Jan 29	Sold goods on account to Belmont, Inc., $24,000. Ignore cost of goods sold.
Jun 1	Received a $24,000, 60-day, 12% note from Belmont, Inc., in satisfaction of its past-due account receivable.
Jul 31	Collected the Belmont, Inc., note at maturity. Use a 360-day year for interest computation and round to the nearest dollar.

Requirement

1. Record the transactions in Jonah Enterprises' journal.

E7-28A. Quick ratio and current ratio (*Learning Objective 7*) 15–20 min.

Consider the following data:

COMPANY	A	B	C	D
Cash	$ 60,000	$ 75,000	$25,000	$105,000
Short-term Investments	58,000	20,000	14,000	24,000
Net Receivables	160,000	115,000	26,000	150,000
Total current assets	320,000	230,000	80,000	315,000
Current Liabilities	180,000	95,000	45,000	340,000

Requirements

1. Calculate the quick assets and the quick ratio for each company.

2. Calculate the current ratio for each company.

3. Which of the companies should be concerned about its liquidity?

E7-29A. Quick ratio, current ratio, and accounts receivable turnover (*Learning Objective 7*) 15–20 min.

Cherokee Equipment reported the following items on December 31, 2014 (amounts in thousands, with last year's amounts also given as needed):

Accounts Payable	$ 450	Accounts Receivable, Net:	
Cash	220	December 31, 2014	$ 250
Inventory:		December 31, 2013	170
December 31, 2014	200	Cost of Goods Sold	1,100
December 31, 2013	140	Short-term Investments	168
Net Credit Sales	1,911	Other Current Assets	60
Long-term Assets	400	Other Current Liabilities	130
Long-term Liabilities	10		

Requirements

1. Compute Cherokee Equipment's (a) quick ratio, (b) current ratio, and (c) accounts receivable turnover for 2014.

2. Evaluate each ratio value as strong or weak. Assume Cherokee Equipment sells on terms of net 30.

MyAccountingLab

Exercises (Group B)

E7-30B. Bank reconciliation adjustments (*Learning Objective 1*) 10–15 min.

Calculate the answers for the missing data:

BANK			BOOKS	
Bal, Dec 31		$ 1,060	Bal, Dec 31	(c)
Add:			Add:	
Deposit in transit		680	Bank collection	425
		(a)	Interest revenue	35
				(d)
Less:			Less:	
Outstanding checks		(b)	Service charge	(45)
Adjusted bank balance		$1,340	Adjusted book balance	$1,340

E7-31B. Prepare a bank reconciliation and journal entries (*Learning Objective 1*) 20–25 min.

Cliff's Construction's checkbook lists the following:

Date	Check No.	Item	Check	Deposit	Balance
4/1					$1,385
5	922	Westin Kitchen	$ 10		1,375
10		Dividends received		$ 325	1,700
14	923	Best Products	41		1,659
15	924	Fergus (payment on account)	67		1,592
19	925	Cash	163		1,429
27	926	Office Supply	186		1,243
28	927	James Town Properties	527		716
30		Monthly Sales		2,890	3,606

Cliff's Construction's April bank statement shows the following:

Bal, Apr 1				$1,385
Deposits:				325
Checks:	No.	Amount		
	922	$ 10		
	923	41		
	924	76*		
	925	163		(290)
Other Charges:				
Printed checks			$32	
Service charge			25	(57)
Bal, Apr 30				$1,363

*This amount is correct for check no. 924.

Requirements

1. Prepare Cliff's Construction's bank reconciliation on April 30, 2014. How much cash does Cliff's Construction actually have on April 30?

2. Prepare all necessary journal entries for Cliff's Construction to update the Cash account as a result of the bank reconciliation.

E7-32B. **Prepare a bank reconciliation** (*Learning Objective 1*) 20–25 min.

Information from Addison Picture Frames' Cash account as well as the November bank statement are presented next.

Cash			
Nov 1	1,600	Check #210	33
Nov 30	2,700	Check #211	400
		Check #212	113
		Check #213	300
		Check #214	150
Pre-adjusted			
Bal @ Nov 30	3,304		

Bank Statement:				
Bal, Nov 1				$ 1,600
Deposits:				
EFT—rent				410
Checks:	No.	Amount		
	210	330		
	211	400		
	212	113		(843)
Other Charges:				
Service charge			$ 23	
Check printing			14	
NSF check #201			100	(137)
Bal, Nov 30				$ 1,030

Check #210 was written for $330 to pay salaries expense.

Requirements

1. Prepare the bank reconciliation on November 30.

2. Prepare all necessary journal entries for Addison Picture Frames to update the Cash account as a result of the bank reconciliation.

E7-33B. **Direct write-off method** (*Learning Objective 4*) 5–10 min.

Fesler Industries uses the direct write-off method to account for bad debts. Record the following transactions that occurred during the year:

May	3	Provided $1,300 of services to Beth Wilson on account.
Nov	8	Wrote off Beth Wilson's $1,300 account as uncollectible.
Dec	10	Unexpectedly collected $1,150 from Beth Wilson on the account that had been written off. Fesler Industries does not expect to collect the remaining balance.

E7-34B. Percent of sales allowance method (*Learning Objective 4*) **10–15 min.**

Teck Automotive ended December 2013 with Accounts Receivable of $30,000 and a credit balance in Allowance for Uncollectible Accounts of $4,000. During January 2014, Teck Automotive completed the following transactions:

a. Sales of $158,000, which included $98,000 in credit sales and $60,000 of cash sales. Ignore cost of goods sold.
b. Cash collections on account, $77,000.
c. Write-offs of uncollectible receivables, $900.
d. Bad debt expense, estimated as 1% of credit sales.

Requirements

1. Prepare journal entries to record sales (ignore cost of goods sold), collections, write-offs of uncollectibles, and bad debt expense by the percent-of-sales method.

2. Calculate the ending balances in Accounts Receivable, Allowance for Uncollectible Accounts, and net Accounts Receivable at January 31, 2014. How much does Teck Automotive expect to collect?

E7-35B. Aging of accounts receivable allowance method (*Learning Objective 4*) **15–20 min.**

On October 31, 2014, the Accounts Receivable balance of Richards Manufacturing is $307,000. The Allowance for Uncollectible Accounts has a $4,200 credit balance. Richards Manufacturing prepares the following aging schedule for its accounts receivable:

	Age of Accounts			
	1–30 Days	31–60 Days	61–90 Days	Over 90 Days
Accounts Receivable.............................	$125,000	$80,000	$61,000	$7,000
Estimated Percentage Uncollectible........	0.3%	4.0%	6.0%	55%

Requirements

1. Journalize the year-end adjusting entry for uncollectible accounts on the basis of the aging schedule. Calculate the resulting ending balance of the Allowance account based on the account aging. Show the T-account for the Allowance on October 31, 2014.

2. Assume that instead of a $4,200 credit balance, there is a $1,300 debit balance in the Allowance account prior to adjustment. Journalize the year-end adjusting entry for uncollectible accounts on the basis of the aging schedule. Calculate the resulting ending balance of the Allowance account based on the account aging. Show the T-account for the Allowance on October 31, 2014.

E7-36B. Percent of sales and aging of accounts receivable allowance methods (*Learning Objective 4*) **15–20 min.**

Outerbanks, Inc., uses the allowance method to account for uncollectible accounts. On December 31, 2014, Allowance for Uncollectible Accounts has a $1,300 credit balance. Journalize the year-end adjusting entry for uncollectible accounts assuming the following *independent* scenarios:

1. Outerbanks, Inc., estimates uncollectible accounts as 3/4 of 1% of net credit sales. Net credit sales for the year equal $800,000.

2. Based on an aging of Accounts Receivable, Outerbanks, Inc. estimates that uncollectible accounts will equal $2,650.

E7-37B. Accounting for notes receivable (*Learning Objective 6*) 15–20 min.

On July 31, 2014, Texas State Bank loaned $475,000 to Gina Baldwin on a one-year, 6% note.

Requirements

1. Compute the interest for the years ended December 31, 2014 and 2015, on the Baldwin note. Round interest calculations to the nearest dollar.

2. Which party has
    a. a note receivable?
    b. a note payable?
    c. interest revenue?
    d. interest expense?

3. How much in total would Baldwin pay the bank if she pays off the note early on January 31, 2015?

E7-38B. Accounting for notes receivable (*Learning Objective 6*) 15–20 min.

Journalize the following transactions of Baltic, Inc., which ends its accounting year on September 30:

May 1	Loaned $16,000 cash to Steve Franklin on a one-year, 6% note.
Sep 17	Sold goods to Findlay, Corp., receiving a 90-day, 10% note for $12,000. Ignore cost of goods sold.
30	Made a single entry to accrue interest revenue on both notes. Use a 360-day year for interest computations and round to the nearest dollar.

E7-39B. Accounting for notes receivable (*Learning Objective 6*) 15–20 min.

Sanchez Enterprises sells on account. When a customer account becomes four months old, Sanchez converts the account to a note receivable. During 2014, Sanchez completed these transactions:

Jan 31	Sold goods on account to Jitterz Coffee, 12,000. Ignore cost of goods sold.
Jun 1	Received a $12,000, 60-day, 7% note from Jitterz Coffee, in satisfaction of its past-due account receivable.
Jul 31	Collected the Jitterz Coffee, note at maturity. Use a 360-day year for interest computation and round to the nearest dollar.

Requirement

1. Record the transactions in Sanchez Enterprises' journal.

E7-40B. Quick ratio and current ratio (*Learning Objective 7*) 15–20 min.

Consider the following data:

COMPANY	A	B	C	D
Cash	$ 95,000	$ 67,000	$20,000	$103,000
Short-term Investments	85,000	30,000	14,000	53,000
Net Current Receivables	120,000	113,000	50,000	145,000
Total Current Assets	325,000	224,000	96,000	368,000
Current Liabilities	200,000	255,000	60,000	260,000

```
┌─────────────────────────────────────────────┐
│              PETTY CASH TICKET                │
│   Date  Jun 21                                │
│   Amount  $25                                 │
│   For  Envelopes                              │
│   Debit  Office Supplies                      │
│   Received by  Jim Dirks    Fund Custodian  SK│
└─────────────────────────────────────────────┘
```

Exhibit 7A-1 ▲

Replenishing the Petty Cash Fund

Payments deplete the petty cash fund, so it must be replenished periodically. On July 31 the petty cash fund of Inland Equipment holds the following:

- $108 cash on hand
- $90 in petty cash tickets: office supplies, $53; delivery expense, $37

Notice that when the $108 of cash on hand is added to the $90 of petty cash tickets, the total comes to $198, which is $2 less than the fund balance of $200. The $2 difference signifies that $2 was misplaced from the fund. The petty cash fund can be reconciled as follows:

Cash on Hand	$108
+ Petty Cash Tickets	90
=	198
+ Cash Shortage	2
= Fund Balance	$200

To replenish the petty cash fund and make the cash on hand equal to $200 again, the company writes a check, payable to Petty Cash, for the $92 ($200 – $108) difference between the cash on hand and the fund balance. The fund custodian cashes this check and puts $92 back in the fund. Now the fund holds $200 cash as required. The following journal entry would be made to record the issuance of the check:

DATE	ACCOUNTS	POST REF.	DR.	CR.
Jul 31	Office Supplies Expense		53	
	Delivery Expense		37	
	Cash Short and Over		2	
	Cash			92
	Replenish the petty cash fund.			

The accounts debited in the entry represent the expense accounts associated with the items that the petty cash funds were used to purchase. The cash shortage is debited to an account titled Cash Short and Over. Notice that the journal entry included a credit to Cash, not Petty Cash. This is because the money to replenish the petty cash fund was taken from the Cash account. The Petty Cash account is only affected when:

- The petty cash fund is established.
- The petty cash fund balance is increased or decreased.

Changing the Petty Cash Fund

Imagine that Inland Equipment wants to increase the size of its fund from $200 to $300 on August 1. The business writes a $100 check payable to Petty Cash, and the custodian cashes it and places the money in the fund. In this case, the journal entry to record this $100 increase will look like the following:

DATE	ACCOUNTS	POST REF.	DR.	CR.
Aug 1	Petty Cash		100	
	Cash			100
	Increase petty cash fund balance.			

Accounting Practice

Short Exercises

S7A-1. Petty cash transactions (*Learning Objective 8*) 5–10 min.

Record the following petty cash transactions of Wilson Supply in the journal; explanations are not required.

Nov	1	Established a petty cash fund with a $100 balance.
	30	The petty cash fund had $26 in cash and $74 in petty cash tickets that were issued to pay for postage. Replenished the fund with cash.

S7A-2. Petty cash transactions (*Learning Objective 8*) 5–10 min.

Record the following petty cash transactions of Apex, Inc., in the journal; explanations are not required.

Sep	1	Established a petty cash fund with a $250 balance.
	30	The petty cash fund had $56 in cash and $187 in petty cash tickets that were issued to pay for office supplies ($112) and entertainment expense ($75). Replenished the fund.
	30	Increased the petty cash fund balance to $300.

Exercises (Group A)

E7A-3A. Petty cash transactions (*Learning Objective 8*) 10–15 min.

Lori's Music School created a $200 petty cash fund on May 1. During the month, the fund custodian authorized and signed petty cash tickets as follows:

Petty Cash			
Ticket No.	**Item**	**Account Debited**	**Amount**
1	Delivery of programs to customers	Delivery Expense	$10
2	Mail package	Postage Expense	50
3	Newsletter	Supplies Expense	22
4	Key to closet	Miscellaneous Expense	40
5	Computer diskettes	Supplies Expense	25

Requirements

1. Record the journal entry to create the petty cash fund.

2. Assuming that the cash in the fund totals $52 on May 31, make the journal entry to replenish the petty cash fund.

E7A-4A. Petty cash transactions (*Learning Objective 8*) **10–15 min.**

Janson, Corp., maintains a petty cash fund of $225. On July 31, the fund holds $14 cash and petty cash tickets for office supplies, $172, and delivery expense, $32.

Requirements

1. Make the journal entry to replenish the petty cash fund.

2. Janson, Corp., decided to increase the petty cash fund by $25. Prepare the journal entry.

MyAccountingLab ## Exercises (Group B)

E7A-5B. Petty cash transactions (*Learning Objective 8*) **10–15 min.**

Lynn's Music School created a $250 petty cash fund on August 1. During the month, the fund custodian authorized and signed petty cash tickets as follows:

Petty Cash			
Ticket No.	Item	Account Debited	Amount
1	Delivery of programs to customers	Delivery Expense	$12
2	Mail package	Postage Expense	47
3	Newsletter	Supplies Expense	25
4	Key to closet	Miscellaneous Expense	41
5	Computer diskettes	Supplies Expense	30

Requirements

1. Record the journal entry to create the petty cash fund.

2. Assuming that the cash in the fund totals $99 on August 31, make the journal entry to replenish the petty cash fund.

E7A-6B. Petty cash transactions (*Learning Objective 8*) **10–15 min.**

Elm Street Motors maintains a petty cash fund of $200. On December 31, the fund holds $12 cash, and petty cash tickets for office supplies totalling $121 and delivery expense totalling $55.

Requirements

1. Make the journal entry to replenish the petty cash fund.

2. Elm Street Motors decided to increase the petty cash fund by $80. Prepare the journal entry.

MyAccountingLab ## Problems (Group A)

P7A-7A. Petty cash transactions (*Learning Objective 8*) **10–15 min.**

On March 1, The Party Place creates a petty cash fund with a balance of $325. During March, Sue Bemis, the fund custodian, signs the following petty cash tickets:

Petty Cash Ticket Number	Item	Amount
101	Office supplies	$102
102	Cab fare for executive	42
103	Delivery of package across town	21
104	Dinner money for president and a potential customer	106

On March 31, prior to replenishment, the fund contains these tickets plus cash of $23. The accounts affected by petty cash payments are Office Supplies Expense, Travel Expense, Delivery Expense, and Entertainment Expense.

Requirements

1. Record the journal entry to create the petty cash fund.

2. Record the journal entry to replenish the petty cash fund on March 31. Do you have any concerns regarding the Cash Short and Over account?

3. Make the April 1 entry to increase the fund balance to $350. Include an explanation, and briefly describe what the custodian does when the balance is increased.

Problems (Group B)

P7A-8B. Petty cash transactions (*Learning Objectives 8*) 10–15 min.

On August 1, City Delivery creates a petty cash fund with a balance of $450. During August, Eva Unger, the fund custodian, signs the following petty cash tickets:

Petty Cash Ticket Number	Item	Amount
101	Office supplies	$92
102	Cab fare for executive	29
103	Delivery of package across town	15
104	Dinner money for president and a potential customer	70

On August 31, prior to replenishment, the fund contains these tickets plus cash of $209. The accounts affected by petty cash payments are Office Supplies Expense, Travel Expense, Delivery Expense, and Entertainment Expense.

Requirements

1. Record the journal entry to create the petty cash fund.

2. Record the journal entry to replenish the petty cash fund on August 31. Do you have any concerns over the Cash Short and Over account?

3. Make the entry on September 1 to decrease the fund balance to $400. Include an explanation, and briefly describe what the custodian does when the balance is decreased.

Long-Term and Other Assets

Business, Accounting, and You

Drive or walk up to an AT&T store. You want to purchase a phone and arrange phone service. You look up and see a building with a big AT&T sign. Now think about AT&T's business. What do you see? You see a lot of land, buildings, computers, satellites, and much more. AT&T needs a lot of assets that have a life longer than one year. These long-term assets are needed to attract customers and deliver the goods and services customers want. Without these assets, no sale will occur. These assets are at the heart of AT&T's success.

Businesses such as AT&T need long-term assets such as land, buildings, and equipment. But the assets are often very expensive. As the business uses these assets, the assets depreciate. If the business needs to sell these assets, it is sometimes difficult to find a buyer. As such, investing money in these assets is risky and must be done carefully.

Learning Objectives

1. Describe the differences between fixed assets, intangible assets, and natural resources

2. Calculate and record the cost of acquiring fixed assets

3. Calculate and record the depreciation of fixed assets

4. Account for repairs to fixed assets

5. Account for the disposal of fixed assets

6. Account for intangible assets

7. Account for natural resources

8. Account for other assets

9. Report long-term assets on the balance sheet

10. Calculate the return on assets and the fixed asset turnover

So how do accountants recognize, measure, record, and report long-term asset transactions? As an accountant or manager, you need to understand how a business accounts for long-term assets. It affects a business's net income and value.

 ## Real World Accounting Video

In the Real World Accounting video, Jason Berry of Rosa Mexicano Restaurants talks about managing a successful business. Look at the video. Think about what Jason is saying. Now realize how important long-term assets are to a successful business like the one Jason manages.

What Are the Different Types of Long-Term Assets?

 Describe the differences between fixed assets, intangible assets, and natural resources

Fixed assets Tangible assets such as buildings and equipment; also called **plant assets**.

Tangible assets Assets that are physical in form. They can be seen, touched, or held.

Intangible assets Assets with no physical form. They are valuable because of the special rights they carry. Examples include patents and copyrights.

Natural resources Assets that come from the earth. Examples include minerals, gas, oil, and timber.

Most businesses will own at least one of the following types of long-term assets:

- **Fixed assets.** **Fixed assets**, often called **plant assets**, are "physical assets"—meaning they can be seen, touched, or held. This includes assets such as land, buildings, vehicles, desks, and equipment. Fixed assets are also sometimes referred to as **tangible assets**.
- **Intangible assets.** Patents, trademarks, and goodwill are examples of **intangible assets**. Unlike fixed assets, intangible assets cannot be seen, touched, or held. For example, even though there may a piece of paper that provides written evidence of a patent, the paper is not the patent. The patent (the intangible asset) is actually the specific rights that are conveyed to the owner of the patent.
- **Natural resources.** Assets that come from the earth and can ultimately be used up are called **natural resources**. Timber, oil, minerals, and coal are all examples of natural resources.

As we learned in Chapter 3, the cost of a long-term asset must be allocated to an expense as the asset is used up. Although the process of cost allocation is similar for the different types of assets, the terminology used to describe the process is different for each type of asset. **Exhibit 8-1** summarizes the different asset types and the cost allocation terminology used with each.

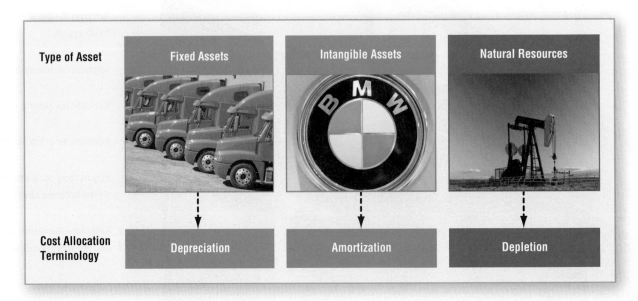

Exhibit 8-1 ▲

The cost allocation methods for each type of asset will be covered later in the chapter. Companies may also own assets that are classified as *other assets*. Other assets typically consist of investments made by a business. These will be discussed near the end of the chapter.

How Is the Cost of a Fixed Asset Calculated?

2 | **Calculate and record the cost of acquiring fixed assets**

Generally Accepted Accounting Principles (GAAP) require that the *cost principle*, which we learned about in Chapter 1, be applied when determining the cost of a fixed asset. Therefore, the actual amount paid for an asset is to be used as the asset's cost. The amount paid for an asset should include all amounts paid to acquire the asset and to prepare it for its intended purpose. These costs vary depending on the type of fixed asset being purchased, so let's discuss each asset type individually.

Land and Land Improvements

The cost of land includes, but is not limited to, the following amounts paid by the purchaser:

- Purchase price
- Realtor commissions
- Survey and legal fees
- Unpaid property taxes owed on the land
- Fees associated with transferring the ownership (title) on the land
- Cost of clearing the land and removing unwanted buildings

The cost of land does *not* include the following costs:

- Fencing
- Paving
- Sprinkler systems
- Lighting
- Signs

Land improvements
Depreciable improvements to land, such as fencing, sprinkler systems, paving, signs, and lighting.

These costs are recorded as separate fixed assets called **land improvements**.

Suppose that Apex Industries purchases land for $75,000 by signing a note payable for the same amount. Apex Industries also pays cash as follows: $2,500 in realtor commission, $1,200 in transfer fees, a $1,700 survey fee, $4,500 to remove an old building, $2,200 to have the land graded and leveled, $6,300 to have the land fenced, $1,300 for a sprinkler system, and $2,700 for outdoor lighting. What amount would Apex Industries record as the cost of the land? How much would Apex record as land improvements? Apex Industries would assign the following costs to land and land improvements:

Cost Incurred	Land	Land Improvements
Purchase price	$75,000	
Realtor commission	2,500	
Transfer fees	1,200	
Survey fee	1,700	
Building removal	4,500	
Grading	2,200	
Fencing		$ 6,300
Sprinkler system		1,300
Lighting		2,700
Total cost	$87,100	$10,300

The purchase of the land and the subsequent cash payments are recorded as:

DATE	ACCOUNTS	POST REF.	DR.	CR.
	Land		75,000	
	Note Payable			75,000
	Purchased land on a note payable.			
	Land		12,100	
	Land Improvements		10,300	
	Cash			22,400
	Paid cash for land and land improvements.			

Capitalized The process of debiting (increasing) an asset account for the cost of an asset.

We would say that Apex Industries *capitalized* the cost of the land at $87,100 ($75,000 + $12,100) and the land improvements at $10,300. **Capitalized** means that an asset account is debited (increased) for the cost of an asset. Notice that Land and Land Improvements are two entirely separate assets. Land is a special fixed asset because it is never really used up. Therefore, land is not depreciated. However, the cost of land improvements *is* depreciated over the useful life of the improvements.

Buildings

The cost of a building depends on whether the building is constructed or whether an existing building is purchased. If a building is constructed, the cost of the building includes the following:

* Architectural fees
* Building permit fees
* Contractor charges
* Payments for material, labor, and overhead

The time to complete a building can be months, even years. If a company constructs its own assets, the cost of a building may also include interest charged during the time of construction on any borrowed money.

If a company purchases an existing building, the cost of the building includes:

* Purchase price
* Realtor commissions
* Appraisal and legal fees
* Unpaid property taxes owed on the building
* Fees associated with transferring the ownership (title) on the building
* Costs of repairing and renovating the building for its intended use

Machinery and Equipment

The cost of machinery and equipment includes:

* Purchase price (less any discounts)
* Transportation (delivery) charges
* Insurance while in transit
* Sales and other taxes
* Purchase commission
* Installation costs
* Cost of testing the asset before it is used

After the asset is up and running, the company no longer debits insurance, taxes, and maintenance costs to the Equipment account. From that point on, insurance, taxes, repairs, and maintenance costs are recorded as expenses.

Furniture and Fixtures

Furniture and fixtures include desks, chairs, file cabinets, display racks, shelving, and so forth. The cost of furniture and fixtures includes the basic cost of each asset (less any discounts), plus all other costs to ready the asset for its intended use. For example, for a desk, this may include the costs to ship the desk to the business and the cost paid to someone to assemble the desk.

Exhibit 8-2 summarizes the costs associated with the different types of fixed assets.

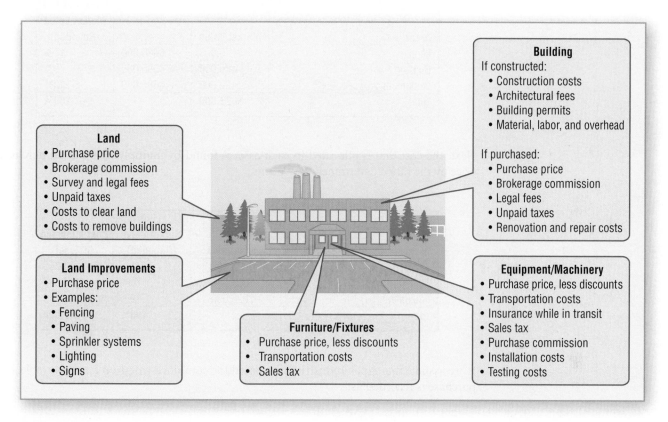

Exhibit 8-2 ▲

Lump-Sum (Basket) Purchase of Assets

Lump-sum purchase Purchase of multiple assets for one price; also called a **basket purchase**.

When a company pays a single price for several assets as a group it is referred to as a **lump-sum purchase,** or **"basket" purchase.** For example, Apex Industries may pay one price ($625,000) for land, a building, and equipment. For accounting, the company must allocate a portion of the total cost to each individual asset, as shown in the following diagram:

The total cost is allocated to the different assets based on their relative market values. Let's assume that an appraisal revealed that the land's market value is $75,000, the building's market value is $480,000, and the equipment's market value is $130,000. Apex Industries got a good deal, paying only $625,000 for assets with a combined market value of $685,000 ($75,000 + $480,000 + $130,000). In order to allocate the total purchase price to the different assets, Apex Industries must first determine the ratio of each asset's market value to the total market value for all assets combined:

Asset	Market Value		Percent of Total Market Value (Rounded)
Land	$ 75,000	÷ $685,000	11%
Building	480,000	÷ $685,000	70%
Equipment	130,000	÷ $685,000	19%
Total	$685,000		100%

Next, the cost that is allocated to each asset is found by multiplying the total purchase price by the ratios determined previously.

Asset	Total Purchase Price	×	Percent of Total Market Value (Rounded)	Cost Allocated to Asset
Land	$625,000	×	11%	$ 68,750
Building	$625,000	×	70%	437,500
Equipment	$625,000	×	19%	118,750
Total			100%	$625,000

If we assume that Apex Industries purchased the combined assets on a note payable, the purchase is recorded as:

DATE	ACCOUNTS	POST REF.	DR.	CR.
	Land		68,750	
	Building		437,500	
	Equipment		118,750	
	Note Payable			625,000
	Purchased land, building, and equipment on a note payable.			

How Are Fixed Assets Depreciated?

3 Calculate and record the depreciation of fixed assets

As we saw in Exhibit 8-1, the process of allocating a fixed asset's cost to expense over its useful life is referred to as depreciation. Depreciation matches the asset's expense against the revenue generated from using the asset, thereby adhering to the matching principle. In accounting, the "using up" of a fixed asset is also referred to as depreciation. For example, a delivery truck can only go so many miles before it is worn out, or used up. As the truck is driven, it depreciates, or is used up. Physical factors, like age and weather, will also contribute to the depreciation of assets. So, depreciation refers to the "using up" of a fixed asset as well as to the process of allocating the asset's cost to expense over the asset's useful life.

Let's contrast this with what depreciation is **not**.

- **Depreciation is not a process of valuation.** Businesses do not record depreciation based on changes in the asset's market (sales) value.
- **Depreciation does not mean that the business sets aside cash to replace an asset when it is used up.** Depreciation has nothing to do with cash.

Accounting in Your World

Have you ever bought a new car or know someone who has? If so, then you have probably heard people comment on how much the car "depreciated" the minute it was driven off the car lot. These people were referring to the fact that the resale value of the car was most likely less than what had been paid for it. In everyday life, the term *depreciation* is commonly used to describe a decrease in the market value of an asset, such as a car. However, from an accounting point of view, the car had not depreciated merely because it was driven off the lot. In accounting, depreciation refers to the allocation of the cost of an asset to expense during the life of the asset rather than to a decline in the market value of the asset.

Measuring Depreciation

Depreciation of a fixed asset is based on three factors:

1. Cost

2. Estimated useful life

3. Estimated residual value

Cost is known and, as mentioned earlier in this chapter, includes all amounts incurred to prepare the asset for its intended purpose. The other two factors are estimates.

Estimated **useful life** represents the expected life of an asset during which it is anticipated to generate revenues. Useful life may be measured in years or in units of output. For example, a building's life is usually stated in years, a truck's in the number of miles it can be driven, and a photocopier's in the number of copies it can make. For each asset, the goal is to define the estimated useful life that best measures the "using up" of the asset.

Useful life The expected life of an asset during which it is anticipated to generate revenues. May be expressed in years or units of output.

Some assets, such as computers and software, may become obsolete before they wear out. An asset is obsolete when a newer asset can perform the job more efficiently. As a result of obsolescence, an asset's useful life may be determined to be shorter than its physical life. In all cases, an asset's cost is depreciated over its useful life.

Estimated **residual value**—also called **salvage value**—is the asset's expected cash value at the end of its useful life. A delivery truck's useful life may be 150,000 miles. When the truck has driven that distance, the company will sell or scrap it. The expected cash value at the end of the truck's life is the truck's estimated residual value. Because the estimated residual value represents a portion of the asset's cost that will be recovered, it is *not* depreciated. The residual value is subtracted from the cost of the asset to arrive at the asset's **depreciable cost**.

Residual value Expected cash value of an asset at the end of its useful life; also called **salvage value**.

Depreciable cost The cost of a fixed asset minus its estimated residual value.

$$
\begin{array}{l}
\text{Cost} \\
- \text{ Residual value} \\
= \text{Depreciable cost}
\end{array}
$$

A business will use past experience as well as information obtained from other sources to make the best estimates it can of useful life and residual value.

Depreciation Methods

The most commonly used depreciation methods are as follows:

- Straight-line
- Units-of-production
- Double-declining-balance

These methods work differently in *how* the yearly depreciation amount is calculated, but they all result in the same total depreciation over the useful life of the asset. To demonstrate the different depreciation methods, let's assume that Apex Industries purchased and placed in service a new delivery truck on January 1. The data related to Apex Industries' new delivery truck is presented next:

Purchase price (cost)..	$43,000
Estimated residual (salvage) value...	$ 4,000
Estimated useful life...	5 years

Straight-Line Method

Straight-line (SL) depreciation method Depreciation method in which an equal amount of depreciation expense is assigned to each year of asset use.

The **straight-line (SL) depreciation method** allocates an equal amount of depreciation to each year. Apex Industries might want to use this method for the truck if it thinks time is the best indicator of the truck's depreciation. The equation to find yearly depreciation using straight-line depreciation is:

$$
\text{Straight-line depreciation} = \frac{\text{Cost} - \text{Residual value}}{\text{Estimated useful life in years}} = \frac{\text{Depreciation}}{\text{expense per year}}
$$

The yearly depreciation expense for Apex Industries' delivery truck is:

$$
\frac{\text{Cost} - \text{Residual value}}{\text{Estimated useful life}} = \frac{\$43,000 - \$4,000}{5} = \$7,800 \text{ per year}
$$

Because Apex Industries purchased the delivery truck on January 1, an entire year's worth of depreciation will be recorded for the first year on December 31:

DATE	ACCOUNTS	POST REF.	DR.	CR.
Dec 31	Depreciation Expense, Truck		7,800	
	Accumulated Depreciation, Truck			7,800
	Record yearly depreciation.			

Exhibit 8-3 demonstrates a straight-line depreciation schedule that has been prepared for Apex Industries' delivery truck.

Year	Asset Cost	Yearly Depreciation	Accumulated Depreciation	Book Value
0	$43,000			$43,000
1		$7,800	$ 7,800	35,200
2		7,800	15,600	27,400
3		7,800	23,400	19,600
4		7,800	31,200	11,800
5		7,800	39,000	4,000

Exhibit 8-3 ▲

The final column shows the asset's *book value*, which is its cost less accumulated depreciation.

Notice that as an asset is depreciated, its accumulated depreciation increases and its book value decreases. Observe the Accumulated Depreciation and Book Value columns in Exhibit 8-3. At the end of its useful life, the asset is said to be **fully depreciated**. Once an asset has been fully depreciated, its final book value should equal its residual value, $4,000 in this case.

Units-of-Production (UOP) Method

Fully depreciated An asset that has reached the end of its estimated useful life. No more depreciation is recorded for the asset.

Units-of-production (UOP) depreciation method Depreciation method by which a fixed amount of depreciation is assigned to each unit of output produced by an asset.

The **units-of-production (UOP) depreciation method** allocates a fixed amount of depreciation to each unit of output:

$$\text{Units-of-production depreciation} = \frac{\text{Cost} - \text{Residual value}}{\text{Estimated useful life in units}} = \frac{\text{Depreciation}}{\text{expense per unit}}$$

Assume that, instead of straight-line depreciation, Apex Industries depreciates its delivery truck using units-of-production depreciation. Apex Industries might want to use UOP depreciation for the truck if it thinks miles are the best measure of the truck's depreciation. The delivery truck is estimated to be driven 35,000 miles the first year, 30,000 the second, 30,000 the third, 20,000 the fourth, and 15,000 during the fifth (for a total of 130,000 miles). The UOP depreciation each period varies with the number of units (miles, in the case of the truck) the asset produces. The depreciation per unit for Apex Industries' delivery truck is calculated as:

$$\frac{\text{Cost} - \text{Residual value}}{\text{Estimated useful life in units}} = \frac{\$43,000 - \$4,000}{130,000 \text{ miles}} = \$0.30 \text{ per mile}$$

Apex Industries would record $10,500 (35,000 miles × $0.30) of depreciation at December 31 of the first year as:

DATE	ACCOUNTS	POST REF.	DR.	CR.
Dec 31	Depreciation Expense, Truck		10,500	
	Accumulated Depreciation, Truck			10,500
	Record yearly depreciation.			

A depreciation schedule similar to the one prepared for straight-line depreciation is presented in **Exhibit 8-4** for units-of-production depreciation.

Notice once again that the ending book value of the delivery truck, $4,000, equals its residual value as it did with straight-line depreciation.

		Yearly Depreciation				
Year	Asset Cost	Number of Units	Depreciation Per Unit	Depreciation Expense	Accumulated Depreciation	Book Value
0	$43,000					$43,000
1		35,000 miles ×	$0.30 =	$10,500	$10,500	32,500
2		30,000 miles ×	$0.30 =	9,000	19,500	23,500
3		30,000 miles ×	$0.30 =	9,000	28,500	14,500
4		20,000 miles ×	$0.30 =	6,000	34,500	8,500
5		15,000 miles ×	$0.30 =	4,500	39,000	4,000

Exhibit 8-4 ▲

Double-declining-balance (DDB) method An accelerated depreciation method that computes annual depreciation by multiplying the asset's decreasing book value by a constant percent that is two times the straight-line rate.

Accelerated depreciation method A depreciation method that writes off more of the asset's cost near the start of its useful life than the straight-line method does.

Double-Declining-Balance Method

The **double-declining-balance (DDB)** method is known as an **accelerated depreciation method.** An accelerated depreciation method writes off more depreciation near the start of an asset's life and less at the end. Although DDB depreciation is generally used for income tax purposes, it can be used for "book" purposes. The use of DDB by Apex Industries would be appropriate if Apex anticipates the delivery truck will be significantly more productive in its early years. The DDB method multiplies the asset's decreasing book value by a constant rate that is twice the straight-line depreciation rate. DDB amounts can be computed using the following formula:

$$\text{Double-declining-balance depreciation} = \frac{1}{\text{Estimated useful life in years}} \times 2 \times \frac{\text{Book value at the}}{\text{beginning of the year}} = \text{Depreciation expense per year}$$

Note that residual value is not included in the formula. Unlike with straight-line and units-of-production, with double-declining-balance depreciation, residual value is ignored until the end of an asset's life.

For the first year of the delivery truck, the calculation would be:

$$\frac{1}{5} \times 2 = 2/5 \times \$43,000 = \$17,200$$

Exhibit 8-5 reflects a depreciation schedule for the delivery truck using double-declining-balance depreciation.

Under double-declining-balance, the depreciation schedule is altered in the final years to prevent the asset from being depreciated below the residual value. In the case of Apex Industries' delivery truck, the residual value was given as $4,000. In the DDB schedule in Exhibit 8-5, notice that after year 4, the truck's book value is $5,573. In year 5, depreciation expense calculated using DDB would reduce the book value below the residual value. Therefore, in the final year, the depreciation expense is reduced to $1,573, which is the book value of $5,573 less the $4,000 residual value. If the residual value is high enough, it is possible that the second-to-last year's depreciation expense could be reduced and there would be no depreciation in the final year.

Year	Asset Cost	Yearly Depreciation			Accumulated Depreciation	Book Value
		DDB Rate*	Book Value	Depreciation Expense		
0	$43,000					$43,000
1		2/5 ×	$43,000 =	$17,200	$17,200	25,800
2		2/5 ×	25,800 =	10,320	27,520	15,480
3		2/5 ×	15,480 =	6,192	33,712	9,288
4		2/5 ×	9,288 =	3,715**	37,427	5,573
5				1,573***	39,000	4,000

*1/5 × 2 = 2/5
**rounded
***5,573 − 4,000 = 1,573

Exhibit 8-5 ▲

Some companies change to the straight-line method during the last years of an asset's life to "level off" the yearly depreciation expense in the final years. The yearly depreciation when switching to straight-line is calculated as:

$$\frac{\text{Remaining book value} - \text{Residual value}}{\text{Remaining useful life}} = \text{Depreciation expense per year}$$

Exhibit 8-6 reflects a depreciation schedule for the delivery truck using double-declining-balance depreciation with a switch to straight-line after year 3.

Year	Asset Cost	Yearly Depreciation			Accumulated Depreciation	Book Value
		DDB Rate	Book Value	Depreciation Expense		
0	$43,000					$43,000
1		2/5 ×	$43,000 =	$17,200	$17,200	25,800
2		2/5 ×	25,800 =	10,320	27,520	15,480
3		2/5 ×	15,480 =	6,192	33,712	9,288
4				2,644*	36,356	6,644
5				2,644*	39,000	4,000

*(9,288 − 4,000) ÷ 2 = 2,644

Exhibit 8-6 ▲

Comparing Depreciation Methods

Let's compare the depreciation methods. Annual amounts vary, but total accumulated depreciation equals $39,000 for all three methods.

	Depreciation per Year		
Year	**Straight-Line**	**Units-of-Production**	**Double-Declining-Balance**
1	$ 7,800	$10,500	$17,200
2	7,800	9,000	10,320
3	7,800	9,000	6,192
4	7,800	6,000	3,715
5	7,800	4,500	1,573
Total Depreciation	$39,000	$39,000	$39,000

Which method is best? That depends on the asset. A business should match an asset's expense against the revenue that the asset produces. Here are some guidelines:

- **Straight-Line.** For an asset that generates revenue evenly over time, the straight-line method follows the matching principle. Each period shows an equal amount of depreciation. For example, the straight-line method would be good for depreciating a building.
- **Units-of-Production.** The UOP method works best for an asset whose use varies from year to year. More use causes greater depreciation. For example, UOP might be good for depreciating copy machines, vehicles, and machinery.
- **Double-Declining-Balance.** The DDB method works best for assets that produce more revenue in their early years and less in their later years. Higher depreciation in the early years is matched against the greater revenue. For example, DDB might be good for depreciating computers. DDB is also often chosen for federal income tax purposes. The increased depreciation in the early years of an asset's life lowers the income in those years and, therefore, lowers the income tax paid.

Partial Year Depreciation

In the examples for Apex Industries' delivery truck, it was assumed that the truck was purchased on January 1 and used for an entire year. However, most assets are not purchased on the first day of the year and used for the entire year. When an asset is not used for an entire year, the depreciation expense for that year must be prorated for the number of months the asset was actually used during the year. If an asset is in service for more than one half of the month, it is considered to be in service for the entire month. The formula for prorating the depreciation expense is:

$$\text{Depreciation expense for the entire year} \times \frac{\text{\# of months asset was used}}{12} = \text{Prorated yearly depreciation expense}$$

Let's return to our example using Apex Industries' delivery truck. Assume that, instead of purchasing the delivery truck on January 1, Apex Industries purchased the delivery truck on May 1. **Exhibits 8-7** and **8-8** reflect new depreciation schedules for Apex Industries' delivery truck using straight-line and double-declining-balance depreciation, respectively.

Year	Asset Cost	Yearly Depreciation	Accumulated Depreciation	Book Value
0	$43,000			$43,000
1		$7,800 × 8/12* = $5,200	$ 5,200	37,800
2		7,800	13,000	30,000
3		7,800	20,800	22,200
4		7,800	28,600	14,400
5		7,800	36,400	6,600
6		$7,800 × 4/12** = 2,600	39,000	4,000

*Prorated for May through December
**Prorated for January through April

Exhibit 8-7 ▲

Year	Asset Cost	Yearly Depreciation			Accumulated Depreciation	Book Value
		DDB Rate	Book Value	Depreciation Expense*		
0	$43,000					$43,000
1		2/5 ×	$43,000 =	$17,200×8/12**=$11,467	$11,467	31,533
2		2/5 ×	31,533 =	12,613	24,080	18,920
3		2/5 ×	18,920 =	7,568	31,648	11,352
4		2/5 ×	11,352 =	4,541	36,189	6,811
5		2/5 ×	6,811 =	2,724	38,913	4,087
6				(4,087 − 4,000) = 87	39,000	4,000

*Rounded
**Prorated for May through December

Exhibit 8-8 ▲

Notice that both schedules now reflect six years, even though the delivery truck has a five-year life. Because the truck was only depreciated for eight months in the first year instead of twelve, the sixth year is added to "pick up" the final four months of depreciation. With units-of-production depreciation, there is no need to prorate the depreciation for partial years. This is because UOP is based on the quantity of units produced by an asset, regardless of how many months the asset was in service during the year.

Changing the Useful Life of a Depreciable Asset

Estimating the useful life and residual value of a fixed asset can be difficult. Sometimes, as the asset is used, a business may determine that it needs to revise the useful life and/ or the residual value of the asset. For example, at the end of year 3, Apex Industries may find that its delivery truck is expected to last seven years instead of five. Accounting changes like this are not uncommon because the original estimates are not based on perfect foresight. Assuming straight-line depreciation is used, the formula used to calculate the new yearly depreciation amount, if the useful life or residual value is changed, looks like this:

$$\frac{(\text{Remaining book value} - \text{New residual value})}{(\text{New estimated useful life} - \text{Number of years already depreciated})} = \text{Revised annual depreciation}$$

In effect, the asset's remaining depreciable book value is spread over the asset's remaining life.

Let's return to our Apex Industries' example. If we look back at Exhibit 8-3, we see that the remaining book value for Apex Industries' delivery truck after year 3 is $19,600. Now let's suppose that, in addition to revising the estimated useful life from five to seven years, the residual value is also revised from $4,000 to $3,000. Apex Industries would calculate the new yearly depreciation as:

$$\frac{(\$19,600 - \$3,000)}{(7 \text{ years} - 3 \text{ years})} = \frac{\$16,600}{4} = \$4,150$$

A new straight-line depreciation schedule reflecting the changes in estimates appears in **Exhibit 8-9**.

Year	Yearly Depreciation	Accumulated Depreciation	Book Value
0			$43,000
1	$7,800	$ 7,800	35,200
2	7,800	15,600	27,400
3	7,800	23,400	19,600
4	4,150	27,550	15,450
5	4,150	31,700	11,300
6	4,150	35,850	7,150
7	4,150	40,000	3,000

Exhibit 8-9 ▲

Using Fully Depreciated Assets

As explained earlier in the chapter, a fully depreciated asset is one that has reached the end of its *estimated* useful life. No more depreciation is recorded for the asset. If the asset is no longer useful, it is disposed of. If the asset is still useful, the company may continue using it. The asset account and its accumulated depreciation remain on the books, but no additional depreciation is recorded. In short, the asset never goes below residual value.

Decision Guidelines

Decision	Guideline	Analyze
Which depreciation method should a business use?	The choice of depreciation method depends upon the specific asset being depreciated as well as what the intended use of that asset is. The best method is one that most closely matches the cost of an asset against the future revenues it generates.	Straight-line depreciation is best for assets that will be used evenly throughout their lives and that will incur repair and maintenance costs evenly.

Units-of-production depreciation is best for assets that will be utilized on an irregular basis throughout their lives.

Double-declining-balance depreciation is best for assets that will be utilized significantly more in the early years of their lives. It is also best for assets that will require significantly more repair and maintenance expenditures in the later years of the asset's life. |

Stop and Think...

After reviewing the year-end balance sheet, the company president called the controller to her office for a meeting. In the meeting, the company president questioned why the book value of the company's equipment was so high. "After all," she explained, "there is no way that the company could sell the equipment for that much money." How should the controller answer the president?

Answer

The controller should explain that the book value of the equipment is not meant to reflect the resale value of the equipment. The book value reflects the cost of the equipment less the depreciation expense that has been taken on the equipment during its life so far. He should explain that depreciation is the process of allocating the cost of an asset to the periods that the asset will be used to generate revenue. So, book value reflects the amount of the asset's cost that has not been expensed.

How Are Costs of Repairing Fixed Assets Recorded?

 Account for repairs to fixed assets

When a business has to repair an existing fixed asset, the method of accounting for the expenditure is determined by the type of repair that occurred. Repairs are generally broken down into three types:

- Ordinary repairs
- Extraordinary repairs
- Betterments

Ordinary Repairs

Ordinary repair Repair work that is necessary to maintain an asset in normal operating condition.

Expenditures incurred to maintain an asset in proper working order are called **ordinary repairs.** For example, the cost of repairing the radiator, changing the oil and filter, or replacing the tires on a company vehicle would be considered to be ordinary repairs. Ordinary repairs do not extend the useful life of an asset beyond its original useful life, nor do they increase the productivity of the asset. They simply keep the asset running. Ordinary repairs are recorded as an expense (usually by debiting Repairs and Maintenance Expense) in the period in which they are incurred. Ordinary repairs are also called **revenue expenditures** because the repair expense is matched against the revenues for the period.

Revenue expenditure Expenditure that is debited to an expense account.

Extraordinary Repairs

Extraordinary repair Repair work that extends the useful life of an asset.

When an expenditure extends the useful life of an asset, it is called an **extraordinary repair.** Replacing the engine on a four-year-old company vehicle is an example of an extraordinary repair. This extraordinary repair would extend the vehicle's useful life past its original expected life. Extraordinary repairs are not expensed when they are incurred because they provide value beyond the current period. Instead, the expenditure is capitalized by debiting the cost of the repair to the account of the repaired asset. The asset is then depreciated over its remaining useful life.

Betterments

Betterment Expenditure that increases the capacity or productivity of an asset.

Capital expenditure Expenditure that increases the capacity or productivity of an asset or extends its useful life. Capital expenditures are debited to an asset account.

Expenditures that increase an asset's capacity or productivity are called **betterments**. An addition to an existing building is an example of a betterment. As with extraordinary repairs, betterments provide value that extends beyond the current period. The cost of a betterment is capitalized (debited to an asset account) and depreciated over the life of the betterment. Both extraordinary repairs and betterments are referred to as **capital expenditures**.

Treating a capital expenditure as an expense, or vice versa, creates an accounting error. Suppose Mackay Machine Works replaces the engine in a company vehicle. This would be an extraordinary repair because it increases the vehicle's life. If Mackay Machine Works expenses the cost by debiting Repair and Maintenance Expense, rather than capitalizing it (debiting an asset), Mackay Machine Works makes an accounting error. This error would:

- overstate Repair and Maintenance Expense.
- understate Net Income and therefore, Retained Earnings.
- understate Assets on the balance sheet.

Incorrectly capitalizing an expense creates the opposite error. Assume a minor repair, such as replacing the alternator on a vehicle, was incorrectly debited to an asset account. The error would result in expenses being understated and Net Income (and therefore Retained Earnings) being overstated. Furthermore, the balance sheet would overstate assets by the amount of the repair bill. Knowingly capitalizing an ordinary repair or expensing a capital expenditure is a violation of proper ethical behavior!

What Happens When a Fixed Asset Is Disposed?

5 Account for the disposal of fixed assets

In addition to acquiring and depreciating fixed assets, businesses often dispose of fixed assets. This may happen before, or after, the asset has reached the end of its useful life. The following are the most common ways that fixed assets are disposed.

1. The asset is discarded (thrown out).

2. The asset is sold.

3. The asset is exchanged for another asset. This occurs most often when an asset is used as a trade-in toward the purchase of another asset.

Regardless of the method of disposal, it is important to ensure that depreciation expense on the asset is up to date prior to recording the disposal. Therefore, for any asset that has not been fully depreciated, a business must record the current period's depreciation expense before recording the disposal of the asset. In many cases, the depreciation needs to be prorated because the asset is not in service for the entire year in which it is disposed. Prorating depreciation was covered earlier in the chapter in the discussion of partial-years depreciation.

Once depreciation is up to date, the disposal of an asset is recorded using the following steps.

Step 1 *Record "what you got."* In other words, if you received any cash as part of the disposal transaction, then you would debit Cash for the amount of cash received. If you received a piece of equipment, then you would debit the Equipment account for the fair value (cost) of the equipment you received.

Step 2 *Record "what you gave up."* You need to remove the asset that was disposed of from your books by debiting Accumulated Depreciation and crediting the Asset account (i.e., Office Equipment) for the respective amounts associated with the disposed-of asset. Then, if you paid out any cash, you would credit Cash. If you gave a note payable, you would credit Notes Payable.

Step 3 *Record any gain or loss recognized on the transaction.* You will recognize (debit) a loss if the value of "what you got" in the transaction is less than "what you gave up." You will recognize (credit) a gain if the value of "what you got" is more than the value of "what you gave up" in the transaction. In effect, the debit or credit needed in this part of the entry will equal the amount necessary to make the entire entry balance.

Prior to 2005, GAAP required that a business determine if an exchange of fixed assets involved assets that were similar in their function, a **like-kind exchange,** or dissimilar in their function. Like-kind exchanges were accounted for differently than exchanges of dissimilar assets. Since 2005, the distinction of *similar versus dissimilar* has been abandoned by GAAP with regard to exchanges.[1] GAAP now requires that exchanges be evaluated to determine whether the exchange has "commercial substance." If an exchange lacks "commercial substance," then no gain on the exchange is recognized. Due to the complex nature of how "commercial substance" is calculated, extended coverage of this topic will be deferred to more advanced accounting courses. All examples in this chapter will assume that fixed asset exchanges have "commercial substance." As a result, new fixed assets received should be recorded at fair value (cost) with the appropriate recognition of gains and losses.

Let's demonstrate asset disposals by once again using the Apex Industries' delivery truck as an example. At the end of its useful life, the delivery truck is represented in the books as:

> **Like-kind exchange** Exchanging one fixed asset for another fixed asset that has similar functionality.

Truck		Accumulated Depreciation, Truck	
43,000			39,000

Consider these three situations in which Apex Industries disposes of the delivery truck. All disposals are assumed to take place after the delivery truck has been fully depreciated.

Situation A: The truck is completely worthless and is scrapped for $0.

Situation B: Apex Industries sells the truck for $5,000 cash.

Situation C: Apex Industries trades the delivery truck in on a new truck that costs $48,000. Apex is granted a trade-in allowance of $5,500 and pays for the difference in cash.

Situation A: The truck is completely worthless and is scrapped for $0. Let's apply the three steps for disposal outlined previously to demonstrate this:

Step 1 Record "what you got." In this case, Apex Industries received nothing for the truck so there will be nothing to record.

Step 2 Record "what you gave up." In this case, Apex Industries gave up the old delivery truck and should remove it from the books. To remove the asset, we must zero out both the Asset and Accumulated Depreciation accounts. To do this, we will need to debit the Accumulated Depreciation, Truck account for $39,000 and credit the Truck account for $43,000.

Step 3 Record any gain or loss on the transaction. This is a loss on disposal because Apex Industries received nothing for a truck that had a net book value (cost – accumulated depreciation) of $4,000. Apex Industries will debit Loss on disposal of Truck for $4,000.

---

[1]For more information see pre-codification FASB 153 and FASB ASC 845.

Apex Industries will record the disposal as:

DATE	ACCOUNTS	POST REF.	DR.	CR.
	Accumulated Depreciation, Truck		39,000	
	Loss on Disposal of Truck		4,000	
	Truck			43,000
	Record discarding of truck.			

Notice that the debit to the loss account equals the amount needed to bring the entire entry into balance.

Situation B: Apex Industries sells the truck for $5,000 cash. The three steps for disposal outlined previously can be applied to this situation as follows:

Step 1 Record "what you got." In this case Apex Industries received $5,000 for the truck, so Cash will be debited for $5,000.

Step 2 Record "what you gave up." Once again, Apex Industries gave up the old delivery truck and should remove it from the books. Accumulated Depreciation, Truck is debited for $39,000 and the Truck account is credited for $43,000.

Step 3 Record any gain or loss on the transaction. This is a gain on sale because Apex Industries received $5,000 for a truck that had a net book value (cost − accumulated depreciation) of $4,000. Apex Industries will credit Gain on Sale of Truck for $1,000.

Apex Industries will record the disposal as:

DATE	ACCOUNTS	POST REF.	DR.	CR.
	Cash		5,000	
	Accumulated Depreciation, Truck		39,000	
	Truck			43,000
	Gain on Sale of Truck			1,000
	Record sale of truck.			

Observe that the credit to the gain account equals the amount needed to bring the entire entry into balance.

Situation C: Apex Industries trades the delivery truck in on a new truck that costs $48,000. Apex is granted a trade-in allowance of $5,500 and pays for the difference in cash. Here again we will apply the three-step process to record the disposal.

Step 1 Record "what you got." In this transaction, Apex Industries received a $48,000 new truck. So, Truck (new) will be debited for $48,000.

Step 2 Record "what you gave up." As in the previous situations, Apex Industries gave up the old delivery truck and should remove it from the books. Accumulated Depreciation, Truck is debited for $39,000 and the Truck (old) account is credited for $43,000. In addition to giving up the truck, Apex Industries paid cash in the amount of $42,500, so Cash is also credited for $42,500. With a trade-in, the amount of cash paid is determined by subtracting the trade-in allowance from the purchase price of the new asset. So, the $48,000 cost of the new truck less the $5,500 trade-in allowance equals the $42,500 cash paid. This same process is used to determine the amount of a note payable if a note is given instead of cash.

Step 3 Record any gain or loss on the transaction. A gain on the exchange occurs because Apex Industries received a truck with a cost of $48,000 for assets worth $46,500 (a truck that had a net book value of $4,000 plus cash of $42,500). Apex Industries will credit Gain on Exchange for $1,500.

Apex Industries will record the disposal as:

DATE	ACCOUNTS	POST REF.	DR.	CR.
	Truck (New)		48,000	
	Accumulated Depreciation, Truck		39,000	
	Truck (Old)			43,000
	Cash			42,500
	Gain on Exchange of Assets			1,500
	Record trade-in of old truck on a new truck.			

Once again, the gain equals the amount necessary to bring the entry into balance.

Try It...

A piece of equipment that was originally purchased for $42,000 and had accumulated depreciation of $35,000 was sold for $8,000. How much gain or loss would be recognized on the sale?

Answer

$8,000 was received for a piece of equipment with a book value of $7,000 ($42,000 − $35,000) so a gain of $1,000 should be recognized on the sale.

How Do You Account for Intangible Assets?

6 Account for intangible assets

Amortization Systematic reduction of an intangible asset's carrying value on the books. An expense that applies to intangible assets in the same way depreciation applies to fixed assets and depletion to natural resources.

As we saw earlier, *intangible assets* have no physical form. Instead, in most cases, these assets convey special rights to their owner. Intangible assets include patents, copyrights, trademarks, and other creative works. The process of allocating the cost of an intangible asset to expense is called **amortization**. Amortization applies to intangible assets exactly as depreciation applies to fixed assets and depletion to natural resources.

Amortization is computed over the intangible asset's estimated useful life—usually by the straight-line method. The residual value of most intangible assets is zero. Also, obsolescence can sometimes cause an intangible asset's useful life to be shortened from its original expected length. Amortization expense for an intangible asset is usually credited directly to the asset account instead of using an accumulated amortization account.

Specific Intangibles

Patents

Patent An intangible asset that is a federal government grant conveying an exclusive 20-year right to produce and sell a process, product, or technology.

A **patent** is an intangible asset that is a federal government grant conveying an exclusive 20-year right to produce and sell an invention. The patent may cover a product, process, or technology. The useful life of a patent is often much less than 20 years because newer, better products and processes are invented, rendering the patent obsolete. When an intangible asset is acquired, the acquisition cost is debited to an asset account.

Suppose Apex Industries pays $160,000 on January 1 to acquire a patent on a new manufacturing process. Apex Industries believes this patent's useful life is only five years because it is likely that a new, more efficient process will be developed within that time.

Amortization expense is $32,000 per year ($160,000/5 years). The acquisition and year-end amortization entries for this patent are:

DATE	ACCOUNTS	POST REF.	DR.	CR.
Jan 1	Patents		160,000	
	Cash			160,000
	Purchase patent.			
Dec 31	Amortization Expense		32,000	
	Patents			32,000
	Record yearly amortization.			

At the end of the first year, Apex Industries will report this patent at $128,000 ($160,000 minus first-year amortization of $32,000), the next year at $96,000, and so forth. Each year for five years the value of the patent will be reduced by $32,000 until the end of its five-year life, at which point its net book value will be $0.

Copyrights

Copyright Exclusive right to reproduce and sell a book, musical composition, film, other work of art, or computer program. Issued by the federal government, copyrights extend 70 years beyond the author's life.

A **copyright** is the exclusive right to reproduce and sell a book, musical composition, film, or other work of art or intellectual property. Copyrights also protect computer software programs such as **Microsoft Windows 7**. Copyrights are issued by the federal government and extend 70 years beyond the author's life, although the useful life of most copyrights is relatively short. A copyright is accounted for in the same manner as a patent.

Trademarks and Brand Names

Trademarks Rights to use distinctive identifications of a product or service.

Brand names Rights to use distinctive identifications of a product or service; also called **trade names**.

Trademarks and **brand names** (also known as **trade names**) convey the exclusive right to utilize a symbol, slogan, or name that represents a distinctive product or service such as **Sony's® Blu-ray Disc**^{TM} and **Intel's® Core**^{TM}. One of the most widely recognized legally protected slogans is **Verizon Wireless**'s "Can you hear me now?"[2] The cost of a trademark or trade name is amortized over its useful life.

Franchises and Licenses

Franchises Privileges granted by a private business or a government to sell a product or service under specified conditions.

Licenses Privileges granted by a private business or a government to sell a product or service under specified conditions.

Franchises and **licenses** are privileges granted by a private business or a government to sell goods or services under specified conditions. The **Seattle Mariners** baseball team is a franchise granted by **Major League Baseball**. **Subway** restaurants and **Midas Muffler** centers are well-known business franchises. The acquisition cost of a franchise or license is amortized over its useful life.

Goodwill

Goodwill Excess of the cost of an acquired company over the market value of its net assets (assets minus liabilities).

Goodwill in accounting has a different meaning from the everyday phrase "goodwill among men." In accounting, **goodwill** refers to the excess of the cost to purchase another company over the market value of its net assets (assets minus liabilities).

Suppose Apex Industries acquires Mackay Machine Works for $1,350,000. At the time of the purchase, the market value of Mackay Machine Works' assets is $1,750,000 and the market value of its liabilities total $500,000. In this case, Apex Industries pays $100,000 above the market value of Mackay Machine Works' net assets of $1,250,000 ($1,750,000 − $500,000). The extra $100,000 is considered to be goodwill and is recorded as:

---

[2] Verizon's slogan "Can you hear me now?" Reprinted with permission of Verizon Wireless.

DATE	ACCOUNTS	POST REF.	DR.	CR.
	Assets (Cash, Accounts Receivable, Equipment, etc. recorded at market value)		1,750,000	
	Goodwill		100,000	
	Liabilities (Account Payable, Notes Payable, Accrued Liabilities, etc.)			500,000
	Cash			1,350,000
	To record purchase of Mackay Machine Works.			

Goodwill has some unique features unlike other intangible assets.

1. Goodwill is recorded only by an acquiring company when it purchases another company. An outstanding reputation may create goodwill, but that company never records goodwill for its own business.

2. According to GAAP, goodwill is *not* amortized. Instead, the acquiring company measures the fair value of its goodwill each year. If the goodwill has increased in fair value, there is nothing to record. But if goodwill's fair value has decreased, then the company records an impairment loss and writes the goodwill down. For example, suppose Apex Industries' goodwill—which it acquired in the purchase of Mackay Machine Works—has a fair value of $80,000 a year after the purchase. In this case, Apex Industries would make the following entry:

DATE	ACCOUNTS	POST REF.	DR.	CR.
	Loss on Impairment of Goodwill		20,000	
	Goodwill ($100,000 – $80,000)			20,000
	To record decrease in fair value of goodwill.			

Apex Industries would then report this goodwill at its reduced fair value of $80,000.

Accounting for Research and Development Costs

Research and development (R&D) costs are the lifeblood of companies such as **Sony**, **Johnson & Johnson**, **IBM**, and **Ford**. In general, companies don't report R&D costs as assets on their balance sheets because GAAP requires companies to expense R&D costs as they are incurred.

How Are Natural Resources Accounted For?

7   **Account for natural resources**

Natural resources are assets that come from the earth. Examples include minerals, oil, natural gas, precious metals, coal, and timber. As stated earlier in the chapter, the process of allocating the cost of a natural resource to an expense is called **depletion.** Depletion expense is that portion of the cost of a natural resource that is used up in a particular period. Depletion expense is computed in a manner almost identical to units-of-production depreciation. The formula used to calculate the depletion per unit of natural resource is:

$$\text{Depletion per unit of natural resource} = \frac{\text{Cost}}{\text{Estimated total units of natural resource}} = \text{Depletion expense per unit}$$

Notice that, unlike UOP depreciation, there is no residual value in the calculation of depletion expense. This is because when a natural resource is used up, there is nothing left to sell.

To illustrate, let's assume that Pegusus Gold owns gold reserves that cost $8,500,000. A geological study estimates that the reserves hold 20,000 ounces of gold. Pegusus Gold would calculate the depletion per ounce of gold as:

$$\frac{\$8,500,000}{20,000 \text{ ounces}} = \$425 \text{ per ounce}$$

Depletion Systematic reduction of a natural resource's carrying value on the books. Expense that applies to natural resources in the same way depreciation applies to fixed assets and amortization to intangible assets. It is computed in a similar fashion as units-of-production depreciation.

If 600 ounces of gold are removed and sold during the month, depletion is $255,000 (600 ounces × $425 per ounce) and would be recorded as:

DATE	ACCOUNTS	POST REF.	DR.	CR.
	Depletion Expense		255,000	
	Accumulated Depletion—Gold Reserves			255,000
	Record monthly depletion.			

Accumulated Depletion is a contra-account similar to Accumulated Depreciation. It is deducted from the cost of the natural resource to determine the net book value of the natural resource.

What Are Other Assets?

8 Account for other assets

Marketable securities Readily tradable equity or debt securities.

Other assets may consist of any assets a business owns that we have not already discussed. Two common assets that a business might own are real estate (land or buildings) that is being held for resale rather than for use and investments in **marketable securities**. Marketable securities are investments, such as stocks, also known as equity securities, and bonds, also called debt securities. Bonds will be discussed more in Chapter 9; basically, buying bonds is a way of loaning money to an entity. Marketable securities are classified as current assets if management intends to sell them, or they mature, within a year. However, if they are not intended to be sold, or they do not mature, within a year they are shown as other long-term assets.

A company investing in marketable securities earns income when it receives dividends on stock or interest on bonds that it holds. Also, changes in the market value of a security can affect a company's income in two ways:

- Realized gains and losses occur when a security is sold for an amount different from its cost.
- Unrealized gains and losses occur when a security's market value changes while the company still owns it. These are considered "unrealized" because the company won't actually gain or lose money until it sells the investment.

The accounting procedures followed for marketable securities depend on the type of investment and on management's intention for the investment. Marketable securities are classified as trading securities, held-to-maturity securities, or available-for-sale securities.

Trading securities Equity or debt securities that are actively managed in order to maximize profit.

- **Trading securities** include equity or debt securities that are actively managed in order to maximize profit as a result of short-term changes in price. These are shown as current assets on the balance sheet at their market value as of the balance sheet date. Any increase or decrease in price during the period is shown as an unrealized gain or loss on the income statement. Any interest or dividends earned during the period are also reported as income on the income statement.

Held-to-maturity securities Debt securities that a company intends and is able to hold until maturity.

- **Held-to-maturity securities** are debt securities that a company intends and is able to hold until they mature. These are reported at their cost on the balance sheet as either current or long-term assets based on their maturity date. Any interest income earned on these securities is reported on the income statement.

Available-for-sale securities Equity or debt securities that cannot be classified as either trading securities or held-to-maturity securities.

- **Available-for-sale securities** include equity or debt securities that cannot be classified as trading or held-to-maturity securities. These are reported at their current market value on the balance sheet date. Any interest or dividends earned during the period are included in net income on the income statement. However, increases or decreases in market value during the period are not reported as part of net income on the income statement. Instead, they are shown as separate changes in stockholders' equity for the period.

How Are Long-Term Assets Reported on the Balance Sheet?

9 Report long-term assets on the balance sheet

In Chapter 4, we learned that current assets appear first on a classified balance sheet. Following the current assets, a business will report its long-term assets. Fixed assets are usually the first long-term asset reported and are often shown as "Property, Plant, and Equipment." Property, Plant, and Equipment includes the original cost, accumulated depreciation, and book value of assets such as land, buildings, and equipment. Natural resources are typically shown after the fixed assets and include the original cost, accumulated depletion, and book value of any natural resources the business owns. A business may choose to show only the net book value of fixed assets and natural resources on the balance sheet. In this case, the business will disclose the costs and accumulated depreciation or depletion for each asset group in the financial statement footnotes.

When a business has intangible assets, the balance sheet will typically show the amount for intangible assets after the fixed assets and the natural resources. The footnotes to the financial statements will include a description of the intangible asset and its estimated useful life. Other long-term assets are typically shown last in the long-term assets section of a balance sheet. **Exhibit 8-10** illustrates a typical long-term assets section of a balance sheet:

Total Current Assets			$ 165,000
Long-Term Assets			
Property, Plant, and Equipment:			
Land	$ 175,000		
Buildings	680,000		
Equipment	240,000		
	1,095,000		
Less: Accumulated Depreciation	385,000		
Net Property, Plant, and Equipment		$710,000	
Gold Reserves, Net of Accumulated Depletion of $260,000		620,000	
Patents		80,000	
Other Long-Term Assets		145,000	
Total Long-Term Assets			1,555,000
Total Assets			$1,720,000

Exhibit 8-10 ▲

Focus on Decision Making

"How Does a Business Manage Assets?"

Investing in assets is a very important decision. Some assets like accounts receivable are easy to convert to cash. Some assets like buildings are not easy to convert into cash. There is a lot of risk in investing in long-term assets. So why invest in risky, long-term assets? The answer is that great risk typically means great profits. Without long-term assets, such as buildings and equipment, a business would have no place to operate. Think of AT&T trying to sell phones without a building. Think of John Deere trying to manufacture tractors and farm equipment without a factory. It can't be done. Businesses need the right blend of long- and short-term assets for employees to use and earn a profit.

10 Calculate the return on assets and the fixed asset turnover

So, how does a business decide whether to invest in assets? The business looks at the investment, estimates the future profits from the investment, and determines whether the profits create enough value to justify the investment. Think about AT&T opening a new store. Does the investment in inventory, buildings, and other assets earn enough profit to justify lenders and owners taking risk over time?

A business can have too little or too much invested in assets. If a business has too few assets, it cannot meet the demand for its product and loses sales and profits. If a

Return on assets (ROA) The ratio of net income divided by average total assets, which indicates the profit earned on each dollar invested in total assets.

business has too much invested in assets, it also loses profits and value. Assets, both short- and long- term, are expensive to maintain and finance. So how do managers and other decision makers determine if the business has the right amount of assets? Two measures often used are return on assets (ROA) and fixed asset turnover.

Return on Assets (ROA) and Fixed Asset Turnover

Walk into an AT&T store. Look around and see the cash in the register, the inventory, the building, and the equipment. Think of all the assets that it takes to operate an AT&T store. Now ask yourself, how much profit do owners earn for each dollar invested in assets? One way to answer that question is to compute the return on assets. **Return on assets (ROA)** is the ratio of net income divided by average total assets. The formula for ROA is:

$$\text{Return on Assets (ROA)} = \frac{\text{Net Income}}{\text{Average Total Assets}}$$

Now walk into the office of the AT&T store manager. Ask the manager how his or her supervisor evaluates the store's performance. You'll likely hear numerous measures, including ROA.

A measure often used to evaluate the productivity, or output, of tangible, physical assets is the fixed asset turnover. Fixed assets are land, buildings, and equipment. Fixed assets are tangible and can be seen and touched. The **fixed asset turnover** is the ratio of sales to average fixed assets. The formula for the fixed asset turnover is:

Fixed asset turnover The ratio of sales to average fixed assets, which indicates the sales generated for every dollar invested in fixed assets.

$$\text{Fixed Asset Turnover} = \frac{\text{Sales}}{\text{Average Fixed Assets}}$$

The ROA and fixed asset turnover are usually computed for an annual period, so the net income and sales figures are the amounts for the entire year. Average total assets and average fixed assets are computed by adding the beginning balance and ending balance of each and dividing the total by two. Remember that balance sheet items, such as fixed assets and total assets, carry their balances from one period to the next. For example, the ending fixed assets for one year become the beginning fixed assets for the next year.

Let's look at an example. Assume MacKay Industries has sales of $500,000, net income of $60,000, beginning fixed assets of $200,000, ending fixed assets of $300,000, beginning total assets of $500,000, and ending total assets of $700,000. The ROA of MacKay Industries is calculated as:

$$\text{Return on Assets (ROA)} = \frac{\$60,000}{((\$500,000 + \$700,000)/2)} = 10\%$$

The fixed asset turnover for MacKay Industries is calculated as:

$$\text{Fixed Asset Turnover} = \frac{\$500,000}{((\$200,000 + \$300,000)/2)} = 2.0$$

The higher the ROA and fixed asset turnover, the more efficiently the business is utilizing its assets. The assets are more productive in generating net income and sales. MacKay Industries is generating net income of $0.10 for every dollar invested in assets and $2.00 of sales for every dollar invested in fixed assets.

How They Do It: A Look at Business

Let's look at two businesses, AT&T and John Deere (Deere & Co.).

It takes a lot of fixed assets to operate AT&T. AT&T has made a large investment in assets such as computers, satellites, and buildings. At December 31, 2012, AT&T

had $272.3 billion invested in total assets and $109.8 billion invested in long-term, fixed assets. AT&T's ROA for the fiscal year ended December 31, 2012, was 2.8%. Its fixed asset turnover for the fiscal year ended December 31, 2012, was 1.2 times a year.

Next we'll look at John Deere, the manufacturer of farm and lawn equipment. It takes a lot of fixed assets to manufacture a tractor. John Deere has made a large investment in assets, particularly land, factories, and equipment. At October 31, 2012, John Deere had $56.3 billion invested in total assets and $5 billion invested in long-term, fixed assets. John Deere's ROA for the fiscal year ended October 31, 2012, was 5.9%. Its fixed asset turnover for the fiscal year ended October 31, 2012, was 7.2 times a year.

Now think about and compare AT&T and John Deere. John Deere appears to generate more net income for every dollar invested in fixed assets. However, to fully understand this, we must look at what the fixed assets are and how the value of the assets are measured. Think about it. Are the fixed assets old or new? Does the conservative historical cost reported in the balance sheet reflect the market value and cost of replacing the assets? How is depreciation measured? Measuring and evaluating how a business manages its fixed assets is complicated.

MyAccountingLab

Summary

Here is what you should know after reading this chapter. MyAccountingLab will help you identify what you know and where to go when you need practice.

Key Points	Key Accounting Terms
1 Describe the differences between fixed assets, intangible assets, and natural resources	Long-term assets consist of: • Fixed, or plant, assets. • Intangible assets. • Natural resources.	**Basket purchase** (p. 357) **Capitalized** (p. 356) **Fixed assets** (p. 354) **Intangible assets** (p. 354) **Land improvements** (p. 355) **Lump-sum purchase** (p. 357) **Natural resources** (p. 354) **Plant assets** (p. 354) **Tangible assets** (p. 354)
2 Calculate and record the cost of acquiring fixed assets		
3 Calculate and record the depreciation of fixed assets	Fixed assets are depreciated using these methods: • Straight-line. • Units-of-production. • Double-declining-balance.	**Accelerated depreciation method** (p. 362) **Depreciable cost** (p. 360) **Double-declining-balance (DDB) method** (p. 362) **Fully depreciated** (p. 361) **Residual value** (p. 360) **Salvage value** (p. 360) **Straight-line (SL) depreciation method** (p. 360) **Units-of-production (UOP) depreciation method** (p. 361) **Useful life** (p. 359)

		Key Points	Key Accounting Terms
4	**Account for repairs to fixed assets**	Repairs to fixed assets are classified as: • Ordinary repairs, which are expensed when incurred. • Extraordinary repairs, which are debited to an asset account and depreciated. • Betterments, which are debited to an asset account and depreciated.	**Betterment** (p. 368) **Capital expenditure** (p. 368) **Extraordinary repair** (p. 367) **Ordinary repair** (p. 367) **Revenue expenditure** (p. 367)
5	**Account for the disposal of fixed assets**	The disposal of fixed assets is accounted for by recording: • "What you got." • "What you gave up." • Any gain or loss recognized on the transaction.	**Like-kind exchange** (p. 369)
6	**Account for intangible assets**	Intangible assets include the following: • Patents • Copyrights • Trademarks • Franchises • Goodwill • Are amortized using a method similar to straight-line depreciation (except goodwill).	**Amortization** (p. 371) **Brand names** (p. 372) **Copyright** (p. 372) **Franchises** (p. 372) **Goodwill** (p. 372) **Licenses** (p. 372) **Patent** (p. 371) **Trade names** (p. 372) **Trademarks** (p. 372)
7	**Account for natural resources**	Natural resources include the following: • Minerals • Oil • Gas • Coal • Timber • Are depleted using a method similar to units-of-production depreciation.	**Depletion** (p. 373)
8	**Account for other assets**	Other assets include the following: • Assets such as land or buildings being held for resale. • Investments in marketable securities.	**Available-for-sale securities** (p. 374) **Held-to-maturity securities** (p. 374) **Marketable securities** (p. 374) **Trading securities** (p. 374)

	Key Points	Key Accounting Terms
9 Report long-term assets on the balance sheet	Long-term assets are reported on the balance sheet after current assets in the following order: • Fixed assets • Natural resources • Intangible assets • Other long-term assets	
10 Calculate the return on assets and the fixed asset turnover	Ratios are often used to help make decisions: • The return on assets measures how much profit a company generates for each dollar of assets it has. • The fixed asset turnover measures how efficiently a company is using its fixed assets to generate sales.	**Fixed asset turnover** (p. 376) **Return on assets (ROA)** (p. 376)

Accounting Practice

Discussion Questions

1. When a company makes an expenditure, it can either capitalize or expense the cost, depending on the nature of the expenditure. What does it mean to capitalize an expenditure? What determines whether an expenditure can be capitalized?

2. If a company were to purchase a piece of land with a building on it that it demolishes to make room for its new building, in which account would the cost of demolition be recorded (Land, Building, Demolition Expense, or something else)? Why?

3. What is a lump-sum purchase of assets? How does a company determine how much to allocate to each asset purchased in a lump-sum purchase?

4. What is depreciation, and why is it used in accounting?

5. Are useful life and physical life the same thing relative to fixed assets? Provide some examples that illustrate your answer.

6. Which depreciation method would be most appropriate for each of the following assets?

   a. This machine is used as a backup to the other machines in the production process. As a result, there are some years where it sees a lot of action and others where it is seldom used. It is not a high-tech machine. It will not become obsolete in the foreseeable future.

   b. Typically this machine will work very effectively and with few repairs for the first three years, but will be down for maintenance quite a bit during its final four years of use.

   c. This machine is expected to run constantly over the entire period it is used. It requires regular maintenance over its lifetime in order to maintain its expected steady level of production.

7. What makes a repair "extraordinary" (as opposed to ordinary)? Give an example of an extraordinary and an ordinary repair. What is the financial statement effect of recording a repair as an extraordinary repair instead of an ordinary repair?

8. What is the book value of an asset? How is gain or loss on disposal of assets calculated?

9. If a machine that cost $10,000 was estimated to have a salvage value of zero after a useful life of 10 years and was sold for $4,500 after it had been owned for 6 complete years, what would be the amount of gain or loss recognized on the sale?

10. Complete the following analogies. What are some similarities and differences between the two concepts involved in each?

    a. Depreciation is to fixed assets as _____ is to intangible assets.
    b. Depreciation is to fixed assets as _____ is to natural resources.

Self Check

1. Which cost is *not* recorded as part of the cost of a building?

   a. Construction materials, labor, and overhead
   b. Annual building maintenance
   c. Earthmoving for the building's foundation
   d. Real estate commission paid to buy the building

2. Northwest Airways bought four used Boeing 737 airplanes. Each plane had a selling price of $40 million, but Northwest bought the combination for $144 million. How much is Northwest Airways' cost of each plane?

    a. $144 million

    b. $36 million

    c. $160 million

    d. $40 million

3. How should a capital expenditure for a long-term asset be recorded?

    a. Debit a liability

    b. Debit an expense

    c. Debit capital

    d. Debit an asset

4. Which depreciation method usually produces the most depreciation expense in the first year?

    a. Straight-line

    b. Double-declining-balance

    c. Units-of-production

    d. All produce the same amount of depreciation for the first year.

5. An airplane costs $75 million and is expected to fly 750 million miles during its 12-year life. Residual value is expected to be zero because the plane was used when acquired. If the plane travels 45 million miles the first year, how much depreciation expense should be recorded under the units-of-production method?

    a. $6.25 million

    b. $10 million

    c. $4.5 million

    d. Cannot be determined from the data given

6. Which depreciation method is generally preferable for income tax purposes? Why?

    a. Double-declining-balance because it gives higher depreciation deductions in earlier years

    b. Straight-line because it is simplest

    c. Double-declining-balance because it gives the most total depreciation over the asset's life

    d. Units-of-production because it best tracks the asset's use

7. A copy machine cost $36,000 when new and has accumulated depreciation of $34,000. Suppose Sun Graphics and Designs Center junks this machine, receiving nothing in return. What is the result of the disposal transaction?

    a. Loss of $36,000

    b. Gain of $34,000

    c. Loss of $2,000

    d. Gain of $2,000

8. Using information from the preceding question, suppose Sun Graphics and Designs Center sold the machine for $6,000. What is the result of this disposal transaction?

    a. Loss of $4,000

    b. Gain of $4,000

    c. Gain of $6,000

    d. Gain of $2,000

9. Depletion is calculated in a manner similar to which depreciation method?

    a. Double-declining-balance method

    b. Units-of-production method

    c. Straight-line method

    d. Accelerated method

10. Which intangible asset is recorded only as part of the acquisition of another company?

   a. Franchise

   b. Patent

   c. Goodwill

   d. Copyright

11. According to the Real World Accounting Video, a quantitative expression of a plan is called a _____.

   a. directive

   b. scheme

   c. budget

   d. dream

12. According to the Real World Accounting Video, the cost of a fixed asset minus its estimated residual value is called an asset's _____.

   a. cost

   b. depreciable cost

   c. liquidation value

   d. depreciation expense

Answers are given after Written Communication.

MyAccountingLab

Short Exercises

S8-1. Long-term asset terms (*Learning Objective 1*) 5–10 min.

Identify each of the following assets as a fixed asset (F) or an intangible asset (I):

_____ 1. Franchises

_____ 2. Vehicles

_____ 3. Buildings

_____ 4. Furniture

_____ 5. Patents

_____ 6. Copyrights

_____ 7. Trademarks

_____ 8. Land improvements

S8-2. Long-term asset terms (*Learning Objective 1*) 5–10 min.

For each of the following long-term assets, identify the type of expense that will be incurred to allocate the asset's cost as depreciation expense (DR), depletion expense (DL), amortization expense (A), or none of these (NA).

_____ 1. Franchises

_____ 2. Land

_____ 3. Buildings

_____ 4. Furniture

_____ 5. Patents

_____ 6. Copyrights

_____ 7. Trademarks

_____ 8. Land improvements

_____ 9. Gold ore deposits

S8-3. Land or Land Improvements (*Learning Objective 2*) 5–10 min.

Identify each of the following as land (L) or land improvements (LI):

_____ 1. Survey fees

_____ 2. Fencing

_____ 3. Lighting

_____ 4. Clearing land

_____ 5. Parking lot

S8-4. Lump-sum purchase (*Learning Objective 2*) 5–10 min.

Peterson purchased land having a current market value of $110,000, a building with a market value of $88,000, and equipment with a market value of $22,000. Journalize the lump-sum purchase of the three assets purchased for a total cost of $210,000 in exchange for a note payable.

S8-5. Errors in accounting for long-term assets (*Learning Objective 4*) 5–10 min.

Noxon, Inc., repaired a piece of equipment at a cost of $3,000, which Noxon, Inc., paid in cash. Noxon, Inc., erroneously capitalized this cost as part of the cost of the equipment.

Requirements

1. Journalize both the incorrect entry the accountant made to record this transaction and the correct entry that the accountant should have made.

2. How will this accounting error affect Noxon, Inc.'s net income? Ignore depreciation.

S8-6. Concept of depreciation (*Learning Objective 3*) 10–15 min.

Jody Martin just slept through the class in which Professor Ibanez explained the concept of depreciation. Because the next test is scheduled for Wednesday, Jody Martin telephones Hanna Svensen to get her notes from the lecture. Hanna Svensen's notes are concise: "Depreciation—Sounds like Greek to me." Jody Martin next tries Tim Lake, who says he thinks depreciation is what happens when an asset wears out. David Coe is confident that depreciation is the process of building up a cash fund to replace an asset at the end of its useful life. Explain the concept of depreciation for Jody Martin. Evaluate the explanations of Tim Lake and David Coe. Be specific.

S8-7. Depreciation methods (*Learning Objective 3*) 10–15 min.

At the beginning of the year, Titan Trucking purchased a used Kenworth truck at a cost of $48,000. Titan Trucking expects the truck to remain useful for four years (800,000 miles) and to have a residual value of $8,000. Titan Trucking expects the truck to be driven 160,000 miles the first year and 280,000 miles the second year.

Requirements

1. Compute Titan Trucking's first-year depreciation expense on the truck using the following methods:
   a. Straight-line
   b. Units-of-production
   c. Double-declining-balance

2. Show the truck's book value at the end of the first year under the straight-line method.

S8-17. Other long-term assets (*Learning Objective 8*) 5–10 min.

Specify how each of the following items would be reported in the financial statements of Cunnington Enterprises for its current fiscal year. Also specify the amount that would appear on the statement. Some items may be reported on more than one financial statement. In these cases, specify the amount that would appear on each statement.

Income Statement (IS)

Balance Sheet (BS)

Change in Stockholders' Equity (SE)

1. Cunnington Enterprises received $143 of dividends during the year on stock it owned in Haskins, Inc.
2. At year-end, Cunnington Enterprises owned a $5,000 US Treasury Bond.
3. Cunnington Enterprises sold stock for $580 cash that had been held as an available-for-sale security. The stock had been purchased for $520 and hadn't changed in value until the time of its sale.
4. Stock that Cunnington Enterprises purchased for $875 during the year as an available-for-sale security has a market value of $940 at the year-end balance sheet date.
5. Stock that Cunnington Enterprises purchased for $640 during the year as a trading security had a market value of $655 at the year-end balance sheet date.
6. $280 of interest earned on a bond that Cunnington Enterprises purchased from the State of Washington.

MyAccountingLab

Exercises (Group A)

Quick solution:

Land = $338,800; Land Improvements = $73,000; Building = $800,000

E8-18A. Capitalized costs for long-term assets (*Learning Objective 2*) 10–15 min.

Pierce Systems purchased land, paying $65,000 cash as a down payment and signing a $260,000 note payable for the balance. In addition, Pierce Systems paid delinquent property tax of $3,500, title insurance costing $1,500, and an $8,800 charge for leveling the land and removing an unwanted building. The company constructed an office building on the land at a cost of $800,000. It also paid $55,000 for a fence around the property, $8,000 for the company sign near the entrance, and $10,000 for special lighting of the grounds.

Requirements

1. Determine the cost of the company's land, land improvements, and building.
2. Which of the assets will Pierce depreciate?

E8-19A. Capitalized costs for long-term assets (*Learning Objective 2*) 10–15 min.

Ramirez Transfer manufactures conveyor belts. Early in August 2015, Ramirez Transfer constructed its own building at a materials, labor, and overhead cost of $1,250,000. Ramirez Transfer paid cash for the construction costs. Ramirez Transfer also paid for architect fees and building permits of $82,000.

Requirements

1. How much should Ramirez Transfer record as the cost of the building in 2015?
2. Record Ramirez Transfer's transactions related to the construction of the building.

E8-20A. Capitalized costs for long-term assets (*Learning Objective 2*) **10–15 min.**

Sunshine Tanning Salon bought three tanning beds in a $13,000 lump-sum purchase. An independent appraiser valued the tanning beds as follows:

Tanning Bed	Appraised Value
1	$2,000
2	6,000
3	8,000

Sunshine Tanning Salon paid $6,500 in cash and signed a note payable for $6,500. Record the purchase in the journal, identifying each tanning bed's cost by number in a separate Tanning Bed account. Round decimals to three places.

E8-21A. Errors in accounting for long-term assets (*Learning Objectives 3 & 4*) **15–20 min.**

On January 1 of year 1, Ramsco, Inc., purchased equipment at a cost of $85,000. Management expects the equipment to remain in service for five years, with zero residual value. Ramsco, Inc., uses the straight-line depreciation method. Through an accounting error, Ramsco, Inc., accidentally expensed the entire cost of the equipment at the time of purchase.

Requirement

1. Prepare a schedule to show the overstatement or understatement in the following items at the end of each year over the five-year life of the equipment.
   a. Equipment, net
   b. Net income

E8-22A. Depreciation methods (*Learning Objective 3*) **15–20 min.**

Wellness Medical Center bought equipment on January 2, 2014, for $24,000. The equipment was expected to remain in service for four years and to perform 700 operations. At the end of the equipment's useful life, Wellness estimates that its residual value will be $3,000. The equipment performed 70 operations the first year, 210 the second year, 280 the third year, and 140 the fourth year.

Requirements

1. Prepare a schedule of depreciation expense per year for the equipment under the three depreciation methods. After two years under double-declining-balance depreciation, the company switched to the straight-line method. Show your computations.
2. Which method tracks the wear and tear on the equipment most closely?
3. Which method would Wellness prefer to use for income-tax purposes in the first years of the equipment's life? Explain in detail why a taxpayer prefers this method.

E8-23A. Straight-line depreciation (*Learning Objective 3*) **10–15 min.**

Hanson Freight purchased a building for $3,200,000 and depreciated it on a straight-line basis over a 30-year period. The estimated residual value was $380,000. After using the building for 15 years, Hanson realized that wear and tear on the building would force the company to replace it before 30 years. Starting with the sixteenth year, Hanson began depreciating the building over a revised total life of 25 years and increased the estimated residual value to $430,000. Record depreciation expense on the building for years 15 and 16.

E8-24A. Straight-line depreciation and long-term asset disposal (*Learning Objectives 3 & 5*) 15–20 min.

On January 2, 2014, Sparkle Lighting purchased showroom fixtures for $20,000 cash, expecting the fixtures to remain in service for 10 years. Sparkle Lighting has depreciated the fixtures on a straight-line basis, with zero residual value. On June 30, 2015, Sparkle Lighting sold the fixtures for $14,500 cash. Record both the depreciation expense on the fixtures for 2015 and the sale of the fixtures on June 30, 2015. Round intermediate calculations to the nearest cent and final answers to the nearest whole dollar.

E8-25A. Disposition of long-term assets (*Learning Objective 5*) 10–15 min.

Assume that Excell Corporation's comparative balance sheet reported these amounts:

	December 31	
	2013	**2012**
Plant and Equipment..	$ 645,000	$ 610,000
Less: Accumulated Depreciation...	137,400	120,600
Net Plant and Equipment..	$ 507,600	$ 489,400

Requirement

1. Assume that on January 2, 2014, Henry sold 1/6 of its plant and equipment for $122,000 in cash. Journalize this transaction for Excell.

E8-26A. Trade-in on purchase of new asset (*Learning Objectives 3 & 5*) 15–20 min.

Essex County Transport is a large trucking company. Essex County Transport uses the units-of-production (UOP) method to depreciate its trucks. In 2013, Essex County Transport acquired a Mack truck costing $400,000 with a useful life of 10 years or 937,500 miles. Estimated residual value was $25,000. The truck was driven 76,000 miles in 2013, 126,000 miles in 2014, and 166,000 miles in 2015. After 60,000 miles in 2016, Essex County Transport traded in the Mack truck for a new Freightliner that cost $460,000. Essex County Transport received a $245,000 trade-in allowance for the old truck and paid the difference in cash. Journalize the entry to record the purchase of the new truck.

E8-27A. Patents (*Learning Objective 6*) 10–15 min.

Part 1. Hamilton Printing manufactures high-speed printers. Hamilton Printing recently paid $380,000 for a patent on a new laser printer. Although it gives legal protection for 20 years, the patent is expected to provide a competitive advantage for only eight years. Using the straight-line method of amortization, make journal entries to record (a) the purchase of the patent and (b) amortization for year 1. Assume the patent is purchased on January 1 of year 1.

Part 2. After using the patent for three years, Hamilton Printing learns at an industry trade show that another company is designing a more efficient printer. On the basis of this new information, Hamilton Printing decides, starting with year 4, to amortize the remaining cost of the patent over two remaining years, giving the patent a total useful life of five years. Record amortization for year 4.

E8-28A. Goodwill (*Learning Objective 6*) 10–15 min.

Rauscher, Corp., aggressively acquires other companies. Assume that Rauscher, Corp., purchased Lancer, Inc., for $12 million cash. The market value of Lancer's assets is $14 million, and it has liabilities with a market value of $3.5 million.

Requirements

1. Compute the cost of goodwill purchased by Rauscher, Corp.
2. Record the purchase of Lancer, Inc., by Rauscher, Corp.

E8-29A. Depletion (*Learning Objective 7*) 10–15 min.

Brimhall Mining paid $1,276,000 for the right to extract mineral assets from an 800,000-ton mineral deposit. In addition to the purchase price, Brimhall Mining also paid a $1,500 filing fee, an $8,500 license fee to the state of Colorado, and $58,000 for a geological survey of the property. Because the company purchased the rights to the minerals only, the company expected the asset to have zero residual value when fully depleted. During the first year, Brimhall Mining removed and sold 83,000 tons of minerals. Using the Mineral Assets account, make journal entries to record the following:

a. Purchase of the minerals

b. Payment of fees and other costs

c. Depletion expense for the first year.

E8-30A. Balance sheet disclosure of long-term assets (*Learning Objective 9*) 10–15 min.

At the end of 2014, Zorro, Corp., had total assets of $11 million and total liabilities of $8 million. Included in the assets were property, plant, and equipment with a cost of $9 million and accumulated depreciation of $3 million. Also included in the assets were $246,000 of patents, $1,200,000 of goodwill, and $345,000 of other long-term assets. During 2014, Zorro, Corp., earned total revenues of $23 million and had total expenses of $21 million.

Requirements

1. Show how Zorro, Corp., reported long-term assets on its balance sheet on December 31, 2014.

2. What was the book value of property, plant, and equipment on that date?

E8-31A. Return on assets (ROA) and fixed asset turnover ratio (*Learning Objective 10*) 5–10 min.

The following is selected data for Edwards Equipment, Inc., for the current year:

Sales	$774,000
Net income	66,000
Total current assets, beginning	121,000
Total current assets, ending	115,000
Property, plant and equipment, beginning	276,000
Property, plant and equipment, ending	298,000
Total assets, beginning	397,000
Total assets, ending	413,000

Requirement

1. Calculate the return on assets (ROA) and the fixed asset turnover ratio for Edwards Equipment for the current year. Round your answers to two decimal places.

Exercises (Group B)

E8-32B. Capitalized costs for long-term assets (*Learning Objective 2*) 10–15 min.

Specialty Systems purchased land, paying $65,000 cash as a down payment and signing a $235,000 note payable for the balance. In addition, Specialty Systems paid delinquent property tax of $6,300, title insurance costing $2,800, and a $5,500 charge for leveling the land and removing an unwanted building. The company constructed an office building on the land at a cost of $840,000. It also paid $36,000 for a fence around the property, $16,700 for the company sign near the entrance, and $7,100 for special lighting of the grounds.

Requirements

1. Determine the cost of the company's land, land improvements, and building.
2. Which of the assets will Specialty depreciate?

E8-33B. Capitalized costs for long-term assets (*Learning Objective 2*) 10–15 min.

Chance Brothers manufactures conveyor belts. Early in July 2015, Chance Brothers constructed its own building at a materials, labor, and overhead cost of $940,000. Chance Brothers paid cash for the construction costs. Chance Brothers also paid for architect fees and building permits of $78,000.

Requirements

1. How much should Chance Brothers record as the cost of the building in 2015?
2. Record Chance Brothers' transactions related to the construction of the building.

E8-34B. Capitalized costs for long-term assets (*Learning Objective 2*) 10–15 min.

Desert Sun Tanning Salon bought three tanning beds in a $21,000 lump-sum purchase. An independent appraiser valued the tanning beds:

Tanning Bed	Appraised Value
1	$ 9,000
2	6,000
3	8,000

Desert Sun Tanning Salon paid $11,000 in cash and signed a note payable for $10,000. Record the purchase in the journal, identifying each tanning bed's cost by number in a separate Tanning Bed account. Round decimals to three places.

E8-35B. Errors in accounting for long-term assets (*Learning Objectives 3 & 4*) 15–20 min.

Assume that on January 1 of year 1, Middleton Company purchased equipment at a cost of $470,000. Management expects the equipment to remain in service for five years, with zero residual value. Middleton Company uses the straight-line depreciation method. Through an accounting error, Middleton Company accidentally expensed the entire cost of the equipment at the time of purchase.

Requirement

1. Prepare a schedule to show the overstatement or understatement in the following items at the end of each year over the five-year life of the equipment:
   a. Equipment, net
   b. Net income

E8-36B. Depreciation methods (*Learning Objective 3*) 15–20 min.

Mercy Medical Center bought equipment on January 2, 2014, for $38,000. The equipment was expected to remain in service for four years and to perform 800 operations. At the end of the equipment's useful life, Mercy estimates that its residual value will be $2,000. The equipment performed 90 operations the first year, 250 the second year, 240 the third year, and 220 the fourth year.

Requirements

1. Prepare a schedule of depreciation expense per year for the equipment under the three depreciation methods. After two years under double-declining-balance depreciation, the company switched to the straight-line method. Show your computations.
2. Which method tracks the wear and tear on the equipment most closely?
3. Which method would Mercy prefer to use for income-tax purposes in the first years of the equipment's life? Explain in detail why a taxpayer prefers this method.

E8-37B. Straight-line depreciation (*Learning Objective 3*) 10–15 min.

Pembrook Freight purchased a building for $1,000,000 and depreciated it on a straight-line basis over a 30-year period. The estimated residual value was $130,000. After using the building for 15 years, Pembrook realized that wear and tear on the building would force the company to replace it before 30 years. Starting with the sixteenth year, Pembrook began depreciating the building over a revised total life of 20 years and increased the estimated residual value to $205,000. Record depreciation expense on the building for years 15 and 16.

E8-38B. Straight-line depreciation and long-term asset disposal (*Learning Objectives 3 & 5*) 15–20 min.

On January 2, 2014, Lithonia Lighting purchased showroom fixtures for $18,000 cash, expecting the fixtures to remain in service for eight years. Lithonia Lighting has depreciated the fixtures on a straight-line basis, with zero residual value. On August 31, 2015, Lithonia Lighting sold the fixtures for $13,200 cash. Record both the depreciation expense on the fixtures for 2015 and the sale of the fixtures on August 31, 2015. Round intermediate calculations to the nearest cent and final answers to the nearest whole dollar.

E8-39B. Disposition of long-term assets (*Learning Objective 5*) 10–15 min.

Assume that Hardigan Corporation's comparative balance sheet reported these amounts:

	December 31	
	2013	**2012**
Plant and Equipment	$ 645,000	$ 638,000
Less: Accumulated Depreciation	175,000	155,000
Net Plant and Equipment	$ 470,000	$ 483,000

Requirement

1. Assume that on January 2, 2014, Hardigan sold 1/2 of its plant and equipment for $252,000 in cash. Journalize this transaction for Hardigan.

E8-40B. Trade-in on purchase of new asset (*Learning Objectives 3 & 5*) 15–20 min.

Maple Valley Transport is a large trucking company. Maple Valley Transport uses the units-of-production (UOP) method to depreciate its trucks. In 2013, Maple Valley Transport acquired a Mack truck costing $385,000 with a useful life of six years or 1,500,000 miles. Estimated residual value was $85,000. The truck was driven 182,000 miles in 2013, 263,000 miles in 2014, and 254,000 miles in 2015. After 62,000 miles in 2016, Maple Valley Transport traded in the Mack truck for a new Freightliner that costs $422,000. Maple Valley Transport received a $243,000 trade-in allowance for the old truck and paid the difference in cash. Journalize the entry to record the purchase of the new truck.

E8-41B. Patents (*Learning Objective 6*) 10–15 min.

Part 1. Morris Printing manufactures high-speed printers. On January 1 of year 1, Morris Printing recently paid $700,000 for a patent on a new laser printer. Although it gives legal protection for 20 years, the patent is expected to provide a competitive advantage for only eight years. Using the straight-line method of amortization, make journal entries to record (a) the purchase of the patent and (b) amortization for year 1.

Part 2. After using the patent for five years, Morris Printing learns at an industry trade show that another company is designing a more efficient printer. On the basis of this new information, Morris Printing decides, starting with year 6, to amortize the remaining cost of the patent over two remaining years, giving the patent a total useful life of seven years. Record amortization for year 6.

E8-42B. Goodwill (*Learning Objective 6*) 10–15 min.

Dillon, Corp., aggressively acquired other companies. Assume that Dillon, Corp., purchased Simmons, Inc., for $16 million cash. The market value of Simmons's assets is $22 million, and it has liabilities with a market value of $8 million.

Requirements

1. Compute the cost of goodwill purchased by Dillon, Corp.
2. Record the purchase of Simmons, Inc., by Dillon, Corp.

E8-43B. Depletion (*Learning Objective 7*) 10–15 min.

Whalen Mining paid $615,000 for the right to extract mineral assets from a 500,000-ton mineral deposit. In addition to the purchase price, Whalen Mining also paid a $1,400 filing fee, a $3,600 license fee to the state of Colorado, and $45,000 for a geological survey of the property. Because the company purchased the rights to the minerals only, the company expected the asset to have zero residual value when fully depleted. During the first year, Whalen Mining removed and sold 80,000 tons of minerals. Using the Mineral Assets account, make journal entries to record the following:

a. Purchase of the minerals
b. Payment of fees and other costs
c. Depletion expense for the first year (assume all the minerals extracted were sold during the year)

E8-44B. Balance sheet disclosure of long-term assets (*Learning Objective 9*) 10–15 min.

At the end of 2014, Jamison, Corp., had total assets of $14 million and total liabilities of $9 million. Included in the assets were property, plant, and equipment with a cost of $12 million and accumulated depreciation of $3 million. Also included in the assets were $210,000 of patents, $1,400,000 of goodwill, and $318,000 of other long-term assets. During 2014, Jamison, Corp., earned total revenues of $9 million and had total expenses of $7 million.

Requirements

1. Show how Jamison, Corp., reported long-term assets on its balance sheet on December 31, 2014.

2. What was the book value of property, plant, and equipment on that date?

E8-45B. Return on assets (ROA) and fixed asset turnover ratio
(*Learning Objective 10*) 5–10 min.

The following is selected data for Richardson Equipment, Inc., for the current year:

Sales	$821,000
Net income	63,000
Total current assets, beginning	103,000
Total current assets, ending	122,000
Property, plant and equipment, beginning	305,000
Property, plant and equipment, ending	314,000
Total assets, beginning	408,000
Total assets, ending	436,000

Requirement

1. Calculate the return on assets (ROA) and the fixed asset turnover ratio for Richardson Equipment for the current year. Round your answers to two decimal places.

MyAccountingLab   ## Problems (Group A)

P8-46A. Long-term asset costs and partial year depreciation
(*Learning Objectives 2 & 3*) 20–25 min.

Tri-State Manufacturing incurred the following costs in acquiring land, making land improvements, and constructing and furnishing a new building.

a.	Purchase price of four acres of land	$193,000
b.	Additional dirt and earthmoving	9,400
c.	Fence around the boundary of the property	17,500
d.	Attorney fee for title search on the land	1,100
e.	Unpaid property taxes on the land to be paid by Tri-state	5,900
f.	Company signs at the front of the property	4,700
g.	Building permit for the building	2,100
h.	Architect's fee for the design of the building	20,900
i.	Labor to construct the building	498,000
j.	Materials used to construct the building	401,000
k.	Landscaping	6,700
l.	Parking lot and concrete walks	29,100
m.	Lights for the parking lot and walkways	10,500
n.	Salary of construction supervisor (85% to building; 15% to parking lot and concrete walks)	60,000
o.	Furniture for the building	106,000
p.	Transportation and installation of furniture	1,900

Tri-State Manufacturing depreciates buildings over 30 years, land improvements over 20 years, and furniture over eight years, all on a straight-line basis with zero residual value.

Requirements

1. Set up columns for Land, Land Improvements, Building, and Furniture. Show how to account for each cost by listing the cost under the correct account. Determine the total cost of each asset.

2. All construction was complete and assets were placed in service on September 1. Record partial-year depreciation for the year ended December 31. Round intermediate calculations to the nearest cent and final answers to the nearest whole dollar.

P8-47A. **Journalize long-term asset transactions** (*Learning Objectives 2, 3, & 5*) **20–25 min.**

Fidelity Freightway provides freight service. The company's balance sheet includes Land, Buildings, and Motor-Carrier Equipment. Fidelity Freightway uses a separate accumulated depreciation account for each depreciable asset. During 2014, Fidelity Freightway completed the following transactions:

Jan 1	Traded in motor-carrier equipment with accumulated depreciation of $112,000 (cost of $151,000) for new equipment with a cash cost of $187,000. Fidelity Freightway received a trade-in allowance of $46,000 on the old equipment and paid the remainder in cash.
Jul 1	Sold a building that cost $740,000 and had accumulated depreciation of $360,000 through December 31 of the preceding year. Depreciation is computed on a straight-line basis. The building has a 40-year useful life and a residual value of $50,000. Fidelity Freightway received $100,000 cash and a $420,000 note receivable.
Oct 31	Purchased land and a building for a cash payment of $700,000. An independent appraisal valued the land at $277,500 and the building at $472,500.
Dec 31	Recorded depreciation as follows: New motor-carrier equipment has an expected useful life of 1 million miles and an estimated residual value of $27,000. Depreciation method is the units-of-production method. During the year, Fidelity Freightway drove the truck 295,000 miles. Depreciation on buildings is straight-line. The new building has a 40-year useful life and a residual value equal to $81,000.

Requirement

1. Record the transactions in Fidelity Freightway's journal.

P8-48A. **Capitalize long-term asset costs and several depreciation methods** (*Learning Objectives 2, 3, & 9*) **20–25 min.**

On January 3, 2015, Azul Enterprises, Inc., paid $281,000 for equipment used in manufacturing automotive supplies. In addition to the basic purchase price, the company paid $700 transportation charges, $300 insurance for the equipment while in transit, $11,000 sales tax, and $2,000 for a special platform on which to place the equipment in the plant. Azul Enterprises, Inc., management estimates that the equipment will remain in service for five years and have a residual value of $35,000. The equipment will produce 60,000 units the first year, with annual production decreasing by 5,000 units during each of the next four years (i.e., 55,000 units in year 2, 50,000 units in year 3, and so on for a total of 250,000 units). In trying to decide which depreciation method to use, Azul Enterprises, Inc., requested a depreciation schedule for each of the three depreciation methods (straight-line, units-of-production, and double-declining-balance).

Requirements

1. For each depreciation method, prepare a depreciation schedule showing asset cost, depreciation expense, accumulated depreciation, and asset book value for each year of the asset's life. For the units-of-production method, round depreciation per unit to three decimal places.

2. Azul Enterprises, Inc., prepares financial statements using the depreciation method that reports the highest income in the early years of asset use. For income tax purposes, the company uses the depreciation method that minimizes income taxes in the early years. Consider the first year Azul Enterprises, Inc., uses the equipment. Identify the depreciation methods that meet Azul Enterprises' objectives, assuming the income tax authorities permit the use of any method.

3. Show how Azul Enterprises, Inc., would report equipment on the December 31, 2015, balance sheet for each depreciation method.

P8-49A. Disposing of an asset (*Learning Objective 5*) **15–20 min.**

Quick solution:

a. *$5,000 loss;*
b. *$2,000 gain;*
c. *$4,500 gain;*
d. *$2,300 loss*

Palmer Industries had a piece of equipment that cost $62,000 and had accumulated depreciation of $57,000.

Requirement

1. Record the disposition of the equipment assuming the following independent situations:
    a. Palmer discarded the equipment, receiving $0.
    b. Palmer sold the equipment for $7,000 cash.
    c. Palmer traded the equipment in on a new piece of equipment costing $77,000. Palmer was granted a $9,500 trade-in allowance for the old equipment and paid the difference in cash.
    d. Palmer traded the equipment in on a new piece of equipment costing $83,000. Palmer was granted a $2,700 trade-in allowance for the old equipment and signed a note payable for the difference.

P8-50A. Goodwill (*Learning Objective 6*) **15–20 min.**

Carl's Restaurants acquired Welcome Diners. The financial records of Welcome Diners included:

Book Value of Assets	$2.4 million
Market Value of Assets	2.8 million
Market Value of Liabilities	1.3 million

Requirements

1. Make the journal entry to record Carl's Restaurants' purchase of Welcome Diners for $2.6 million cash, including any goodwill.

2. How should Carl's Restaurants account for this goodwill after acquiring Welcome Diners? Explain in detail.

P8-51A. Depletion (*Learning Objective 7*) **20–25 min.**

Ewing Oil Company's balance sheet includes three assets: Natural Gas, Oil, and Coal Reserves. Suppose Ewing Oil Company paid $4.8 million in cash for the right to work a mine with an estimated 400,000 tons of coal. Assume the company paid $40,000 to remove unwanted buildings from the land and $55,000 to prepare the surface for mining. Further, assume that Ewing Oil Company signed a $65,000 note payable to a company that will return the land surface to its original condition after the mining ends. During the first year, Ewing Oil Company removed 68,000 tons of coal, which it sold on account for $22 per ton. Operating expenses for the first year totaled $315,000, all paid in cash.

Requirements

1. Record all of Ewing Oil Company's transactions, including depletion, for the first year.

2. Prepare the company's income statement for its coal operations for the first year.

P8-52A. Return on assets (ROA) and fixed asset turnover ratio
(*Learning Objective 10*) 10–15 min.

The following is selected data for Halo Industries:

	2014	2013	2012
Sales	$1,373,000	$1,346,000	$1,268,000
Net income	128,000	117,000	114,000
Total, current assets, ending	173,000	176,000	156,000
Property, plant and equipment, ending	688,000	676,000	685,000
Total assets, ending	861,000	852,000	841,000

Requirements

1. Calculate the return on assets (ROA) and the fixed asset turnover ratio for Halo Industries for 2013 and 2014. Round your answers to two decimal places.

2. Have the ratios improved or deteriorated? Comment on the trend in both ratios.

MyAccountingLab ## Problems (Group B)

P8-53B. Long-term asset costs and partial year depreciation
(*Learning Objectives 2 & 3*) 20–25 min.

Prescott Manufacturing incurred the following costs in acquiring land, making land improvements, and constructing and furnishing a new building.

a.	Purchase price of four acres of land	$210,000
b.	Additional dirt and earthmoving	9,300
c.	Fence around the boundary of the property	14,000
d.	Attorney fee for title search on the land	1,400
e.	Unpaid property taxes on the land to be paid by Prescott	6,700
f.	Company signs at the front of the property	11,400
g.	Building permit for the building	2,900
h.	Architect's fee for the design of the building	26,000
i.	Labor to construct the building	414,000
j.	Materials used to construct the building	377,000
k.	Landscaping	9,300
l.	Parking lot and concrete walks	34,600
m.	Lights for the parking lot and walkways	8,700
n.	Salary of construction supervisor (85% to building; 15% to parking lot and concrete walks)	30,000
o.	Furniture for the building	63,000
p.	Transportation and installation of furniture	1,200

Prescott Manufacturing depreciates buildings over 40 years, land improvements over 15 years, and furniture over eight years, all on a straight-line basis with zero residual value.

Requirements

1. Set up columns for Land, Land Improvements, Building, and Furniture. Show how to account for each cost by listing the cost under the correct account. Determine the total cost of each asset.

2. All construction was complete and the assets were placed in service on November 1. Record partial-year depreciation for the year ended December 31. Round intermediate calculations to the nearest cent and final answers to the nearest whole dollar.

P8-54B. Journalize long-term asset transactions (*Learning Objectives 2, 3, & 5*)
20–25 min.

Russell Freightway provides freight service. The company's balance sheet includes Land, Buildings, and Motor-Carrier Equipment. Russell uses a separate accumulated depreciation account for each depreciable asset. During 2012, Russell Freightway completed the following transactions:

Jan	1	Traded in motor-carrier equipment with accumulated depreciation of $85,000 (cost of $132,000) for new equipment with a cash cost of $174,000. Russell received a trade-in allowance of $64,000 on the old equipment and paid the remainder in cash.
Jul	1	Sold a building that cost $570,000 and had accumulated depreciation of $240,000 through December 31 of the preceding year. Depreciation is computed on a straight-line basis. The building has a 40-year useful life and a residual value of $80,000. Russell received $100,000 cash and a $590,000 note receivable.
Oct	31	Purchased land and a building for a cash payment of $900,000. An independent appraisal valued the land at $331,200 and the building at $703,800.
Dec	31	Recorded depreciation as follows: New motor-carrier equipment has an expected useful life of 800,000 miles and an estimated residual value of $22,000. Depreciation method is the units-of-production method. During the year, Russell drove the truck 100,000 miles. Depreciation on buildings is straight-line. The new building has a 40-year useful life and a residual value equal to $60,000.

Requirement

1. Record the transactions in Russell Freightway's journal. Round your depreciation expense to the nearest whole dollar.

P8-55B. Capitalize long-term asset costs and several depreciation methods (*Learning Objectives 2, 3, & 9*) 20–25 min.

On January 4, 2015, Sunbelt Systems, Inc., paid $287,700 for equipment used in manufacturing automotive supplies. In addition to the basic purchase price, the company paid $2,800 transportation charges, $800 insurance for the equipment while in transit, $25,800 sales tax, and $2,900 for a special platform on which to place the equipment in the plant. Sunbelt Systems, Inc., management estimates that the equipment will remain in service for five years and have a residual value of $40,000. The equipment will produce 60,000 units the first year, with annual production decreasing by 5,000 units during each of the next four years (i.e., 55,000 units in year 2, 50,000 units in year 3, and so on for a total of 250,000 units). In trying to decide which depreciation method to use, Sunbelt Systems, Inc., requested a depreciation schedule for each of the three depreciation methods (straight-line, units-of-production, and double-declining-balance).

Requirements

1. For each depreciation method, prepare a depreciation schedule showing asset cost, depreciation expense, accumulated depreciation, and asset book value for each year of the asset's life. For the units-of-production method, round depreciation per unit to three decimal places.

2. Sunbelt Systems, Inc., prepares financial statements using the depreciation method that reports the highest income in the early years of asset use. For income tax purposes, the company uses the depreciation method that minimizes income taxes in the early years. Consider the first year Sunbelt Systems, Inc., uses the equipment. Identify the depreciation methods that meet Sunbelt Systems' objectives, assuming the income tax authorities permit the use of any method.

3. Show how Sunbelt Systems, Inc., would report equipment on the December 31, 2015, balance sheet for each depreciation method.

P8-56B. Disposing of an asset (*Learning Objective 5*) **15–20 min.**

Alvery Industries had a piece of equipment that cost $31,000 and had accumulated depreciation of $30,000.

Requirement

1. Record the disposition of the equipment assuming the following independent situations:
   a. Alvery discarded the equipment receiving $0.
   b. Alvery sold the equipment for $6,000 cash.
   c. Alvery traded the equipment in on a new piece of equipment costing $35,000. Alvery was granted a $5,500 trade-in allowance for the old equipment and paid the difference in cash.
   d. Alvery traded the equipment in on a new piece of equipment costing $23,000. Alvery was granted a $500 trade-in allowance for the old equipment and signed a note payable for the difference.

P8-57B. Goodwill (*Learning Objective 6*) **15–20 min.**

Cottage Cafe acquired Don's Diners. The financial records of Don's Diners included:

Book Value of Assets	$2.6 million
Market Value of Assets	2.7 million
Market Value of Liabilities	1.3 million

Requirements

1. Make the journal entry to record Cottage Cafe's purchase of Don's Diners for $1.8 million cash, including any goodwill.

2. How should Cottage Cafe account for this goodwill after acquiring Don's Diners? Explain in detail.

P8-58B. Depletion (*Learning Objective 7*) **20–25 min.**

O'Brien Oil Company's balance sheet includes three assets: Natural Gas, Oil, and Coal Reserves. Suppose O'Brien Oil Company paid $1.8 million cash for the right to work a mine with an estimated 150,000 tons of coal. Assume the company paid $66,000 to remove unwanted buildings from the land and $46,000 to prepare the surface for mining. Further, assume that O'Brien Oil Company signed a $32,000 note payable to a company that will return the land surface to its original condition after the mining ends. During the first year, O'Brien Oil Company removed 38,000 tons of coal, which it sold on account for $28 per ton. Operating expenses for the first year totaled $250,000, all paid in cash.

Requirements

1. Record all of O'Brien Oil Company's transactions, including depletion, for the first year.

2. Prepare the company's income statement for its coal operations for the first year.

P8-59B. Return on assets (ROA) and fixed asset turnover ratio
(*Learning Objective 10*) 10–15 min.

The following is selected data for Ibanez Industries:

	2014	2013	2012
Sales	$1,468,000	$1,582,000	$1,427,000
Net income	142,000	151,000	129,000
Total, current assets, ending	158,000	153,000	165,000
Property, plant and equipment, ending	768,000	764,000	736,000
Total assets, ending	926,000	917,000	901,000

Requirements

1. Calculate the return on assets (ROA) and the fixed asset turnover ratio for Ibanez Industries for 2013 and 2014. Round your answers to two decimal places.

2. Have the ratios improved or deteriorated? Comment on the trend in both ratios.

Continuing Exercise

This exercise continues our accounting for Cole's Yard Care, Inc., from previous chapters. In this exercise, we will account for the annual depreciation expense for Cole's Yard Care, Inc. In the Continuing Exercise in Chapter 2, we learned that Cole's Yard Care, Inc., had purchased a lawn mower and a weed whacker on April 3 and that they were expected to last four years.

Requirements

1. Calculate the annual depreciation expense amount for each asset assuming both assets are depreciated using straight-line depreciation.

2. Record the entry for the partial year's depreciation for 2014. Date it December 31, 2014. Assume that no depreciation has been recorded yet in 2014.

Continuing Problem

This problem continues our accounting for Aqua Magic, Inc., from Chapter 7. During 2014, Aqua Magic made the following purchases:

- On May 3, Aqua Magic, Inc., purchased a copy machine for $1,800 cash. The copy machine has an estimated useful life of five years and no salvage value. Aqua Magic uses double-declining-balance depreciation for the copy machine.
- On May 18, Aqua Magic, Inc., purchased a $36,200 truck financed by a note payable bearing 6% annual interest. The truck has an estimated useful life of 250,000 miles and a residual value of $3,700. The truck was driven 26,000 miles in 2014 and is depreciated using the units-of-production method.
- On June 2, Aqua Magic, Inc., paid $25,000 for land.
- On June 22, $4,000 of furniture was purchased on account. The furniture has a six-year life and a residual value of $400. Furniture is depreciated using straight-line depreciation.
- On August 10, $1,800 of furniture was purchased. The furniture has a five-year life and no residual value and is depreciated using straight-line depreciation.
- On August 25, $6,000 of equipment was purchased. The equipment has a four-year life and a $1,500 residual value and is depreciated using the straight-line method.

- On September 1, Aqua Magic, Inc., purchased a building for $150,000 financed by a mortgage bearing 4% annual interest. The building has an estimated salvage value of $30,000 and is being depreciated over 40 years using the straight-line method.

Requirements

1. Calculate the depreciation expense as of December 31, 2014, for all assets purchased in 2014.

2. Assuming these are Aqua Magic's only assets, how will fixed assets be reflected on the balance sheet at December 31, 2014?

Continuing Financial Statement Analysis Problem

Return to Target's 2012 annual report. For instructions on how to access the report online, see the Continuing Financial Statement Analysis Problem in Chapter 2. On page 33 of the annual report, you'll find Target's income statement for the year ending February 2, 2013 (called the Consolidated Statement of Operations). On page 35, you'll find Target's balance sheet as of February 2, 2013 (called the Consolidated Statement of Financial Position). Now answer the following questions:

1. Look at Target's balance sheet. What long-term assets does Target own? How much has Target invested in each type of long-term asset as of February 2, 2013, and January 28, 2012?

2. Look over footnotes 14, 15, and 16 of the financial statements. These footnotes start on page 45 of the financial statements, found in Target's 2012 annual report. Why does Target have tangible and intangible assets?

3. Look over footnotes 14 and 16 of the financial statements. These footnotes start on page 45 of the financial statements, found in Target's 2012 annual report. How is Target depreciating its property and equipment and amortizing its intangible assets?

4. Look at Target's balance sheet and income statement. What is Target's return on assets (ROA) and fixed asset turnover for the year ending February 2, 2013? What do these ratios tell you?

5. Looking back over your answers to question 1 through 4, how do you think Target is performing? What do you think of Target's management of assets?

Apply Your Knowledge

Ethics in Action

Case 1. Luca Hanson owns Luca's Limousine, which operates a fleet of limousines and shuttle buses. Upon reviewing the most recent financial statements, he became confused over the recent decline in net income. He called his accountant and asked for an explanation. The accountant told Luca that the numerous repairs and maintenance expenses, such as oil changes, cleaning, and minor engine repairs, had totaled up to a large amount. Further, because several drivers were involved in accidents, the fleet insurance premiums had also risen sharply. Luca told his accountant to simply capitalize all the expenses related to the vehicles rather than expensing them. These capitalized repair costs could then be depreciated over the next 10 to 20 years. By capitalizing those expenses, the net income would be higher, as would property and equipment assets; therefore, both the income statement and balance sheet would look better. His accountant, however, disagreed because the costs were clearly routine maintenance and because they did not extend the fleet's useful life. Luca then told his accountant that the estimated useful life of the vehicles needed to be changed from 5 years to 15 years to lower the amount of depreciation expense. His accountant responded that capitalizing costs that should be expensed and extending the estimated lives of assets just to increase the reported net income was unethical and wrong. Luca said that it was his business and, therefore, demanded that the financial statements be changed to show more net income. As a result, the accountant told Luca to pick up his files and find another accountant. What ethical concerns did the accountant have? If the total amount of repairs and maintenance was so large, couldn't a case be made that the amount should be capitalized? Is it unethical to change the estimated life of an asset? Was it unethical for the accountant to sever the business relationship? Do you have any suggestions?

Case 2. Panco Corporation purchased Apex Unlimited for $12 million. The fair market value of Apex Unlimited's net assets at the time was $9 million, so Panco Corporation recorded $3 million of goodwill. Included in the purchase was a patent valued at $1.5 million with an estimated remaining life of eight years. To comply with GAAP, the goodwill was not amortized, but the patent was amortized over the remaining eight-year life. However, the Apex Unlimited business was not as profitable as anticipated, and as a result, the accountant for Panco Corporation stated that the goodwill needed to be written off. Further, the accountant discovered that the remaining life of the patent was only six years and that it should be amortized over the remaining six-year life rather than the eight-year life originally estimated. The CEO became concerned because these adjustments would cause net income to be extremely low for the year. As a result, he told the accountant to wait before writing off the goodwill because of the possibility that the purchase could be profitable in the future. Also, he argued, the life of the patent should be left alone because it was originally based upon what was thought to be an eight-year life. After much debate, the CEO then agreed with the accountant as long as the amount of goodwill was not completely written off in the current year. What ethical concerns are involved? Should the accountant change the amortizable life of an intangible asset? Should the accountant completely write off the goodwill account in the current year? Does the CEO's concern for higher net income create any ethical problems when the accountant agrees to not completely write off the goodwill? Do you have any other thoughts?

Know Your Business

Financial Analysis

Purpose: To help familiarize you with the financial reporting of a real company in order to further your understanding of the chapter material you are learning.

This case addresses the long-term assets of Columbia Sportswear. The majority of these assets consist of property and equipment and intangible assets. In the text, you learned how most long-term tangible assets used in business are capitalized and depreciated over their estimated useful lives. Further, you learned that certain intangible assets are amortized over time while others are not. In this case, you will not only see and understand the classification and presentation of these assets, but also explore the methods used by Columbia Sportswear to depreciate and amortize them. Refer to Columbia Sportswear's financial statements in Appendix A. Also, consider the information presented in footnote 2, under the headings Property, plant, and equipment and Intangible assets and goodwill, footnote 6 titled Property, Plant, and Equipment, Net, and footnote 7 titled Intangible Assets, Net and Goodwill.

Requirements

1. What was the balance of net property, plant, and equipment on December 31, 2012? What was the balance of net property, plant, and equipment on December 31, 2011? Did the amount of ending net property, plant, and equipment increase or decrease? Assume Columbia Sportswear removed $492,000 of fully depreciated assets from fixed assets in 2012. What effect did this have on the value of the net property, plant, and equipment balance? Explain your answer.

2. What methods of depreciation were used by Columbia Sportswear? What were the estimated useful lives? What kinds of intangible assets does Columbia Sportswear have? Which intangible assets are amortized by Columbia Sportswear, and which are not? Why?

3. What was the percentage of net property, plant, and equipment compared to the total assets on December 31, 2012? What was the percentage of net property, plant, and equipment compared to the total assets on December 31, 2011? Did the percentage increase or decrease during the year?

4. Columbia Sportswear lists "Leasehold improvements" and "Construction in progress" as part of Property, Plant, and Equipment. Although these assets are not discussed in the textbook, can you describe what these assets represent?

Industry Analysis

Purpose: To help you understand and compare the performance of two companies in the same industry.

Find the Columbia Sportswear Company Annual Report located in Appendix A and go to the Notes to the Consolidated Financial Statements starting on page 659. Now access the 2012 Annual Report for Under Armour, Inc., from the Internet. For instructions on how to access the report online, see the Industry Analysis in Chapter 1. The Notes to Audited Consolidated Financial Statements start on page 53.

Requirement

1. Find the section in the notes for each company where the company discusses its Property and Equipment or its Property, Plant, and Equipment. Also find the section where the company discusses Intangible Assets. Compare the two and note any major differences.

Small Business Analysis

Purpose: To help you understand the importance of cash flows in the operation of a small business.

You've made an appointment to take your year-end financial statements down to the bank. You know that your banker is usually concerned about two things, your net income and the amount of cash you have. You are a little concerned because you know that your current year net income was down a little bit from the prior year. You figure that a significant cause for the decline was due to a large equipment purchase you made early in the year, which resulted in a lot of depreciation expense. However, as you look at your balance sheet, it shows that cash increased from last year to this year. That's a little puzzling, but you're hoping the banker can figure it out.

A couple of days later, you get a call from the banker. You're expecting him to tell you the bank won't be able to extend any more credit to you because your net income has declined. Imagine your surprise when he tells you how pleased he is with your financial performance this year and that he doesn't anticipate any problems extending more credit to you. You want to know what he saw in your financial statements that you didn't see, so you say to him, "Bob, thanks for the good news and the good report on my financial condition. Even though our cash increased this year, I was afraid that the decline in our income might cause you some concern. How come it didn't?"

Requirement

1. What kind of response do you think you might get from the banker regarding your net income as it relates to cash flow?

Written Communication

A client of yours notified you that she just closed a deal to purchase an existing business. It's a pretty hefty purchase. As part of the purchase of the business, she received the land, the building, all the equipment, and the entire merchandise inventory of the company purchased. Your client e-mailed you a copy of the closing statement along with the breakdown of the purchase price shown below. In the e-mail, your client expressed concern about how to account for the $1,800,000 paid for the land and building. She also wanted to know the proper way to account for the merchandise inventory and the goodwill that was purchased.

Asset List	
Description	**Amount**
Land and Building	$1,800,000
Equipment...	725,000
Inventory...	450,000
Goodwill..	300,000
Total Purchase Price	$3,275,000

Requirement

1. Prepare an e-mail to your client explaining how the $1,800,000 should be allocated between the land and building as well as how the merchandise inventory and goodwill should be accounted for.

Self Check Answers
1. b 2. b 3. d 4. b 5. c 6. a 7. c 8. b 9. b 10. c 11. c 12. b

9

Current Liabilities and Long-Term Debt

Business, Accounting, and You

Learning Objectives

1 Distinguish between known, estimated, and contingent liabilities

2 Account for current liabilities of a known amount

3 Account for liabilities of an uncertain amount

4 Account for contingent liabilities

5 Account for long-term debt

6 Report liabilities on the balance sheet

7 Compute the debt ratio and interest coverage ratio

8 (Appendix 9A) Account for payroll (Located online only at www.pearsonhighered.com/kemp)

Ford has cash, accounts receivable, inventory, land, and buildings. It takes a lot of assets to operate Ford. But how does Ford purchase or fund these assets? It takes money to make money.

Remember your accounting equation: Assets equal liabilities plus stockholders' equity. The owners of Ford, the stockholders, provide money. But Ford also uses money obtained with debt, called liabilities. Liabilities are amounts owed to lenders, such as a bank, or other creditors, such as a supplier.

By agreement, some liabilities need to be paid quickly. Suppliers deliver inventory to Ford with the understanding that Ford will pay the supplier within 30 to 60 days. Employees provide labor to Ford believing Ford will pay them within a few weeks. But by agreement, some liabilities are to be paid over long periods of time. Think about Ford spending millions of dollars to build a factory. If Ford borrows this money from a bank or other lender, Ford would probably want to repay that money over many years. That long period of time also means Ford will pay interest to the lender.

Understanding liabilities is very important. Remember that if a business cannot pay its liabilities, it has taken too much risk and will fail. You need to know how accountants recognize, measure, record, and report liabilities. As an accountant or manager, you need to understand how and when a business borrows money and repays money.

▶ Real World Accounting Video

In the Real World Accounting video, Bill Mencer, Controller of Sheffield Pharmaceuticals, talks about borrowing money and accounting for liabilities (debt). Look at the video. Think about what Bill is saying. Think about the role of debt and the challenges in accounting for debt.

What Are the Differences Among Known, Estimated, and Contingent Liabilities?

1 **Distinguish between known, estimated, and contingent liabilities**

Liabilities can generally be broken down into three categories:

- **Known liabilities:** The majority of a company's liabilities fall into this category. Known liabilities can be defined as known obligations of known amounts. In other words, the business knows that it owes something and it knows how much it owes. Examples of known liabilities include accounts payable, notes payable, unearned revenues, and accrued liabilities, such as interest or taxes payable.
- **Estimated liabilities:** An estimated liability is defined as a known obligation of an unknown amount. A business will sometimes encounter a situation where it knows that a liability exists but does not know the exact amount of the liability. In these situations, the amount of the liability must be estimated. A typical example is estimated warranties payable, which is common for companies like **Ford** and **Apple**.
- **Contingent liabilities:** A **contingent liability** is a unique liability that differs from all other types of liabilities. A contingent liability arises because of a *past* event, but it is dependent upon the outcome of a *future* event. In other words, whether or not a company has an obligation depends upon the result of an event that has not yet occurred. In addition, the amount of a contingent liability may be either known or unknown. Current or pending litigation is an example of a contingent liability.

Contingent liability A potential liability that depends on the outcome of a future event.

As we learned in Chapter 4, a liability is classified as a current liability if the obligation will be settled within one year, or the operating cycle if the cycle is longer than one year. All liabilities not classified as current liabilities are classified as long-term debt. It is possible for known, estimated, and contingent liabilities to be classified as either current or long-term. We will begin our discussion of accounting for liabilities by looking at current liabilities of a known amount.

How Do You Account for Current Liabilities of a Known Amount?

2 Account for current liabilities of a known amount

A large portion of liabilities for most companies will be made up of known liabilities that are due within one year. In the following paragraphs, we will learn how to account for the majority of the types of current liabilities of a known amount that most companies are likely to encounter.

Accounts Payable

As we have learned in previous chapters, amounts owed for purchases on account are known as accounts payable. Because accounts payable are typically due in 30 to 45 days, they are classified as current liabilities. The largest portion of accounts payable for most merchandising companies is related to the purchase of inventory on account. Merchandising and service businesses also incur accounts payable when they purchase items such as supplies, electricity, or telephone service on account. Accounts payable transactions are recorded by debiting the related asset or expense account and crediting Accounts Payable. For example, assume that Mackay Industries receives a utility bill for $680. The bill represents prior electricity usage and is not due for 30 days. Mackay Industries would record the receipt of the bill as:

DATE	ACCOUNTS	POST REF.	DR.	CR.
	Utilities Expense		680	
	Accounts Payable			680
	Record utility bill due in 30 days.			

When Mackay Industries pays the utility bill, it will record the payment on account as:

DATE	ACCOUNTS	POST REF.	DR.	CR.
	Accounts Payable		680	
	Cash			680
	Record payment on account.			

Notes Payable

When a business borrows money, usually from a financial institution, the signing of a promissory note is generally required. Businesses also often finance purchases of long-term assets through the use of notes payable. Any note payable that must be paid within one year from the balance sheet date is classified as a current liability. All notes not classified as a current liability are classified as long-term debt (discussed later in the chapter).

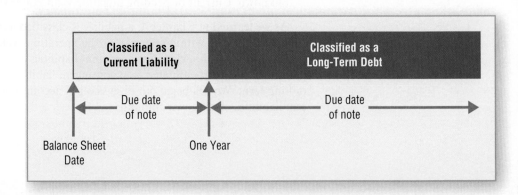

In Chapter 7, we learned about promissory notes when we studied notes receivable. The terms and concepts we learned about then will also apply to notes payable. However, we are now learning about the promissory note transaction from the opposite perspective. To illustrate a note payable, assume that on September 1, 2014 Mackay Industries borrows $8,000 from First State Bank on a nine-month, 6% note payable. Mackay Industries would record the transaction as follows on September 1:

DATE	ACCOUNTS	POST REF.	DR.	CR.
Sep 1	Cash		8,000	
	Notes Payable			8,000
	Record 6%, nine-month note.			

Assuming Mackay Industries uses a calendar year, at December 31, 2014, it is necessary for Mackay Industries to accrue interest expense for the four months from September to December (remember the matching principle). The accrued interest is recorded as:

DATE	ACCOUNTS	POST REF.	DR.	CR.
Dec 31, 2014	Interest Expense		160*	
	Interest Payable			160
	Accrue four months' interest expense.			

*$160 = ($8,000 × 0.06 × 4/12)

The interest accrual at December 31, 2014, allocated $160 of the interest on this note to 2014. The remaining $200 ($8,000 × 0.06 × 5/12) of interest expense on this note will be allocated to 2015 at the time the note is paid off as follows:

DATE	ACCOUNTS	POST REF.	DR.	CR.
Jun 1, 2014	Notes Payable		8,000	
	Interest Payable		160	
	Interest Expense		200	
	Cash			8,360
	Repay 6%, nine-month note plus interest.			

Notice that the $160 debit to Interest Payable zeros out the amount that was accrued in the liability account at December 31, 2014. The $8,000 debit to Notes Payable removes the note from Mackay Industries' books. The $200 debit to Interest Expense records the interest expense for 2015. In addition, the $8,360 credit to Cash reflects the payment of the entire maturity value of the note. If the term of the note had not spanned the end of the accounting period, no adjusting entry to accrue interest would have been necessary. If this had been the case for Mackay Industries in the previous example, the final entry to repay the note would look like this:

DATE	ACCOUNTS	POST REF.	DR.	CR.
	Notes Payable		8,000	
	Interest Expense		360	
	Cash			8,360
	Repay 6%, nine-month note plus interest.			

Notice that Interest Expense is debited for the full amount of the interest on the note, $360. There is also no debit to Interest Payable because no interest had been accrued on the note.

Sales Tax Payable

Most states levy sales tax on retail sales. Retailers collect the sales tax from their customers in addition to the price of the item sold. The sales tax collected must then be remitted, or paid, to the state on a periodic basis, usually monthly or quarterly. Sales Tax Payable is a current liability because the retailer must pay the state in less than a year. Let's apply this to Mackay Industries.

Suppose December's taxable sales for Mackay Industries totaled $22,000. Assume that Mackay Industries is required to collect an additional 8% sales tax, which would equal $1,760 ($22,000 × 0.08). Mackay Industries would record December sales (ignoring cost of goods sold) as:

DATE	ACCOUNTS	POST REF.	DR.	CR.
	Accounts Receivable or Cash		23,760	
	Sales Revenue			22,000
	Sales Tax Payable			1,760
	Record December sales.			

The entry recorded when Mackay Industries remits the sales tax to the state looks like this:

DATE	ACCOUNTS	POST REF.	DR.	CR.
	Sales Tax Payable		1,760	
	Cash			1,760
	Remit sales tax.			

Accrued Expenses (Accrued Liabilities)

In Chapter 3, we learned that an accrued expense is any expense that has been incurred but has not yet been paid. That's why accrued expenses are also called accrued liabilities. Most businesses will often have accrued liabilities for one or more of the following:

- Interest
- Salaries and wages
- Payroll taxes
- Income taxes

Accrued liabilities are recorded by debiting the related expense account and crediting a liability account. For example, the entry to record $700 of accrued income tax would be:

DATE	ACCOUNTS	POST REF.	DR.	CR.
	Income Tax Expense		700	
	Income Tax Payable			700
	Record accrued income tax expense.			

Unearned Revenues

As we saw in Chapter 3, unearned revenues, also called deferred revenues, arise when a business receives cash in advance of providing goods or services. As a result, the business has an obligation to provide goods or services to the customer in the future. Unearned revenues are typically classified as current liabilities because customers do not usually pay for more than one year's worth of goods or services in advance.

Current Portion of Long-Term Debt

Current portion of long-term debt The principal portion of a long-term liability that is payable within one year.

Many long-term debt obligations (discussed later in this chapter) are paid in installments. The principal amount of these obligations, due within one year from the balance sheet date, is referred to as **current portion of long-term debt**. Because it is due within one year from the balance sheet date, current portion of long-term debt is classified as a current liability on the balance sheet. Let's assume that Mackay Industries signs a $30,000, 6% note payable on June 1, 2014. The note requires that annual installments of $6,000, plus interest, be paid on June 1 of each of the next five years. On Mackay Industries' December 31, 2014, balance sheet, what amount will be reflected as current portion of long-term debt? Because the $6,000 payment that is due on June 1, 2015, is due within one year from the balance sheet date, it will be classified as current portion of long-term debt. The remaining $24,000 ($30,000 − $6,000) will be classified as long-term.

Stop and Think...

Jill and Alan work in the accounting department of a large retail business that has a significant amount of long-term debt. Jill was commenting to Alan how important it is to ensure that the current portion of the company's long-term debt be properly classified as such on the balance sheet. Alan argued that it really doesn't matter how the debt was classified as long as the correct total amount of debt was included somewhere on the balance sheet. Is Alan's point of view correct?

Answer

No, Jill's point of view is correct. In Chapter 7, we learned that the current ratio is one of the most widely used tools investors, creditors, and suppliers use to evaluate a company's ability to pay its current obligations as they become due. So, even though a company includes the correct amount of total liabilities on the balance sheet, if the liabilities are not properly classified as current versus long-term, the current ratio will not be correct. As a result, investors, creditors, and suppliers will be unable to correctly assess the ability of a business to pay its current obligations as they come due. Therefore, it is very important for a business to analyze all of its long-term debt at the end of each accounting period to ensure that it is being properly classified as current versus long-term.

How Do You Account for Current Liabilities of an Uncertain Amount?

3 **Account for liabilities of an uncertain amount**

Warranty A guarantee that a product or service is free from defect.

A business may know that a liability exists but not know the exact amount of the liability. It cannot simply ignore the liability. The liability must be reported on the balance sheet. Although there are other types of estimated liabilities, the most common example occurs when a company guarantees its products or services against defects under a **warranty** agreement. Therefore, we will focus our attention on accounting for estimated warranties.

Estimated Warranty Liability

It is common for companies to provide either 90-day or one-year warranties on the goods or services they sell. The matching principle requires that warranty expense be recorded in the same period the revenue related to the warranty is recorded. The expense, therefore, is recorded when sales are made, not when warranty claims are settled. At the time of sale, the company does not know how many warranty claims will be filed. Therefore, the amount of warranty expense for a period is unknown and must be estimated.

Assume that Mackay Industries makes sales of $75,000 during the month of August and that Mackay Industries extends to its customers a 90-day warranty on all products sold. Mackay Industries estimates that 2% of its products will require warranty repairs.

The company would record sales (ignoring cost of goods sold) and warranty expense for the month of August as:

DATE	ACCOUNTS	POST REF.	DR.	CR.
	Accounts Receivable or Cash		75,000	
	Sales Revenue			75,000
	Record monthly sales.			
	Warranty Expense		1,500	
	Estimated Warranty Payable			1,500
	Record estimated warranty expense.			

Now assume that during September Mackay Industries paid $450 to settle warranty claims filed by customers. Mackay would make the following entry to record payment of the warranty claims:

DATE	ACCOUNTS	POST REF.	DR.	CR.
	Estimated Warranty Payable		450	
	Cash			450
	Settled warranty claims.			

If, instead of paying cash to settle the warranty claims, Mackay Industries had replaced the defective goods with new items, the entry would have been:

DATE	ACCOUNTS	POST REF.	DR.	CR.
	Estimated Warranty Payable		450	
	Inventory			450
	Settled warranty claims.			

Estimated liabilities are generally current liabilities. However, if the estimated liability is expected to be settled more than one year from the balance sheet date, it would be classified as long-term.

How Do You Account for a Contingent Liability?

Account for contingent liabilities

As stated earlier, although a contingent liability arises as the result of a *past* event, it is dependent upon the outcome of a *future* event. Therefore, a contingent liability represents a potential, rather than an actual obligation. The outcome of the future event will determine whether a company will incur an obligation. Examples of contingent liabilities are:

* Pending, or current, legal action
* Potential fines resulting from investigations conducted by regulatory agencies, such as the Environmental Protection Agency (EPA) or the Occupational Safety and Health Administration (OSHA)
* Loan guarantees that occur when one entity cosigns a note payable for another entity

Suppose Mackay Industries is being sued by a former employee for wrongful termination. The lawsuit represents a contingent liability because it is the result of a past event (the termination) but is dependent upon the outcome of a future event (settlement of the lawsuit).

The accounting treatment of a contingent liability depends on the likelihood of an actual obligation occurring. **Exhibit 9-1** outlines the accounting treatment of contingent liabilities.

Likelihood of Obligation Occurring	Accounting Treatment
Remote (very unlikely)	No action is necessary.
Reasonably Possible (it could occur)	Disclose the existence of the contingent liability in the financial statement footnotes. An explanation of the circumstances related to the contingent liability should be included in the footnote.
Probable (more likely than not)	If the amount of the potential obligation is known (or can be reasonably estimated), the contingent liability should be recorded. The circumstances related to the contingent liability should also be disclosed in the financial statement footnote.
	If the amount of the obligation is not known and cannot be reasonably estimated, then only footnote disclosure is required.

Exhibit 9-1 ▲

Let's return to our example of the lawsuit from earlier. If Mackay Industries' legal counsel believes the lawsuit is without merit and the chance of Mackay losing the suit is remote, no action is required. However, if instead it is determined that it is reasonably possible that Mackay Industries will lose the lawsuit, Mackay Industries should disclose the lawsuit as a contingent liability in the notes to its financial statements. Finally, if it is determined that it is probable Mackay will lose the lawsuit, the lawsuit should be disclosed in the financial statement notes. In addition, the amount that the lawsuit is expected to cost Mackay should be recorded in the accounting records if it can be reasonably estimated. The contingent liability would be recorded by debiting a loss account and crediting a liability account. Contingent liabilities are classified as current versus long-term based upon when the liability is expected to be paid.

How Do You Account for Long-Term Debt?

5 | **Account for long-term debt**

The long-term debt of most companies is composed of the following types of obligations:

- Notes payable
- Bonds payable
- Leases payable

There are many similarities in the accounting for these different obligations. However, there are also some unique differences. Therefore, we will examine each of the three separately.

Notes Payable

Mortgage A long-term note payable that is secured by real estate.

Collateral Assets pledged to secure repayment of a loan. In the case of nonpayment by the borrower, the lender has the right to take the collateral.

As discussed previously, a note payable is a debt obligation that is supported by a promissory note. Notes payable that are due to be repaid more than one year from the balance sheet date are classified as long-term debt. Most long-term notes payable represent loans taken out for the purchase of land, buildings, or both that are repaid over a long-term period. A note payable used to purchase land or buildings where the asset is used as collateral is a special type of note called a **mortgage.** A mortgage is an example of a secured note because it gives the lender the right to take specified assets, called **collateral,** if the borrower is unable to repay the loan.

Accounting in Your World

If you have ever borrowed money to purchase a car, then you probably know that you do not get clear title to the car until the loan has been paid off. The vehicle title represents legal ownership of the vehicle. Lenders often secure car loans by using the car as collateral for the loan and placing a lien on the title. This means that if the borrower fails to repay the loan, the lender has the right to repossess, or take back, the car to compensate it for the unpaid loan. Once the loan has been repaid, the lender will release the lien on the title. This conveys full legal ownership of the car to the borrower. The title to a vehicle is often referred to as the "pink slip." So, if someone asks you if you have the pink slip to your car, he or she is asking if you owe any money on the car.

A mortgage is typically paid off through installment payments that include both principal and interest. The entries required to record mortgage note transactions are similar to those for note payable transactions. Let's assume that Mackay Industries issues a $155,000, 8%, 20-year mortgage note on January 1, 2014, to finance the purchase of a new building. Payments of $7,831 on the mortgage will be made semi-annually on June 30 and December 31 of each year. The purchase of the building is recorded as:

DATE	ACCOUNTS	POST REF.	DR.	CR.
Jan 1	Buildings		155,000	
	Mortgage Payable			155,000
	Issued mortgage to purchase building.			

In order to keep track of the portion of each payment that is allocated to principal and to interest, an amortization schedule is usually prepared. **Exhibit 9-2** illustrates an amortization schedule for the first four years of Mackay Industries' mortgage:

	A	B	C	D
Date	Payment	Interest (D × 0.08 × 1/2)*	Principal (A − B)	Loan Balance (D − C)
1/01/2014				$155,000
6/30/2014	$7,831	$6,200	$1,631	153,369
12/31/2014	7,831	6,135	1,696	151,673
6/30/2015	7,831	6,067	1,764	149,909
12/31/2015	7,831	5,996	1,835	148,074
6/30/2016	7,831	5,923	1,908	146,166
12/31/2016	7,831	5,847	1,984	144,182
6/30/2017	7,831	5,767	2,064	142,118
12/31/2017	7,831	5,685	2,146	139,972

*Rounded

Column B is calculated by multiplying the loan balance from the prior period (column D) by the interest rate (8%) and then multiplying by 1/2 to account for the fact that the payment is made semiannually.

Column C is calculated by subtracting the interest (column B) from the payment (column A).

Column D is calculated by subtracting the principal portion of the payment (column C) from the loan balance from the prior period (column D).

Exhibit 9-2 ▲

Based on information found in Exhibit 9-2, Mackay Industries will record the June 30, 2014, loan payment as:

DATE	ACCOUNTS	POST REF.	DR.	CR.
Jun 30	Interest Expense		6,200	
	Mortgage Payable		1,631	
	Cash			7,831
	Record semiannual loan payment.			

As discussed previously in the chapter, the principal portion of any mortgage payments due within one year from the balance sheet date will be classified under current portion of long-term debt on the balance sheet.

Bonds Payable

In addition to using notes payable to acquire needed cash, a business may obtain money by issuing **bonds payable.** Bonds payable are long-term, interest-bearing debt issued to lenders called bondholders. By issuing bonds, it is often possible for a business to borrow hundreds of thousands (or even millions) of dollars. Instead of depending on one large loan from a single bank or lender, with bonds, a large number of smaller amounts are borrowed, often from different investors. For example, Mackay Industries could raise $1,000,000 by borrowing $1,000 each from 1,000 different investors.

Before we move on, let's explore some of the terminology associated with bonds.

- **Term bonds** all mature at the same specified time. For example, $500,000 of term bonds may all mature 10 years from today. With term bonds, the company issuing the bonds will have to repay all $500,000 at one time.
- **Serial bonds** are bonds from the same bond issuance that mature at different times. For example, a $1,500,000 serial bond issuance may specify that one-third of the bonds mature in 10 years, one-third mature in 15 years, and one-third mature in 20 years.
- **Secured bonds** are bonds that are backed with some form of collateral. Secured bonds give the bondholders the right to take specified assets of the issuer if the issuer fails to pay principal or interest.

Bonds payable Long-term, interest-bearing debt issued to lenders called bondholders.

Term bonds Bonds that all mature at the same time.

Serial bonds Bonds from the same bond issuance that mature at different times.

Secured bonds Bonds that give bondholders the right to take specified assets of the issuer if the issuer fails to pay principal or interest.

Unsecured bonds Bonds that are backed only by the general credit of the company issuing the bond; also called **debentures**.

Convertible bonds Bonds that may be converted into the common stock of the issuing company at the option of the investor.

Callable bonds Bonds that the issuer may call, or pay off, at a specified price before maturity.

Principal amount The amount a borrower must pay back to the bondholders on the maturity date; also called **par value** or **maturity value**.

Maturity date The date on which the bond issuer (the borrower) must repay the principal amount to the bondholders.

Stated interest rate Interest rate that determines the amount of cash interest the borrower pays and the investor receives each year.

Market interest rate Interest rate investors are expecting to receive for similar bonds of equal risk at the current time.

Discount Excess of a bond's maturity value over its issue price; also called a *bond discount*.

Premium Excess of a bond's issue price over its maturity value; also called *bond premium*.

- **Unsecured bonds** are bonds that are not backed by any assets. They are backed only by the general credit of the company issuing the bond. Unsecured bonds are also called **debentures**.
- **Convertible bonds** are bonds that give the bondholder the option of exchanging the bond for common stock in the company.
- **Callable bonds** are bonds that may be bought back and retired (called) by the bond issuer at a pre-arranged price.
- **Principal amount** is the amount the borrower must pay back to the bondholders on the maturity date. The principal amount is also called **maturity value**, or **par value**.
- **Maturity date** is the date on which the borrower must repay the principal amount to the bondholders.
- **Stated interest rate** determines the amount of cash interest the bond issuer pays each year. The stated interest rate is printed on the bond and *does not change* from year to year. For example, if a $1,000 bond has a stated interest rate of 9%, the bond issuer pays $90 of interest annually on the bond.
- **Market interest rate** is the rate of interest investors are expecting to receive for similar bonds of equal risk at the current time. Bonds are often issued with a stated interest rate that differs from the market interest rate. This is due to the time gap between when the stated rate is determined and when the bonds are actually issued.

Bond Prices

A bond can be issued (sold) at a price that is equal to the par value of the bond, below the par value of the bond, or above the par value of the bond. Whether a bond sells at par, below par, or above par depends on the relationship between the stated interest rate on the bond and the current market rate of interest at the time the bond is sold. Bonds sold at a price equal to par value are said to be sold "at par." Bonds sold at a price below par are said to be sold "at a **discount**," and bonds sold at a price above par are said to be sold "at a **premium**."

To illustrate, let's assume that Mackay Industries issues 6% bonds when the market rate for similar bonds of equal risk is higher, say 6.5% or 7%. Mackay Industries will have a hard time attracting investors to buy its bonds when investors can earn a higher interest rate on similar bonds of other companies. Therefore, to attract investors, Mackay Industries will offer to sell its bonds at a price less than maturity value, or at a discount. So, for example, Mackay Industries may offer to sell its $1,000, 6% bonds for only $920 each. Mackay Industries will pay the investors yearly interest payments equal to $60 ($1,000 par value × 6% stated interest) on each bond. However, because the investors only paid $920 for each bond, the $60 interest payment represents a return of approximately 6.5% ($60 interest/$920 invested).

On the other hand, if the market interest rate is 5% or 5.5%, Mackay Industries' 6% bonds will be so attractive that investors will pay more than maturity value, or a premium, for them. So, for example, Mackay Industries may offer to sell its $1,000, 6% bonds for $1,085 each. Mackay Industries will still pay the investors yearly interest payments equal to $60 ($1,000 par value × 6% interest) on each bond. However, because the investors paid $1,085 for each bond, the $60 interest payment represents a return of approximately 5.5% ($60 interest/$1,085 invested). The actual selling price of a bond represents a price that makes the return on the bond effectively the same as the market rate of interest at the time the bond is sold. **Exhibit 9-3** illustrates the relationship between the stated interest rate and the market interest rate and how it affects the sales price of a bond.

The issue price of a bond determines the amount of cash the company receives when it issues the bond. However, the issue price of a bond does not affect the required payment at maturity. A company must always pay the maturity value (par value) of the bonds when they mature.

Relationship of Stated Interest Rate to Current Market Interest Rate	Bond Is Sold At	Why?
Stated rate = Market rate	Par	Investors are willing to pay the full maturity value for the bond because it offers the same interest rate as similar bonds with equal risk.
Stated rate < Market rate	Discount	Investors are willing to pay a lower price for the bond because they will receive a lower rate of interest from this bond than from similar bonds with equal risk.
Stated rate > Market rate	Premium	Investors are willing to pay a higher price for the bond because they will receive a higher rate of interest from this bond than from similar bonds with equal risk.

Exhibit 9-3 ▲

After bonds have been issued, investors may buy and sell them on the bond market just as they buy and sell stocks on the stock market.

Bond prices are quoted as a percentage of maturity value. For example,

- a $1,000 bond quoted at 100 is bought or sold for 100% of maturity value, ($1,000 × 1.00).
- a $1,000 bond quoted at 96.4 has a price of $964 ($1,000 × 0.964).
- a $1,000 bond quoted at 102.8 has a price of $1,028 ($1,000 × 1.028).

Issuing Bonds Payable at Par

The journal entry to record the issuance of bonds payable depends on whether the bond is issued at par, at a discount, or at a premium. Let's assume that on April 1, 2014, Mackay Industries issues $500,000 of 8% bonds payable that mature in 10 years. The bonds will pay interest semi-annually on March 31 and September 30. First, let's assume that the market rate of interest on April 1, 2014, is 8%. Because the stated interest rate equals the market interest rate, Mackay Industries will issue these bonds at maturity (par) value. The journal entry to record the receipt of cash and issuance of bonds payable is:

DATE	ACCOUNTS	POST REF.	DR.	CR.
Apr 1	Cash		500,000	
	Bonds Payable			500,000
	Issued bonds at par.			

Interest payments occur on March 31 and September 30 each year. Mackay Industries' first semiannual interest payment on September 30, 2014, is journalized as:

DATE	ACCOUNTS	POST REF.	DR.	CR.
Sep 30	Interest Expense		20,000*	
	Cash			20,000
	Paid semiannual interest.			

*$500,000 × 0.08 × 1/2

S9-8. Determining the issue price for bonds (*Learning Objective 5*) 5–10 min.

Determine whether the following bonds payable will be issued at par, at a premium, or at a discount:

a. The market interest rate is 5%. Wilson, Corp., issues bonds payable with a stated rate of 6 1/2%.

b. Apex, Inc., issued 6 1/2% bonds payable when the market rate was 7 1/4%.

c. Huntwood Corporation issued 9% bonds when the market interest rate was 9%.

d. Billings Company issued bonds payable that pay cash interest at the stated rate of 5%. At the date of issuance, the market interest rate was 6 1/4%.

S9-9. Analyzing bond terms (*Learning Objective 5*) 10–15 min.

Allison Supply, Inc. is planning to issue long-term bonds payable to borrow for a major expansion. For each of the following questions, identify whether the bond price involves a discount, a premium, or par value.

a. The stated interest rate on the bonds is 6%, and the market interest rate is 7%. What type of price can Allison Supply, Inc., expect for the bonds?

b. Allison Supply, Inc., could raise the stated interest rate on the bonds to 8% (market rate is 7%). In that case, what type of price can Allison Supply, Inc., expect for the bonds?

c. At what type of bond price will Allison Supply, Inc., have total interest expense equal to the cash interest payments?

d. At which type of price will Allison Supply, Inc.'s total interest expense be less than the cash interest payments?

e. At which type of price will Allison Supply, Inc.'s total interest expense be greater than the cash interest payments?

S9-10. Accounting for bonds (*Learning Objective 5*) 15–20 min.

Wilson, Corp., issued 6.5%, 10-year bonds payable with a maturity value of $30,000 on January 1, 2014. Journalize the following transactions and include an explanation for each entry. The market rate of interest equaled the stated rate at the date of issuance.

a. Issuance of the bond payable at par on January 1, 2014.

b. Payment of semiannual interest on July 1, 2014.

c. Payment of the bonds payable at maturity; give the date.

S9-11. Accounting for bonds (*Learning Objective 5*) 15–20 min.

Allied, Corp., issued 8%, five-year bonds payable with a maturity value of $50,000 at a price of $48,200 on January 1, 2014. Journalize the following transactions for Allied, Corp. Include an explanation for each entry.

a. Issuance of the bond payable on January 1, 2014.

b. Payment of semiannual interest and amortization of bond discount on July 1, 2014. Use the straight-line method to amortize the discount.

S9-12. Accounting for bonds (*Learning Objective 5*) 15–20 min.

Allied, Corp., issued 8%, five-year bonds payable with a maturity value of $50,000 at a price of $52,420 on January 1, 2014. Journalize the following transactions for Allied, Corp. Include an explanation for each entry.

a. Issuance of the bond payable on January 1, 2014.

b. Payment of semiannual interest and amortization of bond premium on July 1, 2014. Use the straight-line method to amortize the premium.

S9-13. Accounting for bonds (*Learning Objective 5*) 15–20 min.

Allied, Corp., issued 8%, five-year bonds payable with a maturity value of $50,000 at par on May 1, 2014. Assume that the fiscal year ends on December 31. Journalize the following transactions and include an explanation for each entry. Round calculations to the nearest dollar.

a. Issuance of the bonds payable on May 1, 2014.

b. Payment of the first semiannual interest amount on November 1, 2014.

c. Accrual of interest expense on December 31, 2014.

S9-14. Classification of liability accounts as current or long-term. (*Learning Objective 6*) 5–10 min.

Identify the section of the balance sheet in which the following accounts would be located: Current Assets (CA), Long-Term Assets (LTA), Current Liabilities (CL), or Long-Term Liabilities (LTL).

_____ 1. Bonds Payable (due in 4 years)

_____ 2. Interest Payable

_____ 3. Leased Equipment

_____ 4. Discount on Bonds Payable

_____ 5. Accumulated Depreciation on Leased Equipment

_____ 6. Lease Payable (due in four years)

_____ 7. Mortgage Notes Payable (due in 10 years)

S9-15. Balance sheet disclosure of long-term liabilities (*Learning Objective 6*) 5–10 min.

Wildflower Magazine, Inc., includes the following selected accounts in its general ledger at December 31, 2014:

Mortgage Notes Payable (due in 15 years)	$180,000	Accounts Payable....................	$42,500
Lease Payable, Long-Term............................	32,000	Discount on Bonds Payable	14,000
Bonds Payable (due in 10 years)...................	420,000		
Interest Payable (due next year)...................	1,350		

Prepare the liabilities section of Wildflower Magazine's balance sheet at December 31, 2014, to show how the company would report these items. Report a total for current liabilities.

MyAccountingLab   # Exercises (Group A)

E9-16A. Sales tax payable (*Learning Objective 2*) 5–10 min.

Make journal entries to record the following transactions. Explanations are not required.

May 31	Recorded cash sales of $263,000 for the month, plus sales tax of 9% collected for the state of Washington. Ignore cost of goods sold.
Jun 6	Sent May sales tax to the state.

E9-17A. Accounting for notes payable (*Learning Objective 2*) 5–10 min.

Record the following note payable transactions of Cigliano, Corp., in the company's journal. Explanations are not required.

2014

Nov 1 Purchased equipment costing $28,000 by issuing a one-year, 9% note payable.
Dec 31 Accrued interest on the note payable.

2015

Nov 1 Paid the note payable at maturity.

E9-18A. Subscriptions (*Learning Objective 2*) 5–10 min.

Pugliese Publishing Company completed the following transactions during 2014:

Sep 1 Sold 36 six-month subscriptions, collecting cash of $1,800, plus sales tax of 7%.
Oct 15 Remitted the sales tax to the state of Idaho.
Dec 31 Made the necessary adjustment at year-end to record the amount of subscription revenue earned during the year.

Requirements

1. Journalize these transactions. Explanations are not required.
2. What amounts would Pugliese Publishing Company report on the balance sheet at December 31, 2014?

Quick solution:

2. December 31, 2014 balance in Estimated Warranty Payable = $20,990

E9-19A. Warranties (*Learning Objective 3*) 5–10 min.

The accounting records of Stevens Auto Repair showed a balance of $6,000 in Estimated Warranty Payable at December 31, 2013. In the past, Stevens's warranty expense has been 9% of sales. During 2014, Stevens made sales of $311,000 on account and paid $13,000 to satisfy warranty claims.

Requirements

1. Journalize Stevens's sales, warranty expense, and cash payments made to satisfy warranty claims during 2014. Explanations are not required. Ignore cost of goods sold.
2. What balance of Estimated Warranty Payable will Stevens report on its balance sheet at December 31, 2014? What amount of warranty expense will Stevens report on its income statement for the year ended December 31, 2014?

E9-20A. Accounting for mortgages (*Learning Objective 5*) 10–15 min.

Clearwater, Corp., issued a $825,000, 5% mortgage on January 1, 2014, to purchase warehouses.

Date	Payment	Interest	Principal	Loan Balance
Jan 1, 2014				$825,000
Jun 30, 2014	$26,692			
Dec 31, 2014				
Jun 30, 2015				
Dec 31, 2015				
Jun 30, 2016				

1. Complete the amortization schedule for Clearwater, Corp., assuming payments are made semiannually. Round amounts to the nearest dollar.
2. Record the journal entries for (a) issuance of mortgage on January 1, 2014, and (b) the first semiannual payment on June 30, 2014.

Learning Objective 5) **15–20 min.**

%, 20-year bonds payable with a maturity value of
bonds were issued at par and pay interest on January 31
ce of the bonds on January 31, (b) payment of interest on
rest on December 31.

arning Objective 5) **15–20 min.**

issues 6%, 20-year bonds payable with a maturity value
96 and pay interest on January 1 and July 1. Penestrie,
unt or premium by the straight-line method.

onds on January 1.

st payment and amortization of any bond discount or

ng Objective 5) **15–20 min.**

0-year, 5% bonds payable on January 1. Lincoln,
d July 1 and amortizes any discount or premium
Inc., can issue its bonds payable under various

en the market rate was above 5%
en the market rate was below 5%

bonds and first semiannual interest payment
not required.
interest expense for Lincoln, Inc.? Explain in

ent or long-term
n.

,500,000 on July 1, 2014, by issuing a 7%
in three equal annual installments plus inter-

how Associated Physicians Group would

December 31		
14	2015	2016
	$	$

SFCC CAMPUS STORE

SPRING 2016 FAQ'S

www.sfccbooks.com

I have been advised to read this document and will comply with its terms.

Please review your receipt for accuracy. All claims must be made within 10 days of purchase.

Cashier

PLEASE KEEP YOUR RECEIPT

Duplicate receipts cannot be provided.

☑ HOW DO I GET MY REFUND?

Did you know the payment method you use to purchase or rent an item affects the type of refund you will receive?

CREDIT CARD/DEBIT PAYMENT: Refunds are credited to the credit card account on which you made the purchase. Please note it may take several business days for a credit to appear on your account and several billing cycles for the credit to appear on your statement. You will need the credit card that was used for the purchase to process the return.

FINANCIAL AID PAYMENT: A refund will be credited to your student account for the appropriate action to be taken if you used Student Financial Aid. Please bring your **SFCC BLUECARD**. Financial aid charging dates are as follows: **January 4—21** for 16 week & 1st 8 week classes; **January 25—29** for 12 week classes; and **March 7—28** for 2nd 8 week classes.

CASH AND CHECK PAYMENT: A refund will be credited to your student account and a check will be mailed to you within 4 weeks.

Thank you for shopping at your
SFCC Campus Store!

	543.78
TOTAL	543.78
SFA - SFCC BLUECARD	

Refunds for financial aid purchases

E9-25A. Balance sheet disclosure of liabilities (*Learning Objective 6*) **15–20 min.**

At December 31, 2014, Dior Drapes owes $53,000 on accounts payable, plus salaries payable of $15,000 and income tax payable of $10,000. Dior Drapes also has $230,000 of notes payable that requires payment of a $45,000 installment in 2015 and the remainder in later years. The notes payable also requires an interest payment of $6,000 on January 1, 2015. Report Dior Drapes' liabilities on its December 31, 2014, classified balance sheet.

E9-26A. Debt ratio and interest coverage ratio (*Learning Objective 7*) **5–10 min.**

Sizemore Industrial Supply had the following balances as of December 31, 2014:

Total Current Assets	$ 85,000
Total Long-Term Assets	360,000
Total Current Liabilities	51,000
Total Long-Term Liabilities	237,000
Total Stockholders' Equity	157,000
Earnings Before Interest and Taxes	41,700
Interest Expense	12,200
Income Tax Expense	7,300
Net Income	22,200

Requirement

1. Calculate Sizemore Industrial Supply's debt ratio as of December 31, 2014.

2. Calculate Sizemore Industrial Supply's interest coverage ratio for 2014. Round your answer to two decimal places.

Exercises (Group B)

E9-27B. Sales tax payable (*Learning Objective 2*) **5–10 min.**

Make journal entries to record the following transactions. Explanations are not required.

May 31	Recorded cash sales of $630,000 for the month, plus sales tax of 7% collected for the state of Mississippi. Ignore cost of goods sold.
Jun 6	Sent May sales tax to the state.

E9-28B. Accounting for notes payable (*Learning Objective 2*) **5–10 min.**

Record the following note payable transactions of Conway, Corp., in the company's journal. Explanations are not required.

2014

Feb 1	Purchased equipment costing $55,000 by issuing a one-year, 6% note payable.
Dec 31	Accrued interest on the note payable.

2015

Feb 1	Paid the note payable at maturity.

E9-29B. Subscriptions (*Learning Objective 2*) 5–10 min.

Ozark Publishing Company completed the following transactions during 2014:

Nov	1	Sold 50 six-month subscriptions, collecting cash of $2,400, plus sales tax of 4%.
Dec	15	Remitted the sales tax to the state of Alabama.
	31	Made the necessary adjustment at year-end to record the amount of subscription revenue earned during the year.

Requirements

1. Journalize these transactions. Explanations are not required.
2. What amounts would Ozark Publishing Company report on the balance sheet at December 31, 2014?

E9-30B. Warranties (*Learning Objective 3*) 5–10 min.

The accounting records of Tim's Auto Repair showed a balance of $1,600 in Estimated Warranty Payable at December 31, 2013. In the past, Tim's warranty expense has been 3% of sales. During 2014, Tim's made sales of $386,000 on account and paid $9,420 to satisfy warranty claims.

Requirements

1. Journalize Tim's sales, warranty expense, and cash payments made to satisfy warranty claims during 2014. Explanations are not required. Ignore cost of goods sold.
2. What balance of Estimated Warranty Payable will Tim's report on its balance sheet at December 31, 2014? What amount of warranty expense will Tim's report on its income statement for the year ended December 31, 2014?

E9-31B. Accounting for mortgages (*Learning Objective 5*) 10–15 min.

Venus, Corp., issued a $460,000, 8%, mortgage on January 1, 2014, to purchase warehouses.

Date	Payment	Interest	Principal	Loan Balance
Jan 1, 2014				$460,000
Jun 30, 2014	$26,602			
Dec 31, 2014				
Jun 30, 2015				
Dec 31, 2015				
Jun 30, 2016				

Requirements

1. Complete the amortization schedule for Venus, Corp., assuming payments are made semiannually. Round amounts to the nearest dollar.
2. Record the journal entries for (a) issuance of mortgage on January 1, 2014, and (b) the first semiannual payment on June 30, 2014.

E9-32B. Accounting for bonds (*Learning Objective 5*) 15–20 min.

Rigby Corporation issued 6%, 15-year bonds payable with a maturity value of $850,000 on May 31. The bonds were issued at par and pay interest on May 31 and November 30.

Requirements

1. Record the issuance of the bonds on May 31.
2. Record the payment of interest on November 30 and accrual of interest on December 31.

E9-33B. Accounting for bonds (*Learning Objective 5*) 15–20 min.

On January 1, Doherty, Corp., issues 5%, 10-year bonds payable with a maturity value of $90,000. The bonds sell at 95 and pay interest on January 1 and July 1. Doherty, Corp., amortizes any bond discount or premium by the straight-line method. Record (a) the issuance of the bonds on January 1, and (b) the semiannual interest payment and amortization of any bond discount or premium on July 1.

E9-34B. Accounting for bonds (*Learning Objective 5*) 15–20 min.

Peterson Machine Tool, Inc., issued $475,000 of 10-year, 7% bonds payable on January 1. Peterson Machine Tool, Inc., pays interest each January 1 and July 1 and amortizes any discount or premium by the straight-line method. Peterson Machine Tool, Inc., can issue its bonds payable under various conditions:

a. Issuance at par value

b. Issuance at a price of $460,000 when the market rate was above 7%

c. Issuance at a price of $493,000 when the market rate was below 7%

Requirements

1. Journalize Peterson's issuance of the bonds and first semiannual interest payment for each situation. Explanations are not required.

2. Which condition results in the most interest expense for Peterson Machine Tool, Inc.? Explain in detail.

E9-35B. Classifying notes payable as current or long-term (*Learning Objectives 5 & 6*) 10–15 min.

Orthopedic Medical Group borrowed $2,100,000 on July 1, 2014, by issuing a 9% long-term note payable that must be paid in three equal annual installments plus interest each July 1 for the next three years.

Requirement

1. Insert the appropriate amounts to show how Orthopedic would report its current and long-term liabilities.

	December 31		
	2014	**2015**	**2016**
Current Liabilities:			
Current Portion of Long-Term Note Payable	$	$	$
Interest Payable			
Long-Term Liabilities:			
Long-Term Note Payable			

E9-36B. Balance sheet disclosure of liabilities (*Learning Objective 6*) 15–20 min.

At December 31, 2014, Padilla Industrial owes $37,000 on accounts payable, plus salaries payable of $8,500 and income tax payable of $11,700. Padilla Industrial also has $180,000 of notes payable that requires payment of a $22,000 installment in 2015 and the remainder in later years. The notes payable also requires an interest payment of $9,000 on January 1, 2015. Report Padilla Industrial's liabilities on its December 31, 2014, classified balance sheet.

E9-37B. Debt ratio and interest coverage ratio (*Learning Objective 7*) 5–10 min.

Sanchez Industrial Supply had the following balances as of December 31, 2014:

Total Current Assets	$ 80,000
Total Long-Term Assets	320,000
Total Current Liabilities	20,000
Total Long-Term Liabilities	200,000
Total Stockholders' Equity	180,000
Earnings Before Interest and Taxes	73,800
Interest Expense	18,700
Income Tax Expense	21,900
Net Income	33,200

Requirements

1. Calculate Sanchez Industrial Supply's debt ratio as of December 31, 2014.

2. Calculate Sanchez Industrial Supply's interest coverage ratio for 2014. Round your answer to two decimal places.

MyAccountingLab

Problems (Group A)

P9-38A. Accounting for several current liabilities (*Learning Objectives 2 & 3*) 20–25 min.

The following transactions of Dalton's Marine Supply occurred during 2014 and 2015:

2014		
Feb	3	Purchased equipment for $26,000, signing a six-month, 5% note payable.
	28	Recorded the week's sales of $87,000, one-third for cash, and two-thirds on account. All sales amounts are subject to a 7% sales tax. Ignore cost of goods sold.
Mar	7	Sent last week's sales tax to the state.
Apr	30	Borrowed $225,000 on a four-year, 8% note payable that calls for annual payment of interest each April 30.
Aug	3	Paid the six-month, 5% note at maturity.
Nov	30	Purchased inventory at a cost of $7,200, signing a three-month, 6% note payable for that amount.
Dec	31	Accrued warranty expense, which is estimated at 1.5% of total sales of $812,000.
	31	Accrued interest on all outstanding notes payable. Accrued interest for each note separately.
2015		
Feb	28	Paid off the 6% inventory note, plus interest, at maturity.
Apr	30	Paid the interest for one year on the long-term note payable.

Requirement

1. Record the transactions in the company's journal. Explanations are not required.

P9-39A. Accounting for several current and long-term liabilities (*Learning Objectives 2, 3, & 5*) **20–25 min.**

Following are pertinent facts about events during the current year at Zepher Snowboards.

a. December sales totaled $404,000, and Zepher collected sales tax of 7%. The sales tax will be sent to the state of Washington early in January.

b. Zepher owes $80,000 on a long-term note payable. At December 31, 6% interest for the year plus $20,000 of principal are payable within one year.

c. On August 31, Zepher signed a six-month, 7% note payable to purchase a machine costing $60,000. The note requires payment of principal and interest at maturity.

d. Sales of $997,000 were covered by the Zepher product warranty. At January 1, estimated warranty payable was $11,700. During the year, Zepher recorded warranty expense of $27,500 and paid warranty claims of $30,300.

e. On October 31, Zepher received cash of $5,232 in advance for the rent on a building. This rent will be earned evenly over six months.

Requirement

1. For each item, indicate the account and the related amount to be reported as a current liability on Zepher's December 31 balance sheet.

P9-40A. Accounting for mortgages (*Learning Objective 5*) **20–25 min.**

Allez, Corp., completed the following transactions in 2014:

Jan 1 Purchased a building costing $315,000 and signed a 7%, 20-year mortgage note payable for the same amount.

Jun 30 Made the first semiannual payment on the mortgage note payable.

Dec 1 Signed a five-year lease to rent a warehouse for $4,800 per month due at the end of each month. The lease is considered an operating lease.

31 Paid for one month's rent on the warehouse.

31 Leased 8 copiers and signed a four-year lease with the option to buy the copiers at the end of the fourth year at a bargain price. Under terms of the lease, monthly lease payments do not start until January 31, 2016. The present value of the lease payments is $43,500.

31 Made the second semiannual payment on the mortgage note payable.

Requirements

1. Complete the following amortization schedule for the first four mortgage payments on the $315,000 mortgage note, assuming semiannual payments of $14,751. Round amounts to the nearest dollar.

Date	Payment	Interest	Principal	Loan Balance
Jan 1, 2014				$315,000
Jun 30, 2014	$14,751			
Dec 31, 2014				
Jun 30, 2015				
Dec 31, 2015				

2. Record the journal entries for the 2014 transactions.

3. Prepare the long-term liabilities section of the balance sheet on December 31, 2014.

P9-41A. Analyzing bond terms and accounting for bonds (*Learning Objective 5*)
20–25 min.

Assume that on April 1, 2014, Pacific, Corp., issues 5%, 10-year bonds payable with a maturity value of $900,000. The bonds pay interest on March 31 and September 30, and Pacific amortizes any premium or discount by the straight-line method. Pacific's fiscal year-end is December 31.

Requirements

1. If the market interest rate is 3.5% when Pacific, Corp., issues its bonds, will the bonds be priced at par, at a premium, or at a discount? Explain.

2. If the market interest rate is 6% when Pacific, Corp., issues its bonds, will the bonds be priced at par, at a premium, or at a discount? Explain.

3. Assume that the issue price of the bonds is $954,000. Journalize the following bonds payable transactions:
   a. Issuance of the bonds on April 1, 2014.
   b. Payment of interest and amortization of premium on September 30, 2014.
   c. Accrual of interest and amortization of premium on December 31, 2014.
   d. Payment of interest and amortization of premium on March 31, 2015.

P9-42A. Analyzing bond terms and accounting for bonds (*Learning Objective 5*)
20–25 min.

On January 1, 2014, Sun Meadow Resorts issued $450,000 of 20-year, 8% bonds payable. The bonds were sold for $432,000. The bonds pay interest each June 30 and December 31, and any discount or premium is amortized using straight-line amortization.

Requirements

1. Fill in the blanks to complete these statements:
   a. Sun Meadow Resorts' bonds are priced at (express the price as a percentage) _____.
   b. When Sun Meadow Resorts issued its bonds, the market interest rate was (higher than, lower than, or equal to) _____ 8%.
   c. The amount of bond discount or premium is $_____.

2. Record the following transactions:
   a. Issuance of the bonds payable on January 1, 2014.
   b. Payment of interest (and amortization of discount or premium if any) on June 30, 2014.
   c. Payment of interest (and amortization of discount or premium if any) on December 31, 2014. Explanations are not required.

3. At what amount will Sun Meadow Resorts report the bonds on its balance sheet at December 31, 2014?

Quick solution:

Total current liabilities = $111,000;
total long-term liabilities =
$297,000

P9-43A. Balance sheet disclosure of long-term liabilities (*Learning Objective 6*)
15–20 min.

The accounting records of Brown Industrial, Inc., include the following items at December 31, 2014:

Salaries Payable........................	$15,000	Accounts Payable...................	$ 51,000
Mortgage Notes Payable,		Mortgage Note Payable,	
Current Portion	25,000	Long-Term........................	105,000
Discount on Bonds Payable	8,000	Interest Payable	11,000
Income Tax Payable	9,000	Bonds Payable (Due 2017)	200,000

Requirement

1. Report these liabilities on Brown Industrial's balance sheet at December 31, 2014, including headings.

P9-44A. Calculation of debt ratio and interest coverage ratio (*Learning Objective 7*)
10–15 min.

The classified balance sheet and selected income statement data for Barnett, Inc., as of
December 31, 2014, are presented next.

Barnett, Inc. Balance Sheet December 31, 2014					
Current Assets:			**Current Liabilities:**		
Cash		$ 21,000	Accounts Payable		$ 1,200
Accounts Receivable		5,000	Salaries Payable		2,700
Supplies		300	Unearned Service Revenue		1,000
Prepaid Rent		4,200	Note Payable		20,000
Total Current Assets		30,500	Total Current Liabilities		24,900
Fixed Assets:			**Long-Term Debt:**		
Land		50,000	Mortgage Note Payable		25,000
Equipment	$ 62,000		Bonds Payable		130,000
Less Accumulated			Total Long-Term Debt		155,000
Depreciation, Equipment	8,000	54,000			
			Stockholders' Equity:		
Building	245,000		Common Stock		25,000
Less Accumulated			Retained Earnings		149,600
Depreciation, Building	25,000	220,000	Total Stockholders' Equity		174,600
Total Fixed Assets		324,000	Total Liabilities and		
Total Assets		$354,500	Stockholders' Equity		$354,500

Selected Income Statement Data

Gross Profit	$268,600
Operating Expenses	147,400
Earnings Before Interest and Taxes	121,200
Interest Expense	14,800
Income Tax Expense	30,300
Net Income	76,100

Requirements

1. Calculate Barnett, Inc.'s debt ratio and interest coverage ratio as of December 31,
   2014. Round to two decimal places.

2. What percentage of Barnett, Inc.'s assets belong to the stockholders?

3. Would you be willing to extend credit to Barnett, Inc.? Why or why not?

MyAccountingLab **Problems (Group B)**

P9-45B. Accounting for several current liabilities (*Learning Objectives 2 & 3*)
20–25 min.

The following transactions of Handy Andy's stores occurred during 2014 and 2015:

2014	
Feb 3	Purchased equipment for $10,000, signing a six-month, 11% note payable.
28	Recorded the week's sales of $48,000, one-third for cash, and two-thirds on account. All sales amounts are subject to a 7% sales tax. Ignore cost of goods sold.
Mar 7	Sent last week's sales tax to the state.
Apr 30	Borrowed $120,000 on a four-year, 6% note payable that calls for annual payment of interest each April 30.
Aug 3	Paid the six-month, 11% note at maturity.
Nov 30	Purchased inventory at a cost of $6,000, signing a three-month, 5% note payable for that amount.
Dec 31	Accrued warranty expense, which is estimated at 6% of total sales of $580,000.
31	Accrued interest on all outstanding notes payable. Accrued interest for each note separately.
2015	
Feb 28	Paid off the 5% note, plus interest, at maturity.
Apr 30	Paid the interest for one year on the long-term note payable.

Requirement

1. Record the transactions in the company's journal. Explanations are not required.

P9-46B. Accounting for several current and long-term liabilities (*Learning Objectives 2, 3, & 5*) 20–25 min.

Following are pertinent facts about events during the current year at Snowking Snowboards.

a. December sales totaled $371,000, and Snowking collected sales tax of 7%. The sales tax will be sent to the state of Montana early in January.

b. Snowking owes $90,000 on a long-term note payable. At December 31, 6% interest for the year plus $25,000 of principal are payable within one year.

c. On August 31, Snowking signed a six-month, 7% note payable to purchase a machine costing $126,000. The note requires payment of principal and interest at maturity.

d. Sales of $1,276,000 were covered by a Snowking product warranty. At January 1, estimated warranty payable was $9,200. During the year, Snowking recorded warranty expense of $31,400 and paid warranty claims of $33,800.

e. On October 31, Snowking received cash of $13,500 in advance for the rent on a building. This rent will be earned evenly over six months.

Requirement

1. For each item, indicate the account and the related amount to be reported as a current liability on Snowking's December 31 balance sheet.

P9-47B. Accounting for mortgages (*Learning Objective 5*) 20–25 min.

Paiscik, Corp., completed the following transactions in 2014:

Jan 1	Purchased a building costing $180,000 and signed an 11%, 30-year mortgage note payable for the same amount.
Jun 30	Made the first semiannual payment on the mortgage note payable.
Dec 1	Signed a five-year lease to rent a warehouse for $12,000 per month due at the end of each month. The lease is considered an operating lease.
31	Paid for one month's rent on the warehouse.
31	Leased 10 copiers and signed a four-year lease with the option to buy the copiers at the end of the fourth year at a bargain price. Under terms of the lease, monthly lease payments do not start until January 31, 2016. The present value of the lease payments is $33,000.
31	Made the second semiannual payment on the mortgage note payable.

Requirements

1. Complete the following amortization schedule for the first four mortgage payments on the $180,000 mortgage note, assuming semiannual payments of $13,077. Round amounts to the nearest dollar.

Date	Payment	Interest	Principal	Loan Balance
Jan 1, 2014				$180,000
Jun 30, 2014	$13,077			
Dec 31, 2014				
Jun 30, 2015				
Dec 31, 2015				

2. Record the journal entries for the 2014 transactions.

3. Prepare the long-term liabilities section of the balance sheet on December 31, 2014.

P9-48B. Analyzing bond terms and accounting for bonds (*Learning Objective 5*) 20–25 min.

Assume that on March 1, 2014, Simmons, Corp., issued 8%, 10-year bonds payable with maturity value of $900,000. The bonds pay interest on February 28 and August 31, and Simmons amortizes any premium or discount by the straight-line method. Simmons' fiscal year-end is September 30.

Requirements

1. If the market interest rate is 7.25% when Simmons, Corp., issues its bonds, will the bonds be priced at par, at a premium, or at a discount? Explain.

2. If the market interest rate is 9.5% when Simmons, Corp., issues its bonds, will the bonds be priced at par, at a premium, or at a discount? Explain.

3. Assume that the issue price of the bonds is $924,000. Journalize the following bonds payable transactions:
   a. Issuance of the bonds on March 1, 2014.
   b. Payment of interest and amortization of premium on August 31, 2014.
   c. Accrual of interest and amortization of premium on September 30, 2014.
   d. Payment of interest and amortization of premium on February 28, 2015.

P9-49B. **Analyzing bond terms and accounting for bonds (*Learning Objective 5*)**
20–25 min.

On January 1, 2014, The Meadows Golf Course issued $450,000 of 15-year, 6% bonds payable. The bonds were sold for $477,000. The bonds pay interest each June 30 and December 31, and any discount or premium is amortized using straight-line amortization.

Requirements

1. Fill in the blanks to complete these statements:
   a. The Meadows Golf Course's bonds are priced at (express the price as a percentage) _____.
   b. When The Meadows Golf Course issued its bonds, the market interest rate was (higher than, lower than, or equal to) _____ 6%.
   c. The amount of bond discount or premium is $ _____.

2. Record the following transactions:
   a. Issuance of the bonds payable on January 1, 2014. Explanations are not required.
   b. Payment of interest (and amortization of discount or premium if any) on June 30, 2014. Explanations are not required.
   c. Payment of interest (and amortization of discount or premium if any) on December 31, 2014. Explanations are not required.

3. At what amount will The Meadows Golf Course report the bonds on its balance sheet at December 31, 2014?

P9-50B. **Balance sheet disclosure of long-term liabilities (*Learning Objective 6*)**
15–20 min.

The accounting records of Romero, Corp., include the following items at December 31, 2014:

Salaries Payable	$ 7,350	Accounts Payable	$ 23,450
Mortgage Note Payable, Current Portion	16,500	Mortgage Note Payable, Long-Term	126,000
Discount on Bonds Payable	12,000	Interest Payable	9,800
Income Tax Payable	18,840	Bonds Payable (Due 2017)	235,000

Requirement

1. Report these liabilities on Romero's balance sheet at December 31, 2014, including headings.

P9-51B. Calculation of debt ratio and interest coverage ratio (*Learning Objective 7*)
10–15 min.

The classified balance sheet and selected income statement data for Quinn, Inc., as of
December 31, 2014, are presented next.

Quinn, Inc. Balance Sheet December 31, 2014					
ASSETS			**LIABILITIES**		
Current Assets:			Current Liabilities:		
Cash		$ 10,000	Accounts Payable		$ 1,500
Accounts Receivable		3,000	Salaries Payable		2,700
Supplies		500	Unearned Service Revenue		300
Prepaid Rent		3,500	Note Payable		56,500
Total Current Assets		$ 17,000	Total Current Liabilities		61,000
Fixed Assets:			Long-Term Debt:		
Land		60,000	Mortgage Note Payable		25,000
Equipment	$ 55,000		Bonds Payable		148,000
Less: Accumulated			Total Long-Term Debt		173,000
Depreciation, Equipment	5,000	50,000			
Building	220,000		**STOCKHOLDERS' EQUITY**		
Less: Accumulated			Common Stock		30,000
Depreciation, Building	22,000	198,000	Retained Earnings		61,000
Total Fixed Assets		308,000	Total Stockholders' Equity		91,000
			Total Liabilities and		
Total Assets		$325,000	Stockholders' Equity		$325,000

Selected Income Statement Data

Gross Profit	$163,400
Operating Expenses	135,600
Earnings Before Interest and Taxes	27,800
Interest Expense	18,700
Income Tax Expense	2,900
Net Income	6,200

Requirements

1. Calculate Quinn's debt ratio and interest coverage ratio as of December 31, 2014.
   Round to two decimal places.

2. What percentage of Quinn's assets belong to the stockholders?

3. Would you be willing to extend credit to Quinn, Inc.? Why or why not?

Continuing Exercise

In this exercise, we will continue the accounting for Cole's Yard Care, Inc. Assume that on October 31, 2014, Cole's Yard Care, Inc., borrowed $12,000 from Central Bank, signing a nine-month, 9.5% note. The fiscal year-end is December 31.

Requirement

1. Prepare the journal entries required on October 31, 2014, December 31, 2014, and July 31, 2015, to record the transactions related to the note. Round your answers to the nearest dollar.

Continuing Problem

This continues the Aqua Magic, Inc., example from the Continuing Problem in Chapter 8. Aqua Magic, Inc., purchased some of its long-term assets during 2014 using long-term debt. The following table summarizes the nature of this long-term debt. Assume the fiscal year ends on December 31.

Date	Item	Annual Interest Rate	Amount	Payment Terms
May 18	Note payable	6%	$36,200	Five equal annual payments of principal plus accrued interest are due on May 18 of each year.
Sep 1	Mortgage payable	4%	$150,000	Semiannual payments of $4,315 due on March 1 and September 1 of each year.

Requirements

1. Calculate the interest expense that Aqua Magic, Inc., should accrue as of December 31, 2014. Round your answer to the nearest dollar. Use 365 days for the note payable.

2. Prepare the balance sheet presentation at December 31, 2014, for all long-term debt indicating the portion that should be classified as current and the portion that should be classified as long-term.

Continuing Financial Statement Analysis Problem

Return to Target's 2012 annual report. For instructions on how to access the report online, see the Continuing Financial Statement Analysis Problem in Chapter 2. On page 33 of the annual report, you'll find Target's income statement for the year ending February 2, 2013 (called the Consolidated Statement of Operations). On page 35, you'll find Target's balance sheet as of February 2, 2013 (called the Consolidated Statement of Financial Position). Now answer the following questions:

1. Look at Target's balance sheet. What liabilities does Target owe as of February 2, 2013, and January 28, 2012? For these two years, how much of Target's liabilities are current and how much are long-term, non-current?

2. Look over footnotes 17, 18, 19, 20, 22, 23, and 24 of the financial statements. These footnotes start on page 47 of the financial statements found in Target's 2012 annual report. What are the different types of liabilities that Target owes?

3. Look at Target's balance sheet and income statement. What are Target's debt ratio and interest coverage ratio for the year ending February 2, 2013? What do these ratios tell you?

4. Looking back over your answers to questions 1 through 3, how do you think Target is performing? What do you think of how Target finances its assets?

Apply Your Knowledge

Ethics in Action

Case 1. Transco, Inc., was the largest company in the state specializing in rebuilding automobile transmissions. Every transmission rebuilt by the business was covered by a nine-month warranty. The owner, Don Adams, was meeting with his accountant to go over the yearly financial statements. In reviewing the balance sheet, Don became puzzled by the large amount of current liabilities being reported, so he asked his accountant to explain them. The accountant said that most of the current liabilities were the result of accruals, such as the estimated warranty payable, some additional wages payable, and interest accrued on the note owed to the bank. The employees were not actually paid until the first week of the new year, so some of their wages had to be recorded and properly matched against revenues in the current period. Also, several months of interest expense had to be accrued on a bank loan, but the largest amount of the accrued liabilities was due to the estimated warranty expense. Don asked whether the wages payable and the interest payable could be removed because they would be paid off shortly after the year ended. The accountant stated that accrued liabilities had to be properly recognized in the current accounting period, and, thus, they could not be removed. Don agreed but then asked about the large accrued liability based upon the estimated warranty amounts. Again, the accountant stated that, in previous years, the actual warranty cost had been about 4% of the total sales and, therefore, in the current year the estimate was accrued at 4%. Don then informed the accountant that a new conditioning lubricant had been added to each transmission rebuilt, which dramatically reduced the amount of rebuilt transmissions being returned under warranty. As a result, Don strongly felt that the warranty estimate should be reduced to only 3% of total sales and, thereby, the accrued warranty liability and related expense would also be reduced. The accountant argued that the only reason Don wanted to reduce the estimated percentage was to improve the financial statements, which would be unethical and inappropriate.

Requirements

1. What is the impact of accrued liabilities on the financial statements? Should the accrued liabilities for wages and interest payable be removed from the balance sheet?

2. Does Don have a valid reason for wanting to reduce the estimated warranty liability? Are the concerns expressed by the accountant valid?

3. What ethical issues are involved?

Case 2. Sherry Talbot, the CEO of Talbot Corporation, was meeting with the company controller to discuss a possible major lease of a new production facility. Talbot Corporation had a large amount of debt, and Sherry was concerned that adding more debt to acquire the production facility would worry the stockholders. Sherry knew that if the production facility could be classified as an operating lease rather than a capital lease, the lease obligation would not have to be reported on the balance sheet. Thus, the company could have a new production facility without having to report any additional debt. The accountant told Sherry that if the title to the production facility transferred automatically to Talbot at the end of the lease term, then the lease would have to be classified as a capital lease. Also, if the lease had a bargain purchase option, such that Talbot Corporation could simply purchase the facility at the end of the lease term for a small amount, it would also be classified as a capital lease. Sherry said not to worry because she would make sure that the lease contract would not contain any title transfer or bargain purchase option. The accountant then said that the facility had a 25-year life and the lease was for 20 years, which was more than 75% of the economic life of the asset, so it would have to be classified as a capital lease. Sherry then said she would change the lease term to 18 years, so the lease term would be less than the 75% of the economic life of the facility. The accountant then computed the present value of all the lease payments, and the total was more than 90% of the market value of the facility. Again, Sherry said she would make any needed changes so that the total present value of the lease payments would be 89% of the current market value of the facility. At this point, the accountant became frustrated and told Sherry that the rules of accounting used to determine the proper classification of a lease were not meant to be used in order to misclassify a leased asset and, thereby, provide misleading information. Sherry then said the rules simply served as a guide for structuring the lease and that she was merely using the rules to allow the lease to be classified as an operating lease and, thus, the lease obligation would not have to be recorded. The accountant said that intentionally avoiding the rules was unethical and wrong.

Requirements

1. Why does Sherry want to have the lease classified as an operating lease rather than a capital lease?

2. Does the accountant have a legitimate argument? Does Sherry have a legitimate argument?

3. What ethical issues are involved?

4. Do you have any other thoughts?

Know Your Business

Financial Analysis

Purpose: To help familiarize you with the financial reporting of a real company in order to further your understanding of the chapter material you are learning.

This case focuses on the liabilities of Columbia Sportswear Company. Current liabilities are those obligations that will become due and payable within the next year or operating cycle (whichever is longer), while long-term liabilities are those that are due and payable more than one year from the balance sheet date. It is important to properly classify and report these liabilities because they affect liquidity. We will now consider the current and long-term liabilities of Columbia Sportswear Company. Refer to the Columbia Sportswear Company financial statements found in Appendix A. Also, consider notes 8, 9, 10, and 11 in the footnotes included in the annual report.

Requirements

1. What was the balance of total current liabilities at December 31, 2012? What was the balance of total current liabilities at December 31, 2011? Did the amount of ending total current liabilities increase or decrease? What caused the biggest change in total current liabilities?

2. Look at the balance of accrued liabilities at December 31, 2012 and December 31, 2011. Then look at the footnote that provides the breakdown of the total accrued liabilities. What makes up the accrued liabilities, and why would they be included in the current liability section? Which liability made up the biggest portion of the accrued liabilities?

3. Look at the financing activities section of the Consolidated Statements of Cash Flows. Can you see the amount of additions to short-term and long-term debt over the past three years? Can you see the amount of reductions of short-term and long-term debt over the last three fiscal years? Does it appear that Columbia Sportswear Company is borrowing more than it repays or repaying more than it borrows?

4. Compare the total amount of current liabilities to the total amount of long-term liabilities at December 31, 2012. Is the amount of total current liabilities more than or less than the total long-term liabilities? What do these results mean? Is the amount of total stockholders' equity more than or less than the total of all the liabilities at December 31, 2012? What does this result mean?

5. Examine the long-term liabilities section of the balance sheet. Can you determine what deferred income taxes are? Why does income taxes payable appear in both the current liabilities and long-term liabilities sections of the balance sheet?

Industry Analysis

Purpose: To help you understand and compare the performance of two companies in the same industry.

Find the Columbia Sportswear Company Annual Report located in Appendix A and go to the Consolidated Financial Statements starting on page 659. Now access the 2012 Annual Report for Under Armour, Inc., from the Internet. For instructions on how to access the report online, see the Industry Analysis in Chapter 1. The company's financial statements start on page 48.

Requirement

1. Calculate the debt ratio for both companies for 2012 and 2011. Generally speaking, what does a debt ratio tell you? Specifically, what does the difference between the debt ratios for these two companies for the two years tell you?

Small Business Analysis

Purpose: To help you understand the importance of cash flows in the operation of a small business.

Your business has been doing pretty well since you first opened the doors five years ago. You've been thinking, for the past six months or so, about expanding the business. There is some property right next door that fits your expansion plans. It would take some renovations to the building, but in order to continue to grow, you know you're going to need more room. But here's the problem: How are you going to pay for the building and the renovations? Your cash account is in pretty good shape, but you remember the sage advice of the business consultant that helped you when you were just getting started. That advice was to always have enough available cash to cover three months' worth of expenses just in case of some unexpected business interruption. Your available cash and short-term investments of $100,000 is right at that benchmark.

Some preliminary investigation into the property next door indicates that the existing owner would probably be willing to accept $200,000 for the property. You also have a discussion with a contractor associate who tells you that the renovations to your specifications would cost about $50,000. So your dilemma is: How are you going to come up with $250,000? You figure that the best place to start is with a visit to your banker.

At the meeting with the banker, he tells you:

"Frank, we would be pleased to help you out with your expansion plans. We would require you to take out a mortgage on the building, and we would need a 20% down payment of the total amount up front. So the balance that we would be lending you would be 80% of the total you need, or $200,000. Your down payment amount would be $50,000. At 8% for 20 years, your monthly payments would be $1,672.88."

You are somewhat pleased with the outcome of the meeting, but you tell the banker you will get back to him in a day or two. You know that this is big step and a long-term investment for the business.

Requirements

1. After thinking through the details of the plan the banker gave you, what are your thoughts? Because the down payment is going to use up about half of your available cash, how does that concern you? What about the long-term commitment of 20 years?

2. Assuming you go ahead with the mortgage and the purchase and renovation of the property, journalize the transactions to acquire the property and make the renovations. Where will the building and the renovations show up on your financial statements? Where will the mortgage show up on your financial statements? If the interest portion of your first payment is going to be $1,333.33, journalize the transaction to make your first mortgage payment.

Written Communication

Your boss has just asked you to write a short note to one of his clients that had expressed some concerns about the difference between liabilities that are of an unknown amount versus contingent liabilities. The client is in the midst of a lawsuit with a governmental agency that its attorney thinks has about a 50–50 chance of winning. However, if the company loses, it could cost a substantial amount of money. The client is wondering if it needs to account for the lawsuit, and if so, how?

Requirement

1. Write a note to the client explaining the difference between a liability of an unknown amount and a contingent liability. Also, make a suggestion as to how this particular situation might need to be accounted for.

Self Check Answers
1. b 2. c 3. d 4. b 5. b 6. c 7. b 8. b 9. a 10. a 11. d 12. c

Company name

Stockholder name

Number of shares owned by the stockholder

Exhibit 10-1 ▲

Outstanding stock Stock in the hands of stockholders.

Stock that is held by the stockholders is said to be **outstanding stock**. The outstanding stock of a corporation represents 100% of its ownership. The number of outstanding shares cannot exceed the number of authorized shares and is usually less than the number of authorized shares.

Corporations dominate business activity in the United States. Proprietorships and partnerships are more numerous, but corporations do much more business and are usually larger. Most well-known companies, such as **General Motors** and **Best Buy**, are corporations. Their full names include *Corporation* or *Incorporated* (abbreviated *Corp.* and *Inc.*) to show that they are corporations—for example, **General Motors Corporation** and **Best Buy, Inc.** The corporate form of organization is attractive for many reasons. Exhibit 10-2 summarizes some of the advantages and disadvantages of the corporate form of business.

Advantages	Disadvantages
• Stockholders have limited liability because the corporation is a separate legal entity.	• Government regulation is cumbersome and expensive.
	• Double taxation.
• Corporations can raise more money than a proprietorship or partnership.	
• A corporation has a continuous life.	
• The transfer of corporate ownership is easy.	

Exhibit 10-2 ▲

What Makes Up the Stockholders' Equity of a Corporation?

2 Describe the two sources of stockholders' equity and the different classes of stock

Recall from Chapter 1 that the stockholders' equity of a corporation is divided into two categories:

- Paid-in capital (also called contributed capital) represents amounts received from the stockholders. Common stock, discussed in Chapter 1, is the main source of paid-in capital. This is *externally* generated capital and results from transactions with outsiders.
- Retained earnings represents capital that has been earned by profitable operations and not paid out as dividends. This is *internally* generated capital and results from internal corporate decisions and earnings.

Stockholders' Rights

There are four basic rights a stockholder may have:

1. **Vote.** Stockholders participate in management by voting on corporate matters. This is the only way in which a stockholder can help to manage the corporation. Normally, each share of common stock carries one vote.

2. **Dividends.** Stockholders receive a proportionate part of any dividend. Each share of stock receives an equal dividend, so, for example, a shareholder who owns 1% of the total shares in the company receives 1% of any dividend.

3. **Liquidation.** Stockholders receive their proportionate share of any assets remaining after the corporation pays its debts and liquidates (goes out of business).

4. **Preemption.** Stockholders can maintain their proportionate ownership in the corporation. Suppose you own 5% of a corporation's stock. If the corporation issues 100,000 new shares of stock, it must offer you the opportunity to buy 5% (5,000) of the new shares. Most states require that preemptive rights be specifically set forth in the corporate charter. For most companies, preemptive rights are the exception rather than the rule.

Classes of Stock

Common stock The most typical kind of stock. It usually has voting rights, the right to receive dividends, and the right to receive assets if the company liquidates.

Every corporation must issue **common stock**, which represents the basic ownership of the corporation. The real "owners" of the corporation are the common stockholders. Some companies issue Class A common stock, which carries the right to vote, and Class B common stock, which is non-voting. There must be at least one voting "class" of stock. However, there is no limit to the number or types of classes of stock that a corporation may issue. Each class of stock has a separate account.

Preferred stock Stock that gives its owners certain advantages over common stockholders, such as the right to receive dividends before the common stockholders and the right to receive assets before the common stockholders if the corporation liquidates.

In addition to common stock, a corporation may also issue **preferred stock**. Preferred stock gives its owners certain advantages over the owners of common stock. Most notably, preferred stockholders receive dividends before the common stockholders. They also receive assets before common stockholders if the corporation liquidates. Corporations pay a fixed dividend on preferred stock, which is printed on the face of the preferred stock certificate. Investors usually buy preferred stock to earn those fixed dividends. With these advantages, preferred stockholders take less investment risk than common stockholders.

Owners of preferred stock may also have the four basic stockholders' rights, unless a right is withheld. The right to vote, however, is usually withheld from preferred stock. Companies may issue different series of preferred stock (Series A and Series B, for example). Each series is recorded in a separate account.

Par Value, Stated Value, and No-Par Stock

Par value Arbitrary amount assigned to a share of stock.

Stock may carry a par value, a stated value, or it may be no-par stock. **Par value** is an arbitrary amount assigned by a company to a share of its stock. The par value of **Johnson & Johnson**'s common stock is $1 per share. **Dell, Inc.,** has common stock with a par value of $0.01 (1 cent) per share. Par value is arbitrary and is assigned when the organizers file the corporate charter with the state. There is no real "reason" for why par values vary. It is simply a choice made by the organizers of the corporation.

Stated value An arbitrary amount that is similar to par value but is assigned after a corporation is organized.

A company may also issue stock that has a **stated value**. Stated value is an arbitrary amount similar to par value. Instead of being assigned when the corporate charter is filed, the stated value is assigned at a later date, such as when the company decides to issue stock. Most companies set par, or stated, value low to avoid legal difficulties that can occur if their stock is issued for a price below the par, or stated, value.

It is also possible for a company to issue stock that has no par (or stated) value, known as *no-par stock*. In addition to its $1 par common stock, **Johnson & Johnson** has preferred stock with no par value.

Let's review some stock issuance examples to illustrate accounting for par, stated, and no-par stock.

Try It...

John and Nancy are working on an assignment their accounting instructor gave them to do over the weekend. In the assignment, they are asked to record the issuance of 200,000 shares of $5 par value stock by a corporation for $30 per share. While working on the assignment, John commented to Nancy that he couldn't believe any investor would be dumb enough to pay a company $30 for a share of stock that is only worth $5. How should Nancy respond to John's comment?

Answer

Nancy should explain to John that the $5 par value has nothing to do with the worth of each share of stock. Par value is an arbitrary amount assigned to each share of stock by the organizers of the corporation. Arbitrary means that the amount was determined by individual preference or convenience, rather than by any underlying logic.

How Is the Issuance of Stock Recorded?

Journalize the issuance of stock

Underwriter A firm, such as Morgan Stanley Smith Barney, that usually agrees to buy all the stock a company wants to issue if the firm cannot sell the stock to its clients.

Corporations such as **IBM** and **Goodyear Tire** need huge quantities of money to operate. They cannot finance all their operations through borrowing, so they raise capital by issuing stock. A company can sell its stock directly to stockholders, or it can use the services of an **underwriter**, such as the brokerage firm Morgan Stanley Smith Barney. An underwriter usually agrees to buy all the stock it cannot sell to its clients.

When a company sells its stock directly to stockholders or to an underwriter, the sale occurs in what is known as the primary market. Once a company's stock is in the hands of the stockholders, it can be traded (bought and sold) in the secondary market. It is important to note that when a company's stock is traded in the secondary market there is no direct financial impact on the company.

Issue price The initial selling price for a share of stock.

The price per share that the corporation receives from issuing stock is called the **issue price.** Usually, the issue price exceeds par value because par value is normally set quite low. In the following sections, we use Mackay Industries as an example to show how to account for the issuance of stock.

Issuing Common Stock

Issuing Common Stock at Par

Suppose Mackay Industries' common stock carried a par value of $1 per share. The entry to record the issuance of 500,000 shares of stock at par value on January 1 would be:

DATE	ACCOUNTS	POST REF.	DR.	CR.
Jan 1	Cash (500,000 × $1)		500,000	
	Common Stock			500,000
	Issued 500,000 shares of common stock for $1 per share.			

Issuing Common Stock above Par

Paid-in Capital in Excess of Par Paid-in capital that represents the amount by which the issue price of stock exceeds its par value; also called **Additional Paid-in Capital**.

As stated previously, most corporations set par value low and issue common stock for a price above par. Let's assume that the 500,000 shares of Mackay Industries' stock are issued for $15 a share on January 1. The $14 difference between the issue price ($15) and par value ($1) represents another type of paid-in capital account called **Paid-in Capital in Excess of Par**. It is also called **Additional Paid-in Capital**. Additional paid-in capital on the sale of common stock is not a gain, income, or profit for the corporation because the company is dealing with its own stock. This situation illustrates one of the fundamentals of accounting: a company can have no profit or loss when buying or selling its own stock.

With a par value of $1, Mackay Industries' entry to record the issuance of its stock at $15 per share on January 1 is:

DATE	ACCOUNTS	POST REF.	DR.	CR.
Jan 1	Cash (500,000 × $15)		7,500,000	
	Common Stock (500,000 × $1 par)			500,000
	Paid-in Capital in Excess of Par—Common			
	[500,000 × ($15 − $1)]			7,000,000
	Issued 500,000 shares of common stock for $15 per share.			

The total paid-in capital should equal the amount of cash received. Altogether, it is the sum of the following:

Total Paid-in Capital = Common Stock + Paid-in Capital in Excess of Par
$7,500,000   = $500,000   + $7,000,000

Issuing No-Par Stock

When a company issues no-par stock, there can be no paid-in capital in excess of par because there isn't any par of which to be in excess. Assume that, instead of $1 par value, Mackay Industries' common stock was no-par. How would that change the recording of the issuance of 500,000 shares for $15 on January 1? The entry to record the issuance of 500,000 shares of no-par stock for $15 per share would be:

DATE	ACCOUNTS	POST REF.	DR.	CR.
Jan 1	Cash (500,000 × $15)		7,500,000	
	Common Stock			7,500,000
	Issued 500,000 shares of no-par common stock for			
	$15 per share.			

With no-par stock, Cash is debited and Common Stock is credited for the cash received, regardless of the stock's price. Notice that the total paid-in capital of $7,500,000 remains the same as when there was a par value per share:

Total Paid-in Capital = Common Stock + Paid-in Capital in Excess of Par

$7,500,000 = $7,500,000 + $0

Issuing No-Par Stock with a Stated Value

Accounting for stock with a stated value is almost identical to accounting for par value stock. The only difference is that stock with a stated value uses an account titled Paid-in Capital in Excess of *Stated* Value to record amounts received above the stated value.

Issuing Stock for Assets Other than Cash

A corporation may issue stock for assets other than cash. It records the assets received at their current market value and credits the stock accounts accordingly. The assets' prior book value is irrelevant. Now, let's reconsider the January 1 entry for Mackay Industries. Assume that, instead of cash, Mackay Industries received a building with a fair market value of $7,500,000 in exchange for the 500,000 shares of its $1 par common stock on January 1. How would the entry change?

DATE	ACCOUNTS	POST REF.	DR.	CR.
Jan 1	Building (fair market value)		7,500,000	
	Common Stock (500,000 × $1 par)			500,000
	Paid-in Capital in Excess of Par—Common			
	($7,500,000 − $500,000)			7,000,000
	Issued 500,000 shares of common stock in exchange for a building.			

As you can see, the only change is in the asset received; the Building account is debited instead of Cash.

Issuing Preferred Stock

Accounting for preferred stock is similar to the process illustrated for issuing common stock. Let's assume that Mackay Industries decides to issue 10,000 shares of its $20 par, 10% preferred stock on February 15 for $25 per share. The entry to record the issuance would be:

DATE	ACCOUNTS	POST REF.	DR.	CR.
Feb 15	Cash (10,000 × $25)		250,000	
	Preferred Stock (10,000 × $20)			200,000
	Paid-in Capital in Excess of Par—Preferred			
	[10,000 × ($25 − $20)]			50,000
	Issued 10,000 shares of preferred stock for $25 per share.			

As with common stock, preferred stock can also be issued at par or it can be no-par stock.

How Are Cash Dividends Accounted For?

4   **Account for cash dividends**

As discussed in Chapter 1, a profitable corporation may distribute cash to the stockholders in the form of dividends. Dividends cause a decrease in both Assets and Stockholders' Equity (Retained Earnings). Most states prohibit using the portion of

Legal capital The portion of stockholders' equity that cannot be used for dividends.

paid-in capital that is represented by the total par or stated value of stock for dividends. Accountants, therefore, use the term legal capital to refer to the portion of stockholders' equity that cannot be used for dividends. Corporations declare cash dividends from Retained Earnings and then pay them with cash.

Dividend Dates

A corporation declares a dividend before paying it. There are three dates associated with the declaration and payment of a cash dividend.

1. **Declaration date.** On the declaration date—say, March 5—the board of directors announces the intention to pay the dividend. The declaration of a cash dividend creates an obligation (liability) for the corporation.

2. **Date of record.** Those stockholders holding the stock at the end of business on the date of record—usually a week or two after declaration, say, March 19—will receive the dividend check.

3. **Payment date.** Payment of the dividend usually follows the record date by a week or two—say, March 31.

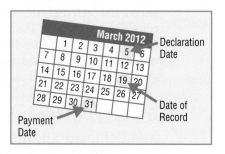

Declaring and Paying Dividends

The annual dividend rate on *preferred stock* is often expressed as a percentage of the preferred stock's par value, such as 10%. But sometimes annual cash dividends on preferred stock are expressed as a flat dollar amount per share, such as $2 per share. Therefore, preferred dividends are computed two ways, depending on how the preferred stock dividend rate is expressed. Let's look at the two ways to compute preferred dividends, using Mackay Industries' 10,000 outstanding shares of 10%, $20 par preferred stock. (Mackay Industries' flat rate instead of 10% could be stated as $2 per share.)

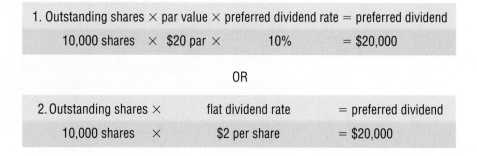

Cash dividends on *common stock* are computed the second way because those cash dividends are not expressed as a percentage.

Remember from Chapter 3 that the Dividends account is closed to Retained Earnings at the end of the year. So, instead of using the Dividends account, companies can record the declaration of a dividend by debiting the Retained Earnings account instead of Dividends. This practice will be used in this chapter. In this case, there will be no entry required at year-end to close the Dividends account. To account for Mackay Industries' declaration of a cash dividend, we debit Retained Earnings (or Dividends) and credit Dividends Payable on the date of declaration:

DATE	ACCOUNTS	POST REF.	DR.	CR.
Mar 5	Retained Earnings (or Dividends)		20,000	
	Dividends Payable			20,000
	Declared a cash dividend.			

On the date of record, no journal entry is required. On the payment date, Mackay Industries will record the payment of the dividend:

DATE	ACCOUNTS	POST REF.	DR.	CR.
Mar 31	Dividends Payable		20,000	
	Cash			20,000
	Paid cash dividend.			

When a company has issued only common stock, the common stockholders will receive any dividend that is declared. However, if both preferred and common stock are issued, the preferred stockholders get their dividends first. The common stockholders receive dividends only if the total dividend declared is larger than the amount of dividends due to the preferred stockholders. In other words, the common stockholders get the leftovers. Let's see how dividends are divided between preferred and common stockholders.

Dividing Dividends Between Preferred and Common Shareholders

Assume that Mackay Industries has 500,000 shares of $1 par common stock outstanding and 10,000 shares of $20 par, 10% preferred stock outstanding at December 31, 2012. We calculated earlier that Mackay Industries' annual preferred dividend was $20,000. So, total declared dividends must exceed $20,000 for the common stockholders to get anything. Exhibit 10-3 shows the division of dividends between preferred and common for two situations at December 31, 2012.

Situation A—Total Dividend of $15,000:	
Preferred dividend (the full $15,000 goes to the preferred stockholders because the annual preferred dividend is $20,000)	$15,000
Common dividend (none because the total dividend did not cover the preferred annual dividend)	0
Total dividend	$15,000
Situation B—Total Dividend of $30,000:	
Preferred dividend (10,000 shares × $20 par × 10%)	$20,000
Common dividend ($30,000 − $20,000)	10,000
Total dividend	$30,000

Exhibit 10-3 ▲

If Mackay Industries' dividend is large enough to cover the preferred dividend (Situation B), the preferred stockholders get their regular dividend ($20,000) and the common stockholders get the remainder ($10,000). But if the year's dividend falls below the annual preferred amount (Situation A), the preferred stockholders will receive the entire dividend and the common stockholders get nothing that year.

Dividends on Cumulative and Noncumulative Preferred Stock

Preferred stock can be either:

* cumulative or
* noncumulative.

Preferred stock is assumed to be cumulative unless it's specifically designated as noncumulative. Most preferred stock is cumulative. Let's see what effect the cumulative versus noncumulative designation has on the payment of dividends.

As we saw with Mackay Industries in Situation A in Exhibit 10-3, a corporation may pay only part of the annual preferred dividend. This may happen if, for example, the company does not have enough cash to fund the entire dividend. This is called *passing the dividend*, and the dividends are called **dividends in arrears**. With **cumulative preferred stock**, shareholders must receive all dividends in arrears plus the current year dividend before the common stockholders get any dividend.

The preferred stock of Mackay Industries is cumulative. How do we know this? Because it is not labeled as noncumulative.

Suppose Mackay Industries passed the entire 2012 preferred dividend of $20,000. Before paying any common dividend in 2013, Mackay Industries must first pay preferred dividends of $20,000 for 2012 and $20,000 for 2013, a total of $40,000. In 2013, Mackay Industries declares a $75,000 dividend. How much of this dividend goes to preferred? How much goes to common? The allocation of this $75,000 dividend is:

Total dividend		$75,000
Preferred stockholders get:		
2012 dividend (10,000 × $20 × 10%)	$20,000	
2013 dividend (10,000 × $20 × 10%)	20,000	
Total to preferred		40,000
Common stockholders get the remainder		$35,000

If Mackay Industries declared the $75,000 dividend on November 10, 2013, it would make the following entry:

DATE	ACCOUNTS	POST REF.	DR.	CR.
Nov 10	Retained Earnings (or Dividends)		75,000	
	Dividends Payable—Preferred			40,000
	Dividends Payable—Common			35,000
	Declared a cash dividend.			

If the preferred stock is *noncumulative*, the corporation is not required to pay any unpaid dividends from prior years. Suppose Mackay Industries' preferred stock was noncumulative and the company passed the 2012 dividend. The preferred stockholders would lose the 2012 dividend of $20,000 forever. Then, before paying any common dividends in 2013, Mackay Industries would only have to pay the 2013 preferred dividend of $20,000, which would leave $55,000 for the common stockholders.

Dividends in arrears are *not* a liability. A liability for dividends arises only after the board of directors declares a dividend. It is possible that the board may never declare another dividend. However, a corporation does report cumulative preferred dividends in arrears in the notes to the financial statements. This shows the common stockholders how big the declared dividend will need to be for them to get any dividends in the future.

Dividends in arrears Cumulative, unpaid dividends on cumulative preferred stock.

Cumulative preferred stock Preferred stock whose owners must receive all dividends in arrears plus the current year dividend before the corporation pays dividends to the common stockholders.

Stop and Think...

Jeffrey and Sandi were discussing cumulative preferred dividends one day after their accounting class. Jeffrey commented that dividends in arrears were a liability of the corporation and, as such, should appear on the company's balance sheet. Sandi disagreed, saying that dividends in arrears are not a liability of the corporation and therefore are not reported on the company's balance sheet. Who is correct?

Answer

Sandi is correct. When a company declares dividends, it is obliged to pay any dividends in arrears to the preferred stockholders before it can pay any dividends to common stockholders. However, the company is under no obligation to ever declare another dividend again. Until it declares a dividend, it has no obligation to pay either the preferred or common stockholders, so it does not have a liability.

Decision Guidelines

Decision		Guideline		Analyze
When is payment of a cash dividend appropriate?		Consider the amount of available cash, retained earnings, and the future needs of the business.		A cash dividend is a distribution of earnings to the company's stockholders. So, a company cannot declare and distribute dividends unless the balance in retained earnings (counting the current year's earnings) exceeds the amount of the desired dividend. In addition, the company must have the cash available to pay the dividend if it is declared. A business should carefully analyze its future cash needs so that it does not deplete its cash with a dividend and end up with cash flow issues in the future.

How Are Stock Dividends and Stock Splits Accounted For?[1]

Stock Dividends

5 **Account for stock dividends and stock splits**

Stock dividend A distribution by a corporation of its own stock to stockholders.

A **stock dividend** is a distribution of a corporation's own stock to its stockholders. Unlike cash dividends, with stock dividends, a company is not required to give any of its assets to the stockholders. Stock dividends:

- Affect only stockholders' equity accounts (including Retained Earnings and Common Stock).
- Have no effect on total stockholders' equity.
- Have no effect on assets or liabilities.

---

[1]The number of shares authorized to be issued is a part of the corporation's Articles of Incorporation. When a company (by action of its Board of Directors) increases the number of shares outstanding with stock dividend or positive stock split, it must have a sufficient number of authorized shares. If the company does not have sufficient number of shares authorized, then it must go through the process of increasing the number of authorized shares by amending its Articles of Incorporation. Amending the Articles of Incorporation must be approved by a vote of the company's shareholders. When a company does a reverse stock split, the numbers of shares decrease.

A corporation distributes stock dividends to stockholders in proportion to the number of shares of stock they already own. Suppose you own 5,000 shares of Mackay Industries' common stock. If Mackay Industries distributes a 5% stock dividend, you would receive 250 (5,000 × .05) additional shares. You would now own 5,250 shares of the stock. All other Mackay Industries' stockholders also receive additional shares equal to 5% of the amount of stock they currently hold. Because the amount of stock every stockholder has increases by 5%, the stockholders would all own the same percentage share of Mackay Industries' stock as they did before the stock dividend.

Companies issue stock dividends for several reasons including:

1. To continue a history of declaring dividends while conserving cash. A company may wish to continue dividends to keep stockholders happy but need to keep its cash for operations. A stock dividend is a way to do so without using any cash.

2. To reduce the market price of its stock. A stock dividend will usually cause the company's stock price to fall. This happens because, after the stock dividend, there will be more shares representing the same total amount of market value. Suppose that a share of Mackay Industries' stock traded at $40 recently. Increasing the shares outstanding by issuing a 10% stock dividend would likely drop Mackay Industries' stock market price to around $36 per share. The objective behind a stock dividend is to make the stock less expensive and, therefore, more available and attractive to investors.

3. To reward investors. Investors often feel like they've received something of value when they get a stock dividend.

Recording Stock Dividends

As with a cash dividend, there are three dates associated with a stock dividend:

- Declaration date
- Date of record
- Distribution date

The board of directors announces the stock dividend on the declaration date. The date of record determines who will receive the additional shares. The distribution date is the date the additional shares are distributed to the stockholders. Unlike with a cash dividend, the declaration of a stock dividend does *not* create a liability. This is because the corporation is not obligated to distribute any assets to the stockholders; recall that a liability is a claim on assets. With a stock dividend, the corporation has simply declared its intention to distribute more of its stock. A stock dividend affects the following accounts:

- Retained Earnings is reduced (or Dividends is increased) by debiting an amount equal to the number of shares being distributed times the current market price per share of the company's stock.
- Common Stock is increased (credited) by an amount equal to the number of shares being distributed times the par value per share of the company's stock.
- Paid-in Capital in Excess of Par—Common is increased (credited) for the remainder.

The net effect of a stock dividend is to transfer an amount equal to the market value of the dividend from Retained Earnings into Paid-in Capital.

Assume that Mackay Industries has the following stockholders' equity on June 15, prior to declaring a stock dividend:

Mackay Industries, Inc. Stockholders' Equity June 15	
Paid-in Capital:	
Preferred Stock, 10%, $20 par, 500,000 shares authorized,	
10,000 shares issued and outstanding	$ 200,000
Paid-in Capital in Excess of Par—Preferred	50,000
Common Stock, $1 par, 2,000,000 shares authorized,	
500,000 shares issued and outstanding	500,000
Paid-in Capital in Excess of Par—Common	7,000,000
Total Paid-in Capital	7,750,000
Retained Earnings	2,000,000
Total Stockholders' Equity	$9,750,000

Now, assume Mackay Industries declares and distributes a 5% common stock dividend on June 15 when the market value of Mackay Industries' common stock is $40 per share. Although the declaration and distribution dates are normally different, we will assume they occurred on the same date for this example. Mackay would record the declaration and distribution of the stock dividend as:

DATE	ACCOUNTS	POST REF.	DR.	CR.
Jun 15	Retained Earnings (or Dividends) (500,000 × 0.05 × $40 market value)		1,000,000	
	Common Stock (500,000 × 0.05 × $1 par)			25,000
	Paid-in Capital in Excess of Par—Common			975,000
	Declared and distributed stock dividend.			

As we did with cash dividends, we debited Retained Earnings directly instead of using the Dividends account. Remember that a stock dividend does not affect assets, liabilities, or total stockholders' equity. A stock dividend merely rearranges the balances in the equity accounts, leaving total equity unchanged. Immediately after the stock dividend, Mackay Industries' stockholders' equity looks like this:

Mackay Industries, Inc. Stockholders' Equity June 15	
Paid-in Capital:	
Preferred Stock, 10%, $20 par, 500,000 shares authorized,	
10,000 shares issued and outstanding	$ 200,000
Paid-in Capital in Excess of Par—Preferred	50,000
Common Stock, $1 par, 2,000,000 shares authorized,	
525,000 shares issued and outstanding	525,000
Paid-in Capital in Excess of Par—Common	7,975,000
Total Paid-in Capital	8,750,000
Retained Earnings	1,000,000
Total Stockholders' Equity	$9,750,000

Note that the number of issued and outstanding shares is now 525,000 [500,000 + (500,000 × 0.05)]. Note also that total stockholders' equity is still $9,750,000. The effect of the stock dividend was simply to transfer $1,000,000 from Retained Earnings to Paid-in Capital.

Stock Splits

Stock split An increase in the number of authorized, issued, and outstanding shares of stock coupled with a proportionate reduction in the par value per share of the stock.

Both a stock dividend and a **stock split** will increase the number of shares of stock issued and outstanding. However, a stock split is fundamentally different from a stock dividend. A stock split increases not only the number of issued and outstanding shares of stock, but also the number of authorized shares. A stock split also decreases the par value per share, whereas stock dividends do not affect the par value per share or the number of authorized shares. For example, if Mackay Industries splits its common stock 2-for-1, the number of outstanding shares is doubled and par value per share is cut in half. A stock split also decreases the market price of the stock.

Assume the market price of a share of Mackay Industries common stock has been approximately $40. If Mackay Industries initiates a 2-for-1 split of its common stock on August 1, the market price per share will drop to around $20. A 2-for-1 stock split means that Mackay Industries will have twice as many shares of stock authorized, issued, and outstanding after the split as before. Each share's par value is also cut in half. **Exhibit 10-4** shows the before and after of how a 2-for-1 split affects Mackay Industries' stockholders' equity.

Study the exhibit and you'll see that a 2-for-1 stock split does the following:

- Cuts par value per share in half.
- Doubles the number of shares of stock authorized, issued, and outstanding.
- Leaves all account balances and total equity unchanged.

Mackay Industries, Inc. **Stockholders' Equity—Before Split** August 1	
Paid-in Capital:	
Preferred Stock, 10%, $20 par, 500,000 shares authorized, 10,000 shares issued and outstanding	$ 200,000
Paid-in Capital in Excess of Par—Preferred	50,000
Common Stock, $1 par, 2,000,000 shares authorized, 525,000 shares issued and outstanding	525,000
Paid-in Capital in Excess of Par—Common	7,975,000
Total Paid-in Capital	8,750,000
Retained Earnings	1,000,000
Total Stockholders' Equity	$9,750,000

Mackay Industries, Inc. **Stockholders' Equity—After Split** August 1	
Paid-in Capital:	
Preferred Stock, 10%, $20 par, 500,000 shares authorized, 10,000 shares issued and outstanding	$ 200,000
Paid-in Capital in Excess of Par—Preferred	50,000
Common Stock, $0.50 par, 4,000,000 shares authorized, 1,050,000 shares issued and outstanding	525,000
Paid-in Capital in Excess of Par—Common	7,975,000
Total Paid-in Capital	8,750,000
Retained Earnings	1,000,000
Total Stockholders' Equity	$9,750,000

Exhibit 10-4 ▲

Accounting in Your World

Robert invited three friends over to watch a football game and share a "take-and-bake" pizza he had purchased. On game day, Robert pulled the pizza out of the oven and was just about to slice it into eight pieces (two slices for each of them) when he began to wonder if there was enough pizza. Robert had an idea. He figured that if he cut the pizza into twelve slices instead of eight slices, each person would get three slices of pizza instead of two. Robert knew that each person would still receive the same amount of pizza, but he figured that his friends would feel more satisfied if they received three slices instead of only two slices. It worked; no one complained that they did not get enough to eat.

The logic behind a stock split is similar to the logic behind Robert slicing the pizza into more pieces. When a company splits its stock, each shareholder still owns the same amount of the company (think the whole pizza). However, the shareholders' ownership is now represented by more shares of stock (think slices of pizza). For example, after a 3-for-2 stock split, each shareholder would own the same amount of the company. Each shareholder would just own three shares of stock now for every two shares he or she used to own.

Memorandum entry A journal entry that "notes" a significant event but that has no debit or credit amount.

Because the stock split does not affect any account balances, no formal journal entry is needed to record a stock split. Instead, the split is recorded in a **memorandum entry,** a journal entry that "notes" a significant event but that has no debit or credit amount. Here is an example of a memorandum entry:

DATE	ACCOUNTS	POST REF.	DR.	CR.
Aug 1	Split the common stock 2-for-1.			
	OLD: 2,000,000 shares authorized; 525,000 shares			
	issued and outstanding, $1 par			
	NEW: 4,000,000 shares authorized; 1,050,000 shares			
	issued and outstanding, $0.50 par			

Stock Dividends and Stock Splits Compared

Stock dividends and stock splits have some similarities and some differences. **Exhibit 10-5** summarizes the effects of each on stockholders' equity. Cash dividends have also been included in the exhibit for comparison purposes.

Event	Common Stock	Paid-In Capital in Excess of Par	Retained Earnings	Total Stockholders' Equity
Cash dividend	No effect	No effect	Decrease	Decrease
Stock dividend	Increase	Increase	Decrease	No effect
Stock split	No effect	No effect	No effect	No effect

Exhibit 10-5 ▲

How Is Treasury Stock Accounted For?

6 **Account for treasury stock**

Treasury stock A corporation's own stock that it has issued and later reacquired.

After a company has issued stock, it is possible for that company to reacquire, or buy back, some of its stock at a later date. The reacquired shares are called **treasury stock** because they are, in effect, held in the company's treasury. A corporation such as Mackay Industries may purchase treasury stock for several reasons:

1. Management hopes to buy the stock when the price is low and sell it when the price goes higher.

2. Management wants to support the company's stock price.

3. Management wants to avoid a takeover by an outside party. If the company purchases the available shares, the shares are not available for others to purchase.

4. Management wants to reward valued employees with stock. Treasury stock can be given to employees as a reward.

   Treasury stock transactions are common among larger corporations.

Treasury Stock Basics

Before we see how treasury stock is accounted for, let's review some basic concepts related to treasury stock:

- The Treasury Stock account is a contra-equity account. Therefore, Treasury Stock has a debit balance, which is the opposite of the other equity accounts.
- Treasury Stock is recorded at cost (par value is ignored).
- The Treasury Stock account is reported beneath Retained Earnings on the balance sheet as a reduction to total stockholders' equity.

Although shares of treasury stock are still considered to be issued shares, they decrease the company's stock that is outstanding. This is because the shares are no longer held by outsiders (the stockholders). We compute outstanding stock as:

Outstanding stock = Issued stock − Treasury stock

Outstanding shares are important because only outstanding shares have voting rights and receive dividends. Treasury stock doesn't have voting rights, and it gets no dividends[2]. Now, let's illustrate how to account for treasury stock, continuing with Mackay Industries.

---

[2]In some cases, it is permissible for a company to issue stock dividends on treasury stock. In this text, stock dividends are assumed to be issued on outstanding shares only.

Purchase of Treasury Stock

Mackay Industries' stockholders' equity, after the stock split discussed earlier in the chapter, appears in **Exhibit 10-6**.

Mackay Industries, Inc. Stockholders' Equity August 1	
Paid-in Capital:	
Preferred Stock, 10%, $20 par, 500,000 shares authorized,	
10,000 shares issued and outstanding	$ 200,000
Paid-in Capital in Excess of Par—Preferred	50,000
Common Stock, $0.50 par, 4,000,000 shares authorized,	
1,050,000 shares issued and outstanding	525,000
Paid-in Capital in Excess of Par—Common	7,975,000
Total Paid-in Capital	8,750,000
Retained Earnings	1,000,000
Total Stockholders' Equity	$9,750,000

Exhibit 10-6 ▲

Assume that on August 10, Mackay Industries purchased 5,000 shares of the company's issued common stock, paying $25 per share. To record the purchase, debit Treasury Stock and credit Cash:

DATE	ACCOUNTS	POST REF.	DR.	CR.
Aug 10	Treasury Stock (5,000 × $25)		125,000	
	Cash			125,000
	Purchased 5,000 shares of treasury stock.			

After posting the entry, the Treasury Stock account would look like this:

Treasury Stock	
8/10 125,000	

Sale of Treasury Stock

Companies buy their treasury stock hoping to sell it at a later date for more than they paid for it. However, companies may sell treasury stock at, above, or below what they paid for it.

Sale at Cost

If treasury stock is sold for cost, the same price the corporation paid for it, then there is no difference between cost and sale price to journalize. Let's assume Mackay Industries sells 500 of the treasury shares on September 5 for $25 each. The entry is:

DATE	ACCOUNTS	POST REF.	DR.	CR.
Sep 5	Cash (500 × $25)		12,500	
	Treasury Stock			12,500
	Sold 500 shares of treasury stock.			

After posting the entry, the Treasury Stock account would look like this:

Treasury Stock			
8/10	125,000	9/5	12,500

Sale Above Cost

If treasury stock is sold for more than cost, the difference is credited to a new account, Paid-in Capital, Treasury Stock. This excess is additional paid-in capital because it came from the company's stockholders. It has no effect on net income. Suppose Mackay Industries resold 500 of its treasury shares for $28 per share on October 2. (Recall that cost was $25.) The entry to sell treasury stock for a price above cost is:

DATE	ACCOUNTS	POST REF.	DR.	CR.
Oct 2	Cash (500 × $28)		14,000	
	Treasury Stock (500 × $25)			12,500
	Paid-in Capital, Treasury Stock (difference)			1,500
	Sold 500 shares of treasury stock.			

Paid-in Capital, Treasury Stock is reported with the other paid-in capital accounts on the balance sheet, beneath Common Stock and Paid-in Capital in Excess of Par. After posting the entry, the Treasury Stock and Paid-in Capital, Treasury Stock accounts would look like this:

Treasury Stock					Paid-in Capital, Treasury Stock		
8/10	125,000	9/5	12,500			10/2	1,500
		10/2	12,500				

Sale Below Cost

The resale price of treasury stock can be less than cost. The shortfall is debited first to Paid-in Capital, Treasury Stock. If this account's balance is too small, then Retained Earnings is debited for the remaining amount. To illustrate, let's assume Mackay Industries had two additional treasury stock sales. First, on October 28, Mackay Industries sold 1,000 treasury shares for $24 each. The entry to record the sale is:

DATE	ACCOUNTS	POST REF.	DR.	CR.
Oct 28	Cash (1,000 × $24)		24,000	
	Paid-in Capital, Treasury Stock (difference)		1,000	
	Treasury Stock (1,000 × $25)			25,000
	Sold 1,000 shares of treasury stock.			

The total difference between the cost and the selling price of the treasury shares is $1,000. Mackay Industries had sufficient paid-in capital from treasury stock transactions on the books from the October 2nd sale to absorb this $1,000 difference.

Now what happens if Mackay Industries sells an additional 1,500 treasury shares for $22 each on November 1?

DATE	ACCOUNTS	POST REF.	DR.	CR.
Nov 1	Cash (1,500 × $22)		33,000	
	Paid-in Capital, Treasury Stock ($1,500 − $1,000)		500	
	Retained Earnings		4,000	
	Treasury Stock (1,500 × $25)			37,500
	Sold 1,500 shares of treasury stock.			

The difference between the cost and the selling price of the treasury stock is $4,500 [($25 cost per share minus $22 sales price per share) × 1,500 shares]. Only $500 remains in the Paid-in Capital, Treasury Stock account, so Mackay debits this account for $500. The remaining $4,000 ($4,500 – $500) is debited to Retained Earnings.

So, what's left in stockholders' equity for Mackay Industries after the treasury stock transactions? First, let's post the treasury stock activity to the affected accounts:

Treasury Stock			
8/10	125,000	9/5	12,500
		10/2	12,500
		10/28	25,000
		11/1	37,500
Bal	37,500		

Paid-in Capital, Treasury Stock			
		10/2	1,500
10/28	1,000		
11/1	500		
		Bal	-0-

Retained Earnings			
11/1	4,000	8/1	1,000,000
		Bal	996,000

Now, we can show the revised stockholders' equity for Mackay Industries in Exhibit 10-7:

Mackay Industries, Inc. Stockholders' Equity November 1		
Paid-in Capital:		
Preferred Stock, 10%, $20 par, 500,000 shares authorized,		
10,000 shares issued and outstanding		$ 200,000
Paid-in Capital in Excess of Par—Preferred		50,000
Common Stock, $0.50 par, 4,000,000 shares authorized,		
1,050,000 shares issued, 1,048,500 shares outstanding		525,000
Paid-in Capital in Excess of Par—Common		7,975,000
Total Paid-in Capital		8,750,000
Retained Earnings		996,000
Subtotal		9,746,000
Less: Treasury Stock at cost (1,500 shares @ $25)		37,500
Total Stockholders' Equity		$9,708,500

Exhibit 10-7 ▲

How Is Stockholders' Equity Reported on the Balance Sheet?

7 | **Report stockholders' equity on the balance sheet**

Companies often report their stockholders' equity on the balance sheet in ways that differ from the examples we have shown in this chapter. In most cases, the information is less detailed because it is assumed that investors understand the details. Two common differences are:

1. The heading Paid-in Capital does not usually appear. It is commonly understood that Preferred Stock, Common Stock, and Additional Paid-in Capital are elements of paid-in capital.

2. All additional paid-in capital accounts are often combined and reported as a single amount labeled Additional Paid-in Capital. The Additional Paid-in Capital is most often reported following Common Stock.

Also, many companies often report a separate statement of stockholders' equity in addition to the regular financial statements. This statement is used to show investors the significant changes in all of the equity categories that occurred during the year. An example of a statement of stockholders' equity is presented in Exhibit 10-8.

			Common Stock	Additional Paid-in Capital	Retained Earnings	Treasury Stock	Total
		Example Company **Statement of Stockholders' Equity** Year Ended December 31, 2014					
		Balance, December 31, 2013	$120,000	$190,000	$160,000	$(25,000)	$445,000
		Issuance of Stock	20,000	90,000			110,000
		Net Income			66,000		66,000
		Cash Dividends			(40,000)		(40,000)
		Stock Dividends	13,000	28,000	(41,000)		0
		Purchase of Treasury Stock				(18,000)	(18,000)
		Sale of Treasury Stock		10,000		9,000	19,000
		Balance, December 31, 2014	$153,000	$318,000	$145,000	$(34,000)	$582,000

Exhibit 10-8 ▲

If a company has preferred stock, the statement would also include a column for Preferred Stock. Many companies will also have a column titled "Accumulated Other Comprehensive Income," which reflects changes in stockholders' equity from things such as unrealized gains on available-for-sale securities (which were discussed in Chapter 8).

Focus on Decision Making

"What's in It for the Stockholders?"

Why would stockholders put, or invest, money in a business? The answer is that they seek value. They seek value from profits. They seek profits that reward them for letting a business use their money over time and for taking risks.

So how does an owner or manager determine whether profits are adequate to reward stockholders? People start with return on equity.

8 | **Evaluate return on stockholders' equity**

Return on Equity (ROE)

Return on equity (ROE) is the ratio of net income divided by average stockholders' equity. The formula for computing return on equity is:

$$\text{Return on Equity} = \frac{\text{Net Income}}{\text{Average Stockholders' Equity}} = \frac{\text{Net Income}}{((\text{Beginning Stockholders' Equity} + \text{Ending Stockholders' Equity})/2)}$$

Return on equity (ROE) Net income divided by average stockholders' equity. It is a measure of profitability; also called *rate of return on stockholders' equity*.

Let's look at an example. Mackay Industries had net income of $136,000, beginning stockholders' equity of $825,000, and ending stockholders' equity of $943,000. Mackay Industries' return on stockholders' equity is computed as:

$$\text{Return on Equity} = \frac{\$136,000}{((\$825,000 + \$943,000)/2)} = \frac{\$136,000}{\$884,000} = 15.38\%$$

For every dollar, on average, stockholders provided Mackay Industries, the company earned its stockholders net income of a little over $0.15.

How They Do It: A Look at Business

What is a good ROE? It depends on the risk associated with a company. A higher-risk company should have a higher ROE than a company with lower risk.

Let's look at two businesses, Apple, Inc., and Dominion Resources, Inc.

First let's look at Apple, the groundbreaking technology company. Apple creates and sells a wide range of best-selling products, including iPads, iPhones and computers. Apple is considered a leader in the ever-changing, high-risk, but very profitable technology business. For the fiscal year ending September 29, 2012, Apple's return on equity was 42.9%.

Secondly, let's look at Dominion Resources, the large utility company that sells electricity and natural gas in the mid-Atlantic area of the United States. Dominion Resources is a very successful power company. Its sales, costs, profits, and cash flow are very stable and predictable. All businesses have risks, but Dominion Resources is a very well-run company that is considered to be a low-risk business. For the fiscal year ending December 31, 2012, Dominion's return on equity was 2.7%.

Now let's compare Apple and Dominion Resources. As expected, Apple's ROE was higher than Dominion Resources' ROE. Apple's higher ROE can be attributed to a higher level of earnings relative to the amount of stockholders' equity, when compared to Dominion Resources. Because Apple has a higher level of risk than Dominion Resources, Apple's higher ROE compensates stockholders for the additional risk assumed.

Summary

MyAccountingLab

Here is what you should know after reading this chapter. MyAccountingLab will help you identify what you know and where to go when you need practice.

	Key Points	Key Accounting Terms
1 Review the characteristics of a corporation **2** Describe the two sources of stockholders' equity and the different classes of stock **3** Journalize the issuance of stock	Corporations can raise money by selling: • Common stock, which comes with voting rights. • Preferred stock, which typically does not come with voting rights but which provides preferential treatment regarding dividends and asset distribution upon liquidation.	**Additional Paid-in Capital** (p. 457) **Articles of incorporation** (p. 453) **Authorized stock** (p. 453) **Capital stock** (p. 453) **Common stock** (p. 455) **Corporate charter** (p. 453) **Issue price** (p. 456) **Outstanding stock** (p. 454) **Paid-in Capital in Excess of Par** (p. 457) **Par value** (p. 456) **Preferred stock** (p. 455) **Share** (p. 453) **Stated value** (p. 456) **Stock certificates** (p. 453) **Underwriter** (p. 456)
4 Account for cash dividends	Cash dividends: • Represent a return of earnings to the stockholders. • Decrease a company's cash and its retained earnings. Preferred dividends may be: • Cumulative, which means that any dividends not paid in a given year go into "arrears" and must be paid before any dividends can be paid to common stockholders. • Noncumulative, which means that any dividends not paid in a given year are lost.	**Cumulative preferred stock** (p. 461) **Dividends in arrears** (p. 461) **Legal capital** (p. 459)
5 Account for stock dividends and stock splits	Stock dividends and stock splits: • Increase the number of issued and outstanding shares of a corporation's stock. • Reduce the market value per share of a corporation's stock.	**Memorandum entry** (p. 466) **Stock dividend** (p. 462) **Stock split** (p. 465)

		Key Points	Key Accounting Terms
6	**Account for treasury stock**	Treasury stock: • Represents a company's own issued stock that is repurchased and held for future sale. • Is a contra-stockholders' equity account whose balance is subtracted from other stockholders' equity accounts in order to arrive at total stockholders' equity.	**Treasury stock** (p. 467)
7	**Report stockholders' equity on the balance sheet**	Many companies often report a separate statement of stockholders' equity in addition to their other financial statements.	
8	**Evaluate return on stockholders' equity**	A ratio often used to help make decisions is return on equity, which measures the percentage of the average stockholders' equity that is earned as net income during the year.	**Return on equity (ROE)** (p. 472)

Accounting Practice

Discussion Questions

1. What are the four basic rights of stockholders?

2. Assume that you are a CFO of a company that is attempting to raise additional capital to finance an expansion of its production facility. You are considering either issuing bonds or additional stock. What are some of the differences in the two options?

3. What accounts are involved in the journal entry to record the issuance of stock at a price above the par value of the stock?

4. What accounts, if any, are involved in the journal entries to record the events associated with each of the following dates associated with cash dividends?

   a. Declaration date
   b. Date of record
   c. Payment date

5. With which type of stock would dividends in arrears be associated? Why?

6. What accounts are affected by the declaration and distribution of a stock dividend? What is the effect of a stock dividend on

   a. Total Stockholders' Equity?
   b. Total Assets?
   c. Total Liabilities?
   d. Cash?

7. What are some of the reasons for issuing a stock dividend?

8. What kind of account is Treasury Stock? What is its normal balance? Where would it be reported on the financial statements?

9. What could you reasonably conclude if a company reports more shares of stock issued than outstanding?

10. When considering whether to invest in a company, why would an investor want to examine the company's return on equity?

Self Check

1. Which characteristic of a corporation is considered to be an advantage?

   a. Limited stockholder liability
   b. Indefinite life
   c. Ease of transferring ownership
   d. All of the above

2. Which of the following is a disadvantage of organizing as a corporation?

   a. Limited ability to raise capital
   b. Separate legal entity
   c. Double taxation
   d. Limited stockholder liability

3. What are the two basic sources of corporate capital?

   a. Common stock and preferred stock
   b. Paid-in capital and retained earnings
   c. Retained earnings and dividends
   d. Stock and bonds

4. Suppose House and Garden Furniture issued 250,000 shares of its $5 par common stock at $6 per share. Which journal entry correctly records the issuance of this stock?

DATE	ACCOUNTS	POST REF.	DR.	CR.
a.	Common Stock		1,500,000	
	Cash			1,250,000
	Paid-in Capital in Excess of Par			250,000
b.	Cash		1,500,000	
	Common Stock			1,500,000
c.	Cash		1,500,000	
	Common Stock			1,250,000
	Paid-in Capital in Excess of Par			250,000
d.	Common Stock		1,500,000	
	Cash			1,500,000

5. Hallery Corporation has 15,000 shares of 5%, $1 par, cumulative preferred stock and 53,000 shares of common stock outstanding. Hallery Corporation declared no dividends in 2014. In 2015, Hallery Corporation declares a total dividend of $31,000. How much of the dividend goes to the common stockholders?

   a. $750
   b. $1,500
   c. $29,500
   d. None; it all goes to preferred.

6. Theodore Company has 12,000 shares of $6 par common stock outstanding, which Theodore Company issued at $10 per share. Theodore Company also has retained earnings of $84,000. How much is Theodore Company's total stockholders' equity?

   a. $ 48,000
   b. $ 120,000
   c. $ 204,000
   d. $ 72,000

7. What is the term for a company's own stock that it has issued and repurchased?

   a. Outstanding stock
   b. Treasury stock
   c. Stock dividend
   d. Issued stock

8. What does a 10% stock dividend do?

   a. Increases Common Stock
   b. Has no effect on total equity
   c. Decreases Retained Earnings
   d. All of the above

9. What happens with a 2-for-1 stock split?

   a. Decreases the par value of the stock
   b. Increases the number of shares of stock issued
   c. Both a and b
   d. None of the above

10. Assume that TJ's Wholesale pays $9 per share to purchase 1,100 of its $1 par common stock as treasury stock. What is the effect of purchasing the treasury stock?

    a. Decreases total stockholders' equity by $1,100
    b. Decreases total stockholders' equity by $9,900
    c. Increases total stockholders' equity by $9,900
    d. Increases total stockholders' equity by $1,100

11. In the Real World Accounting Video, Howard Greenstone talks about the challenges of operating a business. According to Greenstone, what is the objective of a business?

    a. Create sales

    b. Create jobs

    c. Create value

    d. Create preferred dividends

12. According to the Real World Accounting Video, there are two types of stock a company can use to finance its assets and operations. The two types of stock are

_____.

    a. common stock and uncommon stock

    b. preferred stock and designated stock

    c. common stock and preferred stock

    d. designated stock and common stock

Answers are given after Written Communication.

MyAccountingLab

Short Exercises

S10-1. Stockholders' equity terminology (*Learning Objectives 1 & 2*) 10–15 min.

Match the following terms with the correct definition.

a. Common stock	_____ 1. Paid-in capital plus retained earnings.
b. Paid-in capital	_____ 2. Capital from investments by the stockholders.
c. Dividends	
d. Legal capital	_____ 3. Capital earned through profitable operation of the business.
e. Outstanding stock	
f. Par value	_____ 4. The basic form of capital stock.
g. Preferred stock	_____ 5. Stock in the hands of stockholders.
h. Retained earnings	_____ 6. Distributions by a corporation to its stockholders.
i. Treasury stock	
j. Stockholders' equity	_____ 7. Stock that gives its owners certain advantages over common stockholders, such as the right to receive dividends before the common stockholders.
	_____ 8. Arbitrary amount assigned to a share of stock at the time of incorporation.
	_____ 9. The portion of stockholders' equity maintained for the protection of creditors.
	_____10. A corporation's own stock that it reacquires.

S10-2. Stock issuance (*Learning Objective 3*) 5–10 min.

Sullivan, Corp., issued stock above par on July 31. Answer the following questions about Sullivan, Corp.

    1. Sullivan, Corp., received $6 million for the issuance of its stock. The par value of the Sullivan, Corp., stock was only $4.5 million. Was the excess amount of $1,500,000 a profit to Sullivan, Corp.? Did the excess affect net income? If not, what was it?

    2. Suppose the par value of the Sullivan, Corp., stock had been $2 per share, $5 per share, or $10 per share. Would a change in the par value of the company's stock affect Sullivan's total paid-in capital? When issuing stock, what does affect total paid-in capital?

S10-3. Issuance of stock for cash and noncash assets (*Learning Objective 3*) 10–15 min.

This exercise shows the similarity and the difference between two ways to acquire plant assets.

Case A—Issue stock and buy the assets in separate transactions:

Apex, Inc., issued 10,000 shares of its $10 par common stock for cash of $600,000. In a separate transaction, Apex, Inc. purchased a building for $475,000 and equipment for $125,000. Journalize the two transactions.

Case B—Issue stock to acquire the assets:

Apex, Inc., issued 10,000 shares of its $10 par common stock to acquire a building with a fair market value of $475,000 and equipment with a fair market value of $125,000. Journalize this single transaction.

Compare the balances in all accounts after making both sets of entries. Are the account balances similar or different?

S10-4. Stock issuance (*Learning Objectives 2 & 3*) 5–10 min.

Buckeye, Inc., reported the following on its balance sheet at December 31, 2014:

Common Stock, $3.00 par value, 550,000 shares authorized, 400,000 shares issued and outstanding	$ 1,200,000
Paid-in Capital in Excess of Par	425,000
Retained Earnings	2,640,000

1. Assume Buckeye, Inc., issued all of its stock during 2014 in one transaction. Journalize the company's issuance of the stock for cash.

2. Was Buckeye, Inc.'s main source of stockholders' equity paid-in capital or profitable operations? How can you tell?

S10-5. Analyzing stockholders' equity (*Learning Objectives 2 & 3*) 5–10 min.

At December 31, 2014, Sugarland Company reported the following on its comparative balance sheet, which included 2013 amounts for comparison (adapted, with all amounts in millions except par value per share):

	December 31	
	2014	**2013**
Common Stock, $2.25 par value, 550,000 shares authorized, 400,000 shares issued and outstanding in 2014: 399,000 shares in 2013	$ 900,000	$ 897,750
Paid-in Capital in Excess of Par	395,500	362,000
Retained Earnings	2,400,000	2,175,000

1. How much did Sugarland Company's total paid-in capital increase during 2014? What caused total paid-in capital to increase? How can you tell?

2. Did Sugarland Company have a profit or a loss for 2014? How can you tell?

E10-21A. Accounting for stock dividends (*Learning Objectives 5 & 7*) 10–15 min.

The stockholders' equity for Dunelit, Inc., on December 31, 2013, follows:

Stockholders' Equity	
Paid-in Capital:	
Common Stock, $1 par, 450,000 shares authorized,	
50,000 shares issued and outstanding	$ 50,000
Paid-in Capital in Excess of Par	550,000
Total Paid-in Capital	$600,000
Retained Earnings	290,000
Total Stockholders' Equity	$890,000

On January 31, 2014, the market price of Dunelit's common stock was $17 per share and the company distributed a 20% stock dividend.

Requirements

1. Journalize the declaration and distribution of the stock dividend.

2. Prepare the stockholders' equity section of the balance sheet after the stock dividend.

E10-22A. Accounting for cash and stock dividends (*Learning Objectives 4 & 5*) 10–15 min.

Cassel, Inc., is authorized to issue 700,000 shares of $2 par common stock. The company issued 80,000 shares at $9 per share, and all 80,000 shares are outstanding. When the market price of common stock was $20 per share, Cassel, Inc., declared and distributed a 10% stock dividend. Later, Cassel, Inc., declared and paid a $0.25 per share cash dividend.

Requirements

1. Journalize the declaration and distribution of the stock dividend.

2. Journalize the declaration and the payment of the cash dividend.

E10-23A. Accounting for stock splits (*Learning Objectives 5 & 7*) 10–15 min.

Tour Dejour, Inc., had the following stockholders' equity at January 31:

Stockholders' Equity	
Paid-in Capital:	
Common Stock, $5 par, 500,000 shares authorized,	
30,000 shares issued and outstanding	$ 150,000
Paid-in Capital in Excess of Par	450,000
Total Paid-in Capital	$ 600,000
Retained Earnings	550,000
Total Stockholders' Equity	$1,150,000

On February 28, Tour Dejour, Inc., split its common stock 2-for-1.

Requirements

1. Make any necessary entry to record the stock split.

2. Prepare the stockholders' equity section of the balance sheet immediately after the split.

E10-24A. Accounting for stock issuance, splits, and treasury stock
(*Learning Objectives 3, 5, & 6*) 20–25 min.

Consider each of the following transactions separately from every other transaction:

a. Issuance of 40,000 shares of $8 par common at $12.

b. Purchase of 2,100 shares of treasury stock (par value $0.75) at $2 per share.

c. Issuance of a 15% stock dividend. Before the dividend, 300,000 shares of $5 par common stock were outstanding; market value was $7 at the time of the dividend.

d. Sale of 450 shares of $3 par treasury stock for $7 per share. Cost of the treasury stock was $5 per share.

e. Split stock 4-for-1. Prior to the split, 120,000 shares of $4 par common were outstanding.

Requirement

1. Identify whether each transaction increased, decreased, or did not change total stockholders' equity.

E10-25A. Accounting for treasury stock (*Learning Objectives 3 & 6*) 20–25 min.

Journalize the following transactions of All Sports, Inc., a chain of sports stores:

May 4	Issued 29,000 shares of no-par common stock at $5 per share.
Jul 22	Purchased 1,000 shares of treasury stock at $4 per share.
Nov 22	Sold 500 shares of treasury stock at $7 per share.

E10-26A. Accounting for treasury stock (*Learning Objectives 6 & 7*) 20–25 min.

Swanson, Inc., had the following stockholders' equity on November 30:

Stockholders' Equity	
Paid-in Capital:	
Common Stock, $2 par, 750,000 shares authorized,	
70,000 shares issued and outstanding	$140,000
Paid-in Capital in Excess of Par	420,000
Total Paid-in Capital	$560,000
Retained Earnings	370,000
Total Stockholders' Equity	$930,000

On December 24, Swanson, Inc., purchased 12,000 shares of treasury stock at $8 per share.

Requirements

1. Journalize the purchase of the treasury stock.

2. Prepare the stockholders' equity section of the balance sheet at December 31.

E10-27A. Balance sheet disclosure of stockholders' equity (*Learning Objective 7*) 10–15 min.

Oulette Manufacturing, Co., has the following selected account balances at August 31, 2014.

Common Stock, no par with $4 stated value, 40,000 shares authorized, issued, and outstanding	$160,000	Inventory	$146,000
		Machinery and Equipment	105,000
		Preferred Stock, 10%, $25 par, 20,000 shares authorized, 8,000 shares issued and outstanding	200,000
Accumulated Depreciation, Machinery and Equipment	101,000		
Retained Earnings	125,000	Paid-in Capital in Excess of Stated Value—Common	50,000
		Cost of Goods Sold	76,000

Requirement

1. Prepare the stockholders' equity section of the company's balance sheet.

E10-28A. Accounting for various stockholders' equity transactions (*Learning Objective 7*) 20–25 min.

At December 31, 2013, Dungy Corp. reported the following stockholders' equity:

Paid-in Capital:	
Common Stock, $4 par, 200,000 authorized, 80,000 shares issued	$ 320,000
Additional Paid-in Capital	130,000
Total Paid-in Capital	$ 450,000
Retained Earnings	645,000
Subtotal	$1,095,000
Less: Treasury Stock, 2,600 shares at cost	(93,600)
Total Stockholders' Equity	$1,001,400

During 2014, Dungy Corp. completed these transactions and events in this order:

a. Sold 800 shares of treasury stock for $48 per share; the cost of these shares was $36 per share.

b. Issued 1,200 shares of common stock at $26 per share.

c. Net income for the year was $212,000.

d. Declared and paid cash dividends of $160,000.

Requirement

1. Prepare Dungy's statement of stockholders' equity for the year ended December 31, 2014.

E10-29A. Accounting for various stockholders' equity transactions (*Learning Objectives 3, 5, & 7*) 20–25 min.

Oxford Communications, Inc., began 2014 with 2.8 million shares of $1 par common stock issued and outstanding. Beginning Paid-in Capital in Excess of Par was $6.5 million, and retained earnings was $7.5 million. In February 2014, Oxford Communications, Inc., issued 180,000 shares of stock at $9 per share. In October, when the stock's market price was $17 per share, the board of directors distributed a 10% stock dividend.

Requirements

1. Make the journal entries for the issuance of stock for cash and for the declaration and distribution of the 10% stock dividend.

2. Prepare the company's statement of stockholders' equity for the year ended December 31, 2014. Ignore net income.

E10-30A. Calculating return on equity (*Learning Objective 8*) 10–15 min.

Assume that Simmons, Inc., has the following data:

Net income for 2014	$ 136,400
Preferred dividends for 2014	$ 21,800
Total stockholder's equity, 12/31/2014	$1,640,000
Total stockholder's equity, 12/31/2013	$1,590,000
Common stockholder's equity, 12/31/2014	$1,440,000
Common stockholder's equity, 12/31/2013	$1,350,000

Requirements

1. Calculate Simmons' return on equity for 2014.

2. Comment on Simmons' performance during 2014.

MyAccountingLab **Exercises (Group B)**

E10-31B. Stock issuance (*Learning Objective 3*) 10–15 min.

TDR Systems completed the following stock issuance transactions:

Sep 19	Issued 1,500 shares of $6 par common stock for cash of $11.50 per share.
Oct 3	Sold 250 shares of $4.00, no-par preferred stock for $12,000 cash.
11	Received inventory with a market value of $27,000 and equipment with a market value of $16,000. Issued 3,500 shares of the $6 par common stock in exchange.

Requirements

1. Journalize the transactions. Explanations are not required.

2. How much paid-in capital did these transactions generate for TDR Systems?

E10-32B. Stock issuance (*Learning Objectives 3 & 7*) 10–15 min.

The charter for Zoom, Inc., authorizes the company to issue 900,000 shares of $3, no-par preferred stock and 1,400,000 shares of common stock with $6 par value. During its start-up phase, Zoom, Inc., completed the following transactions:

2012	
Oct 6	Issued 300 shares of common stock to the promoters who organized the corporation, receiving cash of $9,000.
12	Issued 500 shares of preferred stock for cash of $26,000.
14	Issued 1,600 shares of common stock in exchange for land with a market value of $18,000.

Requirements

1. Record the transactions in the journal.
2. Prepare the stockholders' equity section of the Zoom's balance sheet at December 31, 2014. Assume that the company earned net income of $32,000 during this period.

E10-33B. Stock issuance (*Learning Objective 3*) 10–15 min.

Hastings, Corp., issued 12,000 shares of no-par common stock for $18 per share.

Requirements

1. Record issuance of the stock if the stock:
   a. is no-par stock.
   b. has a stated value of $10 per share.
2. Which type of stock issuance results in more total paid-in capital?

E10-34B. Issuance of stock for cash and noncash assets (*Learning Objective 3*) 10–15 min.

Alley, Co., recently organized. The company issued no-par common stock to an attorney in exchange for his patent with a market value of $55,000. In addition, Alley, Co., received cash for 3,500 shares of its $50 par preferred stock sold at par value and for 9,000 shares of its no-par common stock sold at $6 per share. Retained earnings at the end of the first year was $39,000.

Requirement

1. Without making journal entries, determine the total paid-in capital created by these transactions.

E10-35B. Accounting for cash dividends (*Learning Objective 4*) **10–15 min.**

Tri State Supply, Inc., has the following stockholders' equity:

Tri State Supply, Inc. Stockholders' Equity	
Paid-in Capital:	
Preferred Stock, 8%, $12 par, 100,000 shares authorized, 25,000 shares issued and outstanding	$ 300,000
Common Stock, $1.00 par, 500,000 shares authorized, 280,000 shares issued and outstanding	280,000
Paid-in Capital in Excess of Par-Common	410,000
Total Paid-in Capital	990,000
Retained Earnings	216,000
Total Stockholders' Equity	$1,206,000

Requirement

1. Assume the preferred stock is cumulative. Compute the amount of dividends to preferred and common shareholders for 2014 and 2015 if total dividends are $18,600 in 2014 and $42,800 in 2015.

E10-36B. Accounting for cash dividends (*Learning Objective 4*) **10–15 min.**

The following elements of stockholders' equity are adapted from the balance sheet of Sandler Corporation.

Stockholders' Equity	$ Thousands
Preferred Stock, cumulative, $2 par (Note 7), 65,000 shares issued and outstanding	$130
Common Stock, $0.10 par, 8,750,000 shares issued and outstanding	875

Note 7. Preferred Stock: Designated annual cash dividend per share, $0.75.

Sandler Corporation paid no preferred dividends in 2014, but paid the designated amount of cash dividends per share to preferred shareholders in all prior years.

Requirement

1. Compute the dividends to preferred and common shareholders for 2015 if total dividends are $175,000.

E10-37B. Accounting for stock dividends (*Learning Objectives 5 & 7*) **10–15 min.**

The stockholders' equity for Shamrock, Inc., on December 31, 2013, follows:

Stockholders' Equity	
Paid-in Capital:	
Common Stock, $10 par, 900,000 shares authorized,	
25,000 issued and outstanding	$250,000
Paid-in Capital in Excess of Par	160,000
Total Paid-in Capital	410,000
Retained Earnings	175,000
Total Stockholders' Equity	$585,000

On August 31, 2014, the market price of Shamrock, Inc.'s common stock was $21 per share and the company distributed a 15% stock dividend.

Requirements

1. Journalize the declaration and distribution of the stock dividend.

2. Prepare the stockholders' equity section of the balance sheet after the stock dividend.

E10-38B. Accounting for cash and stock dividends (*Learning Objectives 4 & 5*) **10–15 min.**

Inland Machine Tool, Inc., is authorized to issue 700,000 shares of $5 par common stock. The company issued 71,000 shares at $5 per share, and all 71,000 shares are outstanding. When the market price of common stock was $9 per share, Inland Machine Tool, Inc., declared and distributed a 15% stock dividend. Later, Inland Machine Tool, Inc., declared and paid a $0.40 per share cash dividend.

Requirements

1. Journalize the declaration and distribution of the stock dividend.

2. Journalize the declaration and the payment of the cash dividend.

E10-39B. Accounting for stock splits (*Learning Objectives 5 & 7*) **10–15 min.**

Schmitz Construction, Inc., had the following stockholders' equity at January 31:

Stockholders' Equity	
Paid-in Capital:	
Common Stock, $2 par, 800,000 shares authorized,	
60,000 shares issued and outstanding	$120,000
Paid-in Capital in Excess of Par	48,000
Total Paid-in Capital	$168,000
Retained Earnings	214,000
Total Stockholders' Equity	$382,000

On February 28, Schmitz Construction, Inc., split its common stock 4-for-1.

Requirements

1. Make any necessary entry to record the stock split.

2. Prepare the stockholders' equity section of the balance sheet immediately after the split.

E10-40B. Accounting for stock issuance, splits, and treasury stock (*Learning Objectives 3, 5, & 6*) **20–25 min.**

Consider each of the following transactions separately from every other transaction:

a. Issuance of 58,000 shares of $14 par common at $22.

b. Purchase of 1,100 shares of treasury stock (par value at $0.50) at $6 per share.

c. Issuance of a 10% stock dividend. Before the dividend, 550,000 shares of $1 par common stock were outstanding; market value was $3 at the time of the dividend.

d. Sale of 300 shares of $1 par treasury stock for $7 per share. Cost of the treasury stock was $4 per share.

e. Split stocks 4-for-1. Prior to the split, 90,000 shares of $3 par common stock were outstanding.

Requirement

1. Identify whether each transaction increased, decreased, or did not change total stockholders' equity.

E10-41B. Accounting for treasury stock (*Learning Objectives 3 & 6*) **20–25 min.**

Journalize the following transactions of Sinclair Sports, Inc., a chain of sports stores:

Mar 4	Issued 20,000 shares of no-par common stock at $10 per share.
May 22	Purchased 1,500 shares of treasury stock at $6 per share.
Sep 22	Sold 600 shares of treasury stock at $9 per share.

E10-42B. Accounting for treasury stock (*Learning Objectives 6 & 7*) **20–25 min.**

Frontier, Inc., had the following stockholders' equity on November 30:

Stockholders' Equity	
Paid-in Capital:	
Common Stock, $4 par, 500,000 shares authorized,	
90,000 shares issued and outstanding	$ 360,000
Paid-in Capital in Excess of Par	450,000
Total Paid-in Capital	810,000
Retained Earnings	550,000
Total Stockholders' Equity	$1,360,000

On December 10, Frontier purchased 2,000 shares of treasury stock at $13 per share.

Requirements

1. Journalize the purchase of the treasury stock.

2. Prepare the stockholders' equity section of the balance sheet at December 31.

E10-43B. Balance sheet disclosure of stockholders' equity (*Learning Objective 7*) 10–15 min.

Mackay Manufacturing, Co., has the following selected account balances at January 31, 2014.

Common Stock, no par with $8 stated value, 50,000 shares authorized, issued, and outstanding	$400,000	Inventory	$ 16,000
		Machinery and Equipment	121,000
		Preferred Stock, 7%, $12 par, 20,000 shares authorized, 10,000 shares issued and outstanding	120,000
Accumulated Depreciation, Machinery and Equipment...	57,000		
Retained Earnings	123,000	Paid-in Capital in Excess of Stated Value—Common.....	65,000
		Cost of Goods Sold	82,000

Requirement

1. Prepare the stockholders' equity section of the company's balance sheet.

E10-44B. Accounting for various stockholders' equity transactions (*Learning Objective 7*) 20–25 min.

At December 31, 2013, Fernandes, Corp., reported the following stockholders' equity.

Paid-in Capital:	
Common Stock, $6 par, 200,000 shares authorized, 140,000 shares issued	$ 840,000
Additional Paid-in Capital	145,000
Total Paid-in Capital	985,000
Retained Earnings	670,000
Subtotal	1,655,000
Less: Treasury stock, 2,200 shares at cost	(63,800)
Total Stockholders' Equity	$1,591,200

During 2014, Fernandes completed these transactions and events in this order:

a. Sold 500 shares of treasury stock for $35 per share; the cost of these shares was $29 per share.

b. Issued 1,100 shares of common stock at $20 per share.

c. Net income for the year was $203,000.

d. Declared and paid cash dividends of $40,000.

Requirement

1. Prepare Fernandes's statement of stockholders' equity for the year ended December 31, 2014.

E10-45B. Accounting for various stockholders' equity transactions (*Learning Objectives 3, 5, & 7*) 20–25 min.

Global Communications, Inc., began 2014 with 3 million shares of $2 par common stock issued and outstanding. Beginning Paid-in Capital in Excess of Par was $9.7 million, and Retained Earnings was $8 million. In June 2014, Global Communications, Inc., issued 120,000 shares of stock at $12 per share. In October, when the stock's market price was $14 per share, the board of directors distributed a 5% stock dividend.

Requirements

1. Make the journal entries for the issuance of stock for cash and for the declaration and distribution of the 5% stock dividend.

2. Prepare the company's statement of stockholders' equity for the year ended December 31, 2014. Ignore net income.

E10-46B. Calculating return on equity (*Learning Objective 8*) 10–15 min.

Assume that Hanson Industrial Supply, Inc., has the following data:

Net income for 2014	$ 251,875
Preferred dividends for 2014	$ 5,875
Total stockholders' equity, 12/31/2014..	$1,750,000
Total stockholders' equity, 12/31/2013..	$1,500,000
Common stockholders' equity, 12/31/2014	$1,590,000
Common stockholders' equity, 12/31/2013	$1,410,000

Requirements

1. Calculate Hanson Industrial Supply's return on equity for 2014.

2. Comment on Hanson Industrial Supply's performance during 2014.

MyAccountingLab

Problems (Group A)

P10-47A. Stock issuance (*Learning Objectives 3 & 7*) 10–15 min.

Partners Pat and Quincy wish to avoid the unlimited personal liability of the partnership form of business, so they are incorporating the company as P & Q Services, Inc. The charter from the state of Texas authorizes the corporation to issue 25,000 shares of 5%, $100 par preferred stock and 300,000 shares of no-par common stock. In its first month, P & Q Services, Inc., completed the following transactions:

Jan	3	Issued 6,100 shares of common stock to Pat and 3,600 shares to Quincy, both for cash of $5 per share.
	12	Issued 900 shares of preferred stock to acquire a patent with a market value of $90,000.
	22	Issued 1,400 shares of common stock to other investors for $5 cash per share.

Requirements

1. Record the transactions in the journal.

2. Prepare the stockholders' equity section of the P & Q Services, Inc.'s balance sheet at December 31. The ending balance of Retained Earnings is $59,000.

P10-48A. Analyzing stockholders' equity (*Learning Objectives 2, 3, 4, & 7*) 20–25 min.

Comstock Corporation was organized in 2013. At December 31, 2013, Comstock Corporation's balance sheet reported the following stockholders' equity:

Stockholders' Equity	
Paid-in Capital:	
Preferred Stock, 5%, $8 par, 30,000 shares authorized, none issued	$ 0
Common Stock, $2 par, 120,000 shares authorized, 12,000 shares issued and outstanding	24,000
Paid-in Capital in Excess of Par—Common	51,000
Total Paid-in Capital	$75,000
Retained Earnings (deficit)	(4,500)
Total Stockholders' Equity	$70,500

Requirements

Answer the following questions and make journal entries as needed:

1. What does the 5% mean for the preferred stock? After Comstock Corporation issues preferred stock, how much in annual cash dividends would Comstock Corporation expect to pay on 5,000 shares?

2. At what average price per share did Comstock Corporation issue the common stock during 2013?

3. Were first-year operations profitable? Give your reason.

4. During 2014, the company completed the following selected transactions. Journalize each transaction. Explanations are not required.
   a. Issued for cash 3,000 shares of preferred stock at par value.
   b. Issued for cash 2,600 shares of common stock at a price of $8.50 per share.

5. Prepare the stockholders' equity section of the Comstock Corporation balance sheet at December 31, 2014. Assume net income for the year is $73,000.

P10-49A. Analyzing stockholders' equity (*Learning Objectives 2, 3, & 4*) 20–25 min.

Malton Hotel, Inc., included the following stockholders' equity on its year-end balance sheet at December 31, 2014, with all dollar amounts, except par value per share, adapted and in millions:

Stockholders' Equity	$ Millions
Paid-in Capital:	
Preferred Stock, 8% cumulative, par value $10 per share;	$ 62
50,000,000 shares authorized, 6,200,000 shares issued and outstanding	
Common Stock, par value $3 per share; 750,000,000 shares	
authorized, 239,000,000 shares issued and outstanding	717
Paid-in Capital in Excess of Par—Common	68
Total Paid-in Capital	$ 847
Retained Earnings	302
Total Stockholders' Equity	$1,149

Requirements

1. Identify the different issues of stock that Malton Hotel, Inc., has outstanding.

2. Give the two entries to record issuance of the Malton Hotel, Inc.'s stock. Assume that all the stock was issued for cash. Explanations are not required.

3. Assume that preferred dividends are in arrears for 2013 and 2014. Record the declaration of a $40 million cash dividend on December 30, 2015. Assume no change in the preferred stock account in 2015. Use separate Dividends Payable accounts for preferred and common stock. Round to the nearest $1 million. An explanation is not required.

P10-50A. Accounting for cash dividends (*Learning Objective 4*) 15–20 min.

Conway Consulting, Inc., has 10,000 shares of $4.50, no-par preferred stock and 30,000 shares of no-par common stock outstanding for 2012–2014. Conway Consulting, Inc., declared and paid the following dividends during a three-year period: 2012, $27,000; 2013, $86,000; and 2014, $116,000.

Requirements

1. Compute the total dividends to preferred stockholders and to common stockholders for each of the three years if:
   a. preferred is noncumulative.
   b. preferred is cumulative.

2. For case 1(b), journalize the declaration of the 2014 dividends on December 28, 2014, and the payment of the dividends on January 17, 2015. Use separate Dividends Payable accounts for preferred and common stock.

P10-51A. Accounting for various stockholders' equity transactions (*Learning Objectives 4, 5, & 6*) 20–25 min.

Littleton Corporation completed the following selected transactions during 2014:

Jan 6	Declared a cash dividend on the 12,000 shares of $2.25, no-par preferred stock outstanding. Declared a $0.10 per share dividend on the 9,000 shares of common stock outstanding. The date of record is January 17, and the payment date is January 20.
Jan 20	Paid the cash dividends.
Mar 21	Split common stock 2-for-1 by calling in the 9,000 shares of $10 par common stock and issuing new stock in its place.
Apr 18	Declared and distributed a 15% stock dividend on the common stock. The market value of the common stock was $34 per share.
Jun 18	Purchased 1,000 shares of treasury common stock at $30 per share.
Dec 22	Sold 500 shares of treasury common stock for $33 per share.

Requirement

1. Record the transactions in the journal.

P10-52A. Accounting for various stockholders' equity transactions (*Learning Objectives 5, 6, & 7*) 20–25 min.

The balance sheet of Britton, Inc., at December 31, 2013, reported 900,000 shares of $2 par common stock authorized with 180,000 shares issued and outstanding. Paid-in Capital in Excess of Par had a balance of $265,000. Retained Earnings had a balance of $226,000. During 2014, the company completed the following selected transactions:

Feb 15	Purchased 8,000 shares of treasury stock at $6 per share.
Mar 8	Sold 2,000 shares of treasury stock for $13 per share.
Sep 28	Declared and distributed a 10% stock dividend on the 174,000 shares of *outstanding* common stock. The market value of Britton's common stock was $12 per share.

Requirements

1. Record the transactions in the journal. Explanations are not required.

2. Prepare the stockholders' equity section of the balance sheet at December 31, 2014, assuming the company earned $84,000 of net income during the year.

P10-53A. Analyzing stockholders' equity (*Learning Objective 7*) 15–20 min.

Market Analysts, Inc., reported the following statement of stockholders' equity for the year ended September 30, 2014:

Market Analysts, Inc.
Statement of Stockholders' Equity
Year Ended September 30, 2014

(Dollar amounts in thousands)	COMMON STOCK	ADDITIONAL PAID-IN CAPITAL	RETAINED EARNINGS	TREASURY STOCK	TOTAL
Balance, September 30, 2013	$171	$2,118	$1,704	$(20)	$3,973
Net Income			519		519
Cash Dividends			(117)		(117)
Issuance of Stock (4,000 shares)	15	51			66
Stock Dividend	24	93	(117)		0
Sale of Treasury Stock		7		9	16
Balance, September 30, 2014	$210	$2,269	$1,989	$(11)	$4,457

Requirements

1. What is the par value of the company's common stock?
2. At what price per share did the company issue its common stock during the year?
3. What was the cost of treasury stock sold during the year? What was the selling price of the treasury stock sold? What was the increase in total stockholders' equity from selling the treasury stock?
4. What overall effect did the stock dividend have on total stockholders' equity?

Quick solution:

1. $3.75 per share; 2. $16.50 per share; 3. Selling price of treasury stock = $16,000; 4. No effect

Problems (Group B)

P10-54B. Stock issuance (*Learning Objectives 3 & 7*) 10–15 min.

Partners Rodriguez and Salizar wish to avoid the unlimited personal liability of the partnership form of business, so they are incorporating the company as R & S Services, Inc. The charter from the state of Texas authorizes the corporation to issue 100,000 shares of 6%, $80 par preferred stock and 500,000 shares of no-par common stock. In its first month, R & S Services, Inc., completed the following transactions:

Jan	3	Issued 4,800 shares of common stock to Rodriguez and 3,600 shares to Salizar, both for cash of $12 per share.
	12	Issued 1,200 shares of preferred stock to acquire a patent with a market value of $96,000.
	22	Issued 1,500 shares of common stock to other investors for $14 cash per share.

Requirements

1. Record the transactions in the journal.
2. Prepare the stockholders' equity section of the R & S Services, Inc.'s balance sheet at December 31. The ending balance of Retained Earnings is $103,000.

P10-55B. Analyzing stockholders' equity (*Learning Objectives 2, 3, 4, & 7*)
20–25 min.

Mackay, Inc., was organized in 2013. At December 31, 2013, Mackay, Inc.'s balance sheet reported the following stockholders' equity:

Stockholders' Equity	
Paid-in Capital:	
Preferred Stock, 6%, $8 par, 70,000 shares authorized,	
none issued	$ 0
Common Stock, $1 par, 140,000 shares authorized,	
12,000 shares issued and outstanding	12,000
Paid-in Capital in Excess of Par	33,000
Total Paid-in Capital	$45,000
Retained Earnings (deficit)	(4,000)
Total Stockholders' Equity	$41,000

Requirements

Answer the following questions and make journal entries as needed:

1. What does the 6% mean for the preferred stock? After Mackay, Inc., issues preferred stock, how much in annual cash dividends would Mackay, Inc., expect to pay on 1,500 shares?

2. At what average price per share did Mackay, Inc., issue the common stock during 2013?

3. Were the first-year operations profitable? Give your reasons.

4. During 2014, the company completed the following selected transactions. Journalize each transaction. Explanations are not required.
   a. Issued for cash 5,000 shares of preferred stock at par value.
   b. Issued for cash 2,000 shares of common stock at a price of $7 per share.

5. Prepare the stockholders' equity section of the Mackay, Inc.'s balance sheet at December 31, 2014. Assume net income for the year was $75,000.

this year. You're certain that the important stockholders would understand if the corporation had to forego paying a dividend this year. Or would they? You decide to have a meeting with the controller to discuss the situation.

Requirement

1. What would be the most viable suggestion that your controller might make to you as an alternative to paying out a cash dividend this year? What are the implications of your recommendation?

Written Communication

You just got off the telephone with one of your clients who wants to start a new business as a corporation. His question to you was concerning the different types of stock that can be issued to the potential stockholders of this new corporation. You had explained it to him during the telephone call, but you thought you should follow up your conversation with a letter.

Requirement

1. Prepare a letter to your client explaining the different types or classes of stock that can be issued and the characteristics of each different type.

Self Check Answers
1. d 2. c 3. b 4. c 5. c 6. c 7. b 8. d 9. c 10. b 11. c 12. c

The Statement of Cash Flows

Business, Accounting, and You

Close your eyes and imagine that you are the head accountant at Delta Airlines. Head accountants are often called controllers. As Delta Airlines' controller, what is your role in the company? Your job is to provide understandable, relevant, and reliable information to decision makers. Many of those decisions deal with cash. Delta Airlines needs cash for a lot of things, including operating, investing in assets, and paying debts.

Decisions about cash are very important. As noted in Chapter 7, a business must have enough cash to operate and pay its bills. But where does a business get cash, and how does it use cash? How does cash flow in and out of a business like Delta Airlines? You cannot tell by looking at the balance sheet. The balance sheet only tells how much cash a business has at a point in time. You cannot tell by looking at the income statement. Income statements are based on accrual accounting, where

Learning Objectives

1 Identify the purposes and importance of the statement of cash flows

2 Differentiate between cash flows from operating, investing, and financing activities

3 Prepare the statement of cash flows using the indirect method

4 Prepare the statement of cash flows using the direct method

5 Evaluate a company's performance with respect to cash

revenues and expenses are recognized when they occur and not when the cash is received or paid. So accountants need to provide information in addition to a balance sheet and an income statement. They need to create a statement that reports where and when the business gets and uses cash during a period of time.

Where does a business get and use cash? Well, where do you get and use cash? Everyone, including you and Delta Airlines, gets cash and uses cash from one of three activities: operating, investing, and financing.

Operating activities Day-to-day activities that create revenues or expenses.

First, let's look at your **operating activities**. Operating activities relate to the receipt and payment of cash for the revenues and expenses reported in the income statement. You go to work. You earn a salary. But you also have expenses. Let's say you earn $500 for working a week. However, you have to wait an additional week before being paid. After finishing your work, you have a $500 receivable from your employer that will be paid in one week's time. But you also have to pay for the gas you used to go to work. For the days you worked, you charged $100 on your credit card for gas. Your charge would be considered a payable. You'll pay the $100 payable when you get your credit card bill at the end of the month. At the end of the week of work, your accrued net income is $400, $500 in revenue less $100 in expenses. However, you will not have any "cash flows" until you receive your paycheck and pay your credit card bill. Your cash flows occurred after the recognition of your net income of $400.

Investing activities Activities that increase or decrease long-term assets.

Second, we'll look at **investing activities**. Investing activities relate to the payment and receipt of cash to buy and sell long-term assets such as buildings and equipment. When you buy a car, you pay cash. When you sell a car, you receive cash. Buying and selling assets that last more than one year are investing activities.

Financing activities Activities related to the issuance of, and repayment of, long-term debt, the issuance of stock, and the payment of dividends.

Third, let's look at **financing activities**. Financing activities relate to the receipt and payment of cash for: (1) long-term liabilities and (2) stockholders' equity. When a business borrows money, it receives cash. When a business repays the liability, it uses cash. When a business sells stock, it receives cash. When the business pays a dividend, it uses cash.

An example of a financing activity is borrowing cash from a bank and agreeing to make loan payments for three years. This is a financing activity. You receive cash when you borrow the money and use cash when you repay the loan.

Statement of cash flows A financial statement that shows all of the sources and all of the uses of cash for an accounting period; also called the **cash flow statement**.

Now look at business. Accountants at Delta Airlines and other businesses need to report how much cash their businesses have. The amount of cash they have is reported on their balance sheet. But they also need to report how cash changed during a period of time. Accountants need to report the activities of a business that provide and use cash and whether these activities are operating, investing, or financing activities. Accountants do this with the **statement of cash flows**.

 # Real World Accounting Video

In the Real World Accounting Video, Peter Kranes, managing director of Fishs Eddy, talks about managing a growing business. Listen to what Peter is saying. Think about cash coming in and going out of the business. Think about managing so there is always enough cash to pay the bills and meet other needs.

What Is the Statement of Cash Flows?

Identify the purposes and importance of the statement of cash flows

Cash is often considered to be the "lifeblood" of a business. As we have seen throughout this book, the balance sheet reports the amount of cash a business has at the end of the accounting period. Remember from Chapter 7, this cash balance typically includes cash as well as cash equivalents. When a balance sheet reports two consecutive years of data, readers of the information can see that cash increased or decreased from one point in time to another. However, a comparative balance sheet does not show *why* cash increased or decreased. Therefore, a statement of cash flows, or a **cash flow statement,** is usually prepared to show why the amount of cash changed during the year. The statement of cash flows reports:

- All sources of cash during the period. In other words, it shows where a company got its cash during the year from operating, investing, and financing activities.
- All uses of cash during the period. In other words, it shows where a company spent its cash during the year on operating, investing, and financing activities.
- How the sources and uses of cash net to equal the change in the amount of cash a business holds between the beginning of the period and the end of the period.

Accounting in Your World

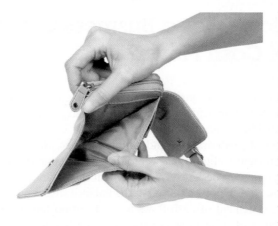

Think about going to college. It's a major step that requires hard work and sacrifice. However, it also takes money to pay for tuition, textbooks, and other items. Going to school requires a big cash outflow. Now think about where you'll get the cash to pay for all these items. You begin to think of the past, the present, and the future. Do you already have cash that you can use to pay the bills? Can you go to work, earn a salary, and use your paycheck to pay the bills? Can you borrow the money to pay the bills? Can you sell an asset, such as your car or entertainment system, to pay the bills? What are you doing? You are thinking about cash flow.

Most people look at cash flow by looking at the cash in their purse or wallet, checking accounts, or saving accounts. They methodically take the beginning balance, add the deposits, and subtract the withdrawals, which results in the ending balance. They then analyze the deposits and withdrawals, separating them into categories such as paycheck and living expenses, big purchases, like cars, and borrowing and repaying debt.

Businesses are like you; they worry about cash flow. Businesses need a statement that explains where they got and used cash. That statement is the statement of cash flows. The statement of cash flows shows:

1. The beginning cash balance,

2. The sources of cash,

3. The uses of cash, and

4. How these add up and become the ending cash balance.

In showing the sources and uses of cash, the statement of cash flows categorizes the sources and uses into operating, investing, and financing activities.

Stop and Think...

Bob Hanson, the CEO of Allied Industrial Supply, was concerned. He was looking over the Income Statement for the second quarter of the year and it showed that Allied Industrial Supply had net income of $84,000. He thought to himself: "How can this be? There isn't any money in the bank to pay bills with." What are some things that could cause Allied Industrial Supply to be low on cash even though it earned $84,000 for the quarter?

Answer

It is important to remember that net income for most companies is calculated on the accrual basis instead of the cash basis, which means that the amount of net income for the period does not represent cash flow. There are many things that could cause Allied Industrial Supply to be low on cash even though it had $84,000 of net income for the quarter. For example, it could have had a significant amount of sales on account that have not yet been collected. This would increase the net income during the period without providing any cash. Allied Industrial Supply could have made a cash purchase of a substantial amount of inventory at the end of the quarter. This would reduce cash but have no effect on net income until the inventory is sold. Or, Allied Industrial Supply could have repaid a significant amount of the principal portion of debt during the period. Repaying principal on debt uses cash but does not affect the net income for the period (only the payment of interest affects net income).

How Does a Business Create a Statement of Cash Flows?

2 Differentiate between cash flows from operating, investing, and financing activities

Individuals and businesses need to understand cash flow. The method businesses use to create a statement of cash flows is different from the method used by individuals. Unlike individuals, businesses do not go to their cash account and look at the beginning balance, deposits, withdrawals, and ending balance. Businesses use the balance sheet and income statement to figure out where their cash came from and went. A business's statement of cash flows is designed to supplement the balance sheet and income statement and to show how transactions reported in the balance sheet and income statement affect cash. As such, the statement of cash flows is a very important statement in giving the user a complete picture of a business's operations. The balance sheet and income statement use accrual accounting to reflect the business's assets, liabilities, stockholders' equity, revenue, and expenses. The balance sheet and income statement reflect transactions when they occur, even though it may take time before cash is affected. The cash flow statement takes the

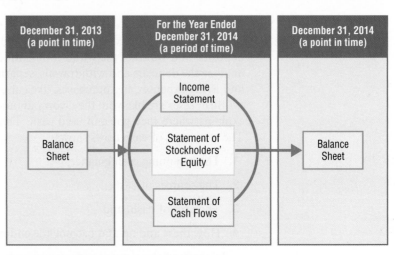

Exhibit 11-1 ▲

information on the balance sheet and income statement and shows how these transactions affect or do not affect cash. In essence, the cash flow statement is the communicating link between the accrual-based balance sheet and income statement and the cash reported on the balance sheet. **Exhibit 11-1** illustrates the relationships between the balance sheet, the income statement, the statement of stockholders' equity, and the statement of cash flows.

The Logic of How the Statement of Cash Flows Is Prepared

Unlike the balance sheet and income statement, the statement of cash flows does not have any unique accounts. It uses the accounts in the balance sheet and income statement to explain the change in cash over a period of time.

Now, consider these points:

- Balance sheets balance.
- If you take a business's balance sheet at the beginning of a period and its balance sheet at the end of that period, you can compute the change in each account. Each change is the net of all the transactions that occurred in that account during that period of time.
- Given the beginning and ending balance sheets balance, the net change in the accounts must balance, just as with the accounting equation. The changes in the assets must equal the changes in the liabilities plus the changes in the stockholders' equity.
- Take the change in the cash account out of the change in assets. What happens? No longer does the change in assets equal the change in liabilities plus the change in stockholders' equity. This imbalance is equal to the change in cash.

A business prepares a statement of cash flows by analyzing the changes in the balance sheet accounts. The impact of these changes is reflected in the operating, investing, and financing sections of the statement of cash flows. We will explore the methods of preparation in more detail in the next section.

Sources and Uses of Cash: Categorizing Changes as Operating, Investing, or Financing

What makes cash go up, and what makes cash go down? What are the sources of cash and uses of cash?

Sources of Cash

Let's look first at the *sources* of cash. A business gets cash from one of the following three activities:

- Operating the business
- Selling long-term assets for cash
- Long-term borrowing of cash or having stockholders invest cash in the business

When a business provides goods or services, it ultimately receives cash from its customers. If a business sells an asset such as a building, it typically receives cash. If a business borrows money, it receives cash. If a business issues stock to its stockholders, it receives cash.

Uses of Cash

Now let's look at how a business *uses* cash. A business uses cash in one of the following three activities:

- Operating the business
- Buying long-term assets with cash
- Repaying long-term loans with cash, paying cash dividends, or repurchasing its stock with cash

A business incurs expenses in order to provide goods or services. Those expenses must ultimately be paid for with cash. If a business buys an asset such as a building, it typically pays cash for part, or all, of the purchase. If a business repays a loan, it pays cash. If a business pays a cash dividend or repurchases its stock (treasury stock), it pays cash.

The statement of cash flows categorizes sources and uses of cash as operating, investing, and financing activities. Exhibit 11-2 shows the various parts of the balance sheet that the operating, investing, and financing cash flows affect. Operating cash flows affect the current asset and current liability accounts. Operating cash flows also affect stockholders' equity through net income. Investing cash flows affect the long-term assets. Financing cash flows affect long-term liabilities and stockholders' equity.

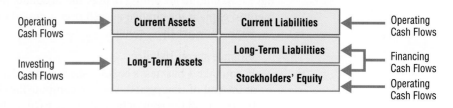

Exhibit 11-2 ▲

Operating Activities

The net cash flow from operating activities is equal to cash basis net income or loss. Cash basis net income or loss is computed as follows:

- Accrual basis net income or loss *(from the income statement)*.
- Plus noncash expenses and losses *(from the income statement)*.
- Minus noncash revenues and gains *(from the income statement)*.
- Plus decreases in noncash current assets *(from the balance sheet)*.
- Minus increases in noncash current assets *(from the balance sheet)*.
- Plus increases in current liabilities *(from the balance sheet)*.
- Minus decreases in current liabilities *(from the balance sheet)*.

If the net result is positive, operating activities are a source of cash. If the net result is negative, operating activities are a use of cash. Look at Exhibit 11-2 and visualize what are operating activities. What are you doing when you adjust net income for noncash items and changes in current assets and liabilities? You are converting accrual-based net income to cash-based net income. An example is adjusting net income for the change in Accounts Receivable. Adding or subtracting the change in Accounts Receivable recognizes that all revenue is not cash revenue. Another example is Accounts Payable. Adding or subtracting the change in Accounts Payable recognizes that all expenses are not cash expenses. Cast your mind back to the $500 you were owed from work. You had an Accounts Receivable. Now also think about the $100 you owed for gas. You also had an Accounts Payable. Although you earned $400 net income ($500 − $100), you had zero operating cash flows until you received the cash from your employer ($500) and paid the credit card bill ($100).

Investing Activities

Investing activities occur when a business buys and sells long-term assets such as buildings, equipment, intangible assets, and long-term receivables. Cash flows from investing activities are computed as follows:

- Increase or decrease in long-term assets *(from the balance sheet)*.
- Plus or minus noncash transactions that affect long-term assets *(from the income statement and balance sheet)*.

If the net result is positive, investing activities are a use of cash. If the net result is negative, investing activities are a source of cash. Look at Exhibit 11-2 and visualize what are investing activities. Think about trading in your old car for a new car. You own a car that has a book value of $2,000. You go to the car dealer who offers to buy your car for

$2,000 if you buy a new car for $10,000. You agree. You give the car dealer your old car and $8,000 in cash. The dealer gives you a new car worth $10,000. Your long-term assets have increased by $8,000 and you used $8,000 of cash.

Financing Activities

Cash flows from financing activities occur when a business borrows money, repays loans, sells stock, repurchases stock (treasury stock), or pays dividends. Cash flows from financing activities are computed as:

- Increase or decrease in long-term liabilities *(from the balance sheet)*.
- Plus the increase in common and preferred stock accounts when common or preferred stock is issued for cash *(from the balance sheet)*.
- Minus the increase in treasury stock when the company repurchases its stock for cash *(from the balance sheet)*.
- Minus the decrease in retained earnings due to paying cash dividends *(from the balance sheet)*.

If the net result is positive, financing activities are a source of cash. If the net result is negative, financing activities are a use of cash. Look at Exhibit 11-2 and visualize what are financing activities. Think about the cash involved when borrowing and repaying money, selling stock, and paying dividends.

Statement of Cash Flows: Two Formats

Indirect method Format of the operating activities section of the statement of cash flows; it starts with net income and reconciles to net cash provided by operating activities.

Direct method Format of the operating activities section of the statement of cash flows; it lists the cash receipts and cash payments resulting from a company's day-to-day operations.

A business can use two formats to create the statement of cash flows, the indirect and direct methods. Investing and financing activities are formatted the same in both the indirect and direct methods. The difference between the indirect and direct methods is the format of operating activities. Both the indirect and direct methods report the same net cash flow from operations, but the format is different.

- The **indirect method** starts with net income and adjusts it to net cash provided by operating activities. Most businesses use the indirect method because the user can more easily see how the income statement ties to the balance sheet and the change in cash.
- The **direct method** shows all cash receipts and all cash payments from operating activities. The direct method restates each (accrual-based) item on the income statement to a cash basis.

Decision Guidelines

Decision	Guideline	Analyze
Is it important where a business gets and how it spends its cash?	Understanding where a business gets and how it spends its cash can be important in determining the financial health of a company. Look at the statement of cash flows to determine where a business got (sources) and spent (used) its cash during the period.	The statement of cash flows is divided into three areas: Operating activities—shows the cash flow from business operations. Investing activities—shows the cash flow from buying and selling long-term assets. Financing activities—shows the cash flow from borrowing and repaying long-term debt, as well as from stockholders' equity transactions. For a business to remain successful, operating activities must be the main source of its cash over the long run.

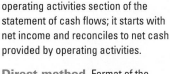

How Is the Statement of Cash Flows Prepared Using the Indirect Method?

Prepare the statement of cash flows using the indirect method

Most businesses prefer to use the indirect method because its format makes it easier to reconcile net income to the net cash flow from operating activities for the period. In order to prepare the statement of cash flows, you will need to have the other financial statements, as well as some supplemental information about the company's operations. The format for the indirect method statement of cash flows for Mackay Industries is presented in Exhibit 11-3.

Mackay Industries, Inc.
Statement of Cash Flows
Year Ended December 31, 2014

Cash flows from operating activities:
  Net Income
  Adjustments to reconcile net income to net cash
    provided by operating activities:
      + Depreciation / amortization expense
      + Loss on sale of long-term assets
      − Gain on sale of long-term assets
      − Increases in current assets other than cash
      + Decreases in current assets other than cash
      + Increases in current liabilities
      − Decreases in current liabilities
  Net cash provided by (used for) operating activities
± **Cash flows from investing activities:**
  + Cash receipts from sales of long-term assets
    (investments, land, building, equipment, and so on)
  − Purchases of long-term assets
  Net cash provided by (used for) investing activities
± **Cash flows from financing activities:**
  + Cash receipts from issuance of stock
  + Sale of treasury stock
  − Purchase of treasury stock
  + Cash receipts from issuance of notes or bonds
    payable (borrowing)
  − Payment of notes or bonds payable
  − Payment of dividends
  Net cash provided by (used for) financing activities
= **Net increase (decrease) in cash during the year**
  + Cash at December 31, 2013
  = Cash at December 31, 2014

Exhibit 11-3 ▲

Mackay Industries' financial statements are presented in Exhibit 11-4.

Exhibit 11-4 ▲

Mackay Industries, Inc.
Income Statement
Year Ended December 31, 2014

	Revenue:		
	Sales Revenue	$268,000	
	Interest Revenue	13,000	
	Dividend Revenue	5,000	
	Total Revenues		$286,000
	Expenses:		
	Cost of Goods Sold	$137,000	
	Salaries Expense	48,000	
B	Depreciation Expense	18,000	
	Other Operating Expense	12,000	
	Interest Expense	11,000	
	Income Tax Expense	9,000	
C	Loss on Sale of Fixed Assets	3,000	
	Total Expenses		238,000
A	Net Income		$ 48,000

Mackay Industries, Inc.
Statement of Retained Earnings
Year Ended December 31, 2014

	Retained Earnings, December 31, 2013	$121,000
	Add: Net Income for the Year	48,000
	Subtotal	169,000
M	Less: Dividends	23,000
	Retained Earnings, December 31, 2014	$146,000

Mackay Industries, Inc.
Balance Sheet
December 31, 2013 and 2014

			2014	2013	INCREASE (DECREASE)
	ASSETS				
	Current:				
		Cash	$ 18,000	$ 11,000	$ 7,000
D		Accounts Receivable	76,000	93,000	(17,000)
E		Inventory	132,000	124,000	8,000
		Total Current Assets	226,000	228,000	(2,000)
H/I	Fixed Assets, Net		385,000	315,000	70,000
	Total Assets		$611,000	$543,000	$ 68,000
	LIABILITIES				
	Current:				
F		Accounts Payable	$ 84,000	$ 96,000	$(12,000)
G		Accrued Liabilities	12,000	8,000	4,000
		Total Current Liabilities	96,000	104,000	(8,000)
J/K	Long-Term Notes Payable		147,000	98,000	49,000
		Total Liabilities	243,000	202,000	41,000
	STOCKHOLDERS' EQUITY				
L	Common Stock		240,000	220,000	20,000
A/M	Retained Earnings		146,000	121,000	25,000
N	Less: Treasury Stock		(18,000)	0	(18,000)
		Total Stockholders' Equity	368,000	341,000	27,000
	Total Liabilities and Stockholders' Equity		$611,000	$543,000	$ 68,000

Using these financial statements, let's prepare Mackay Industries' statement of cash flows one section at a time. To make things easier to follow, each item on the statement of cash flows has been cross-referenced to the financial statements by a letter.

Cash Flows from Operating Activities

The operating activities section of Mackay Industries' statement of cash flows would look like this:

		Cash flows from operating activities:		
A		Net Income		$48,000
		Adjustments to reconcile net income to net cash		
		provided by operating activities:		
B		Depreciation Expense	$ 18,000	
C		Loss on sale of fixed assets	3,000	
D		Decrease in Accounts Receivable	17,000	
E		Increase in Inventory	(8,000)	
F		Decrease in Accounts Payable	(12,000)	
G		Increase in Accrued Liabilities	4,000	22,000
		Net cash provided by operating activities		70,000

Operating cash flows begin with net income, taken from the income statement.

A Net Income

The statement of cash flows—indirect method—begins with net income because revenues and expenses, which affect net income, produce cash receipts and cash payments. Revenues bring in cash receipts, and expenses must be paid. But net income is accrual based, and the accrual basis of revenues and expenses don't always equal the cash flows (cash basis net income). For example, sales *on account* are revenues that increase net income, but the company hasn't yet collected cash from those sales. Accrued expenses decrease your net income, but you haven't paid cash *if the expenses are accrued.*

To go from net income to net cash flow from operating activities, we must make some adjustments to Net Income on the statement of cash flows. These additions and subtractions follow net income and are labeled "Adjustments to reconcile net income to net cash provided by operating activities."

B Depreciation, Depletion, and Amortization Expenses

These expenses are added back to net income to reconcile it to net cash flow from operations. Let's see why. Depreciation expense is recorded as:

DATE	ACCOUNTS	POST REF.	DR.	CR.
	Depreciation Expense		18,000	
	Accumulated Depreciation			18,000

You can see that depreciation expense does not affect cash because there's no Cash account in the journal entry. However, depreciation, like all the other expenses, decreases net income. Therefore, to go from net income to cash flows, we must add the depreciation expense back to net income.

Example: Suppose you had only two transactions during the period:

- $50,000 cash sale
- Depreciation expense of $20,000

Accrual basis net income is $30,000 ($50,000 − $20,000). But net cash flow from operations is $50,000. To reconcile the net income of $30,000 to the net cash flow from operations of $50,000, add back the $20,000 of depreciation expense. You would also add back depletion and amortization expenses because they are noncash expenses similar to depreciation.

ⓒ Gains and Losses on the Sale of Assets

Sales of long-term assets such as land and buildings are investing activities. The total cash proceeds from these sales are included in the investing section of the statement of cash flows. However, these sales usually result in a gain or a loss, which is included in net income. Gains and losses do not represent cash flows. Gains and losses are simply the difference between the cash proceeds and the book value of the asset sold. Therefore, gains and losses must be removed from net income on the statement of cash flows.

Mackay Industries' income statement includes a loss on the sale of fixed assets. During 2014, Mackay Industries sold fixed assets resulting in a loss of $3,000 on the sale. Because the loss reduces net income, it is added back to net income to arrive at net cash flow from operating activities. On the other hand, a gain on the sale of fixed assets would increase net income. So, it would be subtracted from net income to arrive at net cash flow from operating activities.

ⓓ, ⓔ, ⓕ, & ⓖ Changes in the Current Assets and the Current Liabilities

Most current assets and current liabilities result from operating activities. For example,

- Accounts receivable result from sales,
- Inventory and accounts payable relate to cost of goods sold,
- Prepaid assets and accrued liabilities relate to operating expenses, and so on.

Changes in the current asset and current liability accounts create adjustments to net income on the cash flow statement:

1. **A decrease in a current asset other than cash causes an increase in cash.** Mackay Industries' Accounts Receivable decreased by $17,000 ⓓ. What caused the decrease? During the year, Mackay Industries must have collected more cash from credit customers than the current year's credit sales. This means that $17,000 more was collected from customers than what is represented by the Revenues on the income statement. Therefore, the $17,000 decrease in Accounts Receivable is added to net income to arrive at net cash flow from operating activities. A decrease in any current asset other than cash will be added to net income to arrive at net cash flow from operating activities.

2. **An increase in a current asset other than cash causes a decrease in cash.** It takes cash to acquire assets. If Accounts Receivable, Inventory, or Prepaid Expenses increase, then Cash decreases. Therefore, subtract the increase in the current asset from net income to get net cash flow from operations. For example, Mackay Industries' Inventory went up by $8,000 ⓔ. The $8,000 increase in inventory is not reflected in Cost of Goods Sold on the income statement. However, this increase required the payment of cash so it is deducted from net income to arrive at net cash flow from operating activities. An increase in any current asset other than cash will be subtracted from net income to arrive at net cash flow from operating activities.

3. **A decrease in a current liability causes a decrease in cash.** Mackay Industries' Accounts Payable went down $12,000 ⓕ. This means that Mackay Industries paid $12,000 more on its payables than it charged during the current year. However, the amount that Mackay Industries charged on its payables is what is reflected in Cost of Goods Sold and Operating Expenses on the income statement. So, the $12,000 decrease in Accounts Payable is subtracted from net income to arrive at

net cash flow from operating activities. A decrease in any current liability will be subtracted from net income to arrive at net cash flow from operating activities.

4. **An increase in a current liability causes an increase in cash.** Mackay Industries' Accrued Liabilities increased by $4,000 **G**. This means that $4,000 of the operating expenses on the income statement have not yet been paid for. Accordingly, even though net income was reduced by $4,000, cash was not reduced. Therefore, the $4,000 increase in accrued liabilities is added to net income to arrive at net cash flow from operations. An increase in any current liability will be added to net income to arrive at net cash flow from operating activities.

During 2014, Mackay Industries' operations provided net cash flow of $70,000. This amount exceeds net income (due to the various adjustments discussed previously). However, to fully evaluate a company's cash flows, we must also examine its investing and financing activities.

Cash Flows from Investing Activities

As shown in Exhibit 11-2, investing activities affect long-term assets, such as Fixed Assets and Investments. The investing section of Mackay Industries' statement of cash flows is presented next:

		Cash flows from investing activities:		
	H	Acquisition of fixed assets	$(195,000)	
	I	Proceeds from sale of fixed assets	104,000	
		Net cash used in investing activities		(91,000)

Computing Acquisitions and Sales of Fixed Assets

Companies usually keep a separate account for each type of fixed asset. However, for computing investing cash flows, it is helpful to combine all the fixed assets into a single Fixed Assets account. We subtract Accumulated Depreciation from the assets' cost in order to work with a single net figure for fixed assets, such as Fixed Assets, net, $385,000. This simplifies the computations.

To illustrate, observe that Mackay Industries' financial statements presented in Exhibit 11-4 show the following:

- The balance sheet reports Fixed Assets, Net of $385,000 at the end of 2014 and $315,000 at the end of 2013.
- The income statement shows depreciation expense of $18,000 and a $3,000 loss on sale of fixed assets.

The increase in the net amount of fixed assets tells us that Mackay Industries acquired fixed assets during 2014. Let's assume that Mackay Industries' acquisitions of fixed assets during 2014 consisted of $195,000 of cash purchases. The $195,000 of cash used to purchase the fixed assets will be reported as a cash outflow **H** in the investing section of the statement of cash flows. If any portion of the purchase of fixed assets is financed with notes payable, the amount financed is not included in the cash outflow.

The loss on sale of assets reported on the income statement indicates that Mackay Industries sold some older fixed assets. This gives us an incomplete T-account:

Fixed Assets, Net			
12/31/13 Bal	315,000	2012 Depr exp	18,000
Acquisitions	195,000	Sales	?
12/31/14 Bal	385,000		

We can now solve for the net book value of the assets that were sold:

12/31/2013 Balance	+ Acquisitions	− Depreciation Expense	− Sales? = 12/31/2014 Balance
$315,000	+ $195,000 −	$ 18,000	− Sales? = $385,000
		$492,000	− Sales? = $385,000
			Sales = $107,000

Our completed T-account now looks like this:

Fixed Assets, Net

12/31/13 Bal	315,000	2014 Depr exp	18,000
Acquisitions	195,000	Sales	107,000
12/31/14 Bal	385,000		

Once we know the book value of the assets sold, we can calculate the amount of cash received from selling fixed assets by using the journal entry approach:

DATE	ACCOUNTS	POST REF.	DR.	CR.
	Cash		??????	
	Loss of Sale of Fixed Assets		3,000	
	Fixed Assets, Net			107,000

So, we compute the cash receipt from the sale as:

$$\text{Cash} = \text{Fixed assets, net} - \text{loss}$$
$$\text{Cash} = \$107,000 - \$3,000$$
$$\text{Cash} = \$104,000$$

The cash receipt from the sale of fixed assets of $104,000 is shown as item **1** in the investing activities section of the statement of cash flows. **Exhibit 11-5** summarizes the computation of the investing cash flows from the acquisition and sale of fixed assets. Items to be computed are shown in blue.

The investing section of the statement of cash flows will also include cash outflows for the purchase of investments and for any amounts lent to others under long-term notes receivable. Cash inflows reported in the investing section of the statement of cash flows will include proceeds from the sale of investments and any payments received on long-term notes receivable.

As we can see, Mackay Industries used $91,000 in investing activities. Now let's examine the financing section of the statement of cash flows.

Cash Receipts

| From sale of fixed assets | Beginning fixed assets (net) | + | Acquisition | − | Depreciation Expense | − | Book value of assets sold | = | Ending fixed assets (net) |

$$\text{Cash receipt} = \text{Book value of assets sold} \begin{cases} + & \text{Gain on sale} \\ \text{or} & \\ - & \text{Loss on sale} \end{cases}$$

Cash Payments

| For acquisition of fixed assets | Beginning fixed assets (net) | + | Acquisition* | − | Depreciation Expense | − | Book value of assets sold | = | Ending fixed assets (net) |

*Any portion of the acquisition that is financed by a note payable must be deducted from the amount of cash paid.

Exhibit 11-5 ▲

Cash Flows from Financing Activities

As shown in Exhibit 11-2, financing activities affect the long-term liability and stock-holders' equity accounts, such as Long-Term Notes Payable, Bonds Payable, Common Stock, and Retained Earnings (excluding net income). The financing section of Mackay Industries' statement of cash flows is presented next:

		Cash flows from financing activities:		
J		Proceeds from issuance of long-term notes payable	$ 75,000	
L		Proceeds from issuance of common stock	20,000	
K		Payment of long-term notes payable	(26,000)	
M		Payment of dividends	(23,000)	
N		Purchase of treasury stock	(18,000)	
		Net cash provided by financing activities		28,000

Computing Issuances and Payments of Long-Term Notes Payable

The beginning and ending balances of Notes Payable or Bonds Payable are found on the balance sheet. If either the amount of new issuances or payments is known, the other amount can be computed. For Mackay Industries, Inc., let's assume that during 2014, $75,000 was borrowed on a long-term note payable. We can use the amount of the note proceeds and the beginning and ending balances of Notes Payable from Mackay Industries' balance sheet in Exhibit 11-4 to create the following incomplete T-account:

Long-Term Notes Payable			
		12/31/13 Bal	98,000
Note payments	?	New notes	75,000
		12/31/14 Bal	147,000

Then solve for the missing payments value:

12/31/13 Bal	+ New notes issued	– Note payments?	= 12/31/14 Bal
$98,000	+ $ 75,000	– Note payments?	= $147,000
	$173,000	– Note payments?	= $147,000
		Note payments	= $ 26,000

The completed T-account looks like this:

Long-Term Notes Payable			
		12/31/13 Bal	98,000
Note payments	26,000	New notes	75,000
		12/31/14 Bal	147,000

The $75,000 cash received is reflected as a cash inflow **J** in the financing section of the statement of cash flows. The payment of $26,000 is reflected as a cash outflow **K** in the financing section of the statement of cash flows.

Computing Issuances of Stock

Cash flows for these financing activities can be determined by analyzing the stock accounts. We can see from looking at the data in Exhibit 11-4 that the balance in the Common Stock account increased by $20,000. Because we were not told about any stock retirements, we can assume there were none. Therefore, the $20,000 change in the Common Stock balance must be due to new stock issuances. We will assume the stock was issued in exchange for cash, so the $20,000 will be reflected as a cash inflow **L** in the financing section of the statement of cash flows.

Computing Dividend Payments

The amount of dividends that were declared during the year can be found on the statement of retained earnings. From the statement of retained earnings in Exhibit 11-4, we see that Mackay Industries declared $23,000 of dividends during 2014. Remember, a stock dividend has *no* effect on Cash and is, therefore, *not* reported on the statement of cash flows. We will assume that all of Mackay Industries' dividends were cash dividends. Because there were no beginning or ending balances in Dividends Payable on the balance sheet, we can conclude that the entire $23,000 (and no more) was paid during 2014. Therefore, the $23,000 will be reflected as a cash outflow **M** in the financing section of the statement of cash flows.

If the statement of retained earnings is unavailable, the amount of dividends declared can be computed by analyzing the Retained Earnings account. Remember, Retained Earnings increases when companies earn net income. Retained Earnings also decreases when companies have a net loss and when they declare dividends. We can use the amount of the Net Income and the beginning and ending balances of Retained Earnings (from Mackay Industries' financial statements in Exhibit 11-4) to create an incomplete T-account:

Retained Earnings			
		12/31/13 Bal	121,000
Dividends	?	Net income	48,000
		12/31/14 Bal	146,000

Then solve for the missing amount of dividends declared:

$$
\begin{aligned}
\text{12/31/13 Bal} + \text{Net income} - \text{Dividends?} &= \text{12/31/14 Bal} \\
\$121,000 + \$48,000 - \text{Dividends?} &= \$146,000 \\
\$169,000 - \text{Dividends?} &= \$146,000 \\
\text{Dividends} &= \$23,000
\end{aligned}
$$

The completed T-account looks like this:

Retained Earnings			
		12/31/13 Bal	121,000
Dividends	23,000	Net income	48,000
		12/31/14 Bal	146,000

Purchases and Sales of Treasury Stock

The last item that changed on Mackay Industries' balance sheet was Treasury Stock. Because we were not told that any treasury stock was sold, we must assume that 100% of the account change represents new acquisitions of treasury stock. So, $18,000 is shown as a cash outflow in the financing section of the cash flow statement for the purchase of treasury stock **N**.

Net Change in Cash and Cash Balances

The cash provided by or used in operating, investing, and financing activities is totaled to arrive at the net increase of $7,000 in cash. Next, the beginning cash of $11,000 from December 31, 2013, is listed. The net increase of $7,000 is added to the beginning cash of $11,000 to get the ending cash balance on December 31, 2014, of $18,000. The completed statement of cash flows for Mackay Industries, Inc., is presented in **Exhibit 11-6**.

You can see why the statement of cash flows is so valuable. It explains why the cash balance for Mackay Industries increased by only $7,000, even though the company reported net income for the year of $48,000.

Noncash Investing and Financing Activities

The operating, investing, and financing sections of the statement of cash flows only reflect activity that results from the exchange of cash. But companies may make investments that do not require cash. They may also obtain financing for other reasons than to acquire cash. These types of transactions are called *noncash investing and financing activities*. Although these transactions do not affect cash, they still affect the long-term assets, long-term liabilities, and stockholders' equity of a business. In order to provide financial statement users with complete information, all noncash investing and financing activities are reported. Noncash investing and financing activities can be reported in a separate schedule that accompanies the statement of cash flows or disclosed in a financial statement footnote.

Mackay Industries
Statement of Cash Flows
Year Ended December 31, 2014

	Cash flows from operating activities:		
A	Net Income		$ 48,000
	Adjustments to reconcile net income to net cash provided by operating activities:		
B	Depreciation Expense	$ 18,000	
C	Loss on sale of fixed assets	3,000	
D	Decrease in Accounts Receivable	17,000	
E	Increase in Inventory	(8,000)	
F	Decrease in Accounts Payable	(12,000)	
G	Increase in Accrued Liabilities	4,000	22,000
	Net cash provided by operating activities		70,000
	Cash flows from investing activities:		
H	Acquisition of fixed assets	(195,000)	
I	Proceeds from sale of fixed assets	104,000	
	Net cash used in investing activities		(91,000)
	Cash flows from financing activities:		
J	Proceeds from issuance of long-term notes payable	75,000	
L	Proceeds from issuance of common stock	20,000	
K	Payment of long-term notes payable	(26,000)	
M	Payment of dividends	(23,000)	
N	Purchase of treasury stock	(18,000)	
	Net cash provided by financing activities		28,000
	Net increase in cash:		7,000
	Cash balance, December 31, 2013		11,000
	Cash balance, December 31, 2014		$ 18,000

Exhibit 11-6 ▲

Our Mackay Industries example did not include noncash transactions because the company did not have any transactions of this type during the year. So, to illustrate the reporting of noncash transactions, let's consider the following three noncash transactions for Tucker Enterprises.

1. Tucker Enterprises issues $450,000 of no-par common stock in exchange for a building. The journal entry to record the purchase would be:

DATE	ACCOUNTS	POST REF.	DR.	CR.
	Building		450,000	
	Common Stock			450,000
	Exchanged stock for a building.			

The purchase of the building is an investing activity. The issuance of common stock is a financing activity. However, this transaction is not reported in the investing and financing sections of the statement of cash flows because no cash is exchanged. Instead, this transaction is reported as a *noncash investing and financing activity.*

2. Tucker Enterprises acquired $120,000 of land by issuing a note. The journal entry to record the purchase would be:

DATE	ACCOUNTS	POST REF.	DR.	CR.
	Land		120,000	
	Notes Payable			120,000
	Purchased land.			

The purchase of the land is an investing activity. The issuance of the note is a financing activity. Once again, this transaction is not reported in the investing and financing sections of the statement of cash flows because no cash is exchanged. Instead, this transaction is reported as a *noncash investing and financing activity.*

3. Tucker Enterprises issued $80,000 of no-par common stock to settle a debt. The journal entry to record the transaction would be:

DATE	ACCOUNTS	POST REF.	DR.	CR.
	Notes Payable		80,000	
	Common Stock			80,000
	Settled note payable by issuing common stock.			

The settlement of the note and the issuance of the common stock are both financing activities. But, because no cash is involved, this transaction will not be reported in the financing section of the statement of cash flows. It is reported as a *noncash investing and financing activity.*

Exhibit 11-7 illustrates how the noncash investing and financing activities for Tucker Enterprises would be presented.

Tucker Enterprises Statement of Cash Flows—Partial Year Ended December 31, 2014		
Noncash investing and financing activities:		
Issued 10,000 shares of common stock in		
exchange for a building		$450,000
Issued a note payable in exchange for land		120,000
Issued 1,800 shares of common stock		
to settle note payable		80,000

Exhibit 11-7 ▲

Try It...

Alpine Manufacturing purchased a new piece of equipment costing $45,000. Alpine paid $5,000 cash down and signed a long-term note for the remainder. What types of activities (operating, financing, or investing) are represented by this transaction? How would this transaction be reported in Alpine Manufacturing's statement of cash flows?

Answer

Because this transaction involves both the purchase of new fixed assets and the issuance of a long-term note payable, it represents both an investing activity and a financing activity. However, on Alpine Manufacturing's statement of cash flows, only $5,000 will be reflected in the investing section as an outflow of cash for the purchase of fixed assets. The remaining $40,000 will be reflected as a noncash investing and financing activity in a separate schedule.

How Is the Statement of Cash Flows Prepared Using the Direct Method?

4 **Prepare the statement of cash flows using the direct method**

Although most companies utilize the indirect method of reporting cash flows from operating activities, the Financial Accounting Standards Board (FASB) prefers the direct method. The direct method provides clearer information about the sources and uses of cash from operating activities than the indirect method. Investing and financing cash flows are presented exactly the same under both direct and indirect methods.

To illustrate how the operating section of the statement of cash flows differs for the direct method, we will be using the Mackay Industries, Inc., data we used with the indirect method. The format for the direct method statement of cash flows for Mackay Industries is presented in Exhibit 11-8.

Mackay Industries, Inc.
Statement of Cash Flows
Year Ended December 31, 2014

Cash flows from operating activities:
    Receipts:
        Collections from customers
        Interest received
        Dividends received on investments
            Total cash receipts
    Payments:
        To suppliers
        To employees
        For interest
        For income taxes
            Total cash payments
    Net cash provided by (used for) operating activities
± **Cash flows from investing activities:**
  + Cash receipts from sales of long-term assets
      (investments, land, building, equipment, and so on)
  − Purchases of long-term assets
  Net cash provided by (used for) investing activities
± **Cash flows from financing activities:**
  + Cash receipts from issuance of stock
  + Sale of treasury stock
  − Purchase of treasury stock
  + Cash receipts from issuance of notes or bonds
      payable (borrowing)
  − Payment of notes or bonds payable
  − Payment of dividends
  Net cash provided by (used for) financing activities
= **Net increase (decrease) in cash during the year**
  + Cash at December 31, 2013
  = Cash at December 31, 2014

Exhibit 11-8 ▲

Mackay Industries' completed direct method statement of cash flows for 2014 is presented in Exhibit 11-9.

Mackay Industries			
Statement of Cash Flows			
Year Ended December 31, 2014			
Cash flows from operating activities:			
Receipts:			
A Collections from customers		$ 285,000	
B Interest received		13,000	
C Dividends received		5,000	
Total cash receipts			$ 303,000
Payments:			
D To suppliers		(165,000)	
E To employees		(48,000)	
F For interest		(11,000)	
G For taxes		(9,000)	
Total cash payments			(233,000)
Net cash provided by operating activities			70,000
Cash flows from investing activities:			
Acquisition of fixed assets		(195,000)	
Proceeds from sale of fixed assets		104,000	
Net cash used in investing activities			(91,000)
Cash flows from financing activities:			
Proceeds from issuance of long-term notes payable		75,000	
Proceeds from issuance of common stock		20,000	
Payment of long-term notes payable		(26,000)	
Payment of dividends		(23,000)	
Purchase of treasury stock		(18,000)	
Net cash provided by financing activities			28,000
Net increase in cash:			7,000
Cash balance, December 31, 2013			11,000
Cash balance, December 31, 2014			$ 18,000

Exhibit 11-9 ▲

Now, we'll explain how we calculated each number.

Cash Flows from Operating Activities

In the indirect method, we start with net income and then adjust it to "cash-basis" through a series of adjusting items. In the direct method, we convert each line item on the income statement from accrual to cash basis. So, in essence, the operating activities section of the direct method statement of cash flows is really just a cash-basis income statement.

Depreciation, Depletion, and Amortization Expense

As these expenses do not require the payment of cash, they are *not* reported on the direct method statement of cash flows.

A   Cash Collections from Customers

The first item on the income statement is Sales Revenue of $268,000. Sales Revenue represents the total of all sales, whether for cash or on account. The balance sheet accounts related to Sales Revenue are Accounts Receivable and Unearned Revenues. Accounts Receivable decreased $17,000 from $93,000 at December 31, 2013 to $76,000 at December 31, 2014. A decrease in Accounts Receivable means that Mackay Industries collected more cash than it made in sales during the current year. This means that the cash receipts from customers during the year are $17,000 greater than Sales Revenues. The balance sheet shows no unearned revenues, so no adjustment is needed for unearned revenues. We can calculate the cash received from customers:

Sales Revenue...	$268,000
Plus decrease in Accounts Receivable	17,000
Cash receipts from customers.......................	$285,000

B   Cash Receipts of Interest

The second item on the income statement is Interest Revenue of $13,000. The balance sheet account related to Interest Revenue is Interest Receivable. Because there is no Interest Receivable account on the balance sheet, the Interest Revenue must have all been received in cash. So, the cash flow statement shows Interest Received of $13,000. Had there been Interest Receivable in either year, the accrual basis Interest Revenue would have been converted to cash basis in a manner similar to that used for Sales Revenue and Accounts Receivable.

C   Cash Receipts of Dividends

Dividend Revenue is the third item reported on the income statement of $5,000. The balance sheet account related to Dividend Revenue is Dividends Receivable. As with the interest, there is no Dividends Receivable on the balance sheet. Therefore, the Dividend Revenue must have all been received in cash. So, the cash flow statement shows cash received from dividends of $5,000.

D   Payments to Suppliers

Payments to suppliers include all payments for:

* Inventory and
* Operating expenses except employee compensation, interest, and income taxes.

Suppliers are those entities that provide the business with its inventory and essential services. The accounts related to payments to suppliers for inventory are Cost of Goods Sold, Inventory, and Accounts Payable. Cost of Goods Sold on the income statement was $137,000. Inventory increased from $124,000 at 12/31/13 to $132,000 at 12/31/14. The $8,000 ($132,000 − $124,000) increase in Inventory means that Mackay Industries purchased more inventory than it sold during the year. This means that the total amount of inventory purchased during the year would be $145,000.

Cost of Goods Sold.......................	$137,000
Plus increase in Inventory..............	8,000
Total inventory purchased.............	$145,000

Next, we need to consider the change in Accounts Payable to determine the total cash payments for inventory purchased during the year. Accounts Payable decreased from $96,000 at 12/31/13 to $84,000 at 12/31/14. The $12,000 decrease ($96,000 − $84,000) in Accounts Payable means that Mackay Industries paid $12,000 more during the year than the amount of inventory purchased. So, the cash payments for inventory purchased during the year can be calculated as:

Total inventory purchased............................	$145,000
Plus decrease in Accounts Payable..............	12,000
Cash payments for inventory........................	$157,000

The accounts related to payments for other operating expenses are Other Operating Expenses, Prepaid Expenses, and Accrued Liabilities. Other Operating Expenses on the income statement were $12,000. There are no Prepaid Expenses on the balance sheet, so no adjustment is needed for changes in Prepaid Expenses. Accrued Liabilities increased from $8,000 at 12/31/13 to $12,000 at 12/31/14. This means that Mackay Industries incurred more operating expenses than it paid for during the year. By subtracting the $4,000 ($12,000 − $8,000) from the operating expenses, we get the amount of cash payments for other operating expenses:

Other Operating Expenses.................................	$12,000
Less increase in Accrued Liabilities	4,000
Cash payments for other operating expenses	$ 8,000

Finally, by adding the cash paid to suppliers for inventory to the cash paid to suppliers for other operating expenses, we get the total cash paid to suppliers of $165,000.

Cash payments for inventory.............................	$157,000
Cash payments for other operating expenses	8,000
Total cash payments to suppliers......................	$165,000

▪E Payments to Employees

This category includes payments for salaries, wages, and other forms of employee compensation. The accounts related to employee payments are Salaries Expense from the income statement and Salaries Payable from the balance sheet. Because there aren't any Salaries Payable on the balance sheet, the Salaries Expense account must represent all amounts paid in cash to employees. So, the cash flow statement shows cash payments to employees of $48,000. Had there been any Salaries Payable, the Salaries Expense account would have been adjusted to arrive at the cash paid to employees in a manner similar to how other operating expenses were adjusted for accrued liabilities previously.

▪F Payments for Interest Expense

These cash payments are reported separately from the other expenses. The accounts related to interest payments are Interest Expense from the income statement and Interest Payable from the balance sheet. Because there is no Interest Payable on the balance sheet, the Interest Expense from the income statement must represent all amounts paid in cash for interest. So, the cash flow statement shows cash payments for interest of $11,000.

▪G Payments for Income Tax Expense

Like interest expense, these cash payments are reported separately from the other expenses. The accounts related to income tax payments are Income Tax Expense from the income statement and Income Tax Payable from the balance sheet. Again, because there is no Income Tax Payable on the balance sheet, the Income Tax Expense from the income statement must represent all amounts paid in cash for income tax. Therefore, the cash flow statement shows cash payments for income tax of $9,000.

Gains and Losses on the Sale of Fixed Assets

The last item on the income statement is a loss on sale of fixed assets of $3,000. Remember that gains and losses do not represent cash flows. The cash flow related to the sale of a fixed asset equals the proceeds from the sale of the asset. As with the indirect method, the proceeds from the sale of the asset are reported in the investing section, not the operating section.

Net Cash Provided by Operating Activities

To calculate net cash provided by operating activities using the direct method, we add all the cash receipts and cash payments described previously and find the difference. For Mackay Industries, Inc., total Cash receipts were $303,000. Total Cash payments were $233,000. So, net cash provided by operating activities is $70,000. If you refer back to the indirect method cash flow statement shown in Exhibit 11-6, you will find that it showed the same $70,000 for net cash provided by operating activities—only the method by which it was calculated was different.

The remainder of Mackay Industries' cash flow statement using the direct method is exactly the same as what we calculated using the indirect method. (See Exhibit 11-6.)

Focus on Decision Making

"How Do Businesses Manage Cash Flow?"

A business needs cash. If it doesn't have enough cash, it will fail. However, it may also have too much cash. Managing and financing the asset cash is expensive. The benefits of holding cash should exceed the costs. So how do businesses look at and manage cash flow? They often use two measures, free cash flow and the cash conversion cycle.

Free Cash Flow

5 Evaluate a company's performance with respect to cash

Free cash flow The amount of cash available from operations after paying for investments in long-term assets.

The statement of cash flows is a useful tool for examining the sources and uses of cash during an accounting period. However, investors may want to know how much cash a company anticipates it can "free up" for new opportunities, to reduce debt, or to pay dividends. **Free cash flow** is the amount of cash available from operations after paying for investments in long-term assets. Free cash flow is fundamentally net cash flow from operations minus cash payments for investments in long-term assets. Free cash flow can be computed as:[1]

Free Cash Flow = Net Cash Flow from Operations − Cash Payments for Investments in Long-Term Assets

Many companies use free cash flow to manage their operations. Suppose Tucker Enterprises has net cash provided by operations of $160,000 during the year. Tucker Enterprises also spent $85,000 to purchase new equipment. In this case, Tucker Enterprises' free cash flow would be $75,000 ($160,000 − $85,000). If a good investment opportunity comes along (or an anticipated need for cash), Tucker Enterprises should have $75,000 of free cash available. It could also use the $75,000 to pay off debts or to pay dividends.

---

[1]Free cash flow is often used to value a business. To do so, financial analysts measure free cash flow differently. Financial analysts add back the after-tax cost of interest to operating cash flow, producing an adjusted operating cash flow free of all transactions dealing with debt or stockholders' equity. The revised free cash flow is then computed by subtracting investments in long-term assets from this adjusted operating cash flow. The total value of the business, both debt and stockholders' equity, is then estimated using this revised free cash flow.

Cash conversion cycle
A measurement of the amount of time a company's cash is tied up in its operations.

Cash Conversion Cycle

The **cash conversion cycle** represents the time it takes a company to sell its inventory and collect its receivables, less the time it takes the company to pay its payables. In other words, the cash conversion cycle represents the number of days a company's cash is "tied up" in the operations of the business. The cash conversion cycle is calculated as:

Cash Conversion Cycle = (Days-Sales-In-Inventory) + (Receivable Collection Period) − (Accounts Payable Payment Period)

Days-sales-in-inventory tells you how many days it takes to convert inventory into a sale. Look back at Chapter 5 and see how to compute days-sales-in-inventory. The receivable collection period tells you how many days it takes to convert the accounts receivable into cash. Look back at Chapter 7 and see how to compute the receivable collection period. The accounts payable payment period tells you how many days it takes to pay accounts payable. The accounts payable payment period is calculated as:

$$\text{Accounts Payable Payment Period} = \frac{\text{Average Accounts Payable}}{(\text{Cost of Goods Sold}/365 \text{ Days})}$$

Average accounts payable is computed by adding the beginning and ending accounts payable and dividing the total by two. Remember that balance sheet accounts, such as accounts payable, carry their balances from one period to the next. The ending accounts payable for one year becomes the beginning accounts payable for the next year.

Let's assume that Tucker Enterprises has a days-sales-in-inventory of 52 days, a receivable collection period of 34 days, and an accounts payable payment period of 39 days. Tucker Enterprises' cash conversion cycle would equal 47 days (52 + 34 − 39). This means that, on average, Tucker Enterprises' cash is tied up for 47 days. Generally, the lower the cash conversion cycle, the healthier the company. This is because cash is the lifeblood of a business, and the shorter the length of time it is "tied up," the better. Over time, if the cash conversion cycle for a business grows longer, it can be a sign that the business may be facing a pending cash flow "crunch."

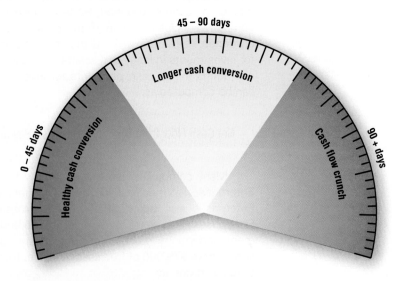

How They Do It: A Look at Business

Let's look at two businesses, Delta Airlines and Procter & Gamble.

First, let's look at Delta Airlines. Delta uses its airplanes to fly people all over the world. It buys its planes with long-term financing, both debt and stockholders' equity.

It then buys fuel and other supplies, using accounts payable. It does not pay cash. It charges passengers, like you and me, for flying us from one place to another. Typically, we do not pay cash. We pay Delta, or a travel agency such as Expedia, with a credit card, a promise of cash in the near future. If we pay a travel agency, then the travel agency collects the cash and pays Delta eventually. Delta then pays its accounts payable to suppliers, employees, and other operating obligations (renting of airport gates). This process creates operating cash flow that can then be used to make planned investments in long-term assets, such as new planes. What results is free cash flow. For the year ending December 31, 2012, Delta's days-sales-in-inventory was 8.2 days, receivable collection period was 16.2 days, and accounts payable payment period was 20.6 days. Delta's cash conversion cycle was 3.8 days (8.2 days + 16.2 days – 20.6 days = 3.8 days).

Procter & Gamble (P&G) manufactures household products such as Cover Girl cosmetics, Gillette razors, Crest toothpaste, Duracell batteries, and Tide detergent. It buys ingredients and makes products. These ingredients and products are P&G's inventory. It then sells its inventory to retailers such as Kroger food stores. However, Kroger does not immediately pay P&G, and P&G has a receivable from Kroger. When Kroger pays P&G, cash is received and the receivable goes away. P&G then is obligated to pay cash to pay its suppliers. This process creates operating cash flow that can then be used to make planned investments in long-term assets, such as new factories. What results is free cash flow. For the fiscal year ending June 30, 2012, P&G's days-sales-in-inventory was 60.7 days, receivable collection period was 26.9 days, and accounts payable payment period was 68.6 days. P&G's cash conversion cycle was 18.9 days (60.7 days + 26.9 days – 68.6 days = 19.0 days).

Now think about Delta and P&G. Think about what they do and how they do it. Delta's cash conversion cycle was 3.8 days versus P&G's cash conversion cycle which was 19 days. P&G had more cash "tied up" in operations than Delta. Why the difference? It's all about how they manage inventory, receivables, and payables.

The Statement of Cash Flows: Putting It All Together

The old adage that "cash is king" is true. A business that cannot manage its cash flows will fail. Managers and other decision makers need to understand a business's cash flows. Remember that accrual accounting reports transactions when they occur, regardless if cash is received or paid. Remember that net income is not cash.

So, how do accountants help managers and other decision makers understand where a business gets and uses its cash? The answer is that accountants create a statement that explains why a business's cash increased or decreased during a period of time. This statement is called the statement of cash flows.

The statement of cash flows shows the impact on cash of transactions reported on the income statement and balance sheet. The statement categorizes transactions affecting cash into either operating, investing, or financing activities. Operating activities relate to the receipt and payment of cash for the revenues and expenses reported in the income statement. Investing activities relate to the receipt and payment of cash to buy and sell long-term assets, such as buildings and equipment. Financing activities relate to the receipt and payment of cash from and to the providers of long-term financing, both lenders and stockholders.

So, think about managing a business. Think about how the income statement, balance sheet, and statement of cash flows combine to create a complete picture of a business's operations. Think about how accountants provide managers and other decision makers a complete picture of how a business generates value.

Summary

Here is what you should know after reading this chapter. MyAccountingLab will help you identify what you know and where to go when you need practice.

	Key Points	Key Accounting Terms
1 Identify the purposes and importance of the statement of cash flows	The statement of cash flows is the report created to explain why a business's cash changed in a period of time.	**Cash flow statement** (p. 506) **Statement of cash flows** (p. 506)
2 Differentiate between cash flows from operating, investing, and financing activities	The statement of cash flows is created to show the sources and uses of cash from operating activities, investing activities, and financing activities. Operating activities relate to cash receipts from revenues and cash payments for expenses. Investing activities relate to cash transactions for the purchase and sale of long-term assets. Financing activities relate to cash transactions for the borrowing and repayment of long-term liabilities, the issuance of stock, the repurchase of stock, and the payments of dividends.	**Direct method** (p. 511) **Financing activities** (p. 506) **Indirect method** (p. 511) **Investing activities** (p. 506) **Operating activities** (p. 506)
3 Prepare the statement of cash flows using the indirect method	Businesses typically use the indirect method to create the statement of cash flows. The indirect method starts by reporting operating activities as net income, adjusted for noncash revenues/gains and expenses/losses, changes in noncash current assets, and changes in current liabilities. Investing activities are reported as changes in long-term assets, adjusted for noncash transactions. Financing activities are reported as changes in long-term liabilities and stockholders' equity accounts, adjusted for noncash transactions. The payment of dividends is included as a financing activity.	
4 Prepare the statement of cash flows using the direct method	Sometimes businesses create a statement of cash flows using the direct method. Investing and financing activities are reported just like with the indirect method. All that differs is how operating activities are reported. The cash provided by and used by the individual elements of the income statement are reported separately in the direct method, showing the cash provided and used by sales, cost of goods sold, operating expense, etc.	
5 Evaluate a company's performance with respect to cash	Cash is a critical resource of the business. A business cannot exist in the long term if it cannot pay its obligations. Thus, where a business gets and uses its cash is very important. The statement of cash flows helps address this concern.	**Cash conversion cycle** (p. 528) **Free cash flow** (p. 527)

Accounting Practice

Discussion Questions

1. What are some of the reasons why a statement of cash flows may be important to users of financial statements?

2. A company used cash to build a new factory and received cash when it sold off the machines in the old factory. In which section of the statement of cash flows would the cash flows from these activities be reported?

3. A company used cash to pay employees and received cash from performing services. In which section of the statement of cash flows would the cash flows from these activities be reported?

4. A company issued bonds during the year. Would this be reported as a source or use of cash on the statement of cash flows? In which section would it be reported?

5. Why is net income a good place to start when attempting to determine the cash flows from operating activities using the indirect method? Why is it not the same as the net cash flow from operating activities?

6. When using the indirect method, why are gains on the sale of fixed assets subtracted from net income in the operating activities section of the statement of cash flows? Why are losses on the sale of fixed assets added to net income?

7. Assuming the indirect method is used, how does an increase in accounts receivable during the year affect the statement of cash flows (if at all)? Why?

8. Why would a decrease in accounts payable be shown as a decrease in cash when using the indirect method of calculating the cash flows from operating activities?

9. How would the sale of treasury stock that was acquired three years ago appear in the statement of cash flows (if at all)?

10. A company's cash conversion cycle increased from 55 days in year 1 to 68 days in year 3. What are the implications of this increase? What do you think happens to the cash conversion cycles of companies during a recession?

Self Check

1. The three main categories of cash flows reported on a cash flow statement are
   a. current, long-term, and fixed.
   b. short-term, long-term, and equity.
   c. direct, indirect, and hybrid.
   d. operating, investing, and financing.

2. Operating activities are most closely related to:
   a. long-term assets.
   b. current assets and current liabilities.
   c. long-term liabilities and stockholders' equity.
   d. net income and dividends.

3. Financing activities are most closely related to
   a. long-term assets.
   b. current assets and current liabilities.
   c. long-term liabilities and stockholders' equity.
   d. net income and dividends.

4. Which item does not appear on a statement of cash flows prepared by the indirect method?

   a. Net income
   b. Gain on sale of land
   c. Collections from customers
   d. Depreciation expense

5. Finlay, Inc., earned net income of $63,000 after deducting depreciation expense of $12,000 and all other expenses. Current assets increased by $11,000, and current liabilities decreased by $13,000. Using the indirect method, how much was Finlay, Inc.'s net cash flow from operating activities?

   a. $37,000
   b. $39,000
   c. $51,000
   d. $27,000

6. The Fixed Assets account of Hamilton, Inc., shows:

Fixed Assets, Net			
Beginning balance	91,000	Depreciation expense	30,000
Purchase	365,000	Sale	?
Ending balance	376,000		

   Hamilton, Inc., sold fixed assets at an $18,000 gain. How much should Hamilton, Inc., report for the sale?

   a. Cash flows from investing activities, $18,000
   b. Cash flows from investing activities, $68,000
   c. Cash flows from investing activities, $32,000
   d. Cash flows from investing activities, $50,000

7. Minot Corporation borrowed $14,000, issued common stock of $11,000, and paid dividends of $16,000. What was Minot Corporation's net cash provided or used by financing activities?

   a. $(5,000)
   b. $16,000
   c. $9,000
   d. $41,000

8. Which item appears on a statement of cash flows prepared by the indirect method?

   a. Payment of income tax
   b. Payment to suppliers
   c. Collections from customers
   d. Net income

9. SRS Systems, Inc., had accounts receivable of $27,000 at the beginning of the year and $56,000 at year-end. Revenue for the year totaled $106,000. How much cash did SRS Systems collect from customers?

   a. $189,000
   b. $162,000
   c. $77,000
   d. $133,000

10. Elliot Enterprises had operating expenses of $51,000. At the beginning of the year, Elliot Enterprises owed $10,000 on accrued liabilities. At year-end, accrued liabilities were $17,000. How much cash did Elliot Enterprises pay for operating expenses?

   a. $41,000

   b. $44,000

   c. $61,000

   d. $58,000

11. According to the Real World Accounting Video, a _____ is a business that sells product to other businesses for resale.

   a. retail business

   b. wholesale business

   c. mixed business

   d. flow-through

12. According to the Real World Accounting Video, Fishs Eddy uses a(n) _____ to help finance its operations when there is a temporary need for cash.

   a. stock sale

   b. bond

   c. accounts payable

   d. line of credit

Answers are given after Written Communication.

MyAccountingLab

Short Exercises

S11-1. Purpose of the statement of cash flows (*Learning Objective 1*) 5–10 min.

Describe how the statement of cash flows helps investors and creditors perform each of the following functions:

   1. Predict future cash flows

   2. Evaluate management decisions

   3. Predict the ability to make debt payments to lenders and pay dividends to stockholders

S11-2. Basics of statement of cash flows (*Learning Objective 2*) 5–10 min.

Answer these questions about the statement of cash flows:

   1. What is the "check figure" for the statement of cash flows? Where do you get this check figure?

   2. List the categories of cash flows in order of importance.

   3. What is the first dollar amount reported using the indirect method?

S11-3. Purpose of statement of cash flows (*Learning Objective 1*) 5–10 min.

Icemountain, Inc., experienced an unbroken string of 10 years of growth in net income. Nevertheless, the business is facing bankruptcy. Creditors are calling all of Icemountain's outstanding loans for immediate payment, and Icemountain, Inc., has no cash available to make these payments because managers placed undue emphasis on net income and gave too little attention to cash flows.

Write a brief memo in your own words to explain to the managers of Icemountain, Inc., the purposes of the statement of cash flows.

S11-4. Classification of items as operating, investing, or financing (*Learning Objective 2*) 10–15 min.

Identify each of the following transactions as one of the following:

- Operating activity (O)
- Investing activity (I)
- Financing activity (F)
- Noncash investing and financing activity (NIF)

For each item, indicate whether it represents an increase (+) or a decrease (–) in cash. The indirect method is used to report cash flows from operating activities.

a. _____ Cash sale of land

b. _____ Issuance of long-term note payable in exchange for cash

c. _____ Depreciation expense of equipment

d. _____ Purchase of treasury stock

e. _____ Issuance of common stock for cash

f. _____ Increase in Accounts Payable

g. _____ Net income

h. _____ Payment of cash dividend

i. _____ Decrease in Accrued Liabilities

j. _____ Loss on sale of land

k. _____ Acquisition of building by issuance of notes payable

l. _____ Payment of long-term debt

m. _____ Acquisition of building by issuance of common stock

n. _____ Decrease in Accounts Receivable

o. _____ Decrease in Inventory

p. _____ Increase in prepaid expenses

S11-5. Classification of items as operating, investing, or financing (*Learning Objective 2*) 10–15 min.

Indicate whether each of the following transactions would result in an operating activity, an investing activity, a financing activity, or a transaction that does not affect cash for a statement of cash flows prepared by the indirect method.

DATE	ACCOUNTS	POST REF.	DR.	CR.
a.	Equipment		13,000	
	Cash			13,000
b.	Cash		7,500	
	Long-Term Investment			7,500
c.	Bonds Payable		500,000	
	Cash			500,000
d.	Building		180,000	
	Notes Payable, Long-Term			180,000
e.	Loss on Disposal of Equipment		1,000	
	Equipment			1,000
f.	Dividends Payable		15,000	
	Cash			15,000
g.	Cash		80,000	
	Common Stock			80,000
h.	Treasury Stock		10,000	
	Cash			10,000
i.	Cash		65,000	
	Sales Revenue			65,000
j.	Land		83,500	
	Cash			83,500
k.	Depreciation Expense		9,200	
	Accumulated Depreciation			9,200

S11-6. Operating activities—indirect method (*Learning Objective 3*) 10–15 min.

Matrix, Inc., reported the following data for 2014:

Income statement:	Net Income	$42,000
	Depreciation Expense	8,000
Balance sheet:	Increase in Accounts Receivable	14,000
	Decrease in Accounts Payable	6,000

Compute Matrix, Inc.'s net cash provided by operating activities according to the indirect method.

S11-7. Operating activities—indirect method (*Learning Objective 3*) 10–15 min.

Trident Equipment's accountants assembled the following data for the year ended April 30, 2014.

Net Income	$72,000	Purchase of equipment with cash	$58,000
Proceeds from issuance of common stock	6,000	Decrease in current liabilities	4,000
Payment of dividends	5,000	Payment of long-term note payable	38,000
Increase in current assets other than cash	35,000	Proceeds from sale of land	63,000
Purchase of treasury stock	7,000	Depreciation Expense	23,000

Prepare Trident Equipment's statement of cash flows for the year ended April 30, 2014, using the indirect method. The cash balance for Trident Equipment, Inc., at April 30, 2013, was $11,000.

S11-8. Operating activities—direct method (*Learning Objective 4*) 5–10 min.

Nemo's Spas began 2014 with cash of $32,000. During the year, Nemo's Spas earned service revenue of $610,000 and collected $572,000 from customers. Expenses for the year totaled $449,000, of which Nemo's Spas paid $417,000 in cash to suppliers and employees. Nemo's Spas also paid $84,000 to purchase equipment and paid a cash dividend of $57,000 to its stockholders during 2014. Prepare the company's statement of cash flows for the year ended December 31, 2014. Format cash flows from operating activities by the direct method.

S11-9. Operating activities—direct method (*Learning Objective 4*) 5–10 min.

Juarez Equipment, Inc., assembled the following data related to its cash transactions for the year ended June 30, 2014:

Payment of dividends	$ 16,000
Proceeds from issuance of stock	21,000
Collections from customers	213,000
Proceeds from sale of land	61,000
Payments to suppliers	92,000
Purchase of equipment with cash	38,000
Payments to employees	67,000
Payment of long-term note payable	41,000

Prepare Juarez Equipment's statement of cash flows for the year ended June 30, 2014, using the direct method. Juarez Equipment's cash balance at June 30, 2013, was $23,000.

S11-10. Calculate certain operating information for direct method (*Learning Objective 4***) 5–10 min.**

Inland Medical Supply, Inc., reported the following financial statements for 2014:

Inland Medical Supply, Inc. **Income Statement** Year Ended December 31, 2014		
Revenue:		(in thousands)
Sales Revenue		$684
Expenses:		
Cost of Goods Sold	$334	
Depreciation Expense	61	
Other Expenses	192	
Total Expense		587
Net Income		$ 97

Inland Medical Supply, Inc.
Comparative Balance Sheet
December 31, 2014 and 2013

(in thousands) ASSETS	2014	2013	LIABILITIES	2014	2013
Current:			Current:		
Cash	$ 25	$ 10	Accounts Payable	$ 55	$ 32
Accounts Receivable	63	43	Salaries Payable	21	11
Inventory	77	84	Accrued Liabilities	4	9
Prepaid Expenses	10	4	Long-Term Notes Payable	62	75
Long-Term Investments	72	91			
Fixed Assets, Net	226	180	**STOCKHOLDERS' EQUITY**		
			Common Stock	41	30
			Retained Earnings	290	255
			Total Liabilities and		
Total Assets	$473	$412	Stockholders' Equity	$473	$412

Use the information in Inland Medical Supply, Inc.'s financial statements to compute the following:

1. Collections from customers

2. Payments for inventory

S11-11. Calculate certain investing and financing information from financial statements (*Learning Objective 3***) 10–15 min.**

Use the Inland Medical Supply, Inc., data in S11-10 to compute the amount of fixed assets acquired by Inland Medical Supply, Inc., assuming Inland sold no fixed assets in 2014.

S11-12. Calculate certain investing and financing information from financial statements (*Learning Objective 3*) 10–15 min.

Use the Inland Medical Supply, Inc., data in S11-10 to compute the following amounts for 2014:

1. Borrowing or payment of long-term notes payable, assuming Inland had only one long-term note payable transaction during the year

2. Issuance of common stock, assuming Inland had only one common stock transaction during the year

3. Payment of cash dividends

MyAccountingLab   **Exercises (Group A)**

E11-13A. Operating activities—indirect method (*Learning Objective 3*) 10–15 min.

The accounting records of Morton, Inc., reveal:

Net Income	$19,000
Depreciation Expense	8,000
Sales Revenue	22,000
Decrease in current liabilities	26,000
Loss on sale of land	3,000
Increase in current assets other than Cash	11,000
Acquisition of land	43,000

Requirements

1. Compute cash flows from operating activities by the indirect method. Use the format of the operating activities section shown in Exhibit 11-3.

2. Evaluate the operating cash flow of Morton, Inc. Give the reason for your evaluation.

E11-14A. Operating activities—indirect method (*Learning Objective 3*) 10–15 min.

The July accounting records of Carlson & Associates include these accounts:

Cash			
Jul 1	13,000	Payments	500,000
Receipts	497,000		
Jul 31	10,000		

Accounts Receivable			
Jul 1	15,000	Collections	497,000
Sales	489,000		
Jul 31	7,000		

Inventory			
Jul 1	17,000	Cost of goods sold	335,000
Purchases	347,000		
Jul 31	29,000		

Accounts Payable			
Payments	345,000	Jul 1	19,000
		Purchases	347,000
		Jul 31	21,000

Accumulated Depreciation		
	Jul 1	53,000
	Depreciation expense	7,000
	Jul 31	60,000

Retained Earnings			
Dividends	19,000	Jul 1	64,000
		Net income	61,000
		Jul 31	106,000

Requirement

1. Compute Carlson & Associates' net cash provided by operating activities during July. Use the indirect method.

E11-15A. Prepare statement of cash flows—indirect method (*Learning Objective 3*)
20–25 min.

The income statement and additional data of Sunbelt Services, Inc., follow:

Sunbelt Services, Inc.
Income Statement
Year Ended September 30, 2014

Revenues:		
Sales Revenue	$307,000	
Dividend Revenue	6,000	
Total Revenues		$313,000
Expenses:		
Cost of Goods Sold	$112,000	
Salaries Expense	56,000	
Depreciation Expense	18,000	
Advertising Expense	7,000	
Interest Expense	1,000	
Income Tax Expense	12,000	
Total Expenses		206,000
Net Income		$107,000

Additional data follows:

a. Acquisition of fixed assets totaled $131,000. Of this amount, $106,000 was paid in cash and a $25,000 note payable was signed for the remainder.

b. Proceeds from sale of land totaled $23,000. No gain or loss was recognized on the sale.

c. Proceeds from issuance of common stock totaled $37,000.

d. Payment of long-term note payable was $13,000.

e. Payment of dividends was $9,000.

f. Data from the comparative balance sheet follow:

September 30	2014	2013
Current Assets:		
Cash	$87,000	$23,000
Accounts Receivable	43,000	59,000
Inventory	33,000	29,000
Current Liabilities:		
Accounts Payable	$31,000	$25,000
Accrued Liabilities	12,000	23,000

Requirements

1. Prepare Sunbelt Services' statement of cash flows for the year ended September 30, 2014, using the indirect method.

2. Calculate Sunbelt Services' free cash flow for the year ended September 30, 2014.

3. Evaluate Sunbelt Services' cash flows for the year. In your evaluation, mention all three categories of cash flows as well as free cash flow and give the reason for your evaluation.

E11-16A. Calculate cash conversion cycle (*Learning Objective 5*) **5–10 min.**

Use the data for Sunbelt Services from E11-15A.

Requirements

1. Calculate the cash conversion cycle for Sunbelt Services. Round all calculations to two decimal places. Assume all sales on credit.

2. Comment on Sunbelt Services' cash conversion cycle assuming that it was 76.39 days for the prior year.

E11-17A. Calculate certain investing and financing information from financial statements (*Learning Objective 3*) **10–15 min.**

Requirements

Compute the following items for the statement of cash flows:

1. The beginning and ending Retained Earnings balances are $47,000 and $82,000, respectively. Net income for the period is $61,000. How much are cash dividends?

2. The beginning and ending net Fixed Assets balances are $106,000 and $114,000, respectively. Depreciation expense for the period is $17,000, and acquisitions of new fixed assets total $38,000. Fixed assets were sold at a $2,000 loss. What were the cash proceeds of the sale?

Quick solution:

1. Cash dividends = $26,000

2. Cash proceeds from sale = $11,000

E11-18A. Operating activities—direct method (*Learning Objective 4*) **10–15 min.**

The accounting records of The Picket Fence, Inc., reveal:

Net Income	$ 41,000	Payment of	
Payment of income tax	20,000	salaries and wages..............	$30,000
Collection of		Depreciation Expense..............	10,000
dividend revenue...............	6,000	Payment of interest..................	22,000
Payment to suppliers	36,000	Payment of	
Collections from customers ...	133,000	dividends.............................	6,000

Requirements

1. Compute cash flows from operating activities by the direct method.

2. Evaluate the operating cash flow of The Picket Fence, Inc. Give the reason for your evaluation.

E11-19A. Prepare statement of cash flows—direct method (*Learning Objective 4*)
20–25 min.

The income statement and additional data of Sunbelt Services, Inc., follow:

	Sunbelt Services, Inc. **Income Statement** Year Ended September 30, 2014		
	Revenues:		
	Sales Revenue	$307,000	
	Dividend Revenue	6,000	
	Total Revenues		$313,000
	Expenses:		
	Cost of Goods Sold	$112,000	
	Salaries Expense	56,000	
	Depreciation Expense	18,000	
	Advertising Expense	7,000	
	Interest Expense	1,000	
	Income Tax Expense	12,000	
	Total Expenses		206,000
	Net Income		$107,000

Additional data follow:

a. Collections from customers are $16,000 more than sales.

b. Payments to suppliers are the sum of cost of goods sold plus advertising expense.

c. Payments to employees are $9,000 more than salaries expense.

d. Dividend revenue, interest expense, and income tax expense equal their cash amounts.

e. Acquisition of fixed assets for cash is $106,000.

f. Proceeds from sale of land total $23,000.

g. Proceeds from issuance of common stock for cash total $37,000.

h. Payment of long-term note payable is $13,000.

i. Payment of dividends is $9,000.

j. Cash balance, September 30, 2013, was $23,000.

Requirement

1. Prepare Sunbelt Services' statement of cash flows for the year ended September 30, 2014. Use the direct method.

E11-20A. Calculate certain information for direct method (*Learning Objective 4*)
10–15 min.

Requirements

Compute the following items for the statement of cash flows:

1. The beginning and ending Accounts Receivable balances are $30,000 and $32,000, respectively. Credit sales for the period total $60,000. How much are cash collections?

2. Cost of Goods Sold is $100,000. Beginning Inventory balance is $23,000, and ending Inventory balance is $17,000. Beginning and ending Accounts Payable are $15,000 and $13,000, respectively. How much are cash payments for inventory?

E11-21A. Calculate certain information for direct method (*Learning Objective 4*) 20–25 min.

Good Life, Inc., a nationwide insurance chain, reported the following selected amounts in its financial statements for the year ended December 31, 2014 (adapted, in millions):

Income Statement

	2014	2013
Net Sales	$27,391	$22,173
Cost of Goods Sold	19,412	15,842
Depreciation Expense	276	237
Other Operating Expenses	4,853	4,012
Income Tax Expense	742	541
Net Income	2,108	1,541

Balance Sheet

	2014	2013
Cash and Cash Equivalents	$ 16	$ 7
Accounts Receivable	798	612
Inventories	1,644	1,439
Property and Equipment, Net	3,171	2,863
Accounts Payable	1,397	1,277
Accrued Liabilities	932	854
Long-Term Liabilities	205	196
Common Stock	590	480
Retained Earnings	2,505	2,114

Requirement

1. Determine the following for Good Life, Inc., during 2014. (Enter all amounts in millions.)
   a. Collections from customers
   b. Payments for inventory
   c. Payments of operating expenses
   d. Acquisitions of property and equipment; no sales were made during 2014
   e. Long-term borrowing, assuming Good Life, Inc., made no payments on long-term liabilities
   f. Proceeds from issuance of common stock
   g. Payment of cash dividends

MyAccountingLab

Exercises (Group B)

E11-22B. Operating activities—indirect method (*Learning Objective 3*) 10–15 min.

The accounting records of Elite Talent Agency reveal:

Net Income	$40,000
Depreciation Expense	3,000
Sales Revenue	13,000
Decrease in current liabilities	24,000
Loss on sale of land	2,000
Increase in current assets other than Cash	15,000
Acquisition of land	39,000

Requirements

1. Compute cash flows from operating activities by the indirect method. Use the format of the operating activities section shown in Exhibit 11-3.

2. Evaluate the operating cash flow of Elite Talent Agency. Give the reason for your evaluation.

E11-23B. Operating activities—indirect method (*Learning Objective 3*) 10–15 min.

The March accounting records of Penestrie, Inc., include these accounts:

Cash			
Mar 1	8,000	Payments	451,000
Receipts	448,000		
Mar 31	5,000		

Accounts Receivable			
Mar 1	18,000	Collections	460,000
Sales	454,000		
Mar 31	12,000		

Inventory			
Mar 1	19,000	Cost of goods sold	264,000
Purchases	278,000		
Mar 31	33,000		

Accounts Payable			
Payments	283,000	Mar 1	7,000
		Purchases	294,000
		Mar 31	18,000

Accumulated Depreciation			
		Mar 1	63,000
		Depreciation expense	9,000
		Mar 31	72,000

Retained Earnings			
Dividends	25,000	Mar 1	84,000
		Net income	73,000
		Mar 31	132,000

Requirement

1. Compute Penestrie, Inc.'s net cash provided by operating activities during March. Use the indirect method.

E11-24B. Prepare statement of cash flows—indirect method (*Learning Objective 3*) 20–25 min.

The income statement and additional data of Snyder Services, Inc., follow:

Snyder Services, Inc.		
Income Statement		
Year Ended November 30, 2014		
Revenues:		
Sales Revenue	$275,000	
Dividend Revenue	11,000	
Total Revenues		$286,000
Expenses:		
Cost of Goods Sold	$103,000	
Salaries Expense	45,000	
Depreciation Expense	19,000	
Advertising Expense	7,000	
Interest Expense	7,000	
Income Tax Expense	12,000	
Total Expenses		193,000
Net Income		$ 93,000

Additional data follows:

a. Acquisition of fixed assets totaled $102,000. Of this amount, $87,000 was paid in cash and a $15,000 note payable was signed for the remainder.

b. Proceeds from the sale of land totaled $19,000. No gain or loss was recognized on the sale.

c. Proceeds from issuance of common stock total $50,000.

d. Payment of long-term note payable was $15,000.

e. Payment of dividends was $16,000.

f. Data from the comparative balance sheet follow:

November 30	2014	2013
Current Assets:		
Cash..	$71,000	$11,000
Accounts Receivable..	40,000	55,000
Inventory...	38,000	24,000
Current Liabilities:		
Accounts Payable..	$36,000	$27,000
Accrued Liabilities...	12,000	25,000

Requirements

1. Prepare Snyder Services' statement of cash flows for the year ended November 30, 2014, using the indirect method.

2. Calculate Snyder Services free cash flow for the year ended November 30, 2014.

3. Evaluate Snyder Services' cash flows for the year. In your evaluation, mention all three categories of cash flows as well as free cash flow and give the reason for your evaluation.

E11-25B. Calculate cash conversion cycle (*Learning Objective 5*) 5–10 min.

Use the data for Snyder Services from E11-24B.

Requirements

1. Calculate the cash conversion cycle for Snyder Services. Round all calculations to two decimal places. Assume all sales on credit.

2. Comment on Snyder Services' cash conversion cycle assuming that it was 66.82 days for the prior year.

E11-26B. Calculate certain investing and financing information from financial statements (*Learning Objective 3*) 10–15 min.

Requirements

Compute the following items for the statement of cash flows:

1. The beginning and ending Retained Earnings balances are $29,000 and $80,000, respectively. Net income for the period is $62,000. How much are cash dividends?

2. The beginning and ending net Fixed Assets balances are $101,000 and $110,000, respectively. Depreciation expense for the period is $16,000, and acquisitions of new fixed assets total $42,000. Fixed assets were sold at a $3,000 gain. What were the cash proceeds of the sale?

P11-33A. Prepare statement of cash flows—indirect method (*Learning Objective 3*)
20–25 min.

The 2014 comparative balance sheet and income statement of Charleston Medical
Supply, Inc., are:

			2014	2013	INCREASE (DECREASE)
	Current Assets:				
		Cash and Cash Equivalents	$ 6,900	$ 5,100	$ 1,800
		Accounts Receivable	24,300	26,500	(2,200)
		Inventory	91,700	89,400	2,300
	Fixed Assets:				
		Land	88,400	60,600	27,800
		Equipment, Net	54,600	49,200	5,400
	Total Assets		$265,900	$230,800	$ 35,100
	Current Liabilities:				
		Accounts Payable	$ 29,700	$ 35,800	$ (6,100)
		Accrued Liabilities	31,400	28,200	3,200
	Long-Term Liabilities:				
		Notes Payable	77,000	100,000	(23,000)
	Stockholders' Equity:				
		Common Stock	88,500	64,100	24,400
		Retained Earnings	39,300	2,700	36,600
	Total Liabilities and Stockholders' Equity		$265,900	$230,800	$ 35,100

Charleston Medical Supply, Inc.
Comparative Balance Sheet
December 31, 2014 and 2013

Charleston Medical Supply, Inc.
Income Statement
Year Ended December 31, 2014

Revenues:			
	Sales Revenue	$207,000	
	Interest Revenue	7,800	
	Total Revenues		$214,800
Expenses:			
	Cost of Goods Sold	$ 70,900	
	Salaries Expense	27,200	
	Depreciation Expense	5,100	
	Other Operating Expenses	11,300	
	Interest Expense	12,400	
	Income Tax Expense	28,600	
	Total Expenses		155,500
Net Income			$ 59,300

Charleston Medical Supply, Inc., had no noncash investing and financing transactions during 2014. During the year, Charleston Medical Supply, Inc., made no sales of land or equipment, no issuance of notes payable, no retirement of stock, and no treasury stock transactions.

Requirements

1. Prepare the 2014 statement of cash flows, formatting operating activities by the indirect method.

2. How will what you learned in this problem help you evaluate an investment in Charleston Medical Supply, Inc.?

P11-34A. Prepare statement of cash flows—direct method (*Learning Objective 4*) 20–25 min.

The accounting records for T. Houton Associates, Inc., for the year ended April 30, 2014, contain the following information:

a. Purchase of fixed assets for cash, $49,000

b. Proceeds from issuance of common stock, $45,000

c. Payment of dividends, $44,400

d. Collection of interest, $7,500

e. Payment of salaries, $95,000

f. Proceeds from sale of fixed assets, $27,000

g. Collections from customers, $609,000

h. Cash receipt of dividend revenue, $5,500

i. Payments to suppliers, $368,500

j. Depreciation expense, $59,000

k. Proceeds from issuance of long-term notes, $39,100

l. Payments of long-term notes payable, $49,000

m. Interest expense and payments, $13,500

n. Income tax expense and payments, $43,000

o. Cash balances: April 30, 2013, $40,100; April 30, 2014, $110,800

Requirement

1. Prepare T. Houton Associates' statement of cash flows for the year ended April 30, 2014. Use the direct method for cash flows from operating activities.

P11-35A. Prepare statement of cash flows—direct method (*Learning Objective 4*) 20–25 min.

Use the Charleston Medical Supply, Inc., data from P11-33A. The cash amounts for Interest Revenue, Salaries Expense, Interest Expense, and Income Tax Expense are the same as the accrual amounts for these items.

Requirements

1. Prepare the 2014 statement of cash flows by the direct method.

2. How will what you learned in this problem help you evaluate an investment in Charleston Medical Supply, Inc.?

P11-36A. Prepare statement of cash flows—direct method (*Learning Objective 4*)
20–25 min.

To prepare the statement of cash flows, accountants for C. Harrison, Inc., summarized 2014 activity in the Cash account as:

Cash			
Beginning balance	100,400	Payment on accounts payable	300,000
Receipts of interest	23,300	Payment of dividends	22,000
Collections from customers	492,300	Payment of salaries and wages	143,800
Issuance of common stock	90,000	Payment of interest	21,600
		Payment for equipment	9,900
		Payment of operating expenses	31,000
		Payment of notes payable	79,000
		Payment of income tax	16,800
Ending balance	81,900		

Requirement

1. Prepare the statement of cash flows of C. Harrison, Inc., for the year ended December 31, 2014, using the direct method for operating activities.

Problems (Group B)

P11-37B. Prepare statement of cash flows—indirect method (*Learning Objective 3*)
20–25 min.

Carlson Corporation accountants assembled the following data for the year ended December 31, 2014:

Carlson Corporation		
December 31	2014	2013
Current Assets:		
Cash and Cash Equivalents	$82,600	$27,000
Accounts Receivable	69,700	64,800
Inventory	80,300	83,500
Current Liabilities:		
Accounts Payable	$57,200	$55,600
Income Tax Payable	14,500	16,500

Transaction Data for 2014:	
Net Income	$ 57,300
Purchase of treasury stock	14,200
Issuance of common stock for cash	36,900
Loss on sale of equipment	10,500
Payment of cash dividends	18,300
Depreciation Expense	21,900
Issuance of long-term note payable in exchange for cash	34,600
Purchase of building for cash	124,000
Retirement of bonds payable by issuing common stock	66,000
Sale of equipment for cash	53,000

Requirement

1. Prepare Carlson Corporation's statement of cash flows using the indirect method to report operating activities. List noncash investing and financing activities on an accompanying schedule.

P11-38B. Prepare statement of cash flows—indirect method (*Learning Objective 3*)
20–25 min.

Data from the comparative balance sheet of Marsing Company at March 31, 2014, follow:

March 31	2014	2013
Current Assets:		
Cash and Cash Equivalents	$15,300	$ 5,600
Accounts Receivable	14,400	21,600
Inventory	54,500	52,800
Current Liabilities:		
Accounts Payable	$31,700	$28,300
Accrued Liabilities	14,200	16,300
Income Tax Payable	8,600	4,800

Marsing Company's transactions during the year ended March 31, 2014, included:

Payment of cash dividend	$42,000	Depreciation Expense	$18,300
Purchase of equipment for cash	29,400	Purchase of building for cash	99,200
Issuance of long-term note payable in exchange for cash	60,000	Net Income	76,400
		Issuance of common stock	15,000

Requirements

1. Prepare Marsing Company's statement of cash flows for the year ended March 31, 2014, using the indirect method to report cash flows from operating activities.

2. Evaluate Marsing Company's cash flows for the year. Mention all three categories of cash flows and give the reason for your evaluation.

P11-39B. Prepare statement of cash flows—indirect method (*Learning Objective 3***)**
20–25 min.

The 2014 comparative balance sheet and income statement of Kahl Medical Supplies
follow:

Kahl Medical Supplies
Comparative Balance Sheet
December 31, 2014 and 2013

			2014	2013	INCREASE (DECREASE)
	Current Assets:				
		Cash and Cash Equivalents	$ 6,600	$ 6,000	$ 600
		Accounts Receivable	25,000	26,800	(1,800)
		Inventory	91,900	89,600	2,300
	Fixed Assets:				
		Land	89,200	60,400	28,800
		Equipment, Net	53,900	49,500	4,400
	Total Assets		$266,600	$232,300	$ 34,300
	Current Liabilities:				
		Accounts Payable	$ 30,300	$ 35,800	$ (5,500)
		Accrued Liabilities	30,900	28,300	2,600
	Long-Term Liabilities:				
		Notes Payable	73,000	101,000	(28,000)
	Stockholders' Equity:				
		Common Stock	88,500	64,400	24,100
		Retained Earnings	43,900	2,800	41,100
	Total Liabilities and Stockholders' Equity		$266,600	$232,300	$ 34,300

Kahl Medical Supplies
Income Statement
Year Ended December 31, 2014

	Revenues:			
		Sales Revenue	$213,000	
		Interest Revenue	8,300	
		Total Revenues		$221,300
	Expenses:			
		Cost of Goods Sold	$ 70,500	
		Salaries Expense	27,700	
		Depreciation Expense	4,600	
		Other Operating Expenses	10,300	
		Interest Expense	11,400	
		Income Tax Expense	29,000	
		Total Expenses		153,500
	Net Income			$ 67,800

Kahl Medical Supplies had no noncash investing and financing transactions during 2014. During the year, Kahl Medical Supplies made no sales of land or equipment, no issuance of notes payable, no retirement of stock, and no treasury stock transactions.

Requirements

1. Prepare the 2014 statement of cash flows, formatting operating activities by the indirect method.

2. How will what you learned in this problem help you evaluate an investment in Kahl Medical Supplies?

P11-40B. Prepare statement of cash flows—direct method (*Learning Objective 4*) 20–25 min.

The accounting records for Inez, Inc., for the year ended September 30, 2014, contain the following information:

a. Purchase of fixed assets, $82,300

b. Proceeds from issuance of common stock, $55,000

c. Payment of dividends, $41,300

d. Collection of interest, $7,600

e. Payments of salaries, $87,400

f. Proceeds from sale of fixed assets, $17,800

g. Collections from customers, $637,000

h. Cash receipt of dividend revenue, $4,800

i. Payments to suppliers, $381,900

j. Depreciation expense, $63,400

k. Proceeds from issuance of long-term notes, $23,500

l. Payments of long-term notes payable, $46,800

m. Interest expense and payments, $13,200

n. Income tax expense and payments, $38,600

o. Cash balance: September 30, 2013, $26,700; September 30, 2014, $80,900

Requirement

1. Prepare Inez, Inc.'s statement of cash flows for the year ended September 30, 2014. Use the direct method for cash flows from operating activities.

P11-41B. Prepare statement of cash flows—direct method (*Learning Objective 4*) 20–25 min.

Use the Kahl Medical Supplies data from P11-39B. The cash amounts for Interest Revenue, Salaries Expense, Interest Expense, and Income Tax Expense are the same as the accrual amounts for these items.

Requirements

1. Prepare the 2014 statement of cash flows by the direct method.

2. How will what you learned in this problem help you evaluate an investment in Kahl Medical Supplies?

P11-42B. Prepare statement of cash flows—direct method (*Learning Objective 4*)
20–25 min.

To prepare the statement of cash flows, accountants for Nelson Industrial, Inc., summarized 2014 activity in the Cash account as:

Cash			
Beginning balance	63,800	Payment on accounts payable	276,900
Receipts of interest	8,200	Payment of dividends	10,700
Collections from customers	461,300	Payment of salaries and wages	62,300
Issuance of common stock	58,500	Payment of interest	21,400
		Payment for equipment	21,800
		Payment of operating expenses	27,900
		Payment of notes payable	72,000
		Payment of income tax	7,600
Ending balance	91,200		

Requirement

1. Prepare the statement of cash flows of Nelson Industrial, Inc., for the year ended December 31, 2014, using the direct method for operating activities.

Continuing Exercise

This exercise continues the accounting for Cole's Yard Care, Inc., from the Continuing Exercise in Chapter 10. Assume that Cole's Yard Care, Inc., had the following comparative balance sheet at the end of 2015, its second year of operations.

Cole's Yard Care, Inc.
Comparative Balance Sheet
December 31, 2015 and 2014

	2015	2014
ASSETS		
Cash	$23,020	$18,400
Accounts Receivable	1,230	800
Lawn Supplies	210	170
Equipment	5,200	1,600
(Less Accumulated Depreciation)	(1,400)	(300)
Total Assets	$28,260	$20,670
LIABILITIES		
Accounts Payable	$ 180	$ 330
Notes Payable (long-term)	$ 7,000	12,000
STOCKHOLDERS' EQUITY		
Common Stock	4,300	2,000
Retained Earnings	16,780	6,340
Total Liabilities and Stockholders' Equity	$28,260	$20,670

Requirement

1. Prepare the statement of cash flows for Cole's Yard Care, Inc., for the year ending December 31, 2015 using the indirect method. The following additional information applies to 2015:
   • Common stock was issued at par value.
   • No dividends were declared or paid during the year.
   • No equipment was sold during the year, and all purchases of equipment were for cash.

Continuing Problem

In this problem, we continue our accounting for Aqua Magic, Inc., from Chapter 10. We will assume that Aqua Magic, Inc., is now in its second year of operations.

Assume that the comparative balance sheet for Aqua Magic, Inc., at July 31, 2015, and the income statement for the month ended July 31, 2015, are:

Aqua Magic, Inc. **Comparative Balance Sheets** July 31 and June 30, 2015		
	July 31	**June 30**
ASSETS		
Cash	$ 8,126	$ 9,246
Accounts Receivable, net	91,647	82,403
Inventory	18,241	16,857
Supplies	164	227
Total Current Assets	118,178	108,733
Fixed Assets	357,600	244,800
Less: Accumulated Depreciation	(9,003)	(8,529)
Net Fixed Assets	348,597	236,271
Total Assets	$466,775	$345,004
LIABILITIES		
Accounts Payable	$ 2,060	$ 1,280
Unearned Revenue	6,800	2,700
Salaries Payable	950	875
Interest Payable	621	180
Payroll Taxes Payable	543	—
Dividend Payable	300	800
Current Portion of Long-Term Debt	11,673	9,896
Total Current Liabilities	22,947	15,731
Notes Payable	59,260	28,960
Mortgage Payable	228,685	148,685
Total Liabilities	310,892	193,376
STOCKHOLDERS' EQUITY		
Preferred Stock	16,000	16,000
Paid-in Capital in Excess of Par, Preferred	12,000	12,000
Common Stock	95,000	95,000
Paid-in Capital in Excess of Par, Common	7,000	7,000
Retained Earnings	25,883	21,628
Total Stockholders' Equity	155,883	151,628
Total Liabilities & Stockholders' Equity	$466,775	$345,004

Aqua Magic, Inc.
Income Statement
Month Ended July 31, 2015

Revenue	$45,691
Expenses:	
Cost of Goods Sold	34,276
Depreciation Expense	474
Rent Expense	1,050
Interest Expense	843
Insurance Expense	240
Supplies Expense	122
Salaries Expense	2,746
Payroll Taxes Expense	543
Bank Service Fees	15
Net Income*	$ 5,382

*Income taxes ignored

Additional information follows:

During the month, Aqua Magic, Inc., purchased a $32,800 truck financed with a note payable; it purchased an $80,000 building site financed with a mortgage payable; and it did not sell any fixed assets during the month.

Requirement

1. Prepare the statement of cash flows using the indirect method for the month of July.

Continuing Financial Statement Analysis Problem

Return to Target's 2012 annual report. For instructions on how to access the report online, see the Continuing Financial Statement Analysis Problem in Chapter 2. On page 33 of the annual report, you'll find Target's income statement for the year ending February 2, 2013 (called the Consolidated Statement of Operations). On page 35, you'll find Target's balance sheet as of February 2, 2013 (called the Consolidated Statement of Financial Position). On page 36, you'll find Target's Consolidated Statement of Cash Flows. Now answer these questions:

1. Look at Target's balance sheet, income statement, and statement of cash flows. Find net income on the income statement and statement of cash flows for the year ending February 2, 2013. Find the ending balance of cash and cash equivalents on the balance sheet as of February 2, 2013, and January 28, 2012. How does the statement of cash flows for the year ending February 2, 2013 tie these amounts together? Show how Target's statement of cash flows ties Target's income statement and balance sheet together.

2. Look over Target's statement of cash flows for the last two years. What are Target's net cash flows from operating, investing, and financing activities? How have these cash flows changed over the last two years?

3. Look at Target's balance sheet and income statement. What is Target's cash conversion cycle for the year ending February 2, 2013? What does this cash conversion cycle tell you? Assume all sales are on account and ignore credit card revenue.

4. Looking back over your answers to questions 1 through 3, how do you think Target is performing? What do you think of Target's management of cash and cash flow?

Apply Your Knowledge

Ethics In Action

Case 1. Design Incorporated experienced a downturn in December sales. To make matters worse, many of the recent sales were on account, and because many customers were not paying on their accounts, the ending balance of Accounts Receivable at December 31 was higher than the beginning balance. Because the business had a dramatic need for cash, a prime piece of land owned by the company was sold for cash in December at a substantial gain. Design had purchased the land 10 years earlier and properly classified it as a long-term investment. The CEO, Jim Shady, was looking over the financial statements and saw the company's weak operating cash flows. He approached the accountant to ask why the December cash flows provided from operations were so weak, given that the land had been sold. The accountant explained that because the indirect method was used in preparing the cash flow statement, certain adjustments to net income were required. To begin with, the increase in accounts receivable was a decreasing adjustment made in arriving at the net cash provided from operating activities. Next, the large gain recognized on the sale of land had to be adjusted by subtracting it from the net income in arriving at the cash provided by operating activities. These large negative adjustments drastically reduced the reported cash provided from that category of cash flows. The accountant then explained that all the cash proceeds from the land sale were included as cash inflows in the investing activities section.

Jim became worried because he remembered the bank telling him about the importance of strong operating cash flows, so he told the accountant to redo the statement but not to reduce the net income by the accounts receivable increase or the gain on the land sale. The accountant refused because these adjustments were necessary in order to properly arrive at the net cash provided from operating activities. If these adjustments were not made, then the net change in cash could not be reconciled. Jim finally agreed but then told the accountant to just include the cash proceeds from the sale of land in the operating activities rather than in the investing activities. The accountant said that would be wrong. Besides, everyone would know that proceeds from the sale of land should be an investing activity. Jim then suggested listing it as "other" in the operating section so no one would ever know that it wasn't an operating cash flow.

Why didn't Jim want the accountant to decrease the net income by the increase in accounts receivable and the gain on the land sale? Why do you think Jim finally agreed with the accountant? Could the operating cash flows be increased by including the cash proceeds from the sale but listing them as "other" rather than as land sale proceeds? What ethical concerns are involved? Do you have any other thoughts?

Case 2. Kevin Sailors, the CEO of Candle Corporation, was discussing the financial statements with the company accountant. Weak cash flows had resulted in the company borrowing a lot of money. Kevin wanted to know why the money borrowed was included as cash inflows in the financing section of the statement of cash flows but the interest paid on the amounts borrowed was not. The accountant replied that the interest paid on loans was an expense included in the calculation of net income, which was in the operating activities section. Kevin then asked why the dividends Candle Corporation paid to stockholders were included as an outflow of cash in the financing section. The accountant then explained that dividends paid, unlike interest paid, were a return to stockholders and not an expense; therefore, they would not be included in net income, nor would they appear in the operating activities section. Kevin replied that he did not care and instructed the accountant to include both the interest paid and the dividends paid in the financing section. The accountant said that such a move would not be proper. Kevin then said to not provide the statement of cash flows at all because too many people would see the weakening operating cash flows. He further stated that investors and creditors who really analyzed the income statements and balance sheets would be able to understand the company without the need for a statement of cash flows spelling out the net changes in cash flows.

Why would Kevin want the interest paid to be included in the financing activities section? Why would the accountant state that interest paid should not be included in the financing activities section? Can the statement of cash flows be omitted? What ethical issues are involved? Do you have any additional thoughts?

Know Your Business

Financial Analysis

Purpose: To help to familiarize you with the financial reporting of a real company in order to further your understanding of the chapter material you are learning.

This case focuses on the cash flows of Columbia Sportswear. Recall that inflows and out-flows of cash are classified as operating activities, investing activities, or financing activities. The statement of cash flows presents cash flows from each of these three activities. It is, therefore, important to understand the information provided in this revealing financial statement. The statement of cash flows and additional related information for Columbia Sportswear are disclosed in its annual report found in Appendix A.

Requirements

1. Look at the operating activities section of the statements of cash flows. Compare the net cash provided by operating activities to the net income for each of the three years presented. Are the net income amounts reported on the cash flow statement the same as on the income statement? How does the net cash flow provided by operations compare to the net income? Why do they differ? Is this difference good or bad? Have the net cash flows provided by operations been increasing or decreasing? Why are depreciation and amortization added back each year?

2. Look at the investing activities section of the statements of cash flows. What has created the largest inflows and outflows of cash related to investing activities in each of the three years presented? Can you determine whether Columbia Sportswear has been spending money to purchase more property and equipment? Did investing activities provide or use cash for the three years presented?

3. Look at the financing activities section of the statements of cash flows. Did financing activities provide or require cash for the three fiscal years presented? What is the significance of this information? What are the stock repurchase and dividend trends? What was the largest item in the financing section for the most recent year?

4. How do you feel about the overall sufficiency of cash flows? Does the net cash provided from operations cover the net cash required for investing activities for each of the three years? Does the net cash provided from operations cover the net cash required for financing activities for each of the three years?

5. What was the net change in cash and cash equivalents for the most recent fiscal year? Does the ending cash amount agree with the cash and cash equivalents reported on the balance sheet? Do you have any other observations about the statement of cash flows?

Industry Analysis

Purpose: To help you understand and compare the performance of two companies in the same industry.

Find the Columbia Sportswear Company Annual Report located in Appendix A and go to the Consolidated Statements of Cash Flows on page 661. Now access the 2012 Annual Report for Under Armour, Inc., from the Internet. For instructions on how to access the report online, see the Industry Analysis in Chapter 1. The company's Consolidated Statements of Cash Flows is on page 52.

Requirement

1. Which method (direct or indirect) does each of these companies use to prepare their statement of cash flows? How can you tell? Which activities provided cash for each of the companies for each of the three years? Which activities used cash for each of these companies for each of the three years? What conclusions can you draw from these results?

Small Business Analysis

Purpose: To help you understand the importance of cash flows in the operation of a small business.

You just received your year-end financial statements from your CPA. Although receiving the year-end financial package is important every year for your financing institutions and your investors, it is especially important this year because of the potential investment opportunity that just became available to you. Yesterday you got a telephone call from one of your competitors with whom you have been discussing the possibility of a merger. The gist of the conversation was that the board of directors wanted to sell outright to you instead of merging. You're pretty happy about that except for the fact that it could create some potential cash flow problems. The other company wants $1,000,000 cash and it wants to do it soon or the deal is off. You've got that amount of cash and cash equivalents available right now, but you know there are some cash commitments coming up soon for capital expenditures and dividend payments. You decide to call one of your financial investors. She suggests that you calculate free cash flow at the end of the year to determine if that amount of cash is available to complete the deal.

You look at your statement of cash flows and see that net cash flow from operations was $1,725,000 and that cash used to purchase long-term assets was $550,000.

Requirement

1. Define free cash flow and calculate it based on the information previously provided. With your understanding of free cash flow, is this new investment something that this company should pursue?

Written Communication

You have been asked by your accounting professor to prepare a paper outlining the importance of the statement of cash flows, the details of what is included in each of the three sections of the statement, and how it provides a link between the income statement and the balance sheet.

Self Check Answers
1. d 2. b 3. c 4. c 5. c 6. b 7. c 8. d 9. c 10. b 11. b 12. d

Comprehensive Problem

The Accounting Cycle and Preparation of Financial Statements Including a Statement of Cash Flows

Haskins Supply, Inc., supplies industrial tools to local businesses. Haskins Supply's November 30, 2014 Balance Sheet appears as:

Haskins Supply, Inc.
Balance Sheet
November 30, 2014

ASSETS		
Current Assets:		
Cash		$ 26,487
Accounts Receivable, net of allowance for doubtful accounts of $2,140		43,350
Inventory		87,244
Supplies		682
Prepaid Insurance		4,800
Total Current Assets		162,563
Long-term assets:		
Office Equipment	19,460	
Less: Accumulated Depreciation, Office Equipment	4,880	14,580
Total Assets		$177,143
LIABILITIES		
Current Liabilities:		
Accounts Payable		$ 25,673
Salaries Payable		885
Total Current Liabilities		26,558
Long-Term Liabilities:		
Notes Payable, Long-Term		7,500
Total Liabilities		34,058
STOCKHOLDERS' EQUITY		
Common Stock, $10 par value, 100,000 shares authorized, 3,000 shares issued and outstanding.		30,000
Paid-in capital in Excess of Par, Common		10,000
Total paid-in Capital		40,000
Retained Earnings		103,085
Total Stockholders' Equity		143,085
Total Liabilities and Stockholders' Equity		$177,143

During the month of December 2014, Haskins Supply, Inc., had the following transactions:

Dec	2	Paid the balance in Salaries Payable
	3	Purchased $2,450 of inventory on account from Ensco, Inc. Terms, 2/10, n/30, FOB shipping point.
	4	Paid freight charges of $160 on Dec 3 purchase from Ensco, Inc.
	5	Purchased $400 of supplies on account from OfficeMaxx. Terms, 3/15, n/30, FOB destination.
	9	Sold merchandise costing $1,120 to Allied, Inc. on account for $2,760. Terms, 2/10, n/30, FOB destination.
	10	Paid $140 freight charges to deliver goods to Allied, Inc.
	11	Paid amount owed to Ensco, Inc. on the Dec 3 purchase in full.
	12	Sold 1,500 shares of common stock for $22,000
	13	Sold merchandise costing $5,310 to a cash customer for $12,870
	14	Received $4,240 from Noxon, Inc. as payment on a November 16 sale. Terms were n/30.
	15	Granted a $360 allowance to Allied, Inc. on the Dec 9 sale due to damaged merchandise.
	15	Purchased a delivery vehicle for $22,500, paying $5,000 cash and signing a 7%, 5-year, note payable for $17,500. The note requires annual payments of $3,500 plus interest on Dec 15 of each year.
	18	Received payment in full from Allied, Inc., for the Dec 9 sale.
	19	Paid for the supplies purchased on December 5.
	22	Declared a $2 per share cash dividend
	24	Sold office equipment for $1,000. Equipment originally cost $2,300 and had accumulated depreciation of $1,500
	26	Paid $2,360 on account to Donovan, Inc. on a November 8 purchase. Terms were 2/15, net 60.
	27	Wrote off the $980 account of XCR, Inc. as uncollectible.
	28	Paid $7,500 on the long-term note payable plus interest. The note was a 1-year, 6% note dated December 28, 2013. No interest has been recorded to this point.
	30	Paid current month's rent, $1,400.
	31	Paid sales commissions, 1,370.
	31	Paid the dividend declared on Dec 22.

Requirements

1. Open four-column general ledger accounts and enter the balances from the November 30 trial balance.

2. Record each transaction in the general journal. Explanations are not required. Post the journal entries to the general ledger, creating new ledger accounts as necessary. Omit posting references. Calculate the new account balances.

3. Prepare an unadjusted trial balance as of December 31, 2014.

4. Journalize and post the adjusting journal entries based on the following information, creating new ledger accounts as necessary:

    a. Depreciation on office equipment for the month is $146 and on vehicles is $375.

    b. Supplies on hand at December 31, $283.

    c. Accrued salary expense for the office receptionist is $1,025.

    d. Accrue interest on the December 15, $17,500 note payable (round to the nearest dollar).

e. The balance in prepaid insurance represents a six-month insurance policy that was purchased on November 31 of the current year.

f. Based on an aging of Accounts Receivable, Haskins Supply estimates uncollectible accounts will equal $2,830.

5. Prepare an adjusted trial balance as of December 31, 2014. Use the adjusted trial balance to prepare Haskins Supply, Inc.'s multi-step income statement and statement of retained earnings for the month ending December 31, 2014. Also, prepare the comparative balance sheet at December 31, 2014. Use the financial statements and the monthly transaction data to prepare Haskins Supply's statement of cash flows for the month ending December 31, 2014, using the indirect method.

6. Journalize and post the closing entries.

7. Prepare a post-closing trial balance at December 31, 2014.

Financial Statement Analysis

Business, Accounting, and You

In previous chapters, you learned about different types of transactions and how accountants classify those transactions. You learned how these transactions feed into the financial statements in order to show the extent of the business's success to interested parties, creditors, vendors, and investors.

Now let's look at how these interested parties, or stakeholders, use this information in the financial statements. Let's look at how to analyze a business's financial statements to understand what the business is doing and whether the business is successful.

Learning Objectives

1 Understand the purpose and process of financial analysis

2 Perform financial analysis using financial statements

3 Use financial analysis to assess the value of a business

Go back and look over Chapter 1. Remember that businesses exist to create value. Think about the businesses we've looked at in this book: Disney, Google, Target, Kroger, Toys R Us, Hershey, John Deere, Apple, and others. How do you tell if these businesses are doing a good or bad job of creating value? Are these businesses creating enough net income to compensate shareholders for the use of their money over time and for taking risks? Would you buy stock in these companies?

It's time to consider what accountants tell us in the financial statements and how you can use that information to evaluate the value of a business. Accounting information is designed to be used by decision makers to help determine whether to invest, lend, or extend credit. In other words, it's time to learn to analyze financial statements.

Real World Accounting Video

In the Real World Accounting Video, David Drake of LDJ Capital, talks about investing in companies. Listen to what David is saying. Think about analyzing a company and deciding whether to invest in it.

What Is Financial Analysis?

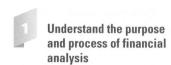

Understand the purpose and process of financial analysis

Financial analysis The process of using a business's financial statements, and other related information, to evaluate whether a business is creating value.

Financial analysts People who perform financial analysis.

Financial analysis is the process of using a business's financial statements, and other related information, to evaluate whether a business is creating value. **Financial analysts**, people who perform financial analysis, use the reports provided by accountants and others to evaluate the past and current performance of a business. Using this evaluation, analysts can begin to predict the future of the business and its value.

Look once more at Chapter 1. Remember that a business exists to create value for all its stakeholders, particularly its owners. So how does a corporation create value for its owners? It creates value for its owners by acquiring money with debt and equity. It then invests that money in assets. Next, the business hires employees to use the assets and create sales. In the process of creating sales, the business incurs operating expenses such as cost of goods sold, salaries, depreciation, and advertising. The net result is an operating profit (Earnings Before Interest and Taxes, or EBIT). This operating profit is first used to pay interest, the cost of debt, and then the taxes that are due to the government. What remains is net income. Net income belongs to the owners, the business's stockholders.

What is the process that analysts, stockholders, and other decision makers use to conduct financial analysis? There is a logical way to look at all the information provided by accountants and others. That logical way is to first figure out the forces that affect a business. Then analysts can look at the financial statements to determine whether a business is operating successfully within these forces.

The process of financial analysis has five steps. These steps are:

1. Understand a business's model and strategy.

2. Understand the environment in which the business operates.

3. Analyze the content of the financial statements and other information, making adjustments if desired.

4. Analyze the business's operations.

5. Use the financial analysis to make decisions.

Step One: Understand a Business's Model and Strategy

Before looking at the financial statements, you need to figure out a business's model and strategy. To do this, you should research and read the comments from management that accompany the financial statements. Financial statements are often a part of a business's annual report. Annual reports typically start with a discussion, by management, of the business's operations, risks, challenges, and opportunities. This discussion by management is called the **management discussion and analysis**, or **MD&A**. The MD&A is followed by the auditor's opinion, the financial statements, and the notes that explain the numbers in the financial statements.

A **business model** describes what a business does, the products it sells, and the customers who buy the products. Different businesses have different business models. Walmart buys and sells household products. This model depends on a lot of inventory and buildings. In contrast, Google creates and sells Internet services and advertising. Unlike Walmart, Google does not depend on inventory or real estate for its business model. A lot of Google's assets are intangible, such as patents. Walmart and Google have different business models.

After figuring out the business's model, you should look at a business's strategy. A **business strategy** is how a business uses its business model to create a competitive advantage. A business's strategy deals with how a business makes customers want to buy their product and not the product of their competitors. Think about it. Walmart, Kmart, and Target are all large discount stores that sell clothing and household products. All three companies have the same business model. Now think. Do you prefer to shop at one over the others? If so, why? Think about what that business does to make you want to shop there. That's strategy.

Understanding a business's model and strategy helps you look for the things that are critical to the success of the business. For example, it's very important that Walmart manages its inventory efficiently because its strategy is based on low prices. However, trying to look at Google's inventory is not important. Instead, you would look at how Google uses its equipment and intangible assets to deliver its search engine. Sound financial analysis starts with a solid understanding of a business's model and strategy.

Step Two: Understand the Environment in Which a Business Operates

Next you should research and examine the environment in which a business operates. The MD&A of a business's annual report is a good place to start when researching this issue. A business's environment has two parts, economic and competitive.

A business's **economic environment** is how the business is affected by the overall economy in which it operates. Let's take a look at Ford and Kroger. When the economy is strong and growing, people have a lot of money and buy automobiles. When the economy is not doing well, people do not have a lot of money and do not buy automobiles. Ford's sales go up and down based on the strength or weakness of the economy. In contrast, Kroger's sales do not fluctuate much based on the strength of the economy. People need and buy food in good and bad times.

Next, you examine a business's competitive environment. A business's **competitive environment** is how a business competes for its customers, supplies, and other critical resources. An example is McDonald's. McDonald's has a lot of competitors. McDonald's must constantly compete for customers by having better products, lower prices, and better facilities. On the other hand, Dominion Resources, the large electric utility, does not have competitors. It's a monopoly. However, it is regulated by state and federal governments. Regulators tell Dominion how much electricity it must produce and how much it can charge its customers for the electricity.

Benchmarking is a technique that helps you understand a business's environment. **Benchmarking** is where an analyst compares a business with similar businesses, often leading competitors. You compare McDonald's to Burger King or to averages that reflect all businesses that operate in the fast food industry. You compare Dominion Resources to Pacific Gas and Electric (PG&E) or to averages that reflect all producers of electricity.

Management discussion and analysis (MD&A) The section of a business's annual report in which a business's management discusses the results of operating the business, risks, challenges, and opportunities.

Business model A description of what a business does, the products it sells, and the customers who buy its products.

Business strategy A description of how a business uses its business model to create a competitive advantage.

Economic environment How a business is affected by the overall economy in which it operates.

Competitive environment How a business competes for its customers, supplies, and other critical resources.

Benchmarking The practice of comparing a company with other companies that are leaders in its industry.

Accounting in Your World

So Just How Badly Did You Do on That Test?

Have you ever received a test or an assignment back and, after looking at your score, were sure you failed? Then you found out your score wasn't so bad after all because there were only 80 points possible. Or perhaps you found out that your score, although low, was higher than the class average. Until you had a point of reference, your raw score did not tell the whole story about your performance. The results of financial statement analysis are similar. The results of financial analysis have limited value without a point of reference. This is why, when conducting financial statement analysis, a company's performance is compared to past performance and to the performance of its competitors.

Step Three: Analyze the Content of the Financial Statements and Other Information, Making Adjustments If Desired

Before using information, you must determine if information is reliable and reflects the operations of the business. How do you do this? First, you look at the audit opinion. Look back in Chapter 6 and review the role of auditors and audit opinions. Do the financial statements conform to Generally Accepted Accounting Principles (GAAP)?

Next, you need to decide whether the GAAP used by the business reflects what you, the analyst, feels is reality. Use the notes to financial statements to figure out which rules of GAAP a business chooses to use and why. An example is a company that purchased a building 20 years ago for $500,000. It is currently being used but is fully depreciated. It has a net value of zero on the company's balance sheet. Analysts may determine through appraisals that the building currently has a market value of $1,000,000. If so, they may want to increase the value of buildings, and thus assets, by $1,000,000. They would also increase stockholders' equity by $1,000,000 to reflect the perceived increase in the value of the business to its stockholders.

Step Four: Analyze the Business's Operations

Financial analysis asks questions about value. That means asking questions about the amount of net income, the time in which the net income is earned, and the risk associated with the net income. Financial analysis looks at how and when a business creates net income. Financial analysis attempts to see how net income changes over time.

Typical questions you should ask are:

- Question 1: Is the business a going concern? In others words, will the business exist in the near future?
- Question 2: How is the business earning a net income or loss?
- Question 3: Where is the business getting its money, and can it pay its debt obligations?

- Question 4: How is the business investing its money, and is it using its assets efficiently?
- Question 5: Is the business generating enough net income to reward the stockholders for the use of their money?

To answer these questions, you need to look at numbers and relationships. The relationships are called ratios. You also need to look at how the numbers and ratios change over time. Analyzing trends over time is very important because change is a major part of risk. You want to understand what a business is doing now and in the past and what has changed. This change helps the analyst forecast the future. Analysts use numbers, ratios, and trends to see if the business is doing a good or bad job acquiring money, investing money, and operating the business.

Step Five: Use the Financial Analysis to Make Decisions

First, you must understand a business's business model, strategy, and environment. Next, you assess the nature of information and make adjustments if they feel appropriate. Then you look at the numbers, ratios, and trends reflected in the financial statements.
   After all that work, it's time to make decisions using these key questions:

- How is the business performing?
- What's the business's value or worth?
- What would you pay for the business?
- Can the business operate more efficiently and improve its value?

Decision Guidelines

Decision	**Guideline**	**Analyze**
How do I know if a business has created value?	The objective of a business is to create value for all its stakeholders, particularly stockholders. Financial analysis is conducted to understand how a business meets this objective.	Look at the balance sheet, income statement, statement of retained earnings, cash flow statement, and other supporting documents such as the auditor's opinion. Now analyze the financial statements using a logical process that captures what a business does and how it does it. Does the business provide enough net income to justify stockholders' investments? Is the net income sufficient to compensate stockholders for the use of their money over time and for accepting risk?

What Measures Does Someone Use to Analyze the Performance of a Business?

2 | **Perform financial analysis using financial statements**

Analysts, which include you, use numbers, ratios, and trends to answer the questions noted earlier in step 4. So let's look at the numbers, ratios, and trends used for each question. Let's use an example to do this. Tucker Enterprises, Inc., buys bicycle parts and resells them to bicycle retailers and repair shops. The business is a corporation with 10,000 shares of common stock outstanding during 2012. The financial statements of Tucker Enterprises, Inc., can be found in **Exhibits 12-1, 12-2, 12-3,** and **12-4.**

Tucker Enterprises, Inc. Income Statement Years Ended December 31, 2014 and 2013		
(in thousands)	**2014**	**2013**
Net Sales	$1,200	$1,000
Cost of Goods Sold	600	400
Gross Profit	600	600
Operating Expenses		
Selling, General, and Administrative	200	200
Depreciation Expense	150	100
Income Before Interest and Taxes	250	300
Interest Expense	100	70
Income Before Taxes	150	230
Income Tax Expense	75	115
Net Income	$ 75	$ 115

Exhibit 12-1 ▲

Tucker Enterprises, Inc. Balance Sheet December 31, 2014 and 2013		
(in thousands)	**2014**	**2013**
Assets		
Current Assets:		
Cash and Cash Equivalents	$ 50	$ 100
Accounts Receivable, Net	100	80
Inventory	250	220
Total Current Assets	400	400
Property, Plant, and Equipment, Net	3,000	2,000
Total Assets	$3,400	$2,400
Liabilities		
Current Liabilities		
Accounts Payable	$ 60	$ 40
Accrued Liabilities	40	25
Total Current Liabilities	100	65
Long-Term Bank Loan	1,500	1,035
Total Liabilities	1,600	1,100
Stockholders' Equity		
Common Stock	550	100
Retained Earnings	1,250	1,200
Total Stockholders' Equity	1,800	1,300
Total Liabilities and Stockholders' Equity	$3,400	$2,400

Exhibit 12-2 ▲

The Techniques of Financial Analysis

Analysts use numbers found on the financial statements. It's important to understand the sales, expenses, and net income of a business. It's important to understand the amount of a business's assets, liabilities, and stockholders' equity. It's important to understand how much cash a business has and where the business obtained and used cash.

However, it's also important to look at relationships called ratios. Let's look at an example. You own two companies, Company A and Company B. This year, Company A earned net income of $1,000 and Company B earned net income of $100. Which company performed the best? Looking only at numbers, you would say Company A outperformed Company B. Company A's net income was 10 times as great as Company B's net income. However, how would your perception change if you knew that Company A had $100,000 in assets and Company B had $100 in assets? The management of Company A only produced $1 of net income for every $100 of assets, while the management of Company B produced $1 of net income for every $1 of assets. The ratio of income to assets was much better for Company B. Given the resources each had, the management of Company B was able to use their assets more effectively and outperformed the management of Company A.

Tucker Enterprises, Inc.
Statement of Retained Earnings
Year Ended December 31, 2014

(in thousands)	
Retained Earnings, January 1, 2014	$1,200
Add: Net Income	75
Subtotal	1,275
Less: Dividends	25
Retained Earnings, December 31, 2014	$1,250

Exhibit 12-3 ▲

Tucker Enterprises, Inc.
Statement of Cash Flows
Year Ended December 31, 2014

(in thousands)		
Cash flows from operating activities:		
Net income		$ 75
Adjustments to reconcile net income to net cash		
provided by operating activities		
Depreciation Expense	$ 150	
Increase in Accounts Receivable	(20)	
Increase in Inventory	(30)	
Increase in Accounts Payable	20	
Increase in Accrued Liabilities	15	135
Net cash provided by operating activities		210
Cash flows from investing activities:		
Acquisition of plant assets	(1,150)	
Net cash used in investing activities		(1,150)
Cash flows from financing activities:		
Proceeds from long-term bank loan	465	
Proceeds from sale of common stock	450	
Payment of dividends	(25)	
Net cash provided by financing activities		890
Net decrease in cash		(50)
Cash balance, December 31, 2013		100
Cash balance, December 31, 2014		$ 50

Exhibit 12-4 ▲

Important parts of financial statement analysis are vertical and horizontal analyses. Let's first look at vertical analysis.

Vertical Analysis

Vertical analysis Analysis of a financial statement that reveals the relationship of each statement item to a specified base amount, which is the 100% figure.

Vertical analysis of a financial statement reflects each item on the financial statement as a percentage of another item (the base amount) on the financial statement. The vertical analysis percentages are calculated as:

$$\text{Vertical analysis percentage} = \frac{\text{Financial statement item \$}}{\text{Base amount \$}} \times 100$$

On the income statement, net sales are used as the base amount and are shown as 100%. On the balance sheet, total assets are used as the base amount and are shown as 100%. Sometimes financial statements are prepared reflecting only the percentages for each line item without any of the actual dollar amounts. These are referred to as **common-size statements**. Formatting financial statements in this way reduces the bias that can occur when analyzing companies of differing sizes. The completed vertical analyses of Tucker Enterprises' 2014 and 2013 income statements and balance sheets are presented in **Exhibits 12-5** and **12-6**.

Common-size statement
A financial statement that reports only percentages (no dollar amounts) for each line item on the financial statement.

Tucker Enterprises, Inc.
Income Statement
Years Ended December 31, 2014 and 2013

(in thousands)	2014	PERCENT	2013	PERCENT
Net Sales	$1,200	100.0%	$1,000	100.0%
Cost of Goods Sold	600	50.0	400	40.0
Gross Profit	600	50.0	600	60.0
Operating Expenses:				
Selling, General, and Administrative	200	16.7	200	20.0
Depreciation Expense	150	12.5	100	10.0
Income Before Interest and Taxes	250	20.8	300	30.0
Interest Expense	100	8.3	70	7.0
Income Before Taxes	150	12.5	230	23.0
Income Tax Expense	75	6.3	115	11.5
Net Income	$ 75	6.3%	$ 115	11.5%

Exhibit 12-5 ▲

A Note About Rounding

An interesting issue often arises when preparing vertical analyses of financial statements. This issue occurs when the calculated percentage amounts are added or subtracted from each other in the same way that was used to prepare the financial statements (i.e., the Cost of Goods Sold percentage is subtracted from the Net Sales percentage to get the Gross Profit percentage, etc.). Some of the percentage amounts arrived at in this manner can differ slightly from the percentage amounts that were initially calculated when doing the vertical analysis. For example, in Exhibit 12-5, for 2014, if the calculated percentage for Income Tax Expense is subtracted from the calculated percentage for Income Before Taxes, the result for Net Income is 6.2 (12.5 – 6.3). This amount differs from the 6.3, which was calculated for Net Income when preparing the vertical analysis of the income statement. These differences are the result of the rounding that took place when calculating the percentages for the vertical analysis. These differences are insignificant and will be ignored for purposes of our discussion of vertical analysis. All of the amounts in the vertical analyses that are performed in this textbook will be based on the calculated percentages.

Tucker Enterprises, Inc.
Balance Sheet
December 31, 2014 and 2013

(in thousands)	2014	PERCENT	2013	PERCENT
Assets				
Current Assets:				
Cash and Cash Equivalents	$ 50	1.5%	$ 100	4.2%
Accounts Receivable, Net	100	2.9	80	3.3
Inventory	250	7.4	220	9.2
Total Current Assets	400	11.8	400	16.7
Property, Plant, and Equipment, Net	3,000	88.2	2,000	83.3
Total Assets	$3,400	100.0%	$2,400	100.0%
Liabilities				
Current Liabilities:				
Accounts Payable	$ 60	1.8%	$ 40	1.7%
Accrued Liabilities	40	1.2	25	1.0
Total Current Liabilities	100	2.9	65	2.7
Long-Term Bank Loan	1,500	44.1	1,035	43.1
Total Liabilities	1,600	47.1	1,100	45.8
Stockholders' Equity				
Common Stock	550	16.2	100	4.2
Retained Earnings	1,250	36.8	1,200	50.0
Total Stockholders' Equity	1,800	52.9	1,300	54.2
Total Liabilities and Stockholders' Equity	$3,400	100.0%	$2,400	100.0%

Exhibit 12-6 ▲

Horizontal Analysis

Horizontal analysis Study of dollar amount and percentage changes in line items on comparative financial statements.

The study of percentage changes in the line items on comparative financial statements is called **horizontal analysis.** Although it can be useful to know if individual financial statement amounts (such as sales, wages expense, or accounts receivable) have increased or decreased from the prior period, the *percentage change* is often more relevant and, therefore, more helpful to know. For example, sales may have increased by $80,000, but considered alone, this fact is not very helpful. For some companies, an $80,000 increase in sales would be significant while for others it would be minor. It is better to know by what percentage sales have increased from the prior year. For instance, knowing that sales have increased by 15% is more meaningful than knowing sales increased by $80,000.

To compute the percentage change in the line items on comparative financial statements,

- Compute the dollar amount of the change from the earlier period to the later period.
- Divide the dollar amount of change by the earlier period amount and multiply by 100. We call the earlier period the **base period.**

Base period The base period is the first and earliest period in computing changes in line items.

To illustrate horizontal analysis, let's consider the comparative income statement and balance sheet for Tucker Enterprises presented in Exhibits 12-1 and 12-2.

The increase in Net Sales is computed as:

Step 1. Compute the dollar amount of change in sales from 2013 to 2014:

$$\frac{\text{2014 amount} - \text{2013 amount} = \text{Dollar change}}{\$1,200 \quad - \quad \$1,000 \quad = \quad \$200}$$

Step 2. Compute the percentage change for the period by dividing the dollar amount of change by the base period (2013) amount and multiplying the result by 100:

$$\text{Percentage change} = \frac{\text{Dollar change}}{\text{Base period amount}} \times 100 = \frac{\$200}{\$1,000} = 20.0\%$$

The percentage changes in the remaining items are computed in the same manner. The completed horizontal analyses for Tucker Enterprises' financial statements are shown in **Exhibits 12-7** and **12-8**.

Exhibit 12-7 ▶

Tucker Enterprises, Inc.
Income Statement
Years Ended December 31, 2014 and 2013

(in thousands)	2014	2013	INCREASE (DECREASE) AMOUNT	PERCENTAGE
Net Sales	$1,200	$1,000	$200	20.0 %
Cost of Goods Sold	600	400	200	50.0
Gross Profit	600	600	—	—
Operating Expenses:				
Selling, General, and Administrative	200	200	—	—
Depreciation Expense	150	100	50	50.0
Income Before Interest and Taxes	250	300	(50)	(16.7)
Interest Expense	100	70	30	42.9
Income Before Taxes	150	230	(80)	(34.8)
Income Tax Expense	75	115	(40)	(34.8)
Net Income	$ 75	$ 115	$ (40)	(34.8)%

Exhibit 12-8 ▶

Tucker Enterprises, Inc.
Balance Sheet
December 31, 2014 and 2013

(in thousands)	2014	2013	INCREASE (DECREASE) AMOUNT	PERCENTAGE
Assets				
Current Assets:				
Cash and Cash Equivalents	$ 50	$ 100	$ (50)	(50.0)%
Accounts Receivable, Net	100	80	20	25.0
Inventory	250	220	30	13.6
Total Current Assets	400	400	—	0.0
Property, Plant, and Equipment, Net	3,000	2,000	1,000	50.0
Total Assets	$3,400	$2,400	$1,000	41.7 %
Liabilities				
Current Liabilities:				
Accounts Payable	$ 60	$ 40	$ 20	50.0
Accrued Liabilities	40	25	15	60.0
Total Current Liabilities	100	65	35	53.8
Long-Term Bank Loan	1,500	1,035	465	44.9
Total Liabilities	1,600	1,100	500	45.5
Stockholders' Equity				
Common Stock	550	100	450	450.0
Retained Earnings	1,250	1,200	50	4.2
Total Stockholders' Equity	1,800	1,300	500	38.5
Total Liabilities and Stockholders' Equity	$3,400	$2,400	$1,000	41.7 %

Trend Percentages

Trend percentages are a form of horizontal analysis. Trends indicate the direction a business is taking. How have sales changed over a five-year period? What trend does net income show? These questions can be answered by looking at trend percentages over a period of time, such as three to five years. To calculate trend percentages, a base year must first be selected. The base year's trend percentage is then set equal to 100%. Next, the amounts for each subsequent year are expressed as a percentage of the base year amount. To compute trend percentages, divide each item for the years following the base year by the base year amount and multiply the result by 100.

$$\text{Trend percentage} = \frac{\text{Any year \$}}{\text{Base year \$}} \times 100$$

Let's assume Tucker Enterprises' Net Sales were $575,000 in 2010 and rose to $1,200,000 in 2014. To illustrate trend analysis, let's review the trend of Net Sales during 2010–2014, with dollars in thousands. The base year is 2010, so that year's trend percentage is set equal to 100. We compute the trend percentages by dividing each year's net sales amount by the 2010 net sales amount and multiplying the result by 100.

(in thousands)	2014	2013	2012	2011	2010
Net Sales..	$1,200	$1,000	$ 725	$ 630	$ 575
Trend Percentage..............................	208.7%	173.9%	126.1%	109.6%	100.0%

The trend analysis shows that Tucker Enterprises' Net Sales increased moderately in 2009 and 2010 and then substantially in 2011 and 2012. You can perform a trend analysis on any one or multiple items you consider important. Trend analysis is widely used to predict future performance.

As you can see, we look at numbers, ratios, and trends to analyze the performance of a business. So let's analyze a business using the five key questions previously discussed.

Question 1: Is the Business a Going Concern?

Will the business exist in the near future? Is the business able to pay its bills and obligations? If it will not, then financial analysis must focus on what lenders and owners will receive when the business stops operating and is liquidated.

To answer this question, analysts look at the business's liquidity. To begin, look at a business's cash and assets that might be easily converted into cash. Look back to Chapters 5, 7, and 8, and refresh your memory regarding Cash, Accounts Receivable, Inventory, and Marketable Securities. Accounts Receivable and Inventory may or may not be easily converted into cash depending on the business's model and strategy.

Besides the amount of cash and assets that can be converted into cash, analysts look at how these items change over time. Analysts use the statement of cash flows to help with this. To review, look at Chapter 11, The Statement of Cash Flows. Analysts also use horizontal analysis to appreciate trends.

To look at liquidity, analysts look at a business's net working capital, current ratio, quick or acid-test ratio, and cash conversion cycle. **Net working capital** represents how much current assets exceed current liabilities and is computed as:

Net Working Capital = Current Assets − Current Liabilities

Current ratio Current assets divided by current liabilities. Measures a business's ability to meet its short-term obligations with its current assets.

The **current ratio** measures a company's ability to meet current obligations with its current assets and is computed as:

$$\text{Current Ratio} = \frac{\text{Current Assets}}{\text{Current Liabilities}}$$

Quick ratio Quick assets (cash, short-term investments, and net current receivables) divided by current liabilities. It measures a company's ability to pay its current liabilities if they came due immediately; also called the *acid-test ratio*.

The **quick ratio** measures a company's ability to use its *near cash* or quick assets to meet its current obligations and is computed as:

$$\text{Quick Ratio} = \frac{\text{Quick Assets (Cash + Net Current Receivables + Short-Term Investments)}}{\text{Current Liabilities}}$$

Analysts also look at a business's cash conversion cycle. Remember from Chapter 11 that the **cash conversion cycle** measures the time between when a company outlays cash for the purchase of inventory and when it collects cash from the sale of the inventory and is computed as:

$$\text{Cash Conversion Cycle} = \text{(Days-Sales-In-Inventory)} + \text{(Receivable Collection Period)} - \text{(Accounts Payable Payment Period)}$$

Cash conversion cycle The number of days it takes to collect cash from the sale of inventory versus the number of days it takes to pay for inventory. It is computed as the days-sales-in-inventory, plus accounts receivable collection period, less the accounts payable payment period.

Where:

$$\text{Days-Sales-In-Inventory} = \frac{\text{Average Inventory}}{\text{(Cost of Goods Sold/365 Days)}}$$

$$\text{Receivable Collection Period} = \frac{\text{Average Net Accounts Receivable}}{\text{(Net Credit Sales/365 Days)}}$$

$$\text{Accounts Payable Payment Period} = \frac{\text{Average Accounts Payable}}{\text{(Cost of Goods Sold/365 Days)}}$$

An Example: Tucker Enterprises, Inc.

First, review Tucker Enterprises' horizontal analysis of the balance sheet presented in Exhibit 12-8. Now look back at Exhibit 12-4 to see Tucker Enterprises' statement of cash flows. Look where Tucker Enterprises is getting and using its cash. Lastly, compute Tucker Enterprises' net working capital, current ratio, quick ratio, and cash conversion cycle. The 2014 net working capital, current ratio, and quick ratio for Tucker Enterprises are computed as:

$$\text{Net Working Capital} = \$400 - \$100 = \$300$$

$$\text{Current Ratio} = \frac{\$400}{\$100} = 4$$

$$\text{Quick Ratio} = \frac{(\$50 + \$100)}{\$100} = 1.5$$

The 2014 cash conversion cycle and related ratios of Tucker Enterprises are computed as (assuming all sales are credit sales):

$$\text{Days-Sales-in-Inventory} = \frac{((\$250 + \$220)/2)}{(\$600/365 \text{ days})} = 143 \text{ Days}$$

$$\text{Receivable Collection Period} = \frac{((\$100 + \$80)/2)}{(\$1200/365 \text{ days})} = 27 \text{ Days}$$

$$\text{Accounts Payable Payment Period} = \frac{((\$60 + \$40)/2)}{(\$600/365 \text{ days})} = 30 \text{ Days}$$

$$\text{Cash Conversion Cycle} = 143 \text{ Days} + 27 \text{ Days} - 30 \text{ Days} = 140 \text{ Days}$$

So what does this tell you? Is Tucker Enterprises a going concern?

Tucker Enterprises has $50,000 in cash at the end of 2014. This is a reduction of 50%, or $50,000 from the end of 2013. This raises a concern. However, in examining Tucker Enterprises' statement of cash flows (Exhibit 12-4), it appears Tucker has used a lot of cash to increase its investment in long-term assets. This implies Tucker Enterprises is preparing to grow.

So is Tucker Enterprises able to pay its bills and stay in business? It appears so. Tucker Enterprises has a strong net cash flow from operations (Exhibit 12-4). It also has good net working capital. Its current and quick ratios are strong. For every dollar of current liabilities, Tucker Enterprises has four dollars of current assets and one and a half dollars of quick assets. Also, as seen in the calculation of its cash conversion cycle, Tucker Enterprises can pay its accounts payable within 30 days.

The bottom line is that it appears Tucker Enterprises is a going concern and analysts can assume it will not be liquidated in the near future. Although we do not have a competitor to benchmark, it appears the business will exist in the future to compete.

Question 2: How Is the Business Earning a Net Income or Loss?

The income statement tells the analyst if, how, and when a business is earning net income or loss. Analysts look at the notes that follow the financial statements to understand how the business is recognizing revenue and expenses.

Before an analyst begins to analyze a business's income, he or she must ask the question, "What is the income measure that should be used?" Sometimes a business experiences items that are not a normal part of its operations. A business may need to shut down permanently and discontinue part of its operations. A business may experience an extraordinary event such as a natural disaster. Analysts may want to evaluate the business by using only the income or loss from the recurring, continuing operations. **Income or loss from continuing operations** excludes the impact of discontinued operations and extraordinary items.

Income or loss from continuing operations Net income excluding the impact of discontinued operations and extraordinary items.

For illustration purposes, consider the income statement for Best Way, Inc., presented in **Exhibit 12-9**:

Best Way, Inc. Income Statement Year Ended December 31, 2014	
Net Sales Revenue	$1,877,000
Cost of Goods Sold	1,145,000
Gross Profit	732,000
Operating Expenses	423,000
Operating Income	309,000
Other Income (Expense):	
Interest Expense	(32,000)
Loss on Sale of Fixed Assets	(14,000)
Income from continuing operations before income tax	263,000
Income tax expense	72,000
Income from continuing operations	191,000
Income from discontinued operations, net of income tax of $26,000	68,000
Income before extraordinary items	259,000
Extraordinary loss from hurricane, net of tax savings of $17,000	(42,000)
Net Income	$ 217,000

Exhibit 12-9 ▲

Income from Continuing Operations

In Exhibit 12-9, the topmost section reports income from continuing operations. Continuing operations consist of business activities that will most likely continue from period to period. Reporting income from continuing operations, therefore, helps investors make predictions about a company's future earnings. The continuing operations of Best Way, Inc., include two items that need explanation:

- *Other income (expense)* includes items that, although a normal part of business operations, fall outside of a company's core business activities. Therefore, these items are not included in sales, cost of goods sold, or operating expenses but are instead reported separately. Gains and losses on the sale of fixed assets, as well as interest income and interest expense, are examples of items reported as part of other income (expense). Best Way, Inc., reported interest expense of $32,000 and a loss on the sale of fixed assets of $14,000.
- *Income tax expense* reflects the income tax expense that is assessed on the company's operating income and other income (expense). Best Way, Inc., was assessed $72,000 of income tax on its operating income.

After continuing operations, an income statement may include the following items:

- Discontinued operations
- Extraordinary gains and losses

Discontinued Operations

Corporations often consist of many different business segments. A business segment is a distinguishable part of a business that is subject to a different set of risks and returns than other parts of the business. Information on any of the company's segments that have been sold (or otherwise discontinued) is reported separately from the results of continuing operations. This is because the discontinued segment will not be part of the company's operations in the future. The results of discontinued operations are generally reported net of income tax expense (or income tax savings in the case of a loss).

Best Way, Inc., reported net income from discontinued operations of $68,000. This amount represents income of $94,000 less income tax expense of $26,000.

Extraordinary Gains and Losses

Extraordinary gains and losses, also called extraordinary items, are both unusual and infrequent in nature. Losses from natural disasters (floods, earthquakes, hurricanes, and tornadoes) and the taking of company assets by a foreign government (expropriation) are examples of extraordinary items. Extraordinary items are generally reported net of their income tax effects and are reported separately from continuing operations because of their infrequent nature. Best Way, Inc., reported an extraordinary loss from a hurricane of $42,000 (net). This amount represents a loss of $59,000, net of tax savings of $17,000.

After determining the net income measure on which they will focus, analysts then look at the individual items in the income statement and how each changed from one year to another. They often divide the income statement into two parts, the operating part and the financing part. The operating part starts with revenue less cost of goods sold, which equals gross profit. Gross profit less operating expenses is **operating income**, often called income from operations or **earnings before interest and taxes (EBIT)**. EBIT is the operating part of the income statement and is created by selling products, hiring people, and using assets. The financing part is EBIT less interest expense, which results in taxable income. After paying taxes, owners get what remains, net income or loss. EBIT provides the return to the providers of the money. Lenders get interest and owners get net income.

Analysts use different measures and techniques to help understand how a business earns net income or loss. Analysts use vertical and horizontal analyses to understand the relationship of sales and expenses through time. A part of this analysis is computing the **gross profit percentage** and **net income percentage**. Look back to Chapter 4. The gross profit percentage measures the percentage of sales left after subtracting cost of goods sold and is computed as:

Operating income Profit or loss from operating the business. Operating income is computed as revenue less cost of goods sold, less operating expenses. Operating income is also called **earnings before interest and taxes (EBIT)**.

Gross profit percentage Sales, less cost of goods sold, divided by net sales.

Net income percentage Net income divided by net sales. Net income percentage is often called *return on sales*.

$$\text{Gross Profit Percentage} = \frac{\text{Gross Profit}}{\text{Net Sales}}$$

The net income percentage measures the percentage of sales left after subtracting cost of goods sold, all operating expenses, interest, and taxes and is computed as:

$$\text{Net Income Percentage} = \frac{\text{Net Income}}{\text{Net Sales}}$$

An Example: Tucker Enterprises, Inc.

Look back at Tucker Enterprises' income statement in Exhibit 12-1 to see how Tucker Enterprises is earning net income. Then look at Exhibits 12-5 and 12-7, which show the vertical and horizontal analyses of Tucker Enterprises' income statement.

Using these statements, you can see how Tucker Enterprises generated its net income and how that process changed over time. So what does this tell you? Is Tucker Enterprises earning a net income or loss? How is Tucker Enterprises doing this? How does Tucker Enterprises compare with similar businesses selling bicycle parts?

Tucker Enterprises is profitable. However, its profitability is dropping. Look at these factors:

1. Per Exhibit 12-7, sales increased 20.0% from $1,000,000 in 2013 to $1,200,000 in 2014. However, net income dropped by 34.8%, or $40,000 (Exhibit 12-7).

2. Tucker Enterprises' gross profit percentage decreased from 60.0% in 2013 to 50.0% in 2014 (Exhibit 12-5).

3. Its net income percentage has decreased from 11.5% in 2013 to 6.3% in 2014 (Exhibit 12-5).

There appears to be a problem with pricing the product and/or controlling expenses. Without a competitor to benchmark, it's hard to determine if this is from Tucker Enterprises' environment or if it is a problem with the business's management.

The bottom line is that Tucker Enterprises is profitable, but the trend is not good. There appears to be risk that Tucker Enterprises' past performance may not be sustained in the future.

Question 3: Where Is the Business Getting Its Money, and Can It Pay Its Debt Obligations?

Financing decision How a business acquires money, debt or equity, to acquire assets.

Where a business decides to get money is called the **financing decision**. A business is financed with debt and stockholders' equity. Both have a cost. The cost of debt is interest. The cost of stockholders' equity is hard to determine but real. Owners will not let a business use their money unless they expect a return. Owners require net income that compensates them for time and risk.

Go back to Chapter 9 and review the sections on liabilities. Analysts look at the balance sheet to determine the amount of, types of, and changes in the debt a business owes. They then read the notes to the financial statements to understand the interest rate being charged on the debt, when the debt is due, and any special features of the debt called covenants. **Debt covenants** are agreements between the lender and borrower. An example of a covenant is where the lender can take ownership of an asset if the borrower does not pay the loan. That asset is called **collateral**.

Debt covenants Conditions, stated in the debt contract, that specify the requirements agreed to by the lender and borrower.

Collateral Assets pledged by a borrower to guarantee the payment of a liability.

Analysts also look at the amount of, types of, and changes in a business's stockholders' equity. They then read the notes to the financial statements to see what is happening in stockholders' equity. Look back in Chapter 10 to refresh your memory regarding common stock, preferred stock, retained earnings, and dividends. Remember that the statement of retained earnings is a reconciliation of how retained earnings changed from the beginning to the end of the period.

The goal of the financing decision is to obtain money at the lowest possible cost. Debt is less expensive than stockholders' equity. However, a business does not want too much debt. A business will fail if it has more debt that it can pay back. To look at how much debt a business has relative to its stockholders' equity, analysts often use vertical analysis. Analysts also use horizontal analysis to see how a business is changing the blend of liabilities and stockholders' equity over time.

Debt ratio Total liabilities divided by total assets. It measures a business's ability to pay liabilities.

To look at critical relationships, analysts use ratios. The first ratio in this area that analysts use is the debt ratio. The **debt ratio** tells the analysts the percentage of assets financed with debt. The debt ratio is computed as:

$$\text{Debt Ratio} = \frac{\text{Total Liabilities}}{\text{Total Assets}}$$

Interest coverage ratio Ratio of income from operations to interest expense. It measures the number of times that operating income can cover interest expense; also called the *times interest earned ratio*.

To see if a business can pay the interest on its debt, analysts look at a business's **interest coverage ratio**. The interest coverage ratio is computed as:

$$\text{Interest Coverage Ratio} = \frac{\text{EBIT}}{\text{Interest Expense}}$$

An Example: Tucker Enterprises, Inc.

Look back at Tucker Enterprises' statement of cash flows presented in Exhibit 12-4 to see how Tucker Enterprises is financing its assets. Then look at the vertical and horizontal analyses of Tucker Enterprises' balance sheet presented in Exhibits 12-6 and 12-8.

Next, look at Exhibit 12-3, Tucker Enterprises' 2014 statement of retained earnings to see what is going in and out of the retained earnings in stockholders' equity.

Lastly, compute Tucker Enterprises' debt ratio and interest coverage ratio. Tucker Enterprises' 2014 debt ratio computes as:

$$\text{Debt Ratio} = \frac{\text{Total Liabilities}}{\text{Total Assets}} = \frac{\$1,600}{\$3,400} = 47.1\%$$

The debt ratio can also be found on the vertical analysis of the balance sheet by looking at the total liabilities line item.

Tucker Enterprises' 2014 interest coverage ratio is computed as:

$$\text{Interest Coverage Ratio} = \frac{\text{EBIT}}{\text{Interest Expense}} = \frac{\$250}{\$100} = 2.5$$

So what does this tell you? Where is Tucker Enterprises getting its money, and can it pay its debt obligations? Tucker Enterprises uses a lot of debt to finance its assets. Per Exhibit 12-6, 47.1% of its assets are financed with debt and 52.9% with equity in 2014. This is approximately the same as in 2013.

Can Tucker Enterprises pay its debt? The answer appears to be yes.

1. It has a strong operating cash flow (Exhibit 12-4).

2. Tucker Enterprises' interest coverage ratio is 2.5, telling the analyst that in 2014 the business generated earnings before interest and taxes (EBIT) that was two and a half times the amount of its interest expense. Even if EBIT fell, Tucker Enterprises appears to have sufficient operating income to cover the interest expense.

The bottom line is that it appears Tucker Enterprises is well financed. It is paying its debts. It appears its risk of defaulting on its debts is low for the foreseeable future. Regardless of how its competitors are financed, Tucker Enterprises appears to be doing well in this area.

Question 4: How Is the Business Investing Its Money, and Is It Using Its Assets Efficiently?

Investing decision How a business uses money to acquire assets.

How a business uses its money to acquire assets is called the **investing decision**. Businesses invest money in assets such as cash, accounts receivable, inventory, buildings, and patents. The goal of the investing decision is to create operating income that rewards lenders and owners for the use of their money adequately.

Analysts want to understand the types of assets in which a business invests and how those investments change over time. Look back at Chapters 5, 7, and 8. Analysts look at the balance sheet to determine the amount of, types of, and changes to the assets a business owns. They then read the notes to the financial statements to gain insights into the assets, such as depreciation assumptions.

Analysts want to understand how the assets come together to produce income. Analysts want to understand the productivity of each asset and combination of all assets. They recognize each asset has a role in earning net income. Businesses use long-term assets, such as buildings, to produce and deliver products. Tangible products are inventory, which are sold for cash or accounts receivable. Inventory and accounts receivable must be converted into cash, which is used to pay debts, dividends, and other needs of the business. All assets, whether current or long-term, have a role in earning net income. However, it's also important to understand how the assets work together.

Analysts use different techniques and measures to understand how a business invests money in assets and uses the assets to earn net income or loss. Analysts often use vertical and horizontal analyses to see the relative importance of each asset through time.

Analysts then compute ratios to see the efficiency or productivity of each asset and assets in total. These ratios include the accounts receivable turnover, the inventory turnover, the fixed asset turnover, the total asset turnover, and return on assets (ROA). The **accounts receivable turnover** measures the ability to collect from credit customers and is computed as:

Accounts receivable turnover Measures a company's ability to collect cash from credit customers. To compute accounts receivable turnover, divide net credit sales by average net accounts receivable.

$$\text{Accounts Receivable Turnover} = \frac{\text{Net Credit Sales}}{\text{Average Net Accounts Receivable}}$$

The **inventory turnover** measures how many times inventory is sold over a period of time and is computed as:

Inventory turnover Measures the number of times a company sells its average level of inventory during a year. To compute inventory turnover, divide cost of goods sold by average inventory.

$$\text{Inventory Turnover} = \frac{\text{Cost of Goods Sold}}{\text{Average Inventory}}$$

The **fixed asset turnover** measures a company's ability to generate sales from fixed assets and is computed as:

Fixed asset turnover A measure of how a business utilizes its property, plant, and equipment to generate sales. Fixed asset turnover is computed as sales divided by average fixed assets.

$$\text{Fixed Asset Turnover} = \frac{\text{Sales}}{\text{Average Fixed Assets}}$$

The **total asset turnover** measures a company's efficiency in using all of its assets to generate sales and is computed as:

Total asset turnover A measure of how a business utilizes its total assets to generate sales. Total asset turnover is computed as sales divided by average total assets.

$$\text{Total Asset Turnover} = \frac{\text{Sales}}{\text{Average Total Assets}}$$

The **return on assets (ROA)** measures the net income earned on each dollar of assets invested and is computed as:

Return on assets (ROA) Ratio of net income to average total assets. It measures a company's effectiveness in using assets to generate earnings; also called *rate of return on total assets*.

$$\text{Return on Assets} = \frac{\text{Net Income}}{\text{Average Total Assets}}$$

An Example: Tucker Enterprises, Inc.

Once again, review Exhibit 12-4 to see how Tucker Enterprises is financing its assets. Then look at Exhibits 12-5, 12-6, 12-7, and 12-8 showing the vertical and horizontal analyses of Tucker Enterprises' financial statements. Lastly, compute Tucker Enterprises' 2014 accounts receivable turnover, inventory turnover, fixed asset turnover, total asset turnover, and return on assets. Tucker Enterprises' accounts receivable turnover is computed as:

$$\text{Accounts Receivable Turnover} = \frac{\text{Net Credit Sales}}{\text{Average Net Accounts Receivable}} = \frac{\$1,200}{((\$100 + \$80)/2)} = 13.33 \text{ times}$$

Tucker Enterprises' inventory turnover is computed as:

$$\text{Inventory Turnover} = \frac{\text{Cost of Goods Sold}}{\text{Average Inventory}} = \frac{\$600}{((\$250 + \$220)/2)} = 2.55 \text{ times}$$

Tucker Enterprises' fixed asset turnover is computed as:

$$\text{Fixed Asset Turnover} = \frac{\text{Sales}}{\text{Average Fixed Assets}} = \frac{\$1,200}{((\$3,000 + \$2,000)/2)} = 0.48 \text{ times}$$

Tucker Enterprises' total asset turnover is computed as:

$$\text{Total Asset Turnover} = \frac{\text{Sales}}{\text{Average Total Assets}} = \frac{\$1,200}{((\$3,400 + \$2,400)/2)} = 0.41 \text{ times}$$

Tucker Enterprises' ROA is computed as:

$$\text{Return on Assets} = \frac{\text{Net Income}}{\text{Average Total Assets}} = \frac{\$75}{((\$3,400 + \$2,400)/2)} = 2.6\%$$

Now what does this tell you? How is Tucker Enterprises investing its money, and is it using its assets efficiently? It's hard to tell without understanding its environment and benchmarking its competitors. However, there are some concerns.

As you can see in Exhibit 12-6, Tucker Enterprises has a lot of assets at the end of 2014 ($3,400,000). During 2014, it increased its investment in assets by 41.7%, from $2,400,000 at the end of 2013 to $3,400,000 at the end of 2014. This increase was from accounts receivable; inventory; and property, plant, and equipment.

But is the investment producing superior results?

1. The accounts receivable turnover is 13.33 times for 2014. Tucker Enterprises is collecting its receivables every 27 days. This appears reasonable given its business model.

2. However, its 2014 inventory turnover is 2.55. After it buys inventory, it takes Tucker Enterprises 143 days to sell the inventory. This appears to be a very low turnover, indicating it has too much inventory.

3. Likewise, its fixed asset turnover is 0.48. Tucker Enterprises has a lot of, maybe too many, fixed assets (property, plant, and equipment) for the sales it generates. This all results in a 2014 ROA of only 2.6%.

The bottom line is that Tucker Enterprises appears to have some room to improve its management of assets. For the sales it generates, it appears to have too many assets. Tucker Enterprises needs to increase ROA by either increasing net income or decreasing assets. This inefficiency creates concern and risk.

Question 5: Is the Business Generating Enough Net Income to Reward the Stockholders for the Use of Their Money?

Analysts want to know if owners are receiving enough benefits to justify their investment in the business. Stockholders invest money in corporations. Corporations use that money to generate net income and eventually pay dividends. But do the net income and dividends reward the stockholders enough for using their money over time and for taking risks?

Analysts will first look at the financial statements using vertical and horizontal analyses. Analysts want to understand how a business generates net income (or loss) and dividends in a period of time and through time.

They will then divide net income by the average number of common shares outstanding to compute the **earnings per share (EPS)**.[1] Earnings per share (EPS) measures the portion of a company's net income allocated to each outstanding share of common stock and is computed as:

Earnings per share (EPS)
Reflects the net income earned for each share of the company's outstanding common stock.

$$\text{Earnings per Share (EPS)} = \frac{\text{Net Income}}{\text{Average Number of Common Shares Outstanding}}$$

---

[1]Some corporations must report two sets of EPS figures, a basic EPS and a diluted EPS. The difference is that basic EPS uses outstanding common shares and diluted EPS uses outstanding common shares plus the additional shares of common stock that would arise if convertible preferred stock (or other dilutive items) were exchanged for common shares. Diluted EPS is always lower than basic EPS.

Dividends per share (DPS)
The dividends a business pays for each share of common stock outstanding. Dividends per share is computed as dividends divided by the average number of shares of common stock outstanding.

Dividend payout ratio
A measure of how much dividends a business is paying in a given period in relationship to the earnings in the same period. The dividend payout ratio is computed as dividends divided by net income.

Return on equity (ROE) Ratio of net income to average stockholders' equity. It is a measure of profitability; also called *rate of return on equity*.

They will also divide dividends by the average number of common shares outstanding to compute the **dividends per share (DPS)**. Dividends per share (DPS) is the amount of the dividend that shareholders receive for each share of common stock they own and is computed as:

$$\text{Dividends Per Share (DPS)} = \frac{\text{Dividends}}{\text{Average Number of Common Shares Outstanding}}$$

To see how dividends and earnings in a given period are related, analysts will compute a dividend payout ratio. The **dividend payout ratio** measures how well earnings support dividend payments and is computed as:

$$\text{Dividend Payout Ratio} = \frac{\text{Dividends}}{\text{Net Income}}$$

Finally, analysts will want to look at the ratio of net income to stockholders' equity. This ratio is called **return on equity (ROE)**. Return on equity (ROE) measures how much profit a company generates with the money shareholders have invested and is computed as:

$$\text{Return on Equity (ROE)} = \frac{\text{Net Income}}{\text{Average Stockholders' Equity}}$$

Return on equity measures the benefits a business earned for its stockholders in relation to the investment made by the stockholders.

ROE is the result of all processes that affect the earning of net income. Let's decompose ROE into a few of its components.

$$\text{ROE} = \text{Net Income/Average Stockholders' Equity}$$
$$= \frac{\text{Net Income}}{\text{Sales}} \times \frac{\text{Sales}}{\text{Average Total Assets}} \times \frac{\text{Average Total Assets}}{\text{Average Stockholders' Equity}}$$

Now, let's think through this equation. Net Income/Sales is the net income percentage and measures how a business operates to earn net income. Sales/Average Total Assets is a measure of the productivity of assets. Average Total Assets/Average Stockholders' Equity is a measure of how the business finances its assets. ROE is a measure that combines all the elements of managing a business, including the financing, investing, and operating decisions.

An Example: Tucker Enterprises, Inc.

Look back at Exhibits 12-1, 12-2, 12-3, and 12-4. Review the vertical and horizontal analyses shown in Exhibits 12-5, 12-6, 12-7, and 12-8. Compute Tucker Enterprises' earnings per share, dividends per share, dividend payout ratio, and return on equity. Tucker Enterprises' 2014 earnings per share is computed as:

$$\text{Earnings per Share (EPS)} = \frac{\text{Net Income}}{\text{Average Number of Common Shares Outstanding}} = \frac{\$75,000}{10,000 \text{ Shares}} = \$7.50 \text{ per Share}$$

In our example, Tucker Enterprises has 10,000 shares of common stock outstanding during 2014. Also remember that the financial statements are stated in thousands of dollars.

Tucker Enterprises' dividends per share is computed as:

$$\text{Dividends per Share (DPS)} = \frac{\text{Dividends}}{\text{Average Number of Common Shares Outstanding}} = \frac{\$25,000}{10,000 \text{ Shares}} = \$2.50 \text{ per Share}$$

Don't forget that dividends are reported in the statement of retained earnings (Exhibit 12-3).

Tucker Enterprises' dividend payout ratio is computed as:

$$\text{Dividend Payout Ratio} = \frac{\text{Dividends}}{\text{Net Income}} = \frac{\$25,000}{\$75,000} = 0.33, \text{ or } 33\%$$

Tucker Enterprises' return on equity is computed as:

$$\text{Return on Equity (ROE)} = \frac{\text{Net Income}}{\text{Average Stockholders' Equity}}$$

$$= \frac{\text{Net Income}}{\text{Sales}} \times \frac{\text{Sales}}{\text{Average Total Assets}} \times \frac{\text{Average Total Assets}}{\text{Average Stockholders' Equity}}$$

$$\text{Return on Equity} = \frac{\text{Net Income}}{\text{Average Stockholders' Equity}} = \frac{\$75}{((\$1,800 + \$1,300)/2)} = 0.048, \text{ or } 4.8\%$$

Breaking down Tucker Enterprises' return on equity, we see the following:

$$\frac{\text{Net Income}}{\text{Sales}} = \frac{\$75}{\$1,200} = 0.062$$

$$\frac{\text{Sales}}{\text{Average Total Assets}} = \frac{\$1,200}{((\$3,400 + \$2,400)/2)} = 0.414$$

$$\frac{\text{Average Total Assets}}{\text{Average Stockholders' Equity}} = \frac{((\$3,400 + \$2,400)/2)}{((\$1,800 + \$1,300)/2)} = 1.871$$

$$\text{Return on Equity} = 0.062 \times 0.414 \times 1.871 = 0.048 = 4.8\%$$

Now what does this tell you? Is Tucker Enterprises generating enough net income to reward the stockholders for the use of their money? It's hard to tell without understanding Tucker Enterprises' environment and benchmarking its competitors. However, there are certain measures to help answer this question.

Tucker Enterprises is profitable. It generated an ROE of 4.8% in 2014. It's good that it was able to compete, stay in business, and pay its bills. However, a 4.8% ROE doesn't appear to be sufficient to justify owners providing money in the long term. Think about it. Tucker Enterprises has significant risks. These risks appear to come from asset and expense management. How much would you pay for a business like Tucker Enterprises that pays you a $2.50 dividend per share and earns a 4.8% ROE? Before you reach your answer, think about your other options, including putting your money in an insured, interest-bearing deposit in a safe bank.

Stop and Think...

Julie and Bryan were discussing the income statement one day after their accounting class. Julie commented that the best way to gauge the future performance of a business was to look at net income because it includes all aspects of a company's performance. Bryan countered that it was better to focus on income from continuing operations when trying to assess the future performance of a business. Who has the strongest argument?

Answer

Bryan has the strongest argument. It is possible for a company's net income to include income/loss from a segment of the business that has been terminated (discontinued operations) or income/loss from an event that was both unusual and infrequent (extraordinary item). Both discontinued operations and extraordinary items are not likely to recur in the future and, therefore, are not good indicators of future performance. Because income from continuing operations excludes both discontinued operations and extraordinary items, it is a better indicator of a company's future performance.

Try It...

Your friend owns a small business and she asks for your advice. For the past couple of years, her company has extended credit to its customers. She wonders how well her company manages its accounts receivable. During the most recent year, your friend's company had net credit sales of $743,000. Net Accounts Receivable at the beginning of the year was $82,000. Ending net Accounts Receivable was $77,000. The company's credit terms are net 30. What should you tell your friend regarding how well accounts receivable is managed?

Answer

In order to analyze how effectively the company is at managing its accounts receivable, you should calculate the accounts receivable turnover. The accounts receivable turnover is calculated as:

$$\frac{\text{Net Credit Sales}}{\text{Average Net Accounts Receivable}} = \frac{\$743,000}{\$79,500} = 9.35$$

With credit terms of 30 days, you would expect to have an accounts receivable turnover of closer to 12 (360 days/30 days) so you should tell your friend that it appears that the company is not managing its accounts receivable very well.

How Do You Put Everything Together to Make Decisions?

Use financial analysis to assess the value of a business

The purpose of financial analysis is to understand how a business creates value. Specifically, financial analysis looks at the financing, investing, and operating decisions that create net income.

Financial analysis is a powerful tool to understand how a business creates value. Look at **Exhibit 12-10** and see all five key questions for analysis and the corresponding ratios with which we've worked. Now reflect on what they tell you, how they are related, and how you can use them to make good business decisions.

Five Key Questions	Ratios used to analyze and make the decision
Is the business a going concern?	Use liquidity ratios to determine the following: $$\textbf{Net Working Capital} = \text{Current Assets} - \text{Current Liabilities}$$ $$\textbf{Current Ratio} = \frac{\text{Current Assets}}{\text{Current Liabilities}}$$ $$\textbf{Quick Ratio} = \frac{\text{Quick Assets (Cash + Net Current Receivables + Short-Term Investments)}}{\text{Current Liabilities}}$$ $$\textbf{Cash Conversion Cycle} = \text{(Days-Sales-In-Inventory)} + \text{(Receivable Collection Period)} - \text{(Accounts Payable Payment Period)}$$ $$\textbf{Days-Sales-In-Inventory} = \frac{\text{Average Inventory}}{\text{(Cost of Goods Sold/365 Days)}}$$ $$\textbf{Receivable Collection Period} = \frac{\text{Average Net Accounts Receivable}}{\text{(Net Credit Sales/365 Days)}}$$ $$\textbf{Accounts Payable Payment Period} = \frac{\text{Average Accounts Payable}}{\text{(Cost of Goods Sold/365 Days)}}$$
How is the business earning a net income or loss?	Use profitability ratios to determine the following: $$\textbf{Gross Profit Percentage} = \frac{\text{Gross Profit}}{\text{Net Sales}}$$ $$\textbf{Net Income Percentage} = \frac{\text{Net Income}}{\text{Net Sales}}$$
Where is the business getting its money and can it pay its debt obligations?	Use solvency ratios to determine the following: $$\textbf{Debt Ratio} = \frac{\text{Total Liabilities}}{\text{Total Assets}}$$ $$\textbf{Interest Coverage Ratio} = \frac{\text{EBIT}}{\text{Interest Expense}}$$
How is the business investing its money and is it using its assets efficiently?	Use asset management ratios to determine the following: $$\textbf{Accounts Receivable Turnover Ratio} = \frac{\text{Net Credit Sales}}{\text{Average Net Accounts Receivable}}$$ $$\textbf{Inventory Turnover Ratio} = \frac{\text{Cost of Goods Sold}}{\text{Average Inventory}}$$ $$\textbf{Fixed Asset Turnover Ratio} = \frac{\text{Sales}}{\text{Average Fixed Assets}}$$ $$\textbf{Total Asset Turnover Ratio} = \frac{\text{Sales}}{\text{Average Total Assets}}$$ $$\textbf{Return on Assets} = \frac{\text{Net Income}}{\text{Average Total Assets}}$$
Is the business generating enough net income to reward the stockholders for the use of their money?	Use market analysis ratios to determine the following: $$\textbf{Earnings per Share (EPS)} = \frac{\text{Net Income}}{\text{Average Number of Common Shares Outstanding}}$$ $$\textbf{Dividends per Share (DPS)} = \frac{\text{Dividends}}{\text{Average Number of Common Shares Outstanding}}$$ $$\textbf{Dividend Payout Ratio} = \frac{\text{Dividends}}{\text{Net Income}}$$ $$\textbf{Return on Equity (ROE)} = \frac{\text{Net Income}}{\text{Average Stockholders' Equity}}$$

Exhibit 12-10 ▲

Seeing the Impact of Decisions

Let's use Tucker Enterprises to examine the impact of decisions. Let's assume the stockholders of Tucker Enterprises believe its ROE is not sufficient to compensate them for the use of their money. The stockholders inform the management of Tucker Enterprises that they will find new management or liquidate the business unless management can improve ROE to at least 7%.

The management of Tucker Enterprises meets and makes four decisions:

1. With better management, Tucker Enterprises can lower expenses and increase net income by $25,000.

2. With better inventory management, Tucker Enterprises can lower its average inventory by $100,000.

3. With better management of accounts receivable, Tucker Enterprises can lower its average accounts receivable by $50,000.

4. With the funds released by lowering inventory and accounts receivable, Tucker Enterprises can declare a one-time dividend, lowering average stockholders' equity by $150,000.

If the management of Tucker Enterprises had made those decisions this past year, what would the ROE be? The components of Tucker Enterprises' revised ROE would be as shown here (in thousands):

$$\frac{100}{1200} \times \frac{1200}{2750} \times \frac{2750}{1400} = 7.1\%$$

The results of better management have been summarized in **Exhibit 12-11**. The actions of Tucker Enterprises' management will create a better return on equity for stockholders.

Tucker Enterprises: Revised Return on Equity (ROE)	
Sales	Unchanged
Net Income	Net Income Increases from $75,000 to $100,000 from lowering expenses
Average Total Assets	Average Total Assets Decrease from $2,900,000 to $2,750,000 from lowering average inventory by $100,000 and average accounts receivable by $50,000
Average Stockholders' Equity	Average Stockholders' Equity Decreases from $1,550,000 to $1,400,000 from the one-time dividend
ROE (Revised)	ROE (Revised) Net Income/Average Stockholders' Equity = $100,000/$1,400,000 = 0.071, or 7.1%

Exhibit 12-11 ▲

What Are Red Flags in Financial Statement Analysis?

In reality, financial analysis looks like a precise science because it uses a lot of numbers. It's not all science. There is a lot of art. That art requires insight and judgment.

Financial analysis often discloses that a problem exists. It provides *red flags* that decision makers must recognize. To understand the causes of the problems may require the analyst to do significant research beyond the financial statements. Recent accounting scandals highlight the importance of these red flags. The following conditions may be cause for concern.

- **Decreased cash flow.** Cash flows from operations validates net income. Is net cash flow from operations consistently lower than net income? If so, the company is in trouble. Are the sales of plant assets a major source of cash? If so, the company may face a cash shortage.
- **Inability to collect receivables.** Is the receivables collection period growing faster than for competitors? A cash shortage may be looming.
- **Buildup of inventories.** Is inventory turnover too slow? If so, the company may have obsolete inventory, or it may be overstating inventory.
- **Movement of sales, inventory, and receivables.** Sales, receivables, and inventory generally move together. Increased sales lead to higher receivables and require more inventory to meet demand. Unexpected or inconsistent movements among sales, inventory, and receivables make the financial statements look suspect.
- **Earnings problems.** Has net income decreased significantly for several years in a row? Has income turned into a loss? Most companies cannot survive consecutive losses year after year.
- **Too much debt.** How does the company's debt ratio compare to that of major competitors? If the debt ratio is too high, the company may be unable to pay its debts.

Based on our financial statement analysis of Tucker Enterprises, the company appears to be in a relatively strong financial condition. One area of concern could be the company's cash position. Tucker Enterprises should monitor its cash position to ensure that it does not encounter any cash flow problems in the future.

Focus on Decision Making

"How Do People Use Financial Analysis to Value a Business?"

There is nothing harder in the financial world than to put a value to a business. Forecasting the future performance of a company is very hard. It's all about trying to use the past and present to see the future. Valuation of a business starts with financial analysis, but ultimately requires making assumptions about whether the future will be better or worse than the past and present.

There are many techniques used to value a business. Analysts will use the past to project the future earnings and free cash flow of the business. They will then estimate how much the future earnings are worth today by using the time value of money noted in Chapter 9. This is a complicated process covered in more advanced texts. However, two measures that are often looked at in valuing a business are dividend yield and price-earnings ratio.

Dividend Yield

Dividends are important. Dividends are the payment of past and present earnings to the stockholders of the business. Although net income is important, stockholders cannot spend net income because it is an accrual measure. Stockholders can spend cash dividends. So why do some businesses pay dividends and others do not? The question is important; the answer is often complicated. However, the logic is based on the question, "What would the business do with the money if it did not pay a dividend?"

Dividends are paid when a business does not have a better use for the money. If a business cannot invest the money and earn a return that adequately compensates the owners for their time and risk, then the business should pay the money to its owners. That payment is a dividend. If a business can invest the money and earn a return that adequately compensates the owners for their time and risk, then the business should retain the money and not pay a dividend. The future profits from the new investment will enable the business to pay bigger dividends in the future.

Dividend yield Ratio of dividends per share of stock to the stock's market price per share. It tells the percentage of a stock's market value that the company returns to stockholders annually as dividends.

A ratio used by analysts and stockholders to compare dividends to what stockholders would currently pay for the stock is called the **dividend yield**. The dividend yield shows how much a company pays out in dividends each year relative to its share price and is computed as:

$$\text{Dividend Yield} = \frac{\text{Dividend per Share}}{\text{Current Market Price per Share of Stock}}$$

A high dividend yield means the stockholder is receiving a large part of his or her return in the form of current dividends. A low dividend yield means the stockholder is receiving a small part of his or her return in the form of current dividends. This means the stockholder is anticipating that he or she will receive larger dividends in the future. Typically, businesses that are experiencing low growth have high dividend yields, and businesses with high growth have low dividend yields.

Let's look at Tucker Enterprises. Analysts believe that the future of Tucker Enterprises is very good. Tucker Enterprises' current stock price is $200 per share. However, Tucker Enterprises has decided to retain all its net income and pay no dividends. Why? Because Tucker Enterprises has a lot of great investment opportunities that should make a lot of net income in the future. To finance these new opportunities, Tucker Enterprises is retaining all its current profits and pays no dividends. Zero dividends mean a zero dividend yield.

Now let's assume Tucker Enterprises' future investment prospects dim. Their future is still good, but the need for money has diminished because the opportunities to invest that money have diminished. Tucker Enterprises decides there isn't a good reason to retain its profits. It begins paying a $2.50 dividend per share. Because Tucker Enterprises' future is not as bright, its stock price drops to $150. Stockholders are buying Tucker Enterprises' stock for the current dividend more than for its bright future. Tucker Enterprises' dividend yield would be 1.7%, calculated as:

$$\text{Dividend Yield} = \frac{\text{Dividend per Share}}{\text{Current Market Price per Share of Stock}} = \frac{\$2.50}{\$150} = 1.7\%$$

Price-Earnings Ratio (PE)

Price-earnings (PE) ratio Ratio of the market price of a share of common stock to the company's earnings per share. It measures the value that the stock market places on $1 of a company's earnings.

The **price-earnings ratio (PE)** is the ratio of the current price of a share of stock divided by the current earnings-per-share of the business. It is a measure of the price paid for a share relative to the annual net income earned by the company per share and is computed as:

$$\text{Price Earnings Ratio (PE)} = \frac{\text{Current Price per Share}}{\text{Current EPS}}$$

A high PE typically indicates that the future of the business is very good. The business is expected to be a high-growth company. A low PE typically indicates the business is not a high-growth company. Its future may be similar or worse than its present.

Let's assume Tucker Enterprises has current EPS of $7.50. Participants in the market believe that the future of Tucker Enterprises is very good. They believe Tucker Enterprises is worth 20 times its current earnings. Tucker Enterprises would have a PE of 20 and a stock price of $150 per share. Now, let's assume something bad happens and the market revises its forecast for Tucker Enterprises. Participants in the market no longer believe the future for Tucker Enterprises is as good as they previously thought. The market revises its forecasts downward. The market now believes that Tucker Enterprises is worth half of what it used to be. Tucker Enterprises' stock price would fall to $75 per share and its PE would decline to 10. Because the market believes the future of Tucker Enterprises is not as good as was expected, the market lowers the price of Tucker Enterprises' stock, which causes the PE to decline.

How They Do It: A Look at Business

Let's look at two companies previously examined: Apple from Chapter 10 and Kroger from Chapter 1.

First is Apple, the company that created the game-changing iPhone and iPad. Because of these successes, Apple is considered a leader in the ever-changing, high-risk, but very profitable technology sector. Apple is a growth company that reinvests most of its profits in new and innovative products. Apple pays a relatively small dividend compared with its net income. On September 29, 2012, Apple's stock price was $667.11 per share. Apple's dividend for the year ending September 29, 2012, was $2.65 per share. Its earnings per share, for the year ending September 29, 2012, was $44.64. Its dividend yield was less than 1%, and its price-earnings ratio was 15.

Second, let's look at Kroger, the large grocery store chain. Kroger is a very profitable seller of groceries. Its sales, costs, profits, and cash flow are very stable and predictable. Kroger is a very well-run company that is considered to be a low-risk, low-growth business. Kroger pays a relatively large dividend relative to its net income. On February 2, 2013, Kroger's stock price was $27.67 per share. Kroger's dividend for the year ending February 2, 2013, was $0.53 per share. Its earnings per share, for the year ending February 2, 2013, was $2.78. Its dividend yield was 1.9%, and its price-earnings ratio was 10.

Think about and compare Apple and Kroger. Both are very successful businesses. Now think what the dividend yield and price-earnings ratio tell you. It appears that investors think the future of both Apple and Kroger is bright, but Apple is expected to grow more than Kroger.

MyAccountingLab

Summary

Here is what you should know after reading this chapter. The Study Plan in MyAccountingLab will help you identify what you know and where to go when you need practice.

Key Points	Key Accounting Terms
1 **Understand the purpose and process of financial analysis**	
Financial analysis is the process of using a business's financial statements, and other related information, to evaluate whether a business is creating value. The process of financial analysis is composed of the following five steps:	**Benchmarking** (p. 567) **Business model** (p. 567) **Business strategy** (p. 567) **Competitive environment** (p. 567) **Economic environment** (p. 567) **Financial analysis** (p. 566) **Financial analyst** (p. 566) **Management discussion and analysis (MD&A)** (p. 567)
1. Understand a business's model and strategy.	
2. Understand the environment in which the business operates.	
3. Analyze the content of the financial statements and other information, making adjustments if desired.	
4. Analyze the business's operations.	
5. Use the financial analysis to make decisions.	

		Key Points	Key Accounting Terms

2 **Perform financial analysis using financial statements**

Key Points

Financial analysis is about asking questions about value. Typical questions you should ask are:

1. Is the business a going concern?
2. How is the business earning net income?
3. Where is the business getting its money, and can it pay its debts?
4. How is the business investing its money, and is it using its assets efficiently?
5. Is the business generating enough net income to reward the stockholders for the use of their money?

Analysts become concerned when they see certain "red flags" such as decreased net cash flow from operations, difficulty in collecting receivables, or too much debt.

Key Accounting Terms

Accounts receivable turnover (p. 582)

Base period (p. 573)

Cash conversion cycle (p. 576)

Collateral (p. 580)

Common-size statement (p. 572)

Current ratio (p. 576)

Debt covenants (p. 580)

Debt ratio (p. 580)

Dividend payout ratio (p. 584)

Dividends per share (DPS) (p. 584)

Earnings before interest and taxes (EBIT) (p. 579)

Earnings per share (EPS) (p. 583)

Financing decision (p. 580)

Fixed asset turnover (p. 582)

Gross profit percentage (p. 579)

Horizontal analysis (p. 573)

Income or loss from continuing operations (p. 577)

Interest coverage ratio (p. 580)

Inventory turnover (p. 582)

Investing decision (p. 581)

Net income percentage (p. 579)

Net working capital (p. 575)

Operating income (p. 579)

Quick ratio (p. 576)

Return on assets (ROA) (p. 582)

Return on equity (ROE) (p. 584)

Total asset turnover (p. 582)

Trend percentages (p. 575)

Vertical analysis (p. 572)

3 **Use financial analysis to assess the value of a business**

There is nothing harder in the financial world than the valuation of a business. The dividend yield and the price-earnings ratio are two measures often looked at in valuing a business.

Dividend yield (p. 590)

Price-earnings (PE) ratio (p. 590)

Accounting Practice

Discussion Questions

1. How is percentage change calculated?

2. Which amount is the base amount for vertical analysis on the income statement?

3. Which amount is the base amount for vertical analysis on the balance sheet?

4. What is the purpose of the common-size financial statement?

5. The Financial Accounting Standards Board and the International Accounting Standards Board have identified the goal of comparability of financial statements as one toward which all companies should strive and consistency as the means toward achieving that goal. How are these characteristics important to horizontal and vertical analysis?

6. What is benchmarking? What should a company that wishes to use benchmarking look for in establishing benchmarks?

7. What are the major goals of each of the following types of ratios?
   a. Liquidity ratios
   b. Asset management ratios
   c. Solvency ratios
   d. Profitability ratios
   e. Market analysis ratios

8. How would you expect a recession to affect asset management ratios?

9. What is a "red flag" with respect to financial statement analysis?

10. A company has experienced increases in accounts receivable and inventory turnover ratios and has net cash flow from operations that exceeds net income. All other things constant, what could you conclude about the company's performance this year relative to last year?

MyAccountingLab

Self Check

1. Net income was $175,000 in 2012, $190,000 in 2013, and $209,000 in 2014. The change from 2013 to 2014 is an
   a. increase of 10%.
   b. increase of 9%.
   c. increase of 8%.
   d. increase of 19%.

2. Horizontal analysis of a financial statement shows
   a. the relationship of each statement item to a specified base.
   b. percentage changes in comparative balance sheets.
   c. percentage changes in comparative income statements.
   d. both b and c.

3. A statement that reports only percentages is called
   a. a comparative statement.
   b. a cumulative statement.
   c. a condensed statement.
   d. a common-size statement.

4. Net working capital is
   a. a measure of the ability to meet short-term obligations with current assets.
   b. defined as current assets minus current liabilities.
   c. defined as current assets divided by current liabilities.
   d. both a and b.

5. Cash is $12,000, net accounts receivable amounts to $18,000, inventory is $21,000, prepaid expenses total $3,000, and current liabilities are $37,500. What is the quick ratio?

   a. 1.44
   b. 1.36
   c. 0.80
   d. 0.88

6. A business's economic environment is

   a. how a business competes for customers, suppliers, and other critical resources.
   b. how a business is affected by the overall economy.
   c. how a business uses its business model to create a competitive advantage.
   d. what a business does, the products it sells, and the customers who buy its products.

7. Rockport Company is experiencing a severe cash shortage due to its inability to collect accounts receivable. Which of the following would most likely identify this problem?

   a. Return on assets
   b. Current ratio
   c. Accounts receivable turnover
   d. Working capital

8. Which of the following statements is *true* of financial statement analysis?

   a. Ratio analysis is more important than either horizontal or vertical analysis.
   b. Vertical analysis involves comparing amounts from one year's financial statements to another year's statements.
   c. Horizontal analysis expresses all items on a financial statement as percentages of a common base.
   d. None of the above

9. Which statement is most likely to be *true*?

   a. An increase in inventory turnover indicates that inventory is not selling as quickly as it was.
   b. A decrease in inventory turnover indicates that inventory is not selling as quickly as it was.
   c. A change in inventory turnover cannot be accurately assessed without considering the change in profit margin.
   d. None of the above

10. How are financial ratios used in decision making?

   a. They can be used as a substitute for consulting financial statements.
   b. They eliminate uncertainty regarding cash flows.
   c. They are only used in evaluating business liquidity.
   d. They help to identify reasons for business success and failure.

11. According to the Real World Accounting Video, a VC is a _____.

   a. veteran communicator
   b. victorious commercialization
   c. venture capitalist
   d. vendor conduit

12. According to the Real World Accounting Video, what is the most important thing investors look at when deciding to invest in a company?

   a. Sales
   b. Management
   c. Competitors
   d. Assets

Answers are given after Written Communication.

Short Exercises

S12-1. Corporate financial statements (*Learning Objective 2*) 5–10 min.

Identify whether each of the following items would be classified as:

- Income from continuing operations (C)
- Income from discontinued operations (D)
- An extraordinary item (E)

_____ **a.** $12,000 insurance proceeds on a fully depreciated piece of equipment that was lost in a hurricane

_____ **b.** $800 gain on the sale of office furniture

_____ **c.** Income tax expense

_____ **d.** $106,000 loss incurred as a result of closing the Walla Walla, Washington store location

_____ **e.** $2,300 loss incurred as a result of a company vehicle being involved in an accident

S12-2. Horizontal analysis (*Learning Objective 2*) 10–15 min.

Wolfe, Inc., had net sales of $212,000 and cost of goods sold of $128,000 in 2012, net sales of $263,000 and cost of goods sold of $161,000 in 2013, and net sales of $325,000 and cost of goods sold of $200,000 in 2014. Round answers to the nearest tenth of a percent.

1. Find the percentage of increase in net sales from 2012 to 2013 and from 2013 to 2014.

2. Find the percentage of increase in gross profit from 2012 to 2013 and from 2013 to 2014.

S12-3. Vertical analysis (*Learning Objective 2*) 10–15 min.

The 2014 accounting records of Sullivan, Inc., showed the following: Cash, $14,400; Net Accounts Receivable, $5,600; Inventory, $23,200; Prepaid Expenses, $2,400; Net Plant and Equipment, $34,400.

Construct a vertical analysis of the asset section of Sullivan, Inc., balance sheet for 2014.

S12-4. Ratio definitions (*Learning Objectives 2 & 3*) 10–15 min.

Match the following terms to their definitions:

1. Tells whether a company can pay all its current liabilities if they become due immediately.

2. Measures a company's success in using assets to earn income.

3. The practice of comparing a company with other companies that are similar.

4. Indicates how rapidly inventory is sold.

5. Shows the proportion of a company's assets that is financed with debt.

6. Tells the percentage of a stock's market value that the company returns to stockholders annually as dividends.

7. Measures a business's ability to pay interest on its debt.

8. Measures a company's ability to collect cash from credit customers.

a. Inventory turnover

b. Interest coverage ratio

c. Quick ratio

d. Dividend yield

e. Return on assets

f. Accounts receivable turnover

g. Benchmarking

h. Debt ratio

S12-5. Purpose of select ratios (*Learning Objective 2*) 10–15 min.

Identify which question each of the following ratios helps answer.

1. Is the business a going concern?
2. How is the business earning a net income or loss?
3. Where is the business getting its money, and can it pay its debt obligations?
4. How is the business investing its money, and is it using its assets efficiently?
5. Is the business generating enough net income to reward the stockholders for the use of their money?

_____ **a.** Inventory turnover

_____ **b.** Debt ratio

_____ **c.** Return on equity

_____ **d.** Fixed asset turnover

_____ **e.** Quick ratio

_____ **f.** Return on assets

_____ **g.** Gross profit percentage

_____ **h.** Accounts receivable turnover

_____ **i.** Current ratio

_____ **j.** Earnings per share

_____ **k.** Interest coverage ratio

_____ **l.** Net income percentage

_____ **m.** Cash conversion cycle

_____ **n.** Dividends per share

_____ **o.** Total asset turnover

S12-6. Accounts receivable turnover, days' sales in accounts receivable, and inventory turnover (*Learning Objective 2*) 10–15 min.

The 2013 and 2014 balance sheets for Flores, Inc., showed net accounts receivable of $13,000 and $17,000, respectively, inventory of $12,000 and $9,000, respectively, and accounts payable of $6,000 and $8,000, respectively. The company's 2014 income statement showed net sales of $189,000 and cost of goods sold of $98,910. Assume all sales on credit. Compute the following ratios for 2014:

1. Accounts receivable turnover
2. Inventory turnover

S12-7. Current ratio and quick ratio (*Learning Objective 2*) 10–15 min.

In addition to the information from S12-6, assume that cash on the 2014 balance sheet was $14,000 and current liabilities totaled $25,000. Compute the following ratios for 2014:

1. Current ratio
2. Quick ratio
3. Cash conversion cycle—round to whole days

S12-8. Return on sales, return on assets, return on common equity, times-interest-earned ratio, and debt ratio (*Learning Objective 2*) 10–15 min.

The 2014 financial statements for Inland Supply, Inc., show total assets of $572,000, total liabilities of $322,500, net sales of $1,276,000, net income of $191,400, income from operations of $227,600, cost of goods sold of $743,600, dividends of $24,600, and interest expense of $18,700. Total assets and total liabilities for 2013 were $513,000 and $314,500, respectively. Compute the following ratios for 2014. Round all answers to two decimal places.

1. Debt ratio
2. Interest coverage ratio
3. Return on assets
4. Dividend payout
5. Return on equity

S12-9. EPS and price-earnings ratio (*Learning Objectives 2 & 3*) 10–15 min.

Using the information from S12-8, a market price of $34 per share, and 50,000 and 60,000 shares of common stock outstanding in 2013 and 2014, respectively, compute the following for 2014. Round answers to two decimal places.

1. Earnings per share
2. Price-earnings ratio

S12-10. Dividend yield (*Learning Objective 3*) 10–15 min.

In 2014, common stockholders received $6 per share in annual dividends. The market price per share for common stock was $24. Compute the dividend yield for common stock.

MyAccountingLab

Exercises (Group A)

E12-11A. Horizontal analysis (*Learning Objective 2*) 15–20 min.

What were the dollar and percentage changes in Meghan's Design Services' net working capital during 2013 and 2014? Is this trend favorable or unfavorable?

	2014	2013	2012
Total Current Assets	$450,000	$400,000	$350,000
Total Current Liabilities	261,000	220,000	200,000

E12-12A. Horizontal analysis (*Learning Objective 2*) 15–20 min.

Below is the comparative income statement of Wellington Supply, Inc.

Wellington Supply, Inc. Comparative Income Statement Years Ended December 31, 2014 and 2013		
	2014	**2013**
Revenue	$515,200	$470,700
Expenses:		
Cost of Goods Sold	223,800	204,900
Selling and General Expenses	96,400	95,600
Interest Expense	51,600	48,100
Income Tax Expense	26,500	21,900
Total Expenses	398,300	370,500
Net Income	$116,900	$100,200

Requirements

1. Prepare a horizontal analysis of the comparative income statement of Wellington Supply, Inc. Round percentage changes to the nearest tenth of a percent.

2. Why did net income increase by a higher percent than total revenues increased during 2014?

E12-13A. Horizontal analysis (*Learning Objective 2*) 15–20 min.

Below are net sales and net income data for a five-year period.

	Year 5	**Year 4**	**Year 3**	**Year 2**	**Year 1**
Net Sales..............	$2,650	$2,625	$2,575	$2,550	$2,500
Net Income	767	728	670	650	650

Requirements

1. Compute trend percentages for net sales and net income for the five-year period, using year 1 as the base year.

2. Which grew faster during the period, net sales or net income?

E12-14A. Vertical analysis (*Learning Objective 2*) 15–20 min.

Peterson Painting, Inc., requested that you perform a vertical analysis of its balance sheet to determine the component percentages of its assets, liabilities, and stockholders' equity. Round to the nearest tenth of a percent.

Peterson Painting
Balance Sheet
December 31, 2014

ASSETS		LIABILITIES	
Total Current Assets	$127,000	Total Current Liabilities	$ 84,000
Long-Term Investments	55,000	Long-Term Debt	189,000
Property, Plant, and		Total Liabilities	273,000
Equipment, Net	331,000		
		STOCKHOLDERS' EQUITY	
		Total Stockholders' Equity	240,000
		Total Liabilities and	
Total Assets	$513,000	Stockholders' Equity	$513,000

E12-15A. Common-size income statement (*Learning Objective 2*) 15–20 min.

Prepare a comparative common-size income statement for Wellington Supply, Inc., using the 2014 and 2013 data of E12-12A. Round percentages to the nearest tenth of a percent.

Quick solution:

a. Current ratio = 1.56; b. Quick ratio = .96 c. Cash conversion cycle = 68 days; d. A/R turnover = 7.50 times; e. Inventory turnover = 5.83 times; f. Gross profit % = 41.7%; g. Net income % = 8.8%

E12-16A. Current ratio, quick ratio, inventory turnover, accounts receivable turnover, and days' sales in accounts receivable (*Learning Objective 2*) 15–20 min.

The financial statements of Voyage, Inc., include the following items:

	Current Year	Previous Year
Balance Sheet		
Cash	$ 20,000	$ 40,000
Short-Term Investments	10,000	30,000
Accounts Receivable, Net	90,000	70,000
Inventory	70,000	50,000
Prepaid Expenses	5,000	10,000
Total Current Assets	195,000	200,000
Accounts Payable	45,000	40,000
Total Current Liabilities	125,000	100,000
Income Statement		
Net Sales	$600,000	
Cost of Goods Sold	350,000	
Net Income	53,000	

Requirement

1. Compute the following ratios for the current year: (a) current ratio, (b) quick ratio, (c) cash conversion cycle, (d) accounts receivable turnover, (e) inventory turnover, (f) gross profit percentage, and (g) net income percentage. Round all calculations to two decimal places, days to full days, and percentages to the nearest tenth of a percent. Assume all sales on credit.

E12-17A. Current ratio, quick ratio, debt ratio, times-interest-earned ratio (*Learning Objective 2*) **15–20 min.**

Prince Clark Winery requested that you determine whether the company's ability to pay its current liabilities and long-term debts improved or deteriorated during 2014. To answer this question, compute the following ratios for 2014 and 2013: (a) current ratio, (b) quick ratio, (c) debt ratio, and (d) interest coverage ratio. Round all ratios to two decimal places. Summarize the results of your analysis.

	2014	2013
Cash..	$ 30,000	$ 40,000
Short-Term Investments...	37,000	18,000
Accounts Receivable, Net...	120,000	140,000
Inventory...	290,000	320,000
Prepaid Expenses..	7,000	10,000
Total Assets	600,000	750,000
Total Current Liabilities	220,000	200,000
Long-Term Note Payable	150,000	185,000
Income From Operations	145,000	180,000
Interest Expense	22,000	26,000

E12-18A. Financial statement analysis (*Learning Objective 2*) **15–20 min.**

Consider the following comparative income statement and additional balance sheet data for Fessler Fashions, Inc.

Fessler Fashions, Inc.
Income Statement
Years Ended December 31, 2014 and 2013

	2014	2013
Net Sales	$236,000	$248,000
Cost of Goods Sold	134,000	142,000
Gross Profit	102,000	106,000
Selling and General Expenses	63,500	61,000
Income From Operations	38,500	45,000
Interest Expense	9,300	8,600
Income Before Income Tax	29,200	36,400
Income Tax Expense	6,600	8,200
Net Income	$ 22,600	$ 28,200

Additional data follow:

	2014	2013	2012
Accounts receivable	23,000	20,000	16,000
Inventory...	13,000	19,000	12,000
Total current assets	44,000	43,000	39,000
Fixed assets	262,000	238,000	217,000
Total Assets	$306,000	$281,000	$256,000

Requirements

1. For 2013 and 2014, compute the five ratios that measure how the business is investing its money and whether it is using its assets efficiently. Round each ratio to two decimal places. Assume all sales on credit.

2. Did the company's performance improve or deteriorate during 2014?

E12-19A. **Financial statement analysis** (*Learning Objective 2*) **15–20 min.**

Evaluate the common stock of Shamrock Incorporated as an investment. Utilize the four ratios that help determine if the business is generating enough net income to reward the stockholders for the use of their money; use this information to determine whether the stock increased or decreased in attractiveness during the past year. Round all ratios to two decimal places.

	2014	2013	2012
Net Income	$ 90,000	$ 80,000	$ 75,000
Total Dividends	50,000	40,000	35,000
Common Stockholders' Equity at Year-End	750,000	720,000	690,000
Number of shares of common stock outstanding at year-end	110,000	100,000	95,000

E12-20A. **Complete financial statement given certain information** (*Learning Objective 2*) **15–20 min.**

The following data (dollar amounts in millions) are adapted from the financial statements of Mountain West, Inc.

Total Current Assets	$18,000
Accumulated Depreciation	2,000
Total Liabilities	22,000
Debt Ratio	40%
Current Ratio	1.2

Requirement

1. Complete the following condensed balance sheet. Report amounts rounded to the nearest $1 million:

Current Assets		$?
Property, Plant, and Equipment	$?	
Less: Accumulated Depreciation	(?)	?
Total Assets		$?
Current Liabilities		$?
Long-Term Liabilities		?
Stockholders' Equity		?
Total Liabilities and Stockholders' Equity		$?

Exercises (Group B)

E12-21B. **Horizontal analysis** (*Learning Objective 2*) **15–20 min.**

What were the dollar and percentage changes in Paw's Pet Shop's net working capital during 2013 and 2014? Is this trend favorable or unfavorable?

	2014	2013	2012
Total Current Assets	$336,250	$328,500	$315,000
Total Current Liabilities	232,705	213,450	185,000

E12-22B. Horizontal analysis (*Learning Objective 2*) 15–20 min.

Below is the comparative income statement of Horton, Inc.

	Horton, Inc. Comparative Income Statement Years Ended December 31, 2014 and 2013		
		2014	**2013**
	Revenue	$595,000	$505,000
	Expenses:		
	Cost of Goods Sold	$270,000	$227,000
	Selling and General Expenses	120,000	110,000
	Interest Expense	48,000	41,000
	Income Tax Expense	30,000	35,000
	Total Expenses	468,000	413,000
	Net Income	$127,000	$ 92,000

Requirements

1. Prepare a horizontal analysis of the comparative income statement of Horton, Inc. Round percentage changes to the nearest tenth of a percent.

2. Why did net income increase by a higher percent than total revenues increased during 2014?

E12-23B. Horizontal analysis (*Learning Objective 2*) 15–20 min.

Below are net sales and net income data for a five-year period.

	Year 5	Year 4	Year 3	Year 2	Year 1
Net Sales..................	$2,714	$2,530	$2,392	$2,346	$2,300
Net Income	660	630	612	606	600

Requirements

1. Compute trend percentages for net sales and net income for the five-year period, using year 1 as the base year.

2. Which grew faster during the period, net sales or net income?

E12-24B. Vertical analysis (*Learning Objective 2*) 15–20 min.

Natalie's Nursing Home requested that you perform a vertical analysis of its balance sheet to determine the component percentages of its assets, liabilities, and stockholders' equity. Round to the nearest tenth of a percent.

Natalie's Nursing Home Balance Sheet December 31, 2014			
ASSETS		**LIABILITIES**	
Total Current Assets	$126,000	Total Current Liabilities	$120,000
Long-Term Investments	90,000	Long-Term Debt	202,000
Property, Plant, and		Total Liabilities	322,000
Equipment, Net	376,000		
		STOCKHOLDERS' EQUITY	
		Total Stockholders' Equity	270,000
		Total Liabilities and	
Total Assets	$592,000	Stockholders' Equity	$592,000

E12-25B. Common-size income statement (*Learning Objective 2*) 15–20 min.

Prepare a comparative common-size income statement for Horton, Inc., using the 2014 and 2013 data of E12-22B. Round percentages to the nearest tenth of a percent.

E12-26B. Current ratio, quick ratio, inventory turnover, accounts receivable turnover, and days' sales in accounts receivable (*Learning Objective 2*) 15–20 min.

The financial statements of Oxford, Inc., include the following items:

	Current Year	Previous Year
Balance Sheet		
Cash	$ 28,000	$ 36,000
Short-Term Investments	20,000	28,000
Accounts Receivable, Net	64,000	70,000
Inventory	77,000	55,000
Prepaid Expenses	6,000	8,000
Total Current Assets	195,000	197,000
Accounts Payable	54,000	48,000
Total Current Liabilities	118,000	92,000
Income Statement		
Net Sales	$488,000	
Cost of Goods Sold	293,000	
Net Income	61,000	

Requirement

1. Compute the following ratios for the current year: (a) current ratio, (b) quick ratio, (c) cash conversion cycle, (d) accounts receivable turnover, (e) inventory turnover, (f) gross profit percentage, and (g) net income percentage. Round all calculations to two decimal places, days to full days, and percentages to the nearest tenth of a percent. Assume all sales on credit.

E12-27B. Current ratio, quick ratio, debt ratio, times-interest-earned ratio (*Learning Objective 2*) 15–20 min.

White Stone Winery requested that you determine whether the company's ability to pay its current liabilities and long-term debts improved or deteriorated during 2014. Round all ratios to two decimal places. To answer this question, compute the following ratios for 2014 and 2013: (a) current ratio, (b) quick ratio, (c) debt ratio, and (d) interest coverage ratio. Round all ratios to two decimal places. Summarize the results of your analysis.

	2014	2013
Cash	$ 40,000	$ 25,000
Short-Term Investments	36,000	22,000
Accounts Receivable, Net	150,000	136,000
Inventory	180,000	192,000
Prepaid Expenses	5,000	4,000
Total Assets	572,000	560,000
Total Current Liabilities	153,000	161,000
Long-Term Note Payable	130,000	165,000
Income From Operations	175,000	158,000
Interest Expense	16,000	19,500

E12-28B. Financial statement analysis (*Learning Objective 2*) **15–20 min.**

Consider the following comparative income statement and additional balance sheet data for Iconic Fashions, Inc.

Iconic Fashions, Inc. Income Statement Years Ended December 31, 2014 and 2013		
	2014	**2013**
Net Sales	$215,000	$200,000
Cost of Goods Sold	118,000	110,000
Gross Profit	97,000	90,000
Selling and General Expenses	41,000	36,500
Income From Operations	56,000	53,500
Interest Expense	18,000	17,500
Income Before Income Tax	38,000	36,000
Income Tax Expense	4,500	4,000
Net Income	$ 33,500	$ 32,000

Additional data follow:

	2014	2013	2012
Accounts receivable	20,000	22,000	19,000
Inventory	7,000	6,000	8,000
Total current assets	31,000	32,000	29,000
Fixed assets	152,000	148,000	146,000
Total Assets	$183,000	$180,000	$175,000

Requirements

1. For 2013 and 2014, compute the five ratios that measure how the business is investing its money and whether it is using its assets efficiently. Round each ratio to two decimal places. Assume all sales on credit.

2. Did the company's performance improve or deteriorate during 2014?

E12-29B. Financial statement analysis (*Learning Objective 2*) **15–20 min.**

Evaluate the common stock of Sharp Systems Incorporated as an investment. Utilize the four ratios that help determine if the business is generating enough net income to reward the stockholders for the use of their money; use this information to determine whether the stock increased or decreased in attractiveness during the past year. Round all ratios to two decimal places.

	2014	2013	2012
Net Income	$110,000	$120,000	$145,000
Total Dividends	45,000	51,000	52,000
Common Stockholders' Equity at Year-End	640,000	603,000	580,000
Number of shares of common stock outstanding at year-end	105,000	100,000	97,000

E12-30B. Complete financial statement given certain information (*Learning Objective 2*) 15–20 min.

The following data (dollar amounts in millions) are adapted from the financial statements of Meadowview, Inc.

Total Current Assets..	$30,000
Accumulated Depreciation	5,000
Total Liabilities..	45,000
Debt Ratio...	60%
Current Ratio...	1.5

Requirement

1. Complete the following condensed balance sheet. Report amounts rounded to the nearest $1 million:

Current Assets		$?
Property, Plant, and Equipment	$?	
Less: Accumulated Depreciation..............................	(?)	?
Total Assets		$?
Current Liabilities..		$?
Long-Term Liabilities		?
Stockholders' Equity		?
Total Liabilities and Stockholders' Equity..................		$?

MyAccountingLab

Problems (Group A)

P12-31A. Horizontal and vertical analysis (*Learning Objective 2*) 20–25 min.

Net sales, net income, and total assets for Columbia Construction, Inc., for a four-year period follow:

(in thousands)	2014	2013	2012	2011
Net Sales..	$570	$550	$510	$500
Net Income	58	56	42	40
Ending Total Assets	345	305	270	250

Requirements

1. Compute trend percentages for each item for 2011–2014. Use 2011 as the base year.

2. Compute the return on assets for 2012–2014, rounding to three decimal places.

3. Columbia's main competitor had a return on assets of just under 18% for the years 2012 through 2014. How does Columbia Construction, Inc.'s return on assets compare with its main competitor?

P12-32A. Common-size financial statements and profitability ratios (*Learning Objective 2*) 20–25 min.

Motion Used Auto Sales asked for your help in comparing the company's profit performance and financial position with the average for the auto sales industry. The proprietor has given you the company's income statement and balance sheet as well as the industry average data for retailers of used autos.

Motion Used Auto Sales Income Statement Compared with Industry Average Year Ended December 31, 2014		
	MOTION	**INDUSTRY AVERAGE**
Net Sales	$952,800	100.0%
Cost of Goods Sold	608,700	62.1%
Gross Profit	344,100	37.9%
Operating Expenses	230,600	27.8%
Operating Income	113,500	10.1%
Other Expenses	6,200	0.4%
Net Income	$107,300	9.7%

Motion Used Auto Sales Balance Sheet Compared with Industry Average December 31, 2014		
	MOTION	**INDUSTRY AVERAGE**
Current Assets	$478,700	70.9%
Fixed Assets, Net	160,600	23.6%
Intangible Assets, Net	7,400	0.8%
Other Assets	42,900	4.7%
Total Assets	$689,600	100.0%
Current Liabilities	$294,800	48.1%
Long-Term Liabilities	118,500	16.6%
Stockholders' Equity	276,300	35.3%
Total Liabilities and Stockholders' Equity	$689,600	100.0%

Requirements

1. Prepare a two-column, common-size income statement and a two-column, common-size balance sheet for Motion Used Auto Sales. The first column of each statement should present Motion Used Auto Sales' common-size statement and the second column should show the industry averages.

2. For the profitability analysis, examine Motion Used Auto Sales' (a) ratio of gross profit to net sales, (b) ratio of operating income to net sales, and (c) ratio of net income to net sales. Compare these figures with the industry averages. Is Motion's profit performance better or worse than the industry average?

3. For the analysis of financial position, examine Motion Used Auto Sales' (a) ratio of current assets to total assets, and (b) ratio of stockholders' equity to total assets. Compare these ratios with the industry averages. Is Motion Used Auto Sales' financial position better or worse than the industry average?

P12-33A. Current ratio, debt ratio, EPS (*Learning Objective 2*) **20–25 min.**

Financial statement data of Southwest Fencing, Inc., include the following items:

Cash..	$ 19,000
Short-Term Investments...	24,000
Accounts Receivable, Net...	80,600
Inventory..	118,300
Prepaid Expenses...	8,400
Total Assets	562,000
Short-Term Notes Payable..	40,000
Accounts Payable...	81,000
Accrued Liabilities..	39,200
Long-Term Notes Payable...	150,600
Other Long-Term Liabilities	32,700
Net Income	64,800
Number of Common Shares Outstanding	55,000

Quick solution:

1. Current ratio = 1.56, Debt ratio = 61.12%, EPS = 1.18; 2. a. Current ratio = 1.45, Debt ratio = 63.82%, EPS = 1.18; 2.b. Current ratio = 2.00, Debt ratio = 54.35%, EPS = 1.05; 2.c. Current ratio = 2.25, Debt ratio = 67.49%, EPS = 1.18; 2.d. Current ratio = 1.56, Debt ratio = 61.12%, EPS = 1.18

Requirements

1. Compute Southwest Fencing's current ratio, debt ratio, and earnings per share. Assume that the company had no preferred stock outstanding. Round all ratios to two decimal places.

2. Compute each of the same three ratios, after evaluating the effect of each independent transaction that follows.
   a. Purchased merchandise of $42,000 on account, debiting Inventory.
   b. Issued 7,000 shares of common stock, receiving cash of $70,000. Use total shares outstanding at year-end instead of average shares outstanding.
   c. Borrowed $110,000 on a long-term note payable.
   d. Received cash on account, $23,000.

P12-34A. Calculate various ratios for analysis (*Learning Objectives 2 & 3*) **20–25 min.**

Comparative financial statement data of Comfort Way Furniture Company follow:

Comfort Way Furniture Company Income Statement Years Ended December 31, 2014 and 2013		
	2014	**2013**
Net Sales	$490,000	$453,000
Cost of Goods Sold	240,000	231,000
Gross Profit	250,000	222,000
Operating Expenses	132,000	133,000
Income from Operations	118,000	89,000
Interest Expense	10,000	16,000
Income Before Income Tax	108,000	73,000
Income Tax Expense	32,000	27,000
Net Income	$ 76,000	$ 46,000

<table>
<tr><td colspan="4" align="center">**Comfort Way Furniture Company**
Balance Sheet
December 31, 2014 and 2013
(Selected 2012 amounts given for computation of ratios)</td></tr>
<tr><td></td><th>2014</th><th>2013</th><th>2012</th></tr>
<tr><td>Current Assets:</td><td></td><td></td><td></td></tr>
<tr><td>Cash</td><td>$105,000</td><td>$109,000</td><td></td></tr>
<tr><td>Accounts Receivable, Net</td><td>76,000</td><td>84,000</td><td>$96,000</td></tr>
<tr><td>Inventory</td><td>168,000</td><td>156,000</td><td>187,000</td></tr>
<tr><td>Prepaid Expenses</td><td>30,000</td><td>22,000</td><td></td></tr>
<tr><td>Total Current Assets</td><td>379,000</td><td>371,000</td><td></td></tr>
<tr><td>Property, Plant, and Equipment, Net</td><td>191,000</td><td>182,000</td><td></td></tr>
<tr><td>Total Assets</td><td>$570,000</td><td>$553,000</td><td></td></tr>
<tr><td></td><td></td><td></td><td></td></tr>
<tr><td>Total Current Liabilities</td><td>$210,000</td><td>$230,000</td><td></td></tr>
<tr><td>Long-Term Liabilities</td><td>129,000</td><td>118,000</td><td></td></tr>
<tr><td>Total Liabilities</td><td>339,000</td><td>348,000</td><td></td></tr>
<tr><td>Common Stockholders' Equity, No Par</td><td>231,000</td><td>205,000</td><td>201,000</td></tr>
<tr><td>Total Liabilities and Stockholders' Equity</td><td>$570,000</td><td>$553,000</td><td></td></tr>
</table>

Other information follows:

a. Market price of common stock was $50.50 at December 31, 2014, and $33.00 at December 31, 2013.

b. Average common shares outstanding were 13,000 during 2014 and 8,000 during 2013.

Requirements

1. Compute the following ratios for 2014 and 2013. Round to two decimal places. Assume all sales on credit.
   a. Current ratio
   b. Inventory turnover
   c. Accounts receivable turnover
   d. Interest coverage ratio
   e. Return on equity
   f. Earnings per share of common stock
   g. Price-earnings ratio

2. Decide: (a) whether Comfort Way Furniture Company's performance improved or deteriorated during 2014; and (b) whether the investment attractiveness of its common stock appears to have increased or decreased.

3. How will what you learned in this problem help you evaluate an investment?

P12-35A. Calculate various ratios for analysis (*Learning Objectives 2 & 3*) **20–25 min.**

Assume you are purchasing an investment and decide to invest in a company in the home remodeling business. You narrow the choice to Remco, Inc., or Home Makeover, Corp. You assemble the following selected data:

Selected income statement data for the current year:

	Remco, Inc.	Home Makeover, Corp.
Net Sales	$198,000	$224,000
Cost of Goods Sold	102,000	141,000
EBIT	88,000	95,000
Interest Expense	17,000	8,000
Net Income	61,000	82,000

Selected balance sheet and market price data at the end of the current year:

	Remco, Inc.	Home Makeover, Corp.
Current Assets:		
Cash	$ 27,000	$ 61,000
Short-Term Investments	32,000	43,000
Accounts Receivable, Net	35,000	26,000
Inventory	51,000	50,000
Prepaid Expenses	6,000	2,000
Total Current Assets	151,000	182,000
Total Assets	246,000	237,000
Total Current Liabilities	73,000	47,000
Total Liabilities	97,000	90,000
Common Stock, $2.00 Par, 6,000 Shares		12,000
$5.00 Par, 5,000 Shares	25,000	
Total Stockholders' Equity	149,000	147,000
Market price per share of common stock	$ 51	$ 54

Selected balance sheet data at the beginning of the current year:

	Remco, Inc.	Home Makeover, Corp.
Accounts Receivable, Net	$ 39,000	$ 13,000
Inventory	73,000	62,000
Total Assets	251,000	174,000
Common Stock, $2.00 Par, 6,000 Shares		12,000
$5.00 Par, 5,000 Shares	25,000	
Total Stockholders' Equity	126,000	167,000

Your investment strategy is to purchase the stock of the company that has a low price-earnings ratio but appears to be in good shape financially. Assume that you analyzed all other factors and your decision depends on the results of the ratio analysis to be performed.

Requirement

1. Compute the following ratios for both companies for the current year and decide which company's stock better fits your investment strategy. Assume all sales on credit.
   a. Quick ratio
   b. Debt ratio
   c. Interest coverage ratio
   d. Accounts receivable turnover
   e. Inventory turnover
   f. Total asset turnover
   g. Return on assets
   h. Return on equity
   i. Earnings per share
   j. Price-earnings ratio

P12-36A. Financial statement ratio analysis (*Learning Objective 2*) 20–25 min.

You have been hired as an investment analyst at Eleanor Regal Securities, Inc. It is your job to recommend investments for your client. You have the following information for two different companies.

Ratio	Madden Sport, Co.	Ultimate Gamer, Inc.
Accounts receivable turnover	13	10
Inventory turnover	14	18
Gross profit percentage	51%	48%
Net income as a percent of sales	11%	14%
Interest coverage ratio	20	18
Return on equity	25%	21%
Return on assets	10%	12%

Requirement

1. Write a memo to your client recommending the company you believe to be a more attractive investment. Explain the reasons for your recommendation.

Problems (Group B)

P12-37B. Horizontal and vertical analysis (*Learning Objective 2*) 20–25 min.

Net sales, net income, and total assets for Regal Clothing Emporium for a four-year period are:

(in thousands)	2014	2013	2012	2011
Net Sales	$1,350	$1,200	$1,150	$1,025
Net Income	82	77	53	49
Ending Total Assets	650	620	550	500

Requirements

1. Compute trend percentages for each item for 2011–2014. Use 2011 as the base year.

2. Compute the return on assets for 2012–2014, rounding to three decimal places.

3. Regal's main competitor had a return on assets of just under 12% for the years 2012 through 2014. How does Regal Clothing Emporium's return on assets compare with its main competitor?

P12-38B. Common-size financial statements and profitability ratios
(*Learning Objective 2*) 20–25 min.

Johnson Auto Sales asked for your help in comparing the company's profit performance and financial position with the average for the auto sales industry. The proprietor has given you the company's income statement and balance sheet, as well as the industry average data for retailers of used autos.

Johnson Auto Sales Income Statement Compared with Industry Average Year Ended December 31, 2014		
	JOHNSON	INDUSTRY AVERAGE
Net Sales	$961,100	100.0%
Cost of Goods Sold	577,800	63.2%
Gross Profit	383,300	36.8%
Operating Expenses	302,400	27.5%
Operating Income	80,900	9.3%
Other Expenses	5,600	0.5%
Net Income	$ 75,300	8.8%

Johnson Auto Sales Balance Sheet Compared with Industry Average December 31, 2014		
	JOHNSON	INDUSTRY AVERAGE
Current Assets	$287,300	71.2%
Fixed Assets, Net	95,900	24.3%
Intangible Assets, Net	2,600	0.7%
Other Assets	20,800	3.8%
Total Assets	$406,600	100.0%
Current Liabilities	$200,500	48.4%
Long-Term Liabilities	75,900	16.1%
Stockholders' Equity	130,200	35.5%
Total Liabilities and Stockholders' Equity	$406,600	100.0%

Requirements

1. Prepare a two-column, common-size income statement and a two-column, common-size balance sheet for Johnson Auto Sales. The first column of each statement should present Johnson Auto Sales' common-size statement and the second column should show the industry averages.

2. For the profitability analysis, examine Johnson Auto Sales': (a) ratio of gross profit to net sales; (b) ratio of operating income to net sales; and (c) ratio of net income to net sales. Compare these figures with the industry averages. Is Johnson Auto Sales' profit performance better or worse than the industry average?

3. For the analysis of financial position, examine Johnson Auto Sales': (a) ratio of current assets to total assets; and (b) ratio of stockholders' equity to total assets. Compare these ratios with the industry averages. Is Johnson Auto Sales' financial position better or worse than the industry average?

P12-39B. Current ratio, debt ratio, EPS (*Learning Objective 2*) **20–25 min.**

Financial statement data of New England Fencing, Inc., include:

Cash	$ 17,000
Short-Term Investments	22,000
Accounts Receivable, Net	103,000
Inventory	119,000
Prepaid Expenses	10,000
Total Assets	660,000
Short-Term Notes Payable	45,000
Accounts Payable	105,000
Accrued Liabilities	40,000
Long-Term Notes Payable	157,000
Other Long-Term Liabilities	34,000
Net Income	75,400
Number of Common Shares Outstanding	35,000

Requirements

1. Compute New England Fencing's current ratio, debt ratio, and earnings per share. Assume that the company had no preferred stock outstanding. Round all ratios to two decimal places.

2. Compute each of the same three ratios after evaluating the effect of each independent transaction that follows:
   a. Purchased merchandise of $26,000 on account, debiting Inventory.
   b. Issued 4,000 shares of common stock, receiving cash of $44,000. Use total shares outstanding at year-end instead of average shares outstanding.
   c. Borrowed $75,000 on a long-term note payable.
   d. Received cash on account, $18,000.

P12-40B. Calculate various ratios for analysis (*Learning Objectives 2 & 3*) **20–25 min.**

Comparative financial statement data of Barton Furniture Company follow:

Barton Furniture Company Income Statement Years Ended December 31, 2014 and 2013		
	2014	**2013**
Net Sales	$492,000	$449,000
Cost of Goods Sold	241,000	231,000
Gross Profit	251,000	218,000
Operating Expenses	143,000	138,000
Income from Operations	108,000	80,000
Interest Expense	10,000	16,000
Income Before Income Tax	98,000	64,000
Income Tax Expense	33,000	22,000
Net Income	$ 65,000	$ 42,000

			2014	2013	2012
	Barton Furniture Company				
	Balance Sheet				
	December 31, 2014 and 2013				
	(Selected 2012 amounts given for computation of ratios)				
	Current Assets:				
	Cash		$ 92,000	$ 98,000	
	Accounts Receivable, Net		86,000	89,000	$102,000
	Inventory		165,000	154,000	191,000
	Prepaid Expenses		31,000	22,000	
	Total Current Assets		374,000	363,000	
	Property, Plant, and Equipment, Net		192,000	174,000	
	Total Assets		$566,000	$537,000	
	Total Current Liabilities		$210,000	$231,000	
	Long-Term Liabilities		128,000	113,000	
	Total Liabilities		338,000	344,000	
	Common Stockholders' Equity, No Par		228,000	193,000	198,000
	Total Liabilities and Stockholders' Equity		$566,000	$537,000	

Other information follows:

1. Market price of common stock was $48.72 at December 31, 2014, and $33.28 at December 31, 2013.

2. Average common shares outstanding were 11,000 during 2014 and 10,000 during 2013.

Requirements

1. Compute the following ratios for 2014 and 2013. Round to two decimal places. Assume all sales on credit.
   a. Current ratio
   b. Inventory turnover
   c. Accounts receivable turnover
   d. Interest coverage ratio
   e. Return on equity
   f. Earnings per share of common stock
   g. Price-earnings ratio

2. Decide: (a) whether Barton Furniture Company's performance improved or deteriorated during 2014; and (b) whether the investment attractiveness of its common stock appears to have increased or decreased.

3. How will what you learned in this problem help you evaluate an investment?

P12-41B. Calculate various ratios for analysis (*Learning Objectives 2 & 3*) **20–25 min.**

Assume you are purchasing an investment and decide to invest in a company in the home remodeling business. You narrow the choice to Here To Stay, Inc., or Dream Home, Corp. You assemble the following selected data. Assume all sales on credit.

Selected income statement data for the current year:

	Here To Stay, Inc.	Dream Home, Corp.
Net Sales	$395,000	$333,000
Cost of Goods Sold	155,000	125,000
EBIT	83,000	63,000
Interest Expense	13,000	11,000
Net Income	43,000	49,000

Selected balance sheet and market price data at the end of the current year:

	Here To Stay, Inc.	Dream Home, Corp.
Current Assets:		
Cash	$ 12,000	$ 13,000
Short-Term Investments	11,000	12,000
Accounts Receivable, Net	28,000	25,000
Inventory	60,000	52,000
Prepaid Expenses	1,000	1,000
Total Current Assets	112,000	103,000
Total Assets	197,000	189,000
Total Current Liabilities	59,000	65,000
Total Liabilities	75,000	74,000
Common Stock, $1.00 Par, 6,000 Shares		6,000
$2.50 Par, 3,000 Shares	7,500	
Total Stockholders' Equity	122,000	115,000
Market price per share of common stock	$ 45	$ 35

Selected balance sheet data at the beginning of the current year:

	Here To Stay, Inc.	Dream Home, Corp.
Accounts Receivable, Net	$ 29,000	$ 24,000
Inventory	53,000	56,000
Total Assets	162,000	155,000
Common Stock, $1.00 Par, 6,000 Shares		6,000
$2.50 Par, 3,000 Shares	7,500	
Total Stockholders' Equity	79,000	118,000

Your investment strategy is to purchase the stock of the company that has a low price-earnings ratio but appears to be in good shape financially. Assume that you analyzed all other factors and your decision depends on the results of the ratio analysis to be performed.

Requirement

1. Compute the following ratios for both companies for the current year and decide which company's stock better fits your investment strategy.
   a. Quick ratio
   b. Debt ratio
   c. Interest coverage ratio
   d. Accounts receivable turnover
   e. Inventory turnover
   f. Total asset turnover
   g. Return on assets
   h. Return on equity
   i. Earnings per share
   j. Price-earnings ratio

P12-42B. **Financial statement ratio analysis** (*Learning Objective 2*) **20–25 min.**

You have been hired as an investment analyst at Walker Securities, Inc. It is your job to recommend investments for your client. You have the following information for two different companies.

Ratio	Anderson Supply, Co.	Mutual Materials, Inc.
Accounts receivable turnover	9.3	13.4
Inventory turnover	8.7	6.4
Gross profit percentage	44%	21%
Net income as a percent of sales	24%	21%
Interest coverage ratio	7.4	9.3
Return on equity	12.2%	16.7%
Return on assets	11.8%	14.1%

Requirement

1. Write a memo to your client recommending the company you believe to be a more attractive investment. Explain the reasons for your recommendation.

Continuing Exercise

This concludes the accounting for Cole's Yard Care, Inc., that we began in Chapter 1. For this exercise, refer to the comparative balance sheet that was presented in the Continuing Exercise in Chapter 11.

Requirements

1. Prepare a horizontal analysis of the balance sheet for Cole's Yard Care, Inc. Round percentages to one-tenth of a percent.

2. Prepare a vertical analysis of the balance sheet for Cole's Yard Care, Inc. Round percentages to one-tenth of a percent.

Continuing Problem

In Chapter 11, we prepared a cash flow statement for Aqua Magic, Inc. Now, we will analyze Aqua Magic's financial statements using the tools we learned in this chapter. Following are the balance sheets for the months ended July 31 and June 30, 2015, and the income statement for the month ended July 31, 2015, for Aqua Magic, Inc.

		JULY 31	**JUNE 30**
Aqua Magic, Inc. **Comparative Balance Sheets** July 31 and June 30, 2015			
Assets			
Cash		$ 8,126	$ 9,246
Accounts Receivable, Net		91,647	82,403
Inventory		18,241	16,857
Supplies		164	227
Total Current Assets		118,178	108,733
Fixed Assets		357,600	244,800
Less: Accumulated Depreciation		(9,003)	(8,529)
Net Fixed Assets		348,597	236,271
Total Assets		$466,775	$345,004
Liabilities			
Accounts Payable		$ 2,060	$ 1,280
Unearned Revenue		6,800	2,700
Salary Payable		950	875
Interest Payable		621	180
Payroll Taxes Payable		543	0
Dividend Payable		300	800
Current Portion of Long-Term Debt		11,673	9,896
Total Current Liabilities		22,947	15,731
Notes Payable		59,260	28,960
Mortgage Payable		228,685	148,685
Total Liabilities		310,892	193,376
Stockholders' Equity			
Preferred Stock		16,000	16,000
Additional Paid-In Capital, Preferred		12,000	12,000
Common Stock		95,000	95,000
Additional Paid-In Capital, Common		7,000	7,000
Retained Earnings		25,883	21,628
Total Stockholders' Equity		155,883	151,628
Total Liabilities & Stockholders' Equity		$466,775	$345,004

Aqua Magic, Inc. Income Statement Month Ended July 31, 2015	
Net Sales	$45,691
Expenses:	
Cost of Goods Sold	34,276
Depreciation Expense	474
Rent Expense	1,050
Interest Expense	843
Insurance Expense	240
Supplies Expense	122
Salaries Expense	2,746
Payroll Taxes Expense	543
Bank Service Fees	15
Net Income*	$ 5,382

*Income taxes ignored

Requirements

1. Prepare a vertical analysis of the income statement using a multi-step income statement. Round percentages to one-tenth of a percent.

2. Calculate the current ratio for Aqua Magic, Inc., at July 31, 2015.

3. Calculate the quick ratio for Aqua Magic, Inc., at July 31, 2015.

4. Why do you think the current and quick ratios are favorable? Do you believe that this is a temporary situation or a long-term situation?

Continuing Financial Statement Analysis Problem

Let's look at Target one last time. Think about Target and all you've learned. Look again at Target's 2012 annual report. For instructions on how to access the report online, see the Continuing Financial Statement Analysis Problem in Chapter 2. Now let's do some financial analysis and answer the following questions:

1. Compute the ratios in Exhibit 12-10 for Target for 2012. Compute the ratios in Exhibit 12-10 for Walmart for 2012. As with Target, Walmart's financial statements can be found in its annual report. You can access the annual report online in the investor relations area of Walmart's web site at www.walmart.com. For both companies, assume that all sales are credit sales. Compare the ratios of Target and Walmart. Which company do you think is doing a better job in managing the following?
   a. Liquidity
   b. Net income or loss
   c. Financing with debt and equity
   d. Investing in assets
   e. Rewarding its stockholders

2. Compute Target's ROE for the year ending February 2, 2013, including the elements of net income/sales, sales/average total assets, and average total assets/average stockholders' equity. What does this analysis tell you about how Target generates its ROE?

3. What are Target's dividends per share and dividend payout ratio for the past two years? Why do you think Target pays a dividend? How do you think Target determines the amount of dividend they will pay?

4. Given Target's stock price was $60 per share at February 2, 2013, what was Target's PE ratio as of that date? If the average PE for companies is 15, what does this tell you the market is saying about Target's future?

5. Looking back over your answers to questions 1 through 4, how do you think Target is performing? Would you buy the stock of Target? If so, why? If not, why not? Do you have any ideas of how to improve Target's performance and its value?

Apply Your Knowledge

Ethics in Action

Case 1. Robin Peterson, the CEO of Teldar Incorporated, was reviewing the financial statements for the first three months of the year. He saw that sales and net income were lower than expected. Because the reported net income and the related earnings per share were below expectations, the price of the stock declined. Robin held a meeting with top management and expressed his concerns over the declining trend in sales and income. He stated that the reduced profitability meant that he needed to formulate a plan to somehow increase the earnings per share. The vice president of marketing suggested that more advertising might help sales increase. Robin stated that spending more money on advertising would not guarantee an increase in sales. Then he announced that the excess company cash would instead be used to buy back shares of outstanding common stock; this move would help increase the earnings per share because fewer shares would be outstanding. Robin reminded everyone that the yearly financial statements would be analyzed and the current year would be compared to previous years' results. He then stated that the treasury stock would lower the total stockholders' equity, which could then provide a stronger EPS so the current year would not look as bad. Finally, Robin reminded everyone that with fewer shares of stock outstanding, the dividend per share could be increased and that would help make Teldar stock more attractive. The CFO argued that buying back stock merely to increase performance measures such as EPS was manipulative and unethical and financial analysts would easily see what Teldar was trying to do.

Why did the CEO want to repurchase shares of Teldar common stock? Would the repurchase of common stock really have any impact on the financial ratios? Would an investor or financial analyst be able to see that financial performance measures were improved because of the stock repurchase? Are any ethical issues involved? Were the concerns expressed by the CFO valid? Do you have any other thoughts?

Case 2. Crane Corporation was in the process of completing the financial statements for the latest fiscal year. Susan Randal, Crane's CEO, was reviewing the comparative financial statements and expressed some concerns. In comparing the current year's income statement against those of the prior years, she noticed that total sales had decreased slightly. Furthermore, the salaries expense had increased while the advertising and research and development expenses had decreased. Although the total operating expenses were essentially the same, Susan was concerned that the increased salaries expense would be questioned by the investors and financial analysts in light of the decreases in advertising and research and development. She knew that the lower sales would be blamed on reduced advertising and less spending on research and development. As a result, Susan ordered the accountants to issue a condensed income statement that would present all operating expenses as a single amount. Also, during the year Crane Corporation had purchased another company for a price higher than the total fair market value of the purchased business. Crane properly recorded the excess cost as goodwill, but the total amount of goodwill had increased substantially because of this purchase. Susan was concerned that this rather large increase in goodwill would be seen as an unnecessary purchase and investors and analysts would become upset. Thus, Susan ordered that the goodwill be lumped in with the other assets rather than listed separately on the balance sheet where it could easily be seen. The accountants argued that attempting to hide these items from investors and analysts would be unethical. They further argued that GAAP required full disclosure and that if Susan insisted on providing condensed statements, details would need to be provided in the footnotes anyway. Susan reluctantly agreed to the disclosure, knowing that often footnotes are not read.

Why would Susan want all the operating expenses lumped together? Why would Susan want the goodwill included as other assets? Were the ethical concerns raised by the accountants valid? Are any ethical issues involved in providing condensed information with the details included in the footnotes? Do you have any additional thoughts?

Know Your Business

Financial Analysis

Purpose: To help familiarize you with the financial reporting of a real company in order to further your understanding of the chapter material.

This case focuses on the financial statement analysis of Columbia Sportswear. Recall from this chapter that stakeholders use numerous ways to analyze and so better understand the financial position and results of operations of a company. Tools such as vertical and horizontal analyses are available; in addition, financial ratios can be used to gain further insight into areas such as liquidity and profitability. Other measures include earnings per share and ratios that consider the share price of the company. Finally, nonfinancial information provides additional insights into the performance and financial position of the company. We will now apply some of the analytical tools contained in the chapter. Refer to the Columbia Sportswear annual report found in Appendix A.

Requirements

1. Perform a vertical analysis on the income statements (Consolidated Statements of Operations) for all three years. Discuss your results. What benefit do you see in performing this analysis? Perform a horizontal analysis of the balance sheets (Consolidated Balance Sheets) for both years. Discuss your results. What benefit do you see in performing this analysis?

2. Look at the income statements (Consolidated Statements of Operations). Can you find the Basic EPS for each fiscal year presented? Has the Basic Earnings per Share increased or decreased each year? Why do you think the Basic EPS has been changing?

3. Determine the liquidity of Columbia Sportswear by computing the net working capital, current ratio, and quick ratio at December 31, 2012, and December 31, 2011. Has Columbia Sportswear's liquidity improved or deteriorated? Compute the return on sales and the return on equity ratio for 2012 and 2011. Use ending equity balance instead of average for 2011. Has Columbia Sportswear's profitability improved or deteriorated?

4. The market price for a share of Columbia Sportswear's common stock was $53.36 on December 31, 2012. Using this price, determine the price-earnings ratio and the dividend yield at December 31, 2012 (the dividends per share can be found on the Consolidated Statements of Stockholders' Equity). What do your results mean? Assume that the industry average PE ratio was 20 times earnings and the dividend yield was 1.8% for the industry. Evaluate your results against the industry averages.

Industry Analysis

Purpose: To help you understand and compare the performance of two companies in the same industry.

Find the Columbia Sportswear Company Annual Report located in Appendix A and go to the Selected Financial Data starting on page 642. Now access the 2012 Annual Report for Under Armour, Inc. from the Internet. For instructions on how to access the report online, see the Industry Analysis in Chapter 1. The company's Selected Financial Data start on page 26.

The Selected Financial Data is the area of the annual report where companies supply the reader of the financial statements with five years of data to analyze. It is then up to the reader to determine the trend of the company.

Requirement

1. In your opinion and based on what you have learned from this chapter, what is the trend of each of these companies? And based on this data, which company would you invest in?

Small Business Analysis

Purpose: To help you understand the importance of cash flows in the operation of a small business.

You just returned from a meeting with your bank loan officer and you were a little taken aback by his comments. You've been doing business with this bank for a number of years, and the officer always seemed happy with your company's performance. This is why you can't understand the bank's hesitation to continue extending credit to your company. At this meeting, you had supplied him with the current year's financial information and even ran some of the financial ratios about which you know the bank asks. You thought the numbers looked decent for the current year; maybe not the best, but respectable. Admittedly, sales had fallen a little bit since the previous year, but they were still fairly sound. So when the discussion turned to a comparison of the last couple of years' financial information with this year's, you had to question why that was relevant: "Why shouldn't each and every year stand by itself?" you asked the banker. His comments to you were, "A company's performance is best evaluated by examining more than one year's data. This is why most financial statements cover at least two periods. In fact, most financial analysis covers trends of up to five years." He also said that a company's performance is best evaluated by comparing it against its own past performance, the performance of competitors, and the industry averages for the industry the company is in.

Requirement

1. Following are some selected financial data from the past four years. Calculate the trend percentages using 2011 as the base year and the return on sales for these four years and see if you can figure out the concern the banker has for the financial health of your company.

	2014	2013	2012	2011
Total Sales	1,010,000	1,050,000	1,080,000	1,000,000
Total Expenses	896,000	888,000	880,000	800,000
Net Income	114,000	162,000	200,000	200,000

Written Communication

Following are selected financial data for your client for the current year and corresponding data for the client's industry.

	Company	Industry
Return on Sales	12.8%	10.7%
Return on Assets	22.1%	19.3%
Current Ratio	1.5	1.4
Inventory Turnover	8.6	7.3
Accounts Receivable Turnover	9.1	12.2
Debt Ratio	58.7%	53.1%

Requirement

1. Write a memo to your client comparing his or her business to the industry averages and explain to the client the value of common-size financial statements.

Self Check Answers
1. a 2. d 3. d 4. d 5. c 6. b 7. c 8. d 9. b 10. d 11. c 12. b

Columbia Sportswear Company

2012

ANNUAL REPORT
TO SHAREHOLDERS

Columbia | montrail | MOUNTAIN HARD WEAR | SOREL

Dear Fellow Shareholders:

One year ago on these pages, following a record-setting warm winter and with Europe in economic quicksand, I wrote that 2012 would be a difficult year for top-line growth.

That turned out to be an accurate prediction, as a second consecutive mild winter in North America and continued macro-economic struggles across Europe offset 11 percent growth in the Latin America/Asia Pacific (LAAP) region and held our 2012 net sales to $1.67 billion, down 1 percent from 2011's record $1.69 billion. Our Columbia, Mountain Hardwear and Montrail brands each generated 2012 sales equal to 2011; only our Sorel footwear brand was unable to fend off the harsh effects of two mild winters, falling 16% after growing nearly 70 percent in 2011. Disciplined discretionary spending throughout the year enabled us to achieve operating margins of 8.0 percent and diluted earnings per share of $2.93, down 3 percent from $3.03 in 2011.

Despite this pause in our growth, we remain resolved to use our powerful portfolio of outdoor brands to drive top-line growth and improved profitability over the long term. Our primary focus is on building the right product, positioned to appeal to a broad range of consumers.

Over the past four years we've focused on reinforcing the Columbia, Mountain Hardwear and Montrail brands as leading innovators in the outdoor, alpine and running segments, respectively. We've introduced numerous innovations, along with significant updates to styling, fit, construction and marketing. Our products increasingly target young, active core outdoor consumers who shop in leading sporting goods, specialty outdoor, fish/hunt/camp, alpine and running shops, and corresponding online channels. At the same time,

we repositioned and elevated the SOREL brand, capturing fashion-forward female consumers and garnering distribution in premium footwear boutiques around the world, benefiting from the brand's growing appeal among film and entertainment icons.

Our pace of innovation and change has been very rapid during the past four years. We succeeded in innovating our technologies and designs, and creating competitive advantages in the battle to offer products that keep consumers warm, dry, cool and protected in the outdoors – any time of year, anywhere in the world.

We believe there remains significant opportunity for growth. Consumer adoption of our new products and brand messaging is beginning to take hold, despite unseasonable weather that temporarily muted demand for cold weather apparel and footwear, and input cost pressures that worked their way through the supply chain into retail prices, revealing additional areas of inelastic consumer demand.

We remain committed to our strategies and intend to focus our efforts for 2013 and beyond on a few primary initiatives:

1. Consolidate and expand our existing innovation platforms –

The innovation platforms we've established help differentiate our products from competitors' and represent valuable growth opportunities. Our product teams and sourcing partners are working to engineer products that make these innovations accessible to a broader base of consumers, while maintaining disciplined distribution in brand-enhancing retail channels. At the same time, we are continually refining our marketing messages and the channels through which we communicate with consumers in order to create awareness, demand and, ultimately, desire for our brands.

2. Grow our warm-weather business –

We currently generate nearly two-thirds of our annual net sales during the second half of the year, relying heavily on winter weather to drive consumer demand. Consumers know and trust our brands to keep them warm and dry in winter, but less so as brands that can keep them cool, dry and protected during their spring and summer outdoor activities. We're working to change that. We offer a full assortment of lightweight layering styles that address outdoor consumers' needs year-round, and we are working closely with our wholesale customers to flow those styles more consistently throughout the year, especially during the "shoulder seasons" of early fall and early spring. In addition, we have extended the SOREL brand's seasonal selling window with a strong assortment of lightweight, less-insulated styles that address the shoulder seasons and, over time, should help reduce reliance on winter weather. For the spring and summer seasons, our Performance Fishing Gear (PFG) sub-brand is our fastest growing product segment. Consumers in the

U.S. Gulf states, and in Central and South America, have embraced PFG apparel as a leading performance and lifestyle icon. We are very excited about the Spring 2013 global launch of our innovative, sweat-activated, visible cooling technology - Columbia's Omni-Freeze® ZERO and Mountain Hardwear's Cool.Q™ ZERO. This launch is being supported by the largest Spring advertising campaign in our history, featuring integrated in-store, print, digital, grassroots guerilla and broadcast elements. Omni-Freeze® ZERO and Cool.Q™ ZERO give outdoor and athletic consumers a powerful reason to seek out our brands year-round for all of their warm climate and/or high-intensity activities.

3. Capitalize on growth opportunities in the LAAP region –

Sales in the LAAP region grew 11 percent in 2012, led by our Japanese and Korean subsidiaries, as well as the efforts of our independent distributors in Latin America and China. We expect this region to be a continued source of growth over the next several years. To drive growth in China, we are laying the groundwork for a new 60/40 joint venture with our current independent distributor, Swire Resources, Ltd., expected to commence January 1, 2014, subject to customary regulatory approvals in China. Swire's efforts as our exclusive distributor over the past decade have already positioned Columbia as a leading premium outdoor brand in this large, growing market. As China's economy and standard of living have increased, so has interest in outdoor activities of all kinds. This joint venture represents an opportunity to add another profitable growth engine to our global business.

4. Continue to build a brand-enhancing direct-to-consumer business –

Direct-to-consumer (DTC) sales represented approximately 29 percent of our global sales in 2012, up from 25 percent in 2011. This part of our business comprises a growing base of branded stores in the U.S., Korea and Japan; outlet stores, primarily in the U.S., that help protect our brands during periods of inventory liquidation; and localized branded ecommerce sites in 12 countries. In 2013, we plan to add outlet stores in the U.S. and more branded stores in Japan and Korea. Plus, the commencement of our China joint venture in 2014 will bring almost 80 additional company-owned branded

stores into our global DTC platform. Creating pure online and brick-and-mortar brand environments allows us to engage directly with consumers and tell our innovation, performance and style stories, helping to drive demand across all channels and geographies.

Michigan Ave.
Chicago, IL
USA

5. Transform our global business processes to drive and support growth –

For us, the word "innovation" refers not only to our product and marketing, but also to how we conduct our business, which has been evolving rapidly as we have invested in long-term growth platforms that are increasingly multi-channel, multi-brand and multi-national. We continue to invest in a multi-year implementation of a new global ERP platform, while simultaneously transforming many of the global processes that support our business. We are investing significant resources in this effort in order to become more nimble in responding to market opportunities, improve delivery and customer service, and drive profitability through better inventory management and operating efficiencies.

We currently expect 2013 net sales to be comparable to 2012, following two consecutive warm winters in North America and with continued macro-economic weakness in Europe. The leadership team remains committed to diligently managing operating expenses while we evolve our brands, the organization and our operations to position us for renewed growth.

However, we know that we cannot cost-cut our way to prosperity and market leadership. We will continue to pursue growth catalysts by investing in our brands, our products, our people and the initiatives that we believe can grow Columbia Sportswear Company into a much larger and more profitable business over time.

We have many tools at our disposal, starting with our brand portfolio and our innovation platforms, all backed by a very strong balance sheet that enables us to stay on offense through periods of slow growth. As we approach Columbia's 75th anniversary in 2013, we are also mindful of the great strength of our heritage as an authentic, innovative, outdoor company.

Thank you for your continued support.

Sincerely,

Timothy P. Boyle
President and Chief Executive Officer

PART I

Item 1. *BUSINESS*

General

Founded in 1938 in Portland, Oregon, as a small, family-owned, regional hat distributor and incorporated in 1961, Columbia Sportswear Company has grown to become a global leader in the design, sourcing, marketing and distribution of active outdoor apparel, footwear, accessories and equipment. Unless the context indicates otherwise, the terms "we", "us", "our", "the Company" and "Columbia" refer to Columbia Sportswear Company and its consolidated subsidiaries.

We design, source, market and distribute active outdoor apparel, footwear, accessories and equipment' under four primary brands: Columbia®, Mountain Hardwear®, Sorel® and Montrail®. As one of the largest outdoor apparel and footwear companies in the world, our products have earned an international reputation for innovation, quality and performance. Our products feature innovative technologies and designs that protect outdoor enthusiasts from the elements, increase comfort and make outdoor activities more enjoyable. Our brands complement each other to address the diverse outdoor performance needs of a wide variety of outdoor consumer segments.

Our brands are distributed through a mix of wholesale distribution channels, our own direct-to-consumer channels (retail stores and e-commerce), independent distributors and licensees. In 2012, our products were sold in approximately 100 countries. We employ creative marketing strategies designed to increase demand, and to create and reinforce consumer awareness of our brands. Substantially all of our products are manufactured by independent factories located outside the United States.

The popularity of outdoor activities, changing design trends and consumer adoption of innovative performance technologies affect consumer demand for our products. Therefore, we seek to influence, anticipate and respond to trends and shifts in consumer preferences by adjusting the mix of available product offerings, developing new products with innovative performance features and designs, and by creating persuasive and memorable marketing communications to drive consumer awareness and demand. Failure to anticipate or respond to consumer needs and preferences in a timely and adequate manner could have a material adverse effect on our sales and profitability.

Our business is subject to many risks and uncertainties that may have a material adverse effect on our financial condition, results of operations or cash flows. Some of these risks and uncertainties are described below under Item 1A, Risk Factors.

Seasonality and Variability of Business

Our business is affected by the general seasonal trends common to the outdoor industry and is heavily dependent upon weather and discretionary consumer spending patterns. Our products are marketed on a seasonal basis and our sales are weighted substantially toward the fall season, while our operating costs are more equally distributed throughout the year. The expansion of our direct-to-consumer operations has increased the proportion of sales and profits that we generate in the fourth calendar quarter. As a result, our sales and profits tend to be highest in the third and fourth calendar quarters. In 2012, approximately 63 percent of our net sales and all of our profitability were realized in the second half of the year, illustrating our dependence upon sales results in the second half of the year, as well as the less seasonal nature of our operating costs.

Results of operations in any period should not be considered indicative of the results to be expected for any future period, particularly in light of persistent volatility in economic conditions. Sales of our products are subject to substantial cyclical fluctuation, the effects of unseasonable weather conditions, the relative popularity of our competitors' brands and the continued popularity of outdoor activities as part of an active lifestyle in key markets. Volatile economic environments in key markets coupled with inflationary or volatile input costs reduce the predictability of our business.

For further discussion regarding the effects of the macro-economic environment on our business, see Part II, Item 7, Management's Discussion and Analysis of Financial Condition and Results of Operations.

Products

We provide high quality apparel, footwear, accessories and equipment for use in a wide range of outdoor activities by men, women and youth, designed to keep the consumer warm or cool, dry and protected. A large percentage of our products are also worn for casual or leisure purposes. The durability and functionality of our products make them ideal for a wide range of outdoor activities. Our products serve a broad range of consumers including elite skiers and mountain climbers, winter outdoor enthusiasts, hunting and fishing enthusiasts, top endurance trail runners, and outdoor-inspired consumers. We also market licensed collegiate apparel and accessories under our Columbia brand.

We develop and manage our merchandise in two principal categories: (1) apparel, accessories and equipment and (2) footwear. The following table presents the net sales and approximate percentages of net sales attributable to each of our principal product categories for each of the last three years ended December 31 (dollars in millions).

	2012		2011		2010	
	Net Sales	% of Sales	Net Sales	% of Sales	Net Sales	% of Sales
Apparel, accessories and equipment..............	$ 1,347.0	80.7%	$ 1,334.9	78.8%	$ 1,213.3	81.8%
Footwear	322.6	19.3	359.1	21.2	270.2	18.2
Total.................	$ 1,669.6	100.0%	$ 1,694.0	100.0%	$ 1,483.5	100.0%

Apparel, accessories and equipment

We design, develop, market and distribute apparel, accessories and equipment for men, women and youth under our Columbia and Mountain Hardwear brands. Our products incorporate the cumulative design, fabrication, fit and construction technologies that we have pioneered over several decades and that we continue to innovate. Our apparel, accessories and equipment are designed to be used during a wide variety of outdoor activities, such as skiing, snowboarding, hiking, climbing, mountaineering, camping, hunting, fishing, trail running, water sports and adventure travel.

Footwear

We design, develop, market and distribute footwear products for men and women under our Columbia, Sorel and Montrail brands and for youth under our Columbia and Sorel brands. Our footwear products seek to address the needs of outdoor consumers who participate in activities that typically involve challenging or unusual terrain in a variety of weather and trail conditions. Our footwear products include durable, lightweight hiking boots, trail running shoes, rugged cold weather boots for activities on snow and ice, sandals for use in amphibious activities, and casual shoes for everyday use. Our Sorel brand primarily offers premium cold weather footwear for men, women and youth along with a Spring offering for men and women, with an increasing focus on young, fashion-conscious female consumers.

Product Design and Innovation

We are committed to designing innovative and functional products for consumers who participate in a wide range of outdoor activities, enabling them to enjoy those activities longer and in greater comfort by keeping them warm or cool, dry and protected. We also place significant value on product design and fit (the overall appearance and image of our products) that, along with technical performance features, distinguish our products in the marketplace.

Our research and development efforts are led by an internal team of specialists who work closely with independent suppliers to develop innovative technologies and products that provide the unique performance benefits needed by consumers during outdoor activities. We have established working relationships with specialists in the fields of chemistry, biochemistry, engineering, industrial design, materials research, graphic design, electronics and related fields. We utilize these relationships, along with consumer feedback, to develop and test innovative performance products, processes, packaging and displays. We believe that these efforts, coupled with our technical innovation efforts, represent key factors in the past and future success of our products.

Intellectual Property

We own many trademarks, including Columbia Sportswear Company®, Columbia®, Sorel®, Mountain Hard Wear®, Montrail®, OutDry®, Pacific Trail®, the Columbia diamond shaped logo, the Mountain Hardwear nut logo and the Sorel polar bear logo, as well as many other trademarks relating to our brands, products, styles and technologies. We believe that our trademarks are an important factor in creating a market for our products, in identifying our Company, and in differentiating our products from competitors' products. We have design, process and utility patents as well as pending patent applications in the United States and other nations. We file applications for United States and foreign patents for inventions, designs and improvements that we believe have commercial value; however, these patents may or may not ultimately be issued or used in our business. We believe our success primarily depends on our ability to continue offering innovative solutions to consumer needs through design, research, development and production advancements rather than our ability to secure patents. The technologies, processes and designs described in our patents are incorporated into many of our most important products and expire at various times. We vigorously protect these proprietary rights against counterfeit reproductions and other infringing activities. Additionally, we license our Columbia trademarks across a range of apparel, footwear, accessories and equipment.

Sales and Distribution

We sell our products through a mix of wholesale distribution channels, our own direct-to-consumer channels, independent distributors and licensees. The majority of our sales are generated through wholesale channels which include small, independently operated specialty outdoor and sporting goods stores, regional, national and international sporting goods chains, and large regional, national and international department store chains. We sell our products to independent distributors in various countries where we generally do not have direct sales operations.

We sell our products directly to consumers through our own network of branded and outlet retail stores and online in each of our geographic segments. Our direct-to-consumer operations are designed to elevate consumer perception of our brands, manage inventory, increase consumer and retailer awareness of and demand for our products, model compelling retail environments for our products and build stronger emotional brand connections with consumers over time. Our branded retail stores and e-commerce sites allow us to showcase a broad selection of products and to support the brand's positioning with fixtures and imagery that may then be replicated and offered for use by our wholesale customers. These stores and sites provide high visibility for our brands and products and help us to monitor the needs and preferences of consumers. In addition, we operate outlet stores, which serve an important role in our overall inventory management by allowing us to sell a significant portion of excess, discontinued and out-of-season products while maintaining the integrity of our brands.

We operate in four geographic segments: (1) the United States, (2) Latin America and Asia Pacific ("LAAP"), (3) Europe, Middle East and Africa ("EMEA"), and (4) Canada, which are reflective of our internal organization, management, and oversight structure. Each geographic segment operates predominantly in one industry: the design, development, marketing and distribution of active outdoor apparel, footwear, accessories and equipment. The following table presents net sales to unrelated entities and approximate percentages of net sales by geographic segment for each of the last three years (dollars in millions):

	2012		2011		2010	
	Net Sales	% of Sales	Net Sales	% of Sales	Net Sales	% of Sales
United States	$ 946.7	56.7%	$ 948.0	56.0%	$ 881.0	59.4%
LAAP	377.6	22.6	341.0	20.1	263.4	17.7
EMEA	230.6	13.8	275.4	16.3	222.4	15.0
Canada	114.7	6.9	129.6	7.6	116.7	7.9
Total	$ 1,669.6	100.0%	$ 1,694.0	100.0%	$ 1,483.5	100.0%

United States

The United States accounted for 56.7% of our net sales for 2012. We sell our products in the United States to approximately 3,400 wholesale customers and through our own direct-to-consumer channels. As of December 31, 2012, we operated 55 outlet retail stores and 8 branded retail stores in various locations in the United States. We also sell Columbia, Mountain Hardwear, Sorel and Montrail products through e-commerce websites. In addition, we earn licensing income in the United States based on our licensees' sale of licensed products.

We distribute the majority of our products sold in the United States from distribution centers that we own and operate in Portland, Oregon and Robards, Kentucky. In some instances, we arrange to have products shipped from the independent factories that manufacture our products through third party logistics vendors and/or directly to wholesale customer-designated facilities in the United States.

LAAP

The LAAP region accounted for 22.6% of our net sales for 2012. We sell our products in the LAAP region to approximately 300 wholesale customers in Japan and Korea and to approximately 14 independent distributors that sell to approximately 700 wholesale customers in locations throughout the LAAP region, including Australia, New Zealand, Latin America and Asia. In addition, as of December 31, 2012, there were 124 and 258 dealer-operated, branded, outlet and shop-in-shop locations in Japan and Korea, respectively. We also sell Columbia, Mountain Hardwear, Sorel and Montrail products through e-commerce websites in Japan and Korea. In addition, we earn licensing income in our LAAP region based on our distributors' production and sale of licensed products.

We distribute our products to wholesale customers, our own retail stores and licensed stores in Japan through an independent logistics company that owns and operates a warehouse located near Tokyo, Japan. We distribute our products to wholesale customers, our own retail stores and licensed stores in Korea from leased warehouse facilities near Seoul, Korea. The majority of sales to our LAAP distributors are shipped directly from the independent factories that manufacture our products.

In August 2012 we entered into an agreement with Swire Resources Limited ("Swire"), our current independent distributor for the China market, to establish a joint venture for purposes of continuing the development of our business in China. The joint venture, in which we will hold a 60% interest, is expected to begin operations in January 2014 upon satisfaction of specified conditions, including receipt of certain governmental approvals from China.

EMEA

Sales in our EMEA region accounted for 13.8% of our net sales for 2012. We sell our products in the EMEA region to approximately 5,700 wholesale customers and to approximately 12 independent distributors that sell to approximately 700 wholesale customers in locations throughout the EMEA region, including Russia, portions of Europe, the Middle East and Africa. In addition, as of December 31, 2012, we operated 7 outlet retail stores and 3 branded retail stores in various locations in Western Europe. We also sell Columbia and Sorel products through e-commerce websites in Austria, Belgium, Finland, France, Germany, Ireland, Italy, Netherlands, Spain and the United Kingdom.

We distribute the majority of our products sold to EMEA wholesale customers and our own retail stores from a distribution center that we own and operate in Cambrai, France. The majority of sales to our EMEA distributors are shipped directly from the independent factories that manufacture our products.

Canada

Sales in Canada accounted for 6.9% of our net sales for 2012. We sell our products in Canada to approximately 1,000 wholesale customers. In addition, as of December 31, 2012, we operated one outlet retail store in Canada. We also sell Columbia and Sorel products through e-commerce websites in Canada.

We distribute the majority of our products sold in Canada through two distribution centers. One is leased in Strathroy, Ontario, and the other is owned in London, Ontario. We plan to consolidate our Canadian distribution functions at our London facility in 2013. In some instances, we arrange to have products shipped directly from the independent factories that manufacture our products to customer-designated facilities in Canada.

Marketing

We believe our brand names and trademarks provide a competitive advantage and help to differentiate our products in the marketplace. Marketing supports our position in the marketplace, helps drive alignment through established seasonal initiatives, builds brand equity, raises global brand relevance and awareness, infuses our brands with excitement and stimulates consumer demand for our products worldwide. During 2012, the cost of our marketing programs represented approximately 4.6% of net sales.

Our integrated marketing efforts are designed to deliver consistent messages about the performance benefits, innovative technologies and styling of our products. We utilize a variety of means to deliver our messages, including online advertising and social media sites; television and print publications; experiential events; branded retail stores in selected high-profile locations; enhanced product displays in partnership with various wholesale customers; and consumer and trade public relations efforts.

We also reinforce our marketing and product innovation messages through selected sponsorships of key outdoor influencers, organizations, events and teams that serve as inspirational models of excellence to customers.

We work closely with our key wholesale customers to reinforce our brand message through cooperative online, television, radio and print advertising campaigns, as well as in stores using branded visual merchandising display tools. We employ a staff of in-store marketing and merchandising coordinators, who visit our customers' retail locations in major cities around the world to ensure that our products are favorably presented.

Our global internet marketing sites are used by consumers to research our products' features and benefits, to interact with content created to inform and entertain about each brand and its technologies, to be directed to nearby retailers where they can purchase our products, and to directly purchase products for delivery in most of our major direct-distribution markets.

Working Capital Utilization

We design, develop, market and distribute our products, but do not own or operate manufacturing facilities. As a result, most of our capital is invested in short-term working capital assets, including cash and cash equivalents, short-term investments, accounts receivable from customers, and finished goods inventory. At December 31, 2012, working capital assets accounted for approximately 77% of total assets. As a result, the degree to which we efficiently utilize our working capital assets can have a significant impact on our profitability, cash flows and return on invested capital. The overall goals of our working capital management efforts are to maintain the minimum level of inventory necessary to deliver goods on time to our customers to satisfy end consumer demand, and to minimize the cycle time from the purchase of inventory from our suppliers to the collection of accounts receivable balances from our customers.

Demand Planning and Inventory Management

As a branded consumer products company, inventory represents one of the largest and riskiest capital commitments in our business model. We design and develop our seasonal product lines 12 to 18 months in advance of their availability to consumers in retail stores. As a result, our ability to forecast and produce an assortment of product styles that match ultimate seasonal wholesale customer and end-consumer demand and to deliver products to our customers in a timely and cost-effective manner can significantly affect our sales, gross margins and profitability. For this reason, we maintain and continue to make substantial investments in information systems, processes and personnel that support our ongoing demand planning efforts. The goals of our demand planning efforts are to develop a collaborative forecast that drives the timely purchase of an adequate amount of inventory to satisfy demand, to minimize transportation and expediting costs necessary to deliver products to customers by their requested delivery dates, and to minimize excess inventory to avoid liquidating excess, end-of-season goods at discounted prices. Failure to achieve our demand planning goals could reduce our revenues and/or increase our costs, which would negatively affect our gross margins, profitability and brand strength.

In order to manage inventory risk, we use incentive discounts to encourage our wholesale customers and independent distributors to place orders at least six months in advance of scheduled delivery. We generally solicit orders from wholesale customers and independent distributors for the fall and spring seasons based on seasonal ordering deadlines that we establish to aid our efforts to plan manufacturing volumes to meet demand for each of our selling seasons.

We use those advance orders, together with forecasted demand from our direct-to-consumer operations, market trends, historical data, customer and sales feedback and other important factors to estimate the volumes of each product to purchase from our suppliers around the world. From the time of initial order through production, receipt and delivery, we attempt to manage our inventory to reduce risk. We typically ship the majority of our advance fall season orders to wholesale customers and independent distributors beginning in June and continuing through November. Similarly, the majority of our advance spring season orders ship to wholesale customers and independent distributors beginning in December and continuing through May. Generally, orders are subject to cancellation prior to the date of shipment.

Our inventory management efforts cannot entirely eliminate inventory risk due to the inherently unpredictable nature of unseasonable weather, consumer demand, the ability of customers to cancel their advance orders prior to shipment, and other variables that affect our customers' ability to take delivery of their advance orders when originally scheduled. To minimize our purchasing costs, the time necessary to fill customer orders and the risk of non-delivery, we place a significant amount of orders for our products with independent factories prior to receiving our customers' advance orders and we maintain an inventory of select products that we anticipate will be in greatest demand. In addition, we build calculated amounts of inventory to support estimated at-once orders from customers and auto-replenishment orders on certain long-lived styles.

Credit and Collection

We extend credit to our customers based on an assessment of each customer's financial condition, generally without requiring collateral. To assist us in scheduling production with our suppliers and delivering seasonal products to our customers on time, we offer customers discounts for placing advance orders and extended payment terms for taking delivery before peak seasonal shipping periods. These extended payment terms increase our exposure to the risk of uncollectable receivables. In order to manage the inherent risks of customer receivables, we maintain and continue to invest in information systems, processes and personnel skilled in credit and collections. In some markets and with some customers we use credit insurance or standby letters of credit to minimize our risk of credit loss.

Sourcing and Manufacturing

We do not own or operate manufacturing facilities and virtually all of our products are manufactured to our specifications by independent factories located outside the United States. We generally do not maintain long-term manufacturing commitments. We believe that the use of independent factories enables us to substantially limit our capital expenditures and avoid the costs and risks associated with owning and operating large production facilities and managing large labor forces. We also believe that the use of independent factories greatly increases our production capacity, maximizes our flexibility and improves our product pricing. We manage our supply chain from a global and regional perspective and adjust as needed to changes in the global production environment, including political risks, factory capacity, import limitations and costs, raw material costs, availability and cost of labor and transportation costs. However, without long-term or reserved commitments, there is no assurance that we will be able to secure adequate or timely production capacity or favorable pricing terms.

Our apparel, accessories and equipment are manufactured in approximately 20 countries, with Vietnam and China accounting for approximately 67% of our 2012 apparel, accessories and equipment production. Our footwear is manufactured in three countries, with China and Vietnam accounting for approximately 93% of our 2012 footwear production.

Our five largest apparel, accessories and equipment factory groups accounted for approximately 25% of 2012 global apparel, accessories and equipment production, with the largest factory group accounting for 9% of 2012 global apparel, accessories and equipment production. Our five largest footwear factory groups accounted for approximately 79% of 2012 global footwear production, with the largest factory group accounting for 34% of 2012 global footwear production. In addition, a single vendor supplies the majority of the zippers used in our products. Most of our largest suppliers have multiple factory locations, thus reducing the risk that unfavorable conditions at a single factory or location will have a material adverse effect on our business.

We maintain 12 manufacturing liaison offices in a total of seven Asian countries. We also maintain a manufacturing liaison office in Richmond, California. Personnel in these manufacturing liaison offices are direct employees of Columbia, and are responsible for overseeing production at our independent factories. We believe that having employees physically located in these regions enhances our ability to monitor factories for compliance with our policies, procedures and standards related to quality, delivery, pricing and labor practices. Our quality assurance process is designed to ensure that our products meet our quality standards. We believe that our quality assurance process is an important and effective means of maintaining the quality and reputation of our products. In addition, independent contractors that manufacture products for us are subject to our Standards of Manufacturing Practices ("SMP"). Columbia sources products around the world and values legal, ethical and fair treatment of people involved in manufacturing our products. Each factory producing products for us is monitored regularly against these standards. Additional information about SMP and corporate responsibility programs may be found at www.columbia.com. The content on our website is not incorporated by reference in this Form 10-K unless expressly noted.

Competition

The markets for apparel, footwear, accessories and equipment are highly competitive. In each of our geographic markets, we face significant competition from numerous and varying competitors, some of which are larger than us and have more marketing resources and operational capabilities with which to compete, and others that are smaller with fewer marketing resources, but deeply entrenched in local markets. Some markets, such as our Asian markets, have grown significantly over the last five years and have attracted a large number of competitive local and global brands. In other markets, such as Europe, we face competition from smaller brands that hold significant market share in one or several European markets, but are not viable competitors in other key markets. Some of our large wholesale customers also market competitive apparel, footwear, accessories and equipment under their own private labels. In addition, our direct-to-consumer channels expose us to branded competitors who operate retail stores in outlet malls and key metropolitan markets, as well as competitors who sell product online. Our licensees also operate in very competitive markets, such as those for apparel, footwear, sunglasses and watches. We believe that the primary competitive factors in the end-use market for active outdoor apparel, footwear, accessories and equipment are brand strength, product innovation, product design, functionality, durability and price.

In addition to competing for end-consumer and wholesale market share, we also compete for manufacturing capacity of independent factory groups, primarily in Asia; for retail store locations in key markets; and for experienced management, staff and suppliers to lead, operate and support our global business processes. Each of these areas of competition requires distinct operational and relational capabilities and expertise in order to create and maintain long-term competitive advantages.

Government Regulation

Many of our international shipments are subject to existing or potential governmental tariff and non-tariff barriers to trade, such as import duties and potential safeguard measures that may limit the quantity of various types of goods that may be imported into the United States and other countries. These trade barriers often represent a material portion of the cost to manufacture and import our products. Our products are also subject to domestic and foreign product safety and environmental standards, laws and other regulations, which are increasingly restrictive and complex. As we strive to achieve technical innovations, we face a greater risk of compliance issues with regulations applicable to products with complex technical features, such as electrical heating components. Although we diligently monitor these standards and restrictions, a state, federal or foreign government may impose new or adjusted quotas, duties, safety requirements, material restrictions, or other restrictions or regulations, any of which could have a material adverse effect on our financial condition, results of operations or cash flows.

Employees

At December 31, 2012, we had 4,166 full-time equivalent employees.

Available Information

We file with the Securities and Exchange Commission ("SEC") our annual report on Form 10-K, quarterly reports on Form 10-Q, current reports on Form 8-K and all amendments to those reports, proxy statements and registration statements. You may read and copy any material we file with the SEC at the SEC's Public Reference Room at 100 F Street, NE, Washington, D.C. 20549. You may also obtain information on the operation of the Public Reference Room by calling the SEC at 1-800-SEC-0330. In addition, the SEC maintains an internet site at http://www.sec.gov that contains reports, proxy and information statements, and other information regarding issuers, including us, that file electronically. We make available free of charge on or through our website at www.columbia.com our annual reports on Form 10-K, quarterly reports on Form 10-Q, current reports on Form 8-K and amendments to these reports filed or furnished pursuant to Section 13(a) or 15(d) of the Exchange Act as soon as reasonably practicable after we file these materials with the SEC.

Item 1A. *RISK FACTORS*

In addition to the other information contained in this Form 10-K, the following risk factors should be considered carefully in evaluating our business. Our business, financial condition, results of operations or cash flows may be materially adversely affected by these and other risks. Please note that additional risks not presently known to us or that we currently deem immaterial may also impair our business and operations.

Our Success Depends on Our Business Strategies

Our business strategies are designed to achieve sustainable, profitable growth by creating innovative products, focusing on product design, utilizing innovations to differentiate our brand from competitors, ensuring that our products are sold through brand enhancing distribution partners around the world, increasing the impact of consumer communications to drive demand for our brands and sell-through of our products, making sure our products are merchandised and displayed appropriately in retail environments and continuing to build a brand enhancing direct-to-consumer business. We intend to pursue these strategies across our portfolio of brands, product categories and geographic markets. We face many challenges in implementing our business strategies. For example, our focus on innovation depends on our ongoing ability to identify, develop or secure rights to product improvements or developments through internal research, joint developments, acquisitions or licenses. Once obtained, these innovations and developments may not be profitable or have the desired effect of increasing demand for our products or enhancing our brands' image. The failure to implement our business strategies successfully could have a material adverse effect on our financial condition, results of operations or cash flows.

To implement our business strategies, we must continue to modify and fund various aspects of our business, to maintain and enhance our information systems and supply chain operations to respond to changes in demand, and to attract, retain and manage qualified personnel. Changes in our business, including efforts to contain costs, may place an increasing strain on management, financial, product design, marketing, distribution, supply chain and other resources, and we may have operating difficulties as a result. For example, in support of our strategic initiatives, we are making significant investments in our business processes and information technology infrastructure that require significant management attention and corporate resources. In addition, we may need to adapt our information technology systems and business processes to integrate business acquisitions. These business initiatives involve many risks and uncertainties that, if not managed effectively, may have a material adverse effect on our financial condition, results of operations or cash flows.

Our business strategies and related increased expenditures could also cause our operating margin to decline if we are unable to offset our increased spending with increased sales or gross margins, or comparable reductions in other operating costs. If our sales or gross margins decline or fail to grow as planned and we fail to sufficiently leverage our operating expenses, our profitability will decline. This could result in a decision to delay, reduce, modify or terminate our strategic business initiatives, which could limit our ability to invest in and grow our business and could have a material adverse effect on our financial condition, results of operations or cash flows.

Initiatives to Upgrade Our Business Processes and Information Technology Infrastructure Involve Many Risks Which Could Result In, Among Other Things, Business Interruptions and Higher Costs

We regularly implement business process improvement initiatives to optimize our performance. Our current business process initiatives include plans to improve business results through standardization of business processes and technology that support our supply chain and go-to-market strategies through implementation of an integrated ERP software solution over the next several years. We may experience difficulties as we transition to these new or upgraded systems and processes, including loss of data, decreases in productivity as our personnel become familiar with new systems and lost revenues. In addition, transitioning to these new or upgraded systems requires significant capital investments and personnel resources. Difficulties in implementing new or upgraded information systems or significant system failures could disrupt our operations and have a material adverse effect on our capital resources, financial condition, results of operations or cash flows.

We expect implementation of this new information technology infrastructure to have a pervasive impact on our business processes and information systems across a significant portion of our operations. As a result, we will experience significant changes in our operational processes and internal controls as our implementation progresses. If we are unable to successfully implement this system, including harmonizing our systems, data and processes, our ability to conduct routine business functions could be negatively impacted and significant disruptions to our business could occur. In addition, we could incur material unanticipated expenses, including additional costs of implementation or costs of conducting business. These risks could result in significant business disruptions and have a material adverse effect on our capital resources, financial condition, results of operations or cash flows.

We Rely on Our Highly Customized Information Management Systems

Our business is increasingly reliant on information technology. Information systems are used across our supply chain and retail operations, from design to distribution and sales, and are used as a method of communication among employees, with our subsidiaries and liaison offices overseas and with our customers and retail stores. We also rely on our information systems to allocate resources, manage product data, develop demand and supply plans, forecast and report operating results and meet regulatory requirements. System failures, breaches of confidential information or service interruptions may occur as the result of a number of factors, including our failure to properly maintain systems redundancy or to protect, repair, maintain or upgrade our systems, computer viruses, programming errors, hacking or other unlawful activities by third parties, and disasters. Any breach or interruption of critical business information systems could have a material adverse effect on our financial condition, results of operations or cash flows.

Our legacy ERP system, on which we currently manage a substantial majority of our business, is highly customized. As a result, the availability of internal and external resources with the expertise to maintain this ERP system is limited. Our legacy ERP system may inhibit our ability to operate efficiently, which could have an adverse effect on our financial condition, results of operations or cash flows. For example, our legacy ERP system may not be compatible with other systems that support desired functionality for our operations. As we transition from our legacy ERP system to a new ERP system and supporting systems that interface with our new ERP system, certain functionality and information from our legacy ERP system may not be fully compatible with the new ERP system. As a result, temporary processes may be required, including manual operations, which could significantly increase the risk of human errors in information used by the business and/or result in business disruptions, which could have a material adverse effect on our capital resources, financial condition, results of operations or cash flows.

System Security Risks, Data Protection Breaches and Cyber Attacks Could Disrupt Our Operations

We manage and store various proprietary information and sensitive or confidential data relating to our business, including sensitive and personally identifiable information. Breaches of our security measures or the accidental loss, inadvertent disclosure or unapproved dissemination of proprietary information or sensitive or confidential data about us, or our customers, including the potential loss or disclosure of such information or data as a result of fraud, trickery or other forms of deception, could expose us, our customers or the individuals affected to a risk of loss or misuse of this information, result in litigation and potential liability for us, damage our brand and reputation or otherwise harm our business. In addition, the cost and operational consequences of implementing further data protection measures could be significant.

Experienced computer programmers and hackers may be able to penetrate our network security and misappropriate or compromise our confidential information or that of third parties, create system disruptions or cause shutdowns. Computer programmers and hackers also may be able to develop and deploy viruses, worms and other malicious software programs that attack or otherwise exploit any security vulnerabilities of our systems. In addition, sophisticated hardware and operating system software and applications that we procure from third parties may contain defects in design or manufacture, including "bugs" and other problems that could unexpectedly interfere with the operation of the system. The costs to us to eliminate or alleviate cyber or other security problems, bugs, viruses, worms, malicious software programs and security vulnerabilities could be significant, and our efforts to address these problems may not be successful and could result in interruptions, delays, cessation of service and loss of existing or potential customers that may impede our sales, manufacturing, distribution or other critical functions.

We Depend on Independent Factories

Our products are manufactured by independent factories worldwide. Although we enter into purchase order commitments with these independent factories each season, we generally do not maintain long-term manufacturing commitments with them. Without long-term or reserve commitments, there is no assurance that we will be able to secure adequate or timely production capacity or favorable pricing if growth or product demand differs from our forecasts. Independent factories may fail to perform as expected or our competitors may obtain production capacities that effectively limit or eliminate the availability of these resources to us. If an independent manufacturer fails to ship orders in a timely manner or to meet our standards or if we are unable to obtain necessary capacities, we may miss delivery deadlines or incur additional costs, which may cause our wholesale customers to cancel their orders, refuse to accept deliveries, or demand a reduction in purchase prices, any of which could have a material adverse effect on our financial condition, results of operations or cash flows.

Reliance on independent factories also creates quality control risks. Independent factories may need to use sub-contracted manufacturers to fulfill demand and these manufacturers may have less experience producing our products or possess lower overall capabilities, which could result in compromised quality of our products. A failure in our quality control program may result in diminished product quality, which in turn could result in increased order cancellations and returns, decreased consumer demand for our products, or product recalls (or other regulatory actions), any of which could have a material adverse effect on our financial condition, results of operations or cash flows.

We also have license agreements that permit unaffiliated parties to manufacture or contract to manufacture products using our trademarks. We impose Standards of Manufacturing Practices on our independent factories and licensees for the benefit of workers and require compliance with our restricted substances list and product safety and other applicable environmental, health and safety laws. We also require our independent factories and licensees to impose these practices, standards and laws on their contractors. If an independent manufacturer or licensee violates labor or other laws, or engages in practices that are not generally accepted as ethical in our key markets, we may experience production disruptions or significant negative publicity that could result in long-term damage to our brands, and in some circumstances parties may attempt to assert that we are liable for the independent manufacturer's or licensee's practices, which could have a material adverse effect on our financial condition, results of operations or cash flows.

We May be Adversely Affected by Volatility in Global Production and Transportation Costs and Capacity

Our product costs are subject to substantial fluctuation based on:

- Availability and quality of raw materials;
- The prices of oil, cotton and other raw materials whose prices are determined by global commodity markets and can be very volatile;
- Changes in labor markets and wage rates paid by our independent factory partners, which are often mandated by governments in the countries where our products are manufactured, particularly in China and Vietnam;
- Interest rates and currency exchange rates;
- Availability of skilled labor and production capacity at independent factories; and
- General economic conditions.

Prolonged periods of inflationary pressure on some or all input costs will result in increased costs to produce our products that may result in reduced gross profit or necessitate price increases for our products that could adversely affect consumer demand for our products.

In addition, since the majority of our products are manufactured outside of our principal sales markets, our products must be transported by third parties over large geographical distances. Shortages in ocean freight capacity, airfreight capacity and volatile fuel costs can result in rapidly changing transportation costs. For example, during 2010, shortages of sourcing and transportation capacity, combined with later-than-optimal production of advance orders, caused us to rely more heavily on airfreight to achieve timely delivery to our customers, resulting in significantly higher freight costs. Because we price our products in advance and changes in transportation and other costs may be difficult to predict, we may not be able to pass all or any portion of these higher costs on to our customers or adjust our pricing structure in a timely manner in order to remain competitive, either of which could have a material adverse effect on our financial condition, results of operations or cash flows.

We May be Adversely Affected by Volatile Economic Conditions

We are a consumer products company and are highly dependent on consumer discretionary spending patterns and the purchasing patterns of our wholesale customers as they attempt to match their seasonal purchase volumes to volatile consumer demand. In addition, as we have expanded our direct-to-consumer operations, we have increased our exposure to the risks associated with volatile and unpredictable consumer discretionary spending patterns. Consumer discretionary spending behavior is inherently unpredictable and consumer demand for our products may not reach our sales targets, or may decline, especially during periods of heightened economic uncertainty in our key markets, particularly markets in North America and the EMEA region. Our sensitivity to economic cycles and any related fluctuation in consumer demand may have a material adverse effect on our financial condition, results of operations or cash flows.

Our Results of Operations Could be Materially Harmed If We Are Unable to Accurately Match Supply Forecast with Consumer Demand for Our Products

Many factors may significantly affect demand for our products, including, among other things, economic conditions, fashion trends, the financial condition of our distributors and wholesale customers, consumer and customer preferences and weather, making it difficult to accurately forecast demand for our products and our future results of operations. To minimize our purchasing costs, the time necessary to fill customer orders and the risk of non-delivery, we place a significant amount of orders for our products with independent factories prior to receiving orders from our customers, and we maintain an inventory of various products that we anticipate will be in greatest demand. In addition, customers are generally allowed to cancel orders prior to shipment.

Factors that could affect our ability to accurately forecast demand for our products include:

- Our reliance, for certain demand and supply planning functions, on manual processes and judgment that are subject to human error;

- Consumer acceptance of our products or changes in consumer demand for products of our competitors;

- Unseasonable weather conditions;

- Unanticipated changes in general market conditions or other factors, which may result in lower advance orders from wholesale customers and independent distributors, cancellations of advance orders or a reduction or increase in the rate of reorders placed by retailers; and

- Weak economic conditions or consumer confidence, which could reduce demand for discretionary items such as our products.

In some cases, we may produce quantities of product that exceed actual demand, which could result in higher inventory levels that we need to liquidate at discount prices. During periods of weak economic conditions we may experience a significant increase in the volume of order cancellations by our customers, including cancellations resulting from the bankruptcy, liquidation or contraction of certain customers' operations. We may not be able to sell all of the products we have ordered from independent factories or that we have in our inventory. Inventory levels in excess of customer demand may result in inventory write-downs and the sale of excess inventory at discounted prices through our owned outlet stores or third-party liquidation channels, which could have a material adverse effect on our brand image, financial condition, results of operations or cash flows.

Conversely, if we underestimate demand for our products or if our independent factories are unable to supply products when we need them, we may experience inventory shortages. Inventory shortages may prevent us from fulfilling customer orders, delay shipments to customers, negatively affect customer relationships, result in increased costs to expedite production and delivery, and diminish our ability to build brand loyalty. Shipments delayed due to limited factory capacity or other factors could result in order cancellations by our customers, which could have a material adverse effect on our financial condition, results of operations or cash flows.

We May be Adversely Affected by Weather Conditions, Including Global Climate Change Trends

Our business is adversely affected by unseasonable weather conditions. A significant portion of the sales of our products is dependent in part on the weather and likely to decline in years in which weather conditions do not stimulate demand for our products. Periods of unseasonably warm weather in the fall or winter or unseasonably cold or wet weather in the spring and summer may have a material adverse effect on our financial condition, results of operations or cash flows. Unintended inventory accumulation by our wholesale customers resulting from unseasonable weather in one season generally negatively affects orders in future seasons, which may have a material adverse effect on our financial condition, results of operations or cash flows.

A significant portion of our business is highly dependent on cold-weather seasons and patterns to generate consumer demand for our cold-weather apparel and footwear. Consumer demand for our cold-weather apparel and footwear may be negatively affected to the extent global weather patterns trend warmer, reducing typical patterns of cold-weather events, or increasing weather volatility, which could have a material adverse effect on our financial condition, results of operations or cash flow.

We May Not Succeed in Realizing the Anticipated Benefits of Our New Joint Venture in China

In August 2012 we entered into an agreement with Swire Resources Limited ("Swire") to establish a joint venture for purposes of continuing the development of our business in China. The joint venture, in which we will hold a 60% interest, will be established upon satisfaction of specified conditions, including receipt of certain governmental approvals from China. These approvals are anticipated to be received prior to January 1, 2014, the anticipated effective date of the joint venture; however, these government approvals may not be obtained as anticipated or at all, and if they are not, we may be forced to abandon the joint venture. Even if we are able to establish it, achieving the anticipated benefits of the joint venture is subject to a number of risks and uncertainties, including the following:

- Our ability to operate the joint venture will be dependent upon, among other things, our ability to attract and retain personnel with the skills, knowledge and experience necessary to carry out the operations of the joint venture. We anticipate that approximately 650 to 700 employees currently working with or for Swire will become employees of, or provide services to, the joint venture. Our ability to effectively operate the joint venture will depend upon our ability to manage the employees of the joint venture, and to attract new employees as necessary to supplement and replace the skills, knowledge and expertise of the existing management team and other key personnel. We face intense competition for these individuals worldwide, including in China. We may not be able to attract qualified new employees or retain existing employees to operate the joint venture. Additionally, turnover in key management positions in China could impair our ability to execute our growth strategy, which may negatively affect the value of our investment in the joint venture and the growth of our sales in China.

- We will be relying on the operational skill of our joint venture partner. Additionally, because our joint venture partner has voting rights with respect to major business decisions of the joint venture, we may experience difficulty reaching agreement as to implementation of certain changes to the joint venture's business. For these reasons, or as a result of other factors, we may not realize the anticipated benefits of the joint venture, and our participation in the joint venture could adversely affect the results of our operations on a consolidated basis.

- Continued sales growth in China is an important part of our expectations for our joint venture business. Although China has experienced significant economic growth in recent years, that growth is slowing. Slowing economic growth in China could result in reduced consumer discretionary spending, which in turn could result in less demand for our products, and thus negatively affect the value of our investment in the joint venture and the growth of our sales in China.

- Although we believe we have achieved a leading market position in China, many of our competitors who are significantly larger than we are and have substantially greater financial, distribution, marketing and other resources, more stable manufacturing resources and greater brand strength are also concentrating on growing their businesses in China. Increased investment by our competitors in this market could decrease our market share and competitive position in China.

Our International Operations Involve Many Risks

We are subject to risks generally associated with doing business internationally. These risks include the effects of foreign laws and regulations, changes in consumer preferences, foreign currency fluctuations, managing a diverse and widespread workforce, political unrest, terrorist acts, military operations, disruptions or delays in shipments, disease outbreaks, natural disasters and changes in economic conditions in countries in which we manufacture or sell products. These factors, among others, may affect our ability to sell products in international markets, our ability to manufacture products or procure materials, and our cost of doing business. For example, unseasonably warm winter weather and a challenging macroeconomic environment in our EMEA region have hampered our ongoing efforts to elevate the Columbia brand in key European markets, where we have significant infrastructure investments. If any of these or other factors make the conduct of business in a particular country undesirable or impractical, our business may be materially and adversely affected. As we expand our operations in geographic scope and product categories, we anticipate intellectual property disputes will increase, making it more expensive and challenging to establish and protect our intellectual property rights and to defend against claims of infringement by others.

In addition, many of our imported products are subject to duties, tariffs or other import limitations that affect the cost and quantity of various types of goods imported into the United States and other markets. Any country in which our products are produced or sold may eliminate, adjust or impose new import limitations, duties, anti-dumping penalties or other charges or restrictions, any of which could have a material adverse effect on our financial condition, results of operations or cash flows.

We May Have Additional Tax Liabilities

As a global company, we determine our income tax liability in various competing tax jurisdictions based on an analysis and interpretation of local tax laws and regulations. This analysis requires a significant amount of judgment and estimation and is often based on various assumptions about the future actions of the local tax authorities. These determinations are the subject of periodic domestic and foreign tax audits. Although we accrue for uncertain tax positions, our accrual may be insufficient to satisfy unfavorable findings. Unfavorable audit findings and tax rulings may result in payment of taxes, fines and penalties for prior periods and higher tax rates in future periods, which may have a material adverse effect on our financial condition, results of operations or cash flows. Changes in tax law or our interpretation of tax laws and the resolution of current and future tax audits could significantly affect the amounts provided for income taxes in our consolidated financial statements.

We earn a significant amount of our operating income from outside the U.S., and any repatriation of funds currently held in foreign jurisdictions may result in higher effective tax rates for Columbia. If we encounter a significant need for liquidity domestically or at a particular location that we cannot fulfill through borrowings, equity offerings or other internal or external sources, we may experience unfavorable tax and earnings consequences as a result of cash transfers. These adverse consequences would occur, for example, if the transfer of cash into the United States is taxed and no offsetting foreign tax credit is available to offset the U.S. tax liability, resulting in lower earnings. Furthermore, foreign exchange ceilings imposed by local governments and the sometimes lengthy approval processes that foreign governments require for international cash transfers may delay or otherwise limit our internal cash transfers from time to time.

We Operate in Very Competitive Markets

The markets for apparel, footwear, accessories and equipment are highly competitive, as are the markets for our licensed products. In each of our geographic markets, we face significant competition from global and regional branded apparel, footwear, accessories and equipment companies.

Retailers who are our customers often pose our most significant competitive threat by designing and marketing apparel, footwear, equipment and accessories under their own private labels. For example, in the United States, several of our largest customers have developed significant private label brands during the past decade that compete directly with our products. These retailers have assumed an increasing degree of inventory risk in their private label products and, as a result, may first cancel advance orders with us in order to manage their own inventory levels downward during periods of unseasonable weather or weak economic cycles.

We also compete with other companies for the production capacity of independent factories that manufacture our products and for import capacity. Many of our competitors are significantly larger than we are and have substantially greater financial, distribution, marketing and other resources, more stable manufacturing resources and greater brand strength than we have. In addition, when our competitors combine operations through mergers, acquisitions or other transactions, their competitive strength may increase.

Increased competition may result in reduced access to production capacity, reductions in display areas in retail locations, reductions in sales, or reductions in our profit margins, any of which may have a material adverse effect on our financial condition, results of operations or cash flows.

We May be Adversely Affected by the Financial Health of our Customers

Sluggish economies and consumer uncertainty regarding future economic prospects in our key markets have had an adverse effect on the financial health of our customers, some of whom have filed or may file for protection under bankruptcy laws, which may in turn have a material adverse effect on our results of operations and financial condition. We extend credit to our customers based on an assessment of the customer's financial condition, generally without requiring collateral. To assist in the scheduling of production and the shipping of seasonal products, we offer customers discounts for placing advance orders and extended payment terms for taking delivery before the peak shipping season. These extended payment terms increase our exposure to the risk of uncollectable receivables. In addition, we face increased risk of order reduction or cancellation or reduced availability of credit insurance coverage when dealing with financially ailing retailers or retailers struggling with economic uncertainty. Some of our significant wholesale customers and distributors have liquidated or reorganized, while others have had financial difficulties in the past and have recently experienced tightened credit markets and sales declines and reduced profitability, which in turn has an adverse effect on our business. We may reduce our level of business with customers and distributors experiencing financial difficulties and may not be able to replace that business with other customers, which could have a material adverse effect on our financial condition, results of operations or cash flows.

We May be Adversely Affected by Global Credit Market Conditions

Economic downturns and economic uncertainty generally affect global credit markets. Our vendors, customers and other participants in our supply chain may require access to credit markets in order to do business. Credit market conditions may slow our collection efforts as customers find it more difficult to obtain necessary financing, leading to higher than normal accounts receivable. This could result in greater expense associated with collection efforts and increased bad debt expense. Credit conditions may impair our vendors' ability to finance the purchase of raw materials or general working capital needs to support our production requirements, resulting in a delay or non-receipt of inventory shipments during key seasons.

Historically, we have limited our reliance on debt to finance our working capital, capital expenditures and investing activity requirements. We expect to fund our future capital expenditures with existing cash, expected operating cash flows and credit facilities, but if the need arises to finance additional expenditures, we may need to seek additional funding. Our ability to obtain additional financing will depend on many factors, including prevailing market conditions, our financial condition, and our ability to negotiate favorable terms and conditions. Financing may not be available on terms that are acceptable or favorable to us, if at all.

We May be Adversely Affected by Retailer Consolidation

When our wholesale customers combine their operations through mergers, acquisitions, or other transactions, their consolidated order volume may decrease while their bargaining power and the competitive threat they pose by marketing products under their own private labels may increase. Some of our significant customers have consolidated their operations in the past, which in turn has had a negative effect on our business. Future customer consolidations could have a material adverse effect on our financial condition, results of operations or cash flows.

We Rely on Innovation to Compete in the Market for our Products

To distinguish our products in the marketplace and achieve commercial success, we rely on product innovations, including new or exclusive technologies, inventive and appealing design, or other differentiating features. Research and development plays a key role in technical innovation. We rely upon specialists in the fields of chemistry, biochemistry, engineering, industrial design, electronics and related fields, guided by consumer feedback, to develop and test innovative performance products. Although we are committed to designing innovative and functional products that deliver relevant performance benefits to consumers who participate in a wide range of competitive and recreational outdoor activities, if we fail to introduce technical innovation in our products that address consumers' performance expectations, demand for our products could decline.

As we strive to achieve product innovations, we face a greater risk of inadvertent infringements of third party rights or compliance issues with regulations applicable to products with technical innovations such as electrical heating components. In addition, technical innovations often involve more complex manufacturing processes, which may lead to higher instances of quality issues, and if we experience problems with the quality of our products, we may incur substantial expense to address the problems and any associated product risks. For example, in recent years we incurred costs in connection with recalls of some of our battery-powered electrically heated apparel. Failure to successfully bring to market innovations in our product lines could have a material adverse effect on our financial condition, results of operations or cash flows.

We Face Risks Associated with Consumer Preferences and Fashion Trends

Changes in consumer preferences or consumer interest in outdoor activities may have a material adverse effect on our business. In addition, changes in fashion trends may have a greater impact than in the past as we expand our offerings to include more product categories in more geographic areas, particularly with the Sorel brand, a product generally more sensitive to fashion trends. We also face risks because our business requires us and our customers to anticipate consumer preferences. Our decisions about product designs often are made far in advance of consumer acceptance. Although we try to manage our inventory risk by soliciting advance order commitments by retailers, we must generally place a significant portion of our seasonal production orders with our independent factories before we have received all of a season's advance orders from customers, and orders may be cancelled by customers before shipment. If we or our customers fail to anticipate and respond to consumer preferences, we may have lower sales, excess inventories and lower profit margins, any of which could have a material adverse effect on our financial condition, results of operations or cash flows.

Our Success Depends on Our Use and Protection of Intellectual Property Rights

Our registered and common law trademarks and our patented or patent-pending designs and technologies have significant value and are important to our ability to differentiate our products from those of our competitors and to create and sustain demand for our products. We also place significant value on our trade dress, the overall appearance and image of our products. We regularly discover products that are counterfeit reproductions of our products or that otherwise infringe on our proprietary rights. Counterfeiting activities typically increase as brand recognition increases, especially in markets outside the United States. Increased instances of counterfeit manufacture and sales may adversely affect our sales and our brand and result in a shift of consumer preference away from our products. The actions we take to establish and protect trademarks and other proprietary rights may not be adequate to prevent imitation of our products by others or to prevent others from seeking to block sales of our products as violations of proprietary rights. In markets outside of the United States, it may be more difficult for us to establish our proprietary rights and to successfully challenge use of those rights by other parties. We also license our proprietary rights to third parties. Failure to choose appropriate licensees and licensed product categories may dilute or harm our brands. In addition to our own intellectual property rights, many of the intellectual property rights in the technology, fabrics and processes used to manufacture our products are generally owned or controlled by our suppliers and are generally not unique to us. In those cases, we may not be able to adequately protect our products or differentiate their performance characteristics and fabrications from those of our competitors. Actions or decisions in the management of our intellectual property portfolio may affect the strength of our brands, which may in turn have a material adverse effect on our financial condition, results of operations or cash flows.

Although we have not been materially inhibited from selling products in connection with patent, trademark and trade dress disputes, as we focus on innovation in our product lines, extend our brands into new product categories and expand the geographic scope of our marketing, we may become subject to litigation based on allegations of infringement or other improper use of intellectual property rights of third parties, including third party trademark, copyright and patent rights. An increasing number of our products include technologies and/or designs for which we have obtained or applied for patent protection. Failure to successfully obtain and maintain patents on these innovations could negatively affect our ability to market and sell our products. Future litigation also may be necessary to defend against claims of infringement or to enforce and protect our intellectual property rights. As we utilize e-commerce and social media to a greater degree in our sales and marketing efforts, we face an increasing risk of patent infringement claims from non-practicing entities and others covering broad functional aspects of internet operations. Intellectual property litigation may be costly and may divert management's attention from the operation of our business. Adverse determinations in any litigation may result in the loss of our proprietary rights, subject us to significant liabilities or require us to seek licenses from third parties, which may not be available on commercially reasonable terms, if at all. Any of these outcomes may have a material adverse effect on our financial condition, results of operations or cash flows.

Our Success Depends on Our Distribution Facilities

Our ability to meet customer expectations, manage inventory, complete sales and achieve objectives for operating efficiencies depends on the proper operation of our existing distribution facilities, the development or expansion of additional distribution capabilities and services, such as the transition of the value added services function from independent factories to our distribution centers, and the timely performance of services by third parties, including those involved in shipping product to and from our distribution facilities. In the United States, we rely primarily on our distribution centers in Portland, Oregon and Robards, Kentucky; in Canada, we have primarily relied on two distribution facilities in Strathroy, Ontario, one of which was transitioned to a facility in London, Ontario in late 2012 and the other of which is expected to be transitioned to this same London, Ontario facility in 2013; in Europe, we rely primarily on our distribution center in Cambrai, France; in Japan, we rely primarily on a third-party logistics distribution provider in Tokyo; and in Korea, we rely primarily on leased distribution facilities near Seoul that we manage and operate.

Our distribution facilities in the United States and France are highly automated, which means that their operations are complicated and may be subject to a number of risks related to computer viruses, the proper operation of software and hardware, electronic or power interruptions, and other system failures. We plan to upgrade our warehouse management system and add automation at our distribution facility in Canada in 2013. Risks associated with upgrading or expanding these facilities may significantly disrupt or increase the cost of our operations. For example, in addition to supporting our traditional wholesale business, our existing distribution facilities have been modified to enable them to also support our e-commerce business in the United States. Failure to successfully maintain and update these modifications could disrupt our wholesale and e-commerce shipments and may have a material adverse effect on our financial condition, results of operations or cash flows.

The fixed costs associated with owning, operating and maintaining these large, highly automated distribution centers during a period of economic weakness or declining sales can result in lower operating efficiencies and financial deleverage. This has occurred in recent years in Europe, where our distribution center is underutilized. This fixed cost structure globally may make it difficult for us to achieve or maintain profitability if sales volumes decline for an extended period of time and could have a material adverse effect on our financial condition, results of operations or cash flows.

Our distribution facilities may also be interrupted by disasters, such as earthquakes, tornadoes or fires. We maintain business interruption insurance, but it may not adequately protect us from the adverse effect that may be caused by significant disruptions in our distribution facilities.

We May be Adversely Affected by Currency Exchange Rate Fluctuations

Although the majority of our product purchases are denominated in U.S. dollars, the cost of these products may be affected by relative changes in the value of the local currencies of our subsidiaries and our manufacturers. Price increases caused by currency exchange rate fluctuations may make our products less competitive or have an adverse effect on our margins. Our international revenues and expenses generally are derived from sales and operations in currencies other than the U.S. dollar. Because the functional currency of many of our subsidiaries is not the U.S. dollar, we are exposed to the potential of material gains or losses from the remeasurement of U.S. dollar monetary transactions into the respective functional currencies. Currency exchange rate fluctuations may also disrupt the business of the independent factories that produce our products by making their purchases of raw materials more expensive and more difficult to finance. As a result, currency fluctuations may have a material adverse effect on our financial condition, results of operations or cash flows.

Our Investments May be Adversely Affected by Market Conditions

Our investment portfolio is subject to a number of risks and uncertainties. Changes in market conditions, such as those that accompany an economic downturn or economic uncertainty, may negatively affect the value and liquidity of our investment portfolio, perhaps significantly. Our ability to find diversified investments that are both safe and liquid and that provide a reasonable return may be impaired, potentially resulting in lower interest income, less diversification, longer investment maturities and/or other-than-temporary impairments.

We May be Adversely Affected by Labor Disruptions

Our business depends on our ability to source and distribute products in a timely manner. While a majority of our own operations are not subject to organized labor agreements, our relationship with our Cambrai distribution center employees is governed by French law, including a formal representation of employees by a Works' Council and the application of a collective bargaining agreement. Labor disputes at independent factories where our goods are produced, shipping ports, transportation carriers, retail stores or distribution centers create significant risks for our business, particularly if these disputes result in work slowdowns, lockouts, strikes or other disruptions during our peak manufacturing, shipping and selling seasons, and may have a material adverse effect on our business, potentially resulting in cancelled orders by customers, unanticipated inventory accumulation, and reduced revenues and earnings.

We Depend on Key Suppliers

Some of the materials that we use may be available from only one source or a very limited number of sources. For example, some specialty fabrics are manufactured to our specification by one source or a few sources, and a single vendor supplies the majority of the zippers used in our products. From time to time, we have difficulty satisfying our raw material and finished goods requirements. Although we believe that we can identify and qualify additional independent factories to produce these materials as necessary, there are no guarantees that additional independent factories will be available. In addition, depending on the timing, any changes in sources or materials may result in increased costs or production delays, which may have a material adverse effect on our financial condition, results of operations or cash flows.

We Depend on Key Personnel

Our future success will depend in part on the continued service of key personnel and our ability to attract, retain and develop key managers, designers, sales and information technology professionals and others. We face intense competition for these individuals worldwide, and there is a significant concentration of well-funded apparel and footwear competitors in and around our headquarters in Portland, Oregon. We may not be able to attract qualified new employees or retain existing employees, which may have a material adverse effect on our financial condition, results of operations or cash flows.

Our Business Is Affected by Seasonality

Our business is affected by the general seasonal trends common to the outdoor industry. Our products are marketed on a seasonal basis and our annual net sales are weighted heavily toward the fall/winter season, while our operating expenses are more equally distributed throughout the year. As a result, the majority, and sometimes all, of our operating profits are generated in the second half of the year. The expansion of our direct-to-consumer operations and sales growth in our winter footwear business (both Sorel and Columbia brands) has increased the proportion of sales and profits that we generate in the fourth calendar quarter. This seasonality, along with other factors that are beyond our control and that are discussed elsewhere in this section, may adversely affect our business and cause our results of operations to fluctuate. As a result, our profitability may be materially affected if management is not able to timely adjust expenses in reaction to adverse events such as unfavorable weather, weak consumer spending patterns or unanticipated levels of order cancellations. Results of operations in any period should not be considered indicative of the results to be expected for any future period.

Our Products Are Subject to Increasing Product Regulations and We Face Risks of Product Liability and Warranty Claims

Our products are subject to increasingly stringent and complex domestic and foreign product labeling and performance and safety standards, laws and other regulations. These requirements could result in greater expense associated with compliance efforts, and failure to comply with these regulations could result in a delay, non-delivery or recall or destruction of inventory shipments during key seasons or in other financial penalties. Significant or continuing noncompliance with these standards and laws could disrupt our business and harm our reputation and, as a result, could have a material adverse effect on our financial condition, results of operations or cash flows.

Our products are used in outdoor activities, sometimes in severe conditions. Product recalls or product liability claims resulting from the failure, or alleged failure, of our products could have a material adverse effect on our financial condition, results of operations or cash flows. Most of our products carry limited warranties for defects in quality and workmanship. We maintain a warranty reserve for future warranty claims, but the actual costs of servicing future warranty claims may exceed the reserve, which may also have a material adverse effect on our financial condition, results of operations or cash flows.

Our Common Stock Price May Be Volatile

The price of our common stock has fluctuated substantially since our initial public offering. Our common stock is traded on the NASDAQ Global Select Market. Factors such as general market conditions, fluctuations in financial results, variances from financial market expectations, changes in earnings estimates or recommendations by analysts, or announcements by us or our competitors may cause the market price of our common stock to fluctuate, perhaps substantially.

Insiders Control a Majority of Our Common Stock and May Sell Shares

Three related shareholders, Timothy Boyle, Gertrude Boyle and Sarah Bany, beneficially own a majority of our common stock. As a result, if acting together, they can effectively control matters requiring shareholder approval without the cooperation of other shareholders. Shares held by these three insiders are available for resale, subject to the requirements of, and the rules under, the Securities Act of 1933 and the Securities Exchange Act of 1934. The sale or the prospect of the sale of a substantial number of these shares may have an adverse effect on the market price of our common stock.

	Year Ended December 31,		
	2012	2011	% Change
	(In millions, except for percentage changes)		
United States	$ 946.7	$ 948.0	—%
LAAP...	377.6	341.0	11%
EMEA...	230.6	275.4	(16)%
Canada	114.7	129.6	(11)%
	$ 1,669.6	$ 1,694.0	(1)%

Net sales in the United States decreased $1.3 million, or less than 1%, to $946.7 million in 2012 from $948.0 million in 2011. The decrease in net sales in the United States consisted of a net sales decrease in our wholesale business across all brands and both product categories, partially offset by a net sales increase in our direct-to-consumer channel across all brands and both product categories. The decrease in net sales in our wholesale business was driven by unseasonably warm winter weather and general consumer caution, resulting in higher cancellations of advance orders and fewer reorders from wholesale customers. The increase in direct-to-consumer net sales was due to a greater number of retail stores operating during 2012 than 2011 and, to a lesser degree, increased sales from existing stores. At December 31, 2012, we operated 63 retail stores, compared with 51 at December 31, 2011.

Net sales in the LAAP region increased $36.6 million, or 11%, to $377.6 million in 2012 from $341.0 million in 2011. Changes in foreign currency exchange rates affected the LAAP net sales comparison by less than one percent. The net sales increase in the LAAP region was led by a net sales increase in apparel, accessories and equipment, followed by a net sales increase in footwear. The LAAP net sales increase was concentrated in the Columbia brand, followed by the Mountain Hardwear brand and the Sorel brand. The LAAP net sales increase was led by Japan, followed by Korea and our LAAP distributor business. The increase in Japan net sales was led by an increase in wholesale net sales, followed by an increase in direct-to-consumer net sales. The increase in Korea net sales was primarily due to a greater number of retail stores operating during 2012 than in 2011, partially offset by the negative effect of foreign currency exchange rates. Net sales to our LAAP distributors increased due to higher demand in key distributor markets, partially offset by a smaller percentage of spring 2013 advance orders shipping in the fourth quarter of 2012 compared to shipments of spring 2012 advance orders in the fourth quarter of 2011.

Net sales in the EMEA region decreased $44.8 million, or 16%, to $230.6 million in 2012 from $275.4 million in 2011. Changes in foreign currency exchange rates negatively affected the EMEA net sales comparison by approximately four percentage points. The decrease in net sales in the EMEA region was led by footwear, followed by apparel, accessories and equipment. The net sales decrease consisted of a net sales decrease in our EMEA direct business reflecting a decline in advance orders due to the effects of the unseasonably warm 2011/2012 winter and a challenging macroeconomic environment, which have hampered our ongoing efforts to revitalize the Columbia brand in key European markets. This decrease was partially offset by a net sales increase in our EMEA distributor business, partially due to higher demand in Russia.

Net sales in Canada decreased $14.9 million, or 11%, to $114.7 million in 2012 from $129.6 million in 2011. Changes in foreign currency exchange rates compared to 2011 affected the Canada net sales comparison by less than one percent. The decrease in net sales was led by apparel, accessories and equipment, followed by footwear, and was led by the Columbia brand, followed by the Sorel and Mountain Hardwear brands. The Canada net sales decrease was primarily a result of a decline in fall 2012 advance orders for Columbia brand products due to the unseasonably warm 2011/2012 winter and retailer consolidation in the region.

Sales by Product Category

Net sales by product category are summarized in the following table:

	Year Ended December 31,		
	2012	**2011**	**% Change**
	(In millions, except for percentage changes)		
Apparel, Accessories and Equipment	$ 1,347.0	$ 1,334.9	1%
Footwear	322.6	359.1	(10)%
	$ 1,669.6	$ 1,694.0	(1)%

Net sales of apparel, accessories and equipment increased $12.1 million, or 1%, to $1,347.0 million in 2012 from $1,334.9 million in 2011. The increase in apparel, accessories and equipment net sales consisted of a net sales increase in the Columbia brand and was led by the LAAP region, followed by the United States, partially offset by net sales decreases in the EMEA region and Canada. The apparel, accessories and equipment net sales increase in the LAAP region was led by Japan, followed by Korea and our LAAP distributor business. The net sales increase in apparel, accessories and equipment in the United States consisted of a net sales increase in our direct-to-consumer business, partially offset by a net sales decrease in our wholesale business.

Net sales of footwear decreased $36.5 million, or 10%, to $322.6 million in 2012 from $359.1 million in 2011. The decrease in footwear net sales was led by the Sorel brand, followed by the Columbia brand. The footwear net sales decrease was led by the EMEA region, followed by the United States and Canada, partially offset by a net sales increase in the LAAP region. The footwear net sales decrease in the EMEA region was primarily concentrated in our EMEA direct business, and was led by the Sorel brand, followed by the Columbia brand. The net sales decrease in footwear in the United States consisted of a net sales decrease in our wholesale business, partially offset by a net sales increase in our direct-to-consumer business. The LAAP footwear net sales increase was led by our LAAP distributor business, followed by Japan and Korea, and was primarily concentrated in the Columbia brand, followed by the Sorel brand.

Sales by Brand

Net sales by brand are summarized in the following table:

	Year Ended December 31,		
	2012	**2011**	**% Change**
	(In millions, except for percentage changes)		
Columbia	$ 1,391.1	$ 1,391.5	—%
Mountain Hardwear	141.5	142.3	(1)%
Sorel	127.0	150.3	(16)%
Other...	10.0	9.9	1%
	$ 1,669.6	$ 1,694.0	(1)%

The net sales decrease in 2012 compared to 2011 primarily consisted of a net sales decrease in the Sorel brand which was unfavorably affected by mild winter weather in both 2011 and 2012 resulting in lower advance orders as well as higher order cancellations and fewer reorders of cold weather footwear from wholesale customers. The Sorel brand net sales decrease was concentrated in the EMEA region, followed by the United States and Canada, partially offset by a net sales increase in the LAAP region.

Gross Profit: Gross profit as a percentage of net sales decreased to 42.9% in 2012 from 43.4% in 2011. Gross margin contraction was primarily due to:

- Lower gross margins on increased promotional selling activities; and
- Higher product input costs;

partially offset by:

- Increased wholesale pricing;
- Lower airfreight costs; and

- Favorable foreign currency hedge rates.

Our gross profit may not be comparable to those of other companies in our industry because some of these companies include all of the costs related to their distribution network in cost of sales while we, like many others, include these expenses as a component of SG&A expense.

Selling, General and Administrative Expense: SG&A expense includes all costs associated with our design, merchandising, marketing, distribution and corporate functions, including related depreciation and amortization.

SG&A expense decreased $18.1 million, or 3%, to $596.6 million, or 35.7% of net sales, in 2012, from $614.7 million, or 36.3% of net sales, in 2011. The SG&A expense decrease was primarily due to:

- The favorable effect of foreign currency translation;
- Reduced advertising spend; and
- Lower variable selling costs;

partially offset by:

- The expansion of direct-to-consumer operations globally; and
- Higher expenses related to information technology initiatives, including our ongoing ERP implementation.

Depreciation and amortization included in SG&A expense totaled $39.9 million in 2012, compared to $42.9 million in 2011.

Net Licensing Income: Net licensing income decreased $2.0 million, or 13%, to $13.8 million in 2012 from $15.8 million in 2011. The decrease in net licensing income was primarily due to decreased licensing income from accessories in the United States and decreased licensing income in the LAAP region, resulting from a timing shift in distributor shipments from the fourth quarter of 2012 into the first quarter of 2013.

Interest Income, Net: Net interest income was $0.4 million in 2012, compared to $1.3 million in 2011. The decrease in interest income was primarily driven by lower average interest rates and lower average cash and investment balances during 2012 compared to 2011. Interest expense was nominal in both 2012 and 2011.

Income Tax Expense: Income tax expense decreased to $34.0 million in 2012 from $34.2 million in 2011. Our effective income tax rate increased to 25.4% from 24.8% in 2011, primarily due to changes in the geographic mix of income, partially offset by increased tax benefits from research and development credits and the resolution of uncertain tax positions.

Net Income: Net income decreased $3.6 million, or 3%, to $99.9 million in 2012 from $103.5 million in 2011. Diluted earnings per share was $2.93 in 2012 compared to $3.03 in 2011.

Year Ended December 31, 2011 Compared to Year Ended December 31, 2010

Net Sales: Consolidated net sales increased $210.5 million, or 14%, to $1,694.0 million in 2011 from $1,483.5 million in 2010. Net sales increased across all geographic regions, in each product category and across all major brands. Changes in foreign currency exchange rates compared with 2010 contributed approximately three percentage points of benefit to the consolidated net sales comparison.

Sales by Geographic Region

Net sales by geographic region are summarized in the following table:

	Year Ended December 31,		
	2011	**2010**	**% Change**
	(In millions, except for percentage changes)		
United States	$ 948.0	$ 881.0	8%
LAAP...	341.0	263.4	29%
EMEA	275.4	222.4	24%
Canada...	129.6	116.7	11%
	$ 1,694.0	$ 1,483.5	14%

Net sales in the United States increased $67.0 million, or 8%, to $948.0 million in 2011 from $881.0 million in 2010. The increase in net sales in the United States by product category was led by apparel, accessories and equipment, followed by a net sales increase in footwear. The net sales increase by brand was led by the Columbia brand, followed by the Sorel brand and the Mountain Hardwear brand. The net sales increase by channel was primarily driven by our direct-to-consumer business, followed by our wholesale business. The increase in net sales in our direct-to-consumer business was driven by strong comparable store sales growth, increased e-commerce sales and the net addition of two outlet stores.

Net sales in the LAAP region increased $77.6 million, or 29%, to $341.0 million in 2011 from $263.4 million in 2010. Changes in foreign currency exchange rates contributed six percentage points of benefit to the LAAP net sales comparison. The net sales increase in the LAAP region by product category was primarily driven by a net sales increase in apparel, accessories and equipment, followed by a net sales increase in footwear. The LAAP net sales increase was concentrated in the Columbia brand and was led by Korea, followed by Japan and our LAAP distributor business. The increase in Korea net sales was primarily due to increased sales from existing stores, a greater number of retail stores operating during 2011 and the favorable effect of foreign currency exchange rates. The increase in Japan net sales was primarily the result of the favorable effect of foreign currency exchange rates and increased wholesale net sales. Net sales to our LAAP distributors increased due to increased demand in key distributor markets coupled with a higher percentage of spring 2012 advance orders shipping in the fourth quarter compared to the spring 2011 season.

Net sales in the EMEA region increased $53.0 million, or 24%, to $275.4 million in 2011 from $222.4 million in 2010. Changes in foreign currency exchange rates contributed four percentage points of benefit to the EMEA net sales comparison. The increase in net sales in the EMEA region by product category was led by footwear, followed by a net sales increase in apparel, accessories and equipment. The net sales increase by channel was led by our EMEA direct business, followed by our EMEA distributors. The increase in EMEA direct net sales was primarily driven by the Sorel brand, followed by the Columbia brand.

Net sales in Canada increased $12.9 million, or 11%, to $129.6 million in 2011 from $116.7 million in 2010. Changes in foreign currency exchange rates compared to 2010 contributed six percentage points of benefit to the Canada net sales comparison. By product category, the increase in net sales was led by apparel, accessories and equipment, followed by a net sales increase in footwear. By brand, the increase in net sales was led by the Columbia brand, followed by the Sorel and Mountain Hardwear brands. The increase in net sales was concentrated in our wholesale business.

Sales by Product Category

Net sales by product category are summarized in the following table:

	Year Ended December 31,		
	2011	**2010**	**% Change**
	(In millions, except for percentage changes)		
Apparel, Accessories and Equipment.....................................	$ 1,334.9	$ 1,213.3	10%
Footwear..	359.1	270.2	33%
	$ 1,694.0	$ 1,483.5	14%

Net sales of apparel, accessories and equipment increased $121.6 million, or 10%, to $1,334.9 million in 2011 from $1,213.3 million in 2010. The increase in apparel, accessories and equipment net sales was primarily concentrated in the

Columbia brand and was led by the LAAP region, followed by the United States, the EMEA region and Canada. The apparel, accessories and equipment net sales increase in the LAAP region was led by Korea, followed by our LAAP distributor business and Japan. The net sales increase in apparel, accessories and equipment in the United States was led by our direct-to-consumer business, partially offset by a net sales decrease in our wholesale business.

Net sales of footwear increased $88.9 million, or 33%, to $359.1 million in 2011 from $270.2 million in 2010. The increase in footwear net sales by brand was led by the Sorel brand, followed by the Columbia brand. The footwear net sales increase by region was led by the United States, followed by the EMEA region, the LAAP region and Canada. The net sales increase in footwear in the United States was primarily driven by our wholesale business, followed by our direct-to-consumer business. The footwear net sales increase in the EMEA region was primarily driven by our EMEA direct business, followed by our EMEA distributor business. The LAAP footwear net sales increase was led by Japan, followed by Korea and our LAAP distributor business.

Sales by Brand

Net sales by brand are summarized in the following table:

	Year Ended December 31,		
	2011	**2010**	**% Change**
	(In millions, except for percentage changes)		
Columbia	$ 1,391.5	$ 1,262.4	10%
Mountain Hardwear	142.3	121.9	17%
Sorel	150.3	89.7	68%
Other	9.9	9.5	4%
	$ 1,694.0	$ 1,483.5	14%

The net sales increase in 2011 compared to 2010 was led by the Columbia brand, followed by the Sorel and Mountain Hardwear brands. Columbia brand net sales increased in both product categories and across all regions, led by the LAAP region, followed by the United States, the EMEA region and Canada. Sorel brand net sales increased across all regions led by the EMEA region, followed by the United States, Canada, and the LAAP region. Mountain Hardwear net sales increased in three regions, led by the United States, the LAAP region and Canada, partially offset by a slight decline in the EMEA region.

Gross Profit: Gross profit as a percentage of net sales increased to 43.4% in 2011 from 42.4% in 2010, driven primarily by lower airfreight costs compared to 2010. Other factors favorably affecting gross margin included:

- Favorable foreign currency hedge rates; and
- A higher proportion of direct-to-consumer sales at higher gross margins;

partially offset by:

- Increased product costs;
- A higher proportion of close-out product sales; and
- An increased proportion of shipments to EMEA and LAAP distributors.

Selling, General and Administrative Expense: SG&A expense increased $80.6 million, or 15%, to $614.7 million, or 36.3% of net sales, in 2011, from $534.1 million, or 36.0% of net sales, in 2010. The SG&A expense increase was primarily due to:

- The expansion of direct-to-consumer operations globally, including a net increase of $3.2 million in store impairment charges;
- Increased advertising expenses;
- Additions to staff and other expenses to support business initiatives and growth;

- Information technology initiatives, including our ERP implementation; and

- The unfavorable effect of foreign currency translation.

Depreciation and amortization included in SG&A expense totaled $42.9 million in 2011, compared to $37.8 million in 2010.

Net Licensing Income: Net licensing income increased $7.8 million, or 98%, to $15.8 million in 2011 from $8.0 million in 2010. The increase in net licensing income was primarily due to increased apparel and footwear licensing in the LAAP region, where a third party distributor is licensed to locally manufacture Columbia brand apparel and footwear for sale in local markets.

Interest Income, Net: Net interest income was $1.3 million in 2011, compared to $1.6 million in 2010. The decrease in interest income was primarily driven by lower average cash and investment balances and lower interest rates in 2011 compared to 2010. Interest expense was nominal in both 2011 and 2010.

Income Tax Expense: Income tax expense increased to $34.2 million in 2011 from $27.9 million in 2010. Our effective income tax rate decreased to 24.8% from 26.6% in 2010, primarily because we earned a higher proportion of our income from foreign jurisdictions with tax rates that are generally lower than the U.S. tax rate.

Net Income: Net income increased $26.4 million, or 34%, to $103.5 million in 2011 from $77.0 million in 2010. Diluted earnings per share was $3.03 in 2011 compared to $2.26 in 2010.

Liquidity and Capital Resources

Our primary ongoing funding requirements are for working capital, investing activities associated with the expansion of our global operations and general corporate needs. At December 31, 2012, we had total cash and cash equivalents of $290.8 million compared to $241.0 million at December 31, 2011. In addition, we had short-term investments of $44.7 million at December 31, 2012 compared to $2.9 million at December 31, 2011. At December 31, 2012, approximately 30% of our cash and short-term investments were held by our foreign subsidiaries where a repatriation of those funds to the United States would likely result in a significant tax expense to the Company. However, based on the capital and liquidity needs of our foreign operations, as well as the status of current tax law, it is our intent to indefinitely reinvest these funds outside the United States. In addition, our United States operations do not require the repatriation of these funds to meet our currently projected liquidity needs.

2012 compared to 2011

Net cash provided by operating activities was $148.7 million in 2012 compared to $63.8 million in 2011. The increase in cash provided by operating activities was primarily due to decreases in accounts receivable and inventory for the year ended December 31, 2012, compared to increases in the prior year; partially offset by a decrease in accounts payable and accrued liabilities for the year ended December 31, 2012 compared to an increase in 2011.

Net cash used in investing activities was $85.0 million in 2012 compared to $12.5 million in 2011. For 2012, net cash used in investing activities primarily consisted of $50.5 million for capital expenditures and $41.7 million for net purchases of short-term investments. For 2011, net cash used in investing activities primarily consisted of $78.4 million for capital expenditures, including the acquisition of a new distribution center and headquarters facility in Canada, partially offset by $65.7 million for net sales of short-term investments.

Net cash used in financing activities was $15.7 million in 2012 compared to $39.2 million in 2011. For 2012, net cash used in financing activities primarily consisted of dividend payments of $29.8 million, partially offset by net proceeds of $13.1 million from the issuance of common stock. For 2011, net cash used in financing activities primarily consisted of dividend payments of $29.1 million and the repurchase of common stock at an aggregate price of $20.0 million, partially offset by net proceeds of $8.0 million from the issuance of common stock.

2011 compared to 2010

Net cash provided by operating activities was $63.8 million in 2011 compared to $23.5 million in 2010. The increase in cash provided by operating activities was primarily due to increased income from operations, combined with a reduction in the rate of growth of accounts receivable and inventory; partially offset by a reduction in the rate of growth of accounts payable and accrued liabilities, an increase in prepaid expenses and an increase in income taxes paid compared to 2010.

Net cash used in investing activities was $12.5 million in 2011 compared to $91.2 million in 2010. For 2011, net cash used in investing activities primarily consisted of $78.4 million for capital expenditures, partially offset by $65.7 million for net sales of short-term investments. For 2010, net cash used in investing activities primarily consisted of $46.1 million for net purchases of short-term investments, $28.8 million for capital expenditures and $16.3 million for acquisitions.

Net cash used in financing activities was $39.2 million in 2011 compared to $82.3 million in 2010. For 2011, net cash used in financing activities primarily consisted of dividend payments of $29.1 million and the repurchase of common stock at an aggregate price of $20.0 million, partially offset by net proceeds of $8.0 million from the issuance of common stock. For 2010, net cash used in financing activities primarily consisted of dividend payments of $75.4 million, including a $50.5 million special dividend paid in December 2010, and the repurchase of common stock at an aggregate price of $13.8 million, partially offset by net proceeds of $6.5 million from the issuance of common stock.

Short-term borrowings and credit lines

We have an unsecured, committed $125.0 million revolving line of credit available to fund our domestic working capital requirements. At December 31, 2012, no balance was outstanding under this line of credit and we were in compliance with all associated covenants. Internationally, our subsidiaries have local currency operating lines of credit in place guaranteed by the parent company with a combined limit of approximately $105.9 million at December 31, 2012, of which $3.7 million is designated as a European customs guarantee. At December 31, 2012, $156,000 was outstanding under these lines of credit.

We expect to fund our future working capital requirements, capital expenditures and our China joint venture obligations with existing cash, operating cash flows and credit facilities. If the need arises, we may need to seek additional funding. Our ability to obtain additional financing will depend on many factors, including prevailing market conditions, our financial condition, and our ability to negotiate favorable terms and conditions. Financing may not be available on terms that are acceptable or favorable to us, if at all.

Our operations are affected by seasonal trends typical in the outdoor apparel industry, and have historically resulted in higher sales and profits in the third and fourth calendar quarters. This pattern has resulted primarily from the timing of shipments of fall season products to wholesale customers and proportionally higher sales from our direct-to-consumer operations in the fourth quarter. We believe that our liquidity requirements for at least the next 12 months will be adequately covered by existing cash, cash provided by operations and existing short-term borrowing arrangements.

Contractual obligations

The following table presents our estimated contractual commitments (in thousands):

| | Year ended December 31, | | | | | | |
	2013	2014	2015	2016	2017	Thereafter	Total
Inventory purchase obligations (1) ..	$255,299	$ —	$ —	$ —	$ —	$ —	$255,299
Operating leases (2).............	42,771	37,477	33,842	32,029	31,203	92,739	270,061

(1)   See *Inventory Purchase Obligations* in Note 13 of Notes to Consolidated Financial Statements.
(2)   See *Operating Leases* in Note 13 of Notes to Consolidated Financial Statements.

We have recorded long-term liabilities for net unrecognized tax benefits related to income tax uncertainties in our Consolidated Balance Sheet at December 31, 2012 of approximately $11.6 million; however, they have not been included in the table above because we are uncertain about whether or when these amounts may be settled. See Note 10 of Notes to Consolidated Financial Statements.

Quantitative and Qualitative Disclosures About Market Risk

In the normal course of business, our financial position and results of operations are routinely subject to a variety of risks. These risks include risks associated with global financial and capital markets, primarily currency exchange rate risk and, to a lesser extent, interest rate risk and equity market risk. We regularly assess these risks and have established policies and business practices designed to mitigate the effect of these risks. We do not engage in speculative trading in any financial or capital market.

Our primary currency exchange rate risk management objective is to mitigate the uncertainty of anticipated cash flows attributable to changes in exchange rates. We focus on mitigating changes in functional currency equivalent cash flows resulting from anticipated U.S. dollar denominated inventory purchases by subsidiaries that use European euros, Canadian dollars, Japanese yen or Korean won as their functional currency. We manage this risk primarily by using currency forward and option contracts. Additionally, we use foreign currency forward and option contracts to hedge net balance sheet exposures related primarily to intercompany transactions and borrowing arrangements.

The net fair value of our derivative contracts was favorable by approximately $5.4 million at December 31, 2012. A 10% exchange rate change in the euro, Canadian dollar, yen and won against the U.S. dollar would have resulted in the net fair value declining by approximately $12.9 million at December 31, 2012. A 10% exchange rate change in the yen against the euro would have resulted in the net fair value declining approximately $2.2 million at December 31, 2012. Changes in fair value resulting from foreign exchange rate fluctuations would be substantially offset by the change in value of the underlying hedged transactions.

Our negotiated credit facilities generally charge interest based on a benchmark rate such as the London Interbank Offered Rate ("LIBOR"). Fluctuations in short-term interest rates cause interest payments on drawn amounts to increase or decrease. At December 31, 2012, our credit facilities had an outstanding balance of $156,000. A 10% interest rate change would be immaterial.

Critical Accounting Policies and Estimates

Management's discussion and analysis of our financial condition and results of operations are based on our consolidated financial statements, which have been prepared in accordance with accounting principles generally accepted in the United States of America. The preparation of these financial statements requires us to make various estimates and assumptions that affect reported amounts of assets and liabilities and related disclosure of contingent assets and liabilities at the date of the consolidated financial statements and the reported amounts of revenue and expenses during the reporting period. We believe that the estimates and assumptions involved in the accounting policies described below have the greatest potential impact on our financial statements, so we consider these to be our critical accounting policies and estimates. Because of the uncertainty inherent in these matters, actual results may differ from the estimates we use in applying these critical accounting policies. We base our ongoing estimates on historical experience and various other assumptions that we believe to be important in the circumstances. Many of these critical accounting policies affect working capital account balances, including the policy for revenue recognition, the allowance for doubtful accounts, the provision for potential excess, closeout and slow moving inventory, product warranty, income taxes and stock-based compensation.

Management regularly discusses with our Audit Committee each of our critical accounting estimates, the development and selection of these accounting estimates, and the disclosure about each estimate in Management's Discussion and Analysis of Financial Condition and Results of Operations. These discussions typically occur at our quarterly Audit Committee meetings and include the basis and methodology used in developing and selecting these estimates, the trends in and amounts of these estimates, specific matters affecting the amount of and changes in these estimates, and any other relevant matters related to these estimates, including significant issues concerning accounting principles and financial statement presentation.

Revenue Recognition

We record wholesale, distributor, e-commerce and licensed product revenues when title passes and the risks and rewards of ownership have passed to the customer. Title generally passes upon shipment to or upon receipt by the customer depending on the terms of sale with the customer. Retail store revenues are recorded at the time of sale.

Where title passes upon receipt by the customer, predominantly in our European wholesale business, precise information regarding the date of receipt by the customer is not readily available. In these cases, we estimate the date of receipt by the customer based on historical and expected delivery times by geographic location. We periodically test the accuracy of these estimates based on actual transactions. Delivery times vary by geographic location, generally from one to five days. To date, we have found these estimates to be materially accurate.

At the time of revenue recognition, we also provide for estimated sales returns and miscellaneous claims from customers as reductions to revenues. The estimates are based on historical rates of product returns and claims, as well as events and circumstances that indicate changes to historical rates of returns and claims. However, actual returns and claims in any future period are inherently uncertain and thus may differ from the estimates. If actual or expected future returns and claims are significantly greater or lower than the reserves that we have established, we will record a reduction or increase to net revenues in the period in which we make such a determination.

Allowance for Uncollectable Accounts Receivable

We make ongoing estimates of the collectability of our accounts receivable and maintain an allowance for estimated losses resulting from the inability of our customers to make required payments. In determining the amount of the allowance, we consider our historical level of credit losses and we make judgments about the creditworthiness of customers based on ongoing credit evaluations. We analyze specific customer accounts, customer concentrations, credit insurance coverage, standby letters of credit, current economic trends, and changes in customer payment terms. Continued uncertainty in credit and market conditions may slow our collection efforts if customers experience difficulty accessing credit and paying their obligations, leading to higher than normal accounts receivable and increased bad debt expense. Because we cannot predict future changes in the financial stability of our customers, actual future losses from uncollectable accounts may differ from our estimates and may have a material effect on our consolidated financial position, results of operations or cash flows. If the financial condition of our customers deteriorates and results in their inability to make payments, a larger allowance may be required. If we determine that a smaller or larger allowance is appropriate, we will record a credit or a charge to SG&A expense in the period in which we make such a determination.

Excess, Close-Out and Slow Moving Inventory

We make ongoing estimates of potential excess, close-out or slow moving inventory. We evaluate our inventory on hand considering our purchase commitments, sales forecasts, and historical experience to identify excess, close-out or slow moving inventory and make provisions as necessary to properly reflect inventory value at the lower of cost or estimated market value. If we determine that a smaller or larger reserve is appropriate, we will record a credit or a charge to cost of sales in the period in which we make such a determination.

Product Warranty

We make ongoing estimates of potential future product warranty costs. When we evaluate our reserve for warranty costs, we consider our product warranty policies, historical claim rates by season, product category and mix, current economic trends, and the historical cost to repair, replace, or refund the original sale. If we determine that a smaller or larger reserve is appropriate, we will record a credit or a charge to cost of sales in the period in which we make such a determination.

Income Taxes

We use the asset and liability method of accounting for income taxes. Under this method, we recognize income tax expense for the amount of taxes payable or refundable for the current year and for the amount of deferred tax liabilities and assets for the future tax consequences of events that have been recognized in our financial statements or tax returns. We make assumptions, judgments and estimates to determine our current provision for income taxes, our deferred tax assets and liabilities, and our uncertain tax positions. Our judgments, assumptions and estimates relative to the current provision for income tax take into account current tax laws, our interpretation of current tax laws and possible outcomes of current and future audits conducted by foreign and domestic tax authorities. Changes in tax law or our interpretation of tax laws and the resolution of current and future tax audits could significantly affect the amounts provided for income taxes in our consolidated financial statements. Our assumptions, judgments and estimates relative to the value of a deferred tax asset take into account predictions of the amount and category of future taxable income. Actual operating results and the underlying amount and category of income in future years could cause our current assumptions, judgments and estimates of recoverable net deferred taxes to be inaccurate. Changes in any of the assumptions, judgments and estimates mentioned above could cause our actual income tax obligations to differ from our estimates, which could materially affect our financial position and results of operations.

Our tax provision for interim periods is determined using an estimate of our annual effective tax rate, adjusted for discrete items, if any, that are taken into account in the relevant period. As the calendar year progresses, we periodically refine our estimate based on actual events and earnings by jurisdiction. This ongoing estimation process can result in changes to our expected effective tax rate for the full calendar year. When this occurs, we adjust the income tax provision during the quarter in which the change in estimate occurs so that our year-to-date provision equals our expected annual effective tax rate.

Stock-Based Compensation

Stock-based compensation cost is estimated at the grant date based on the award's fair value and is recognized as expense over the requisite service period using the straight-line attribution method. We estimate stock-based compensation for stock awards granted using the Black-Scholes option pricing model, which requires various highly subjective assumptions, including volatility and expected option life. Further, we estimate forfeitures for stock-based awards granted, but which are not expected to vest. If any of these inputs or assumptions changes significantly, stock-based compensation expense may differ materially in the future from that recorded in the current period.

Recent Accounting Pronouncements

See "Recent Accounting Pronouncements" in Note 2 of Notes to Consolidated Financial Statements.

Item 8. *FINANCIAL STATEMENTS AND SUPPLEMENTARY DATA*

Our management is responsible for the information and representations contained in this report. The financial statements have been prepared in conformity with accounting principles generally accepted in the United States of America, which we consider appropriate in the circumstances and include some amounts based on our best estimates and judgments. Other financial information in this report is consistent with these financial statements.

Our accounting systems include controls designed to reasonably assure that assets are safeguarded from unauthorized use or disposition and which provide for the preparation of financial statements in conformity with accounting principles generally accepted in the United States of America. These systems are supplemented by the selection and training of qualified financial personnel and an organizational structure providing for appropriate segregation of duties.

The Audit Committee is responsible for appointing the independent registered public accounting firm and reviews with the independent registered public accounting firm and management the scope and the results of the annual examination, the effectiveness of the accounting control system and other matters relating to our financial affairs as they deem appropriate.

Report of Independent Registered Public Accounting Firm

To the Board of Directors and Shareholders
Columbia Sportswear Company
Portland, Oregon

We have audited the accompanying consolidated balance sheets of Columbia Sportswear Company and subsidiaries (the "Company") as of December 31, 2012 and 2011, and the related consolidated statements of operations, comprehensive income, shareholders' equity and cash flows for each of the three years in the period ended December 31, 2012. Our audits also included the financial statement schedule listed in the Index at Item 15. These financial statements and financial statement schedule are the responsibility of the Company's management. Our responsibility is to express an opinion on these financial statements and financial statement schedule based on our audits.

We conducted our audits in accordance with the standards of the Public Company Accounting Oversight Board (United States). Those standards require that we plan and perform the audit to obtain reasonable assurance about whether the financial statements are free of material misstatement. An audit includes examining, on a test basis, evidence supporting the amounts and disclosures in the financial statements. An audit also includes assessing the accounting principles used and significant estimates made by management, as well as evaluating the overall financial statement presentation. We believe that our audits provide a reasonable basis for our opinion.

In our opinion, such consolidated financial statements present fairly, in all material respects, the financial position of Columbia Sportswear Company and subsidiaries as of December 31, 2012 and 2011, and the results of their operations and their cash flows for each of the three years in the period ended December 31, 2012, in conformity with accounting principles generally accepted in the United States of America. Also, in our opinion, such financial statement schedule, when considered in relation to the basic consolidated financial statements taken as a whole, presents fairly, in all material respects, the information set forth therein.

We have also audited, in accordance with the standards of the Public Company Accounting Oversight Board (United States), the Company's internal control over financial reporting as of December 31, 2012, based on the criteria established in *Internal Control—Integrated Framework* issued by the Committee of Sponsoring Organizations of the Treadway Commission, and our report dated February 28, 2013, expressed an unqualified opinion on the Company's internal control over financial reporting.

/s/   DELOITTE & TOUCHE LLP
Portland, Oregon
February 28, 2013

COLUMBIA SPORTSWEAR COMPANY

CONSOLIDATED BALANCE SHEETS
(In thousands)

	December 31, 2012	December 31, 2011
ASSETS		
Current Assets:		
Cash and cash equivalents	$ 290,781	$ 241,034
Short-term investments.	44,661	2,878
Accounts receivable, net (Note 4)	334,324	351,538
Inventories, net (Note 5).	363,325	365,199
Deferred income taxes (Note 10)	50,929	52,485
Prepaid expenses and other current assets	38,583	36,392
Total current assets	1,122,603	1,049,526
Property, plant, and equipment, net (Note 6).	260,524	250,910
Intangible assets, net (Note 7)	37,618	39,020
Goodwill (Note 7)	14,438	14,438
Other non-current assets	23,659	28,648
Total assets.	$ 1,458,842	$ 1,382,542
LIABILITIES AND SHAREHOLDERS' EQUITY		
Current Liabilities:		
Notes payable (Note 8).	$ 156	$ —
Accounts payable	142,240	148,973
Accrued liabilities (Note 9)	105,190	104,496
Income taxes payable (Note 10).	4,406	12,579
Deferred income taxes (Note 10)	67	954
Total current liabilities.	252,059	267,002
Other long-term liabilities (Notes 11, 12).	27,171	23,853
Income taxes payable (Note 10).	11,638	15,389
Deferred income taxes (Note 10)	1,807	1,753
Total liabilities.	292,675	307,997
Commitments and contingencies (Note 13)		
Shareholders' Equity:		
Preferred stock; 10,000 shares authorized; none issued and outstanding.	—	—
Common stock (no par value); 125,000 shares authorized; 34,075 and 33,638 issued and outstanding (Note 14).	24,814	3,037
Retained earnings	1,094,690	1,024,611
Accumulated other comprehensive income (Note 17)	46,663	46,897
Total shareholders' equity.	1,166,167	1,074,545
Total liabilities and shareholders' equity.	$ 1,458,842	$ 1,382,542

See accompanying notes to consolidated financial statements

COLUMBIA SPORTSWEAR COMPANY

CONSOLIDATED STATEMENTS OF OPERATIONS
(In thousands, except per share amounts)

	Year Ended December 31,		
	2012	2011	2010
Net sales	$1,669,563	$1,693,985	$1,483,524
Cost of sales	953,169	958,677	854,120
Gross profit	716,394	735,308	629,404
Selling, general and administrative expenses	596,635	614,658	534,068
Net licensing income	13,769	15,756	7,991
Income from operations	133,528	136,406	103,327
Interest income, net	379	1,274	1,564
Income before income tax	133,907	137,680	104,891
Income tax expense (Note 10)	(34,048)	(34,201)	(27,854)
Net income	$ 99,859	$ 103,479	$ 77,037
Earnings per share (Note 16):			
Basic	$ 2.95	$ 3.06	$ 2.28
Diluted	2.93	3.03	2.26
Cash dividends per share:	$ 0.88	$ 0.86	$ 2.24
Weighted average shares outstanding (Note 16):			
Basic	33,840	33,808	33,725
Diluted	34,132	34,204	34,092

See accompanying notes to consolidated financial statements

COLUMBIA SPORTSWEAR COMPANY

CONSOLIDATED STATEMENTS OF COMPREHENSIVE INCOME
(In thousands)

	Year Ended December 31,		
	2012	2011	2010
Net income	$ 99,859	$ 103,479	$ 77,037
Other comprehensive income (loss):			
Unrealized holding losses on available-for-sale securities (net of tax benefit of $4, $23 and $16, respectively)	(7)	(38)	(28)
Unrealized derivative holding gains arising during period (net of tax (expense) benefit of ($917), ($351) and $725, respectively)	753	3,489	1,167
Reclassification to net income of previously deferred (gains) losses on derivative instruments (net of tax expense (benefit) of $746, ($1,507) and ($269), respectively)	(5,498)	5,432	(1,680)
Foreign currency translation adjustments (net of tax (expense) benefit of ($59), ($315) and $670, respectively)	4,518	(8,701)	3,812
Other comprehensive income (loss)	(234)	182	3,271
Comprehensive income	$ 99,625	$ 103,661	$ 80,308

See accompanying notes to consolidated financial statements

COLUMBIA SPORTSWEAR COMPANY

CONSOLIDATED STATEMENTS OF CASH FLOWS
(In thousands)

	Year Ended December 31,		
	2012	2011	2010
Cash flows from operating activities:			
Net income	$ 99,859	$ 103,479	$ 77,037
Adjustments to reconcile net income to net cash provided by operating activities:. .			
Depreciation and amortization	40,892	43,560	38,430
Loss on disposal or impairment of property, plant, and equipment	1,582	6,485	3,331
Deferred income taxes	7,140	(3,582)	(22,610)
Stock-based compensation	7,833	7,870	6,730
Excess tax benefit from employee stock plans.	(1,016)	(1,828)	(498)
Changes in operating assets and liabilities:			
Accounts receivable	18,166	(54,334)	(69,500)
Inventories.	2,951	(55,223)	(87,265)
Prepaid expenses and other current assets.	(2,025)	(10,186)	3,856
Other assets	(1,259)	(4,520)	(1,566)
Accounts payable	(12,330)	19,081	26,028
Accrued liabilities	(5,199)	17,630	34,224
Income taxes payable	(11,052)	(7,010)	9,018
Other liabilities	3,126	2,374	6,302
Net cash provided by operating activities	148,668	63,796	23,517
Cash flows from investing activities:			
Purchases of short-term investments	(83,969)	(46,349)	(81,671)
Sales of short-term investments	42,319	112,070	35,601
Capital expenditures.	(50,491)	(78,404)	(28,838)
Proceeds from sale of property, plant, and equipment	7,099	168	42
Acquisitions, net of cash acquired	—	—	(16,315)
Net cash used in investing activities	(85,042)	(12,515)	(91,181)
Cash flows from financing activities:			
Proceeds from credit facilities	100,654	119,384	31,680
Repayments on credit facilities	(100,498)	(119,384)	(31,680)
Proceeds from issuance of common stock under employee stock plans	14,600	10,991	7,333
Tax payments related to restricted stock unit issuances.	(1,486)	(2,974)	(853)
Excess tax benefit from employee stock plans.	1,016	1,828	498
Repurchase of common stock.	(206)	(20,000)	(13,838)
Cash dividends paid	(29,780)	(29,075)	(75,439)
Net cash used in financing activities	(15,700)	(39,230)	(82,299)
Net effect of exchange rate changes on cash	1,821	(5,274)	(2,444)
Net increase (decrease) in cash and cash equivalents	49,747	6,777	(152,407)
Cash and cash equivalents, beginning of year.	241,034	234,257	386,664
Cash and cash equivalents, end of year	$ 290,781	$ 241,034	$ 234,257
Supplemental disclosures of cash flow information:			
Cash paid during the year for income taxes	$ 43,696	$ 42,405	$ 34,924
Supplemental disclosures of non-cash investing activities:			
Capital expenditures incurred but not yet paid.	5,313	952	1,001

See accompanying notes to consolidated financial statements

COLUMBIA SPORTSWEAR COMPANY

CONSOLIDATED STATEMENTS OF SHAREHOLDERS' EQUITY
(In thousands)

| | Common Stock | | | Accumulated Other | |
	Shares Outstanding	Amount	Retained Earnings	Comprehensive Income	Total
BALANCE, JANUARY 1, 2010	33,736	$ 836	$ 952,948	$ 43,444	$ 997,228
Net income	—	—	77,037	—	77,037
Other comprehensive income	—	—	—	3,271	3,271
Cash dividends ($2.24 per share)	—	—	(75,439)	—	(75,439)
Issuance of common stock under employee stock plans, net	240	6,480	—	—	6,480
Tax adjustment from stock plans	—	505	—	—	505
Stock-based compensation expense	—	6,730	—	—	6,730
Repurchase of common stock	(293)	(9,499)	(4,339)	—	(13,838)
BALANCE, DECEMBER 31, 2010	33,683	5,052	950,207	46,715	1,001,974
Net income	—	—	103,479	—	103,479
Other comprehensive income	—	—	—	182	182
Cash dividends ($0.86 per share)	—	—	(29,075)	—	(29,075)
Issuance of common stock under employee stock plans, net	353	8,017	—	—	8,017
Tax adjustment from stock plans	—	2,098	—	—	2,098
Stock-based compensation expense	—	7,870	—	—	7,870
Repurchase of common stock	(398)	(20,000)	—	—	(20,000)
BALANCE, DECEMBER 31, 2011	33,638	3,037	1,024,611	46,897	1,074,545
Net income	—	—	99,859	—	99,859
Other comprehensive loss	—	—	—	(234)	(234)
Cash dividends ($0.88 per share)	—	—	(29,780)	—	(29,780)
Issuance of common stock under employee stock plans, net	441	13,114	—	—	13,114
Tax adjustment from stock plans	—	1,036	—	—	1,036
Stock-based compensation expense	—	7,833	—	—	7,833
Repurchase of common stock	(4)	(206)	—	—	(206)
BALANCE, DECEMBER 31, 2012	34,075	$ 24,814	$1,094,690	$ 46,663	$ 1,166,167

See accompanying notes to consolidated financial statements

COLUMBIA SPORTSWEAR COMPANY

NOTES TO CONSOLIDATED FINANCIAL STATEMENTS

NOTE 1—BASIS OF PRESENTATION AND ORGANIZATION

Nature of the business:

Columbia Sportswear Company is a global leader in the design, sourcing, marketing and distribution of active outdoor apparel, footwear, accessories and equipment.

Principles of consolidation:

The consolidated financial statements include the accounts of Columbia Sportswear Company and its wholly owned subsidiaries (the "Company"). All significant intercompany balances and transactions have been eliminated in consolidation.

Estimates and assumptions:

The preparation of financial statements in conformity with accounting principles generally accepted in the United States of America (U.S. GAAP) requires management to make estimates and assumptions that affect the reported amounts of assets and liabilities and disclosure of contingent assets and liabilities at the date of the consolidated financial statements and the reported amounts of revenues and expenses during the reporting period. Actual results may differ from these estimates and assumptions. Some of these more significant estimates relate to revenue recognition, including sales returns and claims from customers, allowance for doubtful accounts, excess, slow-moving and close-out inventories, product warranty, long-lived and intangible assets, income taxes and stock-based compensation.

NOTE 2—SUMMARY OF SIGNIFICANT ACCOUNTING POLICIES

Cash and cash equivalents:

Cash and cash equivalents are stated at fair value or at cost, which approximates fair value, and include investments with original maturities of 90 days or less at the date of acquisition. At December 31, 2012, cash and cash equivalents consisted of cash, money market funds, time deposits, certificates of deposit, repurchase agreements and municipal bonds with original maturities ranging from overnight to less than 90 days. At December 31, 2011, cash and cash equivalents consisted of cash, money market funds and time deposits with original maturities ranging from overnight to less than 90 days.

Investments:

At December 31, 2012, short-term investments consisted of certificates of deposit and municipal bonds with original maturities greater than 90 days, and variable-rate demand notes that generally mature up to approximately 35 years from the purchase date. Investments with maturities beyond one year may be classified as short-term based on their highly liquid nature and because such marketable securities represent the investment of cash that is available for current operations. At December 31, 2011, short-term investments consisted of time deposits with original maturities greater than 90 days. These investments are considered available for use in current operations. All short-term investments are classified as available-for-sale securities and are recorded at fair value with any unrealized gains and losses reported, net of tax, in other comprehensive income. Realized gains or losses are determined based on the specific identification method.

At December 31, 2012 and 2011, long-term investments included in other non-current assets consisted of mutual fund shares held to offset liabilities to participants in the Company's deferred compensation plan. The investments are classified as long-term because the related deferred compensation liabilities are not expected to be paid within the next year. These investments are classified as trading securities and are recorded at fair value with unrealized gains and losses reported in operating expenses, which are offset against gains and losses resulting from changes in corresponding deferred compensation liabilities to participants.

Accounts receivable:

Accounts receivable have been reduced by an allowance for doubtful accounts. The Company makes ongoing estimates of the collectability of accounts receivable and maintains an allowance for estimated losses resulting from the inability of the Company's customers to make required payments.

COLUMBIA SPORTSWEAR COMPANY

NOTES TO CONSOLIDATED FINANCIAL STATEMENTS—(Continued)

Inventories:

Inventories are carried at the lower of cost or market. Cost is determined using the first-in, first-out method. The Company periodically reviews its inventories for excess, close-out or slow moving items and makes provisions as necessary to properly reflect inventory value.

Property, plant, and equipment:

Property, plant and equipment are stated at cost, net of accumulated depreciation. Depreciation is provided using the straight-line method over the estimated useful lives of the assets. The principal estimated useful lives are: buildings and building improvements, 15-30 years; land improvements, 15 years; furniture and fixtures, 3-10 years; and machinery and equipment, 3-5 years. Leasehold improvements are depreciated over the lesser of the estimated useful life of the improvement, which is most commonly 7 years, or the remaining term of the underlying lease.

Improvements to property, plant and equipment that substantially extend the useful life of the asset are capitalized. Repair and maintenance costs are expensed as incurred. Internal and external costs directly related to the development of internal-use software during the application development stage, including costs incurred for third party contractors and employee compensation, are capitalized and depreciated over a 3-7 year estimated useful life.

Impairment of long-lived assets:

Long-lived assets are amortized over their estimated useful lives and are measured for impairment only when events or circumstances indicate the carrying value may be impaired. In these cases, the Company estimates the future undiscounted cash flows to be derived from the asset or asset group to determine whether a potential impairment exists. When reviewing for retail store impairment, identifiable cash flows are measured at the individual store level. If the sum of the estimated undiscounted cash flows is less than the carrying value of the asset, the Company recognizes an impairment loss, measured as the amount by which the carrying value exceeds the estimated fair value of the asset. Impairment charges for long-lived assets are included in selling, general and administrative ("SG&A") expense and were $1,653,000, $6,211,000 and $3,003,000 for the years ended December 31, 2012, 2011 and 2010, respectively. All charges during the three years ended December 31, 2012 were recorded in the United States and EMEA regions.

Intangible assets and goodwill:

Goodwill and intangible assets with indefinite useful lives are not amortized but are periodically evaluated for impairment. Intangible assets that are determined to have finite lives are amortized using the straight-line method over their useful lives and are measured for impairment only when events or circumstances indicate the carrying value may be impaired.

Impairment of goodwill and intangible assets:

The Company reviews and tests its goodwill and intangible assets with indefinite useful lives for impairment in the fourth quarter of each year and when events or changes in circumstances indicate that the carrying amount of such assets may be impaired. The Company's intangible assets with indefinite lives consist of trademarks and tradenames. Substantially all of the Company's goodwill is recorded in the United States segment and impairment testing for goodwill is performed at the reporting unit level. In the impairment test for goodwill, the two-step process first compares the estimated fair value of the reporting unit with the carrying amount of that reporting unit. The Company estimates the fair value of its reporting units using a combination of discounted cash flow analysis, comparisons with the market values of similar publicly traded companies and other operating performance based valuation methods, as necessary. If step one indicates impairment, step two compares the estimated fair value of the reporting unit to the estimated fair value of all reporting unit assets and liabilities, except goodwill, to determine the implied fair value of goodwill. The Company calculates impairment as the excess of carrying amount of goodwill over the implied fair value of goodwill. In the impairment test for trademarks, the Company compares the estimated fair value of the asset to the carrying amount. The fair value of trademarks and tradenames is estimated using the relief from royalty approach, a standard form of discounted cash flow analysis used in the valuation of

COLUMBIA SPORTSWEAR COMPANY

NOTES TO CONSOLIDATED FINANCIAL STATEMENTS—(Continued)

trademarks. If the carrying amount of trademarks exceeds the estimated fair value, the Company calculates impairment as the excess of carrying amount over the estimate of fair value.

If events or circumstances indicate the carrying value of intangible assets with finite lives may be impaired, the Company estimates the future undiscounted cash flows to be derived from the asset or asset group to determine whether a potential impairment exists. If the sum of the estimated undiscounted cash flows is less than the carrying value of the asset the Company recognizes an impairment loss, measured as the amount by which the carrying value exceeds the estimated fair value of the asset.

Impairment charges are classified as a component of SG&A expense. The fair value estimates are based on a number of factors, including assumptions and estimates for projected sales, income, cash flows, discount rates and other operating performance measures. Changes in estimates or the application of alternative assumptions could produce significantly different results. These assumptions and estimates may change in the future due to changes in economic conditions, changes in the Company's ability to meet sales and profitability objectives or changes in the Company's business operations or strategic direction.

Income taxes:

Income taxes are provided on financial statement earnings for financial reporting purposes. Income taxes are based on amounts of taxes payable or refundable in the current year and on expected future tax consequences of events that are recognized in the financial statements in different periods than they are recognized in tax returns. As a result of timing of recognition and measurement differences between financial accounting standards and income tax laws, temporary differences arise between amounts of pre-tax financial statement income and taxable income and between reported amounts of assets and liabilities in the Consolidated Balance Sheets and their respective tax bases. Deferred income tax assets and liabilities reported in the Consolidated Balance Sheets reflect estimated future tax effects attributable to these temporary differences and to net operating loss and net capital loss carryforwards, based on tax rates expected to be in effect for years in which the differences are expected to be settled or realized. Realization of deferred tax assets is dependent on future taxable income in specific jurisdictions. Valuation allowances are used to reduce deferred tax assets to amounts considered likely to be realized. U.S. deferred income taxes are not provided on undistributed income of foreign subsidiaries, where such earnings are considered to be indefinitely invested, or to the extent such recognition would result in a deferred tax asset.

Accrued income taxes in the Consolidated Balance Sheets include unrecognized income tax benefits relating to uncertain tax positions, including related interest and penalties, appropriately classified as current or noncurrent. The Company recognizes the tax benefit from an uncertain tax position if it is more likely than not that the tax position will be sustained on examination by the relevant taxing authority based on the technical merits of the position. The tax benefits recognized in the financial statements from such positions are then measured based on the largest benefit that has a greater than 50% likelihood of being realized upon ultimate settlement with the relevant tax authority. In making this determination, the Company assumes that the taxing authority will examine the position and that they will have full knowledge of all relevant information. The provision for income taxes also includes estimates of interest and penalties related to uncertain tax positions.

Derivatives:

The effective portion of changes in fair values of outstanding cash flow hedges is recorded in other comprehensive income until earnings are affected by the hedged transaction, and any ineffective portion is included in current income. In most cases amounts recorded in other comprehensive income will be released to earnings some time after maturity of the related derivative. The Consolidated Statements of Operations classification of effective hedge results is the same as that of the underlying exposure. Results of hedges of product costs are recorded in cost of sales when the underlying hedged transaction affects earnings. Unrealized derivative gains and losses, which are recorded in assets and liabilities, respectively, are non-cash items and therefore are taken into account in the preparation of the Consolidated Statements of Cash Flows based on their respective balance sheet classifications. See Note 19 for more information on derivatives and risk management.

COLUMBIA SPORTSWEAR COMPANY

NOTES TO CONSOLIDATED FINANCIAL STATEMENTS—(Continued)

is effective for annual and interim impairment tests performed for fiscal years beginning after September 15, 2012, although early adoption is permitted. The Company does not expect the adoption of this standard to have a material effect on the Company's financial position, results of operations or cash flows.

In February 2013, the FASB issued ASU No. 2013-02, *Comprehensive Income (Topic 220): Reporting of Amounts Reclassified Out of Accumulated Other Comprehensive Income*. This ASU requires an entity to disclose additional information with respect to changes in accumulated other comprehensive income (AOCI) balances by component. In addition, an entity is required to present, either on the face of the financial statements or in the notes, significant amounts reclassified out of AOCI by the respective line items of net income, but only if the amount reclassified is required to be reclassified in its entirety in the same reporting period. For amounts that are not required to be reclassified in their entirety to net income, an entity is required to cross-reference to other disclosures that provide additional details about those amounts. This ASU is effective for interim and annual periods beginning after December 15, 2012. The Company does not expect the adoption of this standard to have a material effect on the Company's financial position, results of operations or cash flows, but it will require additional disclosure.

NOTE 3—CONCENTRATIONS

Trade Receivables

No single customer accounted for 10% or more of consolidated accounts receivable at December 31, 2012 or 2011. No single customer accounted for 10% or more of consolidated revenues for any of the years ended December 31, 2012, 2011 or 2010.

Derivatives

The Company uses derivative instruments to hedge the currency exchange rate risk of anticipated transactions denominated in non-functional currencies that are designated and qualify as cash flow hedges. The Company also uses derivative instruments to economically hedge the currency exchange rate risk of certain investment positions, to hedge balance sheet re-measurement risk and to hedge other anticipated transactions that do not qualify as cash flow hedges. At December 31, 2012, the Company's derivative contracts had a remaining maturity of approximately one year or less. The maximum net exposure to any single counterparty, which is generally limited to the aggregate unrealized gain of all contracts with that counterparty, was less than $4,000,000 at December 31, 2012. All of the Company's derivative counterparties have investment grade credit ratings and as a result, the Company does not require collateral to facilitate transactions. See Note 19 for further disclosures concerning derivatives.

Country and supplier concentrations

The Company's products are produced by independent factories located outside the United States, principally in Southeast Asia. Apparel is manufactured in approximately 20 countries, with Vietnam and China accounting for approximately 67% of 2012 global apparel production. Footwear is manufactured in three countries, with China and Vietnam accounting for approximately 93% of 2012 global footwear production. The five largest apparel factory groups accounted for approximately 25% of 2012 global apparel production, with the largest factory group accounting for 9% of 2012 global apparel production. The five largest footwear factory groups accounted for approximately 79% of 2012 global footwear production, with the largest factory group accounting for 34% of 2012 global footwear production. In addition, a single vendor supplies the majority of the zippers used in the Company's products. These companies, however, have multiple factory locations, many of which are in different countries, thus reducing the risk that unfavorable conditions at a single factory or location will have a material adverse effect on the Company.

NOTE 4—ACCOUNTS RECEIVABLE, NET

Accounts receivable, net, is as follows (in thousands):

COLUMBIA SPORTSWEAR COMPANY

NOTES TO CONSOLIDATED FINANCIAL STATEMENTS—(Continued)

	December 31,	
	2012	2011
Trade accounts receivable.	$ 341,701	$ 359,083
Allowance for doubtful accounts	(7,377)	(7,545)
Accounts receivable, net.	$ 334,324	$ 351,538

NOTE 5—INVENTORIES, NET

Inventories, net, consisted of the following (in thousands):

	December 31,	
	2012	2011
Raw materials	$ 1,633	$ 2,044
Work in process.	1,969	1,240
Finished goods	359,723	361,915
	$ 363,325	$ 365,199

NOTE 6—PROPERTY, PLANT, AND EQUIPMENT, NET

Property, plant, and equipment consisted of the following (in thousands):

	December 31,	
	2012	2011
Land and improvements.	$ 20,036	$ 20,690
Building and improvements.	166,365	155,672
Machinery and equipment	206,805	198,387
Furniture and fixtures.	54,914	50,108
Leasehold improvements.	72,426	65,476
Construction in progress	43,021	36,463
	563,567	526,796
Less accumulated depreciation	(303,043)	(275,886)
	$ 260,524	$ 250,910

NOTE 7—INTANGIBLE ASSETS, NET AND GOODWILL

Intangible assets that are determined to have finite lives include patents and purchased technology and are amortized over their estimated useful lives, which is approximately 10 years. Intangible assets with indefinite useful lives include trademarks and tradenames and are not amortized but are periodically evaluated for impairment.

Identifiable intangible assets consisted of the following (in thousands):

	December 31,	
	2012	2011
Intangible assets subject to amortization:		
Gross carrying amount.	$ 14,198	$ 14,198
Accumulated amortization.	(4,001)	(2,599)
Net carrying amount	10,197	11,599
Intangible assets not subject to amortization	27,421	27,421
Intangible assets, net.	$ 37,618	$ 39,020

COLUMBIA SPORTSWEAR COMPANY

NOTES TO CONSOLIDATED FINANCIAL STATEMENTS—(Continued)

Amortization expense for the years ended December 31, 2012, 2011, and 2010 was $1,402,000, $1,403,000 and $553,000, respectively. Annual amortization expense for intangible assets subject to amortization is estimated to be $1,330,000 in 2013 through 2017.

At December 31, 2012, 2011 and 2010, the Company determined that its goodwill and intangible assets were not impaired.

NOTE 8—SHORT-TERM BORROWINGS AND CREDIT LINES

The Company has a domestic credit agreement for an unsecured, committed $125,000,000 revolving line of credit. The maturity date of this agreement is July 1, 2016. Interest, payable monthly, is based on the Company's applicable funded debt ratio, ranging from LIBOR plus 100 to 175 basis points. This line of credit requires the Company to comply with certain financial covenants covering net income, tangible net worth and borrowing basis. If the Company is in default, it is prohibited from paying dividends or repurchasing common stock. At December 31, 2012, the Company was in compliance with all associated covenants. At December 31, 2012 and 2011, no balance was outstanding under this line of credit.

The Company's Canadian subsidiary has available an unsecured and uncommitted line of credit guaranteed by the parent company providing for borrowing up to a maximum of C$30,000,000 (US$30,239,000) at December 31, 2012. The revolving line accrues interest at the bank's Canadian prime rate. At December 31, 2012, $156,000 was outstanding under this line of credit. At December 31, 2011, there was no balance outstanding under this line.

The Company's European subsidiary has available two separate unsecured and uncommitted lines of credit guaranteed by the parent company providing for borrowing up to a maximum of €25,800,000 and €5,000,000, respectively (combined US$40,633,000) at December 31, 2012, of which US$3,694,000 of the €5,000,000 line is designated as a European customs guarantee. These lines accrue interest based on the European Central Bank refinancing rate plus 50 basis points and Euro Overnight Index Average plus 75 basis points, respectively. There was no balance outstanding under either line at December 31, 2012 or 2011.

The Company's Japanese subsidiary has an unsecured and uncommitted line of credit guaranteed by the parent company providing for borrowing up to a maximum of US$5,000,000 at December 31, 2012. The revolving line accrues interest at LIBOR plus 110 basis points. There was no balance outstanding under this line at December 31, 2012 or 2011.

On September 27, 2012, the Company's Korean subsidiary increased the maximum borrowing permitted under its unsecured and uncommitted line of credit agreement to US$30,000,000. The revolving line accrues interest at the Korean three-month CD rate plus 220 basis points. There was no balance outstanding under this line at December 31, 2012 or 2011.

Off-Balance Sheet Arrangements

The Company has arrangements in place to facilitate the import and purchase of inventory through import letters of credit. The Company has available unsecured and uncommitted import letters of credit in the aggregate amount of $5,000,000 subject to annual renewal. At December 31, 2012, no balance was outstanding under these letters of credit.

NOTE 9—ACCRUED LIABILITIES

Accrued liabilities consisted of the following (in thousands):

	December 31,	
	2012	2011
Accrued salaries, bonus, vacation and other benefits	$ 55,728	$ 55,958
Accrued import duties	15,023	11,258
Product warranties	10,209	10,452
Other	24,230	26,828
	$ 105,190	$ 104,496

COLUMBIA SPORTSWEAR COMPANY

NOTES TO CONSOLIDATED FINANCIAL STATEMENTS—(Continued)

A reconciliation of product warranties is as follows (in thousands):

	Year Ended December 31,		
	2012	2011	2010
Balance at beginning of period.	$ 10,452	$ 10,256	$ 12,112
Provision for warranty claims	4,905	4,758	1,371
Warranty claims	(5,272)	(4,468)	(3,104)
Other.	124	(94)	(123)
Balance at end of period.	$ 10,209	$ 10,452	$ 10,256

NOTE 10—INCOME TAXES

Consolidated income from continuing operations before income taxes consisted of the following (in thousands):

	Year Ended December 31,		
	2012	2011	2010
U.S. operations.	$ 73,625	$ 68,412	$ 59,881
Foreign operations	60,282	69,268	45,010
Income before income tax.	$ 133,907	$ 137,680	$ 104,891

The components of the provision (benefit) for income taxes consisted of the following (in thousands):

	Year Ended December 31,		
	2012	2011	2010
Current:			
Federal.	$ 14,365	$ 16,384	$ 24,419
State and local	876	1,995	4,060
Non-U.S.	12,448	19,508	23,253
	27,689	37,887	51,732
Deferred:			
Federal.	5,806	407	(18,405)
State and local	690	229	(1,223)
Non-U.S.	(137)	(4,322)	(4,250)
	6,359	(3,686)	(23,878)
Income tax expense	$ 34,048	$ 34,201	$ 27,854

The following is a reconciliation of the statutory federal income tax rate to the effective rate reported in the financial statements:

	Year Ended December 31,		
	2012	2011	2010
	(percent of income)		
Provision for federal income taxes at the statutory rate	35.0%	35.0%	35.0%
State and local income taxes, net of federal benefit	1.7	1.5	2.7
Non-U.S. income taxed at different rates	(5.4)	(6.5)	(2.3)
Foreign tax credits	—	(1.8)	(3.5)
Reduction of unrecognized tax benefits	(4.3)	(3.5)	(4.0)
Research credits	(1.7)	(0.6)	(0.6)
Other	0.1	0.7	(0.7)
Actual provision for income taxes	25.4%	24.8%	26.6%

COLUMBIA SPORTSWEAR COMPANY

NOTES TO CONSOLIDATED FINANCIAL STATEMENTS—(Continued)

Significant components of the Company's deferred taxes consisted of the following (in thousands):

	December 31,		
	2012		**2011**
Deferred tax assets:			
Non-deductible accruals and allowances	$ 31,139	$	30,307
Capitalized inventory costs.	25,294		25,814
Stock compensation	6,633		6,283
Net operating loss carryforwards	6,198		6,364
Depreciation and amortization	1,568		1,693
Tax credits.	10,398		12,702
Other.	755		1,121
Gross deferred tax assets	81,985		84,284
Valuation allowance	(6,935)		(6,690)
Net deferred tax assets.	75,050		77,594
Deferred tax liabilities:			
Deductible accruals and allowance.	—		(801)
Depreciation and amortization	(16,802)		(12,320)
Foreign currency loss	(2,313)		(2,494)
Other.	(587)		(596)
Gross deferred tax liabilities	(19,702)		(16,211)
Total net deferred taxes	$ 55,348	$	61,383

We record net deferred tax assets to the extent we believe these assets will more likely than not be realized. In making such a determination, we consider all available positive and negative evidence, including future reversals of existing taxable temporary differences, projected future taxable income, tax-planning strategies, and results of recent operations. The Company had net operating loss carryforwards at December 31, 2012 and 2011 in certain international tax jurisdictions of $56,749,000 and $58,272,000, respectively, which will begin to expire in 2015. The net operating losses result in a deferred tax asset of $6,198,000 and $6,364,000 at December 31, 2012 and 2011, respectively, both of which were subject to a 100% valuation allowance. To the extent that the Company reverses a portion of the valuation allowance, the adjustment would be recorded as a reduction to income tax expense.

Non-current deferred tax assets of $6,293,000 and $11,605,000 are included as a component of other non-current assets in the consolidated balance sheet at December 31, 2012 and 2011, respectively.

The Company had undistributed earnings of foreign subsidiaries of approximately $284,611,000 at December 31, 2012 for which deferred taxes have not been provided. Such earnings are considered indefinitely invested outside of the United States. If these earnings were repatriated to the United States, the earnings would be subject to U.S. taxation. The amount of the unrecognized deferred tax liability associated with the undistributed earnings was approximately $70,218,000 at December 31, 2012. The unrecognized deferred tax liability approximates the excess of the United States tax liability over the creditable foreign taxes paid that would result from a full remittance of undistributed earnings.

A reconciliation of the beginning and ending amount of gross unrecognized tax benefits is as follows (in thousands):

COLUMBIA SPORTSWEAR COMPANY

NOTES TO CONSOLIDATED FINANCIAL STATEMENTS—(Continued)

	December 31,		
	2012	2011	2010
Balance at beginning of period	$ 14,316	$ 18,694	$ 20,183
Increases related to prior year tax positions	3,208	43	893
Decreases related to prior year tax positions	(19)	(141)	(27)
Increases related to current year tax positions	2,049	1,388	1,278
Settlements	(1,817)	(649)	—
Expiration of statute of limitations	(5,306)	(5,019)	(3,633)
Balance at end of period	$ 12,431	$ 14,316	$ 18,694

Unrecognized tax benefits of $10,328,000 and $12,735,000 would affect the effective tax rate if recognized at December 31, 2012 and 2011, respectively.

The Company conducts business globally, and as a result, the Company or one or more of its subsidiaries files income tax returns in the U.S. federal jurisdiction and various state and foreign jurisdictions. The Company is subject to examination by taxing authorities throughout the world, including such major jurisdictions as Canada, China, France, Germany, Hong Kong, Italy, Japan, South Korea, Switzerland, the United Kingdom and the United States. The Company has effectively settled U.S. tax examinations of all years through 2008, with the exception of a 2008 income tax refund claim filed in 2012. The Company received a notification from the Internal Revenue Service ("IRS") dated February 15, 2013 indicating that its 2011 United States federal income tax return and its 2008-2010 amended federal income tax returns filed during 2012 have been selected for audit. Internationally, the Company has effectively settled Canadian and Korean tax examinations of all years through 2008, Swiss and French tax examinations of all years through 2009 and Japanese tax examinations of all years through 2010. The Company is not currently under examination in any major jurisdictions. The Company does not anticipate that adjustments relative to ongoing tax audits will result in a material change to its consolidated financial position, results of operations or cash flows.

Due to the potential for resolution of income tax audits currently in progress, and the expiration of various statutes of limitation, it is reasonably possible that the unrecognized tax benefits balance may change within the twelve months following December 31, 2012 by a range of zero to $10,136,000. Open tax years, including those previously mentioned, contain matters that could be subject to differing interpretations of applicable tax laws and regulations as they relate to the amount, timing, or inclusion of revenue and expenses or the sustainability of income tax credits for a given examination cycle.

The Company recognizes interest expense and penalties related to income tax matters in income tax expense. The Company recognized a net reversal of accrued interest and penalties of $357,000 in 2012, a net reversal of accrued interest and penalties of $501,000 in 2011 and net accrued interest and penalties of $780,000 in 2010, all related to uncertain tax positions. The Company had $3,077,000 and $3,434,000 of accrued interest and penalties related to uncertain tax positions at December 31, 2012 and 2011, respectively.

NOTE 11—OTHER LONG-TERM LIABILITIES

Other long-term liabilities consisted of the following (in thousands):

	December 31,	
	2012	2011
Straight-line and deferred rent liabilities	$ 20,395	$ 18,028
Asset retirement obligations	1,849	1,565
Deferred compensation plan liability (Note 12)	4,080	2,521
Other	847	1,739
	$ 27,171	$ 23,853

NOTE 12—RETIREMENT SAVINGS PLANS

COLUMBIA SPORTSWEAR COMPANY

NOTES TO CONSOLIDATED FINANCIAL STATEMENTS—(Continued)

401(k) Profit-Sharing Plan

The Company has a 401(k) profit-sharing plan, which covers substantially all U.S. employees. Participation begins the first day of the quarter following completion of 30 days of service. The Company may elect to make discretionary matching and/or non-matching contributions. All Company contributions to the plan as determined by the Board of Directors totaled $4,966,000, $5,223,000 and $4,443,000 for the years ended December 31, 2012, 2011 and 2010, respectively.

Deferred Compensation Plan

The Company sponsors a nonqualified retirement savings plan for certain senior management employees whose contributions to the tax qualified 401(k) plan would be limited by provisions of the Internal Revenue Code. This plan allows participants to defer receipt of a portion of their salary and incentive compensation and to receive matching contributions for a portion of the deferred amounts. Company contributions to the plan totaled $259,000, $245,000 and $155,000 for the years ended December 31, 2012, 2011 and 2010, respectively. Participants earn a return on their deferred compensation based on investment earnings of participant-selected mutual funds. Changes in the market value of the participants' investment selections are recorded as an adjustment to deferred compensation liabilities, with an offset to compensation expense. Deferred compensation, including accumulated earnings on the participant-directed investment selections, is distributable in cash at participant-specified dates or upon retirement, death, disability or termination of employment. At December 31, 2012 and 2011, the liability to participants under this plan was $4,080,000 and $2,521,000, respectively, and was recorded in other long-term liabilities. The current portion of the participant liability at December 31, 2012 and 2011 was not material.

The Company has purchased specific mutual funds in the same amounts as the participant-directed investment selections underlying the deferred compensation liabilities. These investment securities and earnings thereon, held in an irrevocable trust, are intended to provide a source of funds to meet the deferred compensation obligations, subject to claims of creditors in the event of the Company's insolvency. The mutual funds are recorded at fair value in other non-current assets. At December 31, 2012 and 2011, the fair value of the mutual fund investments was $4,080,000 and $2,521,000, respectively. Realized and unrealized gains and losses on the mutual fund investments are offset against gains and losses resulting from changes in corresponding deferred compensation liabilities to participants.

NOTE 13—COMMITMENTS AND CONTINGENCIES

Operating Leases

The Company leases, among other things, retail space, office space, warehouse facilities, storage space, vehicles and equipment. Generally, the base lease terms are between 5 and 10 years. Certain lease agreements contain scheduled rent escalation clauses in their future minimum lease payments. Future minimum lease payments are recognized on a straight-line basis over the minimum lease term and the pro rata portion of scheduled rent escalations is included in other long-term liabilities. Certain retail space lease agreements provide for additional rents based on a percentage of annual sales in excess of stipulated minimums ("percentage rent"). Certain lease agreements require the Company to pay real estate taxes, insurance, common area maintenance ("CAM"), and other costs, collectively referred to as operating costs, in addition to base rent. Percentage rent and operating costs are recognized as incurred in SG&A expense in the Consolidated Statements of Operations. Certain lease agreements also contain lease incentives, such as tenant improvement allowances and rent holidays. The Company recognizes the benefits related to the lease incentives on a straight-line basis over the applicable lease term.

Rent expense, including percentage rent but excluding operating costs for which the Company is obligated, consisted of the following (in thousands):

COLUMBIA SPORTSWEAR COMPANY

NOTES TO CONSOLIDATED FINANCIAL STATEMENTS—(Continued)

	Year Ended December 31,		
	2012	**2011**	**2010**
Rent expense included in SG&A	$ 51,853	$ 46,869	$ 39,898
Rent expense included in cost of sales..................	1,528	1,429	1,351
	$ 53,381	$ 48,298	$ 41,249

Approximate future minimum payments, including rent escalation clauses and stores that are not yet open, on all lease obligations at December 31, 2012, are as follows (in thousands). Operating lease obligations listed below do not include percentage rent, real estate taxes, insurance, CAM, and other costs for which the Company is obligated. These operating lease commitments are not reflected on the Consolidated Balance Sheets.

2013..	$	42,771
2014..		37,477
2015..		33,842
2016..		32,029
2017..		31,203
Thereafter		92,739
	$	270,061

Inventory Purchase Obligations

Inventory purchase obligations consist of open production purchase orders for sourced apparel, footwear, accessories and equipment, and raw material commitments not included in open production purchase orders. At December 31, 2012 inventory purchase obligations were $255,299,000. To support certain inventory purchase obligations, the Company maintains unsecured and uncommitted lines of credit available for issuing import letters of credit. At December 31, 2012 the Company had no balance outstanding under these letters of credit.

Litigation

The Company is a party to various legal claims, actions and complaints from time to time. Although the ultimate resolution of legal proceedings cannot be predicted with certainty, management believes that disposition of these matters will not have a material adverse effect on the Company's consolidated financial statements.

Indemnities and Guarantees

During its normal course of business, the Company has made certain indemnities, commitments and guarantees under which it may be required to make payments in relation to certain transactions. These include (i) intellectual property indemnities to the Company's customers and licensees in connection with the use, sale and/or license of Company products, (ii) indemnities to various lessors in connection with facility leases for certain claims arising from such facility or lease, (iii) indemnities to customers, vendors and service providers pertaining to claims based on the negligence or willful misconduct of the Company, (iv) executive severance arrangements and (v) indemnities involving the accuracy of representations and warranties in certain contracts. The duration of these indemnities, commitments and guarantees varies, and in certain cases, may be indefinite. The majority of these indemnities, commitments and guarantees do not provide for any limitation of the maximum potential for future payments the Company could be obligated to make. The Company has not recorded any liability for these indemnities, commitments and guarantees in the accompanying Consolidated Balance Sheets.

NOTE 14—SHAREHOLDERS' EQUITY

Since the inception of the Company's stock repurchase plan in 2004 through December 31, 2012, the Company's Board of Directors has authorized the repurchase of $500,000,000 of the Company's common stock. As of December 31, 2012, the Company had repurchased 9,593,278 shares under this program at an aggregate purchase price of approximately

COLUMBIA SPORTSWEAR COMPANY

NOTES TO CONSOLIDATED FINANCIAL STATEMENTS—(Continued)

$441,443,000. During the year ended December 31, 2012, the Company repurchased an aggregate of $206,000 of common stock under the stock repurchase plan. Shares of the Company's common stock may be purchased in the open market or through privately negotiated transactions, subject to market conditions. The repurchase program does not obligate the Company to acquire any specific number of shares or to acquire shares over any specified period of time.

NOTE 15—STOCK-BASED COMPENSATION

The Company's stock incentive plan (the "Plan") provides for issuance of up to 10,400,000 shares of the Company's Common Stock, of which 2,573,748 shares were available for future grants under the Plan at December 31, 2012. The Plan allows for grants of incentive stock options, non-statutory stock options, restricted stock awards, restricted stock units and other stock-based awards. The Company uses original issuance shares to satisfy share-based payments.

Stock-based compensation expense consisted of the following (in thousands):

	Year Ended December 31,		
	2012	2011	2010
Cost of sales	$ 287	$ 282	$ 286
Selling, general and administrative expense	7,546	7,588	6,444
Pre-tax stock-based compensation expense	7,833	7,870	6,730
Income tax benefits	(2,724)	(2,729)	(2,162)
Total stock-based compensation expense, net of tax	$ 5,109	$ 5,141	$ 4,568

No stock-based compensation costs were capitalized for the years ended December 31, 2012, 2011 or 2010.

The Company realized a tax benefit for the deduction from stock-based award transactions of $3,410,000, $4,702,000, and $1,909,000 for the years ended December 31, 2012, 2011 and 2010, respectively.

Stock Options

Options to purchase the Company's common stock are granted at exercise prices equal to or greater than the fair market value of the Company's common stock on the date of grant. Options granted after 2000 and before 2009 generally vest and become exercisable over a period of four years (25 percent on the first anniversary date following the date of grant and monthly thereafter) and expire ten years from the date of the grant, with the exception of most options granted in 2005. Most options granted in 2005 vested and became exercisable one year from the date of grant and expire ten years from the date of grant. Options granted after 2008 generally vest and become exercisable ratably on an annual basis over a period of four years and expire ten years from the date of the grant.

The Company estimates the fair value of stock options using the Black-Scholes model. Key inputs and assumptions used to estimate the fair value of stock options include the exercise price of the award, the expected option term, expected volatility of the Company's stock over the option's expected term, the risk-free interest rate over the option's expected term, and the Company's expected annual dividend yield. The option's expected term is derived from historical option exercise behavior and the option's terms and conditions, which the Company believes provides a reasonable basis for estimating an expected term. The expected volatility is estimated based on observations of the Company's historical volatility over the most recent term commensurate with the expected term. The risk-free interest rate is based on the U.S. Treasury yield approximating the expected term. The dividend yield is based on the anticipated cash dividend payouts. Assumptions are evaluated and revised as necessary to reflect changes in market conditions and the Company's experience. Estimates of fair value are not intended to predict actual future events or the value ultimately realized by people who receive equity awards.

The following table presents the weighted average assumptions for the years ended December 31:

COLUMBIA SPORTSWEAR COMPANY

NOTES TO CONSOLIDATED FINANCIAL STATEMENTS—(Continued)

	2012	2011 [1]	2010
Expected term	4.78 years	5.12 years	4.53 years
Expected stock price volatility	32.20%	30.76%	28.79%
Risk-free interest rate	0.88%	1.84%	1.91%
Expected dividend yield	1.80%	1.31%	1.64%
Weighted average grant date fair value.	$11.57	$16.09	$10.08

[1] During the year ended December 31, 2011, the Company granted two stock option awards totaling 53,720 shares that vest 100% on the fifth anniversary of the grant date. Because the Company did not have sufficient historical exercise data to provide a reasonable basis upon which to estimate the expected term for these grants, the Company utilized the simplified method in developing an estimate of the expected term of these options.

The following table summarizes stock option activity under the Plan:

	Number of Shares	Weighted Average Exercise Price	Weighted Average Remaining Contractual Life	Aggregate Intrinsic Value (in thousands)
Options outstanding at January 1, 2010	1,760,173	$ 42.08	6.25	$ 4,599
Granted	385,924	44.11		
Cancelled.	(77,481)	46.04		
Exercised.	(196,402)	37.34		
Options outstanding at December 31, 2010	1,872,214	42.84	6.33	33,057
Granted	340,973	61.38		
Cancelled.	(40,396)	43.68		
Exercised.	(253,695)	43.32		
Options outstanding at December 31, 2011	1,919,096	46.05	6.25	9,141
Granted	358,169	48.82		
Cancelled.	(172,465)	52.90		
Exercised.	(380,811)	38.34		
Options outstanding at December 31, 2012	1,723,989	$ 47.64	6.15	$ 13,001
Options vested and expected to vest at December 31, 2012	1,672,468	$ 47.51	6.08	$ 12,808
Options exercisable at December 31, 2012	989,092	$ 46.09	4.63	$ 8,708

The aggregate intrinsic value in the table above represents pre-tax intrinsic value that would have been realized if all options had been exercised on the last business day of the period indicated, based on the Company's closing stock price on that day.

Total stock option compensation expense for the years ended December 31, 2012, 2011 and 2010 was $3,180,000, $3,550,000 and $3,348,000, respectively. At December 31, 2012, unrecognized costs related to stock options totaled approximately $5,407,000, before any related tax benefit. The unrecognized costs related to stock options are being amortized over the related vesting period using the straight-line attribution method. Unrecognized costs related to stock options at December 31, 2012 are expected to be recognized over a weighted average period of 2.16 years. The aggregate intrinsic value of stock options exercised was $5,517,000, $4,906,000 and $2,854,000 for the years ended December 31, 2012, 2011 and 2010, respectively. The total cash received as a result of stock option exercises for the years ended December 31, 2012, 2011 and 2010 was $14,600,000, $10,991,000 and $7,333,000, respectively.

Restricted Stock Units

COLUMBIA SPORTSWEAR COMPANY

NOTES TO CONSOLIDATED FINANCIAL STATEMENTS—(Continued)

Service-based restricted stock units are granted at no cost to key employees, and shares granted prior to 2009 generally vest over three years from the date of grant. Service-based restricted stock units granted after 2008 generally vest over a period of four years. Performance-based restricted stock units are granted at no cost to certain members of the Company's senior executive team, excluding the Chairman and the President and Chief Executive Officer. Performance-based restricted stock units granted prior to 2010 generally vest over a performance period of between two and one-half and three years with an additional required service period of one year. Performance-based restricted stock units granted after 2009 generally vest over a performance period of between two and one-half and three years. Restricted stock units vest in accordance with the terms and conditions established by the Compensation Committee of the Board of Directors, and are based on continued service and, in some instances, on individual performance and/or Company performance. For the majority of restricted stock units granted, the number of shares issued on the date the restricted stock units vest is net of the minimum statutory withholding requirements that the Company pays in cash to the appropriate taxing authorities on behalf of its employees. For the years ended December 31, 2012, 2011 and 2010, the Company withheld 30,299, 48,059 and 18,721 shares, respectively, to satisfy $1,486,000, $2,974,000 and $853,000 of employees' tax obligations, respectively.

The fair value of service-based and performance-based restricted stock units is discounted by the present value of the estimated future stream of dividends over the vesting period using the Black-Scholes model. The relevant inputs and assumptions used in the Black-Scholes model to compute the discount are the vesting period, expected annual dividend yield and closing price of the Company's common stock on the date of grant.

The following table presents the weighted average assumptions for the years ended December 31:

	2012	2011	2010
Vesting period.	3.86 years	3.96 years	3.75 years
Expected dividend yield	1.77%	1.33%	1.56%
Estimated average fair value per restricted stock unit granted .	$46.57	$58.37	$43.95

The following table summarizes the restricted stock unit activity under the Plan:

	Number of Shares	Weighted Average Grant Date Fair Value Per Share
Restricted stock units outstanding at January 1, 2010.	286,520	$36.35
Granted	128,525	43.95
Vested	(62,417)	42.95
Forfeited	(23,833)	42.44
Restricted stock units outstanding at December 31, 2010.	328,795	37.63
Granted	145,768	58.37
Vested	(146,951)	38.01
Forfeited	(30,860)	41.79
Restricted stock units outstanding at December 31, 2011.	296,752	47.19
Granted	185,303	46.57
Vested	(91,383)	42.39
Forfeited	(70,114)	46.26
Restricted stock units outstanding at December 31, 2012.	320,558	$48.31

Restricted stock unit compensation expense for the years ended December 31, 2012, 2011 and 2010 was $4,653,000, $4,320,000 and $3,382,000, respectively. At December 31, 2012, unrecognized costs related to restricted stock units totaled approximately $9,570,000, before any related tax benefit. The unrecognized costs related to restricted stock units are being amortized over the related vesting period using the straight-line attribution method. These unrecognized costs at December 31, 2012 are expected to be recognized over a weighted average period of 2.41 years. The total grant date fair value of

COLUMBIA SPORTSWEAR COMPANY

NOTES TO CONSOLIDATED FINANCIAL STATEMENTS—(Continued)

restricted stock units vested during the year ended December 31, 2012, 2011 and 2010 was $3,874,000, $5,586,000 and $2,681,000, respectively.

NOTE 16—EARNINGS PER SHARE

Earnings per share ("EPS"), is presented on both a basic and diluted basis. Basic EPS is based on the weighted average number of common shares outstanding. Diluted EPS reflects the potential dilution that could occur if outstanding securities or other contracts to issue common stock were exercised or converted into common stock. For the calculation of diluted EPS, the basic weighted average number of shares is increased by the dilutive effect of stock options and restricted stock units determined using the treasury stock method.

A reconciliation of the common shares used in the denominator for computing basic and diluted EPS is as follows (in thousands, except per share amounts):

	Year Ended December 31,		
	2012	2011	2010
Weighted average common shares outstanding, used in computing basic earnings per share	33,840	33,808	33,725
Effect of dilutive stock options and restricted stock units	292	396	367
Weighted-average common shares outstanding, used in computing diluted earnings per share	34,132	34,204	34,092
Earnings per share of common stock:			
Basic	$ 2.95	$ 3.06	$ 2.28
Diluted	2.93	3.03	2.26

Stock options and service-based restricted stock units representing 887,186, 452,907 and 480,707 shares of common stock for the years ended December 31, 2012, 2011 and 2010, respectively, were outstanding but were excluded in the computation of diluted EPS because their effect would be anti-dilutive as a result of applying the treasury stock method. In addition, performance-based restricted stock units representing 36,506, 34,448 and 43,323 shares for the years ended December 31, 2012, 2011 and 2010, respectively, were outstanding but were excluded from the computation of diluted EPS because these shares were subject to performance conditions that had not been met.

NOTE 17—ACCUMULATED OTHER COMPREHENSIVE INCOME

Accumulated other comprehensive income, net of applicable taxes, reported on the Company's Consolidated Balance Sheets consists of unrealized gains and losses on available-for-sale securities, unrealized gains and losses on derivative transactions and foreign currency translation adjustments. Accumulated other comprehensive income, net of related tax effects, is as follows (in thousands):

	December 31,		
	2012	2011	2010
Unrealized holding gains (losses) on available-for-sale securities	$ (9)	$ (2)	$ 36
Unrealized holding gains (losses) on derivative transactions	2,505	7,250	(1,671)
Foreign currency translation adjustments	44,167	39,649	48,350
Accumulated other comprehensive income	$ 46,663	$ 46,897	$ 46,715

NOTE 18—SEGMENT INFORMATION

The Company operates in four geographic segments: (1) the United States, (2) Latin America and Asia Pacific ("LAAP"), (3) Europe, Middle East and Africa ("EMEA"), and (4) Canada, which are reflective of the Company's internal

COLUMBIA SPORTSWEAR COMPANY

NOTES TO CONSOLIDATED FINANCIAL STATEMENTS—(Continued)

organization, management, and oversight structure. Each geographic segment operates predominantly in one industry: the design, development, marketing and distribution of active outdoor apparel, footwear, accessories and equipment.

The geographic distribution of the Company's net sales, income before income taxes, interest income (expense), income tax (expense) benefit, and depreciation and amortization expense are summarized in the following tables (in thousands) for the years ended December 31, 2012, 2011 and 2010 and for identifiable assets at December 31, 2012 and 2011. Inter-geographic net sales, which are recorded at a negotiated mark-up and eliminated in consolidation, are not material.

COLUMBIA SPORTSWEAR COMPANY

NOTES TO CONSOLIDATED FINANCIAL STATEMENTS—(Continued)

	2012	2011	2010
Net sales to unrelated entities:			
United States	$ 946,710	$ 947,970	$ 880,990
LAAP	377,545	340,977	263,429
EMEA	230,624	275,416	222,451
Canada	114,684	129,622	116,654
	$ 1,669,563	$ 1,693,985	$ 1,483,524
Income before income taxes:			
United States	$ 68,504	$ 63,847	$ 53,752
LAAP	51,219	46,214	35,635
EMEA	7,993	13,779	5,817
Canada	5,812	12,566	8,123
Interest	379	1,274	1,564
	$ 133,907	$ 137,680	$ 104,891
Interest income (expense), net:			
United States	$ 5,121	$ 4,565	$ 4,664
LAAP	(1,097)	(666)	500
EMEA	293	648	(717)
Canada	(3,938)	(3,273)	(2,883)
	$ 379	$ 1,274	$ 1,564
Income tax (expense) benefit:			
United States	$ (21,961)	$ (19,233)	$ (9,938)
LAAP	(13,792)	(12,163)	(9,325)
EMEA	1,527	(80)	(7,668)
Canada	178	(2,725)	(923)
	$ (34,048)	$ (34,201)	$ (27,854)
Depreciation and amortization expense:			
United States	$ 31,025	$ 33,100	$ 28,634
LAAP	4,214	3,241	2,557
EMEA	4,112	6,292	6,410
Canada	1,541	927	829
	$ 40,892	$ 43,560	$ 38,430
Assets:			
United States	$ 1,031,838	$ 977,792	
LAAP	229,139	242,124	
EMEA	293,878	281,118	
Canada	177,912	179,851	
Total identifiable assets	1,732,767	1,680,885	
Eliminations and reclassifications	(273,925)	(298,343)	
	$ 1,458,842	$ 1,382,542	
Net sales by product category:			
Apparel, accessories and equipment	$ 1,347,005	$ 1,334,883	$ 1,213,301
Footwear	322,558	359,102	270,223
	$ 1,669,563	$ 1,693,985	$ 1,483,524

NOTE 19—FINANCIAL INSTRUMENTS AND RISK MANAGEMENT

In the normal course of business, the Company's financial position and results of operations are routinely subject to a variety of risks. These risks include risks associated with financial markets, primarily currency exchange rate risk and,

COLUMBIA SPORTSWEAR COMPANY

NOTES TO CONSOLIDATED FINANCIAL STATEMENTS—(Continued)

to a lesser extent, interest rate risk and equity market risk. The Company regularly assesses these risks and has established policies and business practices designed to mitigate them. The Company does not engage in speculative trading in any financial market.

The Company actively manages the risk of changes in functional currency equivalent cash flows resulting from anticipated U.S. dollar denominated inventory purchases by subsidiaries that use European euros, Canadian dollars, Japanese yen or Korean won as their functional currency. The Company manages this risk by using currency forward and European-style option contracts formally designated and effective as cash flow hedges. Hedge effectiveness is determined by evaluating the ability of a hedging instrument's cumulative change in fair value to offset the cumulative change in the present value of expected cash flows on the underlying exposures. For forward contracts, the change in fair value attributable to changes in forward points are excluded from the determination of hedge effectiveness and included in current cost of sales. For option contracts, the hedging relationship is assumed to have no ineffectiveness if the critical terms of the option contract match the hedged transaction's terms. Hedge ineffectiveness was not material during the years ended December 31, 2012, 2011 and 2010.

The Company also uses currency forward and option contracts not formally designated as hedges to manage the currency exchange rate risk associated with the remeasurement of non-functional monetary assets and liabilities. Non-functional monetary assets and liabilities consist primarily of cash, intercompany loans and payables.

The following table presents the gross notional amount of outstanding derivative instruments (in thousands):

	December 31,	
	2012	2011
Derivative instruments designated as cash flow hedges:		
Currency forward contracts.	$ 70,000	$ 144,000
Derivative instruments not designated as hedges:		
Currency forward contracts.	121,934	138,807

At December 31, 2012, approximately $3,172,000 of deferred net gains on both outstanding and matured derivatives accumulated in other comprehensive income are expected to be reclassified to net income during the next twelve months as a result of underlying hedged transactions also being recorded in net income. Actual amounts ultimately reclassified to net income are dependent on U.S. dollar exchange rates in effect against the European euro, Canadian dollar, Japanese yen and Korean won when outstanding derivative contracts mature.

At December 31, 2012, the Company's derivative contracts had remaining maturities of approximately one year or less. The maximum net exposure to any single counterparty, which is generally limited to the aggregate unrealized gain of all contracts with that counterparty, was less than $4,000,000 at December 31, 2012. All of the Company's derivative counterparties have investment grade credit ratings and, as a result, the Company does not require collateral to facilitate transactions. The Company does not hold derivatives featuring credit-related contingent terms. In addition, the Company is not a party to any derivative master agreement featuring credit-related contingent terms. Finally, the Company has not pledged assets or posted collateral as a requirement for entering into or maintaining derivative positions.

The following table presents the balance sheet classification and fair value of derivative instruments (in thousands):

COLUMBIA SPORTSWEAR COMPANY

NOTES TO CONSOLIDATED FINANCIAL STATEMENTS—(Continued)

	Balance Sheet Classification	December 31, 2012	December 31, 2011
Derivative instruments designated as cash flow hedges:			
Derivative instruments in asset positions:			
Currency forward contracts	Prepaid expenses and other current assets	$ 2,147	$ 6,591
Currency forward contracts	Other non-current assets	489	1,117
Derivative instruments in liability positions:			
Currency forward contracts	Accrued liabilities	579	824
Currency forward contracts	Other long-term liabilities	—	91
Derivative instruments not designated as hedges:			
Derivative instruments in asset positions:			
Currency forward contracts	Prepaid expenses and other current assets	4,072	645
Derivative instruments in liability positions:			
Currency forward contracts	Accrued liabilities	743	2,962

The following table presents the effect and classification of derivative instruments for the years ended December 31, 2012, 2011 and 2010 (in thousands):

	Statement Of Operations Classification	For the Year Ended December 31, 2012	2011	2010
Currency Forward Contracts:				
Derivative instruments designated as cash flow hedges:				
Gain recognized in other comprehensive income, net of tax	—	$ 753	$3,489	$1,167
Gain (Loss) reclassified from accumulated other comprehensive income to income for the effective portion	Cost of sales	5,908	(6,862)	1,789
Gain reclassified from accumulated other comprehensive income to income as a result of cash flow hedge discontinuance . .	Cost of sales	441	—	—
Loss recognized in income for amount excluded from effectiveness testing and for the ineffective portion	Cost of sales	(40)	(1,889)	(230)
Derivative instruments not designated as hedges:				
Loss recognized in income	Cost of sales	—	—	(130)
Gain (Loss) recognized in income	Selling, general and administrative expense	(1,841)	1,216	(54)

NOTE 20—FAIR VALUE MEASURES

Certain assets and liabilities are reported at fair value on either a recurring or nonrecurring basis. Fair value is defined as an exit price, representing the amount that would be received to sell an asset or paid to transfer a liability in an orderly transaction between market participants, under a three-tier fair value hierarchy which prioritizes the inputs used in measuring fair value as follows:

Level 1 – observable inputs such as quoted prices in active liquid markets;

COLUMBIA SPORTSWEAR COMPANY

NOTES TO CONSOLIDATED FINANCIAL STATEMENTS—(Continued)

Level 2 – inputs, other than the quoted market prices in active markets, which are observable, either directly or indirectly; or observable market prices in markets with insufficient volume and/or infrequent transactions; and

Level 3 – unobservable inputs for which there is little or no market data available, which require the reporting entity to develop its own assumptions.

Assets and liabilities measured at fair value on a recurring basis as of December 31, 2012 are as follows (in thousands):

	Level 1	Level 2	Level 3	Total
Assets:				
Cash equivalents				
Money market funds	$ 70,857	$ —	$ —	$ 70,857
Time deposits	25,035	—	—	25,035
Certificates of deposit	—	2,450	—	2,450
U.S. Government-backed repurchase agreements	—	25,000	—	25,000
U.S. Government-backed municipal bonds	—	5,348	—	5,348
Available-for-sale short-term investments				
Certificates of deposit	—	7,596	—	7,596
Variable-rate demand notes	—	22,640	—	22,640
U.S. Government-backed municipal bonds	—	14,425	—	14,425
Other current assets				
Derivative financial instruments (Note 19)	—	6,219	—	6,219
Non-current assets				
Derivative financial instruments (Note 19)	—	489	—	489
Mutual fund shares	4,080	—	—	4,080
Total assets measured at fair value	$ 99,972	$ 84,167	$ —	$ 184,139
Liabilities:				
Accrued liabilities				
Derivative financial instruments (Note 19)	$ —	$ 1,322	$ —	$ 1,322
Total liabilities measured at fair value	$ —	$ 1,322	$ —	$ 1,322

Assets and liabilities measured at fair value on a recurring basis at December 31, 2011 are as follows (in thousands):

COLUMBIA SPORTSWEAR COMPANY

NOTES TO CONSOLIDATED FINANCIAL STATEMENTS—(Continued)

	Level 1		Level 2		Level 3		Total
Assets:							
Cash equivalents							
Money market funds	$ 55,542	$	—	$	—	$	55,542
Time deposits	10,000		—		—		10,000
Available-for-sale short-term investments							
Time deposits	2,878		—		—		2,878
Other current assets							
Derivative financial instruments (Note 19)	—		7,236		—		7,236
Non-current assets							
Derivative financial instruments (Note 19)	—		1,117		—		1,117
Mutual fund shares	2,521		—		—		2,521
Total assets measured at fair value	$ 70,941	$	8,353	$	—	$	79,294
Liabilities:							
Accrued liabilities							
Derivative financial instruments (Note 19)	$ —	$	3,786	$	—	$	3,786
Other long-term liabilities							
Derivative financial instruments (Note 19)	—		91		—		91
Total liabilities measured at fair value	$ —	$	3,877	$	—	$	3,877

Level 1 instrument valuations are obtained from real-time quotes for transactions in active exchange markets involving identical assets. Level 2 instrument valuations are obtained from inputs, other than quoted market prices in active markets, that are directly or indirectly observable in the marketplace and quoted prices in markets with limited volume or infrequent transactions.

There were no material assets and liabilities measured at fair value on a nonrecurring basis at December 31, 2012 or 2011.

SUPPLEMENTARY DATA—QUARTERLY FINANCIAL DATA (Unaudited)

The following table summarizes the Company's quarterly financial data for the past two years ended December 31, 2012 (in thousands, except per share amounts):

2012	First Quarter	Second Quarter	Third Quarter	Fourth Quarter
Net sales	$ 333,141	$ 290,357	$ 545,005	$ 501,060
Gross profit	147,936	117,868	243,685	206,905
Net income (loss)	3,898	(7,901)	64,375	39,487
Earnings (loss) per share				
Basic	$ 0.12	$ (0.23)	$ 1.90	$ 1.16
Diluted	0.11	(0.23)	1.88	1.15

2011	First Quarter	Second Quarter	Third Quarter	Fourth Quarter
Net sales	$ 333,086	$ 268,030	$ 566,791	$ 526,078
Gross profit	149,536	112,413	249,585	223,774
Net income (loss)	12,770	(13,558)	67,539	36,728
Earnings (loss) per share				
Basic	$ 0.38	$ (0.40)	$ 2.00	$ 1.09
Diluted	0.37	(0.40)	1.98	1.08

Item 9. CHANGES IN AND DISAGREEMENTS WITH ACCOUNTANTS ON ACCOUNTING AND FINANCIAL DISCLOSURE

None.

Item 9A. CONTROLS AND PROCEDURES

Evaluation of Disclosure Controls and Procedures

Our management has evaluated, under the supervision and with the participation of our chief executive officer and chief financial officer, the effectiveness of our disclosure controls and procedures as of the end of the period covered by this report pursuant to Rule 13a-15(b) under the Securities Exchange Act of 1934 (the "Exchange Act"). Based on that evaluation, our chief executive officer and chief financial officer have concluded that, as of the end of the period covered by this report, our disclosure controls and procedures were effective in ensuring that information required to be disclosed in our Exchange Act reports is (1) recorded, processed, summarized and reported in a timely manner, and (2) accumulated and communicated to our management, including our chief executive officer and chief financial officer, as appropriate to allow timely decisions regarding required disclosure.

Design and Evaluation of Internal Control Over Financial Reporting

Report of Management

Our management is responsible for establishing and maintaining adequate internal control over financial reporting. All internal control systems, no matter how well designed, have inherent limitations. Therefore, even those systems determined to be effective can provide only reasonable assurance with respect to financial statement preparation and presentation.

Under the supervision and with the participation of our management, we assessed the effectiveness of our internal control over financial reporting as of December 31, 2012. In making this assessment, we used the criteria set forth by the Committee of Sponsoring Organizations of the Treadway Commission in *Internal Control – Integrated Framework*. Based on our assessment we believe that, as of December 31, 2012, the Company's internal control over financial reporting is effective based on those criteria.

We are implementing an enterprise resource planning ("ERP") system on a worldwide basis, which is expected to impact our business and financial transaction processes. The implementation is expected to occur in phases globally over the next several years, and began with a roll-out to our Canadian subsidiary in April 2012. The implementation of a worldwide ERP system will affect the processes that constitute our internal control over financial reporting and will require continued testing for effectiveness as the implementation progresses.

There has been no change in our internal control over financial reporting that occurred during our fiscal quarter ended December 31, 2012 that has materially affected, or is reasonably likely to materially affect, our internal control over financial reporting.

Our independent auditors have issued an audit report on the effectiveness of our internal control over financial reporting as of December 31, 2012, which is included herein.

Report of Independent Registered Public Accounting Firm
To the Board of Directors and Shareholders
Columbia Sportswear Company
Portland, Oregon

We have audited the internal control over financial reporting of Columbia Sportswear Company and subsidiaries (the "Company") as of December 31, 2012, based on criteria established in *Internal Control — Integrated Framework* issued by the Committee of Sponsoring Organizations of the Treadway Commission. The Company's management is responsible for maintaining effective internal control over financial reporting and for its assessment of the effectiveness of internal control over financial reporting, included in the accompanying "Report of Management". Our responsibility is to express an opinion on the Company's internal control over financial reporting based on our audit.

We conducted our audit in accordance with the standards of the Public Company Accounting Oversight Board (United States). Those standards require that we plan and perform the audit to obtain reasonable assurance about whether effective internal control over financial reporting was maintained in all material respects. Our audit included obtaining an understanding of internal control over financial reporting, assessing the risk that a material weakness exists, testing and evaluating the design and operating effectiveness of internal control based on the assessed risk, and performing such other procedures as we considered necessary in the circumstances. We believe that our audit provides a reasonable basis for our opinion.

A company's internal control over financial reporting is a process designed by, or under the supervision of, the company's principal executive and principal financial officers, or persons performing similar functions, and effected by the company's board of directors, management, and other personnel to provide reasonable assurance regarding the reliability of financial reporting and the preparation of financial statements for external purposes in accordance with generally accepted accounting principles. A company's internal control over financial reporting includes those policies and procedures that (1) pertain to the maintenance of records that, in reasonable detail, accurately and fairly reflect the transactions and dispositions of the assets of the company; (2) provide reasonable assurance that transactions are recorded as necessary to permit preparation of financial statements in accordance with generally accepted accounting principles, and that receipts and expenditures of the company are being made only in accordance with authorizations of management and directors of the company; and (3) provide reasonable assurance regarding prevention or timely detection of unauthorized acquisition, use, or disposition of the company's assets that could have a material effect on the financial statements.

Because of the inherent limitations of internal control over financial reporting, including the possibility of collusion or improper management override of controls, material misstatements due to error or fraud may not be prevented or detected on a timely basis. Also, projections of any evaluation of the effectiveness of the internal control over financial reporting to future periods are subject to the risk that the controls may become inadequate because of changes in conditions, or that the degree of compliance with the policies or procedures may deteriorate.

In our opinion, the Company maintained, in all material respects, effective internal control over financial reporting as of December 31, 2012, based on the criteria established in *Internal Control — Integrated Framework* issued by the Committee of Sponsoring Organizations of the Treadway Commission.

We have also audited, in accordance with the standards of the Public Company Accounting Oversight Board (United States), the consolidated financial statements and financial statement schedule as of and for the year ended December 31, 2012 of the Company, and our report dated February 28, 2013, expressed an unqualified opinion on those financial statements and financial statement schedule.

/s/ DELOITTE & TOUCHE LLP
Portland, Oregon
February 28, 2013

Appendix B

Time Value of Money—Future and Present Value Concepts

Time value of money The concept that states that a dollar today is worth more than a dollar received in the future.

Money earns interest over time, a fact called the **time value of money**. The time value of money idea is based on the thought that $1 today is worth more than $1 received in the future. This is because $1 today can be invested and earn interest and therefore become worth more than $1 at a later date.

Future Value

Future value The amount that a given sum of money will be "worth" at a specified time in the future assuming a certain interest rate.

Future value refers to the amount that a given sum of money will be "worth" at a specified time in the future assuming a certain interest rate. The main application of future value is calculating the future value of an amount invested today (a present value) that earns a constant rate of interest over time. For example, assume that you invest $4,545 and it earns 10% interest per year. After one year, the $4,545 invested grows to a future value of $5,000, as shown next.

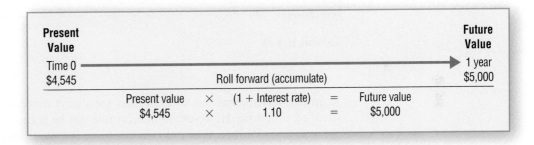

If the money was invested for five years, you would have to perform five such calculations. You would also have to consider the compound interest your investment is earning. **Compound interest** is the interest you earn not only on your principal amount, but also on the interest to date. Most business applications include compound interest. The following table shows the interest calculations for the first two years:

Compound interest Interest earned not only on principal but also on the interest to date.

End of Year	Interest	Future Value
0	—	$4,545
1	$4,545 × 0.10 = $455	5,000
2	5,000 × 0.10 = 500	5,500

Earning 10%, a $4,545 investment grows to $5,000 at the end of one year, to $5,500 at the end of two years, and so on. (Throughout this discussion, we round dollar amounts to the nearest dollar.)

Future-Value Tables

Mathematical tables make computing a future value easy. Exhibit B-1 shows the table used to calculate the future value of $1 for various interest rates over various time periods. Future value depends on three factors:

1. The amount of the investment

2. The length of time the amount is invested

3. The interest rate

The heading in **Exhibit B-1** states that the future value of $1 is being calculated. Future-value and present-value tables are based on $1 because $1 is so easy to work with. Look at the Period column and the interest rate columns from 4% to 16%.

					Future Value of $1					
Period	4%	5%	6%	7%	8%	9%	10%	12%	14%	16%
1	1.040	1.050	1.060	1.070	1.080	1.090	1.100	1.120	1.140	1.160
2	1.082	1.103	1.124	1.145	1.166	1.188	1.210	1.254	1.300	1.346
3	1.125	1.158	1.191	1.225	1.260	1.295	1.331	1.405	1.482	1.561
4	1.170	1.216	1.262	1.311	1.360	1.412	1.464	1.574	1.689	1.811
5	1.217	1.276	1.338	1.403	1.469	1.539	1.611	1.762	1.925	2.100
6	1.265	1.340	1.419	1.501	1.587	1.677	1.772	1.974	2.195	2.436
7	1.316	1.407	1.504	1.606	1.714	1.828	1.949	2.211	2.502	2.826
8	1.369	1.477	1.594	1.718	1.851	1.993	2.144	2.476	2.853	3.278
9	1.423	1.551	1.689	1.838	1.999	2.172	2.358	2.773	3.252	3.803
10	1.480	1.629	1.791	1.967	2.159	2.367	2.594	3.106	3.707	4.411

Exhibit B-1 ▲

In business applications, interest rates are always stated for a one-year period unless specified otherwise. However, an interest rate can be stated for any period, such as 3% per quarter or 5% for a six-month period. For example, an investment may offer a return of 3% per quarter for two years. In that case, you would be working with 3% interest for eight periods (two years multiplied by four quarters per year). It would be incorrect to use 3% for two years because the interest in this case is 3% compounded quarterly, and different future values would result. Take care when calculating future-value and present-value problems to select the proper interest rate and the appropriate number of periods.

Let's demonstrate using the table in Exhibit B-1. The future value of $1.00 invested at 8% for one year is $1.08 ($1.00 × 1.080, which appears at the intersection of the 8% column and the Period 1 row). The future value factor 1.080 includes both the principal (1.000) and the compound interest for one period (0.080).

Suppose you deposit $5,000 in a savings account that pays annual interest of 8%. The account balance at the end of one year will be $5,400. To compute the future value of $5,000 at 8% for one year, multiply $5,000 by 1.080 to get $5,400.

Now suppose you invest $5,000 in a 10-year, 8% certificate of deposit (CD). What will be the future value of the CD at maturity? To compute the future value of $5,000 at 8% for 10 periods, multiply $5,000 by 2.159 (from Exhibit B-1) to get $10,795. This future value of $10,795 indicates that $5,000 earning 8% interest compounded annually grows to $10,795 at the end of 10 years. You can find any present amount's future value at a particular future date.

By
two yea

Amou
Expec
Amou
Expec
Amou

You
amoun
investe
is the s

Prese

We hav
ent val
ease ou
Present

P

Annuities Multiple investments of an equal periodic amount at fixed intervals over the length of the investment.

Exhil

For
the firs
0.909. I
ent val
value o
by 0.90
For
row. W
tation
table, w

Prese

Annuit
the inve

Future Value of an Annuity

In the preceding example, we made an investment of a single amount. Other investments, called **annuities**, include multiple investments of an equal periodic amount at fixed intervals over the length of the investment. Consider the Gomez family members investing for their child's education. Let's assume the Gomez family can invest $4,000 at the end of each year for three years to accumulate a college fund for 15-year-old Daniel. The investment can earn 7% annually until Daniel turns 18—a three-year investment. How much will be available for Daniel on the date of the last investment? The investment will have a future value of $12,860 as calculated next.

End of Year	Annual Investment	+	Interest	=	Increase for the Year	Future Value of Annuity
0	—		—		—	0
1	$4,000		—		$4,000	$ 4,000
2	4,000		+ ($4,000 × 0.07 = $280) =		4,280	8,280
3	4,000		+ ($8,280 × 0.07 = $580) =		4,580	12,860

As with the Future Value of $1 table, mathematical tables make calculating the future value of annuities much easier. **Exhibit B-2**, Future Value of Annuity of $1, gives the future value of a series of investments, each of equal amount, made at regular intervals at the end of each period.

Future Value of Annuity of $1										
Period	4%	5%	6%	7%	8%	9%	10%	12%	14%	16%
1	1.000	1.000	1.000	1.000	1.000	1.000	1.000	1.000	1.000	1.000
2	2.040	2.050	2.060	2.070	2.080	2.090	2.100	2.120	2.140	2.160
3	3.122	3.153	3.184	3.215	3.246	3.278	3.310	3.374	3.440	3.506
4	4.246	4.310	4.375	4.440	4.506	4.573	4.641	4.779	4.921	5.066
5	5.416	5.526	5.637	5.751	5.867	5.985	6.105	6.353	6.610	6.877
6	6.633	6.802	6.975	7.153	7.336	7.523	7.716	8.115	8.536	8.977
7	7.898	8.142	8.394	8.654	8.923	9.200	9.487	10.089	10.730	11.414
8	9.214	9.549	9.897	10.260	10.637	11.028	11.436	12.300	13.233	14.240
9	10.583	11.027	11.491	11.978	12.488	13.021	13.579	14.776	16.085	17.519
10	12.006	12.578	13.181	13.816	14.487	15.193	15.937	17.549	19.337	21.321

Exhibit B-2 ▲

What is the future value of an annuity of three investments of $1 each, made at the end of each year, that earn 7%? The answer is $3.215. The factor can be found in the 7% column and across from 3 in the Period column of Exhibit B-2. This factor can be used to compute the future value of the investment for Daniel's education, as follows:

Amount of Each Periodic Investment	×	Future Value of Annuity of $1 (Exhibit B-2)	=	Future Value of Investment
$4,000	×	3.215	=	$12,860

You can compute the future value of any investment consisting of equal periodic amounts at regular intervals. Businesses make periodic investments to accumulate funds for plant expansion and other uses.

Present value The value on a given date of a future amount, adjusted to reflect the time value of money.

Discounting Computing a present value.

Pre

Ofte
Prese
value
year.
pay t
T

1.

2.

3.

C
less t
Ir
Assu
three
as fo

B
comp

Amc
Exp
Amc

T
equa

If
inves

Prese
Value
Time

$4,132

Consider an investment that promises annual cash receipts of $10,000 to be received at the end of each of three years. Assume that you demand a 12% return on your investment. What is the investment's present value? What would you pay today to acquire the investment? The investment spans three periods, and you would pay the sum of three present values. The computation follows:

Year	Annual Cash Receipt	×	Present Value of $1 at 12% (Exhibit B-3)	=	Present Value of Annual Cash Receipt
1	$10,000	×	0.893	=	$ 8,930
2	10,000	×	0.797	=	7,970
3	10,000	×	0.712	=	7,120
			Total Present Value of Investment =		$24,020

The present value of this annuity is $24,020. By paying this amount today, you will receive $10,000 at the end of each of the three years while earning 12% on your investment.

The example illustrates repetitive computations of the three future amounts. One way to ease the computational burden is to add the three present value factors of $1 from Exhibit B-3, $0.893 + 0.797 + 0.712$, and multiply their sum of 2.402 by the annual cash receipt of $10,000 to obtain the present value of the annuity, $24,020 ($10,000 × 2.402).

An easier approach is to use a present value of an annuity table. **Exhibit B-4** shows the present value of an annuity of $1 to be received at the end of each period for a given number of periods. The present value factor of a three-period annuity at 12% is 2.402, the junction of the Period 3 row and the 12% column. Thus, the present value of $10,000 received annually at the end of each of three years, discounted at 12%, is $24,020 ($10,000 × 2.402).

Present Value of Annuity of $1									
Period	4%	5%	6%	7%	8%	10%	12%	14%	16%
1	0.962	0.952	0.943	0.935	0.926	0.909	0.893	0.877	0.862
2	1.886	1.859	1.833	1.808	1.783	1.736	1.690	1.647	1.605
3	2.775	2.723	2.673	2.624	2.577	2.487	2.402	2.322	2.246
4	3.630	3.546	3.465	3.387	3.312	3.170	3.037	2.914	2.798
5	4.452	4.329	4.212	4.100	3.993	3.791	3.605	3.433	3.274
6	5.242	5.076	4.917	4.767	4.623	4.355	4.111	3.889	3.685
7	6.002	5.786	5.582	5.389	5.206	4.868	4.564	4.288	4.039
8	6.733	6.463	6.210	5.971	5.747	5.335	4.968	4.639	4.344
9	7.435	7.108	6.802	6.515	6.247	5.759	5.328	4.946	4.607
10	8.111	7.722	7.360	7.024	6.710	6.145	5.650	5.216	4.833

Exhibit B-4 ▲

Accounting Practice

Exercises

EB-1A. Calculate present and future values. 10–15 min.

Presented next are four independent situations related to future and present values.

Requirement

1. Using the tables in the appendix, calculate the future or present value of each item as needed.
   a. $8,000 is deposited in the bank today for a period of six years. Calculate the value of the $8,000 at the end of six years assuming it earns 7% interest.
   b. How much must you invest today in order to receive $3,000 at the end of each year for the next four years assuming you can earn 12% interest?
   c. $4,500 will be invested at the end of each year for a period of three years. Calculate the value of the investment at the end of three years assuming it earns 10% interest.
   d. The company you work for wants to purchase a new piece of equipment that is estimated to cost $29,000 ten years from now. How much must they invest today in order to have the $29,000 necessary to purchase the equipment if they can earn 6% interest?

EB-2A. Future value concepts. 15–20 min.

John Resch is considering two plans for building an education fund for his children.

Plan A—Invest $3,000 at the end of each year for ten years. This investment will earn 8% annual interest.

Plan B—Invest $25,000 now, earning 6% annual interest for ten years.

Requirement

1. Before making any calculations, which plan would you expect to provide the larger future amount? Using the tables provided in the appendix, calculate the future value of each plan. Which plan provides the larger amount at the end of ten years?

EB-3A. Present value concepts. 15–20 min.

Hobart Parts, Inc., needs new manufacturing equipment. Two companies can provide similar equipment but under different payment plans:

a. Tanner Manufacturing offers to let Hobart Parts, Inc., pay $55,000 at the end of each year for four years. The payments include interest at 8% per year.

b. Phoenix, Corp., will let Hobart Parts, Inc., make a single payment of $250,000 at the end of four years. This payment includes both principal and interest at 8%.

Requirements

1. Calculate the present value cost of each payment plan.

2. In addition to the present value cost of the equipment, what other factors should Hobart Parts consider when deciding which company to purchase the equipment from?

Company Index

Specialty Systems, 390

Spices and More, Inc., 321

SRS Systems, Inc., 532

Steamed Sensation, Inc., 146

Sterling Company, 548

Stevens and Associates, Inc., 40

Stevens Auto Repair, 434

Stop and Go, 282–283

Subway, 372

Sugarland Company, 478

Sullivan, Corp., 477

Sullivan, Inc., 595

Sullivan Industrial, Inc., 191

Sunbelt Services, Inc., 539–541

Sunbelt Systems, Inc., 397

Sundaze Boats, 430

Sundaze Sunglasses, 238

Sunglass Bungalow, 242

Sun Graphics and Designs Center, 381

Sun Meadow Resorts, 441

Sunshine Tanning Salon, 387

Swanson, Incorporated, 235, 484

Sweet Home Catering, Inc., 133

T

T. Houton Associates, Inc., 550

Talbot Corporation, 448–449

Tanaka's Antique Furniture, 199

Tanner Manufacturing, 627

Target, 3, 7, 49, 73, 98–99, 153, 204, 251–252, 280–281, 292, 343–344, 400, 447–448, 501, 558, 566, 567, 617

Taylor Snowboards, 293

TDR Systems, 486

TDS Corporation, 502

Teck Automotive, 332

Teldar Incorporated, 618

Texas State Bank, 333

Theodore Company, 476

Tiffany & Co., 180, 227–228

Timberview, Inc., 480

Tim's Auto Repair, 437

Tina Dalton, Attorney at Law, Inc., 93

Tiny Tykes Daycare, Inc., 83

Tireboyz Tire, Inc., 195

Titan Realty, Inc., 145

Titan Trucking, 243, 383–384

TJ's Wholesale, 476

Top Flight Airways, 384

Top Line Equipment, 247–248

Top Ten Sporting Goods, 293

Tour Dejour, Inc., 483

Toys R Us, 159–160, 180, 208–209, 227–228, 566

Transco, Inc., 448

Trident, 536

Tri-State Manufacturing, 393–394

Tri State Supply, Inc., 488

Troy, Corp., 144

Tucker Enterprises, Inc., 521–522, 527–528, 569–590

Tucker's Fine Furnishings, 195

TXL Publishing, 384

U

Umbrella.com, 323

Under Armour, Inc., 50, 122–123, 402

Underwater World, 240–241

US Department of Labor, 270

V

Valley Gift and Collectibles, Inc., 192

Venus, Corp., 437

Verizon, 372

Vermont Resources, 238

Voyage, Inc., 599

W

Walker Securities, Inc., 615

Walmart, 6, 23, 314–315, 567

Walsh & Associates, Inc., 83

Walt Disney Company, 102, 122, 566

Washup Plumbing, Inc., 86

Water Works Pool Supply, Inc., 184

Watkins Electric Supply, 280

Watkins Enterprises, 479

Watkins Equipment, 244–245

Watkins Inc., 481

Wave Rider, 29

Waverly, Inc., 129

Bribe. The payment of money in order to influence the conduct of a person, 266

buildings, costs of, 356

Business. A business is a legal organization that attempts to create value by exchanging products with customers for money, 2, 23, 25. *See also* specific types of

  accounting, role in, 1, 11–12

  accounts receivable turnover of, 581–583

  assets, management of, 375–376

  cash flow, management of, 527

  debt covenants of, 580–581

  debt of, 422–423

  defined, 2, 25

  earnings per share of, 583–585

  elements of, 2–3

  environment of, 567

  financing decisions of, 580–581

  for-profit, 6

  goal of, 5

  growing concerns of, 575–577

  income or loss from continuing operations, earning of, 577–580

  investing decisions of, 581–583

  legal forms of, 7–8

  manufacturing, 7

  merchandise, 7

  net income *vs.* loss, earning of, 577–580

  not-for-profit, 7

  operation of, 5–6, 568–569

  organization of, 6–9

  owners of, 4

  performance of, 569–586

  profitability of, 178

  purpose of, 3

  retail, 7

  service, 7

  stakeholders in, 4

  statement of cashflows of, 508–511

  stockholder's investment in, 471–472

  types of, 6–7

  value of, 3–4, 272, 589

  wholesale, 7

Business entity principle. The business entity principle dictates that the financial affairs of a business organization must be kept separate from the personal financial affairs of the business owners, 10

Business model. A description of what a business does, the products it sells, and the customers who buy its products, 567

Business strategy. A description of how a business uses its business model to create a competitive advantage, 567

Business transactions

  accounting, role in reporting, 72–73

  accounts for organizing, 54–56

  double-entry accounting and, 56–58

  financial statements, reporting of, 20–23

  fundamental accounting equation for recording, 13–19

  general journal/ledger for keeping track of, 58–69

  measuring, 12–13

  recognizing, 12

  trial balance and, preparing and using, 69–72

C

Callable bonds. Bonds that the issuer may call, or pay off, at a specified price before maturity, 414

Capital expenditure. Expenditure that increases the capacity or productivity of an asset or extends its useful life. Capital expenditures are debited to an asset account, 368

Capitalized. The process of debiting (increasing) an asset account for the cost of an asset, 356

Capital lease. A lease agreement that is treated as a financed purchase of a long-term asset, 420–421

Capital stock. Represents the individual's ownership of the corporation's capital, 453

Carrying amount. Bonds payable minus the discount or plus the premium, 416

Carrying value. The asset's cost minus its accumulated depreciation, 112

Cash

  balance sheet, reporting on, 300

  conversion cycle for, 528

  customers, collecting from, 525

  internal control of, 291–300

  net change in, 520

  payments with, 292

  purchases with, 162

  receipts for, 291–292, 525

  sources of, 509

  uses of, 509–510

Cash accounting. Accounting that only recognizes business transactions when cash is received or disbursed, 12, 104

Cash-basis accounting. Accounting method that records revenues when cash is received and expenses when cash is paid, 104

Cash conversion cycle. (1) A measurement of the amount of time a company's cash is tied up in its operations. (2) The number of days it takes to collect cash from the sale of inventory *versus* the number of days it takes to pay for inventory. It is computed as the days-sales-in-inventory, plus accounts receivable collection period, less the accounts payable payment period, 528, 576

Cash dividends, 458–462

    declaring, 459–460

    dividend dates for, 459

    paying, 459–460

    on preferred stock, 461

    between shareholders, 460

Cash equivalents. Highly liquid, highly safe investments that so closely resemble cash that they may be shown with cash on the balance sheet, 300

Cash flow statement. (1) A financial statement that reports the sources and uses of cash for a given period of time. (2) A financial statement that shows all of the sources and all of the uses of cash for an accounting period, 22, 506–507

    business, management of, 527

    from financing activities, 518–520

    of inventory, 210–213

    from investing activities, 516–518

    from operating activities, 514–516, 524–527

Cash register schemes. A fraud scheme in which an employee steals cash by processing false refunds, 265

Cash sales, 165, 289

Certified Public Accountant (CPA). An accountant, licensed by a state, who serves the general public by auditing businesses and reporting whether the business's financial statements are in accordance with Generally Accepted Accounting Principles, 268–270

Chart of accounts. A list of all the accounts of a business and the numbers assigned to those accounts, 55

Check tampering. A fraud scheme in which an employee writes a fraudulent check and makes the check payable to himself or herself, or obtains a check intended for an outside party, endorses the check, and then cashes it, 265

Classified balance sheet. A balance sheet that separates assets and liabilities into current and long-term classes, 177

Closing entries. Journal entries that are prepared at the end of the accounting period. Closing entries zero out the revenue, expense, and dividend accounts so accounting can begin for the next period, 117–120

Collateral. (1) Assets pledged to secure repayment of a loan. In the case of nonpayment by the borrower, the lender has the right to take the collateral. (2) Assets pledged by a borrower to guarantee the payment of a liability, 411, 580

Collusion. Two or more individuals working together to commit fraud, 264

Common shareholders, 460

Common-size statement. A financial statement that reports only percentages (no dollar amounts) for each line item on the financial statements, 572

Common stock. (1) The stockholders' equity that is the result of the owners of the business investing money (or other assets) into the business. (2) The most typical kind of stock. It usually has voting rights, the right to receive dividends, and the right to receive assets if the company liquidates, 14, 455, 457–458

Communication of information, 263

Competitive environment. How a business competes for its customers, supplies, and other critical resources, 567

Compound interest. Interest earned not only on principal but also on the interest to date, 689

Compound journal entry. (1) A journal entry that affects more than two accounts. (2) A journal entry affecting more than two accounts; an entry that has more than one debit and/or more than one credit, 66, 165

Conservatism. Accounting principle that states that a business must report all items in the financial statements at amounts that lead to the most cautious immediate results, 220

Consistency principle. Accounting principle that states that a business should use the same accounting methods and procedures from period to period, 219

Contingent liability. A potential liability that depends on the outcome of a future event, 405, 410–411

Contra-account. An account that is linked to another account. A contraaccount will have a normal balance opposite of the account it is linked to, 112

Control account. An account in the general ledger that summarizes the details of an account balance, 303

Control activities. The policies and procedures implemented in an internal control system, 262–263

Control environment. The overall attitude, awareness, and actions of management and staff regarding the internal control system and its importance to the business, 262

Controller. The individual in an organization responsible for the accounting system and financial statements, 293

Convertible bonds. Bonds that may be converted into the common stock of the issuing company at the option of the investor, 414

Copyright. Exclusive right to reproduce and sell a book, musical composition, film, other work of art, or computer program. Issued by the federal government, copyrights extend 70 years beyond the author's life, 372

Corporate charter. Describes the purpose, place, and other details of a corporation, 453

Corporation. A legal entity, chartered under state law, that is empowered to conduct business. The corporation and owners are considered as separate for legal and tax purposes, 7

cash dividends of, 458–462

issuance of stock by, 456–458

organization of, 453–454

stock dividends in, 462–467

stockholder's equity of, 455–456

stock splits in, 462–467

treasury stock in, 467–470

Cost. The amount of money or money substitutes that a business pays to receive an item used in operating a business, 3

actual, 10

average, 210

depreciable, 360

freight, 169–174

of goods, 165, 212

historical, 10

of long-term assets, 355–358

of lump-sum purchase of assets, 357–358

prepaid shipping, 170–173

of repairing long-term assets, 367–368

of research and development, 373

selling, 173

Cost of goods available for sale. The cost of inventory on hand at the beginning of the period plus the net cost of inventory purchased during the period, 212

Cost of goods sold. The cost of the inventory that the business has sold to customers, 165

Cost principle. The cost principle states that when a business acquires assets or services, they should be recorded at their actual cost, 10

Credit. The right side of any account; an entry made to the right side of an account, 15–17, 56

Credit cards, 290–291

Credit memorandum. A document that supports the return of goods from the customer or an allowance for unsatisfactory goods and the adjustment to the customer's account balance, 166–167

Creditor. The entity to whom the debtor promises future payment, 309

Credit purchases, 162

Credit sales, 165–166

Credit terms. The payment terms for customers who buy on account, 163

Cumulative preferred stock. Preferred stock whose owners must receive all dividends in arrears plus the current

year dividend before the corporation pays dividends to the common stockholders, 461

Current assets. (1) Assets that are expected to be converted to cash, sold, or consumed within one year or the business's operating cycle if the cycle is longer than a year. (2) Cash, short-term investments, accounts receivable, inventory, and prepaid expenses, 177, 312, 515–516

Current liabilities. Debts due to be paid with cash or fulfilled with goods and services within one year or the entity's operating cycle if the cycle is longer than a year, 177, 421–422

changes in, 515–516

Current portion of long-term debt. The principal portion of a long-term liability that is payable within one year, 409

Current ratio. (1) The ratio of current assets to current liabilities. (2) Current assets divided by current liabilities. Measures a business's ability to meet its short-term obligations with its current assets, 312–313, 576

Customer. A person or organization that purchases a product from a business, 3

cash, collecting from, 525

relationships with, 160–161

D

Days-sales-in-inventory. The average number of day that it took to sell the average inventory held during the year, 227

Debentures. Bonds that are backed only by the general credit of the company issuing the bond, 414

Debit. The left side of any account; an entry made to the left side of an account, 56

Debit cards, 290–291

Debt

bad, 291

of business, 422–423

long-term, 409, 411–421

Debt covenants. Conditions, stated in the debt contract, that specify the requirements agreed to by the lender and borrower, 580–581

Debtor. The entity that promises future payment, 309

Debt ratio. (1) The ratio of a company's total liabilities (debt) to its total assets. (2) Total liabilities divided by total assets. It measures a business's ability to pay liabilities, 423, 580

Debt securities, 374

Decisions of business

financial statement analysis for making, 569, 586–589

financing, 580–581

investing, 581–583

in ending inventory the last, most recent costs incurred, 210, 214–215

Fiscal year. Any consecutive, 12-month period that a business adopts as its accounting year, 103

Fixed assets. (1) The long-lived assets of a business including land, buildings, furniture, fixtures, and equipment. (2) Tangible assets such as buildings and equipment, 177, 354, 527

Fixed asset turnover. (1) The ratio of sales to average fixed assets, which indicates the sales generated for every dollar invested in fixed assets. (2) A measure of how a business utilizes its property, plant, and equipment to generate sales. Fixed asset turnover is computed as sales divided by average fixed assets, 376, 582

Fixtures, costs of, 357

Footnotes. Disclosures that accompany the financial statements, 222

For-profit business. A business that attempts to create an exchange, or sale, where revenue exceeds expenses, creating a profit, 6

Franchises. Privileges granted by a private business or a government to sell a product or service under specified conditions, 372

Fraud. Deceit or trickery involving intentional actions that cause harm to a business, its stakeholders, or both, 265–267

Fraud triangle. The combination of perceived pressure, rationalization, and perceived opportunity necessary to commit fraud, 266

Free cash flow. The amount of cash available from operations after paying for investments in long-term assets, 527

Free on board (FOB) destination. A shipping term specifying that title to goods passes to the buyer when the goods are received at the buyer's destination; thus, the seller pays the cost of shipping the goods to this destination, 169, 171–172

Free on board (FOB) shipping point. A shipping term specifying that title to goods passes to the buyer when the goods are shipped at the seller's place of business; thus, the buyer pays the cost of shipping the goods to its location, 169, 170–173

Freight charges. The cost of shipping merchandise from the seller to the buyer, 169–174

for delivering goods to customers, 171–173

for receipt of goods from suppliers, 170–171

Full-disclosure principle. Accounting principle that states that a company's financial statements should report enough information for users to make knowledgeable decisions about the company, 222

Fully depreciated. An asset that has reached the end of its estimated useful life. No more depreciation is recorded for the asset, 361, 366

Fundamental accounting equation. The equation that states that total assets equal the sum of total liabilities and total stockholders' equity, 13–19

for recording business transactions, 13–19

for stockholders' equity, 14–19

for transaction analysis, 14

Furniture, costs of, 357

Future value. The amount that a given sum of money will be "worth" at a specified time in the future assuming a certain interest rate, 689–691

G

General and administrative expenses. Office expenses, such as the salaries of the company president and office employees, depreciation of items used in administration, rent, utilities, and property taxes on the office building, 175

General journal. The chronological accounting record of the transactions of a business, 58

for keeping track of business transactions, 58–69

for T-accounts, balancing of, 67–69

for transaction analysis, 60

General ledger. The accounting record summarizing, in accounts, the transactions of a business and showing the resulting ending account balances, 58

for keeping track of business transactions, 58–69

for T-accounts, balancing of, 67–69

for transaction analysis, 60

Generally Accepted Accounting Principles (GAAP). The rules, principles, and concepts established by the accounting profession that govern financial accounting, 9–10, 257

around the world, 259–260

in United States, 258–259

Generally Accepted Auditing Standards (GAAS). The procedures used by CPAs to audit companies, 268

Goods. A good is a physical item that can be touched and felt. Goods are tangible, 2, 209

Goodwill. Excess of the cost of an acquired company over the market value of its net assets (assets minus liabilities), 372–373

Gross margin. Net sales revenue minus cost of goods sold, 175

Gross profit. Net sales revenue minus cost of goods sold, 175

Gross profit method. A way to estimate ending inventory by using the gross profit percentage, 225

Gross profit percentage. (1) A measure of profitability equal to gross profit divided by net sales revenue. (2) Sales, less cost of goods sold, divided by net sales, 179, 579

purchases of, 162–164

sales of, 164–168

shrinkage of, 222

turnover of, 226–227

valuing, 220–222, 224–226

Inventory costing methods, 209–212. *See also* **Inventory**

applying, 212–218

average cost, 216–217

first-in, first-out, 214–215

last-in, first-out, 215–216

net income, effect on, 218–220

specific-identification, 213

Inventory layer. A record of the quantity of and the cost of inventory items made in a single purchase, 211

Inventory shrinkage. The loss of inventory, 222

Inventory turnover. (1) The ratio of cost of goods sold to average inventory. (2) Measures the number of times a company sells its average level of inventory during a year. To compute inventory turnover, divide cost of goods sold by average inventory, 226–227, 582

Investing activities. (1) Decisions made by management to buy and sell long-term assets. (2) Activities that increase or decrease long-term assets, 22, 506, 510–511, 516–518

Investing decision. How a business uses money to acquire assets, 581–583

Issue price. The initial selling price for a share of stock, 456

J

Journalize. Entering a transaction in a journal, 58, 217–218, 299

K

Kickback. The payment of money in order to influence the conduct of a person, 266

Known liabilities, 406–409

L

Land improvements. Depreciable improvements to land, such as fencing, sprinkler systems, paving, signs, and lighting, 355–356

Last-in, first-out (LIFO). Inventory costing method in which the last inventory costs incurred are the first costs to be assigned to cost of goods sold. LIFO leaves in ending inventory the first, oldest costs incurred, 210, 215–216

Leased liabilities, 419–421

Legal capital. The portion of stockholders' equity that cannot be used for dividends, 459

Liabilities. A liability is an amount owed to a lender or other creditor, 5, 405

accounts for, 55

of accounts payable, 406

accrued, 408

contingent, 405, 410–411

current, 177, 421–422, 515–516

estimated, 409–410

known, 406–409

leased, 419–421

long-term, 178, 409

of merchandising business, 177–178

of notes payable, 406–407

of sales tax payable, 408

of unearned revenues, 408

Licenses. Privileges granted by a private business or a government to sell a product or service under specified conditions, 372

Like-kind exchange. Exchanging one fixed asset for another fixed asset that has similar functionality, 369

Limited liability company. A hybrid business entity having characteristics of both a corporation and a partnership, 8

Liquidity. The ability to convert an asset to cash quickly, 177

Liquidity management. The management of cash, specifically the amount and timing of cash receipts and payments, 312

Lock-box system. A system in which customers send payments to a post office box of a business. The bank collects payments from the box and deposits them into the business's account, 295

Long-term assets. (1) Long-lived, tangible assets such as land, buildings, equipment, and furniture used in the operation of a business lasting for more than a year. (2) Assets other than those that are current, 111, 177

balance sheet, reporting of, 375

costs of, calculating of, 355–358

depreciation of, 111–113, 358–367

disposing of, 368–371

recording costs of repairing, 367–368

types of, 354–355

Long-term debt, 411–421

balance sheet, reporting of, 421–422

bonds payable and, 413–419

leased liabilities and, 419–421

liabilities of, 409

notes payable and, 411–413

Useful life. The expected life of an asset during which it is anticipated to generate revenues. May be expressed in years or units of output, 359–360, 365–366

V

Value. The price someone is willing to pay for an item, 3

book, 112, 272

of business, 3–4, 272, 589

carrying, 112

future, 689–691

of inventory, 220–222, 224–226

market, 272

maturity, 309, 414

net, 112

net realizable, 303

no-par stock with stated, 458

par, 414, 456

present, 692–694

residual, 360

salvage, 111, 360

stated, 456

Vertical analysis. Analysis of a financial statement that reveals the relationship of each statement item to a specified base amount, which is the 100% figure, 572

W

Warranty. A guarantee that a product or service is free from defect, 409–410

Whistleblower. A person who reports illegal or unethical behavior, 270

Wholesale business. A business that sells products to other businesses for resale, 7

Wholesalers. Businesses that buy goods from manufacturers and resell them to retailers, 160–161

Work in process. Inventory of partially completed goods, 209

Write off. Removing a customer's receivable from the accounting records because it is considered uncollectible, 301

Photo Credits

Frontmatter: Page v, top: Courtesy of Robert Kemp; bottom: Courtesy of Jeffrey Waybright

Chapter 1: Page 1: © Rick Wilking/Reuters/Corbis; Page 11: © Sergey Turanov/iStockphoto

Chapter 2: Page 53: © Philip Scalia/Alamy; Page 57 top: © Diego_cervo/iStockphoto; bottom left: © BananaStock/JupiterImages; bottom center: © Steve Collender/Shutterstock; bottom right: © Comstock/JupiterImages

Chapter 3: Page 102: © Katja Kreder/Imagebroker/Alamy; Page 109: © Godfried Edelman/iStockphoto

Chapter 4: Page 159: © Patti McConville/Alamy; Page 170: © Photos.com/Jupiter Images

Chapter 5: Page 208: © Jeff Greenberg/Alamy; Page 210: © Photos.com/Jupiter Images

Chapter 6: Page 256: © Bikeriderlondon/Shutterstock; Page 263: © Photos.com/Jupiter Images

Chapter 7: Page 288: © Andrew Clark/Alamy; Page 296: © FreezeFrameStudio/iStockphoto

Chapter 8: Page 353: © World Photo Collection/Alamy; Page 354 left: © Comstock/JupiterImages; center: © DPA Picture Alliance/Alamy; right: © ImagineGolf/iStockphoto; Page 357: left: © Haoliang/Shutterstock; center: © Photos.com/Jupiter Images; right: © Lcholakov/Dreamstime; Page 359: Thinkstock/Jupiter Unlimited

Chapter 9: Page 404: © B. Christopher/Alamy; Page 412: © Scott Rothstein/Shutterstock

Chapter 10: Page 452: © Sergey Nivens/Fotolia; Page 466: © ITStock Free/JupiterImages

Chapter 11: Page 505: © Gunnar Kullenberg/Purestock/Alamy; Page 507: © Razvan/iStockphoto

Chapter 12: Page 565: Newphotoservice/Shutterstock; Page 568: Maxkateusa/Dreamstime